A Programmer's Guide to Java™ Certification

A Programmer's Guide to Java™ Certification

A Comprehensive Primer

Khalid A. Mughal
and
Rolf W. Rasmussen

Addison-Wesley

An imprint of PEARSON EDUCATION
Harlow, England • Reading, Massachusetts • Menlo Park, California • New York • Don Mills, Ontario • Amsterdam • Bonn • Sydney
Singapore • Tokyo • Madrid • San Juan • Milan • Mexico City • Seoul • Taipei

Pearson Education Limited
Head Office:
Edinburgh Gate
Harlow CM20 2JE
Tel: +44 (0) 1279 623623
Fax: +44 (0) 1279 431059

London Office:
128 Long Acre
London WC2E 9AN
Tel: +44 (0)20 7447 2000
Fax: +44 (0)20 7240 5771

Visit us on the World Wide Web at:
www.awl.com/cseng

First published in Great Britain 2000

ISBN 0-201-59614-8

British Library Cataloguing in Publication Data
A catalogue record for this book is available from the British Library.

Library of Congress Cataloging in Publication Data
Mughal, Khalid Azim.
A programmer's guide to Java certification : a comprehensive primer / Khalid Azim Mughal and Rolf Rasmussen.
p. cm.
Includes bibliographical references (p.).
ISBN 0-201-59614-8 (paperback : alk. paper)
1. Electronic data processing personnel--Certification Study guides. 2. Java (Computer program language) I. Rasmussen, Rolf (Rolf W.) II. Title.
QA76.3.M846 1999
005.13'3--dc21 99-40779
CIP

10 9 8 7 6 5

Typeset by CRB Associates, Norfolk.
Printed and bound in the United States of America.

The publishers' policy is to use paper manufactured from sustainable forests.

To the loving memory of my mother, Zubaida Begum,
and my father, Mohammed Azim.
K.A.M.

For Olivia E. Rasmussen and
Louise J. Dahlmo.
R.W.R.

Preface

About this book

This book provides an extensive coverage of the Java programming language and its core APIs, with particular emphasis on its syntax and usage. The book is primarily intended for professionals who want to prepare for the Sun Certified Programmer for Java 2 Platform exam (referred to as the SCPJ2 exam), but it is readily accessible to any programmer who wants to master the language. For both purposes, it provides an in-depth coverage of essential features of the language and its core APIs.

There is a great and increasing demand for certified Java programmers. Sun Microsystems has defined the SCPJ2 exam, which professionals can take to validate their skills. The certification provides the IT industry the standard to use for hiring such professionals, and allows the professionals to turn their Java skills into credentials that are important for career advancement.

The book helps the reader to master all features of the Java language, and this mastering of the language can culminate in accomplishing the exam. It provides an extensive coverage of all the objectives defined for the exam by Sun. Since the exam objectives are selective, they do not cover many of the essential features of Java. The book provides extensive coverage of additional topics that every Java programmer should master in order to be proficient in this field. In this regard, the book is a comprehensive primer for learning the Java programming language.

This book is *not* a *complete reference* for Java, as it does not attempt to list every member of every class from the Java Development Kit (JDK) API documentation. Its purpose is not to document the JDK APIs. It is also *not* a book on *teaching programming techniques*. Its emphasis is on the Java programming language features, their syntax and correct usage.

The book assumes a background in programming. We believe the exam is accessible to any programmer who works through the book. A Java programmer can easily skip over material which is well understood, and concentrate on parts that need reinforcing, whereas a programmer new to Java will find the concepts explained from basic principles.

Each topic is explained and discussed thoroughly with examples, and backed by review questions and exercises to reinforce the concepts. The book is not biased toward any particular platform, but provides platform-specific details where necessary.

Using the book

The reader can choose a linear or a non-linear route through the book depending on his or her programming background. Non-Java programmers wishing to migrate to Java can read Chapter 1, which provides a short introduction to object-oriented programming concepts, and the procedure for compiling and running Java applets and standalone applications. For those preparing for the SCPJ2 exam, the book has a separate appendix providing all the pertinent information on taking the exam.

The objectives defined by Sun are organized into major sections, detailing the curriculum for the examination. These objectives are reproduced in a separate appendix where, for each section of the syllabus, study notes are included to point the reader to topics essential for the exam. The book is organized into chapters that logically follow the order of these major sections. Exam objectives are stated clearly at the start of every chapter, together with any supplementary objectives. Each chapter concludes with a summary of the topics, pointing out the major concepts discussed in the chapter.

Review questions are provided after every major topic, to test and reinforce the material. Programming exercises are provided at the end of each chapter, so that concepts can be tried out in practice. A complete sample exam is provided in a separate appendix, which the reader can try when he or she is ready. Annotated answers to the review questions and solutions to the programming exercises are also provided in separate appendices.

The table of contents, listings of tables, examples and figures, and an extensive index facilitate locating topics discussed in the book.

In order to obtain optimal benefit from using this book in preparing for the SCPJ2 exam, we strongly recommend installing the latest version (at least 1.2) of the JDK and its accompanying API documentation. The book focuses solely on Java 2, and does not acknowledge previous versions. API-related information is highlighted by a gray vertical bar in the book. We encourage experimenting with the code examples and programming exercises, to reinforce the material from the book. These can be downloaded from the book web site.

Book web sites

This book is backed by web sites providing auxiliary material (available directly from Addison-Wesley's site – go to the main entry for this book to access the links):

<URL:`http://www.awl.com/cseng`>

Contents of the web sites include the following:

- Source code for all the examples in the book.
- Mock exam engine.
- Errata.
- Links to miscellaneous Java resources (certification, newsgroups, tools, etc.).

Information about the JDK and its documentation can be found at the following web site:

<URL:`http://java.sun.com/products/jdk/1.2/`>

Conventions used in the book

Code Referencing in the Text

Java code is written in a `mono spaced font`. Lines of code in the examples or in code snippets are referenced in the text by a number, which is specified by using a single-line comment in the code. For example, in the code snippet below, the call to the method `doSomethingInteresting()` hopefully does something interesting at line (1).

```
// ...
doSomethingInteresting();                                    // (1)
// ...
```

API Bar

A vertical gray bar is used to highlight methods, variables and constants found in the classes of the core Java APIs.

Any explanation following the API information is also similarly highlighted.

Java Naming Conventions

Names of classes and interfaces start with an uppercase letter. Names of packages, variables and methods start with a lowercase letter. Constants are all in uppercase letters.

Request for feedback

Considerable effort has been made to ensure the accuracy of the contents of this book. Several Java professionals have proofread the manuscript. All code examples (including code fragments) have been compiled and tested on Windows, Macintosh and Unix platforms.

Any questions, comments, suggestions and corrections are welcome. Whether the book was helpful or detrimental for your purpose, we would like your assessment. Any feedback is valuable. The authors can be reached at:

```
khalid@ii.uib.no
rolfwr@ii.uib.no
```

Authors' background

Khalid A. Mughal is an Associate Professor at the Department of Informatics at the University of Bergen, Norway. The University was one of the first to introduce Java into the curriculum (January 1997). Professor Mughal is responsible for designing and implementing various courses which use Java. In his 18 years at the university, he has taught Programming Languages (Java, C/C++, Pascal), Software Engineering (Object-oriented System Development), Databases (Data Modeling and Database Management Systems) and Compiler Techniques. During the last two years, he has also given numerous courses and seminars at various levels in object-oriented programming and system development using Java and Java-related technology, both at the University and for the IT industry. He is the principal author of the book, responsible for writing the material covering the Java topics.

His primary research is in theory, design and implementation of programming languages and tools (Programming Environments). Recently he has been working on the application of Object Technology in such fields as Marine Information Systems, Bioinformatics, and Distant Learning.

He has spent over three years at the Department of Computer Science, Cornell University, as a Visiting Associate Professor, and will be spending his upcoming sabbatical at Cornell starting Fall 1999.

He is a member of the ACM and of the IEEE Computer Society.

Rolf W. Rasmussen is a Java programmer working on his thesis at the University, relating to Object Technology, Java, UML and the development of CASE tools. He is primarily responsible for developing the review questions and answers, the programming exercises and their solutions, the sample exam, and all the practical aspects relating to taking the SCPJ2 exam.

Apart from finishing his thesis, his research interests include patterns for software development, technologies for descriptive markup of documents, and open source software.

Acknowledgments

A small application for drawing simple shapes is used in the book to illustrate various aspects of GUI building. The idea for this application, as far as we know, first appeared in Appendix D of *Data Structures and Problem Solving Using Java* (M.A. Weiss, Addison-Wesley, 1998).

At Addison-Wesley-Longman (AWL), we would like to thank Emma Mitchell for the support and the guidance she provided us right from the start of this project, Martin Klopstock at AWL for accommodating the non-standard procedure involved in getting the book to the printing press, Clive Birks at CRB Associates for providing the professional look to the contents of this book, and finally, Sally Mortimore at AWL for seeing us over the finishing line. The efforts of other professionals behind the scenes at AWL are also acknowledged.

Many reviewers have been involved during the course of writing this book. First of all, we would like to thank the five anonymous reviewers commissioned by AWL to review the initial draft. Their input was useful in the subsequent writing of this book.

Several people have provided us with feedback on different parts of the material at various stages: Jon Christian Lønningdal, Tord Kålsrud, Kjetil Iversen, Roy Oma and Arne Løkketangen. Their help is hereby sincerely acknowledged.

We are also very grateful to Laurence Vanhelsuwé, Kris Laporte, Anita Jacob, and Torill Hamre for taking on the daunting task of reviewing the final draft, and providing us with extensive feedback at such short notice. We would like to thank Marit Mughal for reading the manuscript with the trained eye of a veteran English schoolteacher.

We now understand why family members are invariably mentioned in a preface. Without our families' love, support and understanding this book would have remained a virtual commodity. Khalid would like to thank Marit, Nina and Laila for their love, and for being his pillars of support, during the writing of this book. Thanks also to the folks in Birmingham for cheering us on. Rolf would like to thank Liv, Rolf V., Knut and Elisabeth for enduring the strange working hours producing this book has entailed. A special thanks to Marit for providing us with scrumptious dinners for consumption at the midnight hour.

Khalid A. Mughal
Rolf W. Rasmussen

March, 1999
Bergen, Norway

Contents

Preface **vii**

About this book vii
Using the book viii
Book web sites ix
Conventions used in the book ix
Request for feedback x
Authors' background x
Acknowledgments xi

1 Basics of Java Programming **1**

1.1 Introduction 2
1.2 Classes 2
Declaring Members: Variables and Methods 3
1.3 Objects 4
Class Instantiation 4
Object References 5
1.4 Instance Members 6
Invoking Methods 6
1.5 Static Members 7
1.6 Inheritance 9
1.7 Aggregation 11
1.8 Tenets of Java 11
Review Questions *12*
1.9 Java Programs 14
1.10 Sample Standalone Java Application 14
Main Elements of a Java Standalone Application 14
Compiling and Running a Standalone Program 15
1.11 Sample Java Applet 16
Main Elements of an Applet 16
Compiling and Running an Applet 17
Review Questions *18*
Chapter Summary *19*

2 Language Fundamentals **20**

2.1 Language Building Blocks 21
Lexical Tokens 21
Identifiers 21
Keywords 21
Literals 22
Integer Literals 22
Floating-point Literals 24
Boolean Literals 24
Character Literals 24
String Literals 26
White Spaces 26
Comments 27
Review Questions *28*
2.2 Primitive Datatypes 28
2.3 Variable Declarations 29
Declaring, Initializing and Using Variables 29
Object Reference Variables 30
2.4 Integers 31
2.5 Characters 31
2.6 Floating-point Numbers 31
2.7 Booleans 32
2.8 Wrapper Classes 32
Review Questions *33*
2.9 Initial Values for Variables 34
Default Values for Member Variables 34
Initializing Local Variables of Primitive Datatypes 35
Initializing Local Reference Variables 36
Review Questions *36*
2.10 Java Source File Structure 37
Review Questions *38*
2.11 The `main()` Method 38
The `main()` Method Modifiers 39
Review Questions *39*
Chapter Summary *39*
Programming Exercises *40*

3 Operators and Assignments **41**

3.1 Precedence and Associativity Rules for Operators 42
3.2 Conversions 43
Casting 43
Narrowing and Widening Conversions 43
Numeric Promotions 44
Type Conversion Contexts 45
3.3 Simple Assignment Operator = 45

Assigning Primitive Values 46
Assigning References 46
Multiple Assignments 46
Numeric Type Conversions on Assignment 47
Review Questions *48*
3.4 Arithmetic Operators: *, /, %, +, - 49
Arithmetic Operator Precedence and Associativity 49
Arithmetic Expression Evaluation 50
Numeric Promotions in Arithmetic Expressions 51
Arithmetic Extended Assignment Operators: *=, /=, %=, +=, -= 53
3.5 The Binary String Concatenation Operator + 54
3.6 Variable Increment and Decrement Operators: ++, -- 54
Increment Operator ++ 54
Decrement Operator -- 55
Review Questions *55*
3.7 Boolean Expressions 58
3.8 Relational Operators: <, <=, >, >= 58
3.9 Equality 59
Primitive Data Value Equality: ==, != 59
Object Reference Equality: ==, != 59
Object Value Equality 60
3.10 Boolean Logical Operators: !, ^, &, | 61
Operand Evaluation for Boolean Logical Operators 62
Boolean Logical Extended Assignment Operators: &=, ^=, |= 62
3.11 Conditional Operators: &&, || 63
Short-circuit Evaluation 64
3.12 Representing Integers 64
Calculating 2's Complement 65
3.13 Integer Bitwise Operators: ~, &, |, ^ 66
Bitwise Extended Assignment Operators: &=, ^=, |= 67
3.14 Shift Operators: <<, >>, >>> 68
The Shift-left Operator << 69
The Shift-right-with-sign-fill Operator >> 70
The Shift-right-with-zero-fill Operator >>> 70
Shift Extended Assignment Operators: <<=, >>=, >>>= 71
3.15 The Conditional Operator ? : 71
3.16 Other Operators: `new`, `[]`, `instanceof` 72
Review Questions *72*
3.17 Parameter Passing 74
3.18 Passing Primitive Data Values 76
3.19 Passing Object Reference Values 77
3.20 Passing Array References 79
3.21 Array Elements as Actual Parameters 80
3.22 `final` Parameters 82
3.23 Program Arguments 82

Review Questions *83*
Chapter Summary *84*
Programming Exercises *85*

4 Declarations and Access Control **86**

4.1 Arrays 87
Declaring Array Variables 87
Constructing an Array 88
Initializing an Array 89
Using an Array 89
Multidimensional Arrays 91
Anonymous Arrays 93
Review Questions *94*
4.2 Defining Classes 97
4.3 Defining Methods 97
Statements 98
Instance Methods and Object Reference `this` 98
Method Overloading 99
4.4 Constructors 100
Default Constructor 101
Overloaded Constructors 103
Review Questions *103*
4.5 Packages 105
Defining Packages 106
Using Packages 107
4.6 Accessibility Modifiers for Classes and Interfaces 108
4.7 Other Modifiers for Classes 109
`abstract` Classes 109
`final` Classes 110
Review Questions *111*
4.8 Scope and Accessibility of Members 112
Class Scope for Members 112
Block Scope for Local Variables 113
4.9 Member Accessibility Modifiers 114
`public` Members 115
`protected` Members 117
Default Accessibility for Members 118
`private` Members 118
Review Questions *120*
4.10 Other Modifiers for Members 121
`static` Members 121
`final` Members 123
`abstract` Methods 124
`synchronized` Methods 124
`native` Methods 125

`transient` Variables 126
`volatile` Variables 126
Review Questions *127*
Chapter Summary *130*
Programming Exercises *131*

5 Flow Control and Exception Handling **132**
5.1 Overview of Flow Control Statements 133
5.2 Selection Statements 133
Simple `if` Statement 133
`if-else` Statement 134
`switch` Statement 136
Review Questions *140*
5.3 Iteration Statements 141
`while` Statement 142
`do-while` Statement 143
`for` Statement 143
5.4 Transfer Statements 145
`break` Statement 145
`continue` Statement 147
`return` Statement 148
Review Questions *149*
5.5 Exception Handling 153
Exception Types 155
5.6 `try`, `catch` and `finally` Blocks 156
`try` Block 157
`catch` Block 157
`finally` Block 159
5.7 `throw` Statement 160
5.8 `throws` Clause 162
Review Questions *164*
Chapter Summary *169*
Programming Exercises *169*

6 Object-oriented Programming **172**
6.1 Inheritance 173
Object-oriented Programming Concepts 175
Review Questions *178*
6.2 Method Overriding and Variable Shadowing 179
Method Overriding 179
Variable Shadowing 181
Overriding vs. Overloading 181
Object Reference `super` 183
Review Questions *185*
6.3 Chaining Constructors using `this()` and `super()` 187

`this()` Constructor Call 188
`super()` Constructor Call 190
Review Questions *193*
6.4 Interfaces 195
Defining Interfaces 195
Implementing Interfaces 197
Extending Interfaces 197
Supertypes 198
Constants in Interfaces 199
Review Questions *199*
6.5 Assigning, Passing and Casting References 201
Reference Assignment Conversions 204
Parameter Passing Conversions 205
Reference Casting and `instanceof` Operator 206
Converting References of Class and Interface Types 209
Review Questions *210*
6.6 Polymorphism and Dynamic Method Lookup 213
Review Questions *216*
6.7 Inheritance vs. Aggregation 217
Encapsulation 217
Choosing between Inheritance and Aggregation 217
Review Questions *220*
Chapter Summary *221*
Programming Exercises *222*

7 Inner Classes 223

7.1 Overview of Nested Classes 224
7.2 Top-level Nested Classes and Interfaces 226
7.3 Non-static Inner Classes 230
Accessing Shadowed Members from Non-static Inner Classes 232
Compiling and Importing Non-static Inner Classes 234
Inheritance and Containment Hierarchy of Non-static Inner Classes 235
Review Questions *236*
7.4 Local Classes 238
Access Rules for Local Classes 240
Instantiating Local Classes 240
7.5 Anonymous Classes 243
Extending an Existing Class 243
Implementing an Interface 245
Instantiating Anonymous Classes 245
Access Rules for Anonymous Classes 246
Review Questions *247*
Chapter Summary *249*
Programming Exercise *249*

8 Object Lifetime **250**
8.1 Garbage Collection 251
Object Lifetime 251
Cleaning Up 251
Object Finalization 252
Finalizer Chaining 253
Invoking Garbage Collection 255
Review Questions *255*
8.2 Initializers 257
Variable Initializer Expressions 257
Static Initializer Blocks 260
Instance Initializer Blocks 262
Constructing Initial Object State 264
Review Questions *267*
Chapter Summary *270*

9 Threads **271**
9.1 Multitasking 272
9.2 Threads 272
Main Thread 273
9.3 Thread Creation 273
Implementing the `Runnable` Interface 273
Extending the `Thread` Class 276
Review Questions *278*
9.4 Synchronization 279
Monitors 279
Synchronized Methods 280
Synchronized Blocks 281
Review Questions *282*
9.5 Thread Transitions 283
Thread States 283
Thread Priorities 284
Thread Scheduler 285
Running and Yielding 285
Sleeping and Waking Up 286
Waiting and Notifying 286
Miscellaneous Methods in the Thread Class 290
Review Questions *292*
Chapter Summary *293*
Programming Exercises *294*

10 Fundamental Classes **295**
10.1 Overview of the `java.lang` package 296
10.2 The `Object` Class 296
Review Questions *298*

10.3 The Wrapper Classes 299
- Common Wrapper Class Constructors 299
- Common Wrapper Class Utility Methods 300
- `Boolean` Class 301
- `Character` Class 301
- Numeric Wrapper Classes 301
- `Void` Class 302
- *Review Questions* 302

10.4 The `Math` Class 303
- Miscellaneous Rounding Functions 303
- Exponential Functions 304
- Trigonometry Functions 305
- Pseudo Random Number Generator 305
- *Review Questions* 305

10.5 The `String` Class 307
- Creating and Initializing Strings 307
- Reading Individual Characters in a String 309
- Comparing Strings 310
- Character Case in a String 311
- Concatenation of Strings 311
- Searching for Characters and Substrings 312
- Extracting Substrings 313
- Conversion of Objects to Strings 313
- *Review Questions* 314

10.6 The `StringBuffer` Class 317
- Constructing String Buffers 317
- Changing and Reading Characters in String Buffers 318
- Constructing Strings from String Buffers 318
- Appending, Inserting and Deleting Characters in String Buffers 318
- Controlling String Buffer Capacity 320
- *Review Questions* 320
- *Chapter Summary* 321
- *Programming Exercises* 322

11 Collections 323

11.1 Collections Framework 324
- Core interfaces 324
- Implementations 325
- Algorithms 326

11.2 Collections 327
- *Review Questions* 329

11.3 Sets 330

11.4 Lists 333
- *Review Questions* 336

11.5 Maps 338

11.6 Sorted Sets and Sorted Maps 341
11.7 Customizing Collections 345
Review Questions *348*
Chapter Summary *349*
Programming Exercise *350*

12 AWT Components **351**
12.1 Overview of the `java.awt` package 352
12.2 Components and Containers 352
`Component` Class 353
`Container` Class 355
`Panel` Class 355
`Applet` Class 355
`Window` Class 355
`Frame` Class 356
`Dialog` Class 357
Review Questions *357*
12.3 GUI Control Components 359
Running the Examples 360
`Button` 361
`Canvas` 362
`Checkbox` and `CheckboxGroup` 363
`Choice` 365
`Label` 366
`List` 367
`Scrollbar` 369
`TextField` and `TextArea` 372
Review Questions *375*
12.4 Menu Components 377
Review Questions *380*
Chapter Summary *381*
Programming Exercise *381*

13 Layout Management **382**
13.1 Layout Management Policies 383
Layout Managers 383
Common Methods for Designing a Layout 384
Communication between Container and Layout Manager 384
Layout and Preferred Size 385
Review Questions *386*
13.2 Running the Example Code 386
13.3 `FlowLayout` Manager 387
Review Questions *388*
13.4 `GridLayout` Manager 389
Review Questions *391*
13.5 `BorderLayout` Manager 392

	Review Questions	*396*
13.6	`CardLayout` Manager	396
	Review Questions	*399*
13.7	`GridBagLayout` Manager	399
	Review Questions	*405*
13.8	Customized Layout	406
13.9	Building Component Hierarchies	407
	Chapter Summary	*411*
	Programming Exercises	*411*
14	**Event Handling**	**412**
14.1	Overview of Event Handling	413
14.2	The Event Hierarchy	413
	`AWTEvent` Classes	414
	Semantic Event Classes	415
	Low-level Events	417
	Review Questions	*420*
14.3	The Event Delegation Model	421
	Review Questions	*427*
14.4	Event Adapters	429
	Event Listeners as Anonymous Inner Classes	432
14.5	Building GUI-based Applications	433
	Review Questions	*439*
14.6	Low-Level Event Processing	441
	Review Questions	*447*
	Chapter Summary	*448*
	Programming Exercises	*448*
15	**Painting**	**450**
15.1	Rendering Graphics	451
	Graphics Context	451
	Drawing Components	451
	The `Graphics` Class	453
15.2	Using Color	454
	Review Questions	*456*
15.3	Rendering Text and Working with Fonts	458
15.4	Drawing Shapes	462
	Drawing Lines	462
	Drawing Rectangles	463
	Drawing Ovals	466
	Drawing Arcs	467
	Drawing Polygons	469
15.5	Clipping	471
	Review Questions	*473*
15.6	The AWT Thread	475

15.7 Organizing Painting and Event Handling 477
Painting Modes 479
15.8 Handling Images 481
Review Questions *485*
Chapter Summary *486*
Programming Exercise *486*

16 Applets **487**

16.1 Creating Applets 488
16.2 Running Applets 488
HTML `APPLET` Element 489
HTML `OBJECT` Element 491
Applet Layout Management Specification 491
Applet Code Specification 493
16.3 Applet Life Cycle 495
Review Questions *496*
16.4 Applets and Threads 497
16.5 Other Useful Methods of the Applet Class 500
16.6 Supplying Applet Parameters 501
16.7 Using Images and Sound in Applets 503
16.8 JAR Files 505
16.9 Applet Security 506
Review Questions *507*
Chapter Summary *508*
Programming Exercises *508*

17 Swing **509**

17.1 Swing Overview 510
Heavyweight and Lightweight Components 511
Swing and the AWT 511
Swing Packages 512
17.2 The Root Pane Container Model 512
17.3 Swing Components 516
Root Containers 517
`JComponent` 518
Labels and Buttons 519
Basic Components 521
Text Components 523
Space-saving Components 525
Components with Complex Models 526
Large Compound Components 529
Review Questions *530*
17.4 Other Swing Topics 531
`BoxLayout` 531
Look and Feel 534

Alternatives to Traditional Event Handling 535
The Single-Thread Rule 538
Review Questions *538*
17.5 Building a GUI with Swing 540
Chapter Summary *547*
Programming Exercise *547*

18 Files and Streams 548

18.1 Input and Output 549
18.2 `File` Class 549
Querying the File System 551
File or Directory Existence 553
Read and Write Access 553
Listing Directory Entries 553
Creating New Files and Directories 554
Renaming Files and Directories 554
Deleting Files and Directories 554
18.3 Byte Streams: Input Streams and Output Streams 555
File Streams 558
Filter Streams 560
I/O of Java Primitive Values 560
Buffered Byte Streams 563
Comparison of Byte Output Streams and Input Streams 564
Review Questions *565*
18.4 Character Streams: Readers and Writers 567
Character Encodings 570
Print Writers 571
Writing Text Files 572
Reading Text Files 574
Buffered Character Streams 575
Using Buffered Writers 575
Using Buffered Readers 576
Terminal I/O 579
Comparison of Character Writers and Readers 581
Comparison of Byte Streams and Character Streams 581
Review Questions *582*
18.5 Random Access for Files 583
Review Questions *586*
18.6 Object Serialization 587
`ObjectOutputStream` Class 587
`ObjectInputStream` Class 588
Review Questions *591*
Chapter Summary *591*
Programming Exercise *592*

19 Javadoc Facility 593

19.1 Javadoc Facility 594
19.2 Using Tags 596
Javadoc Tags for Classes, Interfaces and Members 597
Documenting Classes and Interfaces 599
Documenting Methods 600
Documenting Member Variables 600
Some Documentation Conventions 601
19.3 Running `javadoc` 601
Common Pitfalls when Using Javadoc 604
Review Questions 604
Chapter Summary 606
Programming Exercise 606

A Taking the SCPJ2 Exam 607

Preparing for the programmer exam 607
Registering for the exam 608
Obtaining an exam voucher 608
Signing up for the test 608
Contact information 609
After taking the exam 611
Moving on to the developer exam 611
How the examination is conducted 612
The testing locations 612
Utilizing the allotted time 612
The exam program 612
The questions 613
Forms of answers expected 613
Forms of questions 614
Topics covered by the questions 614

B Objectives for the SCPJ2 Exam 616

C Annotated Answers to Review Questions 623

D Solutions to Programming Exercises 666

E Sample Exam 698

Index 729

List of Tables

1.1	Terminology for Class Members	9
2.1	Keywords in Java	22
2.2	Reserved Keywords not currently in use	22
2.3	Reserved Literals in Java	22
2.4	Examples of Literals	22
2.5	Number Systems	23
2.6	Examples of Octal and Hexadecimal Literals in Java	24
2.7	Examples of Unicode Values	25
2.8	Expressing Character Literals as Unicode Values	25
2.9	Escape Sequences	26
2.10	Range of Integer Values	31
2.11	Range of Character Values	31
2.12	Range of Floating-point Values	31
2.13	Boolean Values	32
2.14	Summary of Primitive Datatypes	33
2.15	Default Values	34
3.1	Operator Precedence and Associativity	42
3.2	Arithmetic Operators	49
3.3	Examples of Arithmetic Expression Evaluation	50
3.4	Arithmetic Extended Assignment Operators	53
3.5	Relational Operators	58
3.6	Primitive Data Value Equality Operators	59
3.7	Reference Equality Operators	60
3.8	Boolean Logical Operators	61
3.9	Truth-values for Boolean Logical Operators	62
3.10	Boolean Logical Extended Assignment Operators	63
3.11	Conditional Operators	63
3.12	Truth-values for Conditional Operators	63
3.13	Representing Signed Integers using 2's Complement	65
3.14	Bitwise Operators	66
3.15	Result-table for Bitwise Operators	67
3.16	Examples of Bitwise Operations	67
3.17	Bitwise Extended Assignment Operators	68

3.18	Shift Operators	68
3.19	Shift Extended Assignment Operators	71
3.20	Parameter Passing	75
4.1	Summary of Accessibility Modifiers for Classes and Interfaces	109
4.2	Summary of Other Modifiers for Classes and Interfaces	111
4.3	Summary of Accessibility Modifiers for Members	119
4.4	Summary of Other Modifiers for Members	127
5.1	`return` Statement	148
6.1	Types	201
7.1	Overview of Classes and Interfaces	225
11.1	Core Interfaces in the Collections Framework	325
11.2	Implementations of the Core Interfaces	325
11.3	Bulk Operations and Set Logic	330
12.1	Components and Containers in AWT	353
12.2	GUI Control Components in AWT	360
13.1	Overview of Layout Managers	383
13.2	Layout Operations	385
13.3	Components in Grid Bag Layout	404
14.1	Semantic Event Handling	422
14.2	Low-Level Event Handling	423
14.3	Semantic Event Listener Interfaces and Their Methods	423
14.4	Low-level Event Listener Interfaces and Their Methods	424
14.5	Low-Level Event Listener Interfaces and Their Adapters	431
14.6	Event Masks and Event Processing Methods	442
17.1	Swing Packages	512
17.2	Swing Root Containers	518
17.3	Label and Button Components	520
17.4	General Lightweight Swing Components	522
17.5	Swing Text Components	524
17.6	Space-saving Components	525
17.7	Components with Complex Models	526
17.8	Large Compound Components	529
18.1	Input Streams	557
18.2	Output Streams	557
18.3	`DataInput` and `DataOutput` Interfaces	561
18.4	Comparing Output Streams and Input Streams	565
18.5	Readers	568
18.6	Writers	569
18.7	Encoding Schemes	570
18.8	Print Methods of the `PrintWriter` Class	572
18.9	Correspondence between Writers and Readers	581
18.10	Correspondence between Byte Streams and Character Streams	581
19.1	Common Javadoc Tags	597
19.2	Common Options for the `javadoc` Utility	601

List of Examples

1.1	Basic Elements of a Class Definition	3
1.2	Static Members in Class Definition	8
1.3	Defining a Subclass	10
1.4	A Standalone Application	14
1.5	A Java Applet	16
2.1	Default Values for Member Variables	34
2.2	Flagging Uninitialized Local Variables of Primitive Datatypes	35
2.3	Flagging Uninitialized Local Reference Variables	36
3.1	Numeric Promotion in Arithmetic Expressions	52
3.2	Passing Primitive Values	76
3.3	Passing Object Reference Values	77
3.4	Passing Arrays	79
3.5	Array Elements as Primitive Data Values	81
3.6	Array Elements as Object Reference Values	81
3.7	Passing Program Arguments	83
4.1	Using Arrays	90
4.2	Using Multidimensional Arrays	92
4.3	Using Anonymous Arrays	94
4.4	Using `this` Reference	99
4.5	Accessibility Modifiers for Classes and Interfaces	108
4.6	Abstract Classes	110
4.7	Class Scope	113
4.8	Public Accessibility of Members	116
4.9	Accessing Static Members	122
4.10	Accessing Final Members	123
4.11	Synchronized Methods	124
5.1	Fall Through in `switch` Statement	138
5.2	Using `break` in `switch` Statement	138
5.3	Nested `switch` Statement	139
5.4	`break` Statement	146
5.5	Labeled `break` Statement	146
5.6	`continue` Statement	147
5.7	Labeled `continue` Statement	148

5.8 The `return` Statement 149
5.9 Default Exception Handling 155
5.10 `try-catch` Construct 158
5.11 `try-catch-finally` Construct 159
5.12 `try-finally` Construct 160
5.13 Throwing Exceptions 161
5.14 `throws` Clause 162
6.1 Extending Classes 173
6.2 Illustrating Inheritance 176
6.3 Overriding and Overloading Methods and Shadowing Variables 179
6.4 Overloaded Method Resolution 182
6.5 Using `super` Keyword 183
6.6 Constructor Overloading 188
6.7 `this()` Constructor Call 189
6.8 `super()` Constructor Call 191
6.9 Interfaces 195
6.10 Variables in Interfaces 199
6.11 Assigning and Passing Reference Values 202
6.12 `instanceof` and cast Operator 207
6.13 Using `instanceof` Operator 208
6.14 Polymorphism and Dynamic Method Lookup 215
6.15 Inheritance and Aggregation 217
7.1 Top-level Nested Classes and Interfaces 226
7.2 Access in Top-level Nested Classes and Interfaces 228
7.3 Defining Non-static Inner Classes 230
7.4 Special Form of `this` and `new` Constructs in Non-static Inner Classes 232
7.5 Importing Inner Classes 234
7.6 Inheritance and Containment Hierarchy 235
7.7 Access in Local Classes 239
7.8 Instantiating Local Classes 241
7.9 Defining Anonymous Classes 243
7.10 Access in Anonymous Classes 246
8.1 Using Finalizers 253
8.2 Initializer Expression Order 258
8.3 Exceptions in Initializer Expressions 259
8.4 Static Initializer Blocks 261
8.5 Instance Initializer Block in Anonymous Class 263
8.6 Exception Handling in Instance Initializer Blocks 264
8.7 Object State Construction 265
8.8 Initialization under Object State Construction 266
9.1 Implementing the `Runnable` Interface 275
9.2 Extending the `Thread` Class 277
9.3 Waiting and Notifying 287
9.4 Usage of `isAlive()` and `join()` Methods 291
10.1 Anonymous Strings 308
10.2 Usage of `length()` and `charAt()` Methods of the `String` Class 309

11.1	Using Sets	331
11.2	Using Lists	335
11.3	Using Maps	339
11.4	Using SortedMaps	344
12.1	Illustrating Button	361
12.2	Illustrating Canvas	362
12.3	Illustrating Checkbox	363
12.4	Illustrating Radio Buttons	364
12.5	Illustrating Choice	366
12.6	Illustrating Labels	367
12.7	Illustrating List	369
12.8	Illustrating Scrollbar	371
12.9	Illustrating Text Field	372
12.10	Illustrating Text Area	373
12.11	Illustrating Text Lines and Variable Pitch Fonts	375
12.12	Illustrating Menus	379
13.1	Demonstrating Flow Layout	388
13.2	Demonstrating Grid Layout	390
13.3	Demonstrating Border Layout – Only North and South Regions	393
13.4	Demonstrating Border Layout – Only East, West and Center Regions	394
13.5	Demonstrating Border Layout – North, South, East, West and Center	395
13.6	Demonstrating Card Layout	397
13.7	Demonstrating Grid Bag Layout	403
13.8	Demonstrating Component Hierarchy	408
14.1	Illustrating Event Delegation Model	425
14.2	Implementing Listener Interfaces	429
14.3	Using Event Adapters	431
14.4	Listeners as Anonymous Classes	432
14.5	GUI + Event Handling	434
14.6	Low-level Event Processing I	443
14.7	Low-level Event Processing II	445
15.1	Color	456
15.2	Standard Font Names	459
15.3	Rendering Text	462
15.4	Drawing Lines	463
15.5	Drawing Rectangles	465
15.6	Drawing Ovals	466
15.7	Drawing Arcs	469
15.8	Drawing Polygons	470
15.9	Drawing Polylines	471
15.10	Clipping Region	472
15.11	Screen Updating	475
15.12	Organizing Painting and Event Handling	478
15.13	Painting Modes	479
15.14	Displaying Images	481
15.15	Image Buffering	483

15.1	Coordinates of a Component	453
15.2	Foreground and Background Color	455
15.3	Standard Fonts (Windows Platform)	459
15.4	Font Measurements	460
15.5	Rendering Text	461
15.6	Drawing Lines	463
15.7	Drawing Rectangles	465
15.8	Bounding Rectangle for Ovals	466
15.9	Drawing Ovals	467
15.10	Measurements for Drawing Arcs	468
15.11	Drawing Arcs	468
15.12	Drawing Polygons and Polylines	470
15.13	Clipping Region	472
15.14	Clip Region set by AWT	476
15.15	Painting and Event Handling	477
15.16	Painting Modes	480
15.17	Displaying Images	482
15.18	Incremental Image Drawing	483
15.19	Image Buffering	483
16.1	Alignment of Applets	492
16.2	Threads in Applets	498
16.3	Using Applet Parameters	502
16.4	GUI for the SoundApplet	504
17.1	Lightweight and Heavyweight Components in AWT	510
17.2	Containment Model	513
17.3	Containment Model for Root Components	513
17.4	Simple Swing Application	514
17.5	Root Containers	518
17.6	Label and Button Components	519
17.7	Text Component Hierarchy	524
17.8	Illustrating Complex Components	528
17.9	Layout to demonstrate Box Layout	532
17.10	Demonstrating Box Layout	533
17.11	Demonstrating Actions	536
17.12	GUI with Windows Look and Feel	540
17.13	GUI with Motif Look and Feel	540
17.14	Component Hierarchy	545
18.1	Byte Stream Inheritance Hierarchies	556
18.2	Stream Chaining	561
18.3	Buffering Byte Streams	564
18.4	Character Stream Inheritance Hierarchies	567
18.5	Setting up a Print Writer	573
18.6	Setting up Readers	574
18.7	Buffered Writers	576
18.8	Buffered Readers	577
18.9	Random Access File Inheritance Hierarchy	583

16.1	Using Threads in Applets	499
16.2	Applet Parameters	502
16.3	Playing Sounds	504
17.1	A Simple Swing Application	514
17.2	Using Complex Components	528
17.3	Using Box Layout	533
17.4	Using Actions and Implementing Models	536
17.5	Building GUI with Swing	541
18.1	Listing Files Under a Directory	554
18.2	Copy a File	559
18.3	Reading and Writing Java Primitive Values	562
18.4	Demonstrating Readers and Writers, and Character Encoding	577
18.5	Demonstrating Terminal I/O	579
18.6	Random Access File	585
18.7	Object Serialization	589
19.1	Using Javadoc Tags	594

List of Figures

1.1 UML Notation for Classes 3
1.2 UML Notation for Objects 5
1.3 Aliases 6
1.4 Class Diagram showing Static Members of a Class 7
1.5 Class Diagram depicting Inheritance Relation 9
1.6 Class Diagram depicting Aggregation 11
1.7 Running an Applet with the Applet Viewer 18
2.1 Primitive Datatypes in Java 29
2.2 Java Source File Structure 37
3.1 Widening Conversions 44
3.2 Numeric Promotion in Arithmetic Expressions 51
3.3 Parameter Passing: Primitive Data Values 77
3.4 Parameter Passing: Object Reference Values 78
3.5 Parameter Passing: Arrays 80
4.1 Array of Arrays 92
4.2 Package Hierarchy 106
4.3 Block Scope 114
4.4 Public Accessibility 116
4.5 Protected Accessibility 117
4.6 Default Accessibility 118
4.7 Private Accessibility 119
5.1 State Diagram for `if` Statements 133
5.2 State Diagram for `switch` Statement 137
5.3 State Diagram for `while` Statement 142
5.4 State Diagram for `do-while` Statement 143
5.5 State Diagram for the `for` Statement 144
5.6 Partial Exception Inheritance Hierarchy 154
5.7 `try-catch-finally` block 157
6.1 Inheritance Hierarchy 174
6.2 Inheritance Relationship between `String` and `Object` Classes 175
6.3 Inheritance Relations 197
6.4 Array Types in Inheritance Hierarchy 202
6.5 Polymorphic Methods 214

6.6 Inheritance and Aggregation
7.1 Top-level Nested Classes and Interfaces
7.2 Outer Object with Associated Inner Objects
9.1 Spawning Threads
9.2 Thread States
9.3 Running and Yielding
9.4 Sleeping and Waking up
9.5 Waiting and Notifying
10.1 Partial Inheritance Hierarchy in the `java.la`
11.1 The Core Interfaces
11.2 The Core Interfaces and their Implementatio
11.3 Bulk Operations on Collections
12.1 Partial Inheritance Hierarchy of Components
12.2 Button
12.3 Canvas
12.4 Checkbox
12.5 Radio Buttons
12.6 Choice
12.7 Labels
12.8 List
12.9 Scrollbars
12.10 Text Field
12.11 Text Area
12.12 Text Lines and Variable Pitch Fonts
12.13 Inheritance Hierarchy of Menu Components ar
12.14 Menus
13.1 Flow Layout
13.2 Grid Layout
13.3 Locations in Border Layout
13.4 Horizontal and Vertical Stretching
13.5 Regions in Border Layout
13.6 Card Layout
13.7 Alignment of Different Size Components in Gric
13.8 Layout Constraints
13.9 Grid Bag Layout
13.10 GUI
13.11 Component Hierarchy
13.12 GUI for Exercise 13.1
13.13 GUI for Exercise 13.2
14.1 Partial Inheritance Hierarchy of Event Classes
14.2 Handling Events
14.3 Event Delegation
14.4 Delegating Events
14.5 GUI + Event Handling
14.6 Low-level Event Processing
14.7 GUI for Exercise 14.1

18.10 Positioning the File Pointer for Direct File Access 584
18.11 Object Stream Chaining 587
19.1 Javadoc Document 603

Basics of Java Programming 1

Supplementary Objectives

- Know the basic terminology and concepts in object-oriented programming: classes, objects, references, members, variables, methods, inheritance.
- Recognize the main elements of a Java program.
- Distinguish between a standalone Java application and a Java applet.
- Know how to compile and run Java programs.

1.1 Introduction

Before embarking on the road to programmer certification in Java, it is important to understand the basic terminology and concepts in object-oriented programming (OOP). Java supports the writing of standalone applications and applets. The basic elements for writing both kinds of programs are introduced. The old adage that practice makes perfect is certainly true when learning a programming language. To encourage programming on the computer, the mechanics of compiling and running Java programs are outlined.

In this chapter, the emphasis is on providing an introduction rather than an exhaustive coverage of the topics mentioned above. In-depth coverage of these topics follows in due course in subsequent chapters of the book.

1.2 Classes

Abstractions are one of the fundamental ways in which people handle complexity. An abstraction denotes the essential properties and behaviors of an object that differentiate it from other objects. The essence of object-oriented programming is modeling abstractions using classes and objects. The hard part in this endeavor is finding the right abstractions.

A *class* models an abstraction by defining the properties and behaviors for the objects represented by the abstraction. A class thus denotes a category of objects, and acts as a blueprint for creating such objects. An object exhibits the properties and behaviors defined by its class. Properties of an object of a class are also called *attributes*, and are defined using *variables* in Java (a.k.a. *fields*). Behaviors of an object of a class are also known as *operations*, and are defined using *methods* in Java. Variables and methods in a class definition are collectively called *class members*.

An important distinction is made between the *contract* and the *implementation* a class provides for its objects. The contract defines *what* services, and the implementation defines *how* these services are provided by the class. Clients (i.e. other objects) only need to know the contract of an object, and not its implementation, in order to avail themselves of the object's services.

By way of example, a class called `CharStack` will be implemented, which models the abstraction of a stack that can push and pop characters. The stack will use an array of characters to store the characters, and a variable to indicate the top element in the stack. Using Unified Modeling Language (UML) notation, the class `CharStack` is graphically depicted in Figure 1.1. Both the variable and the method names are shown in Figure 1.1a.

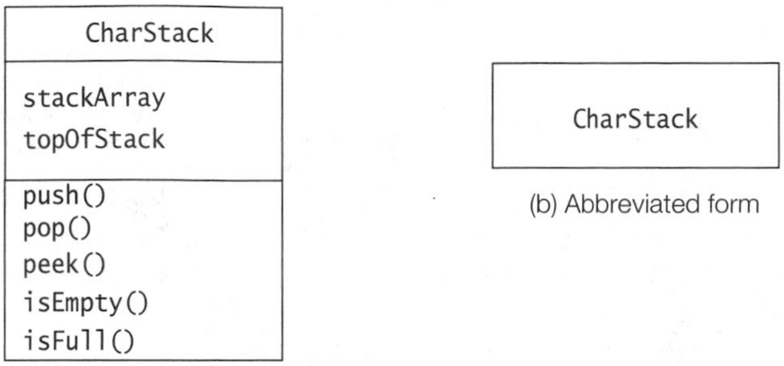

(a) Expanded form

(b) Abbreviated form

Figure 1.1 *UML Notation for Classes*

Declaring Members: Variables and Methods

Example 1.1 shows the class definition implemented in Java for the class depicted in Figure 1.1. It is meant to illustrate the salient features of a class definition in Java, and not effective implementation of stacks. The class `CharStack` has two variables: `stackArray` which is an array to hold the elements of the stack (in this case characters), and `topOfStack` to denote the top element of the stack. The class has five methods (`push()`, `pop()`, `peek()`, `isEmpty()` and `isFull()`), which implement the essential operations on a stack. It also has a special method that has the same name as the class. Such methods are called *constructors*, and their purpose is to initialize the object when it is created from the class. The implementation details in the example are not important for the present discussion.

Example 1.1 *Basic Elements of a Class Definition*

```
class CharStack {                    // Class name
    // Class Declarations:

    // (1) Variables:
    private char[] stackArray;       // The array that implements the stack.
    private int topOfStack;          // The top of the stack.

    // (2) Constructor:
    public CharStack(int n) { stackArray = new char[n]; topOfStack = -1; }

    // (3) Methods:
    public void push(char element) { stackArray[++topOfStack] = element; }
    public char pop() { return stackArray[topOfStack--]; }
    public char peek() { return stackArray[topOfStack]; }
    public boolean isEmpty() { return topOfStack < 0; }
    public boolean isFull() { return topOfStack == stackArray.length - 1; }
}
```

1.3 Objects

Class Instantiation

An *object* is an instance of a class. It is constructed using the class as a blueprint, and is a concrete instance of the abstraction that the class represents. An object must explicitly be created from its class before it can be used in a program. In Java, objects are manipulated through *object references* (also called *reference values* or simply *references*). The process of creating objects usually involves the following steps:

1. Declaration of a reference variable.
   This involves declaring a *reference variable* of the appropriate class to store the reference to the object.

   ```
   // Declaration of two reference variables that will denote
   // two distinct objects, namely two stacks of characters respectively.
   CharStack stack1, stack2;
   ```

2. Creating an object.
   This involves using the `new` operator, together with a call to a constructor of the class, to create an instance of the class.

   ```
   // Create two distinct stacks of chars.
   stack1 = new CharStack(10); // Stack length: 10 chars
   stack2 = new CharStack(5);  // Stack length: 5 chars
   ```

   The `new` operator returns a reference to a new instance of the `CharStack` class. This reference can be assigned to a reference variable of the appropriate class. Each object has a unique identity and has its own copy of the variables declared in the class definition. The two stacks, referenced by `stack1` and `stack2`, will have their own copies of the `stackArray` and `topOfStack` variables.

   The purpose of the constructor call on the right side of the `new` operator is to initialize the newly created object. In this particular case, for each instance created, the constructor creates an array of characters whose length is given by the value of the argument to the constructor, and it also initializes the top of stack.

The declaration and the instantiation can also be combined:

```
CharStack stack1 = new CharStack(10),
          stack2 = new CharStack(5);
```

Figure 1.2 shows the UML notation for objects. The graphical representation of an object is very similar to that of a class. Figure 1.2a shows the canonical notation where the name of the object is prefixed to the class name. If the name of the object is omitted, as in Figure 1.2b, this denotes an anonymous object. Since objects in Java do not have names but are denoted by references, a more elaborate notation is shown in Figure 1.2c, where reference objects of `CharStack` class explicitly refer to `CharStack` objects. In most cases the more compact notation will suffice.

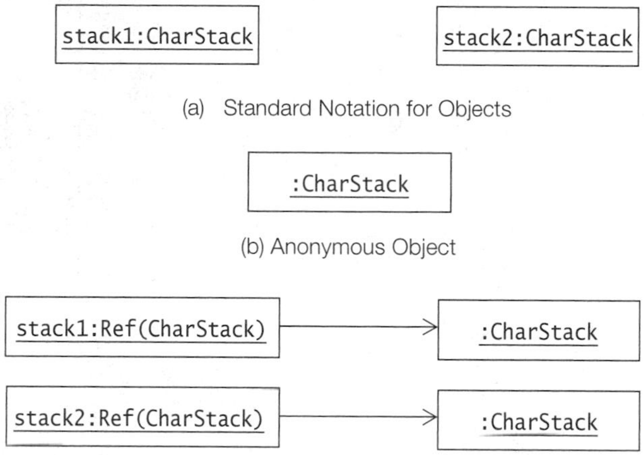

(a) Standard Notation for Objects

(b) Anonymous Object

(c) Explicit References for Java Objects

Figure 1.2 *UML Notation for Objects*

Object References

A reference provides a handle to an object that is created and stored in memory. In Java, objects can only be manipulated via references, which can be stored in variables. An object can have several references, often called its *aliases*. The object can be manipulated via any one of its aliases.

```
// Create two distinct stacks of chars.
CharStack stackA = new CharStack(12); // Stack length: 12 chars
CharStack stackB = new CharStack(6);  // Stack length: 6 chars

stackB = stackA;                      // (1) aliases after assignment
// Stack previously referenced by stackB can now be garbage collected.
```

Two stacks are created in the code above. Before the assignment at (1), the situation is as depicted in Figure 1.3a. After the assignment at (1), reference variables `stackA` and `stackB` will denote the same stack, as depicted in Figure 1.3b. Reference variables `stackA` and `stackB` are aliases after the assignment, as they denote the same object. What happens to the stack object that was denoted by the reference variable `stackB` before the assignment? The answer is that object deletion in Java is taken care of by the runtime system. If necessary, when objects are no longer in use, their memory is reclaimed and reallocated for other objects. This is called *garbage collection*.

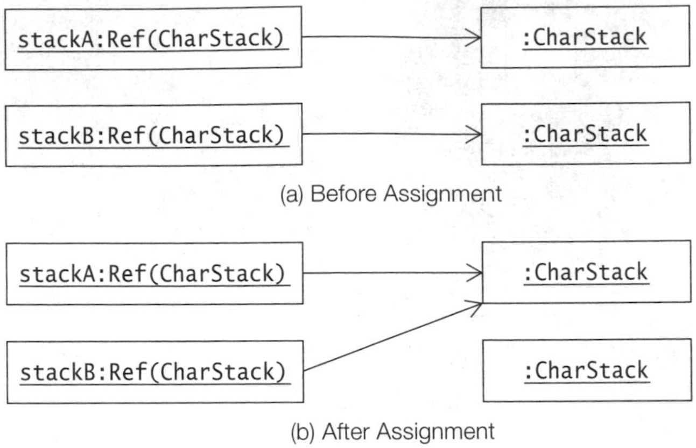

Figure 1.3 *Aliases*

1.4 Instance Members

Each object created will have its own instances of the member variables defined in its class. The values of the variables in an object comprise its *state*. Two distinct objects can have the same state, if their variables have the same values. The methods define the behavior of an object. It is important to note that the methods pertain to each object of the class. This should not be confused with the implementation of the methods, which is shared by all instances of the class. These member variables and methods are called *instance members* (since they belong to instances or objects), to distinguish them from *static members* which only belong to the class. Static members are discussed in the next section.

Invoking Methods

Objects communicate by message passing. This means that an object can be made to exhibit a particular behavior by invoking the appropriate operation on the object. In Java, this is done by *calling* a method on the object using the binary infix dot '.' operator which spells out the complete message: the object which is the receiver of the message, the method to be invoked, and the arguments to the method if any. The method invoked in the receiver can also send information back to the sender via a return value. The method called must be one that is defined for the object.

```
CharStack stack = new CharStack(5);      // Create a stack
stack.push('J');                // (1) Character 'J' pushed
char c = stack.pop();           // (2) One character popped and returned: 'J'
stack.printStackElements();     // (3) Compile Error: No such method in CharStack
```

The sample code above invokes methods on the object denoted by the reference variable `stack`. The method call at (1) pushes one character on the stack, and the method call at (2) pops one character off the stack. Both `push()` and `pop()` methods are defined in class `CharStack`. The `push()` method does not return any value, but the `pop()` method returns the character popped. Trying to invoke a method `printStackElements()` on the stack results in a compile time error, as no such method is defined in the class `CharStack`.

The dot `'.'` notation can also be used with a reference to access instance variables of an object if these variables have the right *accessibility*. The variables of the `CharStack` class have `private` accessibility, meaning that they are not accessible from outside the class.

```
stack.topOfStack++;  // Compile Error: topOfStack is a private variable.
```

1.5 Static Members

There are cases when certain members should only belong to the class, and not be part of any object created from the class. An example of such a situation is when a class wants to keep track of how many objects of the class have been created. Defining a counter as an instance variable in the class definition for tracking the number of objects created does not solve the problem, since this counter will be instantiated for all objects of the class. Which counter should then be updated? The solution is to use a *static variable*. Such a variable belongs to the class, and not to any object of the class. A static variable is initialized when the class is loaded at runtime. Similarly, a class can have static *methods* that belong only to the class and not to any objects of the class. Static members are distinguished from instance variables in a class definition by the keyword `static` in their declaration. Table 1.1 at the end of this section provides a summary of the terminology used in defining members of a class.

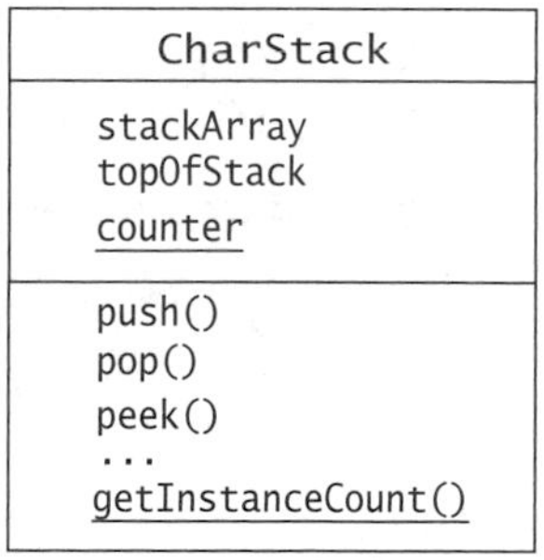

Figure 1.4 *Class Diagram showing Static Members of a Class*

Figure 1.4 shows the definition of the class `CharStack` which has been augmented by two static members which are shown underlined. The augmented definition of the `CharStack` class is implemented in Example 1.2. The variable `counter` is a static variable declared at (1). It will be allocated and initialized to the default value `0` when the class is loaded. Each time an object of the `CharStack` class is created, the constructor at (2) is executed. The constructor explicitly increments the counter in the class. The method `getInstanceCount()` at (3) is a static method belonging to the class. It returns the counter value when called.

Example 1.2 *Static Members in Class Definition*

```
class CharStack {
    // Instance variables
    private char[] stackArray;  // The array that implements the stack.
    private int topOfStack;     // The top of the stack.

    // Static variable
    private static int counter;                                    // (1)

    // Constructor now increments the counter for each object created.
    public CharStack(int capacity) {                               // (2)
        stackArray = new char[capacity];
        topOfStack = -1;
        counter++;
    }

    // Instance methods
    public void push(char element) { stackArray[++topOfStack] = element; }
    public char pop() { return stackArray[topOfStack--]; }
    public char peek() { return stackArray[topOfStack]; }
    public boolean isEmpty() { return topOfStack < 0; }
    public boolean isFull() { return topOfStack == stackArray.length - 1; }

    // Static method                                                  (3)
    public static int getInstanceCount() { return counter; }
}
```

Clients can access static members in the class by using the class name. The following code invokes the `getInstanceCount()` method in the class `CharStack`:

```
int count = CharStack.getInstanceCount(); // Class name to invoke static method
```

Static members can also be accessed via references to objects of the class:

```
CharStack stack1 = new CharStack(10);
int count1 = stack1.getInstanceCount();   // Object reference invokes static method
```

Static members can be accessed by both the class name and objects of the class, but instance members can only be accessed by objects of the class.

Table 1.1 *Terminology for Class Members*

Instance Members	These are instance variables and instance methods of an object. They can only be accessed or invoked through an object reference.
Instance Variable	A variable which is allocated when the class is instantiated, i.e. when an object of the class is created.
Instance Method	A method which belongs to an instance of the class. Objects of the same class share its implementation.
Static Members	These are static variables and static methods of a class. They can be accessed or invoked either using the class name or through an object reference.
Static Variable	A variable which is allocated when the class is loaded. It belongs to the class and not to any object of the class.
Static Method	A method which belongs to the class and not to any object of the class.

1.6 Inheritance

There are two fundamental mechanisms for building new classes from existing ones: *inheritance* and *aggregation*. It makes sense to *inherit* from an existing class `Vehicle` to define a class `Car`, since a car is a vehicle. The class `Vehicle` has several *parts*, therefore it makes sense to define an *aggregate object* of class `Vehicle` which has *constituent objects* of such classes as `Motor`, `Axle` and `GearBox`, which make up a vehicle.

Inheritance is illustrated by way of an example which implements a stack of characters that can print its elements on the terminal. This new stack has all the properties and behaviors of the `CharStack` class, but it also has the additional capability of printing its elements. This printable stack is a stack of characters and can be derived from the `CharStack` class. This relationship is shown in Figure 1.5. The class `PrintableCharStack` is called the *subclass* and the class `CharStack` is called the *superclass*. The `CharStack` class is a *generalization* for all stacks of characters, whereas the class `PrintableCharStack` is a *specialization* of stacks of characters to stacks that can also print their elements.

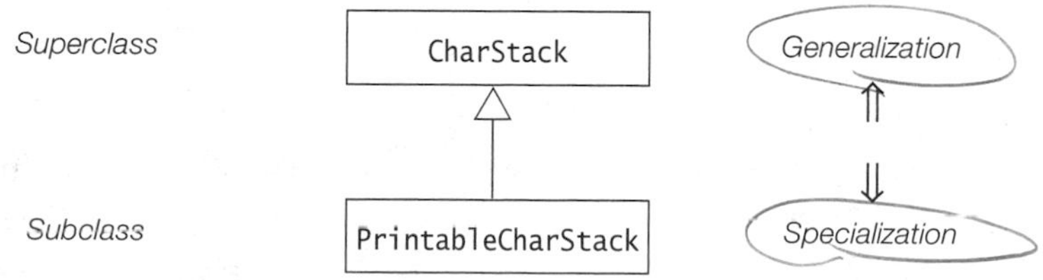

Figure 1.5 *Class Diagram depicting Inheritance Relation*

In Java, deriving a new class from an existing class requires the use of the `extends` clause in the subclass definition. In Java, a subclass can *extend* only one superclass. The subclass inherits members of the superclass. The following code fragment implements the `PrintableCharStack` class:

```
class PrintableCharStack extends CharStack {                          // (1)
    // Instance method
    public void printStackElements() {                                // (2)
        // ... implementation of print ...
    }

    // Constructor calls the constructor of the superclass explicitly.
    public PrintableCharStack(int capacity) { super(capacity); }      // (3)
}
```

The `PrintableCharStack` class extends the `CharStack` class at (1). Implementing the `printStackElements()` method in the `PrintableCharStack` class requires access to the inherited variable `stackArray` from the superclass `CharStack`, but this variable is *private* and therefore not accessible in the subclass. If the accessibility of the instance variables is changed to *protected* in the `CharStack` class, then the subclass can access these variables. In Example 1.3, the implementation of the `printStackElements()` method is shown at (2). The constructor of the `PrintableCharStack` class at (3) calls the constructor of the superclass `CharStack` to initialize the stack properly.

Example 1.3 *Defining a Subclass*

```
class CharStack {
    // Instance variables
    protected char[] stackArray;  // The array that implements the stack.
    protected int topOfStack;     // The top of the stack.

    // The rest of the definition is the same as in Example 1.2.
}

class PrintableCharStack extends CharStack {                          // (1)
    // Instance method
    public void printStackElements() {                                // (2)
        for (int i = 0; i <= topOfStack; i++)
            System.out.print(stackArray[i]); // print each char on terminal
        System.out.println();
    }
    // Constructor calls the constructor of the superclass explicitly.
    public PrintableCharStack(int capacity) { super(capacity); }      // (3)
}
```

Objects of the `PrintableCharStack` class will respond just like the objects of the `CharStack` class, but they will also have the additional functionality defined in the subclass:

```
PrintableCharStack aPrintableCharStack = new PrintableCharStack(3);
aPrintableCharStack.push('H');
aPrintableCharStack.push('i');
aPrintableCharStack.push('!');
aPrintableCharStack.printStackElements();    // Prints "Hi!" on the terminal
```

1.7 Aggregation

When building new classes from existing classes using *aggregation*, an aggregate object is built from other constituent objects that are its parts.

Java supports aggregation of objects by reference, since objects cannot contain other objects explicitly. They can only contain variables of primitive types and references to other objects. Each object of the `CharStack` class has a reference to an array object to hold the characters, and a variable of primitive datatype `int` to denote the top of stack. This is reflected in the definition of the `CharStack` class, which contains an instance variable for each of these parts. In contrast to the constituent objects, the values of constituent variables of primitive types are stored in the aggregate object. The *aggregation* relationship is depicted by the UML diagram in Figure 1.6, showing that each object of the `CharStack` class will have one array object of `char` associated with it.

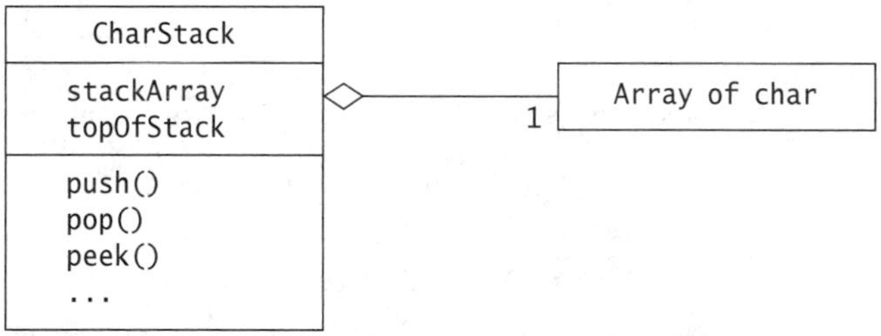

Figure 1.6 *Class Diagram depicting Aggregation*

1.8 Tenets of Java

- Everything in Java must be encapsulated in classes.
- There are two kinds of values in Java: atomic values of primitive types, and reference values.
- References denote objects which are created from classes.
- Objects can only be manipulated via references.
- Objects in Java cannot contain other objects; they can only have references to other objects.
- Deletion of objects is managed by the runtime system.

Review questions

1.1 A method is ...

Select the one right answer.

(a) an implementation of an abstraction.
(b) an attribute defining the property of a particular abstraction.
(c) a category of objects.
(d) an operation defining the behavior for a particular abstraction.
(e) a blueprint for making operations.

1.2 An object is ...

Select the one right answer.

(a) what classes are instantiated from.
(b) an instance of a class.
(c) a blueprint for creating concrete realization of abstractions.
(d) a reference to an attribute.
(e) a variable.

1.3 Which line contains a constructor in this class definition?

```
public class Counter {                                                // (1)
    int current, step;

    public Counter(int startValue, int stepValue) {                   // (2)
        set(startValue);
        setStepValue(stepValue);
    }

    public int get() { return current; }                              // (3)

    public void set(int value) { current = value; }                   // (4)

    public void setStepValue(int stepValue) { step = stepValue; }     // (5)
}
```

Select the one right answer.

(a) Code marked with (1) is a constructor.
(b) Code marked with (2) is a constructor.
(c) Code marked with (3) is a constructor.
(d) Code marked with (4) is a constructor.
(e) Code marked with (5) is a constructor.

1.4 Given that `Thing` is a class, how many objects and reference variables are created by the following code?

```
Thing item, stuff;
item = new Thing();
Thing entity = new Thing();
```

Select all valid answers.

(a) One object is created.
(b) Two objects are created.
(c) Three objects are created.
(d) One reference variable is created.
(e) Two reference variables are created.
(f) Three reference variables are created.

1.5 An instance member ...

Select the one right answer.

(a) is also called a static member.
(b) is always a variable.
(c) is never a method.
(d) belongs to a single instance, not to the class as a whole.
(e) always represents an operation.

1.6 How do objects pass messages in Java?

Select the one right answer.

(a) They pass messages by modifying each other's member variables.
(b) They pass messages by modifying the static member variables of each other's classes.
(c) They pass messages by calling each other's instance member methods.
(d) They pass messages by calling static member methods of each other's classes.

1.7 Given the following code, which statements are true?

```
class A {
    int value1;
}

class B extends A {
    int value2;
}
```

Select all valid answers.

(a) Class `A` extends class `B`.
(b) Class `B` is the superclass of class `A`.
(c) Class `A` inherits from class `B`.
(d) Class `B` is a subclass of class `A`.
(e) Objects of class `A` have a member variable named `value2`.

1.9 Java Programs

Two types of programs can be developed in Java:

- Standalone applications
- Applets

The next two sections provide an example of each type of program, highlighting what constitutes a standalone application and what constitutes an applet.

A Java program is a collection of one or more classes. A Java *source file* can contain more than one class definition. Sun's Java Development Kit (JDK) enforces the rule that at most one class in the source file has `public` accessibility. The name of the source file is comprised of the name of this public class with "`.java`" as extension. Each class definition in a source file is compiled into *Java byte code* and stored in a separate *class file*. The name of this file is comprised of the name of the class with "`.class`" as extension. All programs must be compiled before they can be run. The JDK provides tools for this purpose, as explained in the next two sections.

1.10 Sample Standalone Java Application

A standalone application is what is normally meant by a program: source code that is compiled and directly executed. In order to create a standalone application in Java, the program must define a class with a special method called `main`. The `main()` method in the class is the starting point for the execution of any standalone application.

Main Elements of a Java Standalone Application

Example 1.4 is an example of a standalone application, in which a client uses the `CharStack` class to reverse a string of characters.

Example 1.4 *A Standalone Application*

```
// Example of a standalone application
// Source Filename: Client.java

public class Client {

    public static void main(String args[]) {

        // Create a stack
        CharStack stack = new CharStack(40);

        // Create a string to push on the stack
        String str = "!no tis ot nuf era skcatS";
        int length = str.length();
```

```
            // Push the string char by char onto the stack
            for (int i = 0; i<length; i++) {
                stack.push(str.charAt(i));
            }

            // Pop and print each char from the stack
            while (!stack.isEmpty()) {
                System.out.print(stack.pop());
            }
            System.out.println();
        }
    }

    class CharStack {
        // Same as in Example 1.2.
    }
```

Output from the program:

```
Stacks are fun to sit on!
```

The public class `Client` defines a method with the name `main`. The `main()` method in this public class is invoked by the Java interpreter to start the application. It is important to note how the `main()` method is declared:

```
public static void main(String args[]) {
    // ...
}
```

The `main()` method has `public` accessibility, meaning it is accessible from any class. The keyword `static` means the method belongs to the class. The keyword `void` means that the method does not return any value. The parameter list, `String args[]`, is an array of strings used to pass information to the `main()` method, and hence to the application when the application is started.

Compiling and Running a Standalone Program

Java source files can be compiled using the Java compiler `javac`, which is a part of the JDK.

The source file `Client.java` contains the definitions of both the `Client` class and the `CharStack` class. The source file can be compiled by giving the following input at the command line:

```
javac Client.java
```

This creates two Java class files, `Client.class` and `CharStack.class`, containing the Java byte code corresponding to the two class definitions contained in the source file `Client.java`.

Source file → .java
byte code → .class

Class files can be executed by the Java interpreter `java`, which is also a part of the JDK. The above example can be run by giving the following input at the command line:

```
java Client
```

Note that only the name of the class is specified, resulting in invoking the `main()` method from the specified class. The standalone application in Example 1.4 terminates when the execution of the `main()` method ends.

1.11 Sample Java Applet

Applets are Java programs that must be run in other applications such as web browsers. Most of the well-known web browsers are capable of running Java applets. The *applet viewer* provided with the JDK can be used to test applets. This is often useful, since the Java runtime environment found in web browsers is often not up to date with the latest Java version.

Main Elements of an Applet

Example 1.5 is a Java applet which implements a client that uses the `CharStack` class to reverse a string of characters.

Example 1.5 *A Java Applet*

```
// Source Filename: ClientApplet.java

import java.applet.Applet;     // Import the Applet class
import java.awt.Graphics;      // Import the Graphics class

// An applet must extend the Applet class
public class ClientApplet extends Applet { // (1)

    // Instance variables
    CharStack stack;
    String originalStr;
    String reversedStr;

    // Instance methods
    public void init() {                    // (2) Called when the applet is loaded.

        // Create a stack
        stack = new CharStack(40);

        // Create a string to push on the stack
        originalStr = new String("!no tis ot nuf era skcatS");
        int length = originalStr.length();

        // Push the string char by char onto the stack
        for (int i = 0; i<length; i++) {
            stack.push(originalStr.charAt(i));
        }
```

```
        // Pop and store each char from the stack into a new string
        reversedStr = new String();         // Empty new string
        while (!stack.isEmpty()) {
            reversedStr += stack.pop();     // Concatenate characters
        }
    }

    public void paint(Graphics gfx) {       // (3) Called to draw the applet.
        // A Graphics object is used to render graphics in an applet.
        // Draw the reversed string at the specified coordinates.
        gfx.drawString(reversedStr, 25, 25);
    }
}
class CharStack {
    // Same as in Example 1.2.
}
```

The Applet class in the standard Java class library provides the basic functionality of an applet. The ClientApplet class extends the Applet class at (1), thereby inheriting this functionality. An applet can customize this functionality by redefining certain methods from the Applet class. The ClientApplet class customizes two such methods: the init() and the paint() methods at (2) and (3) respectively. The init() method is called when the applet is loaded by the runtime environment in which the applet is to run. In Example 1.5, the init() method reverses a string using a stack and stores the reversed string in an instance variable, reversedStr. The paint() method is called by the runtime environment to draw the applet on the screen. In Example 1.5, the paint() method draws the reversed string using a Graphics object passed as argument to the method. The import statements specify where the Applet and the Graphics classes can be found in the Java class library. As can be seen, the main() method is not necessary for an applet.

Compiling and Running an Applet

The source code for the applet is compiled just like any other Java program:

```
javac ClientApplet.java
```

The source file ClientApplet.java contains two class definitions, ClientApplet and CharStack. This creates two class files, ClientApplet.class and CharStack.class, containing the Java byte code for the corresponding class definitions contained in the source file ClientApplet.java .

An applet is not run in the same way as a standalone application. Instead, the applet is loaded though an HTML (HyperText Markup Language) page, either in a web browser or using the applet viewer. An HTML file with the relevant information must be created, so that the applet can be loaded and run. This information can be provided in an APPLET element, giving the name of the applet class file and specifying the size of the display area for the applet. The following HTML content is placed in a file called `ClientApplet.html` for the applet above:

```
<applet code="ClientApplet.class" width=200 height=200> </applet>
```

The HTML file `ClientApplet.html` can be loaded in a web browser to run the applet. The applet can also be run from the command line, using the applet viewer provided in the JDK:

```
appletviewer ClientApplet.html
```

Figure 1.7 shows the result of running the applet from Example 1.5.

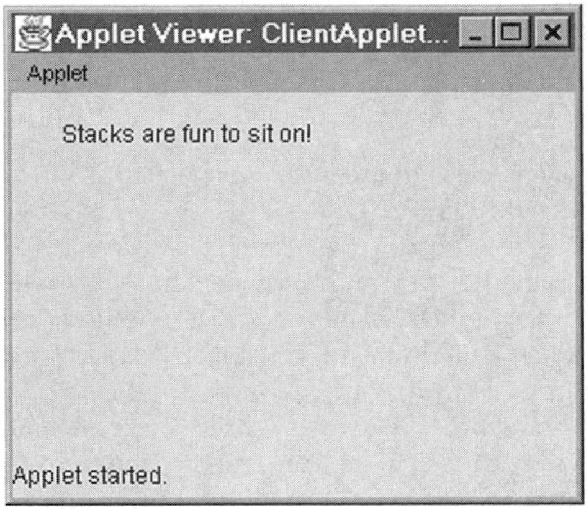

Figure 1.7 *Running an Applet with the Applet Viewer*

Review questions

1.8 If this source code is contained in a file called `SmallProg.java`, what command should be used to compile it using the JDK?

```
public class SmallProg {
    public static void main(String args[]) { System.out.println("Good luck!"); }
}
```

Select the one right answer.

(a) `java SmallProg`
(b) `javac SmallProg`
(c) `java SmallProg.java`
(d) `javac SmallProg.java`
(e) `java SmallProg main`

1.9 What command should be used to run the program from the last question, using the JDK?

Select the one right answer.

(a) `java SmallProg`
(b) `javac SmallProg`
(c) `java SmallProg.java`
(d) `java SmallProg.class`
(e) `java SmallProg.main()`

Chapter summary

The following topics were discussed in this chapter:

- Basic concepts in object-oriented programming and how they are supported in Java.
- Main elements of Java standalone applications and applets.
- Compiling and running Java standalone applications and applets.

2 Language Fundamentals

Exam Objectives

- Identify correctly constructed `package` declarations, `import` statements, class declarations (of all forms, including inner classes), interface declarations and implementations (for `java.lang.Runnable` or other interface described in the test), method declarations (including the `main` method that is used to start execution of a class), variable declarations and identifiers.
  - *For defining and using packages, see Section 4.5.*
  - *For class declarations, see Section 4.2.*
  - *For inner classes, see Chapter 7.*
  - *For interface declarations and implementations, see Section 6.4.*
  - *For method declarations, see Section 4.3.*
- State the correspondence between index values in the argument array passed to a `main` method and command line arguments.
  - *See Section 3.23.*
- Identify all Java programming language keywords and correctly constructed identifiers.
- State the effect of using a variable or array element of any kind, when no explicit assignment has been made to it.
  - *For array elements, see Section 4.1.*
- State the range of all primitive data types, and declare literal values for `String` and all primitive types using all permitted formats, bases and representations.

Supplementary Objectives

- State the wrapper classes for primitive data types.

2.1 Language Building Blocks

Like any other programming language, the Java programming language is defined by *grammar rules* that specify how *syntactically* legal constructs can be formed using the language elements, and by a *semantic definition* that specifies the *meaning* of syntactically legal constructs.

Lexical Tokens

The low-level language elements are called *lexical tokens* (or just *tokens* for short) and are the building blocks for more complex constructs. Identifiers, operators and special characters are all examples of tokens that can be used to build high-level constructs like expressions, statements, methods and classes.

Identifiers

A name in a program is called an *identifier*. Identifiers can be used to denote classes, methods and variables.

In Java an *identifier* is composed of a sequence of characters, where each character can be either a *letter*, a *digit*, a *connecting punctuation* (such as *underscore* _) or any *currency symbol* (such as $, ¢, ¥ or £), and cannot start with a digit. Since Java programs are written in the Unicode character set (p. 24), the definitions of letter and digit are interpreted according to this character set.

Note that Java is case-sensitive, e.g. `price` and `Price` are two different identifiers.

Examples of legal identifiers:

```
number, Number, sum_$, bingo, $$_100, mål, grüß
```

Examples of illegal identifiers:

```
48chevy, all/clear, get-lost-fred
```

Keywords

Keywords are reserved identifiers that are predefined in the language, and cannot be used to denote other entities. Incorrect usage results in compilation errors.

Keywords currently defined in the language are listed in Table 2.1. In addition, three identifiers are reserved as predefined *literals* in the language: `null`, `true`, `false` (Table 2.3). Keywords currently reserved, but not in use, are listed in Table 2.2. All these reserved words cannot be used as identifiers. The index contains references to relevant sections where currently defined keywords are explained.

Table 2.1 *Keywords in Java*

abstract	do	import	public	throws
boolean	double	instanceof	return	transient
break	else	int	short	try
byte	extends	interface	static	void
case	final	long	strictfp	volatile
catch	finally	native	super	while
char	float	new	switch	
class	for	package	synchronized	
continue	if	private	this	
default	implements	protected	throw	

Table 2.2 *Reserved Keywords not currently in use*

const	goto

Table 2.3 *Reserved Literals in Java*

null	true	false

Literals

A *literal* denotes a constant value. This value can be numerical (integer or floating-point), character, boolean or a string. In addition there is the null literal (`null`) which represents the null reference.

Table 2.4 *Examples of Literals*

Integer	2000	0	-7		
Floating-point	3.14	-3.14	.5	0.5	
Character	'a'	'A'	'0'	'*'	')'
Boolean	true	false			
String	"abba"	"3.14"	"for"	"a piece of the action"	

Integer Literals

Integer datatypes are comprised of the following primitive types: `int`, `long`, `byte` and `short`.

The default type of an integer literal is `int`, but it can be specified as `long` by appending the suffix `L` (or `l`) to the integer value; for example `2000L`, `0l`. There is no way to specify a `short` or a `byte` literal.

Octal Numbers and Hexadecimal Numbers

In addition to the decimal number system, integer literals can also be specified in octal (*base* 8) and hexadecimal (*base* 16) number systems. Table 2.5 lists the integers from `0` to `16`, showing their equivalents in the octal and hexadecimal number systems.

Table 2.5 *Number Systems*

Decimal numbers	Octal numbers	Hexadecimal numbers
0	0	0
1	1	1
2	2	2
3	3	3
4	4	4
5	5	5
6	6	6
7	7	7
8	10	8
9	11	9
10	12	a
11	13	b
12	14	c
13	15	d
14	16	e
15	17	f
16	20	10

In Java, octal and hexadecimal numbers are specified with `0` and `0x` prefix respectively. Some examples of octal and hexadecimal literals are shown in Table 2.6.

Converting Octal and Hexadecimal Numbers to Decimals

Octal and hexadecimal numbers can be easily converted to their decimal equivalents:

```
0132 = 1*8^2 + 3*8^1 + 2*8^0 = 64 + 24 + 2 = 90     (1) Octal -> Decimal
0x5a = 5*16^1 + a*16^0 = 80 + 10 - 90              (2) Hex -> Decimal
```

Table 2.6 *Examples of Octal and Hexadecimal Literals in Java*

Decimal	Octal	Hexadecimal
8	010	0x8
10	012	0xa
16	020	0x10
27	033	0x1b
90	0132	0x5a
2147483647	017777777777	0x7fffffff
-2147483648	-017777777777	-0x7fffffff

At (1) an octal number, expressed in base 8, is converted to its equivalent decimal value. Each digit in the octal number contributes to the final decimal value by virtue of its position, starting with position 0 (units) for the rightmost digit in the number. Since hexadecimal numbers have the base 16, this value is used as the base for converting from hexadecimal to decimal in (2).

Floating-point Literals

Floating-point data types come in two flavors: `float` or `double`.

The default type of a floating-point literal is `double`, but this can be explicitly designated by appending the suffix `D` (or `d`) to the value. A floating-point literal can also be specified to be a `float` by appending the suffix `F` (or `f`).

Floating-point literals can also be specified in scientific notation, for example `5E-1` is equivalent to $5*10^{-1}$, i.e. `0.5`, where `E` (or `e`) stands for *Exponent*.

Boolean Literals

Boolean truth-values can be denoted using the reserved literals `true` or `false`.

Character Literals

A character literal is quoted in single-quotes (`'`).

All characters are represented by 16-bit Unicode. The Unicode character set subsumes the 8-bit ISO-Latin-1 and the 7-bit ASCII characters. In Table 2.7, note that digits (`1` to `9`), upper-case letters (`A` to `Z`) and lower-case letters (`a` to `z`) have contiguous Unicode values.

Table 2.7 *Examples of Unicode Values*

Character Literal	Unicode value (using hexadecimal digits)	Character
`' '`	`\u0020`	Space
`'0'`	`\u0030`	0
`'1'`	`\u0031`	1
`'9'`	`\u0039`	9
`'A'`	`\u0041`	A
`'B'`	`\u0042`	B
`'Z'`	`\u005a`	Z
`'a'`	`\u0061`	a
`'b'`	`\u0062`	b
`'z'`	`\u007a`	z
`'Ñ'`	`\u0084`	Ñ
`'å'`	`\u008c`	å
`'ß'`	`\u00a7`	ß

Unicode Literals

Alternatively, a character literal can be defined by quoting the Unicode value, as shown in Table 2.8.

Table 2.8 *Expressing Character Literals as Unicode Values*

Character Literal	Unicode Literal	Character
`' '`	`'\u0020'`	Space
`'0'`	`'\u0030'`	0
`'A'`	`'\u0041'`	A

Escape Sequences

Certain *escape sequences* define special character values as shown in Table 2.9. These escape sequences can be single-quoted to define character literals. For example, the character literals `'\t'` and `'\u0009'` are equivalent.

Table 2.9 *Escape Sequences*

Escape Sequence	Unicode Value	Character
`\b`	`\u0008`	Backspace
`\t`	`\u0009`	Horizontal tabulation
`\n`	`\u000a`	Linefeed
`\f`	`\u000c`	Form feed
`\r`	`\u000d`	Carriage return
`\'`	`\u0027`	Apostrophe-quote
`\"`	`\u0022`	Quotation mark
`\\`	`\u005c`	Backslash

String Literals

A string literal is a sequence of characters, which must be quoted in quotation marks and which must occur on a single line.

Escape sequences as well as Unicode values can appear in string literals:

```
"Here comes a tab.\t And here comes another one\u0009!"   // (1)
"What's on the menu?"                                       // (2)
"\"String literals are double-quoted.\""                    // (3)
```

In (1), the tab character is specified using the escape sequence and the Unicode value respectively. In (2), the single apostrophe need not be escaped in strings, but it would be if specified as a character literal(`'\''`). In (3), the double apostrophes in the string must be escaped. Printing these strings would give the following result:

```
Here comes a tab.    And here comes another one    !
What's on the menu?
"String literals are double-quoted."
```

White Spaces

A white space is a sequence of spaces, tabs, form feeds and line terminator characters. Line terminators can be newline, carriage return or carriage return-newline sequence in a Java source file.

A Java program is a free-format sequence of characters which is *tokenized* by the compiler, i.e. broken into a stream of tokens for further analysis. Separators and operators help to distinguish tokens, but sometimes white space has to be inserted explicitly. For example, the identifier `classRoom` will be interpreted as a single token, unless white space is inserted to distinguish the keyword `class` from the identifier `Room`.

White space aids not only in separating tokens, but also in formatting the program so that it is easy for humans to read. The compiler ignores the white spaces once the tokens are identified.

Comments

A program can be documented by inserting comments at relevant places. These comments are for documentation purposes and are ignored by the compiler.

Java provides three types of comments to document a program:

- A single-line comment
- A multiple-line comment
- A documentation (or Javadoc) comment

Regardless of the type of comment, they cannot be nested. The comment-start sequences (//, /*, /**) are not treated differently from other characters when occurring within comments.

Single-line Comment

All characters after the comment-start sequence // through to the end of the line constitute a single-line comment.

```
// This comment ends at the end of this line.
```

Multiple-line Comment

A multiple-line comment, as the name suggests, can span several lines. Such a comment starts with /* and ends with */.

```
/*  A comment
    on several
    lines.
*/
```

Documentation Comment

A documentation comment is a special-purpose comment which when placed at appropriate places in the program can be extracted and used by the `javadoc` utility to generate HTML documentation for the program. Documentation comments are usually placed in front of class, interface, method and variable definitions. Groups of special tags can be used inside a documentation comment to provide more specific information. Such a comment starts with /** and ends with */:

```
/**
 *  This class implements a gizmo
 *  @author K.A.M.
 *  @version 1.0
 */
```

For a detailed discussion of the `javadoc` utility, see Chapter 19.

Review questions

2.1 Which of the following is not a legal identifier?

Select all valid answers.

(a) `a2z`
(b) `ödipus`
(c) `52pickup`
(d) `_class`
(e) `ca$h`

2.2 Which one of these statements is correct?

Select the one right answer.

(a) `new` and `delete` are keywords in the Java language.
(b) `try`, `catch` and `thrown` are keywords in the Java language.
(c) `static`, `unsigned` and `long` are keywords in the Java language.
(d) `exit`, `class` and `while` are keywords in the Java language.
(e) `return`, `goto` and `default` are keywords in the Java language.
(f) `for`, `while` and `next` are keywords in the Java language.

2.3 Is this a complete and legal comment?

```
/* // */
```

Select the one right answer.

(a) No, the block comment (`/* ... */`) is not ended since the single-line comment (`// ...`) comments out the closing part.
(b) It is a completely valid comment. The `//` part is ignored by the compiler.
(c) This combination of comments is illegal and the compiler will reject it.

2.2 Primitive Datatypes

Figure 2.1 gives an overview of the primitive datatypes in Java.

Primitive datatypes in Java can be divided into three main categories:

- Integral types consisting of integers and characters:
  Integer datatypes are `byte`, `short`, `int` and `long`. They represent signed integers.

  The character datatype is represented by the `char` type. It represents the symbols in the Unicode character set, like letters, digits and special characters.

- Floating-point types:
  This category includes `float` and `double` datatypes. They represent fractional signed numbers.

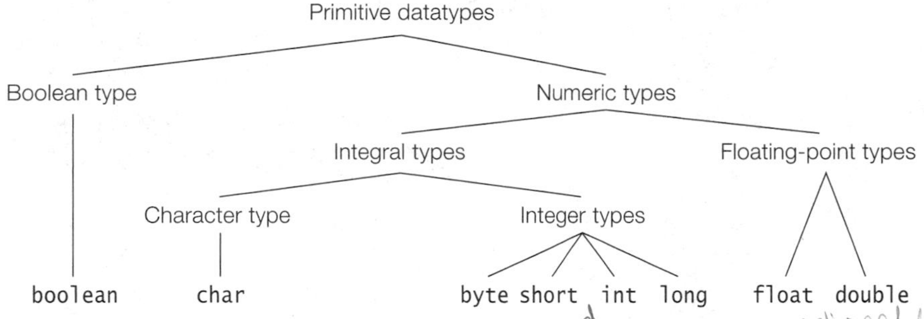

Figure 2.1 *Primitive Datatypes in Java*

- Boolean type:
  The datatype `boolean` represents truth-values `true` and `false`.

Primitive data values are *atomic* and are not objects. Each primitive datatype defines the range of values in the datatype, and operations on these values are defined by special operators in the language.

Each primitive datatype has a corresponding *wrapper* class that can be used to represent a primitive value as an object. Wrapper classes are discussed in Section 10.3.

2.3 Variable Declarations

Declaring, Initializing and Using Variables

Variables in Java come in three flavors:

- *Instance variables* that are members of a class and are instantiated for each object of the class. In other words, all instances, i.e. objects, of the class will have their own instances of these variables, which are local to the object. The values of these variables at any given time constitute the *state* of the object.
- *Static variables* that are also members of a class, but these are not instantiated for any object of the class and therefore belong only to the class (Section 4.10, p. 121).
- *Local variables* (also called *method automatic variables*), which are declared in methods and in blocks, are instantiated for each invocation of the method or block. In Java, local variables must be declared before they can be used (Section 4.8, p. 113).

A *variable* stores values of datatypes. A variable has a name, a type, a particular size and a value associated with it.

A variable declaration, in its simplest form, can be used to specify the name and the type of variables. This implicitly determines their size and the values that can be stored in them.

```
char a, b, c;              // a, b and c are character variables.
double area;               // area is a floating-point variable.
boolean flag;              // flag is a boolean variable.
```

A declaration can also include initialization code to specify an initial value for the variable:

```
int i = 10,                // i is an int variable with initial value 10.
    j = 101;               // j is an int variable with initial value 101.
long big = 2147483648L;   // big is a long variable with specified initial value.
```

In Java, variables can only store values of primitive datatypes and references to objects.

Initializers for initializing member variables in objects, classes and interfaces are discussed in Section 8.2.

Object Reference Variables

An *object reference* provides a handle for an object. References can be stored in variables.

In Java, reference variables must be declared and initialized before they can be used. A reference variable has a name and a type or class associated with it. A reference variable declaration, in its simplest form, can be used to specify the name and the type. This determines what objects a reference variable can denote.

```
Pizza yummyPizza;    // Variable yummyPizza can reference objects of class Pizza.
Hamburger bigOne,    // Variable bigOne can reference objects of class Hamburger,
          smallOne; // and so can variable smallOne.
```

It is important to note that the declarations above do not create objects of class `Pizza` or `Hamburger`. They only create variables which can store references to objects of these classes.

A declaration can also include an initializer to create an object that can be assigned to the reference variable:

```
Pizza yummyPizza = new Pizza("Hot&Spicy"); // Declaration with initializer.
```

The reference variable `yummyPizza` can reference objects of class `Pizza`. The keyword `new`, together with the *constructor call* `Pizza("Hot&Spicy")`, creates an object of class `Pizza`. The reference to this object is assigned to the variable `yummyPizza`. The newly created object of class `Pizza` can now be manipulated through the reference stored in this variable.

2.4 Integers

Table 2.10 *Range of Integer Values*

Datatype	Width (bits)	Minimum value MIN_VALUE	Maximum value MAX_VALUE
`byte`	8	-2^{7} (-128)	$2^{7}-1$ (+127)
`short`	16	-2^{15} (-32768)	$2^{15}-1$ (+32767)
`int`	32	-2^{31} (-2147483648)	$2^{31}-1$ (+2147483647)
`long`	64	-2^{63} (-9223372036854775808L)	$2^{63}-1$ (+9223372036854775807L)

Integer values are represented as signed with 2's complement (Section 3.12, p. 64).

```
int i      = -215;                  // int literal
int max    = 0x7fffffff;            // 2147483647 as hex int literal
int min    = 0x80000000;            // -2147483648 as hex int literal
long isbn  = 05402202647L;          // octal long literal
long phone = 55584152L;             // long literal
```

2.5 Characters

Table 2.11 *Range of Character Values*

Datatype	Width (bits)	Minimum Unicode value	Maximum Unicode value
`char`	16	`0x0`	`0xffff`

The `char` datatype encompasses all the 65536 (2^{16}) characters in the Unicode character set as 16-bit values. The first 128 characters of the Unicode set are the same as the 128 characters of the 7-bit ASCII character set, and the first 256 characters of the Unicode set correspond to the 256 characters of the 8-bit ISO Latin-1 character set. See Section 18.4 on page 570 for a discussion on *character encodings*.

2.6 Floating-point Numbers

Table 2.12 *Range of Floating-point Values*

Datatype	Width (bits)	Minimum value MIN_VALUE	Maximum value MAX_VALUE
`float`	32	1.40129846432481707e-45	3.40282346638528860e+38
`double`	64	4.94065645841246544e-324	1.79769313486231570e+308

Floating-point numbers conform to the IEEE 754-1985 standard. Table 2.12 shows the range of values for positive floating-point numbers, but these apply equally to negative floating-point numbers with the `'-'` sign as prefix. Zero can be either `0.0` or `-0.0`.

Since the size for representation is finite, certain floating-point numbers can only be represented as approximations.

```
float pi = 3.14159F;
double p = 314.159e-2;
double fraction = 1.0/3.0;
```

2.7 Booleans

Table 2.13 *Boolean Values*

Datatype	Width	True value/literal	False value/literal
`boolean`	not applicable	`true`	`false`

The `boolean` datatype is used to represent logical values that can be either the literal `true` or the literal `false`.

Boolean values are returned by all *relational* (Section 3.8), *conditional* (Section 3.11) and boolean logical operators (Section 3.10), and are primarily used to govern the flow of control during program execution.

Note that boolean values cannot be converted to other primitive data values, and vice versa.

2.8 Wrapper Classes

The wrapper classes for primitive datatypes are found in the `java.lang` package, and are summarized in Table 2.14. For each primitive datatype there is a corresponding wrapper class to represent the values of the primitive datatype as an object. These wrapper classes also define useful methods for manipulating both primitive data values and objects. Wrapper classes are discussed in detail in Section 10.3.

The wrapper classes for integers (`Byte`, `Short`, `Integer`, and `Long`) are subclasses of the `java.lang.Number` class, as are the wrapper classes for floating-point numbers (`Float`, `Double`).

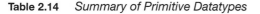

Examples of Primitive Values as Objects:

```
Integer intObj     = new Integer(2010);
Long longObj       = new Long(2030L);

Float floatObj     = new Float(3.14F);
Double doubleObj   = new Double(3.14D);

Character charObj = new Character('\t');
Boolean boolObj    = new Boolean(true);
```

Table 2.14 *Summary of Primitive Datatypes*

Datatype	Width (bits)	Minimum value, Maximum value	Wrapper Class
boolean	not applicable	true, false (no ordering)	Boolean
byte	8	-2^7, 2^7-1	Byte
short	16	-2^{15}, $2^{15}-1$	Short
char	16	0x0, 0xffff	Character
int	32	-2^{31}, $2^{31}-1$	Integer
long	64	-2^{63}, $2^{63}-1$	Long
float	32	±1.40129846432481707e-45, ±3.40282346638528860e+38	Float
double	64	±4.94065645841246544e-324, ±1.79769313486231570e+308	Double

Review questions

2.4 Which of the following does not denote a primitive data value in Java?

Select all valid answers.

(a) `"t"`
(b) `'k'`
(c) `50.5F`
(d) `"hello"`
(e) `false`

2.5 Which of the following lines are valid declarations?

Select all valid answers.

(a) `char a = '\u0061';`
(b) `char \u0061 = 'a';`
(c) `ch\u0061r a = 'a';`

2.6 Which integral type in Java has the exact range from `-2147483648` (-2^{31}) to `2147483647` ($2^{31}-1$), inclusive?

Select the one right answer.

(a) Type `byte`
(b) Type `short`
(c) Type `int`
(d) Type `long`
(e) Type `char`

2.9 Initial Values for Variables

Default Values for Member Variables

Default values for primitive datatypes are listed in Table 2.15.

Table 2.15 *Default Values*

Datatype	Default value
boolean	false
`char`	`'\u0000'`
Integer (`byte`, `short`, `int`, `long`)	`0`
Floating-point (`float`, `double`)	`+0.0F or +0.0D`
Object reference	`null`

Static variables in a class are initialized to default values when the class is loaded, if they are not explicitly initialized.

Instance variables are also initialized to default values when the class is instantiated, if they are not explicitly initialized.

Note that a reference variable is initialized with the value `null`.

Example 2.1 *Default Values for Member Variables*

```
class Light {
    // Static variable
    static int counter;      // Default value 0 when class is loaded.

    // Instance variables
    int noOfWatts = 100;     // Explicitly set to 100.
    boolean indicator;       // Implicitly set to default value false.
    String location;         // Implicitly set to default value null.
```

```
        public static void main(String args[]) {
            Light bulb = new Light();
            System.out.println("Static member counter: " + Light.counter);
            System.out.println("Instance member noOfWatts: " + bulb.noOfWatts);
            System.out.println("Instance member indicator: " + bulb.indicator);
            System.out.println("Instance member location: " + bulb.location);
        }
    }
```

Output from the program:

```
Static member counter: 0
Instance member noOfWatts: 100
Instance member indicator: false
Instance member location: null
```

Example 2.1 illustrates default initialization of member variables. Note that static variables are initialized when the class is loaded the first time, and instance variables are initialized accordingly in *every* object created from the class `Light`.

Initializing Local Variables of Primitive Datatypes

Local variables are *not* initialized when they are instantiated at method invocation. The compiler `javac` reports use of uninitialized local variables.

Example 2.2 *Flagging Uninitialized Local Variables of Primitive Datatypes*

```
public class TooSmartClass {
    public static void main(String args[]) {
        int weight = 10, thePrice;                          // local variables

        if (weight < 10) thePrice = 100;
        if (weight > 50) thePrice = 5000;
        if (weight >= 10) thePrice = weight*10;             // Always executed.

        System.out.println("The price is: " + thePrice);    // (1)
    }
}
```

In Example 2.2, the compiler complains that the local variable `thePrice` in the `println` statement at (1) may not be initialized. However, from the program it can be seen that the local variable `thePrice` gets the value `100` in the last `if`-statement before it is used in the `println` statement. The compiler does not perform a rigorous analysis of the program in this regard. The program will compile correctly if the variable was initialized in the declaration, or if an unconditional assignment is made to the variable in the method.

Initializing Local Reference Variables

Note that the same initialization rules that apply to local variables of primitive datatypes also apply to local reference variables.

Example 2.3 *Flagging Uninitialized Local Reference Variables*

```
public class VerySmartClass {
    public static void main(String args[]) {
        String oneLongString;        // local reference variable

        System.out.println("The string length is: " + oneLongString.length());
    }
}
```

In Example 2.3, the compiler complains that the local variable `oneLongString` in the `println` statement may not be initialized. Objects should be created and their state initialized appropriately (for example, in a constructor) before use. If the variable `oneLongString` is set to the value `null`, the program will compile. However, at runtime, a `NullPointerException` will be thrown since the variable `oneLongString` will not reference any object. The golden rule is to ensure that a reference variable denotes an object before invoking methods via the reference, i.e. it is not `null`.

Arrays and their default values are discussed in Section 4.1 on page 88.

Review questions

2.7 Given the following code, which statement is true?

```
int a, b;
b = 5;
```

Select the one right answer.

(a) Variable `a` is not declared.
(b) Variable `b` is not declared.
(c) Variable `a` is declared but not initialized.
(d) Variable `b` is declared but not initialized.
(e) Variable `b` is initialized but not declared.

2.8 In which of these variable declarations will the variable remain uninitialized unless explicitly initialized?

Select all valid answers.

(a) Declaration of an instance variable of type `int`.
(b) Declaration of a static class variable of type `float`.
(c) Declaration of a local variable of type `float`.
(d) Declaration of a static class variable of type `Object`.
(e) Declaration of an instance variable of type `int[]`.

2.10 Java Source File Structure

A Java source file has the following elements, specified in the following order.

1. An optional `package` definition to specify a package name. The classes and interfaces defined in the file will belong to this package. If omitted, the definitions will belong to the *default package*. Packages are discussed in Section 4.5.
2. Zero or more `import` statements. The `import` statement is discussed in Section 4.5 on page 107.
3. Any number of class and interface definitions. Technically a source file need not have any such definitions, but that is hardly useful. The classes and interfaces can be defined in any order. Note that JDK imposes the restriction that only one `public` class definition per source file can be defined, and it requires that the file name match this `public` class. If the `public` class name is `NewApp` then the file name must be `NewApp.java`. Classes are discussed in Section 4.2, and interfaces are discussed in Section 6.4.

The above structure is depicted by a skeletal source file in Figure 2.2.

```
// Filename: NewApp.java

// PART 1: (OPTIONAL)
// Package name
package com.company.project.fragilePackage;

// PART 2: (ZERO OR MORE)
// Packages used
import java.util.*;
import java.io.*;

// PART 3: (ZERO OR MORE)
// Definitions of classes and interfaces (in any order)
public class NewApp { }
class C1 { }
interface I1 { }
// ...
class Cn { }
interface Im { }
// end of file
```

Figure 2.2 *Java Source File Structure*

Review questions

2.9 What will be the result of attempting to compile this class?

```
import java.util.*;

package com.acme.toolkit;

public class AClass {
    public Other anInstance;
}

class Other {
    int value;
}
```

Select the one right answer.

(a) The class will fail to compile, since the class `Other` has not yet been declared when referenced in class `AClass`.
(b) The class will fail to compile, since `import` statements must never be at the very top of a file.
(c) The class will fail to compile, since the `package` declaration can never occur after an `import` statement.
(d) The class will fail to compile, since the class `Other` must be defined in a file called `Other.java`.
(e) The class will fail to compile, since the class `Other` must be declared `public`.
(f) The class will compile without errors.

2.10 Is an empty file a valid source file?

Answer yes or no.

2.11 The `main()` Method

The Java interpreter executes a method called `main` in the class specified on the command line. This is the standard way in which a standalone application is invoked. The `main()` method has the following signature:

```
public static void main(String args[])
```

The command

```
java TooSmartClass
```

results in a call to the `TooSmartClass.main()` method. Note that any class can have a `main()` method. Only the `main()` method of the class specified to the Java interpreter is executed.

The `main()` Method Modifiers

The `main()` method always has `public` accessibility so that the interpreter can call it (Section 4.9, p. 115). It is a `static` method belonging to the class (Section 4.10, p. 121). It does not return a value, i.e. it is declared `void` (Section 5.4, p. 148). It always has an array of `String` objects as its only formal parameter. This array contains any arguments passed to the program on the command line (Section 3.23, p. 82). All this adds up to the following definition of the `main()` method:

```
...
public static void main(String args[]) {
    // ...
}
...
```

The requirements above do not exclude specification of additional modifiers (Section 4.10, p. 121).

Review questions

2.11 Which of these are valid declarations of the `main()` method in order to start the execution of a Java program?

Select all valid answers.

(a) `static void main(String args[]) { /* ... */ }`
(b) `public static int main(String args[]) { /* ... */ }`
(c) `public static void main(String args) { /* ... */ }`
(d) `final static public void main(String[] arguments) { /* ... */ }`
(e) `public int main(Strings args[], int argc) { /* ... */ }`
(f) `public void main(String args[]) { /* ... */ }`

Chapter summary

The following information was included in this chapter:

- Explanation of identifiers, keywords, literals, white spaces, and comments.
- Explanation of all the primitive datatypes in Java.
- Declaration, initialization and usage of variables, including reference variables.
- Usage of default values for member variables.
- Structure of a Java source file.
- Declaration of `main()` method.

Programming exercises

2.1 The following program has several errors. Modify it so that it will compile and run without errors.

```
import java.util.*;

package com.acme;

public class Exercise1 {
    int counter;

    void main(String args[]) {
        Exercise1 instance = new Exercise1();
        instance.go();
    }

    public void go() {
        int sum;
        int i = 0;
        while (i<100) {
            if (i == 0) sum = 100;
            sum = sum + i;
            i++;
        }
        System.out.println(sum);
    }
}
```

2.2 The following program has several errors. Modify it so that it will compile and run without errors.

```
// Filename: Temperature.java
PUBLIC CLASS temperature {
    PUBLIC void main(string args) {
        double fahrenheit = 62.5;
        */ Convert /*
        double celsius = f2c(fahrenheit);
        System.out.println(fahrenheit + 'F = ' + celsius + 'C');
    }

    double f2c(float fahr) {
        RETURN (fahr - 32) * 5 / 9;
    }
}
```

Operators and Assignments 3

Exam Objectives

- Determine the result of applying any operator, including assignment operators and the `instanceof` operator, to operands of any type, class, scope or accessibility, or any combination of these.
  - *See Section 6.5.*
- Determine the result of applying the boolean `equals(Object)` method to objects of any combination of the classes `java.lang.String`, `java.lang.Boolean` and `java.lang.Object`.
- In an expression involving the operators `&`, `|`, `&&`, `||` and variables of known values, state which operands are evaluated and the value of the expression.
- Determine the effect upon objects and primitive values of passing variables into methods and performing assignments or other modifying operations in that method.

Supplementary Objectives

- Understand the operator precedence and associativity rules.
- Distinguish between conversions involving casting, widening numeric conversions and narrowing numeric conversions.
- State unary numeric promotion and binary numeric promotion rules, and the contexts in which they are applied.
- Understand type conversions for primitive datatypes on assignment, string concatenation, arithmetic expression evaluation and method invocation.
- Understand how signed and unsigned integer numbers are represented using 2's complement.

3.1 Precedence and Associativity Rules for Operators

Precedence and associativity rules are necessary for deterministic evaluation of expressions. The operators, together with their precedence and associativity, are summarized in Table 3.1. They are discussed in subsequent sections in this chapter.

The following remarks apply to Table 3.1:

- The operators are shown with decreasing precedence from the top of the table.
- Operators within the same row have the same precedence.
- Parentheses, `()`, can be used to override precedence and associativity.
- The unary postfix operators and all binary operators, except for the assignment operators, associate from left to right.
- All unary operators (except for unary postfix operators), all assignment operators, and the ternary conditional operator (including object creation and cast) associate from right to left.

Table 3.1 *Operator Precedence and Associativity*

Postfix Operators	`[] . (parameters) expression++ expression--`
Prefix Unary Operators	`++expression --expression +expression -expression ~ !`
Object creation and cast	`new (type)`
Multiplication	`* / %`
Addition	`+ -`
Shift	`<< >> >>>`
Relational Operators	`< <= > >= instanceof`
Equality Operators	`== !=`
bitwise/boolean AND	`&`
bitwise/boolean XOR	`^`
bitwise/boolean OR	`|`
logical AND	`&&`
logical OR	`||`
Conditional Operator	`?:`
Assignment	`= += -= *= /= %= <<= >>= >>>= &= ^= |=`

Precedence rules are used to determine which operator should be applied first if there are two operators with different precedence, and these follow each other in the expression. In such a case, the operator with the highest precedence is applied first.

`2 + 3 * 4` is evaluated as `2 + (3 * 4)` (with the result 14) since `*` has higher precedence than `+`.

Associativity rules are used to determine which operator should be applied first if there are two operators with same precedence, and these follow each other in the expression.

Left associativity implies grouping from left to right:

`1 + 2 - 3` is interpreted as `((1 + 2) - 3)` since the binary operators `+` and `-` both have same precedence and left associativity.

Right associativity implies grouping from right to left:

`- - 4` is interpreted as `(- (- 4))` (with result `4`) since the unary operator `-` has right associativity.

3.2 Conversions

Casting

Java, being a *strongly typed* language, checks for *type compatibility* (i.e. if a type can substitute for another type in a given context) at compile time. However, some checks are only possible at runtime (for example, which type of object a reference actually denotes at runtime), and cases where an operator would have incompatible operands (for example, assigning a `double` to an `int`). In those cases, Java demands that a *cast* be used to explicitly indicate the type conversion. The cast construct has the following syntax:

(<*type*>) <*expression*>

At runtime, a cast results in a new value of <*type*>, which best represents the value of the <*expression*> in the old type. Casting can be applied to primitive values as well as references. Of course, casting between primitive datatypes and reference types is not permitted.

Boolean values cannot be cast to other data values, and vice versa. The same applies to the reference literal `null`, which is not of any type and therefore cannot be cast to any type.

Type conversions involving casts are called *explicit conversions*. In certain contexts, the compiler performs *implicit conversions*, for example when a `char` is assigned to an `int`. Contexts under which conversions occur are mentioned at the end of this section.

Narrowing and Widening Conversions

For the primitive datatypes, a value of a *narrower* datatype can be converted to a value of a *broader* datatype without loss of information. This is called a *widening primitive conversion*. Widening conversions to the next broader type for primitive datatypes are summarized in Figure 3.1. The conversions shown are transitive. For

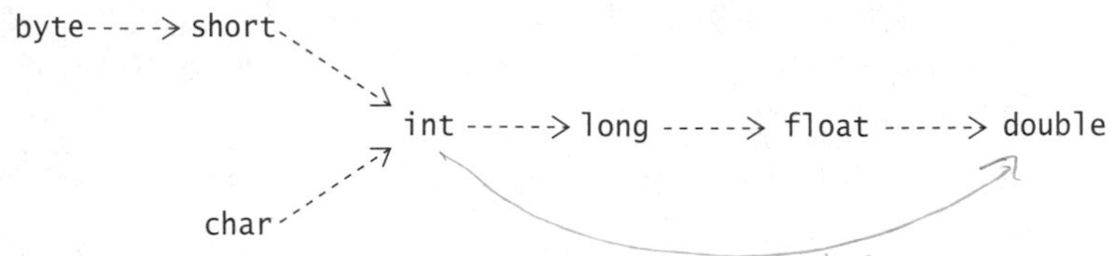

Figure 3.1 *Widening Conversions*

example, an `int` can be directly converted to a `double` without first having to convert it to a `long` and a `float`.

Converting from a broader datatype to a narrower datatype is called a *narrowing primitive conversion*, which can result in loss of information. In fact, any conversion which is not a widening conversion according to Figure 3.1 is a narrowing conversion. Note that all conversions between `char` and the two integer types `byte` and `short` are narrowing conversions.

Widening reference conversions and *narrowing reference conversions* are defined for reference types, and are discussed in Section 6.5. Conversions "up" the *inheritance hierarchy* are called *upcasting*. Conversions "down" the inheritance hierarchy are called *downcasting*, which are narrowing reference conversions.

Both narrowing and widening conversions can be either explicit (i.e. requiring a cast) or implicit.

Numeric Promotions

Numeric operators only allow operands of certain types. Numeric promotion is implicitly applied on the operands to convert them to permissible types. Distinction is made between unary and binary numeric promotion.

Unary Numeric Promotion

Unary numeric promotion states that:

> If the single operand of the operator has a type narrower than `int`, it is converted to `int` by an implicit widening primitive conversion, otherwise it is not converted.

In other words, unary numeric promotion converts operands of `byte`, `short` and `char` to `int` by applying an implicit widening conversion, but operands of other numeric types are not affected.

Unary numeric promotion is applied in the following contexts:

- Operand of the unary arithmetic operators `+` and `-` (Section 3.4, p. 49).
- Operand of the unary integer bitwise complement operator `~` (Section 3.13, p. 66).

- During array creation, for example `new int[20]`, where the dimension expression must evaluate to an `int` value (Section 4.1, p. 88).
- Indexing array elements, for example `table['a']`, where the index expression must evaluate to an `int` value (Section 4.1, p. 89).
- Individual operands of the shift operators `<<`, `>>` and `>>>` (Section 3.14, p. 68).

Binary Numeric Promotion

Binary numeric promotion implicitly applies appropriate widening primitive conversions so that a pair of operands have the broadest numeric type of the two, but which is always at least `int`. Given `T` to be the broadest numeric type of the two operands, the operands are promoted as follows under binary numeric promotion:

> If `T` is broader than `int`, both operands are converted to `T`, otherwise both operands are converted to `int`.

This means that `byte`, `short`, `char` are always converted to at least `int`.

Binary numeric promotion is applied in the following contexts:

- Operands of the arithmetic operators `*`, `/`, `%`, `+` and `-` (Section 3.4, p. 49).
- Operands of the relational operators `<`, `<=`, `>` and `>=` (Section 3.8, p. 58).
- Operands of the numerical equality operators `==` and `!=` (Section 3.9, p. 59).
- Operands of the integer bitwise operators `&`, `^` and `|` (Section 3.13, p. 66).

Type Conversion Contexts

Type conversions occur in the following contexts:

- *Assignments* involving primitive datatypes (Section 3.3, p. 47) and reference types (Section 6.5, p. 201).
- *Method invocation* involving parameters of primitive datatypes (Section 3.17, p. 74) and reference types (Section 6.5, p. 201).
- *Arithmetic expression evaluation* involving numeric types (Section 3.4, p. 51).
- *String concatenation* involving objects of class `String` and other datatypes (Section 3.5, p. 54).

3.3 Simple Assignment Operator =

The assignment statement has the following syntax:

<variable> = *<expression>*

which can be read as "the destination, <*variable*>, gets the value of the source, <*expression*>". The assignment operator = writes over the previous value of the destination variable.

The destination <*variable*> and the source <*expression*> must be type compatible. The destination variable must also have been declared. Since variables can store either primitive data values or object references, <*expression*> evaluates to either a primitive data value or an object reference.

Assigning Primitive Values

The following simple examples illustrate assignment of primitive values:

```
int j, k;
j = 10;           // j gets the value 10.
j = 5;            // j gets the value 5. Previous value is overwritten.
k = j;            // k gets the value 5.
```

The assignment operator has the lowest precedence, allowing the expression on the right-hand side to be evaluated before assignment.

```
int i;
i = 5;            // i gets the value 5.
i = i + 1;        // i gets the value 6. + has higher precedence than =.
i = 20 - i * 2;   // i gets the value 8: (20 - (i * 2))
```

Assigning References

Copying references by assignment creates aliases, which is discussed in Section 1.3 on page 5. The following example recapitulates that discussion:

```
Pizza pizza1 = new Pizza("Hot&Spicy");
Pizza pizza2 = new Pizza("Sweet&Sour");

pizza2 = pizza1;
```

Variable `pizza1` is a reference to a pizza which is hot and spicy, and `pizza2` is a reference to a pizza which is sweet and sour. Assigning `pizza1` to `pizza2` means that now `pizza2` references the same pizza as `pizza1`, i.e. the hot and spicy one. After assignment these references are aliases, and either one can be used to manipulate the hot and spicy `Pizza` object. Assigning references does not copy the *state* of the source object on the right-hand side, only the reference value.

Multiple Assignments

Application of the binary assignment operator returns the value of the expression on the right-hand side as a result of applying the operator.

```
int j, k;
j = 10;           // j gets the value 10 which is returned
k = j;            // k gets the value of j which is 10 which is returned
```

The last two assignments can be written as multiple assignments, illustrating the right associativity of the assignment operator:

```
k = j = 10;         // (k = (j = 10))
```

Multiple assignments are equally valid with references:

```
Pizza pizzaOne, pizzaTwo;
pizzaOne = pizzaTwo = new Pizza("Supreme"); // Aliases.
```

Numeric Type Conversions on Assignment

If the destination and the source are of the same type in an assignment, then obviously the source and the destination are type compatible, and there is no type conversion of the value of the source type. Otherwise, if a widening primitive conversion is permissible, then the widening conversion is applied implicitly, i.e. the source type is promoted to the destination type in an assignment context.

```
// Implicit Widening Primitive Conversions
int small = 1234;
long big = 2000;              // Implicit widening: int to long.
double large = big;           // Implicit widening: long to double.
```

Integer values widened to floating-point values can result in loss of *precision*. *Magnitude* (i.e. how big a value can be represented) must not be confused with *precision* (i.e. significant digits in the number). In the example below, the precision of the least significant bits of the `long` value may be lost when converting to a `float` value:

```
long bigInteger = 98765432112345678L;
float realNo = bigInteger;  // Widening but loss of precision
```

Additionally, implicit narrowing primitive conversions on assignment can occur in cases where the source is an `int` constant expression whose value can be determined to be in the range of the destination type at compile time; the destination type is either `byte`, `short` or `char` type.

```
// Narrowing Primitive Conversions involving int literals
short s = 10;             // int value in range. No cast required.
byte tiny = (byte) 128;   // int value not in range. Cast required.
char symbol = 32;         // int value in range. No cast required.

// Narrowing Primitive Conversions involving int variables
int i = -20;
final int j = 20;
final int k = i;
byte b1 = j;              // final value of j in range. No cast required.
byte b2 = (byte) i;       // Value of i not determinable. Cast required.
byte b3 = (byte) k;       // final value of k not determinable. Cast required.
```

All other narrowing primitive conversions will produce a compile error on assignment, and will explicitly require a cast. Floating-point values are truncated when converted to integral values.

```
// Explicit Narrowing Primitive Conversions
float fast = (float) 100.5D;    // Narrowing: double to float.
int slow = (int) fast;          // Narrowing: float to int. Value truncated.
byte crawl = (byte) slow;       // Narrowing: int to byte. Value truncated.
char c2 = (char) 3.14F;         // Narrowing: float to char. Value truncated.
```

Narrowing conversions between `char` and `byte` (or `short`) values on assignment always require an explicit cast, even if the value is in the range of the destination datatype.

```
short val = (short) 'a';    // Value in range of short but explicit cast required.
byte b = 32;                // int to byte, constant in range. No cast required.
char c = (char) b;          // byte to char but explicit cast required.
```

The above discussion on numeric assignment conversions also applies to numeric parameter values at method invocation (Section 3.18, p. 76), except for the implicit narrowing conversions mentioned above, which also require a cast.

Review questions

3.1 Given `char c = 'A';`

What is the easiest way to convert the character value in `c` into an `int`?

Select the one right answer.

(a) `int i = c;`
(b) `int i = (int) c;`
(c) `int i = Character.getNumericValue(c);`
(d) `int i = (Integer.valueOf(c.toString())).intValue();`
(e) `int i = Integer.parseInt(c.toString());`

3.2 What will be the result of attempting to compile and run the following class?

```
public class Assignment {
    public static void main(String args[]) {
        int a, b, c;
        b = 10;
        a = b = c = 20;
        System.out.println(a);
    }
}
```

Select the one right answer.

(a) The code will fail to compile, since the compiler will recognize that the variable `c` in the assignment "`a = b = c = 20;`" has not been initialized.
(b) The code will fail to compile because the assignment "`a = b = c = 20;`" is illegal.
(c) The code will compile correctly and will display "`10`" when run.
(d) The code will compile correctly and will display "`20`" when run.

3.3 What will be the result of attempting to compile and run the following program?

```
public class MyClass {
    public static void main(String args[]) {
        String a, b, c;
        c = new String("mouse");
        a = new String("cat");
        b = a;
        a = new String("dog");
        c = b;

        System.out.println(c);
    }
}
```

Select the one right answer.

(a) The program will fail to compile.
(b) The program will print "mouse" when run.
(c) The program will print "cat" when run.
(d) The program will print "dog" when run.
(e) The program will randomly print either "cat" or "dog" when run.

3.4 Arithmetic Operators: *, /, %, +, -

Arithmetic Operator Precedence and Associativity

Table 3.2 *Arithmetic Operators*

Unary	+ *Addition*	- *Subtraction*	
Binary	* *Multiplication*	/ *Division*	% *Modulus*
	+ *Addition*	- *Subtraction*	

The arithmetic operators are used to construct mathematical expressions as in algebra. The operands are of numeric type. The binary operator + also acts as *string concatenation* if one of the operands is a string (Section 3.5, p. 54).

In Table 3.2, the precedence of the operators is in decreasing order, starting from the top row, which has the highest precedence. For example, unary subtraction has higher precedence than multiplication. The operators in the same row have the same precedence. For example, binary multiplication, division and modulus operators have the same precedence.

The associativity of the unary operators is from right to left:

```
int value = - -10;              // (-(-10))
```

Notice the blank needed to separate the unary operators, otherwise these would be interpreted as the decrement operator -- (Section 3.6, p. 54).

The associativity of the binary operators is from left to right:

```
int newVal = 10 % 4 + 3;          // ((10 % 4) + 3) which is 5

int iValue = 12 / 5;              // Integer division: 2
double dValue = 12.0 / 5.0;       // Floating-point division: 2.4
```

The modulus operator returns the remainder of the division performed on the operands. Note that the division performed is integer division if the operands have integral values, even if the result will be stored in a floating-point type.

Arithmetic Expression Evaluation

At runtime, the operands are evaluated from left to right before the operators are applied. This behavior is guaranteed in Java for arithmetic expressions. In the expression `a + b * c`, the operand `a` will always be evaluated before `b`, but the multiplication operator `*` will be applied before the addition operator `+`.

Table 3.3 *Examples of Arithmetic Expression Evaluation*

Arithmetic Expression	Evaluation	Result when printed
`3 + 2 - 1`	`((3 + 2) - 1)`	`4`
`2 + 6 * 7`	`(2 + (6 * 7))`	`44`
`-5+7- -6`	`(((-5)+7)-(-6))`	`8`
`2+4/5`	`(2+(4/5))`	`2`
`13 % 5`	`(13 % 5)`	`3`
`11.5 % 2.5`	`(11.5 % 2.5)`	`1.5`
`10 / 0`	`ArithmeticException`	
`2+4.0/5`	`(2.0+(4.0/5.0))`	`2.8`
`4.0 / 0.0`	`(4.0 / 0.0)`	`INF`
`-4.0 / 0.0`	`((-4.0) / 0.0)`	`-INF`
`0.0 / 0.0`	`(0.0 / 0.0)`	`NaN`

Notice the exception `ArithmeticException` that is thrown when attempting integer division with `0`, and the resulting values `INF` (positive infinity) and `-INF` (negative infinity) printed when attempting floating-point division with `0.0`. Both positive and negative infinity are represented by manifest constants, `POSITIVE_INFINITY` and `NEGATIVE_INFINITY`, in the wrapper classes `java.lang.Float` and `java.lang.Double`. Java also defines a not-a-number value represented by the manifest constant `NaN` in the wrapper classes `Float` and `Double`, as illustrated by the last example in Table 3.3.

Numeric Promotions in Arithmetic Expressions

Unary numeric promotion is applied to the single operand of unary arithmetic operators - and +. In other words, when a unary operator is applied to an operand of byte, short or char type, the operand is first promoted to a value of type int, with the evaluation resulting in an int value. Assigning the int result to a variable of these types requires an explicit narrowing conversion, as demonstrated by the following example where the byte operand b is promoted to an int in the expression (-b):

```
byte b = 3;           // int literal in range. Implicit narrowing.
b = (byte) -b;        // Explicit narrowing on assignment required.
```

Binary numeric promotion is applied to operands of binary arithmetic operators in Table 3.2. Its application leads to automatic type promotion for the operands. The result is of the promoted type, which is always at least type int. For the expression at (1) in Example 3.1, numeric promotions proceed as shown in Figure 3.2. Note the integer division performed in evaluating the subexpression (c / s).

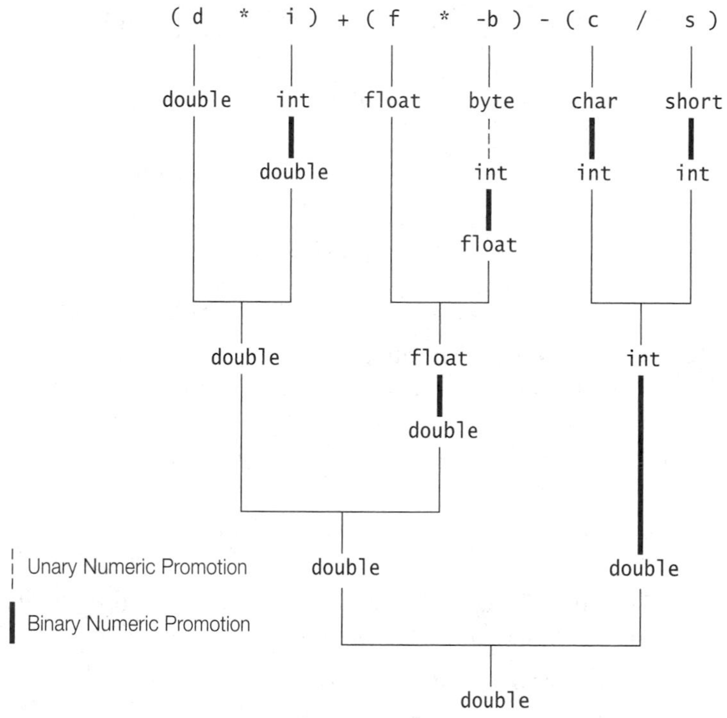

Figure 3.2 *Numeric Promotion in Arithmetic Expressions*

Example 3.1 *Numeric Promotion in Arithmetic Expressions*

```
public class NumPromotion {
    public static void main(String args[]) {
        byte b = 32;
        char c = 'z';
        short s = 256;
        int i = 10000;
        float f = 3.5F;
        double d = 0.5;
        double v = (d * i) + (f * - b) - (c / s);     // (1) 4888.0D
        System.out.println("Value of v: " + v);
    }
}
```

Output from the program:

```
Value of v: 4888.0
```

In addition to the binary numeric promotions in arithmetic expression evaluation, the resulting value can undergo an implicit widening conversion if assigned to a variable.

```
byte b = 10;
short s = 20;
char c = 'z';
int i = s * b;       // Values in s and b converted to int.
long n = 20L + s;    // Value in s converted to long.
float r = s + c;     // Values in s and c promoted to int, followed by implicit
                     // widening conversion of int to float on assignment.
double d = r + i;    // value in i promoted to float, followed by implicit
                     // widening conversion of float to double on assignment.
```

Binary numeric promotion for operands of binary operators implies that each `byte`, `short` or `char` operand of a binary operator is promoted to type `int` or broader numeric type, if necessary. As with unary operators, care must be exercised in assigning the resulting value from applying a binary operator to operands of these types:

```
short h = 40;          // OK: int converted to short
h = h + 2;             // Error: cannot assign an int to short
```

The expression `h + 2` is of type `int`. Although the result of the expression is in the range of `short`, an assignment requires an explicit cast.

```
h = (short) (h + 2);   // OK
```

Notice that applying the cast only to the `int` value `2` does not work:

```
h = h + (short) 2;     // Requires an additional cast.
```

In this case, binary numeric promotion leads to an `int` value as the result of evaluating the expression on the right-hand side, and therefore requires an additional cast to narrow it to a `short` value.

Arithmetic Extended Assignment Operators: *=, /=, %=, +=, -=

An extended assignment operator has the following syntax:

<variable> <op>= <expression>

and the following semantics:

<variable> = (*<type>*) (*<variable> <op>* (*<expression>*))

The type of the *<variable>* is *<type>* and the *<variable>* is evaluated only once. Note the cast and the parentheses implied in the semantics. Here *<op>*= can be any of the extended assignment operators specified in Table 3.1. The extended assignment operators have the lowest precedence of all the operators in Java, allowing the expression on the right-hand side to be evaluated before the assignment. Table 3.4 defines the arithmetic extended assignment operators.

Table 3.4 *Arithmetic Extended Assignment Operators*

Expression:	Given T as the numeric type of x, the expression is evaluated as:
`x *= a`	`x = (T) (x * (a))`
`x /= a`	`x = (T) (x / (a))`
`x %= a`	`x = (T) (x % (a))`
`x += a`	`x = (T) (x + (a))`
`x -= a`	`x = (T) (x - (a))`

The implied cast, `(T)`, in the extended assignments becomes necessary when the result must be narrowed to the destination type. This is illustrated by the following examples:

```
int i = 2;
i *= i + 4;             // (1) Evaluated as i = (int) (i * (i + 4)).

byte b = 2;
b += 10;                // (2) Evaluated as b = (byte) ((int) b + 10).
b = b + 10;             // (3) Will not compile. Explicit cast required.
```

At (1), the source `int` value is assigned to the destination `int` variable, and the cast in this case is an *identity conversion* (i.e. conversion from a type to the same type). Such casts are permitted. However, at (2), the source value is an `int` value because the `byte` value in `b` is promoted to `int` to carry out the addition, and assigning it to a destination `byte` variable requires an implicit narrowing conversion. The situation at (3) with simple assignment will not compile, because implicit narrowing is not applicable.

Implicit narrowing conversions are also applied for increment and decrement operators (Section 3.6, p. 54).

Other extended assignment operators include boolean logical (Section 3.10, p. 62), bitwise (Section 3.13, p. 67) and shift (Section 3.14, p. 71) operators.

3.5 The Binary String Concatenation Operator +

The binary operator + is overloaded in the sense that the operation performed is determined by the type of the operands. When one of the operands is a `String` object, the other operand is implicitly converted to its string representation and string concatenation is performed. For a numeric operand, its value is converted to a `String` object with the string representation of the value. Values like `true`, `false` and `null` are represented by string representations of these words. For a non-`String` object as operand, its string representation is constructed by applying the method `toString()` to the object. The result of the concatenation is always a new `String` object. Discussion of the `toString()` method can be found in Section 10.2. The `String` class is discussed in Section 10.5.

```
String trademark = "Uranium";
trademark = "Pure " + trademark;          // "Pure Uranium"
trademark = 100 + "% " + trademark;       // "100% Pure Uranium"
```

The integer literal `100` is implicitly converted to the string `"100"` before concatenation.

Note that the following statement

```
System.out.println("We put two and two together and get " + 2 + 2);
```

prints `"We put two and two together and get 22"` and not `"We put two and two together and get 4"`. The first integer literal `2` is promoted to a `String` literal `"2"` for the first concatenation, resulting in the `String` literal `"We put two and two together and get 2"`. This result is then concatenated with the `String` literal `"2"`. The whole process proceeds as follows:

```
((("We put two and two together and get ") + 2)+ 2)
```

3.6 Variable Increment and Decrement Operators: ++, --

Variable increment (`++`) and decrement (`--`) operators come in two flavors: *prefix* and *postfix*. These operators have the side-effect of changing the value of the arithmetic operand, which must evaluate to a variable.

These operators are very useful for updating variables in loops where only the side-effect of the operator is of interest.

Increment Operator ++

Prefix increment operator has the following semantics:

`++i` adds `1` to `i` first, then uses the new value of `i` as the value of the expression.

Postfix increment operator has the following semantics:

> `j++` uses the current value of `j` as the value of the expression first, then adds 1 to `j`.

Decrement Operator --

Prefix decrement operator has the following semantics:

> `--i` subtracts 1 from `i` first, then uses the new value of `i` as the value of the expression.

Postfix decrement operator has the following semantics:

> `j--` uses the current value of `j` as the value of the expression first, then subtracts 1 from `j`.

Examples of Increment and Decrement Operators

```
// Prefix order: increment operand before use.
int i = 10;
int j = ++i;           // j is 11, and so is i.
int k = j+ --i;        // (j+ (--i)). k gets the value 21 and i becomes 10.
--i;                   // Only side-effect utilized. i becomes 9.

// Postfix order: increment operand after use.
int i = 10;
int j = i++;           // j is 10, but i becomes 11.
int k = j+ i--;        // (j+ (i--)). k gets the value 21 and i becomes 10.
i++;                   // Only side-effect utilized. i becomes 11.
```

The increment and decrement operators can be applied to operands of `char`, `byte` and `short` datatypes as well. In these cases, both binary numeric promotion and an implicit narrowing conversion are performed to achieve the side-effect of modifying the value of the operand. In the example below, the `int` value of `(++b)`, i.e. 11, is assigned to `int` variable `i`. The side-effect of incrementing the value of `byte` variable `b` requires binary numeric promotion to perform `int` addition, followed by an implicit narrowing conversion of the `int` value to `byte`.

```
byte b = 10;
int i = ++b;          // i is 11, and so is b.
```

Review questions

3.4 What will be the result of attempting to compile and run the following class?

```
public class Integers {
    public static void main(String args[]) {
        System.out.println(0x10 + 10 + 010);
    }
}
```

Select the one right answer.

(a) The code won't compile. The compiler will complain about the expression `0x10 + 10 + 010`.
(b) When run, the program will print "28".
(c) When run, the program will print "30".
(d) When run, the program will print "34".
(e) When run, the program will print "36".
(f) When run, the program will print "101010".

3.5 What is the value of evaluating this expression: `- -1-3 * 10 / 5-1`

Select the one right answer.

(a) –8
(b) –6
(c) 7
(d) 8
(e) 10
(f) None of the above.

3.6 Which of the following statements are true?

Select all valid answers.

(a) The result of the expression `(1 + 2 + "3")` would be the string `"33"`.
(b) The result of the expression `("1" + 2 + 3)` would be the string `"15"`.
(c) The result of the expression `(4 + 1.0f)` would be the `float` value `5.0`.
(d) The result of the expression `(10/9)` would be the `int` value `1`.
(e) The result of the expression `('a' + 1)` would be the `char` value `'b'`.

3.7 What happens when you try to compile and run the following program?

```
public class Prog1 {
    public static void main(String args[]) {
        int k = 1;
        int i = ++k + k++ + + k;
        System.out.println(i);
    }
}
```

Select the one right answer.

(a) The compiler will refuse to compile and will complain about the `"++k + k++ + + k"` expression.
(b) The program will compile and will print the value `3` when run.
(c) The program will compile and will print the value `4` when run.
(d) The program will compile and will print the value `7` when run.
(e) The program will compile and will print the value `8` when run.

3.8 Which is the first incorrect line that will cause a compile time error in the following program?

```
public class MyClass {
    public static void main(String args[]) {
        char c;
        int i;
        c = 'a'; // (1)
        i = c;   // (2)
        i++;     // (3)
        c = i;   // (4)
        c++;     // (5)
    }
}
```

Select the one right answer.

(a) The line labeled (1)
(b) The line labeled (2)
(c) The line labeled (3)
(d) The line labeled (4)
(e) The line labeled (5)
(f) None of the lines are incorrect. The program will compile just fine.

3.9 What happens when you try to compile and run the following program?

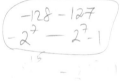

```
public class Cast {
    public static void main(String args[]) {
        byte b = -128;
        int  i = b;
        System.out.println(i);
    }
}
```

Select the one right answer.

(a) The compiler will refuse to compile it, since you cannot assign a `byte` to an `int` without a cast.
(b) The program will compile and will print `-128` when run.
(c) The compiler will refuse to compile it, since `-128` is outside the legal range of values for a `byte`.
(d) The program will compile, but will throw a `ClassCastException` when run.
(e) The program will compile and will print `255` when run.

3.10 Which of these assignments are valid?

Select all valid answers.

(a) `short s = 12;`
(b) `long l = 012;`
(c) `int other = (int) true;`
(d) `float f = -123;`
(e) `double d = 0x12345678;`

3.7 Boolean Expressions

Boolean expressions have `boolean` datatype, and can only evaluate to the values `true` or `false`.

Boolean expressions, when used as conditionals in control statements, allow the control flow in a program to be changed during execution.

Boolean expressions can be formed using *relational operators* (Section 3.8, p. 58), *equality operators* (Section 3.9, p. 59), *logical operators* (Section 3.10, p. 61), *conditional operators* (Section 3.11, p. 63) and the *assignment operator* (Section 3.3, p. 45).

3.8 Relational Operators: <, <=, >, >=

Given that `a` and `b` represent numeric expressions, the relational (also called *comparison*) operators are defined as shown in Table 3.5.

Table 3.5 *Relational Operators*

`a < b`	`a` less than `b`?
`a <= b`	`a` less than or equal to `b`?
`a > b`	`a` greater than `b`?
`a >= b`	`a` greater than or equal to `b`?

All relational operators are binary operators, and their operands are numeric expressions. Binary numeric promotion is applied to the operands of these operators. The evaluation results in a `boolean` value. Relational operators have precedence lower than arithmetic operators, but higher than that of the assignment operators.

```
double hours = 45.5;
boolean overtime = hours >= 35.0;      // true.
boolean order = 'A' < 'a';             // true. Binary numeric promotion applied.
```

Mathematical expressions like $a \le b \le c$ must be written using relational and boolean logical/conditional operators. Since relational operators have left associativity, the evaluation of the expression `a <= b <= c` at (1) in the examples below would proceed as follows: `((a <= b) <= c)`. Evaluation of `(a <= b)` would yield a `boolean` value which is not permitted as an operand of a relational operator, i.e. `(`<*boolean value*> `<= c)` would be illegal.

```
int a = 1, b = 7, c = 10;
boolean valid1 = a <= b <= c;              // (1) Illegal.
boolean valid2 = a <= b && b <= c;         // (2) OK.
```

3.9 Equality

Primitive Data Value Equality: ==, !=

Given that a and b represent operands of primitive datatypes, the primitive data value equality operators are defined as shown in Table 3.6.

Table 3.6 *Primitive Data Value Equality Operators*

`a == b`	a and b are equal? I.e. have the same primitive value? (Equality)
`a != b`	a and b are not equal? I.e. do not have the same primitive value? (Inequality)

The equality operator == and the inequality operator != can be used to compare primitive data values, including `boolean` values. Binary numeric promotion is applied to the non-boolean operands of these equality operators.

```
int year = 1998;
boolean isEven = year % 2 == 0;     // true.
boolean compare = '1' == 1;         // false. Binary numeric promotion applied.
boolean test = compare == false;    // true.
```

Care must be exercised in comparing floating-point numbers for equality, as certain values can only be stored as approximations in a finite number of bits. For example, the expression `(1.0 - 2.0/3.0 == 1.0/3.0)` returns `false`, although mathematically the result should be true.

Analogous to the discussion for relational operators, mathematical expressions like $a = b = c$ must be written using relational and logical/conditional operators. Since equality operators have left associativity, the evaluation of the expression `a == b == c` would proceed as follows: `((a == b) == c)`. Evaluation of `(a == b)` would yield a `boolean` value which *is* permitted as an operand of a data value equality operator, but `(`*<boolean value>* `== c)` would be illegal if c had a numeric type. This is illustrated in the examples below. The expression at (1) is illegal, but those at (2) and (3) are legal.

```
int a, b, c;
a = b = c = 5;
boolean valid1 = a == b == c;          // (1) Illegal.
boolean valid2 = a == b && b == c;     // (2) OK.
boolean valid3 = a == b == true;       // (3) Legal.
```

Object Reference Equality: ==, !=

Given that r and s are reference variables, the reference equality operators are defined as shown in Table 3.7.

The equality operator == and the inequality operator != can be applied to object references to test if they denote the same object. The operands must be type

Table 3.7 *Reference Equality Operators*

`r == s`	r and s are equal? I.e. have the same reference value? (Equality)
`r != s`	r and s are not equal? I.e. do not have the same reference value? (Inequality)

compatible: it must be possible to cast one into the other's type, otherwise it is a compile time error. Type compatibility of references is discussed in Section 6.5.

```
Pizza pizza_A = new Pizza("Sweet&Sour");        // new object
Pizza pizza_B = new Pizza("Sweet&Sour");        // new object
Pizza pizza_C = new Pizza("Hot&Spicy");         // new object

String banner = "Come and get it!";             // new object

boolean test = banner == pizza_A;               // Compile time error.
boolean test1 = pizza_A == pizza_B;             // false
boolean test2 = pizza_A == pizza_C;             // false

pizza_A = pizza_B;                              // Denote the same object
boolean test3 = pizza_A == pizza_B;             // true
```

The comparison `banner == pizza_A` is illegal because `String` and `Pizza` types are not compatible. The values of `test1` and `test2` are `false`, because the three references denote different objects, regardless of the fact that `pizza_A` and `pizza_B` are both sweet and sour pizzas. The value of `test3` is `true`, because now both `pizza_A` and `pizza_B` denote the same object.

The equality and inequality operators are applied to object references to check whether two references denote the same object or not. The state of the objects that the references denote is not compared. This is the same as testing whether the references are aliases, i.e. denoting the same object.

The `null` reference can be assigned to any object reference, and an object reference can be compared for equality with the `null` reference.

```
boolean validObjRef = objRef != null;
```

Object Value Equality

The `Object` class provides the boolean method `equals(Object obj)` which can be *overridden* (Section 6.2, p. 179) to give the right semantics of *object value equality*. The default implementation in the `Object` class returns true only if the object is compared to itself, i.e. as if the equality operator == had been used. This means that if a class does not change the semantics of the `equals()` method in the `Object` class, then object value equality is the same as object reference equality.

Certain classes in the standard API override the `equals()` method, for example `String`, `BitSet`, `Date`, `File` and wrapper classes for the primitive datatypes. For `String` objects, they are equal if they contain the same character sequence. For the wrapper classes, value equality means that the primitive values in the two wrapper objects are equal.

```
// Equality for String objects means same character string
String movie1 = "The Revenge of the Exception Handler";
String movie2 = "High Noon at the Java Corral";
String movie3 = "The Revenge of the Exception Handler";
boolean test0 = movie1.equals(movie2);             // false
boolean test1 = movie1.equals(movie3);             // true

// Equality for Boolean objects means same primitive value
Boolean flag1 = new Boolean(true);
Boolean flag2 = new Boolean(true);
boolean test2 = flag1.equals(flag2);               // true

// Pizza class does not override the equals() method,
// can use either equals (inherited from Object) or ==.
Pizza pizza1 = new Pizza("VeggiesDelight");
Pizza pizza2 = new Pizza("VeggiesDelight");
Pizza pizza3 = new Pizza("CheeseDelight");
boolean test3 = pizza1.equals(pizza2);             // false
boolean test4 = pizza1.equals(pizza3);             // false
boolean test5 = pizza1 == pizza2;                  // false
```

3.10 Boolean Logical Operators: !, ^, &, |

Boolean logical operators can be applied to `boolean` operands, returning a `boolean` value. The operators ^, & and | can also be applied to integral operands to perform *bitwise* logical operations (Section 3.13, p. 66).

Given that x and y represent boolean expressions, the boolean logical operators are defined in Table 3.8.

Table 3.8 *Boolean Logical Operators*

Boolean NOT (NEGATION)	!x	Returns the complement of the truth-value of x.
Boolean AND	x & y	`true` if both operands are true, otherwise `false`.
Boolean OR	x | y	`true` if either or both operands are true, otherwise `false`.
Boolean XOR	x ^ y	`true` if and only if one operand is true, otherwise `false`.

All boolean operators are binary, except for the negation operator. Their operands are all boolean expressions. Their evaluation results in a `boolean` value. These operators always evaluate both the operands, unlike their counterpart conditional operators '&&' and '||' (Section 3.11, p. 63). Truth-values for boolean operators are shown in Table 3.9. Note that the boolean operators '&' and '|' have the same truth-values as their counterpart conditional operators '&&' and '||' respectively.

Table 3.9 *Truth-values for Boolean Logical Operators*

x	y	!x	x & y	x | y	x ^ y
true	true	false	true	true	false
true	false	false	false	true	true
false	true	true	false	true	true
false	false	true	false	false	false

Operand Evaluation for Boolean Logical Operators

In evaluation of boolean expressions involving boolean logical AND, XOR and OR operators, both the operands are evaluated:

```
if (i > 0 & i++ < 10) {/*...*/} // i will be incremented, regardless of value in i.
```

The binary boolean logical operators have precedence lower than arithmetic operators, but higher than assignment, conditional AND and OR operators (Section 3.11, p. 63). This is illustrated in the following examples:

```
boolean b1, b2, b3 = false, b4 = false;
b1 = (4 == 2) & (1 < 4);        // false
b2 = b1 | !(2.5 >= 8);          // true
b3 = b3 ^ b2;                   // true
b4 = b4 | b1 & b2;              // false
```

Order of evaluation is illustrated by the following example:

```
   (b4 | (b1 & b2))
⇒ (false | (b1 & b2))
⇒ (false | (false & b2))
⇒ (false | (false & true))
⇒ (false | false)
⇒ (false)
```

Note that b2 was evaluated although, strictly speaking, it was not necessary. This behavior is guaranteed for boolean logical operators.

Boolean Logical Extended Assignment Operators: &=, ^=, |=

Extended assignment operators for the boolean logical operators are defined in Table 3.10. The left-hand operand must be a boolean variable, and the right-hand operand must be a boolean expression. An identity cast is applied implicitly on assignment. These operators can also be applied to integral operands to perform *bitwise* extended assignments (Section 3.13, p. 67).

Table 3.10 *Boolean Logical Extended Assignment Operators*

<table>
<tr><th>Expression:</th><th>Given <code>b</code> and <code>a</code> are of type <code>boolean</code>, the expression is evaluated as:</th></tr>
<tr><td><code>b &= a</code></td><td><code>b = (b & (a))</code></td></tr>
<tr><td><code>b ^= a</code></td><td><code>b = (b ^ (a))</code></td></tr>
<tr><td><code>b |= a</code></td><td><code>b = (b | (a))</code></td></tr>
</table>

Examples of Boolean Logical Extended Assignment:

```
boolean b1 = false, b2 = false, b3 = false;
b1 |= true;                    // true
b2 ^= b1;                      // true
b3 &= b1 | b2;                 // (1) false. b3 = (b3 & (b1 | b2)).
b3 = b3 & b1 | b2;             // (2) true.  b3 = ((b3 & b1) | b2).
```

It is instructive to note how the assignments at (1) and (2) above are performed, giving different results for the same value of the operands.

3.11 Conditional Operators: &&, ||

Conditional operators are much like boolean logical operators, except that their evaluation is *short-circuited*. Given that `x` and `y` represent values of `boolean` expressions, the *conditional operators* are defined in Table 3.11.

Table 3.11 *Conditional Operators*

<table>
<tr><td>Conditional AND</td><td><code>x && y</code></td><td><code>true</code> if both operands are true, otherwise <code>false</code>.</td></tr>
<tr><td>Conditional OR</td><td><code>x || y</code></td><td><code>true</code> if either or both operands are true, otherwise <code>false</code>.</td></tr>
</table>

Both the conditional operators are binary operators. Contrary to their logical counterparts `&` and `|`, the conditional operators `&&` and `||` can only be applied to `boolean` expressions. Their evaluation results in a `boolean` value. Truth-values for conditional operators are shown in Table 3.12. Not surprisingly, they have the same truth-values as their counterpart logical operators.

Table 3.12 *Truth-values for Conditional Operators*

<table>
<tr><th>x</th><th>y</th><th>x && y</th><th>x || y</th></tr>
<tr><td><code>true</code></td><td><code>true</code></td><td><code>true</code></td><td><code>true</code></td></tr>
<tr><td><code>true</code></td><td><code>false</code></td><td><code>false</code></td><td><code>true</code></td></tr>
<tr><td><code>false</code></td><td><code>true</code></td><td><code>false</code></td><td><code>true</code></td></tr>
<tr><td><code>false</code></td><td><code>false</code></td><td><code>false</code></td><td><code>false</code></td></tr>
</table>

Note that there are no extended assignment operators for the conditional operators.

Short-circuit Evaluation

In evaluation of boolean expressions involving conditional AND and OR, the left operand is evaluated before the right one, and the evaluation is short-circuited, i.e. if the result of the boolean expression can be determined from the left-hand operand, the right-hand operand is not evaluated.

The binary conditional operators have precedence lower than either arithmetic or relational operators, but higher than assignment operators. The following examples illustrate usage of conditional operators:

```
boolean b1 = (4 == 2) && (1 < 4);   // false
boolean b2 = (!b1) || (2.5 > 8);    // true
boolean b3 = !(b1 && b2);           // true
boolean b4 = b1 || !b3 && b2;       // false
```

Order of evaluation for computing the value of boolean variable `b4` proceeds as follows:

```
   (b1 || ((!b3) && b2))
⇒ (false || ((!b3) && b2))
⇒ (false || ((!true) && b2))
⇒ (false || ((false) && b2))
⇒ (false || false)
⇒ (false)
```

Note that `b2` is not evaluated, short-circuiting the evaluation.

3.12 Representing Integers

Integer datatypes in Java represent both positive and negative integer values. Java uses 2's complement to store integer values. For example, `byte` values (–128 to +127) are represented as shown in Table 3.13.

Bits in an integral value are usually numbered from right to left, starting with bit `0` (also called the *rightmost bit*). The number of the most significant bit (also called the leftmost bit), when applying bitwise operators, is dependent on the integral type: bit `31` for `byte`, `short`, `char` and `int`, and bit `63` for `long`. Note the representation of the negative values which have the most significant bit set to `1`. Adding `1` to the maximum `int` value `2147483647` results in the minimum value `-2147483648`, i.e. the values "wrap-around" for integers, and no over- or under-flow is indicated.

Table 3.13 *Representing Signed Integers using 2's Complement*

Decimal value	8-bit Binary representation	Hexadecimal value
127	01111111	0x7f
126	01111110	0x7e
...	...	...
41	00101001	0x29
...	...	...
2	00000010	0x02
1	00000001	0x01
0	00000000	0x0
-1	11111111	0xff
-2	11111110	0xfe
...	...	...
-41	11010111	0xd7
...	...	...
-127	10000001	0x81
-128	10000000	0x80

Converting Binary Numbers to Decimals

Binary numbers can be easily converted to their decimal equivalents:

$$
\begin{aligned}
101001 &= 1*2^5 + 0*2^4 + 1*2^3 + 0*2^2 + 0*2^1 + 1*2^0 \\
&= 32 + 0 + 8 + 0 + 0 + 1 \\
&= 41
\end{aligned}
$$

A binary number is converted to its equivalent decimal value. Each digit in the binary number contributes to the final decimal value by virtue of its position, starting with position 0 (units) for the rightmost digit in the number.

Calculating 2's Complement

Given a positive `byte` value, say `41`, then the binary representation of `-41` can be found as follows:

	Binary representation	Decimal value
Given a value:	00101001	41
Form 1's complement:	11010110	
Add 1:	00000001	
Result is 2's complement:	11010111	-41

Similarly, given a negative number, say `-41`, we can find the binary representation of `41`:

	Binary representation	Decimal value
Given a value:	`11010111`	`-41`
Form 1's complement:	`00101000`	
Add 1:	`00000001`	
Result is 2's complement:	`00101001`	`41`

As can be seen from the discussion above, the negative integers have their most significant bit set. Applying *bitwise operators* (Section 3.13) to integer numbers can thus change the value dramatically.

The above discussion on `byte` values applies equally to other integer types: `short`, `int` and `long`.

Java uses 2's complement for representation of integer values, as integer arithmetic can be performed easily using bit arithmetic on binary representation.

3.13 Integer Bitwise Operators: ~, &, |, ^

The binary bitwise operators manipulate corresponding individual bit values in the operands, which must be of the integral type. Unary numeric promotion is applied to the operand of the unary bitwise complement operator ~, and binary numeric promotion is applied to the operands of the binary bitwise operators. The result is a new integer value of the promoted type, which can only be either `int` or `long`.

Given that `A` and `B` are corresponding bit values in the left-hand and right-hand operands respectively, these bitwise operators are defined as shown in Table 3.14.

Table 3.14 *Bitwise Operators*

Operator Name	Notation	Effect on each bit of the binary representation
Bitwise NOT	`~A`	Invert the bit value. (Complement)
Bitwise AND	`A & B`	1 if both bits are 1, otherwise 0.
Bitwise OR	`A | B`	1 if either or both bits are 1, otherwise 0.
Bitwise XOR	`A ^ B`	1 if and only if one of the bits is 1, otherwise 0.

The result of applying bitwise operators between two corresponding bits in the operands is shown in Table 3.15, where `A` and `B` are corresponding bit values in left-hand and right-hand operands respectively.

Table 3.15 *Result-table for Bitwise Operators*

<table>
<tr><th>A</th><th>B</th><th>~A</th><th>A & B</th><th>A | B</th><th>A ^ B</th></tr>
<tr><td>1</td><td>1</td><td>0</td><td>1</td><td>1</td><td>0</td></tr>
<tr><td>1</td><td>0</td><td>0</td><td>0</td><td>1</td><td>1</td></tr>
<tr><td>0</td><td>1</td><td>1</td><td>0</td><td>1</td><td>1</td></tr>
<tr><td>0</td><td>0</td><td>1</td><td>0</td><td>0</td><td>0</td></tr>
</table>

Examples of Bitwise Operator Application:

```
char v1 = ')';      // 41
byte v2 = 13;
int result;

result = ~v1;       // -42
result = v1 & v2;  // 9
result = v1 | v2;  // 45
result = v1 ^ v2;  // 36
```

Table 3.16 shows how the result is calculated. Unary and binary numeric promotions are applied first, converting the operands to `int` in these cases. Note that the operator is applied to corresponding individual bits, i.e. first bit of left-hand operand and first bit of right-hand operand, then second bit of left-hand operand and second bit of right-hand operand, and so on.

Table 3.16 *Examples of Bitwise Operations*

<table>
<tr><th>~v1</th><th>v1 & v2</th><th>v1 | v2</th><th>v1 ^ v2</th></tr>
<tr><td>~ 0...0010 1001</td><td>0...0010 1001</td><td>0...0010 1001</td><td>0...0010 1001</td></tr>
<tr><td></td><td>& 0...0000 1101</td><td>| 0...0000 1101</td><td>^ 0...0000 1101</td></tr>
<tr><td>= 1...1101 0110</td><td>= 0...0000 1001</td><td>= 0...0010 1101</td><td>= 0...0010 0100</td></tr>
<tr><td>= 0xffffffd6</td><td>= 0x00000009</td><td>= 0x0000002d</td><td>= 0x00000024</td></tr>
<tr><td>= -42</td><td>= 9</td><td>= 45</td><td>= 36</td></tr>
</table>

Bitwise Extended Assignment Operators: &=, ^=, |=

Bitwise extended assignment operators for the bitwise operators are defined in Table 3.17. Type conversions for these operators, when applied to integral operands, are the same as for other extended assignment operators: an implicit narrowing conversion is performed on assignment when the destination datatype is either `byte`, `short` or `char`. These operators can also be applied to boolean operands to perform logical extended assignments (Section 3.10, p. 62).

Table 3.17 *Bitwise Extended Assignment Operators*

<table>
<tr><th>Expression:</th><th>Given T is the integral type of b, the expression is evaluated as:</th></tr>
<tr><td>b &= a</td><td>b = (T) (b & (a))</td></tr>
<tr><td>b ^= a</td><td>b = (T) (b ^ (a))</td></tr>
<tr><td>b |= a</td><td>b = (T) (b | (a))</td></tr>
</table>

Examples of Bitwise Extended Assignment:

```
int v0 = -42;
char v1 = ')';      // 41
byte v2 = 13;

v0 &= 15;           //     1...1101 0110 & 0...0000 1111 => 0...0000 0110 (= 6)
v1 |= v2;           // (1) 0...0010 1001 | 0...0000 1101 => 0...0010 1101 (= 45)
```

At (1) in the examples above, both the `byte` value in `v1` and the `char` value in `v2` are first promoted to `int`. The result is implicitly narrowed to the destination type `char` on assignment.

3.14 Shift Operators: <<, >>, >>>

The binary shift operators form a new value by shifting bits either left or right a specified number of times in a given integral value. The number of shifts (also called the *shift distance*) is given by the right-hand operand, and the value which is to be shifted by the left-hand operand. Note that *unary* numeric promotion is applied to each operand individually. The value returned has the promoted type of the left-hand operand. Also, the value of the left-hand operand is not affected by applying the shift operator. The number of bits shifted is always in the range modulus 32 for an `int` value, and in the range modulus 64 for a `long` value.

Given that `a` contains the value whose bits are to be shifted and `n` is the number of times to shift, the bitwise operators are defined in Table 3.18.

Table 3.18 *Shift Operators*

Shift left	`a << n`	Shift all bits in `a` left `n` times, filling with `0` from the right.
Shift right with sign bit	`a >> n`	Shift all bits in `a` right `n` times but filling with the sign bit from the left.
Shift right with zero fill	`a >>> n`	Shift all bits in `a` right `n` times but filling with `0` from the left.

Since `char`, `byte` and `short` operands are promoted to `int`, the result of applying these bitwise operators is always either an `int` or a `long` value. Care must be taken in employing a cast to narrow the resulting value, as this can result in loss of information as the upper bits are chopped off during conversion.

Bit values shifted out ("falling off") from bit `0` or the most significant bit are lost. Since bits can be shifted both left and right, a positive value when shifted can result in a negative value, and vice versa.

The Shift-left Operator <<

As the bits are shifted left, zeros are always filled in from the right.

```
int i = 12;
int result = i << 4;    // 192
```

The bits in the `int` value for `i` are shifted left 4 places as follows:

```
i << 4
= 0000 0000 0000 0000 0000 0000 0000 1100 << 4
= 0000 0000 0000 0000 0000 0000 1100 0000
= 0x000000c0
= 192
```

Each left-shift corresponds to multiplication of the value by 2. In the above example, $12*2^4$ is 192.

The sign bit of a `byte` or `short` value is extended to fill the higher bits when the value is promoted, as illustrated by the example below:

```
byte b = -42;           // 11010110
int result = b << 4;    // -672
```

The bits in the `byte` value for `b`, after promotion to `int`, are shifted left 4 places:

```
b << 4
= 1111 1111 1111 1111 1111 1111 1101 0110 << 4
= 1111 1111 1111 1111 1111 1101 0110 0000
= 0xfffffd60
= -672
```

In the above example, $-42*2^4$ is `-672`.

Care must also be taken when assigning the result of a shift operator to a narrower datatype.

```
byte a = 32, b;
int j;

j = a << 3;             // 256
b = (byte) (a << 3);    // 0. Cast mandatory.
```

The result of `(a << 3)` is `256`:

```
a << 3
= 0000 0000 0000 0000 0000 0000 0010 0000 << 3
= 0000 0000 0000 0000 0000 0001 0000 0000
= 0x00000100
= 256
```

The value `j` gets is `256`, but the value `b` gets is `0`, as the higher bits are discarded in the explicit narrowing conversion.

The Shift-right-with-sign-fill Operator >>

As the bits are shifted right, the sign bit (the most significant bit) is used to fill in from the left. So, if the left operand is a positive value, zeros are filled in from the left, but if the operand is a negative value, ones are filled in from the left.

```
int i = 12;
int result = i >> 2;     // 3
```

The value for `i` is shifted right with sign-fill 4 places:

```
i >> 2
= 0000 0000 0000 0000 0000 0000 0000 1100 >> 2
= 0000 0000 0000 0000 0000 0000 0000 0011
= 0x00000003
= 3
```

Each right-shift corresponds to division of the value being shifted by 2, but this can give unexpected results if care is not exercised, as bits start falling off. In the above example, $12/2^2$ is `3`.

Similarly when a negative value is shifted right, ones are filled in from the left.

```
byte b = -42;           // 11010110
int result = b >> 4;    // -3
```

The `byte` value for `b`, after promotion to `int`, is shifted right with sign-fill 4 places.

```
b >> 4
= 1111 1111 1111 1111 1111 1111 1101 0110 >> 4
= 1111 1111 1111 1111 1111 1111 1111 1101
= 0xfffffffa
= -3
```

The Shift-right-with-zero-fill Operator >>>

As the bits are shifted right, zeros are filled in from the left, regardless of whether the operand has a positive or a negative value. Obviously, for positive values, the shift-right-with-zero-fill and shift-right-with-sign-fill operators are equivalent.

```
byte b = -42;              // 11010110
int result = b >>> 4;      // 268435453
```

The `byte` value for `b`, after promotion to `int`, is shifted right with zero-fill 4 places.

```
b >>> 4
= 1111 1111 1111 1111 1111 1111 1101 0110 >>> 4
= 0000 1111 1111 1111 1111 1111 1111 1101
= 0x0ffffffd
= 268435453
```

3 bytes for sign-?

Shift Extended Assignment Operators: <<=, >>=, >>>=

Table 3.19 lists shift extended assignment operators. Type conversions for these operators, when applied to integral operands, are the same as for other extended assignment operators: an implicit narrowing conversion is performed on assignment when the destination datatype is either `byte`, `short` or `char`.

Table 3.19 *Shift Extended Assignment Operators*

Expression:	Given T as the integral type of x, the expression is evaluated as:
`x <<= a`	`x = (T) (x << (a))`
`x >>= a`	`x = (T) (x >> (a))`
`x >>>= a`	`x = (T) (x >>> (a))`

Examples of Shift Extended Assignment Operators:

```
int i = -42;
i >>= 4;                  // 1...11010110 >> 4 => 1...11111101 (= -3).

byte a = 12;
a <<= 5;                  // (1) -128. Evaluated as a = (byte)((int)a << 5)
a = a << 5;               // Compile time error. Needs explicit cast.
```

The example at (1) illustrates the truncation that takes place on narrowing to destination type. The `byte` value in `a` is first promoted to `int` (by applying unary numeric promotion in this case), and then shifted left 5 places, followed by implicit narrowing to `byte`:

```
a = (byte) (a << 5)
  = (byte) (0000 0000 0000 0000 0000 0000 0000 1100 << 5)
  = (byte)  0000 0000 0000 0000 0000 0001 1000 0000
  = 1000 0000
  = 0xc0
  = -128
```

3.15 The Conditional Operator ? :

The ternary conditional operator allows conditional expressions to be defined. The operator has the following syntax:

<condition> ? *<expression1>* : *<expression2>*

If the boolean expression *<condition>* is `true` then *<expression1>* is evaluated, otherwise *<expression2>* is evaluated. Of course, *<expression1>* and *<expression2>* must evaluate to values of compatible types. The value of the expression evaluated is returned by the conditional expression.

```
boolean leapYear = false;
int daysInFebruary = leapYear ? 29 : 28; // 28
```

The conditional operator is the expression equivalent of the `if-else` statement. The conditional expression can be nested and the conditional operator associates from right to left:

`(a?b?c?d:e:f:g)` evaluates as `(a?(b?(c?d:e):f):g)`

3.16 Other Operators: `new`, `[]`, `instanceof`

The `new` operator is used to create objects, i.e. instances of classes and arrays. It is used with a constructor to instantiate classes (Section 4.4, p. 100) and with the `[]` notation to create arrays (Section 4.1, p. 87). It is also used to instantiate anonymous arrays (Section 4.1, p. 93) and anonymous classes (Section 7.5, p. 243).

```
Pizza onePizza = new Pizza();       // Create an instance of Pizza class.
```

The `[]` notation is used to declare and construct arrays, and also to access array elements (Section 4.1, p. 87):

```
int[] anArray = new int[5];// Declare and construct an int array of 5 elements.
anArray[4] = anArray[3];   // Element at index 4 gets value of element at index 3.
```

The boolean, binary and infix operator `instanceof` is used to test an object's type (Section 6.5, p. 206).

```
Pizza myPizza = new Pizza();
boolean test1 = myPizza instanceof Pizza;  // True.
boolean test2 = "Pizza" instanceof Pizza;  // Compile error. String is not Pizza.
boolean test3 = null instanceof Pizza;     // Always false. null not an instance.
```

Review questions

3.11 What would be printed during execution of the following program?

```
public class MyClass {
    public static void main(String args[]) {
        test(1<<32, "1<<32");
        test(1<<31, "1<<31");
        test(1<<30, "1<<30");
        test(1,     "1"    );
        test(0,     "0"    );
        test(-1,    "-1"   );
    }

    public static void test(int i, String exp) {
        if ((i >> 1) != (i >>> 1)) System.out.println(exp);
    }
}
```

Select all valid answers.

(a) `"1<<32"`

(b) `"1<<31"`

(c) "1<<30"
(d) "1"
(e) "0"
(f) "-1"

3.12 Which of the following is not an operator in Java?

Select all valid answers.

(a) %
(b) <<<
(c) &
(d) %=
(e) >>>
(f) <=

3.13 Which of the following statements are true?

Select all valid answers.

(a) The modulus operator % can only be used with integer operands.
(b) Identifiers in Java are case-insensitive.
(c) The arithmetic operators *, / and % have the same level of precedence.
(d) A short value ranges from -128 to +127 inclusive.
(e) (+15) is a legal expression.

3.14 Given a variable x of type int (which may contain a negative value), which are correct ways of doubling the value of x, barring any overflow?

Select all valid answers.

(a) `x << 1;`
(b) `x = x * 2;`
(c) `x *= 2;`
(d) `x += x;`
(e) `x <<= 1;`

3.15 Given these declarations, which of the following expressions are valid?

```
byte  b = 1;
char  c = 1;
short s = 1;
int   i = 1;
```

Select all valid answers.

(a) `s = b * 2;`
(b) `i = b << s;`
(c) `b <<= s;`
(d) `c = c + b;`
(e) `s += i;`

3.16 What happens during execution of the following program?

```
public class OperandOrder {
    public static void main(String args[]) {
        int i = 0;
        int[] a = {3,6};
        a[i] = i = 9;
        System.out.println(i + " " + a[0] + " " + a[1]);
    }
}
```

Select the one right answer.

(a) Raises `ArrayIndexOutOfBoundsException`
(b) Prints "9 9 6"
(c) Prints "9 0 6"
(d) Prints "9 3 6"
(e) Prints "9 3 9"

3.17 Which statements about the output of the following program are true?

```
public class Logic {
    public static void main(String args[]) {
        int i = 0;
        int j = 0;

        boolean t = true;
        boolean r;

        r = (t &  0<(i+=1));
        r = (t && 0<(i+=2));
        r = (t |  0<(j+=1));
        r = (t || 0<(j+=2));
        System.out.println(i + " " + j);
    }
}
```

Select all valid answers.

(a) The first digit printed is 1.
(b) The first digit printed is 2.
(c) The first digit printed is 3.
(d) The second digit printed is 1.
(e) The second digit printed is 2.
(f) The second digit printed is 3.

3.17 Parameter Passing

Objects communicate by passing *messages* (Section 1.4, p. 6). A message is implemented as a *method call* to invoke a particular method on an object. Static methods can be invoked on classes in Java. Parameters in the method call provide one way of exchanging information between the caller object and the callee object (which need not be different).

The syntax of a method call can be any one of the following:

<object reference>.*<method name>* (*<actual parameter list>*)

<class name>.*<static method name>* (*<actual parameter list>*)

<method name> (*<actual parameter list>*)

The *<object reference>* must be an expression which evaluates to an object reference. If the caller and the callee are the same, then *<object reference>* can be omitted. See discussion on `this` reference in Section 4.3 on page 98. The *<class name>* can be the *fully qualified name* (Section 4.5, p. 105) of the class. The *<actual parameter list>* is *comma separated* if there is more than one parameter. The parentheses are mandatory even if the actual parameter list is empty. This distinguishes the method call from the construct for accessing member variables and that for specifying fully qualified names for classes and packages using the dot operator.

```
objRef.doIt(time, place);          // Explicit object reference.
int i = java.lang.Math.abs(-1);    // Fully qualified class name.
int j = Math.abs(-1);              // Class name.
someMethod(ofValue);               // Object or class implicitly implied.
someObjRef.make().make().make();   // make() returns an object reference.
```

The dot operator `.` has left associativity. In the last code line, the first call of the `make()` method returns an object reference that indicates the object to execute the next call, and so on.

Actual parameters are parameters passed to the method when the method is invoked by a method call, and can vary from call to call. *Formal parameters* are parameters defined in the *method definition* (Section 4.3, p. 97) and are local to the method.

Actual and formal parameters have to be compatible in the following respects:

- The number of actual parameters must equal the number of formal parameters in the method definition.
- Corresponding individual actual and formal parameters must be *type compatible*. Method invocation conversions for primitive values are discussed in Section 3.18, and those for type references are discussed in Section 6.5.

Table 3.20 *Parameter Passing*

Datatype of the Formal Parameters:	Value passed:
Primitive datatypes	Primitive data value
Class type	Reference value
Array type	Reference value

In Java, all parameters are passed by value. Table 3.20 summarizes what value is passed depending on the type of the formal parameter. In the case of primitive datatypes, the data value of the actual parameter is passed. If the actual parameter is a reference to an object (i.e. instantiation of a class or an array), then the reference value is passed and not the object itself. If the actual parameter is an array element of a primitive datatype, then its data value is passed, and if the array element is a reference to an object, then its reference value is passed.

It should also be stressed that each invocation of a method has its own instances of the formal parameters, as is the case for any local variable in the method.

For expositional purposes, the examples in subsequent sections primarily show method invocation on the same object or the same class. The parameter passing mechanism is no different when different objects or classes are involved.

3.18 Passing Primitive Data Values

When the actual parameter is a variable of a primitive datatype, the value of the variable is copied to the formal parameter at method invocation. Since formal parameters are local to the method, any changes made to the formal parameter value will not be reflected in the actual parameter.

Note that the actual parameter can be an expression that is evaluated first, and the resulting value is then passed.

Type conversions between actual and formal parameters of primitive datatypes are similar to those for numeric assignment conversions (i.e. widening primitive conversions are implicitly applied). However, for parameter passing there are no implicit narrowing conversions for `int` constants (Section 3.3, p. 47).

Example 3.2 *Passing Primitive Values*

```
public class CustomerOne {
    public static void main (String args[]) {
        PizzaFactory pizzaHouse = new PizzaFactory();

        int pricePrPizza = 15;
        double totPrice = pizzaHouse.calcPrice(4, pricePrPizza);      // (1)
       System.out.println("Value of pricePrPizza: " + pricePrPizza); // Unchanged.
    }
}

class PizzaFactory {

    public double calcPrice(int numberOfPizzas, double pizzaPrice) {  // (2)
        pizzaPrice = pizzaPrice/2.0; // Change price.
        return numberOfPizzas * pizzaPrice;
    }
}
```

Output from the program:

```
Value of pricePrPizza: 15
```

In Example 3.2, the method `calcPrice()` is defined in class `PizzaFactory` at (2). It is called from the `CustomerOne.main()` method at (1). The value of the first actual parameter, `4`, is copied to the `int` formal parameter `numberOfPizzas`. Note that the second actual parameter `pricePrPizza` is of type `int`, while the corresponding formal parameter `pizzaPrice` is of type `double`. Before the value of actual parameter `pricePrPizza` is copied to the formal parameter `pizzaPrice`, it is implicitly widened to a `double`. Passing of primitive values is illustrated in Figure 3.3.

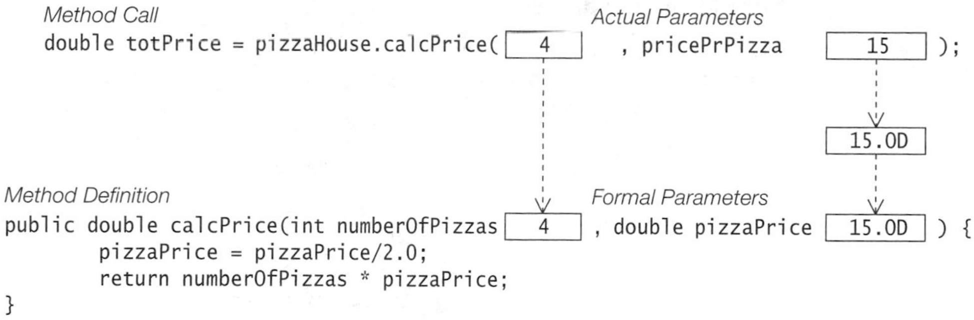

Figure 3.3 *Parameter Passing: Primitive Data Values*

The value of the formal parameter `pizzaPrice` is changed in the `PizzaFactory.calcPrice()` method, but this does not affect the value of the actual parameter `pricePrPizza` on return. It still has the value `15`. The bottom line is that the formal parameter cannot change the value of the actual parameter.

3.19 Passing Object Reference Values

If an actual parameter is a reference to an object, then the reference value of the object is passed. This means that both the actual parameter and the formal parameter are aliases to the same object during the invocation of the method. In particular, this implies that changes made to the object via the formal parameter will be apparent after the call returns. The actual parameter expression must evaluate to an object reference before the reference value can be passed.

Type conversions between actual and formal parameters of reference types are discussed in Section 6.5.

Example 3.3 *Passing Object Reference Values*

```
public class CustomerTwo {
   public static void main (String args[]) {
      Pizza favoritePizza = new Pizza();              // (1)
```

```
        System.out.println("Meat on pizza before baking: " + favoritePizza.meat);
        bake(favoritePizza);                               // (2)
        System.out.println("Meat on pizza after baking: " + favoritePizza.meat);
    }
    public static void bake(Pizza pizzaToBeBaked) { // (3)
        pizzaToBeBaked.meat = "chicken";  // Change the meat on the pizza.
        pizzaToBeBaked = null;                             // (4)
    }
}

class Pizza {                                              // (5)
    String meat = "beef";
}
```

Output from the program:

```
Meat on pizza before baking: beef
Meat on pizza after baking: chicken
```

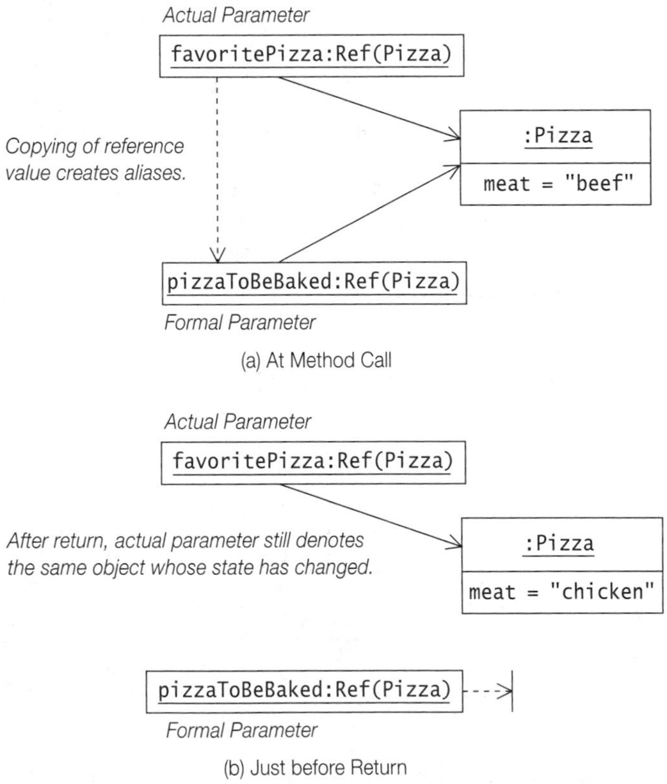

Figure 3.4 *Parameter Passing: Object Reference Values*

In Example 3.3, a `Pizza` object is created at (1). Any object of the class `Pizza` created using the class definition at (5) always results in a beef pizza. In the call to the `bake()` method at (2), the value of the object reference in the actual parameter `favoritePizza` is assigned to the formal parameter `pizzaToBeBaked` in the definition of the `bake()` method at (3). One particular consequence of passing reference values to formal parameters is that any changes made to the object via formal parameters will be reflected back in the calling method when the call returns. In this case, the reference `favoritePizza` will show that chicken has substituted beef on the pizza. Setting the formal parameter `pizzaToBeBaked` to `null` at (4) does not change the reference value in the actual parameter `favoritePizza`. The situation at method invocation and just before return from method `bake` is illustrated in Figure 3.4.

In summary, the formal parameter can only change the *state* of the object whose reference value was passed to the method.

The parameter passing strategy in Java is *call-by-value* and not *call-by-reference*, regardless of the type of the parameter. Call-by-reference would have allowed values in the actual parameters to be changed via formal parameters, i.e. the value in `pricePrPizza` to be halved in Example 3.2 and `favoritePizza` to be set to `null` in Example 3.3. This, however, cannot be directly implemented in Java.

3.20 Passing Array References

Arrays are objects in Java, and discussed in Section 4.1 on page 87. A review of that section is recommended before continuing with this section. The discussion on passing object reference values in the previous section is equally valid for arrays.

Method invocation conversions for array types are discussed along with those for type references in Section 6.5.

Example 3.4 *Passing Arrays*

```
class Percolate {

    public static void main (String args[]) {
        int[] dataSeq = {8,4,6,2,1};    // Create and initialize an array.

        // Write array before percolation.
        for (int i = 0; i < dataSeq.length; ++i)
            System.out.print(" " + dataSeq[i]);
        System.out.println();

        // Percolate.
        int maxIndex = 0;
        for (int index = 1; index < dataSeq.length; ++index)
           if (dataSeq[maxIndex] > dataSeq[index]) {
               swap(dataSeq, maxIndex, index);                       // (1)
               maxIndex = index;
           }
```

```
            // Write array after percolation.
            for (int i = 0; i < dataSeq.length; ++i)
                System.out.print(" " + dataSeq[i]);
            System.out.println();
        }

        public static void swap(int[] table, int i, int j) {          // (2)
            int tmp = table[i]; table[i] = table[j]; table[j] = tmp;
        }
    }
```

Output from the program:

```
 8 4 6 2 1
 4 6 2 1 8
```

In Example 3.4, note that in the definition of the method `swap()` at (2), the formal parameter `table` is an array. This method is called in the `main()` method at (1), where one of the actual parameters is array `dataSeq`. The reference value of variable `dataSeq` is assigned to variable `table` at method invocation. After return from the call to the `swap()` method, array `dataSeq` will reflect the changes made to it via the corresponding formal parameter. This situation is depicted in Figure 3.5 at the first call and return from the `swap()` method, indicating how values of elements at index `0` and `1` in the array have been swapped.

*: Array name are references; Hence the changes in the methods will reflect.

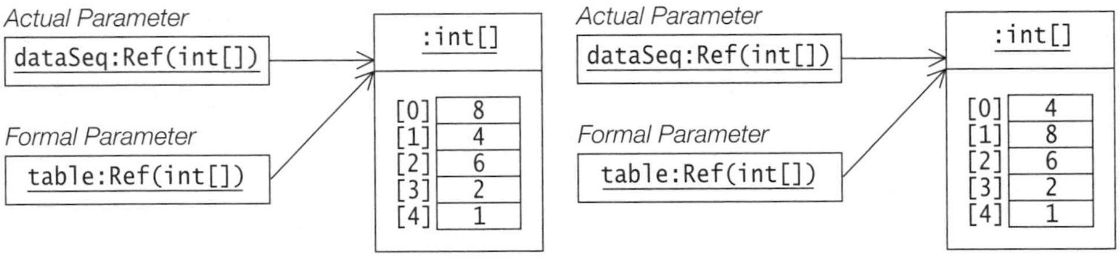

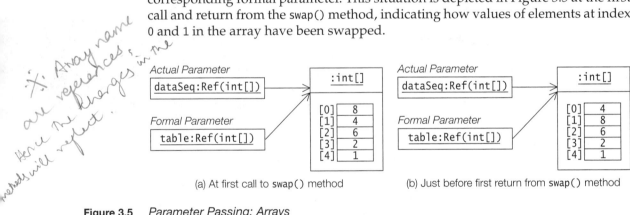

(a) At first call to `swap()` method (b) Just before first return from `swap()` method

Figure 3.5 *Parameter Passing: Arrays*

3.21 Array Elements as Actual Parameters

Array elements, like other variables, can store values of primitive datatypes or object references. In the latter case it means they can also be arrays, i.e. array of arrays (Section 4.1, p. 91). If an array element is of a primitive datatype, then its data value is passed, and if it is a reference to an object, then the reference value is passed.

Example 3.5 *Array Elements as Primitive Data Values*

```
class FindMinimum {

    public static void main(String args[]) {

        int[] dataSeq = {8,4,6,2,1};

        int minValue = dataSeq[0];
        for (int index = 1; index < dataSeq.length; ++index)
            minValue = minimum(minValue, dataSeq[index]);            // (1)

        System.out.println("Minimum value: " + minValue);
    }

    public static int minimum(int i, int j) {                       // (2)
        return (i <= j) ? i : j;
    }
}
```

Output from the program:

```
Minimum value: 1
```

In Example 3.5, note that the value of all but one element of the array `dataSeq` is retrieved and passed consecutively at (1) to the formal parameter `j` of the `minimum()` method defined at (2). The discussion in Section 3.18 on call-by-value applies also to array elements that have primitive values.

Example 3.6 *Array Elements as Object Reference Values*

```
class FindMinimumMxN {

    public static void main(String args[]) {

        int[][] matrix = { {8,4},{6,3,2},{7} };                  // (1)

        int min = findMinimum(matrix[0]);                        // (2)
        for (int i = 1; i < matrix.length; ++i) {
            int minInRow = findMinimum(matrix[i]);               // (3)
            if (min > minInRow) min = minInRow;
        }
        System.out.println("Minimum value in matrix: " + min);
    }

    public static int findMinimum(int[] seq) {                   // (4)
        int min = seq[0];
        for (int i = 1; i < seq.length; ++i)
            min = Math.min(min, seq[i]);
        return min;
    }
}
```

Output from the program:

```
Minimum value in matrix: 2
```

In Example 3.6, note that the formal parameter seq of the findMinimum() method defined at (4) is an array. The variable matrix is an array of arrays declared at (1), simulating a multidimensional array, which has three rows, where each row is an array. The first row, denoted by matrix[0], is passed to the findMinimum() method in the call at (2). Each remaining row is passed by reference value in the call to the findMinimum() method at (3).

3.22 final Parameters

A formal parameter can be declared with the keyword final preceding the parameter declaration in the method definition. A final parameter is also known as a *blank final variable*, i.e. it is blank (uninitialized) until a value is assigned to it at method invocation, for example, and then the value in the variable cannot be changed during the lifetime of the variable. The compiler can treat such blank final variables as constants for code optimization purposes.

The definition of method calcPrice() from Example 3.2 is shown below, with the formal parameter pizzaPrice declared as final.

```
public double calcPrice(int numberOfPizzas, final double pizzaPrice) {  // (2)
    pizzaPrice = pizzaPrice/2.0;                                        // (3)
    return numberOfPizzas * pizzaPrice;
}
```

If this definition of the calcPrice() method is compiled, the compiler will not allow the value of the final parameter pizzaPrice to be changed at (3) in the body of the method.

As another example, the definition of method bake() from Example 3.3 is shown below with the formal parameter pizzaToBeBaked declared as final.

```
public static void bake(final Pizza pizzaToBeBaked) { // (3)
    pizzaToBeBaked.meat = "chicken";                  // (3') Allowed.
    pizzaToBeBaked = null;                            // (4) Not allowed.
}
```

If this definition of the bake() method is compiled, the compiler will not allow the reference value of the final parameter pizzaToBeBaked to be changed at (4) in the body of the method. Note that this applies to the reference value in the final parameter, not the object denoted by this parameter. The state of the object can be changed as before as shown at (3').

3.23 Program Arguments

Any arguments passed to the program on the command line can be accessed in the main() method of the class specified on the command line:

```
java Colors red green blue
```

These arguments are called *program arguments*. Note that the command name, `java`, and the class name `Colors` are not passed to the `main()` method of the class `Colors`.

Since the formal parameter `args` is an array of `String` objects, individual `String` elements can be accessed in the usual way that elements are indexed in any array, by using the `[]` operator.

In Example 3.7, the three arguments `"red"`, `"green"` and `"blue"` can be accessed in the `main()` method of the `Colors` class as `args[0]`, `args[1]` and `args[2]` respectively. The total number of arguments is given by the member variable `length` of the `String` array `args`. Note that program arguments can only be passed as a list of character strings, and must explicitly be converted to other values by the program if necessary.

Program arguments can be used to supply information to the application, which can be used to tailor it according to user requirements.

Example 3.7 *Passing Program Arguments*

```
public class Colors {
    public static void main(String args[]) {
       for (int i = 0; i < args.length; i++)
          System.out.println("Argument no. " + i + " (" + args[i] + ") has " +
                                 args[i].length() + " characters.");
    }
}
```

Output from the program:

```
Argument no. 0 (red) has 3 characters.
Argument no. 1 (green) has 5 characters.
Argument no. 2 (blue) has 4 characters.
```

Review questions

3.18 What will be the result of attempting to compile and run the following class?

```
public class Passing {
    public static void main(String args[]) {
        int a = 0; int b = 0;
        int[] bArr = new int[1]; bArr[0] = b;

        inc1(a); inc2(bArr);

        System.out.println("a=" + a + " b=" + b + " bArr[0]=" + bArr[0]);
    }

    public static void inc1(int x) { x++; }

    public static void inc2(int[] x) { x[0]++; }
}
```

Select the one right answer.

(a) The code will fail to compile, since "`x[0]++;`" is not a legal statement.
(b) The code will compile and will display "`a=1 b=1 bArr[0]=1`" when run.
(c) The code will compile and will display "`a=0 b=1 bArr[0]=1`" when run.
(d) The code will compile and will display "`a=0 b=0 bArr[0]=1`" when run.
(e) The code will compile and will display "`a=0 b=0 bArr[0]=0`" when run.

3.19 Given the class

```
// Filename: Args.java
public class Args {
    public static void main(String args[]) {
        System.out.println(args[0] + " " + args[args.length-1]);
    }
}
```

what would be the result of executing the following on the command line?

```
java Args In politics stupidity is not a handicap
```

Select the one right answer.

(a) The program will throw `java.lang.ArrayIndexOutOfBoundsException`.
(b) The program will print "`java handicap`".
(c) The program will print "`Args handicap`".
(d) The program will print "`In handicap`".
(e) The program will print "`Args a`".
(f) The program will print "`In a`".

Chapter summary

The following information was included in this chapter:

- Explanation of operators in Java, including precedence and associativity rules.
- Explanation of type conversions: casting, narrowing and widening. In addition, the unary and binary numeric promotions are stated, and the context under which they are applied discussed.
- Defining and evaluating arithmetic and boolean expressions.
- Explanation of assigning values and assigning references.
- Explanation of object value equality and object reference equality.
- Explanation of parameter passing, both primitive values and type references, including arrays and array elements. In addition, final parameters are also discussed.
- Explanation of passing program arguments.

Programming exercises

3.1 The program below is supposed to calculate and show the time it takes for light to travel from the sun to the earth. It contains some logical errors. Fix the program so that it will compile and show the intended value when run.

```
// Filename: Sunlight.java
public class Sunlight {
    public static void main(String args[]) {
        // Distance from sun (150 million kilometers)
        int kmFromSun = 150000000;

        int lightSpeed = 299792458; // meters per second

        // Convert distance to meters.
        int mFromSun = kmFromSun * 1000;

        int seconds = mFromSun / lightSpeed;

        System.out.print("Light will use ");
        printTime(seconds);
        System.out.println(" to travel from the sun to the earth.");
    }

    public static void printTime(int sec) {
        int min = sec / 60;
        sec = sec - (min*60);
        System.out.print(min + " minute(s) and " + sec + " second(s)");
    }
}
```

3.2 Create a method that takes an `int` as an argument and returns a `String` object representing the binary representation of the integer. Given the argument `42`, it should return "101010".

3.3 Create a program that will print every other argument given on the command line. If the program was executed with the following on the command line:

```
java ArgumentSkipper one two three a b c d
```

the program would print

```
one
three
b
d
```

Consider how your program would operate when no arguments are given.

4 Declarations and Access Control

Exam Objectives

- Write code that declares, constructs and initializes arrays of any base type using any of the permitted forms, both for declaration and for initialization.
- Declare classes, inner classes, methods, instance variables, static variables and automatic (method local) variables, making appropriate use of all permitted modifiers (such as `public`, `final`, `static`, `abstract` and so forth). State the significance of each of these modifiers both singly and in combination, and state the effect of package relationships on declared items qualified by these modifiers.
  - *For inner classes, see Chapter 7.*
- For a given class, determine if a default constructor will be created, and if so, state the prototype of that constructor.
- State the legal return types for any method, given the declarations of all related methods in this or parent classes.
  - *For method overriding, see Section 6.2.*

Supplementary Objectives

- Defining and using anonymous arrays.
- Usage of `this` reference in instance methods.
- Understand the term *method signature* and state the circumstances under which methods can be overloaded.
- Identify a non-default constructor, and understand how constructors can be overloaded.
- State how the `package` and `import` statements are used to define and use packages.

4.1 Arrays

An *array* is a data structure which defines an ordered collection of a fixed number of homogeneous data elements. This means that all elements in the array have the same data type. The size of an array is fixed and cannot increase to accommodate more elements.

In Java, arrays are objects. Arrays can be of primitive datatypes or reference types. In the former case, all elements in the array are of a specific primitive datatype. In the latter case, all elements are references of a specific reference type. Each array object has an instance variable, `length`, which specifies the number of elements the array can accommodate.

Simple arrays are *one-dimensional arrays*, i.e. a simple list of values. Since arrays can store object references, the objects referenced can also be array objects. This allows implementation of *array of arrays*.

Passing array references as parameters is discussed in Section 3.20. Type conversions for array references on assignment and method invocation are discussed in Section 6.5.

Declaring Array Variables

An array variable declaration has either the following syntax:

<elementType>`[]` *<arrayName>*`;`

or

<elementType> *<arrayName>*`[];`

where *<elementType>* can be a primitive datatype or a reference type (i.e. a class name or an interface name). Note that the array size is not specified.

It is important to understand that the declaration does not actually construct an array. It only declares a reference for an array.

```
int anIntArray[], oneInteger;
Pizza[] mediumPizzas, largePizzas;
```

These two declarations declare `anIntArray` and `mediumPizzas` to be reference variables which can denote arrays of `int` values and arrays of `Pizza` objects respectively. The variable `largePizzas` is also an array of pizzas, but the variable `oneInteger` is not an array.

When the `[]` notation follows the type, all variables in the declaration are arrays. Otherwise the `[]` notation must follow each individual array name in the declaration.

Note that if a member array variable is only declared (i.e. not constructed or initialized) as an instance or static array (i.e. a member of a class), it will be initialized to the default reference value `null`. This default initialization does *not* apply to local reference variables, and therefore does not apply to local arrays as well (Section 2.9, p. 34).

Constructing an Array

An array can be constructed for a specific number of elements of the element type, using the `new` operator. The resulting array reference can be assigned to a variable of the corresponding type:

<*arrayName*> `= new` <*elementType*>`[`<*noOfElements*>`];`

The minimum value of <*noOfElements*> is `0`, i.e. arrays with zero elements can be constructed in Java.

Given the following array declarations:

```
int anIntArray[], oneInteger;
Pizza[] mediumPizzas, largePizzas;
```

the arrays can be constructed as follows:

```
anIntArray = new int[10];          // array for 10 integers
mediumPizzas = new Pizza[5];       // array of 5 pizzas
largePizzas = new Pizza[3];        // array of 3 pizzas
```

The array declaration and construction can be combined:

<*elementType*$_1$> <*arrayName*>`[] = new` <*elementType*$_2$>`[`<*noOfElements*>`];`

However, here array type <*elementType*$_2$>[] must be *assignable* to array type <*elementType*$_1$>[] (Section 6.5, p. 201). When the array is constructed, all its elements are initialized to the default value for <*elementType*$_2$>. This is true for both member and local arrays when they are constructed.

In all the examples below, the code constructs the array and the array elements are implicitly initialized to their default value. For example, the element at index `2` in array `anIntArray` gets the value `0`, and the element at index `3` in array `mediumPizzas` gets the value `null` when the arrays are constructed.

```
int[] anIntArray = new int[10];              // Default element value: 0.

Pizza[] mediumPizzas = new Pizza[5];         // Default element value: null.

// Pizza class extends Object class
Object objArray = new Pizza[3];              // Default element value: null.

// Pizza class implements Eatable interface
Eatable[] eatables = new Pizza[2];           // Default element value: null.
```

The value of the instance variable, `length`, in each array is set to the number of elements specified during the construction of the array; for example, `mediumPizzas.length` has the value `5`.

Initializing an Array

Java provides the means of declaring, constructing and explicitly initializing an array in one language construct:

<elementType>`[]` *<arrayName>* `= {` *<arrayInitializerCode>* `};`

This form of initialization applies to member as well as local arrays.

The initialization code in the block results in the construction and initialization of the array.

```
int[] anIntArray = {1, 3, 49, 2, 6, 7, 15, 2, 1, 5};
```

The array `anIntArray` is declared as an array of `int`s. It is constructed to hold 10 elements (equal to the number of items in the comma-separated list in the block), where the first element is initialized to `1`, the second element to `3`, and so on.

```
// Pizza class extends Object class
Object[] objArray = { new Pizza(), new Pizza(), null };
```

The array `objArray` is declared as an array of `Object` class, constructed to hold three elements. The initialization code sets the first two elements of the array to refer to two `Pizza` objects, while the last element is initialized to the null reference.

The code at (1) in the code below defines an array of four `String` objects, while the code at (2) should make clear that a `String` object is not the same as an array of `char`.

```
// Array with 4 String objects
String[] pets = {"crocodiles", "elephants", "crocophants", "elepodiles"}; // (1)

// Array of 3 characters
char[] charArray = {'a', 'h', 'a'};     // (2) Not the same as "aha".
```

Once an array has been constructed, its elements can also be initialized individually in a loop. Examples in the rest of this section make heavy use of this idiom to loop through the elements of an array for various purposes.

Using an Array

The whole array is referenced by the array name, but individual array elements are accessed using the `[]` operator. Each individual element is treated as a simple variable of the element type. Since the lower bound of an array is always `0`, the upper bound is one less than the number of elements in the array, i.e. (*<arrayName>*`.length-1`). The *index* can be any expression that returns an `int` value. The `i`th element in the array has index `(i-1)`. At runtime, the index value is automatically checked to ensure that it is within bounds. If the index value is less than `0` or greater than or equal to *<arrayName>*`.length`, `ArrayIndexOutOfBoundsException` is thrown. A program can either check the index explicitly, or be prepared to catch the exception (Section 5.5, p. 153).

The array operator `[]` is used to access array elements. The only time this operator is not used is when an array reference is manipulated, for example in an assignment (Section 6.5, p. 201) or when it is passed as an actual parameter in a method call (Section 3.20, p. 79).

Example 4.1 shows traversal of arrays. The loop at (3) initializes the local array `trialArray` declared at (2) five times with pseudorandom numbers (from `0.0` to `100.0`), by calling the method `randomize()` at (5). The minimum value in the array is found by calling the method `findMinimum()` at (6), and is stored in the array `storeMinimum` declared at (1). The loop at (4) prints the minimum values from the trials. The start value of the loop variable is initially set to `0`. The loop condition tests whether the loop variable is less than the length of the array; this guarantees that the index will not go out of bounds.

Example 4.1 *Using Arrays*

```
class Trials {
    public static void main(String args[]) {
        // Declare and construct the local arrays
        double[] storeMinimum = new double[5];               // (1)
        double[] trialArray = new double[15];                // (2)
        for (int j = 0; j < storeMinimum.length; ++j) {      // (3)
            // Initialize the array
            randomize(trialArray);
            // Find and store the minimum value
            storeMinimum[j] = findMinimum(trialArray);
        }
        // Print the minimum values                             (4)
        for (int j = 0; j < storeMinimum.length; ++j) {
            System.out.println(storeMinimum[j]);
        }
    }

    public static void randomize(double[] valArray) {        // (5)
        for (int i = 0; i < valArray.length; ++i)
            valArray[i] = Math.random() * 100.0;
    }

    public static double findMinimum(double[] valArray) {   // (6)
        // Assume the array has at least one element.
        double minValue = valArray[0];
        for (int i = 1; i < valArray.length; ++i)
            minValue = Math.min(minValue, valArray[i]);
        return minValue;
    }
}
```

Possible output from the program:

```
6.756931310985048
5.364063199341363
8.359410202984296
8.858272848258109
9.759950059619849
```

Multidimensional Arrays

Since an array element can be an object reference and arrays are objects, array elements can themselves reference other arrays. In Java, an array of arrays can be defined as follows:

<elementType>`[][]...[]` *<arrayName>*`;`

or

<elementType> *<arrayName>*`[][]...[];`

In fact the sequence of `[]`, indicating the number of dimensions, can be distributed as a postfix to both the element type and the array name.

Arrays of arrays are also loosely called *multidimensional arrays*.

```
int[][] mXnArray;        // 2-dimensional array
```

is equivalent to

```
int[] mXnArray[];        // 2-dimensional array
```

It is customary to combine the declaration with the construction of the multidimensional array.

```
int[][] mXnArray = new int[4][5];    // 4 x 5 matrix of ints
```

The above declaration constructs an array `mXnArray` of four elements, where each element is an array (row) of 5 `int` values. Each row in the matrix is denoted by `mXnArray[i]`, `(0≤i<4)`. The jth element, `(0≤j<5)`, in `mXnArray[i]` is accessed by `mXnArray[i][j]`. The number of rows is given by `mXnArray.length`, in this case `4`, and the number of values in each row is given by `mXnArray[i].length`, `(0≤i<4)`, in this case `5`.

Multidimensional arrays can also be constructed and explicitly initialized using the array initializer discussed for simple arrays. Note that each row is an array which uses array initializers to specify the values:

```
double[][] identityMatrix = {
    {1.0, 0.0, 0.0, 0.0 }, // 1. row
    {0.0, 1.0, 0.0, 0.0 }, // 2. row
    {0.0, 0.0, 1.0, 0.0 }, // 3. row
    {0.0, 0.0, 0.0, 1.0 }  // 4. row
}; // 4 x 4 Floating-point matrix
```

Arrays in a multidimensional array need not have the same length. The array of arrays `pizzaGalore` in the code below will have five rows, but the fifth row is left unconstructed.

```
Pizza[][] pizzaGalore = {
 { new Pizza(), null, new Pizza() },    // 1. row is an array of 3 elements.
 { null, new Pizza()},                  // 2. row is an array of 2 elements.
 new Pizza[1],                          // 3. row is an array of 1 element.
 {},                                    // 4. row is an array of 0 elements.
 null                                   // 5. row is not constructed.
};
```

When constructing multidimensional arrays with the `new` operator, the length of the deeply nested arrays may be omitted. In this case, these arrays are left unconstructed. The code below constructs an array of arrays `matrix`, where the first row has one element, the second row has two elements, and the third row has three elements. Note that the outer array is constructed first. The second dimension is constructed in a loop that constructs the array in each row. The elements in the multidimensional array will be implicitly initialized to the default `double` value (`0.0D`). In Figure 4.1, the array of arrays `matrix` is depicted after the elements have been explicitly initialized.

```
double matrix[][] = new double[3][];        // No. of rows

for (int i = 0; i < matrix.length; ++i)
   matrix[i] = new double[i + 1];           // Construct ith. row
```

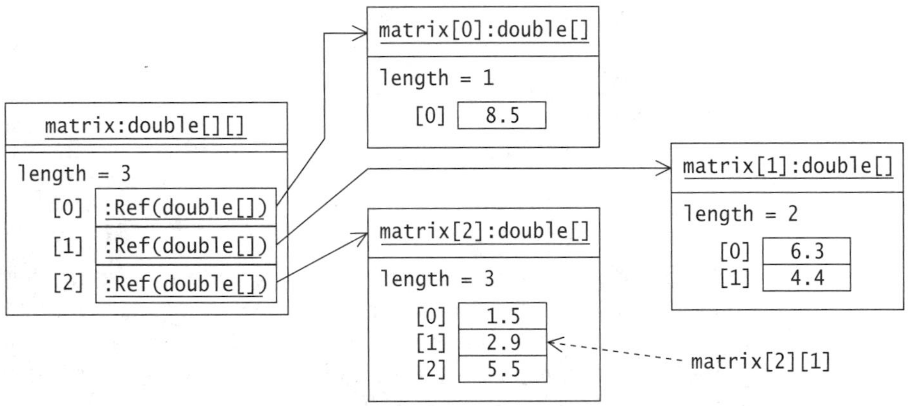

Figure 4.1 *Array of Arrays*

Nested loops are commonly used for manipulating arrays of arrays. In Example 4.2, a 4 x 3 `int` matrix is declared and constructed at (1). The program finds the minimum value in the matrix. The outer loop at (2) traverses the rows (`mXnArray[i]`, `0 ≤ i < mXnArray.length`), and the inner loop at (3) traverses the elements in each row in turn (`mXnArray[i][j]`, `0 ≤ j < mXnArray[i].length`).

Example 4.2 *Using Multidimensional Arrays*

```
class MultiArrays {

    public static void main(String args[]) {
        // Declare and construct the M X N matrix.
        int[][] mXnArray = {                                            // (1)
             {16,  7, 12}, // 1. row
             { 9, 20, 18}, // 2. row
             {14, 11,  5}, // 3. row
             { 8,  5, 10}  // 4. row
         }; // 4 x 3 int matrix
```

```
            // Find the minimum value in a M X N matrix
            int min = mXnArray[0][0];
            for (int i = 0; i < mXnArray.length; ++i)                 // (2)
                // Find min in mXnArray[i], i.e. in the ith. row
                for (int j = 0; j < mXnArray[i].length; ++j)          // (3)
                    min = Math.min(min, mXnArray[i][j]);

            System.out.println("Minimum value: " + min);
        }
    }
```

Output from the program:

```
Minimum value: 5
```

Anonymous Arrays

As shown earlier in this section, the construct

<elementType$_1$>`[]` *<arrayName>* `= new` *<elementType$_2$>*`[`*<noOfElements>*`];`

```
int[] intArray = new int[5];
```

allows creation of arrays given the dimension of the array, but the array elements have to be initialized in some other way. On the other hand, the following construct

<elementType>`[]` *<arrayName>* `= {` *<initialization code>* `};`

```
int[] intArray = {3, 5, 2, 8, 6};
```

both creates and initializes the declared array. In both cases, the array name has to be explicitly specified. Java allows these two constructs to be combined in a concept called *anonymous array*, which initializes an array upon construction:

`new` *<elementType>*`[] {` *<initialization code>* `}`

```
new int[] {3, 5, 2, 8, 6}
```

The construct has enough information to create a nameless array of a specific type. Neither the name of the array nor the dimension of the array is specified. The construct returns an array reference which can be assigned, and passed as parameter. In particular, the following two examples are equivalent:

```
int[] intArray = {3, 5, 2, 8, 6};

int[] intArray = new int[] {3, 5, 2, 8, 6};
```

The concept of anonymous arrays is similar to that of *anonymous classes* (Section 7.5, p. 243): combining the definition and instantiation of classes into one process.

In Example 4.3, an anonymous array is constructed at (1) and passed as parameter to the `static` method `findMinimum()` defined at (2). Note that no array name or array dimension is specified for the anonymous array.

Example 4.3 *Using Anonymous Arrays*

```
class AnonArray {

    public static void main(String args[]) {
        System.out.println("Minimum value: " +
                findMinimum(new int[] {3, 5, 2, 8, 6}));              // (1)
    }

    public static int findMinimum(int[] dataSeq) {                     // (2)
        // Assume the array has at least one element.
        int min = dataSeq[0];
        for (int index = 1; index < dataSeq.length; ++index)
            if (min >= dataSeq[index])
                min = dataSeq[index];
        return min;
    }
}
```

Output from the program:

```
Minimum value: 2
```

Review questions

4.1 Given the following declaration, what is the correct way to get the size of the array, assuming the array has been initialized?

```
int[] array;
```

Select the one right answer.

(a) `array[].length()`
(b) `array.length()`
(c) `array[].length`
(d) `array.length`
(e) `array[].size()`
(f) `array.size()`

4.2 Is it possible to create arrays of length zero?

Select the one right answer.

(a) Yes, you can create arrays of any type with length zero.
(b) Yes, but only for primitive datatypes.
(c) Yes, but only for arrays of object references.
(d) No, you cannot create zero length arrays, but the main method may be passed an array of `String` references that is of length zero if a program is started without any arguments.
(e) No, arrays of length zero do not exist in Java.

4.3 Which of these array declarations and instantiations are not legal?

Select all valid answers.

(a) `int []a[] = new int [4][4];`
(b) `int a[][] = new int [4][4];`
(c) `int a[][] = new int [][4];`
(d) `int []a[] = new int [4][];`
(e) `int[][] a = new int[4][4];`

4.4 Which of these array declarations and initializations are not legal?

Select all valid answers. Ans: b & e

(a) `int[] i[] = { { 1, 2 }, { 1 }, {}, { 1, 2, 3 } };`
(b) `int i[] = new int[2] {1, 2};`
(c) `int i[][] = new int[][] { {1, 2, 3}, {4, 5, 6} };`
(d) `int i[][] = { { 1, 2 }, new int[ 2 ] };`
(e) `int i[4] = { 1, 2, 3, 4 };`

4.5 What would be the result of attempting to compile and run the following program?

```
// Filename: MyClass.java
class MyClass {
    public static void main(String args[]) {
        int size = 20;
        int[] arr = new int[ size ];

        for (int i = 0; i < size; ++i) {
                System.out.println(arr[i]);
        }
    }
}
```

Select the one right answer.

(a) The code will fail to compile, because the `int[]` array declaration is incorrect.
(b) The program will compile, but will throw an `ArrayIndexOutOfBoundsException` when run.
(c) The program will compile and run without error, but will produce no output.
(d) The program will compile and run without error and will type the numbers 0 through 19.
(e) The program will compile and run without error and will type `0` twenty times.
(f) The program will compile and run without error and will type `null` twenty times.

4.6 Given the following program, which statement is true?

```
class MyClass {
    public static void main(String args[]) {
        String[] numbers = { "one", "two", "three", "four" };

        if (args.length == 0) {
           System.out.println("no arguments");
        } else {
           System.out.println(numbers[ args.length ] + " arguments");
        }
    }
}
```

Select the one right answer.

(a) The program will fail to compile.
(b) The program will throw a `NullPointerException` when run with zero arguments.
(c) The program will type "`no arguments`" and "`two arguments`" when called with zero and three arguments respectively.
(d) The program will type "`no arguments`" and "`three arguments`" when called with zero and three arguments respectively.
(e) The program will type "`no arguments`" and "`four arguments`" when called with zero and three arguments respectively.
(f) The program will type "`one arguments`" and "`four arguments`" when called with zero and three arguments respectively.

4.7 What would be the result of trying to compile and run the following program?

```
public class DefaultValuesTest {
    int[] ia = new int[1];
    boolean b;
    int i;
    Object o;

    public static void main(String args[]) {
        DefaultValuesTest instance = new DefaultValuesTest();
        instance.print();
    }

    public void print() {
        System.out.println(ia[0] + " " + b + " " + i + " " + o);
    }
}
```

Select the one right answer.

(a) The program will fail to compile, owing to uninitialized variables.
(b) The program will throw a `java.lang.NullPointerException` when run.
(c) The program will print "`0 false NaN null`".
(d) The program will print "`0 false 0 null`".
(e) The program will print "`null 0 0 null`".
(f) The program will print "`null false 0 null`".

4.2 Defining Classes

A class definition specifies a new type and its implementation. It has the following general syntax:

<class header> {
  <class body>
}

In the class header, the name of the class is preceded by the keyword `class`. In addition, the class header can specify the following information:

- Scope or accessibility modifier (Section 4.6, p. 108).
- Additional class modifiers (Section 4.7, p. 109).
- Any class it extends (Section 6.1, p. 173).
- Any interfaces it implements (Section 6.4, p. 195).

The class body contains variables and methods, collectively called *members*. Members belonging to the class are called *static members*, and those belonging to the objects of the class are called *instance members*. Variable declarations are covered in Section 2.3. Methods and constructors are discussed in Section 4.3 and Section 4.4 respectively. A class body can also contain declarations of other classes and interfaces as members. Such members are called *inner classes* (Section 7.1, p. 224). In addition, a class body can contain *static and instance initializers* (Section 8.2, p. 257).

4.3 Defining Methods

The behavior of objects is specified by the methods of the class. Like member variables, member methods can be characterized as:

- *Instance methods* which are discussed below.
- *Static methods* which are discussed in Section 4.10 on page 121.

The general syntax of a method definition is:

<method header> (*<formal parameter list>*) *<throws clause>* {
  <method body>
}

In addition to the name of the method and the type of the *return value* (Section 5.4, p. 148), the method header can specify the following information:

- Scope or *accessibility modifier* (Section 4.8, p. 112).
- Additional *method modifiers* (Section 4.10, p. 121).

The *formal parameter list*, which is a comma-separated list of parameters, passes information to the method when the method is invoked by a *method call* (Section

3.17, p. 74). Each parameter is a simple variable declaration consisting of its type and name.

Exceptions thrown by the method can be specified using the `throws` clause (Section 5.8, p. 162). The method body specifies the *local declarations* (Section 2.3, p. 29) and the *statements* of the method.

Statements

Statements in Java can be grouped into various categories. Variable declarations with explicit initialization of the variables are called *declaration statements* (Section 2.3, p. 29). Other basic forms of statements are *expression statements* and *flow control statements* (Chapter 5). A statement in Java is terminated by a semicolon (;). An expression statement is an expression terminated by a semicolon. Only certain types of expressions have meaning as statements. They include the following:

- Assignments (Section 3.3, p. 45).
- Increment and decrement operators (Section 3.6, p. 54).
- Method calls (Section 3.17, p. 74).
- Object creation with the `new` operator (Section 3.16, p. 72).

A solitary semicolon denotes the *empty statement* that does nothing. A block, `{}`, is a *compound* statement which can be used to group zero or more local declarations and statements (Section 4.8, p. 113). It can be used in any context where a simple statement is permitted. Statements can also be labelled. For example, see Section 5.4, p. 145.

Instance Methods and Object Reference `this`

Instance methods belong to every object of the class. Instance methods can only be invoked on objects of the class. The body of an instance method can access all members, including static members, defined in the class. The reason is that all instance methods are passed an implicit parameter which is a reference to the object on which the method is being invoked. This object can be referenced in the body of the instance method by the keyword `this`. In the body of the method, the `this` reference can be used like any other object reference to access members of the object. However, the `this` reference cannot be modified.

A local variable can *shadow* (also called *hiding*) a member variable that has the same name. In the example below, the two parameters, `noOfWatts` and `indicator`, of the constructor in the `Light` class have the same names as the instance variables in the class. The example also declares a local variable `location`, which has the same name as an instance member. The reference `this` can be used to distinguish the instance variables from the local variables inside the method. In the constructor using the `this` reference at (1), assignment is made to the instance variable, but without the `this` reference at (2), assignment is made to the parameter, resulting in a logical error. Similarly at (3), without the `this` reference, assignment is made to the local variable and not to the instance variable.

Example 4.4 *Using* `this` *Reference*

```
class Light {
    // Instance variables
    int noOfWatts;          // wattage
    boolean indicator;      // on or off
    String location;        // placement

    // Constructor
    public Light(int noOfWatts, boolean indicator, String site) {
        String location;

        this.noOfWatts = noOfWatts;   // (1) Assignment to instance variable.
        indicator = indicator;        // (2) Assignment to parameter.
        location = site;              // (3) Assignment to local variable.
        this.someAuxilliaryMethod();  // (4)
        someAuxilliaryMethod();       // equivalent to call at (4)
    }

    void someAuxilliaryMethod() { System.out.println(this); }  // (5)
}
```

The simple name `member` is considered a short-hand notation for `this.member`. In particular, the `this` reference can be used explicitly to invoke other methods in the class. This is illustrated at (4) in the example above, where the method `someAuxilliaryMethod()` is called.

If, for some reason, a method needs to pass the object on which it is being invoked to another method, it can do so using the `this` reference. This is illustrated at (5) in the example above, where the object is passed to the `println()` method.

Note that no implicit `this` reference is passed to static methods, as these are not invoked on behalf of any object.

Method Overloading

Each method has a *signature*, which is comprised of the name of the method and the types and order of the parameters in the parameter list. Several methods can have the same name, as long as their signatures differ. *Method overloading* allows a method with the same name but different parameters, thus with different signatures, to have different implementations and return values of different types.

Rather than invent new method names all the time, method overloading can be used when the same operation has different implementations. The JDK APIs make heavy use of method overloading. For example, the class `java.lang.Math` contains an overloaded method `min()`, which returns the minimum of two numeric values:

```
public static double min(double a, double b)
public static float min(float a, float b)
public static int min(int a, int b)
public static long min(long a, long b)
```

In the examples below, five implementations of the method `methodA` are shown:

```
public void methodA(int a, double b) {/* ... */}          // (1)
public int methodA(int a) { return a; }                   // (2)
public int methodA() { return 1; }                        // (3)
public long methodA(double a, int b) { return b; }        // (4)
public long methodA(int x, double y) { return x; }        // (5) Not OK.
```

The corresponding signatures of the methods are as follows:

```
methodA(int, double)                          // (1')
methodA(int)                                  // (2') Number of parameters.
methodA()                                     // (3') Number of parameters.
methodA(double, int)                          // (4') Order of parameters.
methodA(int, double)                          // (5') Same as (1').
```

The first four implementations of the method `methodA` are overloaded correctly, each time with a different parameter list and therefore different signatures. The declaration at (5) has the same signature `methodA(int, double)` as the declaration at (1), and is therefore not a valid overloading of this method.

```
void bake(Cake k) { /* ... */ }               // (1)
void bake(Pizza p) { /* ... */ }              // (2)

int    halfIt(int a) { return a/2; }          // (3)
double halfIt(int a) { return a/2.0; }        // (4) Not OK. Same signature.
```

The method `bake` is correctly overloaded at (1) and (2), with two different signatures. Changing just the return type (as shown at (3) and (4)), or the exceptions thrown, in the implementation is not enough to overload a method, and will be flagged as a compile time error. The parameter list in the definitions must be different. Overloaded methods should be considered as individual methods that just happen to have the same name. Methods with the same name are allowed since methods are identified by their signature. At compile time, the right implementation is chosen based on the signature of the method call. Details of method overloading resolution can be found in Section 6.2 on page 181. Method overloading should not be confused with *method overriding* (Section 6.2, p. 179).

4.4 Constructors

The main purpose of constructors is to set the initial state of an object when the object is created using the `new` operator.

A constructor has the following general syntax:

<constructor header> (*<parameter list>*) {
  <constructor body>
}

Constructors are like member methods, but the constructor header can only contain the following information:

- Scope or accessibility modifier. Accessibility modifiers for methods also apply to constructors (Section 4.9, p. 114).
- Constructor name, which must be the same as the class name.

The following restrictions should be noted:

- Modifiers other than accessibility modifiers are not permitted.
- Constructors cannot return a value.
- Constructors can only be called using the `new` operator.

Chaining of constructors is discussed in Section 6.3 on page 187.

Default Constructor

A *default constructor* is a constructor without any parameters. If a class does not specify *any* constructors, then an *implicit* default constructor is supplied for the class. The implicit default constructor is equivalent to the following implementation:

```
<class name> () { }                    // No parameters. Empty constructor body.
```

In the code below, the class `Light` does not specify any constructors.

```
class Light {
    // Instance variables
    int noOfWatts;          // wattage
    boolean indicator;      // on or off
    String location;        // placement

    // No constructors
    //...
}

class Greenhouse {
    // ...
    Light oneLight = new Light();     // (1) Call of implicit default constructor.
}
```

The following implicit default constructor is generated and employed when a `Light` object is created at (1):

```
Light () { }
```

As can be seen from the definition, the method body is empty. The reference declaration and object creation at (1) result in the instance variables of the object being initialized to their default values. In this case, the instance variables `noOfWatts`, `indicator` and `location` are initialized to `0`, `false` and `null` respectively.

A class can choose to provide an implementation of the default constructor. In the example below, the class `Light` provides an explicit default constructor at (1). Note that it has the name of the class and that it does not have any parameters.

```
class Light {
    // ...
    // Explicit Default Constructor
    Light() {                          // (1)
        noOfWatts = 50;
        indicator = true;
        location = new String("X");
    }
    //...
}

class Greenhouse {
    // ...
    Light extraLight = new Light();   // (2) Call of explicit default constructor.
}
```

Since the class `Light` now provides an implementation of the default constructor, any object of the class `Light` created with `new Light()`, as at (2), will now have its state initialized as follows: its instance variables `noOfWatts`, `indicator` and `location` will be initialized to `50`, `true` and `"X"` respectively when the body of the default constructor is executed.

If a class defines one or more constructors, it cannot rely on the implicit default constructor being generated. If the class requires a default constructor, its implementation must be provided. In the example below, class `Light` only provides a non-default constructor at (1). It is called at (2) when an object of class `Light` is created with the `new` operator. Any attempt to call the default constructor will be flagged as a compile time error as shown at (3).

```
class Light {
    // ...
    // Only non-default Constructor
    Light(int watts, boolean state, String place) {          // (1)
        noOfWatts = watts;
        indicator = state;
        location = place;
    }
    //...
}

class Greenhouse {
    // ...
    Light moreLight = new Light(100,true,"Greenhouse");      // (2) OK.
//  Light firstLight = new Light();                          // (3) Error.
}
```

Overloaded Constructors

Like methods, constructors can also be overloaded. In the example below, class `Light` now provides both an explicit implementation of the default constructor at (1) and a non-default constructor at (2). The constructors are overloaded, as is evident by their signatures. The non-default constructor is called at (3) when an object of class `Light` is created, and the default constructor is likewise called at (4). Overloading of constructors allows appropriate initialization of objects on creation, depending on the constructor invoked. See also Section 6.3.

```
class Light {
    // ...
    // Explicit Default Constructor
    Light() {                                                   // (1)
        noOfWatts = 50;
        indicator = true;
        location = new String("X");
    }

    // Non-default Constructor
    Light(int watts, boolean ind, String loc) {                 // (2)
        noOfWatts = watts;
        indicator = ind;
        location = loc;
    }
    //...
}

class Greenhouse {
    // ...
    Light moreLight = new Light(100,true,"Greenhouse");         // (3) OK.
    Light firstLight = new Light();                             // (4) OK.
}
```

Review questions

4.8 Which of the following code fragments are valid method declarations?

```
void method1         { /* (1) */ }
void method2()       { /* (2) */ }
void method3(void)   { /* (3) */ }
method4()            { /* (4) */ }
method5(void)        { /* (5) */ }
```

Select all valid answers.

(a) The code labeled (1) is a valid method declaration.
(b) The code labeled (2) is a valid method declaration.
(c) The code labeled (3) is a valid method declaration.
(d) The code labeled (4) is a valid method declaration.
(e) The code labeled (5) is a valid method declaration.

4.9 Given the following code, which statements can be placed at the indicated position without causing compile errors?

```
public class ThisUsage {
    int planets;
    static int suns;

    public void gaze() {
        int i;
        // ... insert statements here ...
    }
}
```

Select all valid answers.

(a) `i = this.planets;`
(b) `i = this.suns;`
(c) `this = new ThisUsage();`
(d) `this.i = 4;`
(e) `this.suns = planets;`

4.10 Given the following pairs of method declarations, which of these statements are true?

```
void fly(int distance) {}
int  fly(int time, int speed) { return time*speed; }

void fall(int time) {}
int  fall(int distance) { return distance; }

void glide(int time) {}
void Glide(int time) {}
```

Select all valid answers.

(a) The first pair of methods will compile correctly and overload the method name `fly`.
(b) The second pair of methods will compile correctly and overload the method name `fall`.
(c) The third pair of methods will compile correctly and overload the method name `glide`.
(d) The second pair of methods will not compile correctly.
(e) The third pair of methods will not compile correctly.

4.11 Given a class named `Book`, which of these would be valid definitions of constructors for the class?

Select all valid answers.

(a) `Book(Book b) {}`
(b) `Book Book() {}`
(c) `private final Book() {}`
(d) `void Book() {}`
(e) `public static void Book(String args[]) {}`
(f) `abstract Book() {}`

4.12 Which of these statements are true?

Select all valid answers.

(a) All classes must define a constructor.
(b) A constructor can be declared `private`.
(c) A constructor can declare a return value.
(d) A constructor must initialize all the member variables of a class.
(e) A constructor can access the non-static members of a class.

4.13 What will be the result of attempting to compile the following program?

```
public class MyClass {
    long var;

    public void MyClass(long param) { var = param; }  // (1)

    public static void main(String args[]) {
        MyClass a, b;
        a = new MyClass();                            // (2)
        b = new MyClass(5);                           // (3)
    }
}
```

Select the one right answer.

(a) A compilation error will be encountered at (1), since constructors should not specify a return value.
(b) A compilation error will be encountered at (2), since the class does not have a default constructor.
(c) A compilation error will be encountered at (3), since the class does not have a constructor accepting a single argument of type `int`.
(d) The program will compile correctly.

4.5 Packages

A package in Java is an encapsulation mechanism that can be used to group related classes, interfaces and subpackages.

Figure 4.2 shows a package called `wizard` which contains two other packages: `pandorasBox` and `spells`. The package `pandorasBox` has a class called `Clown` that implements an interface called `Magic`, found in the same package. In addition, the package `pandorasBox` has a class called `LovePotion` and a subpackage called `artifacts` containing a class called `Ailment`. The package `spells` has two classes: `Baldness` and `LovePotion`. The class `Baldness` is a subclass of class `Ailment` found in the subpackage `artifacts` in the package `pandorasBox`.

The dot (`.`) operator is used to uniquely identify package members in the package hierarchy. The class `wizard.pandorasBox.LovePotion` is different from the class `wizard.spells.LovePotion`. The `Ailment` class can be easily identified by the name `wizard.pandorasBox.artifacts.Ailment`. This is called the *fully qualified name* of the

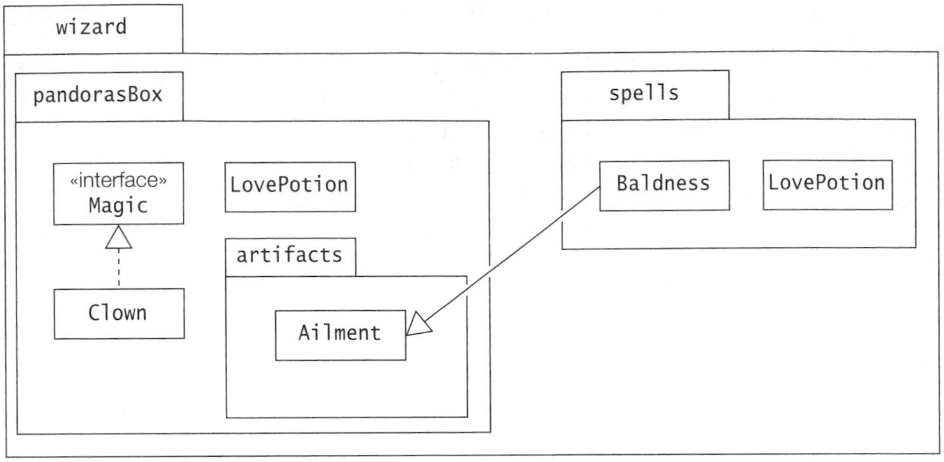

Figure 4.2 *Package Hierarchy*

package member. It is not surprising that certain programming environments reflect the fully qualified name of packages in the underlying (hierarchical) file system. A global naming scheme has been proposed to use the Internet domain names to uniquely identify packages. If the above package `wizard` was implemented by a company called Sorcerers Limited, its fully qualified name would be:

```
com.sorcerersltd.wizard
```

The subpackage `wizard.pandorasBox.artifacts` could easily have been placed elsewhere, as long as it was uniquely identified. Subpackages do not afford anything extra when it comes to accessibility of the members. To all intents and purposes, subpackages are more an *organizational* feature rather than a language feature. Accessibility of members in a package is discussed in Section 4.6. Accessibility of members in classes and interfaces is discussed in Section 4.9.

Defining Packages

A package hierarchy represents the organization of the Java byte code of classes and interfaces. It does *not* represent the source code organization of the classes and interfaces. The source code is of no consequence in this regard. Each Java source file (also called *compilation unit*) can contain zero or more definitions of classes and interfaces, but the compiler produces a separate *class* file containing the Java byte code for each of them. A class or interface can indicate that its Java byte code be placed in a particular package, using a `package` declaration.

The `package` statement has the following syntax:

`package` <*fully qualified package name*>;

At most one package declaration can appear in a source file, and it must be the first statement in the unit. The package name is saved in the Java byte code for the types contained in the package.

Note that this scheme has two consequences. First, all the classes and interfaces in a source file will be placed in the same package. Secondly, several source files can be used to specify the contents of a package.

Example 4.5 illustrates how the package `wizard.pandorasBox` in Figure 4.2 can be defined.

Using Packages

Types in a package must have the right accessibility in order to be referenced from outside the package. Given that a type is accessible from outside a package, a type can be accessed in two ways. The first method is to use the fully qualified name of the type. However, this can become tedious. The second method is a short-hand for specifying the fully qualified name of the type, and involves using the `import` declaration.

The `import` declarations must be the first statement after any `package` declaration in a source file. The simple form of the `import` declaration has the following syntax:

`import` *<fully qualified type name>*`;`

Now, the *simple* name of the type (i.e. its identifier) can be used to access this particular type. Given the following `import` declaration:

```
import wizard.pandorasBox.Clown;
```

the name `Clown` can be used in the source file to refer to the class.

Alternatively, the following form (called *import on demand*) of the `import` declaration can be used:

`import` *<fully qualified package name>*`.*;`

This allows any types from the specified package to be accessed by its simple name.

An `import` declaration does not recursively import subpackages. The declaration does not result in inclusion of the source code of the types. The declaration only imports type names.

The following example illustrates usage of the `import` declaration:

```
package wizard.spells;                           // Package declaration
import wizard.pandorasBox.*;                     // (1)
import wizard.pandorasBox.artifacts.*;           // (2)

class Baldness extends Ailment {                 // (3)
      wizard.pandorasBox.LovePotion tlcOne;      // (4)
      LovePotion tlcTwo;                         // (5)
}

class LovePotion { /*...*/ }
```

The class `Baldness` extends the class `Ailment`, which is in the subpackage `artifacts` of the `wizard.pandorasBox` package. A new `import` declaration at (2) is used to import the types from the subpackage `artifacts`. The class `Baldness` uses two different love potions at (4) and (5). In order to distinguish between them, one of them is specified with the fully qualified name. Such name conflicts can be resolved using variations of the `import` declaration together with fully qualified names.

Example 4.5 provides another example of usage of the `import` declaration.

4.6 Accessibility Modifiers for Classes and Interfaces

Top-level classes and interfaces within a package can be specified as `public`. This means that they are accessible from everywhere, both inside and outside of this package. The access modifier can be omitted (called *package* or *default accessibility*), in which case they are only accessible in the package but not in any subpackages.

Example 4.5 *Accessibility Modifiers for Classes and Interfaces*

```
// File: Clown.java
package wizard.pandorasBox;                 // Package declaration

public class Clown implements Magic {
     LovePotion tlc;
     /*...*/
}

class LovePotion {/*...*/}

interface Magic {/*...*/}
```

```
// File: Ailment.java
package wizard.pandorasBox.artifacts;      // Package declaration

public class Ailment {/*...*/}
```

```
// File: Client.java
import wizard.pandorasBox.*;                // Import of classes.

public class Client {
    Clown performerOne;                     // OK. Abbreviated class name
    wizard.pandorasBox.Clown performerTwo; // OK. Fully qualified class name

//  LovePotion moreTLC;                     // Error. Not accessible
//  Magic magician;                         // Error. Not accessible
}
```

In Example 4.5, compiling the file `Clown.java` results in the two classes `Clown` and `LovePotion`, and the interface `Magic`, being placed in a package called `wizard`.

pandorasBox. The public class Clown is accessible from everywhere. In the file Client.java, the class Client wishing to use the class Clown from the package wizard.pandorasBox can do so in two ways: denote the class by its fully qualified class name, wizard.pandorasBox.Clown, or import the package wizard.pandorasBox and use the abbreviated class name Clown. Since the class LovePotion and interface Magic have default accessibility in the package wizard.pandorasBox, they are only accessible in that package. They are not accessible outside of this package, not even in any packages nested in this package.

In the case of classes, just because the class is accessible, it does not automatically mean that members of the class are also accessible. Member accessibility is governed separately from class accessibility, as explained in Section 4.8. However, if the class is not accessible, its members will not be accessible, regardless of member accessibility.

Table 4.1 *Summary of Accessibility Modifiers for Classes and Interfaces*

Modifiers	Classes and Interfaces
default (No modifier)	Accessible in its package (package accessibility)
public	Accessible anywhere

4.7 Other Modifiers for Classes

abstract Classes

Any class can be specified with the keyword abstract to indicate that it cannot be instantiated. A class might choose to do this if the abstraction it represents is so general that it has to be specialized in order to be of practical use. A class Vehicle might be specified as abstract to represent the general abstraction of a vehicle, and creating instances of the class would not make much sense. Its non-abstract subclasses Car and Bus can make the abstraction more concrete, as creating instances of these classes would make more sense.

A class that has an abstract method (Section 4.10, p. 124) must be declared abstract. Obviously such classes cannot be instantiated, as their implementation is only partial. A class might choose this strategy to dictate certain behavior, but allow its subclasses the freedom to provide the relevant implementation. In other words, subclasses of the abstract class have to take a stand and provide implementations of inherited abstract methods before they can be instantiated. This is illustrated in Example 4.6.

In Example 4.6, the definition of abstract class Light has an abstract method KWHprice at (1). This forces its subclasses to provide the implementation for this method. A subclass which does not provide an implementation of its inherited methods is also abstract. The subclass TubeLight provides an implementation for the method `KWHprice` at (2). The class `Factory` creates an instance of class `TubeLight` at (3). Reference variables of an abstract class can be declared as shown at (4), but an abstract class cannot be instantiated as shown at (5).

Example 4.6 *Abstract Classes*

```
abstract class Light {
    // Instance variables
    int noOfWatts;           // wattage
    boolean indicator;       // on or off
    String location;         // placement

    // Instance methods
    public void switchOn()  { indicator = true; }
    public void switchOff() { indicator = false; }
    public boolean isOn()   { return indicator; }

    // Abstract Instance Method
    abstract public double KWHprice();                // (1) No method-body
}

class TubeLight extends Light {
    // Instance variables
    int tubeLength;
    int color;

    // Implementation of inherited abstract method.
    public double KWHprice() { return 2.75; }        // (2)
}

class Factory {
    TubeLight cellarLight = new TubeLight();          // (3) OK.
    Light spotlight;                                  // (4) OK.
//  Light tableLight = new Light();                   // (5) Compile time error.
}
```

Interfaces just specify the method prototypes and not the implementation; they are, by their nature, implicitly abstract, i.e. they cannot be instantiated. Thus specifying an interface with the keyword `abstract` is not appropriate, and should be omitted.

`final` Classes

A `final` class cannot be extended. In other words, its behavior cannot be changed by subclassing. It marks the lower boundary of its *implementation inheritance hierarchy*. Only a class whose definition is complete (i.e. has implementations of all the methods) can be specified to be `final`.

A final class must be *complete*, whereas an abstract class is considered incomplete. Classes therefore cannot be both abstract and final at the same time.

If it is decided that the class `TubeLight` in Example 4.6 cannot, or should not, be extended, it can be declared as `final`:

```
final class TubeLight extends Light {
    // Instance variables
    int tubeLength;
    int color;

    // Implementation of inherited abstract method.
    public double KWHprice() { return 2.75; }
}
```

The Java API includes many `final` classes, for example `java.lang.String` which cannot be specialized any further by subclassing.

Table 4.2 *Summary of Other Modifiers for Classes and Interfaces*

Modifiers	Classes	Interfaces
`abstract`	Class may contain abstract methods, and thus cannot be instantiated.	Implied.
`final`	The class cannot be extended, i.e. it cannot be subclassed.	Not possible.

Review questions

4.14 Given the following class, which of these are valid ways of referring to the class from outside of the package `net.basemaster`?

```
package net.basemaster;

public class Base {
    // ...
}
```

Select all valid answers.

(a) By simply referring to the class as `Base`.
(b) By simply referring to the class as `basemaster.Base`.
(c) By simply referring to the class as `net.basemaster.Base`.
(d) By importing `net.basemaster.*` and referring to the class as `Base`.
(e) By importing the package `net.*` and referring to the class as `basemaster.Base`.

4.15 Which one of the following class definitions is a legal definition of a class that cannot be instantiated?

Select the one right answer.

(a)
```
class Ghost {
    abstract void haunt();
}
```

(b)
```
abstract class Ghost {
    void haunt();
}
```
(c)
```
abstract class Ghost {
    void haunt() {};
}
```
(d)
```
abstract Ghost {
    abstract void haunt();
}
```
(e)
```
static class Ghost {
    abstract haunt();
}
```

4.16 Which one of these is a proper definition of a class named `Link` that cannot be subclassed?

Select the one right answer.

(a) `class Link { }`
(b) `abstract class Link { }`
(c) `native class Link { }`
(d) `static class Link { }`
(e) `final class Link { }`
(f) `private class Link { }`
(g) `abstract final class Link { }`

4.8 Scope and Accessibility of Members

Member scope rules govern where in the program a variable or a method is accessible. In most cases, Java provides explicit modifiers to control the accessibility of members, but in two areas this is governed by specific scope rules:

- Class scope for members
- Block scope for local variables

Class Scope for Members

Class scope concerns accessing members (including inherited ones) by their simple names from code within a class. Such code can directly access members defined in the class and those inherited into the class. Accessibility of members is primarily governed by the accessibility modifiers (Section 4.9, p. 114). However, static methods can only access static members (Section 4.10, p. 121).

Within a class definition, reference variables of this class's type can be used to access all members regardless of their accessibility modifiers. In Example 4.7, the method `duplicateLight` at (1) in class `Light` has a parameter `oldLight` and a local variable `newLight` that are references of class `Light`. Even though the instance variables of the class are `private`, they are accessible through the two references (`oldLight` and `newLight`) in the method `duplicateLight()` as shown at (2), (3) and (4).

Example 4.7 *Class Scope*

```
class Light {
    // Instance variables
    private int noOfWatts;          // wattage
    private boolean indicator;      // on or off
    private String location;        // placement

    // Instance methods
    public void switchOn()  { indicator = true; }
    public void switchOff() { indicator = false; }
    public boolean isOn()   { return indicator; }

    public static Light duplicateLight(Light oldLight) {        // (1)
        Light newLight = new Light();
        newLight.noOfWatts = oldLight.noOfWatts;                // (2)
        newLight.indicator = oldLight.indicator;                // (3)
        newLight.location = new String(oldLight.location);      // (4)
        return newLight;
    }
}
```

Block Scope for Local Variables

Declarations and statements can be grouped into a *block* using braces, {}. Note that the body of a method is a block. Blocks can be nested and certain scope rules apply to local variable declarations in such blocks. A local declaration can appear anywhere in a block. The general rule is that a variable declared in a block is *in scope* inside the block in which it is declared, but it is not accessible outside of this block. Execution of a block instantiates the local variables declared in the block. These exist until the block finishes executing.

Local variables of a method are comprised of formal parameters of the method and variables that are declared in the method body. The method body is a block. A local variable can exist in different invocations of the same method, with each invocation having its own storage for the local variable.

Figure 4.3 illustrates the salient features of block scope. It is not possible to declare a new variable if a local variable of the same name is already declared in the current scope.

Parameters cannot be redeclared in the method body as shown at (1) in Block 1.

```
public static void main(String args[]) {                  // Block 1
//  String args = "";      // (1) Cannot redeclare parameters.
    char digit = 'z';

    for (int index = 0; index < 10; ++index) {            // Block 2
        switch(digit) {                                   // Block 3
            case 'a':
                int i;     // (2)
            default:
//              int i;     // (3) Already declared in the same block.
        } // switch
        if (true) {                                       // Block 4
            int i;         // (4) OK
//          int digit;     // (5) Already declared in enclosing block 1.
//          int index;     // (6) Already declared in enclosing block 2.
        } //if
    } // for
    int index;             // (7) OK
} // main
```

Figure 4.3 *Block Scope*

A local variable, already declared in an enclosing block and therefore visible in a nested block, cannot be redeclared in the nested block. These cases are shown at (3), (5) and (6).

A local variable in a block can be redeclared in another block if the blocks are disjoint. This is the case for variable `i` at (2) in Block 3 and at (4) in Block 4, as these two blocks are disjoint.

Block scope of a declaration begins from where it is declared in the block and ends where this block terminates. The loop variable `index` is in scope in Block 2 . Even though Block 2 is nested in Block 1, the declaration of the variable `index` at (7) in Block 1 is valid because its scope spans from its declaration to the end of this block, and it does not overlap with that of the loop variable `index` in Block 2.

4.9 Member Accessibility Modifiers

Accessibility modifiers for members help a class to define a *contract* so that clients know exactly what services are offered by the class. By using accessibility modifiers for members, a class can control what information is accessible to clients, i.e. other classes.

Accessibility of members can be one of the following:

- `public`
- `protected`
- default (also called *package accessibility*)
- `private`

In the following discussion on accessibility modifiers for members of a class, it should be kept in mind that the modifier usage has meaning only if the class (or one of its subclasses) is accessible by the client. Also, note that only one access modifier can be specified for a member.

In UML notation, `+`, `#` and `-` as prefix to the member name indicates public, protected and private member access respectively, whereas no prefix indicates default or package access.

`public` Members

Public access is the least restrictive of all the access modifiers. A `public` member is accessible everywhere, both in its class's package and in other packages where its class is visible. This is true for both instance and static members.

Example 4.8 contains two source files, shown at (1) and (6). The information in the source files is depicted in Figure 4.4, showing the two packages `packageA` and `packageB` containing their respective classes. Classes in package `packageB` use classes from package `packageA`. `SuperclassA` in `packageA` has two subclasses: `SubclassA` in `packageA` and `SubclassB` in `packageB`.

Accessibility is illustrated in Example 4.8 by the access modifiers for the instance variable `superclassVarA` and the method `superclassMethodA` at (2) and (3) respectively, defined in class `SuperclassA`. These members are accessed from four different clients in Example 4.8:

- Client 1: From a subclass in the same package, which accesses an inherited instance variable. `SubclassA` at (4) is such a client.
- Client 2: From a non-subclass in the same package, which invokes a method on an instance of the class. `AnyClassA` at (5) is such a client.
- Client 3: From a subclass in another package, which invokes an inherited method. `SubclassB` at (7) is such a client.
- Client 4: From a non-subclass in another package, which accesses an instance variable in an instance of the class. `AnyClassB` at (8) is such a client.

In Example 4.8, the instance variable `superclassVarA` and the method `superclassMethodA` have public accessibility, and are accessible by all the four clients listed above. Subclasses can access their inherited public members directly, and all clients can access public members through an instance of the class. Public accessibility is depicted in Figure 4.4.

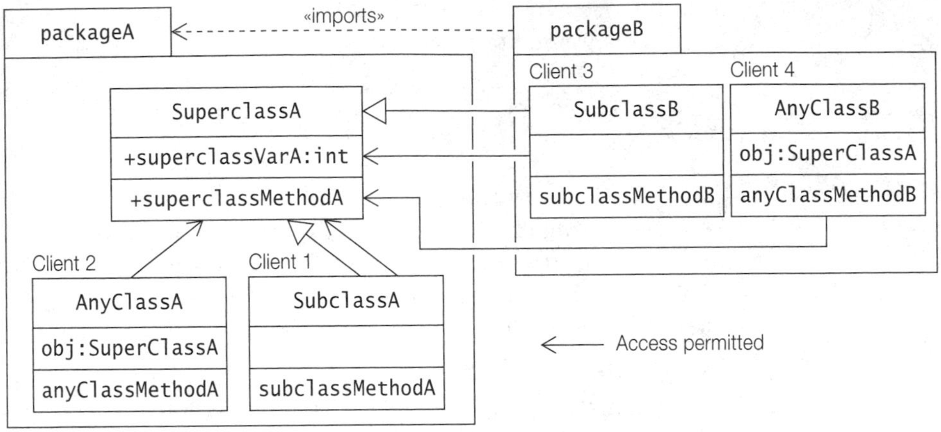

Figure 4.4 *Public Accessibility*

Example 4.8 *Public Accessibility of Members*

```
// Filename: SuperclassA.java                               (1)
package packageA;

public class SuperclassA {
    public int superclassVarA;                            // (2)
    public void superclassMethodA() {/*...*/}             // (3)
}

class SubclassA extends SuperclassA {
    void subclassMethodA() { superclassVarA = 10; }  // (4) OK.
}

class AnyClassA {
    SuperclassA obj = new SuperclassA();
    void anyClassMethodA() {
        obj.superclassMethodA();                          // (5) OK.
    }
}
```

```
// Filename: SubclassB.java                                 (6)
package packageB;
import packageA.*;

public class SubclassB extends SuperclassA {
    void subclassMethodB() { superclassMethodA(); }  // (7) OK.
}

class AnyClassB {
    SuperclassA obj = new SuperclassA();
    void anyClassMethodB() {
        obj.superclassVarA = 20;                          // (8) OK.
    }
}
```

`protected` Members

Protected members are accessible in the package containing this class, and by all subclasses of this class in any package where this class is visible. In other words, non-subclasses in other packages cannot access protected members from other packages. It is less restrictive than the default accessibility.

In Example 4.8, if the instance variable `superclassVarA` and the method `superclassMethodA` have protected accessibility, then they are accessible within package `packageA`, and only accessible by subclasses in any other packages.

```
public class SuperclassA {
    protected int superclassVarA;                    // (2)
    protected void superclassMethodA() {/*...*/}     // (3)
}
```

Client 4 in package `packageB` cannot access these members, as shown in Figure 4.5.

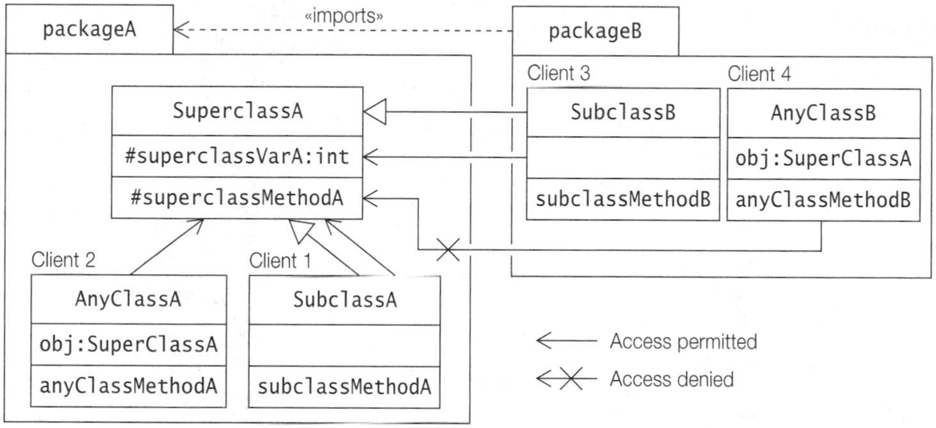

Figure 4.5 *Protected Accessibility*

A subclass in another package can only access protected members in the superclass via references of its own type or a subtype. The following new definition of `SubclassB` in `packageB` from Example 4.8 illustrates the point.

```
public class SubclassB extends SuperclassA {        // In packageB.

    SuperclassA objRefA = new SubclassB();          // (1)
    SubclassB objRefB = new SubclassB();            // (2)

    void subclassMethodB() {
        objRefB.superclassMethodA();                // (3) OK.
        objRefA.superclassVarA = 10;                // (4) Not OK.
    }
}
```

The class `SubclassB` defines two instance variables, one of own type (`objRefB`) and one of its superclass's type (`objRefA`) at (1) and (2) above. As can be seen, access is permitted to a protected member of the `SuperclassA` in `packageA` by a reference of the subclass, but not by a reference of its superclass, as shown at (3) and (4) in the example above. Access to protected members of the superclass would also be permitted via any references of subclasses of `SubclassB`. The above restriction helps to ensure that subclasses in packages different from their superclass can only access protected members of the superclass in their part of the inheritance hierarchy.

Default Accessibility for Members

When no access modifier is specified for a member, it is only accessible by another class in the package where its class is defined. Even if its class is visible in another (possibly nested) package, the member is not accessible there.

In Example 4.8, if the instance variable `superclassVarA` and the method `superclassMethodA` are defined with no access modifier, then they are only accessible within package `packageA`, but not in any other (possibly nested) packages.

```
public class SuperclassA {
    int superclassVarA;                              // (2)
    void superclassMethodA() {/*...*/}               // (3)
}
```

The clients in package `packageB` (i.e. Clients 3 and 4) cannot access these members. This situation is depicted in Figure 4.6.

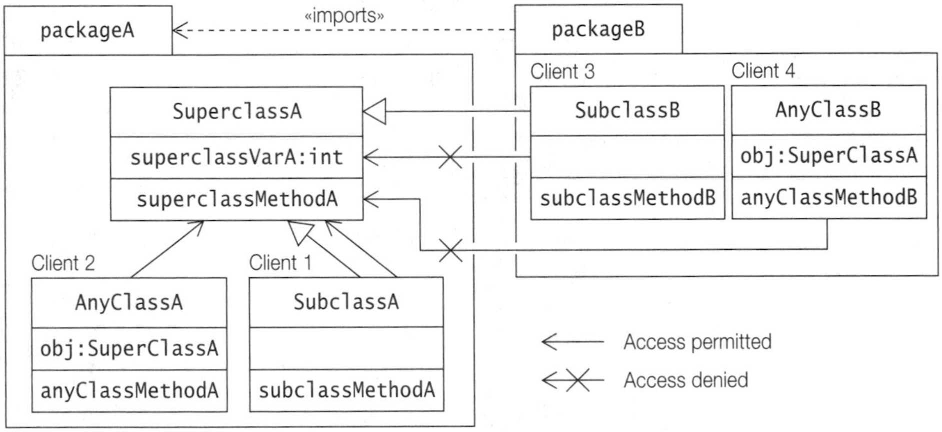

Figure 4.6 *Default Accessibility*

`private` Members

This is the most restrictive of all the access modifiers. Private members are not accessible from any other class. This also applies to subclasses, whether they are in the same package or not. It is not to be confused with inheritance of members by the subclass. Members are still inherited, but they are not accessible in the subclass.

It is a good design strategy to make all member variables private, and provide public accessor methods for them. Auxiliary methods are often declared private, as they do not concern any client.

In Example 4.8, if the instance variable `superclassVarA` and the method `superclassMethodA` have private accessibility, then they are not accessible by any other clients.

```
public class SuperclassA {
    private int superclassVarA;                        // (2)
    private void superclassMethodA() {/*...*/}         // (3)
}
```

None of the clients in Figure 4.7 can access these members.

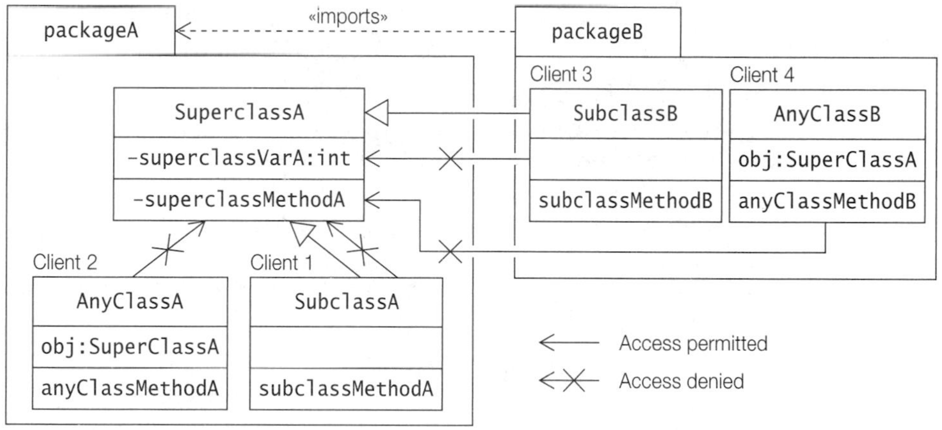

Figure 4.7 *Private Accessibility*

Table 4.3 *Summary of Accessibility Modifiers for Members*

Modifiers	Members
`public`	Accessible everywhere.
`protected`	Accessible by any class in the same package as its class, and accessible only by subclasses of its class in other packages.
default (no modifier)	Only accessible by classes, including subclasses, in the same package as its class (package accessibility).
`private`	Only accessible in its own class and not anywhere else.

Review questions

4.17 Given the following definition of a class, which member variables are accessible from outside the package `com.corporation.project`?

```
package com.corporation.project;

public class MyClass {
              int i;
    public    int j;
    protected int k;
    private   int l;
}
```

Select all valid answers.

(a) Member variable `i`.
(b) Member variable `j`.
(c) Member variable `k`.
(d) Member variable `k`, but only for subclasses.
(e) Member variable `l`.
(f) Member variable `l`, but only for subclasses.

4.18 How restrictive is the default accessibility compared to `public`, `protected` and `private` accessibility?

Select the one right answer.

(a) Less restrictive than `public`.
(b) More restrictive than `public`, but less restrictive than `protected`.
(c) More restrictive than `protected`, but less restrictive than `private`.
(d) More restrictive than `private`.
(e) Less restrictive than `protected` from within a package, and more restrictive than `protected` from outside a package.

4.19 Which of these statements concerning accessibility of members are true?

Select all valid answers.

(a) Private members are always accessible from within the same package.
(b) Private members can only be accessed by code from within the class of the member.
(c) A member with default accessibility can be accessed by any subclass of the class in which it is defined.
(d) Private members cannot be accessed at all.
(e) Package/default accessibility for a member can be declared using the keyword `default`.

4.10 Other Modifiers for Members

Certain characteristics of member variables and/or methods can be specified by using the following keywords:

- `static`
- `final`
- `abstract`
- `synchronized`
- `native`
- `transient`
- `volatile`

`static` Members

The declaration of static members is prefixed by the keyword `static` to distinguish them from instance members.

Static members belong to the class in which they are declared, and are not part of any instance of the class. Depending on the accessibility modifiers of the static members in a class, clients can access these by using the class name, or through object references of the class. The class need not be instantiated to access its static members.

Static variables (also called *class variables*) only exist in the class they are defined in. They are not instantiated when an instance of the class is created. In other words, the values of these variables are not a part of the state of any object. When the class is loaded, static variables are initialized to their default values if no other explicit initialization is provided (Section 8.2, p. 260).

Static methods are also known as *class methods*. A static method in a class can directly access other static members in the class. It cannot access instance (i.e. non-static) members of the class, as there is no object being operated on when a static method is invoked. Note, however, that a static method in a class can always use a reference of the class's type to access its members, regardless of whether these members are static or not.

eg main() method

A typical static method might perform some task on behalf of the whole class and/or for objects of the class. In the example below, the static variable `counter` keeps track of the number of instances of the `Light` class created. Note that the static method `writeCount` can only access static members directly as shown at (2), but not non-static members as shown at (3). The static variable `counter` will be initialized to the value `0` when the class is loaded at runtime. The `main` method at (4) in class `Warehouse` shows how static members of class `Light` can be accessed via the class name and via object references of the class.

Example 4.9 *Accessing Static Members*

```
class Light {
    // Instance variables
    int noOfWatts;          // wattage
    boolean indicator;      // on or off
    String location;        // placement

    // Static variable
    static int counter;     // No. of Light objects created.          (1)

    // Explicit Default Constructor
    Light() {
        noOfWatts = 50;
        indicator = true;
        location = new String("X");
        ++counter;          // Increment counter.
    }

    // Static method
    public static void writeCount() {
         System.out.println("Number of lights: " + counter);      // (2)

         // Error. noOfWatts is not accessible
         // System.out.println("Number of Watts: " + noOfWatts);  // (3)

    }
}

public class Warehouse {
    public static void main(String args[]) {                     // (4)

        Light.writeCount();                       // Invoked using class name

        Light aLight = new Light();               // Create an object
        System.out.println(
            "Value of counter: " + Light.counter  // Accessed via class name
        );
        Light bLight = new Light();               // Create another object
        bLight.writeCount();                      // Invoked using reference
        Light cLight = new Light();               // Create another object
        System.out.println(
            "Value of counter: " + cLight.counter // Accessed via reference
        );

    }
}
```

Output from the program:

```
Number of lights: 0
Value of counter: 1
Number of lights: 2
Value of counter: 3
```

`final` Members

A `final` variable is a constant, and its value cannot be changed once it's initialized. This applies to instance, static and local variables, including parameters that are declared `final`. For `final` variables of primitive datatypes, it means that once the variable is initialized, its value cannot be changed. Variables defined in an interface are implicitly `final` (Section 6.4, p. 195). For a `final` variable of a reference type it means that its reference value cannot be changed, but the state of the object it references may be changed. Note that a `final` variable need not be initialized at its declaration, but it must be initialized once before it is used. These variables are also known as *blank final variables*.

A `final` method in a class is complete (i.e. has an implementation) and cannot be overridden in any subclass (Section 6.2, p. 179). Subclasses are then restricted in changing the behavior of the method.

`Final` variables ensure that values cannot be changed, and `final` methods ensure that behavior cannot be changed. `Final static variables` are commonly used to define *manifest constants*, for example `Integer.MAX_VALUE`, which is the maximum `int` value. Final classes are discussed in Section 4.7.

For `final` members, the compiler is able to perform certain code optimizations because certain assumptions can be made about such members.

In Example 4.10, the class `Light` defines a `final` static variable at (1) and a `final` method at (2). An attempt to change the value of the `final` variable at (3) results in a compile time error. The subclass `TubeLight` attempts to override the `final` method `setKWH` from the superclass `Light` at (4), which is illegal. The class `Warehouse` defines a `final` local reference `aLight` at (5). The state of the object denoted by `aLight` can be changed at (6), but its reference value cannot be changed as attempted at (7).

Example 4.10 *Accessing Final Members*

```
class Light {
    // Final static variable                 (1)
    final public static double KWH_PRICE = 3.25;

    int noOfWatts;

    // Final instance methods                (2)
    final public void setWatts(int watt) {
         noOfWatts = watt;
    }

    public void setKWH() {
      // KWH_PRICE = 4.10;                  // (3) Not OK. Cannot be changed.
    }
}

class TubeLight extends Light {
    // Final method cannot be overriden.
    // This will not compile.
```

```
    /*
    public void setWatts(int watt) {       // (4) Attempt to override.
        noOfWatts = 2*watt;
    }
    */
}

public class Warehouse {
    public static void main(String args[]) {

        final Light aLight = new Light();// (5) Final local variable.
        aLight.noOfWatts = 100;          // (6) OK. Changing object state.
    //  aLight = new Light();            // (7) Not OK. Changing final reference.
    }
}
```

abstract **Methods**

An abstract method has the following syntax:

`abstract` ... *<return type>* *<method name>* (*<parameter list>*) *<throws clause>*;

An abstract method does not have an implementation, i.e. no method body is defined for an `abstract` method, only the method prototype is provided in the class definition. Its class is then `abstract` (i.e. incomplete) and must be explicitly declared as such (Section 4.7, p. 109). Subclasses of an abstract class must then provide the method implementation, otherwise they are also abstract. See Section 4.7, where Example 4.6 also illustrates the usage of `abstract` methods.

A `final` method cannot be `abstract` (i.e. cannot be incomplete), and vice versa. Methods specified in an interface are implicitly `abstract`, as only the method prototypes are defined in an interface (Section 6.4, p. 195).

synchronized **Methods**

Several threads can be executing in a program (Section 9.4, p. 279). They might try to execute the same method on an object simultaneously. If it is desired that only one thread at a time can execute the method, then the method can be specified as `synchronized` in the method definition. Its execution is then mutually exclusive among all threads. At any one time, only one thread can be executing `synchronized` methods on an object. This discussion also applies to `static synchronized` methods of a class.

Example 4.11 *Synchronized Methods*

```
class StackImpl {
    private Object[] stackArray;
    private int topOfStack;
```

```
    // ...
    synchronized public void push(Object elem) { // (1)
        stackArray[++topOfStack] = elem;
    }

    synchronized public Object pop() {           // (2)
        Object obj = stackArray[topOfStack];
        stackArray[topOfStack] = null;
        topOfStack--;
        return obj;
    }
    // Other methods, etc.
    public Object peek() { return stackArray[topOfStack]; }
}
```

In Example 4.11, both the `push()` and the `pop()` methods are `synchronized` in class `StackImpl`. Now at most one thread can execute a `synchronized` method in an object of the class `StackImpl`. This means that it is not possible for the state of an object of the class `StackImpl` to be corrupted, for example, while one thread is pushing an element and another is popping the stack.

`native` Methods

Native methods are also called *foreign methods*. Their implementation is not defined in Java but in another programming language, for example C or C++. Such a method can be a declared member in a Java class definition. Since its implementation appears elsewhere, only the method prototype is specified in the class definition. The method prototype is prefixed with the keyword `native`. The example below shows how native methods are used.

JNI (Java Native Interface) is a special API which allows Java methods to invoke native methods implemented in C.

In the example a `native` method in class `Native` is declared at (2). The class also uses a static initializer (Section 8.2, p. 260) at (1) to load the native library when the class is loaded. Clients of the `Native` class can call the `native` method like another method call as at (3).

```
class Native {

    /*
     * The static block ensures that the native method library
     * is loaded before the native method is called.
     */
    static {
        System.loadLibrary("NativeMethodLib");  // (1) Load native library.
    }

    native void nativeMethod();                 // (2) Native method prototype.
    // ...
}
```

```
class Client {
    //...
    public static void main(String args[]) {

        Native aNative = new Native();
        aNative.nativeMethod();                // (3) Native method call.

    }
    //...
}
```

transient Variables

Objects can be stored, using serialization (Section 18.6, p. 587). Objects can later be retrieved in the same state as when they were serialized, meaning that all their instance variables will have the same values they had at the time of serialization. Such objects are said to be *persistent*.

There are cases where a value of an instance variable in a class will not be persistent when the object is stored. Such an instance variable can be specified as `transient`, indicating that its value need not be saved when objects of its class are put in persistent storage. In the example below, the instance variable `currentTemperature` is declared `transient` at (1), because the current temperature is most likely to have changed when the object is restored at a later date. However, the value of the instance variable `mass`, declared at (2), is likely to remain persistent. When objects of the class `Experiment` are serialized, the value of `currentTemperature` will not be saved, but that of variable `mass` will be, as part of the state of the serialized object.

```
class Experiment implements Serializable {
    // ...

    // The value of currentTemperature will not persist
    transient int currentTemperature;     // (1) Transient value.

    double mass;                          // (2) Persistent value.

}
```

Note that the `transient` modifier should not be specified for `static` variables, as these do not belong to objects.

volatile Variables

During execution, threads might cache the values of member variables for efficiency reasons. Since threads can share a variable, it is then vital that reading and writing of the value in the copies and the master variable do not result in any inconsistencies. As this variable's value could be changed unexpectedly, the `volatile` modifier can be used to inform the compiler that it should not attempt to perform optimizations on the variable.

In the simple example below, the value of the instance variable `clockReading` might be changed unexpectedly by another thread while one thread is performing a task which involves always using the current value of clockReading. Declaring the variable as volatile ensures that a write operation will always be performed on the master variable, and a read operation will always return the correct current value.

```
class VitalControl {
    // ...
    volatile long clockReading;
    // Two successive reads might give different results.
}
```

Table 4.4 *Summary of Other Modifiers for Members*

Modifiers	Variables	Methods
`static`	Defines a class variable.	Defines a class method.
`final`	Defines a constant.	The method cannot be overridden.
`abstract`	Not relevant.	No method body is defined. Its class must be designated abstract.
`synchronized`	Not relevant.	Methods can only be executed by one thread at a time.
`native`	Not relevant.	Declares that the method is implemented in another language.
`transient`	This variable's value will not be persistent if its object is serialized.	Not applicable.
`volatile`	This variable's value can change asynchronously; the compiler should not attempt to optimize it.	Not applicable.

Review questions

4.20 Which of these statements concerning the use of modifiers are true?

Select all valid answers.

(a) If no accessibility modifier (public, protected and private) is given in a member declaration of a class, the member is only accessible for classes in the same package and subclasses of the class.

(b) You cannot specify visibility of local variables. They are always only accessible within the block in which they are declared.

(c) Subclasses of a class must reside in the same package as the class they extend.

(d) Local variables can be declared static.

(e) Objects themselves do not have any visibility, only the references to the object.

4.21 Given the following source code, which one of the lines that are commented out may be reinserted without introducing errors?

```
abstract class MyClass {
    abstract void f();
    final    void g() {}
 // final    void h() {}                                // (1)

    protected static int i;
    private          int j;
}

final class MyOtherClass extends MyClass {
 // MyOtherClass(int n) { m = n; }                      // (2)

    public static void main(String args[]) {
        MyClass mc = new MyOtherClass();
    }

    void f() {}
    void h() {}
 // void k() { i++; }                                   // (3)
 // void l() { j++; }                                   // (4)

    int m;
}
```

Select the one right answer.

(a) `final void h() {}` // (1)
(b) `MyOtherClass(int n) { m = n; }` // (2)
(c) `void k() { i++; }` // (3)
(d) `void l() { j++; }` // (4)

4.22 What would be the result of attempting to compile and run the following program?

```
class MyClass {
    static MyClass ref;
    String[] arguments;

    public static void main(String args[]) {
        ref = new MyClass();
        ref.func(args);
    }

    public void func(String[] args) {
        ref.arguments = args;
    }
}
```

Select the one right answer.

(a) The program will fail to compile, since the static method `main` is trying to call the non-static method `func`.
(b) The program will fail to compile, since the non-static method `func` cannot access the static member variable `ref`.

(c) The program will fail to compile, since the argument `args` passed to the static method `main` cannot be passed on to the non-static method `func`.
(d) The program will fail to compile, since method `func` is trying to assign to the non-static member variable `arguments` through the static member variable `ref`.
(e) The program will compile, but will throw an exception when run.
(f) The program will compile and run successfully.

4.23 Given the following set of member declarations, which statement is true?

```
int a;                            // (1)
static int a;                     // (2)
int f() { return a; }             // (3)
static int f() { return a; }      // (4)
```

Select all valid answers.

(a) Declarations (1) and (3) cannot occur in the same class definition.
(b) Declarations (2) and (4) cannot occur in the same class definition.
(c) Declarations (1) and (4) cannot occur in the same class definition.
(d) Declarations (2) and (3) cannot occur in the same class definition.

4.24 Which of these statements are true?

Select all valid answers.

(a) A static method can call other non-static methods in the same class by using the `this` keyword.
(b) A class may contain both static and non-static variables and both static and non-static methods.
(c) Each object of a class has its own instance of each static member variable.
(d) Instance methods may access local variables of static methods.
(e) All methods in a class are implicitly passed a `this` parameter when called.

4.25 What, if anything, is wrong with the following code?

```
abstract class MyClass {
    transient int j;
    synchronized int k;

    final void MyClass() {}

    static void f() {}
}
```

Select the one right answer.

(a) The class `MyClass` cannot be declared `abstract`.
(b) The variable `j` cannot be declared `transient`.
(c) The variable `k` cannot be declared `synchronized`.
(d) The constructor `MyClass()` cannot be declared `final`.
(e) The method `f()` cannot be declared `static`.
(f) Nothing is wrong with the code, it will compile without errors.

4.26 Which of these are not legal declarations within a class?

Select all valid answers.

(a) `static int a;`
(b) `final Object[] fudge = { null };`
(c) `abstract int t;`
(d) `native void sneeze();`
(e) `final transient static private double PI = 3.14159265358979323846;`

4.27 Which of these statements concerning modifiers are true?

Select all valid answers.

(a) Abstract classes can contain `final` methods.
(b) Variables can be declared `native`.
(c) Non-`abstract` methods can be declared in `abstract` classes.
(d) Classes can be declared `native`.
(e) Abstract classes can be `final`.

4.28 Which of these statements are true?

Select all valid answers.

(a) Transient variables will not be saved during serialization.
(b) Constructors can be declared `abstract`.
(c) The initial state of an array object constructed with the statement `int a[] = new int[10]` will depend on whether the variable `a[]` is a local variable, or a member variable of a class.
(d) Any subclass of a class with an `abstract` method must implement a method body for that method.
(e) Only `static` methods can access `static` members.

Chapter summary

The following information was included in this chapter:

- Explanation of declaration, construction, initialization and usage of both simple and multidimensional arrays, including anonymous arrays.
- Defining classes.
- Defining methods, usage of `this` reference in an instance method, and method overloading.
- Defining constructors, usage of the default constructor and overloading of constructors.
- Defining and using packages.
- Discussion of accessibility (default, `public`) and other modifiers (`abstract`, `final`) for classes and interfaces.

- Explanation of class scope for members, and block scope for local variables.
- Applicability of accessibility (default, `public`, `protected`, `private`) and other modifiers (`static`, `final`, `abstract`, `synchronized`, `native`, `transient`, `volatile`) for members.

Programming exercises

4.1 Imagine you are creating an application that has a number of different tools a user may invoke. These tools need a special context to work in. The context describes the current active selection in the application. The selection consists of a reference to an arbitrary object. We wish to create a class representing an editing context that the tools may use. This class should contain the aforementioned selection reference. We do not want to allow direct manipulation of the reference, but want to have methods in the context class that allow anyone to get and set the current selection.

Write such a class. Be sure to get the accessibility right.

4.2 A wide variety of tools can exist in an application, as described in Exercise 4.1. The only thing they all have in common is that they can all be given an instance of an editing context, and that they are in either an active or an inactive state.

Write an interface that contains methods for giving the tool an editing context instance and querying the tool whether it is active or not.

4.3 Design a class for a bank database. The database should support the following operations:

- depositing a certain amount into an account.
- withdrawing a certain amount from an account.
- return a value specifying the amount (i.e. the balance) in an account.
- transferring an amount from one account to another.

The amount in the transactions is a value of type `long`. The accounts are identified by instances of a class `Account` that resides in a package called `com.megabankcorp.records`. The database object should reside in a package called `com.megabankcorp.system`. The depositing, withdrawing and amount-specifying operations should not have any implementation, but allow subclasses to provide the implementation. The transferring operation should use the depositing and withdrawing operations to implement the transfer. It should not be possible to alter this operation in any subclass, and only classes within the package `com.megabankcorp.system` should be allowed to use this operation. The depositing and withdrawing operations should be available from anywhere. The balance operation should only be available from subclasses and from classes within the package `com.megabankcorp.system`.

5 Flow Control and Exception Handling

Exam Objectives

- Write code using `if` and `switch` statements, and identify legal argument types for these statements.
- Write code using all forms of loops, including labeled and unlabeled use of `break` and `continue`, and state the values taken by loop counter variables during and after loop execution.
- Write code that makes proper use of exceptions and exception handling clauses (`try-catch-finally`), and declares methods and overriding methods that throw exceptions.

Supplementary Objectives

- State the names of the major classes in the inheritance hierarchy of exception classes.
- Distinguish between checked and unchecked exceptions.
- Understand exception propagation through the method activation stack.

5.1 Overview of Flow Control Statements

Flow control statements govern the flow of control in a program during execution. There are three main categories of flow control statements that are discussed in this chapter:

- *Selection* statements: `if`, `if-else` and `switch`.
- *Iteration* statements: `while`, `do-while` and `for`.
- *Transfer* statements: `break`, `continue`, `return` and `try-catch-finally`.

5.2 Selection Statements

Java provides selection statements that allow the program to choose between alternate actions during execution. The choice is based on criteria specified in the selection statement. These selection statements are:

- Simple `if` Statement
- `if-else` Statement
- `switch` Statement

Simple `if` Statement

The simple `if` statement has the following syntax:

`if` (*<conditional expression>*)
    <statement>

It is used to choose whether an action is to be performed, based on a condition. The condition is specified by *<conditional expression>* and the action to be performed is specified by *<statement>*.

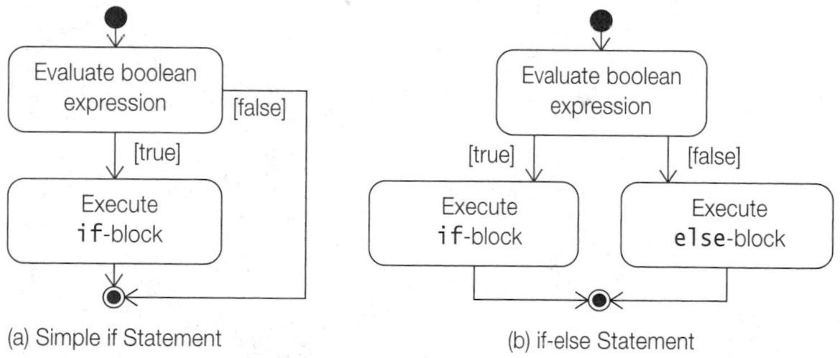

Figure 5.1 *State Diagram for `if` Statements*

The semantics of the simple `if` statement are straightforward. The *<conditional expression>* is evaluated first. If its value is `true`, then *<statement>* is executed and afterwards execution continues with the rest of the program. If the value is `false`, then *<statement>* is skipped and execution continues with the rest of the program. The semantics are illustrated by the state diagram in Figure 5.1a.

Here are some simple examples of the `if` statement. It is assumed that the variables have been declared and the methods defined appropriately:

```
if (emergency) operate(); // emergency is a boolean variable

if (temperature > critical) soundAlarm();

if (isLeapYear() && endOfCentury()) celebrate();

if (catIsAway()) {          // Block
    getFishingRod();
    goFishing();
}
```

Note that *<statement>* can be a *block*, and *<conditional expression>* can be an arbitrary `boolean` expression.

`if-else` Statement

The `if-else` statement has the following syntax:

```
if (<conditional expression>)
    <statement1>
else
    <statement2>
```

It is used to choose between two actions, based on a condition.

The *<conditional expression>* is evaluated first. If its value is `true`, then <*statement*$_1$> (also called the `if` block) is executed and afterwards execution continues with the rest of the program. If the value is `false`, then <*statement*$_2$> (also called the `else` block) is executed and afterwards execution continues with the rest of the program. In other words, one of two mutually exclusive actions is performed. The `else` clause is optional; if omitted, the construct reduces to the simple `if` statement. The semantics are illustrated by the state diagram in Figure 5.1b.

Some examples of the `if-else` statement are given below, where it is assumed that all variables and methods have been declared appropriately:

```
if (emergency)
    operate();
else
    joinQueue();

if (temperature > critical)
    soundAlarm();
else
    businessAsUsual();
```

```
if (catIsAway()) {
    getFishingRod();
    goFishing();
} else
    killCat();
```

Since actions can be arbitrary statements, the `if` statements can be nested:

```
if (temperature >= upperLimit) {          // (1)
    if (danger) soundAlarm();             // (2) Simple if.
    if (critical)                         // (3)
        evacuate();
    else                                  // Goes with if at (3).
        turnHeaterOff();
} else                                    // Goes with if at (1).
        turnHeaterOn();
```

The use of the block notation, {}, can be critical to the meaning of `if` statements. The `if` statements (A) and (B) in the following examples do *not* have the same meaning. The `if` statements (B) and (C) are the same, with extra indentation used in (C) to make the meaning evident. Leaving out the block notation in this case could have catastrophic consequences: the heater could be turned on when the temperature is above the upper limit.

```
// (A)
if (temperature > upperLimit) {          // (1) Block notation.
    if (danger) soundAlarm();            // (2)
} else turnHeaterOn();                   // Goes with if at (1).

// (B)
if (temperature > upperLimit)            // (1) Without block notation.
    if (danger) soundAlarm();            // (2)
else turnHeaterOn();                     // Goes with if at (2).

// (C)
if (temperature > upperLimit)            // (1)
    if (danger)                          // (2)
        soundAlarm();
    else                                 // Goes with if at (2).
        turnHeaterOn();
```

The rule for matching an `else` clause is that an `else` clause always refers to the nearest `if` which is not already associated with another `else` clause. Block notation and proper indentation can be used to make the meaning obvious.

Cascading `if-else` statements are a sequence of nested `if-else` statements where the `if` of the next `if-else` statement is joined to the `else` clause of the previous one. The decision to execute a block is then based on all the conditions evaluated so far.

```
if (temperature >= upperLimit) {                          // (1)
    soundAlarm();
    turnHeaterOff();
} else if (temperature < lowerLimit) {                    // (2)
    soundAlarm();
    turnHeaterOn();
```

```
} else if (temperature == (upperLimit-lowerLimit)/2) {     // (3)
    doingFine();
} else                                                      // (4)
    noCauseToWorry();
```

The block corresponding to the first `if` condition that evaluates to `true` is executed, and the remaining `if`s are skipped. In the example given above, the block at (3) will execute only if the conditions at (1) and (2) are `false` and the condition at (3) is `true`. If none of the conditions are true, the block associated with the last `else` clause is executed, and if there is no last `else` clause then no actions are performed.

`switch` Statement

The `switch` statement can be used to choose one among many alternative actions, based on the value of an integral expression. Its general form is as follows:

```
switch (<integral expression>) {
    case label1:
        <statement1>
    case label2:
        <statement2>
    ...
    case labeln:
        <statementn>
    default:
        <statement>
} // end switch
```

The syntax of the `switch` statement comprises a `switch` expression followed by the `switch` body, which is a block. Its semantics are as follows:

- The integral expression is evaluated first.
- The value of the integral expression is successively compared with the `case` labels. The <*statement*$_i$> associated with the `case` label that is equal to the value of the integral expression is executed. The <*statement*$_i$> can be a sequence of arbitrary statements. After execution of the associated statement, control *falls through* to the *next* statement unless appropriate action is taken. The examples below will make this clear.
- If no `case` label is equal to the value of the integral expression, the statement associated with the `default` label is performed.

Figure 5.2 illustrates the flow of control through a `switch` statement.

There are few other aspects to note about the `switch` statement. All labels are optional. There can be at most one `default` label in a `switch` statement. If it is left out and no valid `case` labels are found, the whole `switch` statement is skipped.

default label is not a must
if present there can be only one default

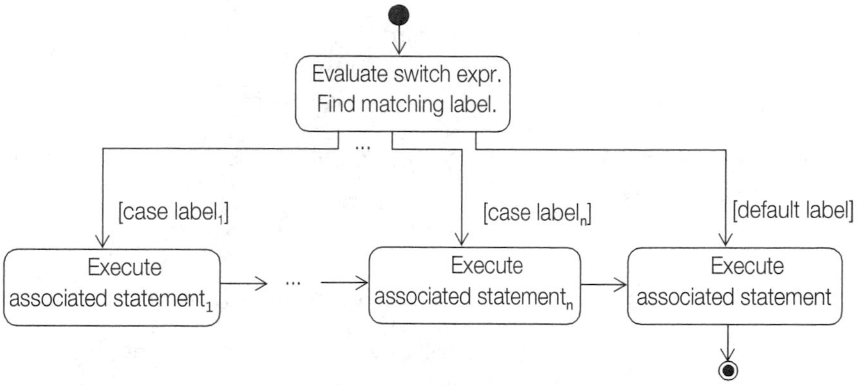

Figure 5.2 *State Diagram for* `switch` *Statement*

The labels (including the `default` label) can be specified in any order in the `switch` body. The `case` labels are constant expressions whose values must be unique, meaning no duplicate values are allowed. Multiple `case` labels can be specified for the same associated statement (Example 5.3).

The type of the integral expression must be `char`, `byte`, `short` or `int`. The `case` label values must be *assignable* to the type of the integral expression (Section 3.3, p. 47). In particular, the `case` label values must be in the range of the type of the integral expression. Note that the type of the `case` label cannot be `boolean`, `long` or floating-point.

In Example 5.1, depending on the value of the `howMuchAdvice` parameter, different advice is printed in the `switch` statement at (1) in the method `dispenseAdvice`. The example shows the output when the value of the `howMuchAdvice` parameter is `LOTS_OF_ADVICE`. In the `switch` statement, the associated statement at (2) is executed, giving one advice. Control then falls through to the statement at (3), giving the second advice. Control falls through to (4), dispensing the third advice, and finally executing the `break` statement at (5) causes control to exit the `switch` statement. Without the `break` statement at (5), control would continue to fall through the remaining labels if there were any. Execution of the `break` statement in a `switch` body transfers control out of the `switch` statement (Section 5.4, p. 145). If the parameter `howMuchAdvice` has the value `MORE_ADVICE`, then the advice at (3) and (4) is given. The value `LITTLE_ADVICE` results in only one advice at (5) being given. Any other value results in the `default` action, which announces that there is no advice.

It is important to note that the associated statement of a `case` label can be a *list* of statements (which need *not* be a statement block). The `case` label is prefixed to the first statement in each `case`. This is illustrated by the associated statement for the `case` label `LITTLE_ADVICE` in Example 5.1, which comprises statements (4) and (5).

Example 5.1 *Fall Through in* `switch` *Statement*

```
public class Advice {
    public static final int LITTLE_ADVICE = 0;
    public static final int MORE_ADVICE = 1;
    public static final int LOTS_OF_ADVICE = 2;

    public static void main(String args[]) {
        dispenseAdvice(LOTS_OF_ADVICE);
    }

    public static void dispenseAdvice(int howMuchAdvice) {
        switch(howMuchAdvice) {                          // (1)
            case LOTS_OF_ADVICE:
                System.out.println("See no evil.");      // (2)
            case MORE_ADVICE:
                System.out.println("Speak no evil.");    // (3)
            case LITTLE_ADVICE:
                System.out.println("Hear no evil.");     // (4)
                break;                                   // (5)
            default:
                System.out.println("No advice.");        // (6)
        }
    }
}
```

Output from the program:

```
See no evil.
Speak no evil.
Hear no evil.
```

Use of the `break` statement in a `switch` statement is a common programming idiom. Example 5.2 illustrates the use of this idiom for converting the `char` value of a digit to its corresponding string. Note that the `break` statement is the last statement in the list of statements associated with each `case` label. It is easy to think that the `break` statement is a part of the `switch` statement syntax, but technically it is not.

Example 5.2 *Using* `break` *in* `switch` *Statement*

```
public class Digits {

    public static void main(String args[]) {
        System.out.println(digitToString('7') + " " +
                           digitToString('8') + " " +
                           digitToString('6'));
    }

    public static String digitToString(char digit) {
        String str = "";
        switch(digit) {
            case '1': str = "one";   break;
            case '2': str = "two";   break;
```

```
                case '3': str = "three"; break;
                case '4': str = "four";  break;
                case '5': str = "five";  break;
                case '6': str = "six";   break;
                case '7': str = "seven"; break;
                case '8': str = "eight"; break;
                case '9': str = "nine";  break;
                case '0': str = "zero";  break;
                default:  System.out.println(digit + " is not a digit!");
            }
            return str;
        }
    }
```

Output from the program:

```
seven eight six
```

Several case labels can have the same associated statement. This is a consequence of control falling through: if there is no associated statement for a case label, then control falls through to the next statement successively. This is illustrated in Example 5.3 for the switch statement at (1). The semantics of the switch statement are the same as before.

Since each action associated with a case label can be an arbitrary statement, it can be another switch statement. In other words, switch statements can be nested. Since a switch statement defines its own local block, the case labels in an inner block do not conflict with any case labels in an outer block. Labels can be redefined in nested blocks, but variables cannot (Section 4.8, p. 113). In Example 5.3, an inner switch statement is defined at (2). This allows further refinement of the action to take on the value of the switch expression, in cases when multiple labels are used in the outer switch statement.

Nested Switch Stmt

Example 5.3 *Nested* switch *Statement*

```
public class Seasons {

    public static void main(String args[]) {
        int monthNumber = 11;
        switch(monthNumber) {                                    // (1) Outer.
            case 12: case 1: case 2:
                System.out.println("Snow in the winter.");
                break;
            case 3: case 4: case 5:
                System.out.println("Green grass in spring.");
                break;
            case 6: case 7: case 8:
                System.out.println("Sunshine in the summer.");
                break;
```

```
            case 9: case 10: case 11:                              // (2)
                switch(monthNumber) { // Nested switch                (3) Inner.
                    case 10:
                        System.out.println("Halloween.");
                        break;
                    case 11:
                        System.out.println("Thanksgiving.");
                        break;
                } // end nested switch
                // Always printed for case labels 9, 10, 11
                System.out.println("Yellow leaves in the fall.");   // (4)
                break;
            default:
                System.out.println(monthNumber + " is not a valid month.");
        }
    }
}
```

Output from the program:

```
Thanksgiving.
Yellow leaves in the fall.
```

Review questions

5.1 What will be the result of attempting to compile and run the following class?

```
public class IfTest {
    public static void main(String args[]) {
        if (true)
        if (false)
        System.out.println("a");
        else
        System.out.println("b");
    }
}
```

Select the one right answer.

(a) The code will fail to compile because the syntax of the `if` statement is incorrect.

(b) The code will fail to compile because the compiler will not be able to determine which `if` the `else` clause belongs to.

(c) The code will compile correctly and will display the letter `a` when run.

(d) The code will compile correctly and will display the letter `b` when run.

(e) The code will compile correctly but will not display any output.

5.2 Which of these statements are true?

Select all valid answers.

(a) The condition expression in an `if` statement can contain method calls.
(b) If `a` and `b` are of type `boolean`, the expression `(a = b)` can be the condition expression of an `if` statement.
(c) An `if` statement can have either an `if` clause or an `else` clause.
(d) The statement `if (false) ; else ;` is illegal.
(e) Only expressions which evaluate to a `boolean` value can be used as the condition in an `if` statement.

5.3 What, if anything, is wrong with the following code?

```
void test(int x) {
    switch (x) {
        case 1:
        case 2:
        case 0:
        default:
        case 4:
    }
}
```

Select the one right answer.

(a) The `x` is not the right type to use as an expression for the `switch` clause.
(b) The `case` label `0` must precede `case` label `1`.
(c) Each `case` section must be ended by a `break` keyword.
(d) The `default` label must be the last label in the `switch` statement.
(e) The body of the `switch` statement must contain at least one statement.
(f) There is nothing wrong with the code.

5.4 Which of these combinations of `switch` expression types and `case` label value types are legal within a `switch` statement?

Select all valid answers.

(a) `switch` expression of type `int` and `case` label value of type `char`.
(b) `switch` expression of type `float` and `case` label value of type `int`.
(c) `switch` expression of type `byte` and `case` label value of type `float`.
(d) `switch` expression of type `char` and `case` label value of type `long`.
(e) `switch` expression of type `boolean` and `case` value of type `boolean`.

5.3 Iteration Statements

Loops allow a block of statements to be executed repeatedly (i.e. iterated). A boolean condition is commonly used to determine when to terminate the loop, called the *loop condition*. The statements executed in the loop constitute the *loop body*. The loop body can be a single statement or a block.

Java provides three language constructs for constructing loops:

- `while` Statement
- `do-while` Statement
- `for` Statement

These loops differ in the order in which they execute the loop body and test the loop condition. The `while` and the `for` loops test the loop condition before executing the loop body, while the `do-while` loop tests the loop condition after execution of the loop body.

`while` Statement

The syntax of the `while` loop is:

```
while (<loop condition>)
   <loop body>
```

The loop condition is evaluated before executing the loop body. The `while` statement executes the loop body as long as the loop condition is `true`. When the loop condition becomes `false`, the loop is terminated and execution continues with the statement immediately following the loop. If the loop condition is `false` to begin with, the loop body is not executed at all. The loop condition must be a `boolean` expression. The flow of control in a `while` statement is shown in Figure 5.3.

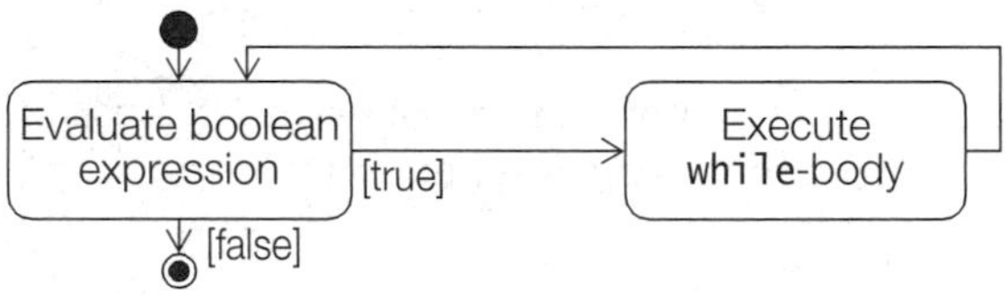

Figure 5.3 *State Diagram for* `while` *Statement*

The `while` statement is normally used when the number of iterations is not known *a priori*:

```
while (noSignOfLife())
    keepLooking();
```

Note that the loop body can be any valid statement, including a block. In particular it can be the empty statement (`;`) or the empty block (`{}`). Inadvertently terminating each line with a semicolon can give unexpected results:

```
while (noSignOfLife());      // Empty statement as loop body!
    keepLooking();           // Statement not in the loop body.
```

`do-while` Statement

The syntax of the `do-while` loop is:

```
do
   <loop body>
while (<loop condition>);
```

The loop condition is evaluated after executing the loop body. The `do-while` statement executes the loop body as long as the loop condition is `true`. When the loop condition becomes `false`, the loop is terminated and execution continues with the statement immediately following the loop. Note that the loop body is executed at least once. Figure 5.4 illustrates the flow of control in a `do-while` statement.

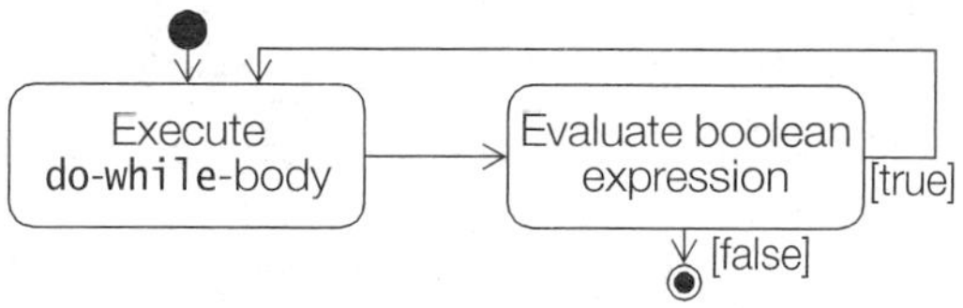

Figure 5.4 *State Diagram for* `do-while` *Statement*

The loop body in a `do-while` loop is invariably a statement block. It is instructive to compare the `while` and the `do-while` loops. In the examples below, the mice might never get to play if the cat is not away, as in the loop at (1). The mice do get to play at least once (at the peril of losing their life) in the loop at (2).

```
while (cat.isAway()) {        // (1)
    mice.play();
}
do {                          // (2)
    mice.play();
} while (cat.isAway());
```

`for` Statement

The `for` loop is the most general of all the loops. It is mostly used for counter-controlled loops, i.e. when the number of iterations is known beforehand.

The syntax of the loop is as follows:

```
for (<initialization>; <loop condition>; <increment expression>)
   <loop body>
```

The *<initialization>* usually declares and initializes a loop variable that controls the execution of the *<loop body>*. The *<loop condition>* is a `boolean` expression, usually involving the loop variable, such that if the loop condition is `true`, the loop body is executed, otherwise execution continues with the statement following the `for` loop. After each iteration, i.e. execution of the loop body, the *<increment expression>* is executed. This usually modifies the value of the loop variable to ensure loop termination. The loop condition is then tested to determine if the loop body should be executed again. Note that the *<initialization>* is only executed once on entry to the loop. The semantics of the `for` loop are illustrated in Figure 5.5, and can be summarized by the following code template:

```
<initialization>
while (<loop condition>) {
    <loop body>
    <increment expression>
}
```

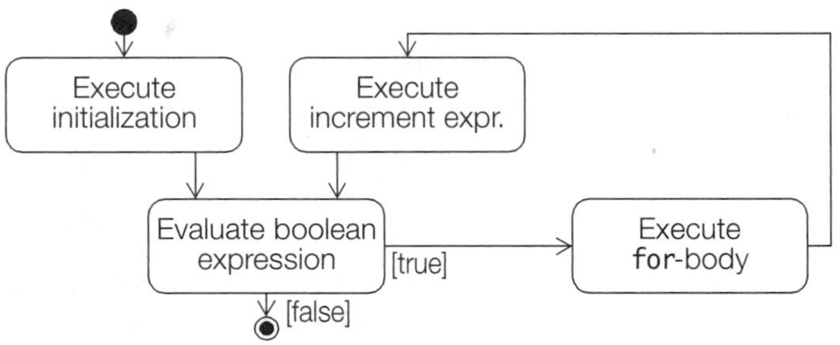

Figure 5.5 *State Diagram for the* `for` *Statement*

```
int sum = 0;
int[] array = {12, 23, 5, 7, 19};
for (int index = 0; index < array.length; index++)
    sum += array[index];
```

In the example above, the variable `index` is declared and initialized in the *<initialization>* section of the loop. The `for` loop defines a local block such that the scope of this declaration is the `for` block, which comprises the *<initialization>*, the *<loop condition>*, the *<loop body>* and the *<increment expression>* sections. The *<increment expression>* can be a comma-separated list of *expression* statements, while the *<initialization>* can be either a comma-separated list of *declaration* statements or expression statements. The following code specifies three declaration statements in the *<initialization>* section, and two expression statements in the *<increment expression>* section (Section 4.3, p. 98):

```
// Legal usage but not recommended.
int[][] sqMatrix = { {3, 4, 6}, {5, 7, 4}, {5, 8, 9} };
for (int i = 0, j = sqMatrix[0].length - 1, asymDiagonal = 0;  // initialization
     i < sqMatrix.length;                                      // loop condition
     i++, j--)                                           // increment expression
     asymDiagonal += sqMatrix[i][j];
```

All variables declared in the *<initialization>* section are local variables in the `for` block and obey the scope rules for local blocks. The *<initialization>* section in the above example is a legal comma-separated list of declaration statements, and such comma-separated declarations cannot be mixed with expression statements in the

<initialization> section as is the case at (1) in the example below. Factoring out the declaration, as at (2), leaves a legal comma-separated list of expression statements only.

```
// (1) Not legal and ugly.
for (int i = 0, System.out.println("This won't do!"); flag; i++) {
    // loop body
}

// (2) Legal but still ugly.
int i;
for (i = 0, System.out.println("This is legal!"); flag; i++) {
    // loop body
}
```

The sections in the `for`-header are optional. Any one of them can be left empty, but the two semicolons are mandatory. In particular, leaving out the *<loop condition>* signifies that the loop condition is `true`. The "crab", `(;;)`, is commonly used to construct an infinite loop, where termination is then achieved by other means:

```
for (;;) Java.programming();       // Infinite loop
```

5.4 Transfer Statements

Java provides four ways of transferring control in a program, which is embodied in the following language constructs:

- `break`
- `continue`
- `return`
- `try-catch-finally`

Note that Java does not have a `goto` statement, although `goto` is a reserved word.

`break` Statement

The `break` statement can be used in *labeled blocks*, loops (`for`, `while`, `do-while`) and `switch` statements, in order to transfer control out of the current context, i.e. the closest enclosing block. In the case of the labeled block, the rest of the block is skipped and execution continues with the statement following the block. For loops, the rest of the loop body is skipped, terminating the loop, with execution continuing with the statement following the loop. For the `switch` statement, the rest of the `switch` statement is skipped and execution continues with the statement following the `switch` statement. In Example 5.4, the `break` statement is used to terminate a `for` loop. Control is transferred to (2) when the value of `i` is equal to `4` at (1), skipping the rest of the loop body and terminating the loop.

Example 5.4 break *Statement*

```
class BreakOut {
    public static void main(String args[]) {
        for (int i = 1; i <= 5; ++i) {
            if (i == 4) break;          // (1) Terminate loop. Control to (2)
            // Rest of loop body skipped when i gets the value 4.
            System.out.println(i + "\t" + Math.sqrt(i));
        } // end for
        // (2) Continue here.
    }
}
```

Output from the program:

```
1    1.0
2    1.4142135623730951
3    1.7320508075688772
```

The break statement can also be used with an optional identifier which is the label of an arbitrary enclosing statement. Control is then transferred to the statement following this enclosing labeled statement. In Example 5.5, two nested for loops are defined at (1) and (2). The outer loop is labeled outer at (1). The break statement at (3) transfers control to (5) when it is executed, i.e. it terminates the inner loop and control is transferred to the statement after the inner loop. The labeled break statement at (4) transfers control to (6) when it is executed, i.e. it terminates both the inner and the outer loop, transferring control to the statement after the loop labeled outer.

Example 5.5 *Labeled* break *Statement*

```
class LabeledBreakOut {
    public static void main(String args[]) {
        int[][] squareMatrix = {{4, 3, 5}, {2, 1, 6}, {9, 7, 8}};
        int sum = 0;

        outer:                                                  // label
        for (int i = 0; i < squareMatrix.length; ++i){          // (1)
            for (int j = 0; j < squareMatrix[i].length; ++j) {  // (2)
                if (j == i) break;          // (3) Terminate this loop.
                                            //     Control to (5).
                System.out.println("Element[" + i + ", " + j + "]: " +
                                    squareMatrix[i][j]);
                sum += squareMatrix[i][j];
                if (sum > 10) break outer;// (4) Terminate both loops.
                                            //     Control to (6).
            } // end inner loop
            // (5) Continue with outer loop.
        } // end outer loop
```

```
            // (6) Continue here.
            System.out.println("sum: " + sum);
        }
    }
```

Output from the program:

```
Element[1, 0]: 2
Element[2, 0]: 9
sum: 11
```

`continue` Statement

The `continue` statement can be used in a `for`, `while` or `do-while` loop to prematurely stop the current iteration of the loop body and to proceed with the next iteration, if possible. In the case of the `while` and `do-while` loops, the rest of the loop body is skipped, i.e. stopping the current iteration, with execution continuing with the *<loop condition>*. In the case of the `for` loop, the rest of the loop body is skipped, with execution continuing with the *<increment expression>*. In Example 5.6, the `continue` statement is used to skip an iteration in a `for` loop. Control is transferred to (2) when the value of `i` is equal to `4` at (1), skipping the rest of the loop body and continuing with the *<increment expression>* in the `for` statement.

Example 5.6 `continue` *Statement*

```
class Skip {
    public static void main(String args[]) {
        for (int i = 1; i <= 5; ++i) {
            if (i == 4) continue;            // (1) Control to (2).
            // Rest of loop body skipped when i gets the value 4.
            System.out.println(i + "\t" + Math.sqrt(i));
            // (2). Continue with increment expression.
        } // end for
    }
}
```

Output from the program:

```
1       1.0
2       1.4142135623730951
3       1.7320508075688772
5       2.23606797749979
```

The `continue` statement can also be used with an optional identifier which is the label of an arbitrary enclosing loop. Control is then transferred to the end of that enclosing labeled loop. In Example 5.7, the `continue` statement at (3) transfers control to (5) when it is executed, i.e. the rest of the loop body is skipped and execution continues with the next iteration of the inner loop. The labeled `continue` statement at (4) transfers control to (6) when it is executed, i.e. it terminates the inner loop but execution continues with the next iteration of the loop labeled `outer`. It is instructive to compare the output from Example 5.5 (labeled `break`) and Example 5.7 (labeled `continue`).

Example 5.7 *Labeled* `continue` *Statement*

```
class LabeledSkip {
    public static void main(String args[]) {
        int[][] squareMatrix = {{4, 3, 5}, {2, 1, 6}, {9, 7, 8}};
        int sum = 0;

        outer:                                                    // label
        for (int i = 0; i < squareMatrix.length; ++i){           // (1)
            for (int j = 0; j < squareMatrix[i].length; ++j) {   // (2)
               if (j == i) continue;                          // (3) Control to (5).
                System.out.println("Element[" + i + ", " + j + "]: " +
                                    squareMatrix[i][j]);
                sum += squareMatrix[i][j];
               if (sum > 10) continue outer;                  // (4) Control to (6).
                // (5) Continue with inner loop.
            } // end inner loop
            // (6) Continue with outer loop.
        } // end outer loop
        System.out.println("sum: " + sum);
    }
}
```

Output from the program:

```
Element[0, 1]: 3
Element[0, 2]: 5
Element[1, 0]: 2
Element[1, 2]: 6
Element[2, 0]: 9
sum: 25
```

`return` Statement

The `return` statement is used to stop execution of the current method and transfer control back to the calling method (a.k.a. the *caller*). The usage of the two forms of the `return` statement is dictated by whether it is used in a `void` or a non-`void` method. The first form does not return any value to the calling program, but the second form does.

Table 5.1 `return` *Statement*

Form of `return` statement	In `void` method	In non-`void` method
`return;`	optional	not allowed
`return` *<expression>*`;`	not allowed	mandatory

The <*expression*> must evaluate to a primitive value or an object reference, and its type must be assignable to the *return type* in the method header (Section 3.3, Section 6.5). As can be seen from Table 5.1, non-`void` methods must return a value. A `void` method need not have a `return` statement – in which case control normally returns to the caller after the last statement in the callee's body has been executed. The first form of the `return` statement can also be used in constructors as these also do not return a value. Example 5.8 illustrates the usage of the `return` statement summarized in Table 5.1.

Example 5.8 *The* `return` *Statement*

```
public class ReturnDemo {

    public static void main (String args[]) { // (1) void method can use return.
        if (args.length == 0) return;
        output(checkValue(args.length));
    }

    static void output(int value) {   // (2) void method need not use return.
        System.out.println(value);
        return 'a';                   // Not OK. Cannot return a value.
    }

    static int checkValue(int i) {    // (3) non-void method must return a value.
        if (i > 3)
           return i;                  // OK.
        else
           return 2.0;                // Not OK. double not assignable to int.
    }
}
```

Review questions

5.5 What will be the result of attempting to compile and run the following code?

```
class MyClass {
    public static void main(String args[]) {
        boolean b = false;
        int i = 1;
        do {
            i++;
            b = ! b;
        } while (b);
        System.out.println(i);
    }
}
```

Select the one right answer.

(a) The code will fail to compile, since `b` is an invalid condition expression for the `do-while` statement.

(b) The code will fail to compile, since the assignment `b = ! b` is not allowed.

(c) The code will compile without error and will print 1 when run.
(d) The code will compile without error and will print 2 when run.
(e) The code will compile without error and will print 3 when run.

5.6 What will be the output when running the following program?

```
public class MyClass {
    public static void main(String args[]) {
        int i=0;
        int j;
        for (j=0; j<10; ++j) { i++; }
        System.out.println(i + " " + j);
    }
}
```

Select all valid answers.

(a) The first number printed will be 9.
(b) The first number printed will be 10.
(c) The first number printed will be 11.
(d) The second number printed will be 9.
(e) The second number printed will be 10.
(f) The second number printed will be 11.

5.7 Which of these for statements are valid?

Select all valid answers.

(a) `int j=10; for (int i=0, j+=90; i<j; i++) { j--; }`
(b) `for (int i=10; i=0; i--) {}`
(c) `for (int i=0, j=100; i<j; i++, --j) {;}`
(d) `int i, j; for (j=100; i<j; j--) { i += 2; }`
(e) `int i=100; for ((i>0); i--) {}`

5.8 What will be the result of attempting to compile and run the following program?

```
class MyClass {
    public static void main(String args[]) {
        int i = 0;
        for (   ; i<10; i++) ;      // (1)
        for (i=0;      ; i++) break; // (2)
        for (i=0; i<10;     ) i++;   // (3)
        for (   ;     ;     ) ;      // (4)
    }
}
```

Select the one right answer.

(a) The code will fail to compile, since the for statement in the line labeled (1) is missing the expression in the first section.
(b) The code will fail to compile, since the for statement in the line labeled (2) is missing the expression in the middle section.

(c) The code will fail to compile, since the for statement in the line labeled (3) is missing the expression in the last section.

(d) The code will fail to compile, since the for statement in the line labeled (4) is invalid.

(e) The code will compile without error and will run and terminate without any output.

(f) The code will compile without error, but will never terminate when run.

5.9 Which of these statements are valid when occurring by themselves?

Select all valid answers.

(a) `while () break;`

(b) `do { break; } while (true);`

(c) `if (true) { break; }`

(d) `switch (1) { default: break; }`

(e) `for (;true;) break;`

5.10 Given the following code fragment, which of the following lines would be a part of the output?

```
outer:
for (int i = 0; i < 3; i++) {
    for (int j = 0; j < 2; j++) {
        if (i == j) {
            continue outer;
        }
        System.out.println("i=" + i + ", j=" + j);
    }
}
```

Select all valid answers.

(a) `i=1, j=0`

(b) `i=0, j=1`

(c) `i=1, j=2`

(d) `i=2, j=1`

(e) `i=2, j=2`

(f) `i=3, j=3`

(g) `i=3, j=2`

5.11 What will be the result of attempting to compile and run the following code?

```
class MyClass {
    public static void main(String args[]) {
        for (int i = 0; i<10; i++) {
            switch(i) {
                case 0:
                    System.out.println(i);
            }
```

```
                    if (i) {
                        System.out.println(i);
                    }
                }
            }
        }
```

Select the one right answer.

(a) The code will fail to compile, owing to an illegal expression in the `switch()` clause.
(b) The code will fail to compile, owing to an illegal expression in the `if()` clause.
(c) The code will compile without error and will print the numbers 0 through 10 when run.
(d) The code will compile without error and will print the number 0 when run.
(e) The code will compile without error and will print the number 0 twice when run.
(f) The code will compile without error and will print the numbers 1 through 10 when run.

5.12 Which of the following implementations of a `max()` method will correctly return the largest value?

```
// (1)
int max(int x, int y) {
    return (if (x > y) { x; } else { y; });
}

// (2)
int max(int x, int y) {
    return (if (x > y) { return x; } else { return y; });
}

// (3)
int max(int x, int y) {
    switch (x < y) {
        case true:
            return y;
        default:
            return x;
    };
}

// (4)
int max(int x, int y) {
    if (x>y) return x;
    return y;
}
```

Select all valid answers.

(a) Implementation labeled (1)
(b) Implementation labeled (2)
(c) Implementation labeled (3)
(d) Implementation labeled (4)

5.13 Given the following code, which of these statements are true?

```
class MyClass {
    public static void main(String args[]) {
        int k=0;
        int l=0;
        for (int i=0; i <= 3; i++) {
            k++;
            if (i == 2) break;
            l++;
        }
        System.out.println(k + ", " + l);
    }
}
```

Select all valid answers.

(a) The program will fail to compile.
(b) The program will print `3, 3` when run.
(c) The program will print `4, 3` when run if `break` is replaced by `continue`.
(d) The program will fail to compile if `break` is replaced by `return`.
(e) The program will fail to compile if `break` is simply removed.

5.14 Which of these statements are true?

Select all valid answers.

(a) `{{}}` is a valid statement block.
(b) `{ continue; }` is a valid statement block.
(c) `block: { break block; }` is a valid statement block.
(d) `block: { continue block; }` is a valid statement block.
(e) The `break` keyword can only be used if there exists an enclosing loop construct (i.e. `while`, `do-while` or `for`).

5.5 Exception Handling

An exception in Java is a signal that indicates the occurrence of some exceptional condition. For example, a requested file cannot be found, or an index is out of bounds, or a network link failed. Manually and continuously testing for such conditions can easily result in incomprehensible code. Java provides a mechanism for systematically dealing with exceptional conditions.

The exception mechanism is built around the throw-and-catch paradigm. To *throw* an exception is to signal that an exceptional condition has occurred. To *catch* an exception is to take appropriate action to deal with the exception. An exception is caught by an *exception handler*, and the exception need not be caught in the same context that it was thrown in. The runtime behavior of the program determines which exceptions are thrown and how they are caught.

Exceptions in Java are objects. All exceptions are derived from the `java.lang.Throwable` class. Figure 5.6 shows a partial hierarchy of classes derived from the `Throwable` class. As the `java.io.IOException` shows, not all exception classes are found in the same package.

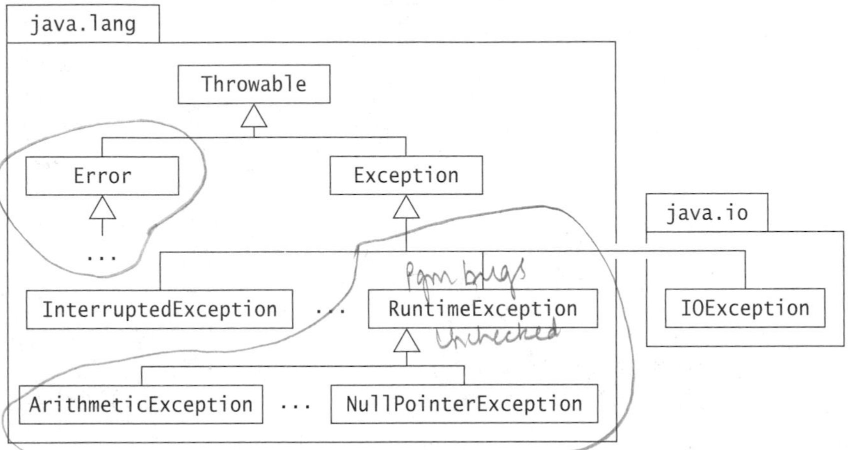

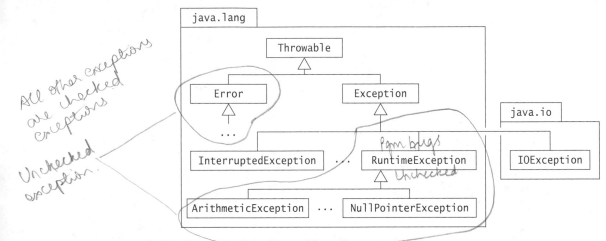

Figure 5.6 *Partial Exception Inheritance Hierarchy*

The `java.lang.Error` class and its subclasses define exceptions that indicate linkage (`LinkageError`), thread (`ThreadDeath`) and virtual machine (`VirtualMachineError`) related problems. These are invariably never explicitly caught, and are usually irrecoverable. All other kinds of exceptions are subclasses of the `java.lang.Exception` class.

Runtime exceptions like out-of-bound array indices (`ArrayIndexOutOfBoundsException`), uninitialized references (`NullPointerException`), illegal casting of references (`ClassCastException`), illegal parameters (`IllegalArgumentException`), division by zero (`ArithmeticException`) and number format (`NumberFormatException`) problems are all subclasses of the `java.lang.RuntimeException` class, which is a subclass of the `Exception` class. As these runtime exceptions are usually due to program bugs that should not occur in the first place, it is more appropriate to treat them as faults in the program design, rather than merely catching them during program execution.

Other subclasses of the `Exception` class define other categories of exceptions, for example I/O-related exceptions (`IOException`, `FileNotFoundException`, `EOFException`) and GUI-related exceptions (`AWTException`).

Except for `RuntimeException`, `Error` and their subclasses, all exceptions are called *checked* exceptions. The compiler ensures that if a method can throw a checked exception, directly or indirectly, then the method must explicitly deal with it. The method must either catch the exception and take the appropriate action, or pass on the exception to its caller (Section 5.8, p. 162).

Exceptions defined by `Error` and `RuntimeException` classes and their subclasses are known as *unchecked* exceptions, meaning that a method is not obliged to deal with these kinds of exceptions.

If an exception is not explicitly caught and handled by the program, it percolates upwards in the *method activation stack*, and is dealt with by the *default exception handler*. The default exception handler usually prints the name of the exception, with an explanatory message, followed by the *stack trace* (which is comprised of the active method calls in the method activation stack) at the time the exception was thrown. An uncaught exception results in the death of the thread in which the exception occurred.

Example 5.9 *Default Exception Handling*

```
public class DefaultExceptionHandlingDemo {

    public void division() {
        int num1 = 10;
        int num2 = 0;

        System.out.println(num1 + " / " + num2 + " = " + (num1/num2));    // (1)
        System.out.println("Returning from division.");                     // (2)
    }

    public static void main(String args[]) {
        new DefaultExceptionHandlingDemo().division();
    }
}
```

Output of program execution:

```
java.lang.ArithmeticException: / by zero
        at DefaultExceptionHandlingDemo.division(DefaultExceptionHandlingDemo.java)
        at DefaultExceptionHandlingDemo.main(DefaultExceptionHandlingDemo.java)
```

Example 5.9 illustrates how exceptions are handled by the default exception handler. Attempting to divide by zero, at (1), resulted in an exception being thrown by the runtime system. The statement at (2) never got executed, as the program was aborted. The stack trace in the output shows which method calls led to the `java.lang.ArithmeticException` being thrown. Also, since the methods on the call stack did not deal with the exception, it was dealt with by the default exception handler, as described above. In this case the exception was thrown by the runtime environment, and not by any explicit action taken by the program.

Exception Types

New exceptions are created by extending the `Exception` class or its subclasses, thereby making them checked. As exceptions are classes, they can define member variables and methods, thus providing more information as to their cause and remedy when they are thrown and caught. The `Throwable` class only provides a

`String` variable that can be set by the inheriting subclasses. Note that the exception class must be instantiated to create an exception object that can be thrown and subsequently caught and dealt with. The code below sketches a class definition for an exception that can include all pertinent information about the exception.

```
public class EvacuateException extends Exception {
    // Data
    Date date;
    Zone zone;
    TransportMode transport;

    // Constructor
    public EvacuateException(Date d, Zone z, TransportMode t) {
        // Call the constructor of the superclass
        super("Evacuation of zone " + z);
        // ...
    }
    // Methods
    // ...
}
```

Several examples illustrate exception handling in the subsequent sections.

5.6 `try`, `catch` and `finally` Blocks

The `try-catch-finally` construct allows handling of exceptions. Its general form is as follows:

```
try {                                               // try block
    <statements>
} catch (<exception type1> <parameter1>) {         // catch block
    <statements>
}
...
  catch (<exception typen> <parametern>) {         // catch block
    <statements>
} finally {                                         // finally block
    <statements>
}
```

Exceptions thrown during execution of the `try` block can be caught and handled in a `catch` block. The code in the `finally` block is always executed.

A few aspects about the syntax of this construct should be noted. The block notation is mandatory. For each `try` block there can be zero or more `catch` blocks, but only one `finally` block. The `catch` blocks and `finally` block must always appear in conjunction with a `try` block, and in the above order. A `try` block must be followed by either at least one `catch` block or one `finally` block. Each `catch` block defines an exception handler. The header of the `catch` block takes exactly one argument, which is the exception its block is willing to handle. The exception must be of the `Throwable` class or one of its subclasses.

Typical control flow through the `try-catch-finally` block is illustrated in Figure 5.7. In a `try-catch-finally` construct, if a `finally` block is specified, then it is guaranteed to be executed, regardless of the cause of exit from the `try` block, or whether any `catch` block was executed.

Note also that the construct can be nested as a block and can contain arbitrary code.

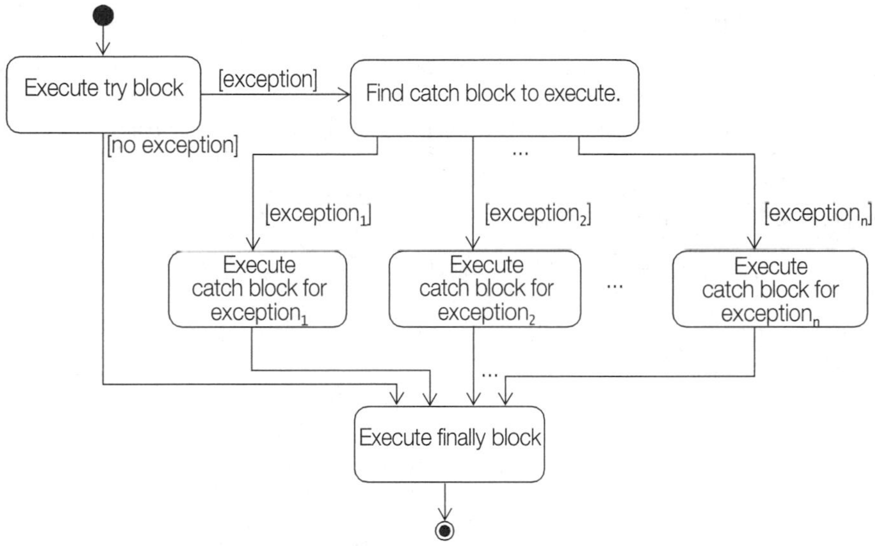

Figure 5.7 `try-catch-finally` *block*

`try` Block

The `try` block establishes a context that wants its termination to be handled. Termination occurs as a result of encountering an exception, or from successful execution of the code in the `try` block.

For all exits from the `try` block, except those due to exceptions, the `catch` blocks are skipped and control is transferred to the `finally` block, if one is specified.

For all exits from the `try` block resulting from exceptions, control is transferred to the `catch` blocks, if any such blocks are specified. If no `catch` block matches the thrown exception, control is transferred to the `finally` block, if one is specified.

`catch` Block

An exit from a `try` block resulting from an exception can transfer control to a `catch` block. A `catch` block can only handle the thrown exception if the exception is assignable to the reference type of the parameter in the `catch` block (Section 6.5, p. 201). The code of the first such `catch` block is executed and all other `catch` blocks are skipped.

After a catch block has been executed, control is always transferred to the finally block, if one is specified. This is always true as long as there is a finally block specified, regardless of whether the catch block itself throws an exception.

On exit from a catch block, if there is any pending exception that has been thrown and not handled, the method is aborted and the exception is propagated as explained earlier (after any finally block has been executed). If the exception has been dealt with in a catch block, normal execution resumes.

In Example 5.10, the exception thrown by the runtime system at (1) is explicitly caught and handled in the catch block at (2). Normal execution of the method continues at (3), as witnessed by the output from the statements at (3) and (4).

Example 5.10 try-catch *Construct*

```
public class DivisionByZero2 {
    public void division() {
        int num1 = 10;
        int num2 = 0;

        try {
            System.out.println(num1 + " / " + num2 + " = " +
                               (num1 / num2));                     // (1)
        } catch (ArithmeticException e) {                          // (2)
            System.out.println("Dealt with " + e);
        }
        System.out.println("Returning from division.");            // (3)
    }

    public static void main(String args[]) {
        new DivisionByZero2().division();
        System.out.println("Returning from main.");                // (4)
    }
}
```

Output from the program:

```
Dealt with java.lang.ArithmeticException: / by zero
Returning from division.
Returning from main.
```

The scope of the argument name in the catch block is the block itself. As mentioned earlier, the type of the exception object must be *assignable* to the type of the argument in the catch block (Section 6.5, p. 201). In the body of the catch block, the exception object can be queried like any other object by using the argument name. The compiler also complains if a catch block for a superclass exception shadows the catch block for a subclass exception, as the catch block of the subclass exception will never be executed. The example below shows incorrect order of the catch blocks at (1) and (2), which will result in a compile time error: the superclass Exception will shadow the subclass ArithmeticException.

```
...
// Compiler complains
catch (Exception e) {                       // (1) superclass
    System.out.println(e);
} catch (ArithmeticException e) {           // (2) subclass
    System.out.println(e);
}
...
```

`finally` Block

If any code in the `try` block is executed, then the `finally` block is guaranteed to be executed, regardless of whether any `catch` block was executed. Since the `finally` block is always executed before control transfers to its final destination, it can be used to specify any clean-up code (for example to free resources like files, net connections, etc.).

Example 5.11 `try-catch-finally` *Construct*

```
public class DivisionByZero3 {

    public void division() {
        int num1 = 10;
        int num2 = 0;

        try {
            System.out.println(num1 + " / " + num2 + " = " +
                      (num1 / num2));                          // (1)
        } catch (ArithmeticException e) {                      // (2)
            System.out.println("Dealt with " + e);
        } finally {                                            // (3)
            System.out.println("Finally done.");
        }
        System.out.println("Returning from division.");        // (4)
    }

    public static void main(String args[]) {
        new DivisionByZero3().division();
        System.out.println("Returning from main.");
    }
}
```

Output from the program:

```
Dealt with java.lang.ArithmeticException: / by zero
Finally done.
Returning from division.
Returning from main.
```

Example 5.11 shows how the exception thrown at (1) in the `try` block is caught and handled by the catch block at (2). Afterwards the `finally` block at (3) is executed, with normal execution continuing at (4).

On exit from the `finally` block, if there is any pending exception, the method is aborted and the exception propagated as explained earlier, otherwise normal execution resumes. This is illustrated in Example 5.12. The method `division` is aborted after the `finally` block at (2) has been executed, as the exception thrown at (1) is not handled. In this case the exception is handled by the default exception handler. Notice the difference in the output from Example 5.11 and Example 5.12.

Example 5.12 `try-finally` *Construct*

```
public class DivisionByZero4 {

    public void division() {
        int num1 = 10;
        int num2 = 0;

        try {
            System.out.println(num1 + " / " + num2 + " = " +
                               (num1 / num2));             // (1)
        } finally {                                        // (2)
            System.out.println("Finally done.");
        }
        System.out.println("Returning from division.");
    }

    public static void main(String args[]) {
        new DivisionByZero4().division();
        System.out.println("Returning from main.");
    }
}
```

Output from the program:

```
Finally done.
java.lang.ArithmeticException: / by zero
        at DivisionByZero4.division(DivisionByZero4.java)
        at DivisionByZero4.main(DivisionByZero4.java)
```

Default exception Handler

Since `catch` and `finally` blocks can contain arbitrary code, exceptions can also be thrown from inside a `catch` and the `finally` block. A `catch` block can rethrow an exception, which is then propagated as explained earlier. An exception which is thrown in a `finally` block overrules any previously unhandled exception, and is propagated in the usual way.

5.7 `throw` Statement

A program can throw an exception, using the `throw` statement. The general format of the `throw` statement is as follows:

`throw` *<object reference expression>*;

The reference is to an object of the `Throwable` class or one of its subclasses. Often the exception object is created in the `throw` statement:

```
throw new DivisionByZeroException("/ by 0");
```

The (checked) exception class `DivisionByZeroException` must be defined, for example:

```
class DivisionByZeroException extends Exception {
    DivisionByZeroException(String msg) { super(msg); }
}
```

When an exception is thrown, normal execution is suspended. The runtime system proceeds to find a `catch` block that can handle the exception. The search starts in the context of the current `try` block, propagating to any enclosing `try` blocks and through the method invocation stack to find a handler for the exception. Any associated `finally` block of a `try` block encountered along the search path is executed. If no handler is found, then the exception is dealt with by the default exception handler at the top level. If a handler is found, execution resumes with the code in its `catch` block.

In Example 5.13, the `try` block at (1) in the `division` method throws an exception at (2) and catches the exception at (4). Note that the rest of the `try` block at (3) is not executed. The statement in the `finally` block at (5) is executed, with execution continuing normally, as shown by the execution of the statements at (6) and (7).

Example 5.13 *Throwing Exceptions*

```
class DivisionByZeroException extends Exception {
    DivisionByZeroException(String msg) { super(msg); }
}

public class DivisionByZero5 {
    public void division() {
        int num1 = 10;
        int num2 = 0;
        try {                                                          // (1)
            if (num2 == 0) throw new DivisionByZeroException("/ by 0"); // (2)
            System.out.println(num1 + " / " + num2 + " = " +
                               (num1 / num2));                         // (3)
        } catch (DivisionByZeroException e) {                          // (4)
            System.out.println("Dealt with " + e);
        } finally {                                                    // (5)
            System.out.println("Finally done.");
        }
      System.out.println("Returning from division.");                  // (6)
    }

    public static void main(String args[]) {
        new DivisionByZero5().division();
        System.out.println("Returning from main.");                    // (7)
    }
}
```

Output from the program:

```
Dealt with DivisionByZeroException: / by 0
Finally done.
Returning from division.
Returning from main.
```

5.8 `throws` Clause

Any method that can cause a checked exception to be thrown, either directly by using the `throw` statement or indirectly by invoking other methods which can throw this exception, must deal with the exception in, usually, one of two ways. Either it can use a `try` block and catch the exception in a handler and deal with it, or it can explicitly propagate the exception to its caller by using the `throws` clause in its method header. This mechanism ensures that, regardless of the path of execution, a checked exception will be monitored. It aids development of robust programs, as allowance can be made for many contingencies. The compiler enforces that a method can only throw those checked exceptions that are specified in its `throws` clause.

In Example 5.14, the method `main` calls the method `division` in a `try` block at (4). At (3), the method `division` throws the checked exception `DivisionByZeroException`, defined at (1). The method `division` does not catch the exception, instead it throws it to its caller, as declared in the `throws` clause in its header at (2). Throwing of the exception `DivisionByZeroException` results in the method `division` being aborted and the exception being propagated to its caller, which in this case is the `main` method. Since the `division` method was called from the context of the `try` block at (4) in the `main` method, the exception is successfully matched with its `catch` block at (5). The exception is handled, with normal execution proceeding with the `finally` block at (6). If the method `main` did not catch the exception, it would have to declare this exception in a `throws` clause. In that case, the exception would end up being taken care of by the default exception handler.

Example 5.14 `throws` *Clause*

```
class DivisionByZeroException extends Exception {                    // (1)
    public DivisionByZeroException(String msg) { super(msg); }
}

public class DivisionByZero6 {
    public void division() throws DivisionByZeroException {          // (2)
        int num1 = 10;
        int num2 = 0;
```

```
            if (num2 == 0) throw new DivisionByZeroException("/ by 0");    // (3)
            System.out.println(num1 + " / " + num2 + " = " + (num1 / num2));
            System.out.println("Returning from division.");
        }

        public static void main(String args[]) {
             try {                                                          // (4)
                 new DivisionByZero6().division();
             } catch (DivisionByZeroException e) {                          // (5)
                System.out.println("In main, dealt with " + e);
             } finally {                                                    // (6)
                 System.out.println("Finally done in main.");
             }
             System.out.println("Returning from main.");                    // (7)
        }
    }
```

Output from the program:

```
In main, dealt with DivisionByZeroException: / by 0
Finally done in main.
Returning from main.
```

The exception type specified in the `throws` clause in the method header can be a superclass type of the actual exceptions thrown, i.e. the exceptions thrown must be assignable to the type of the exceptions specified in the `throws` clause. If a method can throw exceptions of the type `A`, `B` and `C` where these are subclasses of type `D`, then the `throws` clause can either specify `A`, `B` and `C` or just specify `D`. In the `division` method, the method header could specify the superclass `Exception` of the subclass `DivisionByZeroException` in a `throws` clause:

```
public void division() throws Exception { /*...*/ }
```

It is generally not a good programming style to specify exception superclasses in the `throws` clause of the method header, when the actual exceptions thrown in the method are instances of their subclasses. Programmers will be deprived of information about which specific subclass exceptions can be thrown, unless they have access to the source code.

A subclass can *override* a method defined in its superclass by providing a new implementation (Section 6.2, p. 179). What happens when a method with a list of exceptions in its `throws` clause is overridden in a subclass? The method definition in the subclass can only specify all or none, or a subset of the exception classes (including their subclasses) specified in the `throws` clause of the overridden method in the superclass.

```
class A {
    // ...
    protected void superclassMethodX ()
        throws FirstException, SecondException, ThirdException {/* ... */} // (1)
    // ...
}
```

```
class B extends A {
    // ...
    protected void superclassMethodX ()
        throws FirstException, ThirdException { /* ... */ }            // (2)
    // ...
}
```

In the code above, the method superclassMethodX in superclass A is overridden in subclass B. The throws clause of the method in subclass B at (2) is a subset of the exceptions specified for the method in the superclass at (1).

Review questions

5.15 Which digits, and in which order, will be printed when the following program is run?

```
public class MyClass {
    public static void main(String args[]) {
        int k=0;
        try {
            int i = 5/k;
        } catch (ArithmeticException e) {
            System.out.println("1");
        } catch (RuntimeException e) {
            System.out.println("2");
            return;
        } catch (Exception e) {
            System.out.println("3");
        } finally {
            System.out.println("4");
        }
        System.out.println("5");
    }
}
```

Select the one right answer.

(a) The program will print 5.
(b) The program will print 1 and 4, in that order.
(c) The program will print 1, 2 and 4, in that order.
(d) The program will print 1, 4 and 5, in that order.
(e) The program will print 1, 2, 4 and 5, in that order.
(f) The program will print 3 and 5, in that order.

5.16 Given the following program, which of these statements are true?

```
public class Exceptions {
    public static void main(String args[]) {
        try {
            if (args.length == 0) return;
            System.out.println(args[0]);
```

```
            } finally {
                System.out.println("The end");
            }
        }
    }
```

Select all valid answers.

(a) If run with no arguments, the program will produce no output.
(b) If run with no arguments, the program will print "The end".
(c) The program will throw an ArrayIndexOutOfBoundsException.
(d) If run with one argument, the program will simply print the given argument.
(e) If run with one argument, the program will print the given argument followed by "The end".

5.17 What will be the result of attempting to compile and run the following program?

```
public class MyClass {
    public static void main(String args[]) {
        RuntimeException re = null;
        throw re;
    }
}
```

Select the one right answer.

(a) The code will fail to compile, since the main method does not declare that it throws RuntimeException in its declaration.
(b) The program will fail to compile, since it cannot throw re.
(c) The program will compile without error and will throw java.lang.RuntimeException when run.
(d) The program will compile without error and will throw java.lang.NullPointerException when run.
(e) The program will compile without error and will run and terminate without any output.

5.18 Which of these statements are true?

Select all valid answers.

(a) If an exception is uncaught in a method, the method will terminate and normal execution will resume.
(b) An overriding method must declare that it throws the same exception classes as the method it overrides.
(c) The main method of a program can declare that it throws checked exceptions.
(d) A method declaring that it throws a certain exception class may throw instances of any subclass of that exception class.
(e) finally blocks are executed if, and only if, an exception gets thrown while inside the corresponding try block.

5.19 Which digits, and in which order, will be printed when the following program is compiled and run?

```
public class MyClass {
    public static void main(String args[]) {
        try {
            f();
        } catch (InterruptedException e) {
            System.out.println("1");
            throw new RuntimeException();
        } catch (RuntimeException e) {
            System.out.println("2");
            return;
        } catch (Exception e) {
            System.out.println("3");
        } finally {
            System.out.println("4");
        }
        System.out.println("5");
    }

    // InterruptedException is a direct subclass of Exception.
    static void f() throws InterruptedException {
        throw new InterruptedException("Time for lunch.");
    }
}
```

Select the one right answer.

(a) The program will print 5.
(b) The program will print 1 and 4, in that order.
(c) The program will print 1, 2 and 4, in that order.
(d) The program will print 1, 4 and 5, in that order.
(e) The program will print 1, 2, 4 and 5, in that order.
(f) The program will print 3 and 5, in that order.

5.20 Which digits, and in which order, will be printed when the following program is run?

```
public class MyClass {
    public static void main(String args[]) throws InterruptedException {
        try {
            f();
            System.out.println("1");
        } finally {
            System.out.println("2");
        }
        System.out.println("3");
    }

    // InterruptedException is a direct subclass of Exception.
    static void f() throws InterruptedException {
        throw new InterruptedException("Time to go home.");
    }
}
```

Select the one right answer.

(a) The program will print 2 and throw `InterruptedException`.
(b) The program will print 1 and 2, in that order.
(c) The program will print 1, 2 and 3, in that order.
(d) The program will print 2 and 3, in that order.
(e) The program will print 3 and 2, in that order.
(f) The program will print 1 and 3, in that order.

5.21 What is wrong with the following code?

```
public class MyClass {
    public static void main(String args[]) throws A {
        try {
            f();
        } finally {
            System.out.println("Done.");
        } catch (A e) {
            throw e;
        }
    }

    public static void f() throws B {
        throw new B();
    }
}

class A extends Throwable {}

class B extends A {}
```

Select the one right answer.

(a) The `main` method must declare that it throws `B`.
(b) The `finally` block must be below the `catch` block in the `main` method.
(c) The `catch` block in the `main` method must declare that it catches `B` rather than `A`.
(d) A single `try` block cannot be followed by both a `finally` and a `catch` block.
(e) The declaration of class `A` is illegal.

5.22 What is the minimal list of exception classes that the overriding method `f()` in the following code must declare in its `throws` clause before the code will compile correctly?

```
class A {
   // InterruptedException is a direct subclass of Exception.
    void f() throws ArithmeticException, InterruptedException {
        div(5, 5);
    }

    int div(int i, int j) throws ArithmeticException {
        return i/j;
    }
}
```

```
public class MyClass extends A {
    void f() /* throws [...list of exceptions...] */ {
        try {
            div(5, 0);
        } catch (ArithmeticException e) {
            return;
        }
        throw new RuntimeException("ArithmeticException was expected.");
    }
}
```

Select the one right answer.

(a) Does not need to specify any exceptions.
(b) Needs to specify that it throws ArithmeticException.
(c) Needs to specify that it throws InterruptedException.
(d) Needs to specify that it throws RuntimeException.
(e) Needs to specify that it throws both ArithmeticException and InterruptedException.

5.23 What, if anything, would cause the following code not to compile?

```
class A {
    void f() throws ArithmeticException {
        //...
    }
}

public class MyClass extends A {
    public static void main(String args[]) {
        A obj = new MyClass();

        try {
            obj.f();
        } catch (ArithmeticException e) {
            return;
        } catch (Exception e) {
            System.out.println(e);
            throw new RuntimeException("Something wrong here");
        }
    }

    // InterruptedException is a direct subclass of Exception.
    void f() throws InterruptedException {
        //...
    }
}
```

Select the one right answer.

(a) The main method must declare that it throws RuntimeException.
(b) The overriding f() method in MyClass must declare that it throws ArithmeticException, since the f() method in class A declares that it does.
(c) The overriding f() method in MyClass is not allowed to throw InterruptedException, since the f() method in class A is not allowed to throw this exception.

(d) The compiler will complain that the `catch(ArithmeticException)` block overshadows the `catch(Exception)` block.
(e) You cannot throw exceptions from a `catch` block.
(f) Nothing is wrong with the code, it will compile without errors.

Chapter summary

The following information was included in this chapter:

- Explanation of the selection statements: `if`, `if-else`, `switch`.
- Explanation of the iteration statements: `for`, `while`, `do-while`.
- Explanation of the transfer statements: `break`, `continue`, `return`.
- Discussion of exception handling and exception classes in the core APIs.
- Defining new exception types.
- Explanation of the `try-catch-finally` construct and control flow paths through the construct.
- Throwing exceptions with the `throw`-statement.
- Specification of checked exceptions with the `throws` clause.

Programming exercises

5.1 Create different versions of a program that finds all the primes below 100. Create one version that uses only the `for` loop construct (i.e. no `while` or `do-while`). Create another version that uses only the `while` loop construct.

5.2 Here is a skeleton of a system for simulating a nuclear power plant. Implement the methods in the class named `Control`. Modify the method declarations if necessary. The Javadoc comments for each method give a description of what the implementation should do. Some of the methods in the other classes have unspecified implementations. Assume that these methods have been properly implemented and provide hooks to the rest of the system.

```
/** A PowerPlant with a reactor core. */
public class PowerPlant {
    /** Each power plant has a reactor core. This has package
        accessibility so that the Control class which is defined in
        the same package can access it. */
    Reactor core;

    /** Initializes the power plant, creates a reactor core. */
    PowerPlant() {
        core = new Reactor();
    }
```

```
    /** Sound the alarm to evacuate the power plant. */
    public void soundEvacuateAlarm() {
        // ... implementation unspecified ...
    }

    /** Get the level of reactor output that is most desirable at this time.
        (Units are unspecified.) */
    public int getOptimalThroughput() {
        // ... implementation unspecified ...
        return 0;
    }

    /** The main entry point of the program: sets up a PowerPlant
        object and a Control object and lets the Control object run the
        power plant. */
    public static void main(String args[]) {
        PowerPlant plant = new PowerPlant();
        Control ctrl = new Control(plant);
        ctrl.runSystem();
    }
}

/** A reactor core that has a throughput that can be either decreased or
    increased. */
class Reactor {
    /** Get the current throughput of the reactor. (Units are unspecified.) */
    public int getThroughput() {
        // ... implementation unspecified ...
        return 0;
    }

    /** @returns true if the reactor status is critical, false otherwise. */
    public boolean isCritical() {
        // ... implementation unspecified ...
        return false;
    }

    /** Ask the reactor to increase throughput. */
    void increaseThroughput() throws ReactorCritical {
        // ... implementation unspecified ...
    }

    /** Ask the reactor to decrease throughput. */
    void decreaseThroughput() {
        // ... implementation unspecified ...
    }
}

/** This exception class should be used to report that the reactor status is
    critical. */
class ReactorCritical extends Exception {}

/** A controller that will manage the power plant and make sure that the reactor
    runs with optimal throughput. */
class Control {
    PowerPlant thePlant;
```

```
    public Control(PowerPlant p) {
        thePlant = p;
    }

    /** Run the power plant by continuously monitoring the
        optimalThroughput and the actual throughput of the reactor. If
        the throughputs differ by more than 10 units, adjust the reactor
        throughput. If the reactor status becomes critical, the evacuate alarm is
        sounded and the reactor is shut down.
        <p>The runSystem() method can handle the reactor core directly
        but calls methods needAdjustment(), adjustThroughput() and shutdown()
        instead. */
    public void runSystem() {
        // ... provide implementation here ...
    }

    /** Reports whether the throughput of the reactor needs adjusting.
        This method should also monitor and report if the reactor status becomes
        critical.
        @return true if the optimal and actual throughput values
        differ by more than 10 units. */
    public boolean needAdjustment() {
        // ... provide implementation here ...
    }

    /** Adjust the throughput of the reactor by calling increaseThroughput() and
        decreaseThroughput() methods until the actual throughput is within 10
        units of the target throughput. */
    public void adjustThroughput(int target) {
        // ... provide implementation here ...
    }

    /** Shut down the reactor by lowering the throughput to 0. */
    public void shutdown() {
        // ... provide implementation here ...
    }
}
```

6 Object-oriented Programming

Exam Objectives

- State the benefits of encapsulation in object-oriented design, and write code that implements tightly encapsulated classes and the relationships *is-a* and *has-a*.
- Write code to invoke overridden or overloaded methods and parental or overloaded constructors; and describe the effect of invoking these methods.
- Write code to construct instances of any concrete class, including normal top-level classes, inner classes, static inner classes and anonymous inner classes.
  - *For inner classes, see Chapter 7.*

Supplementary Objectives

- Understand the concepts single implementation inheritance, multiple interface inheritance and supertypes, and their implication for object-oriented programming (OOP).
- Understand constructor chaining involving `this()` and `super()` constructs.
- State conversion rules for assigning, casting and passing references.
- Determine at runtime if an object is an instance of a specified class or some subclass of that class, using the `instanceof` operator.
- Understand polymorphism and dynamic method lookup.

6.1 Inheritance

One of the fundamental mechanisms for code reuse in object-oriented programming is *inheritance*. It allows new classes to be derived from an existing class. The new class (a.k.a. *subclass, derived class, child class*) inherits all the members of the old class (a.k.a. *superclass, base class, parent class*). The subclass can add new behavior and properties, and under certain circumstances, modify its inherited behavior.

In Java, inheritance is used for extending classes, i.e. adding new variables and methods, and modifying inherited members (Section 6.2, p. 179). Inheritance of members should not be confused with their declared accessibility. Using appropriate modifiers, the superclass can place restrictions on which inherited members can be accessed by its subclasses (Section 4.9, p. 114).

The superclass is specified using the `extends` clause in the header of the subclass. The definition of the subclass only specifies the additional new and modified members in its class definition. The rest of the definition is inherited. If no `extends` clause is specified in the header of a class definition, then the class implicitly inherits from the `java.lang.Object` class. This implicit inheritance is assumed in the definition of the `Light` class at (1) in Example 6.1. Also in Example 6.1, the subclass `TubeLight` at (2) explicitly uses the `extend` clause and only specifies additional members to what it already inherits from the superclass `Light` (which in turn inherits from the `Object` class).

Example 6.1 *Extending Classes*

```
class Light {                          // (1)
    // Instance variables
    private int noOfWatts;             // wattage
    private boolean indicator;         // on or off
    private String location;           // placement

    // Static variable
    private static int counter;        // no. of Light objects created

    // Constructor
    Light() {
        noOfWatts = 50;
        indicator = true;
        location = new String("X");
    }

    // Instance methods
    public void switchOn()  { indicator = true; }
    public void switchOff() { indicator = false; }
    public boolean isOn() { return indicator; }

    // Static methods
    public static void writeCount() {
         System.out.println("Number of lights: " + counter);
    }
```

```
    //...
}

class TubeLight extends Light {      // (2)
    // Instance variables
    private int tubeLength;
    private int color;

    // Instance method
    public int getTubeLength() { return tubeLength; }
    // ...
}
```

A class in Java can only extend one other class, i.e. it can only have one immediate superclass. This kind of inheritance is sometimes called *simple or linear implementation inheritance*. The name is appropriate, as the subclass inherits the *implementations* of its superclass members. The inheritance relationship can be depicted as an *inheritance hierarchy* (also called *class hierarchy*). Classes higher up in the hierarchy are more *generalized*, as they abstract the class behavior. Classes lower down in the hierarchy are more *specialized*, as they customize the inherited behavior by additional properties and behavior. Figure 6.1 illustrates the inheritance relationship between the class `Light`, which represents the more general abstraction, and its subclasses which are more specialized. The `Object` class is always the root of any inheritance hierarchy, as all classes inherit (either directly or indirectly) from the `Object` class.

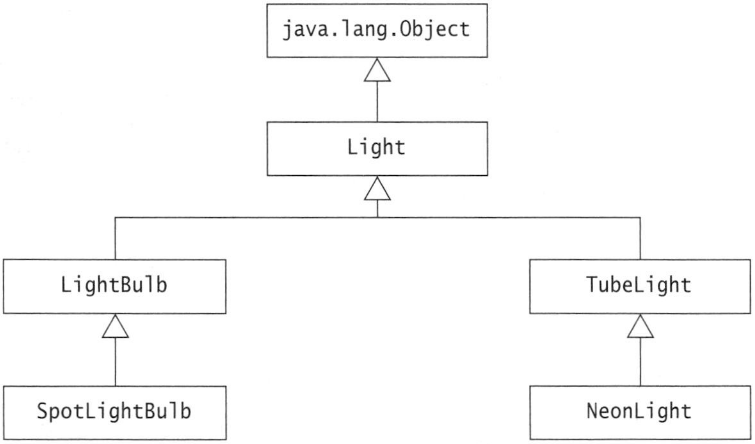

Figure 6.1 *Inheritance Hierarchy*

Inheritance defines the relationship *is-a* (also called *superclass–subclass* relationship) between a superclass and its subclasses. This means that an object of a subclass can be used wherever an object of the superclass can be used. This is often employed as a litmus test for using inheritance. It has particular consequences on how objects can be used. An object of the `TubeLight` class can be used wherever an object of the superclass `Light` can be used. An object of the `LightBulb` class *is-a* object of the superclass `Light`. The inheritance relationship is transitive: if class `B` extends class `A`, then a class `C`, which extends class `B`, will also inherit from class `A` via class `B`. An object of the `SpotLightBulb` class *is-a* object of the class `Light`. The *is-a* relationship does not hold between peer classes: an object of the `LightBulb` class is not an object of the class `TubeLight`, and vice versa.

The other fundamental code reuse mechanism is *aggregation*. Whereas inheritance defines the relationship *is-a* (a.k.a. *superclass–subclass* relationship) between a superclass and its subclasses, aggregation defines the relationship *has-a* (a.k.a. *whole–part* relationship) between an instance of a class and its constituents (a.k.a. *parts*). An instance of class `Light` *has* the following parts: a variable to indicate its wattage (`noOfWatts`), a variable to indicate whether it is on or off (`indicator`), and a `String` object to indicate its location (`location`). In Java, an aggregate object cannot contain other objects. It can only have *references* to its constituent objects. This relationship defines an *aggregation hierarchy* which depicts the *has-a* relationship. In this simple form of aggregation, constituent objects can be shared between objects, and their lifetimes are independent of the lifetime of the aggregate object. Inheritance and aggregation are compared in Section 6.7.

Object-oriented Programming Concepts

The basic concepts of object-oriented programming (OOP) are introduced by way of example, and are elaborated upon in relevant sections in this chapter.

Figure 6.2 shows the inheritance relationship between the class `String` and its superclass `Object`. A client that uses a `String` object is defined in Example 6.2. During the execution of the `main()` method, the `String` object created at (1) is manipulated by using two references: reference `stringRef` of the subclass `String` and reference `objRef` of the superclass `Object`. Walking through the code for the `main()` method reveals salient features of OOP.

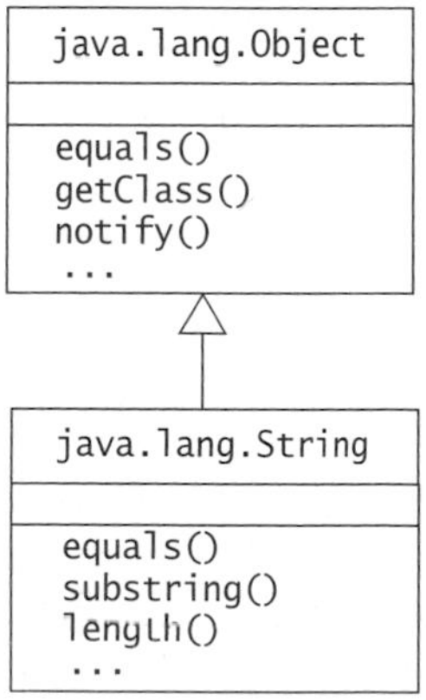

Figure 6.2 *Inheritance Relationship between* `String` *and* `Object` *Classes*

Example 6.2 *Illustrating Inheritance*

```
// String class is a subclass of Object class
class Client {
    public static void main(String args[]) {

        String stringRef = new String("Java");                    // (1)

        System.out.println("(2): " + stringRef.getClass());       // (2)
        System.out.println("(3): " + stringRef.length());         // (3)
        Object objRef = stringRef;                                // (4)
//      System.out.println("(5): " + objRef.length());            // (5) Not OK.
        System.out.println("(6): " + objRef.equals("Java"));      // (6)
        System.out.println("(7): " + objRef.getClass());          // (7)

        stringRef = (String) objRef;                              // (8)
        System.out.println("(9): " + stringRef.equals("C++"));    // (9)
    }
}
```

Output from the program:

```
(2): class java.lang.String
(3): 4
(6): true
(7): class java.lang.String
(9): false
```

Inheriting from the Superclass

The subclass `String` inherits the method `getClass()` from the superclass `Object`. This is immaterial for a client of class `String`, as a client can directly invoke this method on objects of class `String` in the ordinary manner. In Example 6.2, this is illustrated at (2).

```
System.out.println("(2): " + stringRef.getClass());       // (2)
```

Extending the Superclass

The subclass `String` defines the method `length()`, which is not in the superclass `Object`, thereby extending the superclass. In Example 6.2, invocation of this new method on an object of class `String` is shown at (3).

```
System.out.println("(3): " + stringRef.length());         // (3)
```

Upcasting

A subclass reference can be assigned to a superclass reference, because a subclass object can be used where a superclass object can be used. This is called *upcasting*, as references are assigned up the inheritance hierarchy (Section 6.5, p. 201). In Example 6.2, this is illustrated at (4), where the value of the subclass reference `stringRef` is assigned to the superclass reference `objRef`:

```
Object objRef = stringRef;                                // (4)
```

Both references denote the same `String` object after the assignment. One might be tempted to invoke methods exclusive to the `String` subclass via the superclass reference `objRef`, as illustrated at (5):

```
System.out.println("(5): " + objRef.length());          // (5) Not OK.
```

This, however, will not work, as the compiler has no way of knowing what object the reference `objRef` is denoting. It only knows the class of the reference. As the definition of the `Object` class does not have a method called `length()`, this invocation of `length()` at (5) would be flagged as a compile time error.

Method Overriding

In contrast to the situation at (5), the invocation of the `equals()` method at (6) using the superclass reference `objRef` is legal, because the compiler can check that the `Object` class does define a method called `equals()`.

```
System.out.println("(6): " + objRef.equals("Java"));    // (6)
```

Note that this method is redefined in the `String` class with the same signature (i.e. method name and parameters) and the same return type. This is called *method overriding* (Section 6.2, p. 179).

Polymorphism and Dynamic Method Binding

The invocation of the `equals()` method at (6), using the superclass reference `objRef`, does not necessarily invoke the `equals()` method from the `Object` class at runtime. The method invoked is dependent on the actual object denoted by the reference at runtime. The actual method is determined by *dynamic method lookup*. The ability of a superclass reference to denote objects of its own class and its subclasses at runtime is called *polymorphism*. Section 6.6 provides a discussion on how polymorphism and dynamic method lookup can be employed to achieve code reuse.

Under normal program execution, the reference `objRef` will refer to an object of the `String` class at (6), resulting in the `equals()` method from the `String` class being executed, and not the one in the `Object` class.

The situation at (7), where the `getClass()` method is invoked using the superclass reference `objRef`, is allowed at compile time because the `Object` class defines a method called `getClass()`.

```
System.out.println("(7): " + objRef.getClass());        // (7)
```

In this case, under normal program execution, the reference `objRef` will refer to an object of the `String` class at (7). Dynamic method lookup determines which method definition binds to the method signature `getClass()`. Since no `getClass()` method is defined in the `String` class, the method `getClass()` inherited from the `Object` class is thus executed.

Downcasting

Casting the value of a superclass reference to a subclass type is called *downcasting* (Section 6.5, p. 201). This is assigning references down the inheritance hierarchy, and requires explicit casting. The following code from Example 6.2 illustrates downcasting:

```
stringRef = (String) objRef;                               // (8)
System.out.println("(9): " + stringRef.equals("C++"));   // (9)
```

At (8), the source reference `objRef` is of type `Object`, which is the superclass of the class of the destination reference `stringRef`. If the reference `objRef` actually denoted an object of class `String` at runtime, the cast would convert it to the proper subclass type, so that the assignment to the reference `stringRef` would be legal at (8). The reference `stringRef` could then be used to invoke the `equals()` method on this `String` object, as at (9). Not surprisingly, the `equals()` method from the `String` class would be executed.

The cast ensures a correct inheritance relationship between source and destination reference types at compile time. However, the cast can be invalid at runtime. If at runtime the reference `objRef` denotes an object of class `Object` or some unrelated subclass of class `Object`, then obviously casting the value of such a reference to that of subclass `String` would be illegal. In such a case, a `ClassCastException` would be thrown at runtime. The `instanceof` operator (Section 6.5, p. 206) can be used to determine the runtime type of an object before any cast is applied.

Review questions

6.1 Which of the following statements are true?

Select all valid answers.

(a) In Java the `extends` clause is used to specify inheritance.
(b) The subclass of a non-abstract class can be declared `abstract`.
(c) All the members of the superclass are inherited by the subclass.
(d) A `final` class can be `abstract`.
(e) A class, in which all the members are declared `private`, cannot be declared `public`.

6.2 Which of the following statements are true?

Select all valid answers.

(a) Inheritance defines a *has-a* relationship between a superclass and its subclasses.
(b) Every Java object has a method named `equals()`.
(c) Every Java object has a method named `length()`.
(d) A class can extend any number of other classes.
(e) A non-final class can be extended by any number of classes.

6.2 Method Overriding and Variable Shadowing

Method Overriding

Under certain circumstances, a subclass may *override* non-static methods inherited from the superclass. When the method is invoked on an object of the subclass, it is the new method definition in the subclass that is executed. The following aspects about method overriding should be noted:

- The new method definition must have the same *method signature* (i.e. method name and parameters) and the same return type.
- The new method definition, in addition, cannot "narrow" the accessibility of the method, but it can "widen" it (Section 4.9, p. 114).
- The new method definition in the subclass can only specify all or none, or a subset of the exception classes (including their subclasses) specified in the `throws` clause of the overridden method in the superclass (Section 5.8, p. 162).
- Whether parameters in the overriding method should be `final` is at the discretion of the subclass (Section 3.22, p. 82). A method's signature does not encompass the `final` modifier of parameters, only their types and order.

These aspects also apply to interfaces, where a subinterface can override method prototypes from its superinterfaces (Section 6.4, p. 195).

In Example 6.3, the new definition of the `getBill()` method at (4) in the subclass `TubeLight` has the same signature and the same return type as the method at (2) in the superclass `Light`. The new definition specifies a subset of the exceptions (`ZeroHoursException`) thrown by the overridden method (exception class `InvalidHoursException` is a superclass of `NegativeHoursException` and `ZeroHoursException`), and the new definition also "widens" the accessibility (`public`) from what it was in the overridden definition (`protected`). The overriding method also declares the parameter to be `final`. Invocation of the method `getBill()` on an object of subclass `TubeLight` using references of the subclass and the superclass, at (10) and (11) respectively, results in the new definition at (4) being executed. Invocation of the method `getBill()` on an object of superclass `Light` using a reference of the superclass, at (12), results in the overridden definition at (2) being executed. A subclass can also use the keyword `super` to invoke the overridden method in the superclass.

Example 6.3 *Overriding and Overloading Methods and Shadowing Variables*

```
// Exceptions
class InvalidHoursException extends Exception {}
class NegativeHoursException extends InvalidHoursException {}
class ZeroHoursException extends InvalidHoursException {}
```

```
class Light {

    protected String billType = "Small bill";                  // (1)

    protected double getBill(int noOfHours)
              throws InvalidHoursException {                   // (2)
        double smallAmount = 10.0,
               smallBill = smallAmount * noOfHours;
        System.out.println(billType + ": " + smallBill);
        return smallBill;
    }
}

class TubeLight extends Light {

    public String billType = "Large bill";                     // (3) Shadowing.

    public double getBill(final int noOfHours)
           throws ZeroHoursException {                         // (4) Overriding.
        double largeAmount = 100.0,
               largeBill = largeAmount * noOfHours;
        System.out.println(billType + ": " + largeBill);
        return largeBill;
    }

    public double getBill() {                                  // (5)
        System.out.println("No bill");
        return 0.0;
    }
}

public class Client {
    public static void main(String args[])
            throws InvalidHoursException {                     // (6)

        TubeLight tubeLightRef = new TubeLight();              // (7)
        Light lightRef1 = tubeLightRef;                        // (8)
        Light lightRef2 = new Light();                         // (9)

        // Invoke overridden methods
        tubeLightRef.getBill(5);                               // (10)
        lightRef1.getBill(5);                                  // (11)
        lightRef2.getBill(5);                                  // (12)

        // Access shadowed variables
        System.out.println(tubeLightRef.billType);             // (13)
        System.out.println(lightRef1.billType);                // (14)
        System.out.println(lightRef2.billType);                // (15)

        // Invoke overloaded method
        tubeLightRef.getBill();                                // (16)
    }
}
```

Output from the program:

```
Large bill: 500.0
Large bill: 500.0
Small bill: 50.0
Large bill
```

```
Small bill
Small bill
No bill
```

Any `final`, `static` and `private` methods in a class cannot be overridden. A `final` method, of course, cannot be overridden because `final` prevents method overriding. A `static` method is class-specific and not part of any object. Overriding methods are invoked on behalf of objects of the subclass. Accessibility `private` for a method means that it is not accessible outside the class in which it is defined, therefore a subclass cannot override it. However, a subclass can give its own definition of methods which also happen to have the same signature as the methods in its superclass, but doing so would only defeat the purpose of the original definitions.

Variable Shadowing

A subclass cannot override variable members of the superclass, but it can *shadow* them. The subclass can define variable members with the same name as in the superclass. If this is the case, the variable members in the superclass cannot be accessed directly by their simple names in the subclass. A subclass method can use the keyword `super` to access inherited members, including shadowed variables. A client can use a reference of the *superclass* to access members that are shadowed in the subclass, as explained below. Of course, if the shadowed variable is `static`, it can be accessed by the superclass name.

The following distinction between invoking instance methods on an object and accessing instance variables of an object must be noted. When a method is invoked on an object using a reference, it is the *class of the current object* denoted by the reference, not the type of the reference, that determines which method implementation will be executed. In Example 6.3 at (10), (11) and (12), this is evident from invoking the overridden method `getBill()`: the method from the class corresponding to the current object is executed, regardless of the reference type. When a variable of an object is accessed using a reference, it is the *type of the reference*, not the class of the current object denoted by the reference, that determines which variable will actually be accessed. In Example 6.3 at (13), (14) and (15), this is evident from accessing the shadowed variable `billType`: the variable accessed is from the class corresponding to the reference type, regardless of the object denoted by the reference.

Overriding vs. Overloading

Method overriding should not be confused with *method overloading* (Section 4.3, p. 99). Method overriding requires the same method signature (name and parameters) and the same return type, and that the original method is inherited from its superclass. Overloading requires different method signatures, but the method name should be the same. Therefore to overload methods, the parameters must differ in type, order or number. As the return type is not a part of the signature, changing it is not enough to overload methods.

A method can be overloaded in the class it is defined in, or in a subclass of its class. Invoking an overridden method in the superclass from a subclass requires special syntax (for example, the keyword `super`). This is not necessary for invoking an overloaded method in the superclass from a subclass. If the right kinds of arguments are passed in the method call occurring in the subclass, the overloaded method in the superclass will be invoked. In Example 6.3, the method `getBill()` at (2) in class `Light` is overridden in class `TubeLight` at (4) and overloaded at (5). When invoked at (16), the definition at (5) is executed.

Method Overloading Resolution

How is parameter resolution done to choose the right implementation when an overloaded method is invoked? In Example 6.4, the method `testIfOn()` is overloaded at (1) and (2). The call `client.testIfOn(tubeLightRef)` at (3) "satisfies" the parameter lists in both the implementations given at (1) and (2), as the reference `tubeLightRef`, which denotes an object of class `TubeLight`, can also be assigned to a reference of its superclass `Light`. The "most specific" method, i.e. the one at (2), is chosen, resulting in `false` being written on the terminal. The call `client.testIfOn(lightRef)` at (4) only "satisfies" the parameter list in the implementation given at (1), resulting in `true` being written on the terminal.

Example 6.4 *Overloaded Method Resolution*

```
class Light { /* ... */ }

class TubeLight extends Light { /* ... */ }

public class OverloadResolution {
    boolean testIfOn(Light light1) { return true; }                  // (1)
    boolean testIfOn(TubeLight tubeLightRef) { return false; }       // (2)

    public static void main(String args[]) {

        TubeLight tubeLightRef = new TubeLight();
        Light lightRef = new Light();

        OverloadResolution client = new OverloadResolution();
        System.out.println(client.testIfOn(tubeLightRef));           // (3)
        System.out.println(client.testIfOn(lightRef));               // (4)

    }
}
```

Output from the program:

```
false
true
```

Object Reference `super`

The `this` reference is passed as an implicit parameter when an instance method is invoked (Section 4.3, p. 98). It denotes the object on which the method is called. The keyword `super`, on the other hand, can be used in the body of an instance method in a subclass to access variables and invoke methods inherited from the superclass. The keyword `super` provides a reference to the current object as an instance of its superclass. In method invocation with `super`, the method inherited from the superclass is simply invoked regardless of the actual type of the object or whether the current class overrides the method. It is typically used to invoke methods that are overridden, and access variables that are shadowed by the subclass. Unlike the `this` keyword, the `super` keyword cannot be used as an ordinary reference, for example it cannot be assigned to other references or cast to other reference types.

In Example 6.5, the method `demonstrate()` at (7) in class `NeonLight` makes use of the `super` keyword to access members higher up in its inheritance hierarchy. This is the case when the `banner()` method at (8) is invoked. This method is defined in class `Light` and not in the immediate superclass of class `NeonLight`. The overridden method `getBill()` and its overloaded version in class `TubeLight` are invoked, using `super`, at (9) and (10) respectively.

Class `NeonLight` is a subclass of class `TubeLight`, which is a subclass of class `Light`, which has an instance variable `billType` and a method called `getBill()` defined at (1) and (2) respectively. One might be tempted to use the syntax `super.super.getBill(20)` to invoke this method from subclass `NeonLight`, but this is not a valid construct. One might be tempted to cast the `this` reference to the class `Light` and try again as shown at (12). The output shows that the method `getBill()` from class `TubeLight` was executed, not the one from class `Light`. The reason is that a cast only changes the type of the reference (in this case to `Light`), not the class of the object (which is still `NeonLight`). Method invocation is determined by the class of the current object. Dynamic method lookup results in the method `getBill()` from class `TubeLight` being executed. At (13), a similar attempt to access the variable `billType` from class `Light` is successful, because it is the type of the reference that determines the variable accessed. From an instance method in a subclass, it is possible to directly access variables in a class higher up the inheritance hierarchy, by casting the `this` reference. However, casting the `this` reference has no effect on which method is invoked.

Example 6.5 *Using* `super` *Keyword*

```
// Exceptions
class InvalidHoursException extends Exception {}
class NegativeHoursException extends InvalidHoursException {}
class ZeroHoursException extends InvalidHoursException {}
```

```
class Light {

    protected String billType = "Small bill";               // (1)

    protected double getBill(int noOfHours)
              throws InvalidHoursException {                // (2)
        double smallAmount = 10.0,
               smallBill = smallAmount * noOfHours;
        System.out.println(billType + ": " + smallBill);
        return smallBill;
    }

    public void banner() {                                  // (3)
        System.out.println("Let there be light!");
    }
}

class TubeLight extends Light {

    public String billType = "Large bill";                  // (4) Shadowing.

    public double getBill(final int noOfHours)
            throws ZeroHoursException {                     // (5) Overriding.
        double largeAmount = 100.0,
               largeBill = largeAmount * noOfHours;
        System.out.println(billType + ": " + largeBill);
        return largeBill;
    }

    public double getBill() {                               // (6)
        System.out.println("No bill");
        return 0.0;
    }
}

class NeonLight extends TubeLight {
    // ...
    public void demonstrate()
             throws InvalidHoursException {                 // (7)
        super.banner();                                     // (8)
        super.getBill(20);                                  // (9)
        super.getBill();                                    // (10)
        System.out.println(super.billType);                 // (11)
        ((Light) this).getBill(20);                         // (12)
        System.out.println(((Light) this).billType);        // (13)
    }
}

public class Client {
    public static void main(String args[])
                    throws InvalidHoursException {
        NeonLight neonRef = new NeonLight();
        neonRef.demonstrate();
    }
}
```

Output from the program:

```
Let there be light!
Large bill: 2000.0
No bill
Large bill
Large bill: 2000.0
Small bill
```

Review questions

6.3 Which of the following statements are true?

Select all valid answers.

(a) Subclasses must define all the methods that the superclass defines.
(b) It is possible for a subclass to define a method with the same name and parameters as a method that the superclass defines.
(c) It is possible for a subclass to define a member variable with the same name as a member variable that the superclass defines.
(d) It is possible for two classes to be the superclass of each other.

6.4 Given the following classes and declarations, which of these statements are true?

```
// Classes
class Foo {
    private int i;
    public void f() { /* ... */ }
    public void g() { /* ... */ }
}

class Bar extends Foo {
    public int j;
    public void g() { /* ... */ }
}

// Declarations:
// ...
    Foo a = new Foo();
    Bar b = new Bar();
// ...
```

Select all valid answers.

(a) The `Bar` class is a legal subclass of `Foo`.
(b) The statement `b.f();` is legal.
(c) The statement `a.j = 5;` is legal.
(d) The statement `a.g();` is legal.
(e) The statement `b.i = 3;` is legal.

6.5 Which of the following statements are true?

Select all valid answers.

(a) Private methods cannot be overridden in subclasses.
(b) A subclass can override any method in a non-final superclass.
(c) An overriding method can declare that it throws a wider spectrum of exceptions than the method it is overriding.
(d) The parameter list of an overriding method must be a subset of the parameter list of the method that it is overriding
(e) The overriding method can have a different return value than the overridden method.

6.6 Given classes `A`, `B` and `C`, where `B` extends `A` and `C` extends `B` and where all classes implement the instance method `void doIt()`. How can the `doIt()` method in `A` be called from an instance method in `C`?

Select the one right answer.

(a) `doIt();`
(b) `super.doIt();`
(c) `super.super.doIt();`
(d) `this.super.doIt();`
(e) `A.this.doIt();`
(f) `((A) this).doIt();`
(g) It is not possible.

6.7 What would be the result of attempting to compile and run the following code?

```
// Filename: MyClass.java
public class MyClass {
    public static void main(String args[]) {
        C c = new C();
        System.out.println(c.max(13, 29));
    }
}

class A {
    int max(int x, int y) { if (x>y) return x; else return y; }
}

class B extends A{
    int max(int x, int y) { return super.max(y, x) - 10; }
}

class C extends B {
    int max(int x, int y) { return super.max(x+10, y+10); }
}
```

Select the one right answer.

(a) The code will fail to compile, since the `max()` method in `B` passes the arguments to the calling method in the wrong order.

(b) The code will fail to compile, owing to a call to a `max()` method being ambiguous.
(c) The code will compile without errors and will print `13` when run.
(d) The code will compile without errors and will print `23` when run.
(e) The code will compile without errors and will print `29` when run.
(f) The code will compile without errors and will print `39` when run.

6.8 Given the following code, which is the simplest print statement that can be put into the `print` method?

```
// Filename: MyClass.java
public class MyClass extends MySuperclass {
    public static void main(String args[]) {
        MyClass object = new MyClass();
        object.print();
    }

    public void print() {
        // INSERT CODE HERE THAT WILL FIND AND PRINT
        // THE "Hello, world!" STRING FROM THE Message
        // CLASS.
    }
}

class MySuperclass {
    Message msg = new Message();
}

class Message {
    // The message that should be printed:
    String text = "Hello, world!";
}
```

Select the one right answer.

(a) `System.out.println(text);`
(b) `System.out.println(Message.text);`
(c) `System.out.println(msg.text);`
(d) `System.out.println(object.msg.text);`
(e) `System.out.println(super.msg.text);`
(f) `System.out.println(object.super.msg.text);`

6.3 Chaining Constructors using `this()` and `super()`

Constructors are discussed in Section 4.4 on page 100. Other uses of the keywords `this` and `super` can be found in the discussion on method overriding and variable shadowing (Section 6.2, p. 179).

`this()` Constructor Call

Constructors cannot be overridden. They can be overloaded, but only in the same class. In Example 6.6, the class `Light` has three overloaded constructors. In the non-default constructor at (3), the `this` reference is used to access the instance variables shadowed by the parameters. In the `main()` method at (4), the appropriate constructor is invoked depending on the arguments in the constructor call, as illustrated by the program output.

Example 6.6 *Constructor Overloading*

```
class Light {

    // Instance Variables
    private int noOfWatts;          // wattage
    private boolean indicator;      // on or off
    private String location;        // placement

    // Constructors
    Light() {                                     // (1) Explicit default constructor
        noOfWatts = 0;
        indicator = false;
        location = "X";
        System.out.println("Returning from default constructor no. 1.");
    }
    Light(int watts, boolean onOffState) {                          // (2) Non-default
        noOfWatts = watts;
        indicator = onOffState;
        location = "X";
        System.out.println("Returning from non-default constructor no. 2.");
    }
    Light(int noOfWatts, boolean indicator, String location) {  // (3) Non-default
        this.noOfWatts = noOfWatts;
        this.indicator = indicator;
        this.location = new String(location);
        System.out.println("Returning from non-default constructor no. 3.");
    }
}

public class DemoConstructorCall {
    public static void main(String args[]) {                        // (4)
        System.out.println("Creating Light object no.1.");
        Light light1 = new Light();
        System.out.println("Creating Light object no.2.");
        Light light2 = new Light(250, true);
        System.out.println("Creating Light object no.3.");
        Light light3 = new Light(250, true, "attic");
    }
}
```

Output from the program:

```
Creating Light object no.1.
Returning from default constructor no. 1.
Creating Light object no.2.
```

```
Returning from non-default constructor no. 2.
Creating Light object no.3.
Returning from non-default constructor no. 3.
```

Example 6.7 illustrates the idiomatic usage of the `this()` construct, which can lead to *local chaining* of constructors in the class when an instance of the class is created. The first two constructors at (1) and (2) from Example 6.6 have been rewritten using the `this()` construct. The construct can be regarded as being "locally overloaded", since its parameters (and hence its signature) can vary as shown in the body of the constructors at (1) and (2). The `this()` call invokes the constructor with the corresponding parameter list. In the `main()` method at (4), the appropriate constructor is invoked depending on the arguments in the constructor call when each of the three `Light` objects are created. Calling the default constructor to create a `Light` object results in the second and third constructors being executed as well. This is confirmed by the output from the program. In this case, the output shows that the third constructor completed first, followed by the second and finally the default constructor which was called first. Bearing in mind the definition of the constructors, the constructors must have been invoked in the *reverse* order, i.e. invocation of the default constructor immediately leads to invocation of the second constructor by the call `this(0, false)`, and its invocation leads to the third constructor being called immediately by the call `this(watt, ind, "X")`, with the completion of the execution in the reverse order of their invocation. Similarly, calling the second constructor to create an instance of the `Light` class results in the third constructor being executed as well.

Java specifies that when using the `this()` call, it must occur as the *first* statement in a constructor, and it can only be used in a constructor definition. The `this()` call can be followed by any other relevant statements. These restrictions are due to Java's handling of constructor invocation in the superclass when an object of the subclass is created. This mechanism is explained in the next subsection.

Example 6.7 `this()` *Constructor Call*

```
class Light {

    // Instance Variables
    private int       noOfWatts;
    private boolean   indicator;
    private String    location;

    // Constructors
    Light() {                                  // (1) Explicit default constructor
        this(0, false);
        System.out.println("Returning from default constructor no. 1.");
    }
    Light(int watt, boolean ind) {             // (2) Non-default
        this(watt, ind, "X");
        System.out.println("Returning from non-default constructor no. 2.");
    }
```

```
    Light(int noOfWatts, boolean indicator, String location) {  // (3) Non-default
        this.noOfWatts = noOfWatts;
        this.indicator = indicator;
        this.location = new String(location);
        System.out.println("Returning from non-default constructor no. 3.");
    }
}

public class DemoThisCall {
    public static void main(String args[]) {                    // (4)
        System.out.println("Creating Light object no.1.");
        Light light1 = new Light();                             // (5)
        System.out.println("Creating Light object no.2.");
        Light light2 = new Light(250, true);                    // (6)
        System.out.println("Creating Light object no.3.");
        Light light3 = new Light(250, true, "attic");           // (7)
    }
}
```

Output from the program:

```
Creating Light object no.1.
Returning from non-default constructor no. 3.
Returning from non-default constructor no. 2.
Returning from default constructor no. 1.
Creating Light object no.2.
Returning from non-default constructor no. 3.
Returning from non-default constructor no. 2.
Creating Light object no.3.
Returning from non-default constructor no. 3.
```

`super()` Constructor Call

The `super()` construct is used in a subclass constructor to invoke constructors in the *immediate* superclass. This allows the subclass to influence the initialization of its inherited state when an object of the subclass is created. A `super()` call in the constructor of a subclass will result in the execution of the relevant constructor from the superclass, based on the arguments passed.

A constructor in a subclass can access the class's inherited instance members directly, provided accessibility has been granted by the superclasses. The keyword `super` can also be used in a subclass constructor to access inherited instance members via its superclass. One might be tempted to use the `super` keyword in a constructor to specify initial values of inherited instance variables. However, the `super()` construct provides a better solution, using superclass constructors to initialize the inherited state.

In Example 6.8, the non-default constructor at (3) of the class `Light` has a `super()` call (with no arguments) at (4). Although the constructor is not strictly necessary, as the compiler will insert one as explained below, it is included for expositional purposes. The non-default constructor at (6) of class `TubeLight` has a `super()` call (with arguments) at (7). As can be seen, this `super()` call will match the non-default constructor at (3) of superclass `Light`. This is evident from the program output.

Example 6.8 `super()` *Constructor Call*

```
class Light {
    // Instance Variables
    private int       noOfWatts;
    private boolean   indicator;
    private String    location;

    // Constructors
    Light() {                                   // (1) Explicit default constructor
        this(0, false);
        System.out.println(
            "Returning from default constructor no. 1 in class Light");
    }
    Light(int watt, boolean ind) {                               // (2) Non-default
        this(watt, ind, "X");
        System.out.println(
            "Returning from non-default constructor no. 2 in class Light");
    }
    Light(int noOfWatts, boolean indicator, String location) {  // (3) Non-default
        super();                                                 // (4)
        this.noOfWatts = noOfWatts;
        this.indicator = indicator;
        this.location = new String(location);
        System.out.println(
            "Returning from non-default constructor no. 3 in class Light");
    }
}
class TubeLight extends Light {
    // Instance variables
    private int tubeLength;
    private int colorNo;

    TubeLight(int tubeLength, int colorNo) {                     // (5) Non-default
        this(tubeLength, colorNo, 100, true, "Unknown");
        System.out.println(
            "Returning from non-default constructor no. 1 in class TubeLight");
    }

    TubeLight(int tubeLength, int colorNo, int noOfWatts,
              boolean indicator, String location) {              // (6) Non-default
        super(noOfWatts, indicator, location);                   // (7)
        this.tubeLength = tubeLength;
        this.colorNo = colorNo;
        System.out.println(
            "Returning from non-default constructor no. 2 in class TubeLight");
    }
}
```

```
public class Chaining {
    public static void main(String args[]) {
        System.out.println("Creating a TubeLight object.");
        TubeLight tubeLightRef = new TubeLight(20, 5);          // (8)
    }
}
```

Output from the program:

```
Creating a TubeLight object.
Returning from non-default constructor no. 3 in class Light
Returning from non-default constructor no. 2 in class TubeLight
Returning from non-default constructor no. 1 in class TubeLight
```

The `super()` construct has the same restrictions as the `this()` construct: if used, the `super()` call must occur as the *first* statement in a constructor, and it can only be used in a constructor definition. This implies that `this()` and `super()` calls cannot both occur in the same constructor. The `this()` construct is used to "chain" constructors in the *same* class, and the constructor at the end of such a chain can invoke a superclass constructor using the `super()` construct. Just as the `this()` construct leads to chaining of constructors in the same class, the `super()` construct leads to chaining of subclass constructors to superclass constructors. This chaining behavior guarantees that all superclass constructors are called, starting with the constructor of the class being instantiated, all the way up to the root of the inheritance hierarchy, which is always the `Object` class. Note, however, that the body of the constructors is executed in the reverse order to the call order, as `super()` can only occur as the first statement in a constructor. This ensures that the constructor from the `Object` class is executed first, followed by the constructors in the other classes down to the class being instantiated in the inheritance hierarchy. This is called (subclass–superclass) *constructor chaining*. The output from Example 6.8 clearly illustrates this chain of events when an object of class `TubeLight` is created.

If a constructor at the end of such a `this()`-chain (which may not be a chain at all if no `this()` call is invoked) does not have an explicit call to `super()`, then the call `super()` (without the parameters) is implicitly inserted to invoke the default constructor of the superclass. In other words, if a constructor does not have either a `this()` or a `super()` call as its first statement, then a `super()` call to the default constructor in the superclass is inserted. The code

```
class A {
    public A() {}
    // ...
}
class B extends A {
    // no constructors
    // ...
}
```

is equivalent to

```
class A {
    public A() { super(); }       // (1)
    // ...
}
class B extends A {
    public B() { super(); }       // (2)
    // ...
}
```

as the implicit default constructors with calls to the default superclass constructor are inserted in the code.

If a class only defines non-default constructors (i.e. only constructors with parameters), then its subclasses cannot rely on the implicit behavior of a `super()` call being inserted. This will be flagged as a compile time error. The subclasses must then explicitly call a superclass constructor, using the `super()` construct with the right arguments.

```
class NeonLight extends TubeLight {
    // Instance Variable
    String sign;

    NeonLight() {                                  // (1)
        super(10, 2, 100, true, "Roof-top");       // (2) Cannot be commented out.
        sign = "All will be revealed!";
    }
    // ...
}
```

The definition of the subclass `NeonLight` above provides a constructor at (1). The call at (2) of the constructor in the superclass `TubeLight` cannot be omitted. If it is omitted, any insertion of a `super()` call (with no arguments) in this constructor will not match any default constructor in the superclass `TubeLight`, as this superclass does not provide one. The superclass `TubeLight` only provides non-default constructors. The class `NeonLight` will not compile unless an explicit `super()` call (with valid arguments) is inserted at (2).

Subclasses without any declared constructors will fail to compile if the superclass does not have a default constructor (i.e. provides only non-default constructors). This is because the implicit default constructor of the subclass will attempt to call the non-existent default constructor in the superclass.

Review questions

6.9 Given the following code, which of these constructors could be added to the `MySubclass` without causing a compile time error?

```
class MySuper {
    int number;
    MySuper(int i) { number = i; }
}
```

```
class MySub extends MySuper {
    int count;
    MySub(int cnt, int num) {
        super(num);
        count=cnt;
    }

    // INSERT ADDITIONAL CONSTRUCTOR HERE
}
```

Select all valid answers.

(a) `MySub() {}`
(b) `MySub(int cnt) { count = cnt; }`
(c) `MySub(int cnt) { super(); count = cnt; }`
(d) `MySub(int cnt) { count = cnt; super(cnt); }`
(e) `MySub(int cnt) { this(cnt, cnt); }`
(f) `MySub(int cnt) { super(cnt); this(cnt, 0); }`

6.10 Which of these statements are true?

Select all valid answers.

(a) A `super()` or `this()` call must always be provided explicitly as the first statement in the body of a constructor.
(b) If both a subclass and its superclass do not have any declared constructors, the implicit default constructor of the subclass will call `super()` when run.
(c) If neither `super()` or `this()` is declared as the first statement in the body of a constructor, then `this()` will implicitly be inserted as the first statement.
(d) If `super()` is the first statement in the body of a constructor, then `this()` can be declared as the second statement.
(e) Calling `super()` as the first statement in the body of a constructor of a subclass will always work, since all superclasses have a default constructor.

6.11 What will the following program print when run?

```
// Filename: MyClass.java
public class MyClass {
    public static void main(String args[]) {
        B b = new B("Test");
    }
}

class A {
    A() { this("1", "2"); }

    A(String s, String t) { this(s + t); }

    A(String s) { System.out.println(s); }
}

class B extends A {
    B(String s) { System.out.println(s); }
```

```
    B(String s, String t) { this(t + s + "3"); }

    B() { super("4"); };
}
```

Select the one right answer.

(a) It will simply print Test.
(b) It will print Test followed by Test.
(c) It will print 123 followed by Test.
(d) It will print 12 followed by Test.
(e) It will print 4 followed by Test.

6.4 Interfaces

Extending classes using *linear implementation inheritance* creates new (class) types. A superclass reference can polymorphically denote objects of its own type and its subclasses strictly according to the inheritance hierarchy. Because this relationship is linear, it rules out *multiple implementation inheritance*, i.e. a subclass inheriting from more than one superclass. Instead Java provides *interfaces* which not only allow new type names to be introduced and used polymorphically, but also permit *multiple interface inheritance.*

Defining Interfaces

An interface defines a *contract* by specifying prototypes of methods, and not their implementation.

<interface header> {
    <interface body>
}

In the interface header, the name of the interface is preceded by the keyword `interface`. The body of the interface is usually a list of method prototypes. Example 6.9 specifies an interface `IStack` at (1) which contains two method prototypes. The methods in an interface are all `abstract` by virtue of their declaration, and should not be declared `abstract` (Section 4.10, p. 124). An interface is abstract by definition and therefore cannot be instantiated. It should also not be declared `abstract`.

Example 6.9 *Interfaces*

```
interface IStack {                                   // (1)
    void push(Object item);
    Object pop();
}

class StackImpl implements IStack {                  // (2)
    protected Object[] stackArray;
    protected int tos;
```

```
    public StackImpl(int capacity) {
        stackArray = new Object[capacity];
        tos = -1;
    }

    public void push(Object item)                                   // (3)
        { stackArray[++tos] = item; }

    public Object pop() {                                           // (4)
        Object objRef = stackArray[tos];
        stackArray[tos] = null;
        tos--;
        return objRef;
    }

    public Object peek() { return stackArray[tos]; }
}

interface ISafeStack extends IStack {                               // (5)
    boolean isEmpty();
    boolean isFull();
}

class SafeStackImpl extends StackImpl implements ISafeStack {       // (6)

    public SafeStackImpl(int capacity) { super(capacity); }
    public boolean isEmpty() { return tos < 0; }                    // (7)
    public boolean isFull() { return tos == stackArray.length-1; }  // (8)
}

public class StackUser {

    public static void main(String args[]) {                        // (9)
        SafeStackImpl safeStackRef = new SafeStackImpl(10);
        StackImpl stackRef = safeStackRef;
        ISafeStack isafeStackRef = safeStackRef;
        IStack istackRef = safeStackRef;
        Object objRef = safeStackRef;

        safeStackRef.push("Dollars");                               // (10)
        stackRef.push("Kroner");
        System.out.println(isafeStackRef.pop());
        System.out.println(istackRef.pop());
        System.out.println(objRef.getClass());
    }
}
```

Output from the program:

```
Kroner
Dollars
class SafeStackImpl
```

Implementing Interfaces

Any class can elect to implement, wholly or partially, zero or more interfaces. Classes implementing interfaces thus introduce multiple interface inheritance into their linear implementation inheritance hierarchy. A class specifies the interfaces it implements as a comma-separated list using the `implements` clause in the class header. The interface methods will all have `public` accessibility when implemented in the class (or its subclasses). In Example 6.9, the class `StackImpl` implements the interface `IStack` by both specifying the interface name using the `implements` clause in its class header at (2) and providing the implementation for the methods in the interface at (3) and (4). A class can choose to implement only some of the methods of its interfaces, i.e. give a partial implementation of its interfaces. The class must then be declared as `abstract` (Section 4.7, p. 109). Note that interface methods cannot be declared `static`, because they comprise the contract fulfilled by the *objects* of the class implementing the interface and are therefore instance methods.

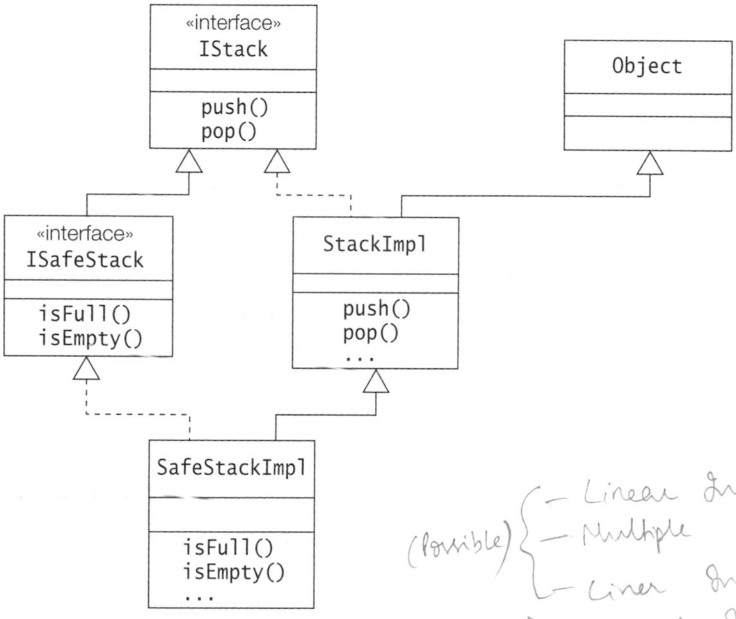

Figure 6.3 *Inheritance Relations*

Extending Interfaces

An interface can extend other interfaces, using the `extends` clause. Unlike extending classes, an interface can extend several interfaces. Unlike the linear implementation hierarchy involving classes, which always has the `Object` class as the single root, multiple inheritance of interfaces can result in an inheritance hierarchy which has multiple roots designated by different interfaces.

Example 6.9 provides an example of multiple inheritance in Java. In Example 6.9, the interface `ISafeStack` extends the interface `IStack` at (5). The class `SafeStackImpl` both extends the `StackImpl` class and implements the `ISafeStack` interface at (6). Both the implementation and interface inheritance hierarchies for classes and interfaces defined in Example 6.9 are shown in Figure 6.3.

In UML, an interface can be depicted similar to a class, but with the interface name in italics. Interface inheritance is shown similar to implementation inheritance, but with a dotted inheritance arrow. It is instructive to note how class `SafeStackImpl` implements the `ISafeStack` interface: it inherits implementations of the `push()` and `pop()` methods from its superclass `StackImpl`, and provides its own implementation of the `isFull()` and `isEmpty()` methods from the `ISafeStack` interface. The interface `ISafeStack` inherits two method prototypes from its superinterface `IStack`. All its methods are implemented by the `SafeStackImpl` class. The class `SafeStackImpl` implicitly implements the `IStack` interface: it implements the `ISafeStack` interface which inherits from the `IStack` interface. This is readily evident from the diamond shape of the inheritance hierarchy in Figure 6.3. There is only one single *implementation* inheritance into the class `SafeStackImpl`. Note that there are three different inheritance relations at work when defining inheritance between classes and interfaces:

- Linear implementation inheritance hierarchy between classes: a class extends another class.
- Multiple inheritance hierarchy between interfaces: an interface extends other interfaces.
- Multiple interface inheritance hierarchy between interfaces and classes: a class implements interfaces.

Supertypes

Interfaces define new types. Although interfaces cannot be instantiated, variables of an interface type can be declared. If a class implements an interface, then references to objects of this class and its subclasses can be assigned to a variable of this interface type. The interfaces that a class implements and the classes it extends, directly or indirectly, are called its *supertypes*. A supertype is thus a reference type. In Example 6.9, an object of the class `SafeStackImpl` is created in the `main()` method of the class `StackUser` at (9). Its reference is assigned to variables of all its supertypes, which are used to manipulate the object. Polymorphic behavior of supertype variables is discussed in Section 6.6.

Interfaces with empty bodies are often used as markers to "tag" classes as having a certain property or behavior. Java APIs provide several examples of such marker interfaces: `java.lang.Cloneable`, `java.util.EventListener` (Section 14.3, p. 421), `java.io.Serializable` (Section 18.6, p. 587).

Accessibility of interfaces is discussed in Section 4.6 on page 108.

Constants in Interfaces

An interface can also define constants. Such constants are considered to be `public`, `static` and `final` regardless of whether these modifiers are specified. An interface constant can be accessed by any client (a class or interface) using its fully qualified name, regardless of whether the client extends or implements its interface. However, if a client is a class that implements this interface or an interface that extends this interface, then the client can also access such constants directly without using the dot (.) notation. Typical usage of constants in interfaces is illustrated in Example 6.10, showing both direct access and using fully qualified names at (1) and (2) respectively.

Extending an interface which has constants is analogous to extending a class having static variables. In particular, these constants can be shadowed by the subinterfaces. In the case of multiple inheritance, any name conflicts can be resolved using fully qualified names for the constants involved.

Example 6.10 *Variables in Interfaces*

```
interface Constants {
    double PI = 3.14;
    String AREA_UNITS = " sq.cm.";
    String LENGTH_UNITS = " cm.";
}

public class Client implements Constants {
    public static void main(String args[]) {
        double radius = 1.5;
        System.out.println("Area of circle is " + (PI*radius*radius) +
                           AREA_UNITS);              // (1) Direct access.
        System.out.println("Circumference of circle is " + (2*PI*radius) +
                           Constants.LENGTH_UNITS); // (2) Fully qualified name.
    }
}
```

Output from the program:

```
Area of circle is 7.0649999999999995 sq.cm.
Circumference of circle is 9.42 cm.
```

Review questions

6.12 Which of these statements about interfaces are true?

Select all valid answers.

(a) Interfaces permit multiple implementation inheritance.
(b) Interfaces can be extended by any number of other interfaces.
(c) Interfaces can extend any number of other interfaces.
(d) Members of an interface are never static.
(e) Members of an interface can always be defined `static`.

6.13 Given the following variable declaration within the definition of an interface, which of these declarations are equivalent to it?

```
int answer = 42;
```

Select all valid answers.

(a) `public static int answer = 42;`
(b) `public final int answer = 42;`
(c) `static final int answer = 42;`
(d) `public int answer = 42;`
(e) `final int answer = 42;`

6.14 Which of these statements concerning interfaces are true?

Select all valid answers.

(a) The keyword `extends` is used to signify that an interface inherits from another interface.
(b) The keyword `extends` is used to signify that a class inherits from an interface.
(c) The keyword `implements` is used to signify that an interface inherits from another interface.
(d) The keyword `implements` is used to signify that a class inherits from an interface.
(e) The keyword `implements` is used to signify that a class inherits from another class.

6.15 What is wrong, if anything, with the following code?

```
// Filename: MyClass.java
abstract class MyClass implements Interface1, Interface2 {
    public void f() { }
    public void g() { }
}

interface Interface1 {
    int VAL_A = 1;
    int VAL_B = 2;

    void f();
    void g();
}

interface Interface2 {
    int VAL_B = 3;
    int VAL_C = 4;

    void g();
    void h();
}
```

Select the one right answer.

(a) `Interface1` and `Interface2` do not match, therefore `MyClass` cannot implement them both.
(b) `MyClass` only implements `Interface1`. Implementation for `void h()` from `Interface2` is missing.
(c) The declarations of `void g()` in the two interfaces clash.
(d) The definitions of `int VAL_B` in the two interfaces clash.
(e) Nothing is wrong with the code, it will compile without errors.

6.5 Assigning, Passing and Casting References

Table 6.1 summarizes the types found in Java. Only primitive data and reference values can be stored in variables.

Table 6.1 *Types*

	Corresponding Types:
Primitive data values	Primitive datatypes.
Reference values	Class, interface or array type (called *reference types*).
Objects	Class or array type.

Arrays are objects in Java. Array types (`boolean[]`, `Object[]`, `StackImpl[]`) implicitly augment the inheritance hierarchy. The inheritance hierarchy depicted in Figure 6.3 is augmented by the corresponding array types, which are shown in Figure 6.4. An array type is shown as a "class" with the `[]` notation appended to the name of the element type. The class `SafeStackImpl` is a subclass of the class `StackImpl`. The corresponding array types, `SafeStackImpl[]` and `StackImpl[]`, have the same relationship in the extended inheritance hierarchy. Figure 6.4 also shows array types corresponding to some of the primitive datatypes.

Variables of array reference types can be declared, and arrays of reference types can be instantiated. All array types implicitly extend the `Object` class. Note the difference between arrays of primitive datatypes and class types. Arrays of class types also extend the array type `Object[]`. An array reference exhibits the same polymorphic behavior as any other reference, subject to its location in the extended inheritance hierarchy.

Reference values, like primitive values, can be assigned, cast and passed as arguments. For values of the primitive datatypes and reference types, conversions occur during:

- Assignment
- Parameter passing
- Explicit casting

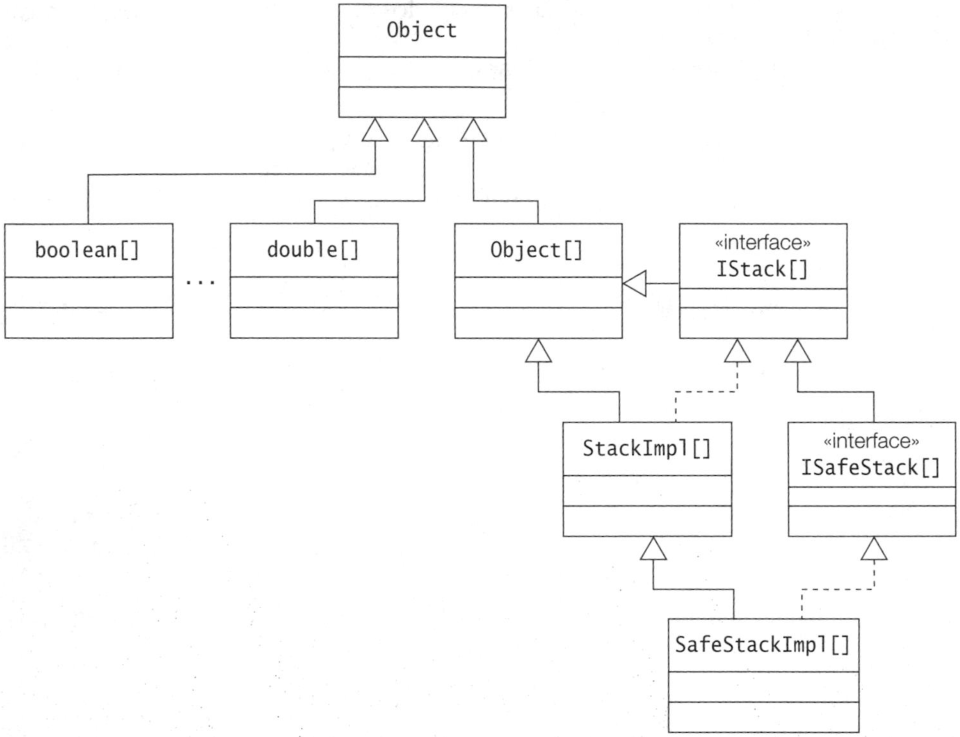

Figure 6.4 *Array Types in Inheritance Hierarchy*

The rule of thumb for the primitive datatypes is that widening conversions are permitted, but narrowing conversions require an explicit cast. The rule of thumb for reference values is that conversions up the inheritance hierarchy are permitted (called *upcasting*), but conversions down the hierarchy require explicit casting (called *downcasting*). In other words, conversions which preserve the inheritance *is-a* relationship are allowed, other conversions require an explicit cast or are illegal. There is no notion of promotion for reference values.

Example 6.11 *Assigning and Passing Reference Values*

```
interface IStack { /* See Example 6.9 for definition */ }
class StackImpl implements IStack { /* See Example 6.9 for definition */ }
interface ISafeStack extends IStack { /* See Example 6.9 for definition */ }
class SafeStackImpl extends StackImpl implements ISafeStack {
    /* See Example 6.9 for definition */
}

public class ReferenceConversion {

    public static void main(String args[]) {

        Object objRef;
        StackImpl stackRef;
```

```
        SafeStackImpl safeStackRef = new SafeStackImpl(10);
        IStack iStackRef;
        ISafeStack iSafeStackRef;

        // SourceType is a class type
        objRef = safeStackRef;       // (1) Always possible
        stackRef = safeStackRef;     // (2) Subclass to superclass assignment
        iStackRef = stackRef;        // (3) StackImpl implements IStack
        iSafeStackRef = safeStackRef;// (4) SafeStackImpl implements ISafeStack

        // SourceType is an interface type
        objRef = iStackRef;          // (5) Always possible
        iStackRef = iSafeStackRef;   // (6) Sub- to super-interface assignment

        // SourceType is an array type.
        Object[] objArray = new Object[3];
        StackImpl[] stackArray = new StackImpl[3];
        SafeStackImpl[] safeStackArray = new SafeStackImpl[5];
        ISafeStack[] iSafeStackArray = new SafeStackImpl[5];
        int[] intArray = new int[10];

        objRef = objArray;           // (7) Always possible
        objRef = stackArray;         // (8) Always possible
        objArray = stackArray;       // (9) Always possible
        objArray = iSafeStackArray;  // (10) Always possible
        objRef = intArray;           // (11) Always possible
    //  objArray = intArray;         // (12) Compile time error
        stackArray = safeStackArray; // (13) Subclass array to superclass array
        iSafeStackArray =
                safeStackArray;      // (14) SafeStackImpl implements ISafeStack

        // Parameter Conversion
        System.out.println("First call:");
        sendParams(stackRef, safeStackRef, iStackRef,
                   safeStackArray,iSafeStackArray);                     // (15)
    //  Call Signature: sendParams(StackImpl, SafeStackImpl, IStack,
    //                             SafeStackImpl[], ISafeStack[]);

        System.out.println("Second call:");
        sendParams(iSafeStackArray, stackRef, iSafeStackRef,
                   stackArray, safeStackArray);                         // (16)
    //  Call Signature: sendParams(ISafeStack[], StackImpl, ISafeStack,
    //                             StackImpl[], SafeStackImpl[]);
    }

    public static void sendParams(Object objRefParam, StackImpl stackRefParam,
            IStack iStackRefParam, StackImpl[] stackArrayParam,
            IStack[] iStackArrayParam) {                                // (17)
    //  Signature: sendParams(Object, StackImpl, IStack, StackImpl[], IStack[])
    //  Print class name of object denoted by the reference at runtime.
        System.out.println(objRefParam.getClass());
        System.out.println(stackRefParam.getClass());
        System.out.println(iStackRefParam.getClass());
        System.out.println(stackArrayParam.getClass());
        System.out.println(iStackArrayParam.getClass());
    }
}
```

Output from the program:

```
First call:
class SafeStackImpl
class SafeStackImpl
class SafeStackImpl
class [LSafeStackImpl;
class [LSafeStackImpl;
Second call:
class [LSafeStackImpl;
class SafeStackImpl
class SafeStackImpl
class [LSafeStackImpl;
class [LSafeStackImpl;
```

Reference Assignment Conversions

Reference assignments are generally permitted "up" the inheritance hierarchy, with implicit conversion of the source reference type to the destination reference type. A reference assignment results in creating a new alias to the object of the source reference type.

The rules for reference assignment are stated based on the following code:

```
SourceType srcRef;
DestinationType destRef = srcRef;
```

The rules are illustrated by code from Example 6.11.

- If `SourceType` is a *class type*, the reference value in `srcRef` may be assigned to the `destRef` reference, provided `DestinationType` is one of the following:
  - `DestinationType` is a superclass of the subclass `SourceType`.
  - `DestinationType` is an interface type which is implemented by the class `SourceType`.

```
objRef = safeStackRef;         // (1) Always possible
stackRef = safeStackRef;       // (2) Subclass to superclass assignment
iStackRef = stackRef;          // (3) StackImpl implements IStack
iSafeStackRef = safeStackRef;  // (4) SafeStackImpl implements ISafeStack
```

- If `SourceType` is an *interface type*, the reference value in `srcRef` may be assigned to the `destRef` reference, provided `DestinationType` is one of the following:
  - `DestinationType` is `Object`.
  - `DestinationType` is a superinterface of subinterface `SourceType`.

```
objRef = iStackRef;         // (5) Always possible
iStackRef = iSafeStackRef; // (6) Subinterface to superinterface assignment
```

- If `SourceType` is an *array type*, the reference value in `srcRef` may be assigned to the `destRef` reference, provided `DestinationType` is one of the following:

- DestinationType is Object.
- DestinationType is an array type, where the element type of SourceType can be converted to the element type of DestinationType.

```
    objRef = objArray;              // (7) Always possible
    objRef = stackArray;            // (8) Always possible
    objArray = stackArray;          // (9) Always possible
    objArray = iSafeStackArray;     // (10) Always possible
    objRef = intArray;              // (11) Always possible
//  objArray = intArray;            // (12) Compile time error
    stackArray = safeStackArray;    // (13) Subclass array to superclass array
    iSafeStackArray =
             safeStackArray;        // (14) SafeStackImpl implements ISafeStack
```

If an assignment is legal, then the reference value of srcRef is said to be *assignable* to a reference of DestinationType. Lastly, note that the above rules for assignment are enforced at compile time, guaranteeing that no type conversion error will occur during assignment at runtime. Such conversions are *type safe*. The reason the rules can be enforced at compile time is that they concern the type of the reference (which is always known at compile time) rather than the actual type of the object being referenced (which is known at runtime).

Parameter Passing Conversions

The rules for reference assignment conversion also apply for *parameter passing conversions*. This is reasonable, as parameters in Java are passed by value (Section 3.19, p. 77), requiring that values of actual parameters must be assignable to formal parameters of compatible types.

In Example 6.11, the method sendParams() at (17) has the following signature indicating the types of the formal parameters:

```
sendParams(Object, StackImpl, IStack, StackImpl[], IStack[])
```

The method call at (15) has the following signature, showing the types of the actual parameters:

```
sendParams(StackImpl, SafeStackImpl, IStack, SafeStackImpl[], ISafeStack[]);
```

Note that the assignment of the values of the actual parameters to the corresponding formal parameters is legal, according to the rules for assignment discussed above. The method call at (16) provides another example of parameter passing conversion. It has the following signature:

```
sendParams(ISafeStack[], StackImpl, ISafeStack, StackImpl[], SafeStackImpl[]);
```

Analogous to assignment, the rules for parameter passing conversions are based on the reference type of the parameters, and are enforced at compile time. The output in Example 6.11 shows the class of the actual objects referenced by the formal parameters at runtime, which turns out to be either SafeStackImpl or SafeStackImpl[] in this case. The characters "[L" in the output indicate an array of a class or interface (see the Class.getName() method in the API documentation).

The parameter passing conversion rules are useful in creating *generic data types* which can handle objects of arbitrary types. The classes in the `java.util` package that manage *collections* make heavy use of `Object` as argument type to implement methods that can take any object as argument.

Reference Casting and `instanceof` Operator

The expression to cast *<reference>* of *<source type>* to *<destination type>* has the following syntax:

(*<destination type>*) *<reference>*

The binary `instanceof` operator has the following syntax:

<reference> `instanceof` *<destination type>*

The `instanceof` operator (note that the keyword is composed of only lowercase letters) returns the value `true` if the left-hand operand (any reference) can be *cast* to the right-hand operand (a class, interface or array type). This is equivalent to saying that the corresponding cast expression is valid. Both the cast and the `instanceof` operators require a compile time check and a runtime check as explained below.

The compile time check determines whether a reference of *<source type>* and a reference of *<destination type>* can denote objects of a class (or its subclasses) where this class is a common subtype of both *<source type>* and *<destination type>* in the inheritance hierarchy. If this is not the case, then obviously there is no relationship between the types, and neither the cast nor the `instanceof` operator application would be valid.

With *<source type>* and *<destination type>* as classes `Light` and `String` respectively, there is no common subtype whose objects could possibly be denoted by the references of `Light` and `String`. The compiler would reject casting a reference of type `Light` to type `String` or applying the `instanceof` operator, as shown at (2) and (3) in Example 6.12. With *<source type>* and *<destination type>* as classes `Light` and `TubeLight` respectively, references of `Light` and `TubeLight` can denote objects of class `TubeLight` (or its subclasses) in the inheritance hierarchy depicted in Figure 6.3. It therefore makes sense to apply the `instanceof` operator or cast a reference of type `Light` to type `TubeLight`, as shown at (4) and (5) respectively in Example 6.12.

At runtime, the result of applying the `instanceof` operator at (4) is `false`, because the reference `light1` of class `Light` will actually denote an object of subclass `LightBulb`, and this object cannot be denoted by a reference of the peer class `TubeLight`. Applying the cast at (5) results in a `ClassCastException` for the same reason. This is the reason why cast conversions are said to be *unsafe*, as they may throw a `ClassCastException` at runtime. Note that if the result of the `instanceof` operator is `false`, then the cast involving the operands will throw a `ClassCastException`.

In Example 6.12, the result of applying the `instanceof` operator at (6) is also `false`, because the reference `light1` will still denote an object of class `LightBulb` whose objects cannot be denoted by a reference of its subclass `SpotLightBulb`. Thus applying the cast at (7) results in a `ClassCastException`.

The situation shown at (8), (9) and (10) illustrates typical usage of the `instanceof` operator to determine what object a reference is denoting, so that it can be cast for the purpose for carrying out some special action. The reference `light1` of class `Light` is initialized to an object of subclass `NeonLight` at (8). The result of the `instanceof` operator at (9) is `true`, because the reference `light1` will denote an object of subclass `NeonLight` whose objects can also be denoted by a reference of its superclass `TubeLight`. By the same token, the cast at (10) is also valid. If the result of the `instanceof` operator is `true`, then the cast involving the operands will always be valid.

Example 6.12 `instanceof` *and cast Operator*

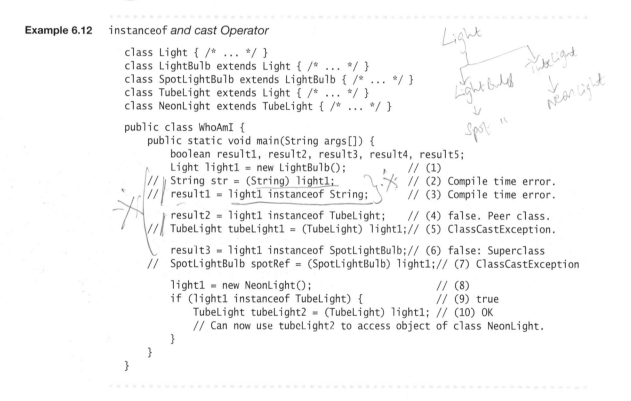

```
class Light { /* ... */ }
class LightBulb extends Light { /* ... */ }
class SpotLightBulb extends LightBulb { /* ... */ }
class TubeLight extends Light { /* ... */ }
class NeonLight extends TubeLight { /* ... */ }

public class WhoAmI {
    public static void main(String args[]) {
        boolean result1, result2, result3, result4, result5;
        Light light1 = new LightBulb();                // (1)
    //  String str = (String) light1;                  // (2) Compile time error.
    //  result1 = light1 instanceof String;            // (3) Compile time error.

        result2 = light1 instanceof TubeLight;     // (4) false. Peer class.
    //  TubeLight tubeLight1 = (TubeLight) light1;// (5) ClassCastException.

        result3 = light1 instanceof SpotLightBulb;// (6) false: Superclass
    //  SpotLightBulb spotRef = (SpotLightBulb) light1;// (7) ClassCastException

        light1 = new NeonLight();                        // (8)
        if (light1 instanceof TubeLight) {               // (9) true
            TubeLight tubeLight2 = (TubeLight) light1; // (10) OK
            // Can now use tubeLight2 to access object of class NeonLight.
        }
    }
}
```

The `instanceof` operator effectively determines whether the object denoted by the reference on the left-hand side is an instance of the class (or of a subclass) that is specified on the right-hand side, or if it is an instance of a class (or of a subclass) that implements the interface specified on the right-hand side. At runtime, it is the actual object denoted by the reference that is compared with the type specified on the right-hand side. In other words, what matters is the class of the actual object denoted by the reference at runtime, not the type of the reference.

Example 6.13 provides more examples of the `instanceof` operator. It is instructive to go through the print statements and understand the results printed out. The literal `null` is not an instance of any reference type, as shown in the print statements (1), (2) and (16). An instance of a superclass is not an instance of its subclass, as shown in the print statement (4). An instance of a class is not an instance of a totally unrelated class, as shown in the print statement (10). An instance of a class cannot be of an interface type which is not implemented by the class of the object, as shown in the print statement (6). Any array of non-primitive type is an instance of both `Object` and `Object[]` types, as shown in the print statements (14) and (15) respectively.

Example 6.13 *Using* `instanceof` *Operator*

```
interface IStack {/* From Example 6.9 */}
class StackImpl implements IStack {/* From Example 6.9 */}
interface ISafeStack extends IStack {/* From Example 6.9 */}
class SafeStackImpl extends StackImpl implements ISafeStack
    {/* From Example 6.9 */}

public class Identification {

    public static void main(String args[]) {
        Object obj = new Object();
        StackImpl stack = new StackImpl(10);
        SafeStackImpl safeStack = new SafeStackImpl(5);
        IStack iStack;

        System.out.println("(1): " +
            (null instanceof Object));       // Always false.
        System.out.println("(2): " +
            (null instanceof IStack));       // Always false.

        System.out.println("(3): " +         // true: instance of subclass of
            (stack instanceof Object));      //       Object.
        System.out.println("(4): " +
            (obj instanceof StackImpl));     // false: Downcasting.
        System.out.println("(5): " +
            (stack instanceof StackImpl));   // true: instance of StackImpl.

        System.out.println("(6): " +         // false: Object does not implement
             (obj instanceof IStack));       //        IStack.
        System.out.println("(7): " +         // true: SafeStackImpl implements
             (safeStack instanceof IStack)); //       IStack.

        obj = stack;                         // Assigning subclass to superclass.
        System.out.println("(8): " +
            (obj instanceof StackImpl));     // true: instance of StackImpl.
        System.out.println("(9): " +         // true: StackImpl implements
            (obj instanceof IStack));        //       IStack.
        System.out.println("(10): " +
             (obj instanceof String));       // false: No relationship.
```

```
        iStack = (IStack) obj; // Cast required: superclass assigned subclass.
        System.out.println("(11): " +         // true: instance of subclass
            (iStack instanceof Object));      //       of Object.
        System.out.println("(12): " +
            (iStack instanceof StackImpl));   // true: instance of StackImpl.

        String[] strArray = new String[10];
    //  System.out.println("(13): " +         // Compile time error,
    //      (strArray instanceof String);     // no relationship.
        System.out.println("(14): " +
            (strArray instanceof Object));    // true: array subclass of Object.
        System.out.println("(15): " +
            (strArray instanceof Object[])); // true: array subclass of Object[].
        System.out.println("(16): " +
            (strArray[0] instanceof Object));// false: strArray[0] is null.
        strArray[0] = "Amoeba strip";
        System.out.println("(17): " +
            (strArray[0] instanceof String));// true: instance of String.

    }
}
```

Output from the program:

```
(1): false
(2): false
(3): true
(4): false
(5): true
(6): false
(7): true
(8): true
(9): true
(10): false
(11): true
(12): true
(14): true
(15): true
(16): false
(17): true
```

Converting References of Class and Interface Types

References of interface type can be declared, and these can denote objects of classes that implement this interface. This is another example of upcasting. Note that converting a reference of interface type to the type of the class implementing the interface requires explicit casting. This is an example of downcasting. The following code illustrates these cases:

```
IStack istackOne = new StackImpl(5);                 // Upcasting
StackImpl stackTwo = (StackImpl) istackOne;          // Downcasting
```

Using the reference `istackOne` of interface type `IStack`, methods of the `IStack` interface can be invoked on objects of the `StackImpl` class which implements this interface, but the additional members of the `StackImpl` class cannot be accessed via this reference:

```
Object obj1 = istackOne.pop();        // OK. Method in IStack interface.
Object obj2 = istackOne.peek();       // Not OK. Method not in IStack interface.
```

Review questions

6.16 Given the following program, which statement is true?

```
// Filename: MyClass.java
public class MyClass {
    public static void main(String args[]) {
        A[] arrA;
        B[] arrB;

        arrA = new A[10];
        arrB = new B[20];
        arrA = arrB;       // (1)
        arrB = (B[]) arrA; // (2)
        arrA = new A[10];
        arrB = (B[]) arrA; // (3)
    }
}

class A {}

class B extends A {}
```

Select the one right answer.

(a) The program will fail to compile, owing to the line labeled (1).
(b) The program will throw a `java.lang.ClassCastException` at the line labeled (2) when run.
(c) The program will throw a `java.lang.ClassCastException` at the line labeled (3) when run.
(d) The program will compile and run without problems, even if the `(B[])` cast in the lines labeled (2) and (3) were removed.
(e) The program compiles and runs without problems, but would not do so if the `(B[])` cast in the lines labeled (2) and (3) were removed.

6.17 Which is the first line that will cause compilation to fail in the following program?

```
// Filename: MyClass.java
class MyClass {
    public static void main(String args[]) {
        MyClass a;
        MySubclass b;

        a = new MyClass();             // (1)
        b = new MySubclass();          // (2)
```

```
            a = b;                          // (3)
            b = a;                          // (4)

            a = new MySubclass();           // (5)
            b = new MyClass();              // (6)
        }
    }

    class MySubclass extends MyClass {}
```

Select the one right answer.

(a) Line labeled (1)
(b) Line labeled (2)
(c) Line labeled (3)
(d) Line labeled (4)
(e) Line labeled (5)
(f) Line labeled (6)

6.18 Given the following definitions and reference declarations, which of the following assignments are legal?

```
// Definitions:
interface I1 {}
interface I2 {}
class C1 implements I1 {}
class C2 implements I2 {}
class C3 extends C1 implements I2 {}

// Reference declarations:
// ...
    C1 obj1;
    C2 obj2;
    C3 obj3;
// ...
```

Select all valid answers.

(a) `obj2 = obj1;`
(b) `obj3 = obj1;`
(c) `obj3 = obj2;`
(d) `I1 a = obj2;`
(e) `I1 b = obj3;`
(f) `I2 c = obj1;`

6.19 Given the following class definitions and the following reference declarations, what can be said about the statement `y = (Sub) x`?

```
// Class definitions:
class Super {}
class Sub extends Super {}
```

```
// Reference declarations
// ...
    Super x;
    Sub y;
// ...
```

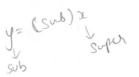

Select the one right answer.

(a) Illegal at compile time.
(b) Legal at compile time, but might be illegal at runtime.
(c) Definitely legal at runtime, but the (Sub) cast was not strictly needed.
(d) Definitely legal at runtime, and the (Sub) cast was needed.

6.20 Given the following class definitions and the following object instantiations, which of these assignments are legal at compile time?

```
// Definitions:
interface A {};
class B {};
class C extends B implements A {};
class D implements A {};

// Object instantiation:
// [...]
    B b = new B();
    C c = new C();
    D d = new D();
// [...]
```

Select all valid answers.

(a) `c = d;`
(b) `d = c;`
(c) `A a = d;`
(d) `d = (D) c;`
(e) `c = b;`

6.21 Which letters will be printed when the following program is run?

```
// Filename: MyClass.java
public class MyClass {
    public static void main(String args[]) {
        B b = new C();
        A a = b;
        if (a instanceof A) System.out.println("A");
        if (a instanceof B) System.out.println("B");
        if (a instanceof C) System.out.println("C");
        if (a instanceof D) System.out.println("D");
    }
}

class A {}
class B extends A {}
class C extends B {}
class D extends C {}
```

Select all valid answers.

(a) `A` will be printed.
(b) `B` will be printed.
(c) `C` will be printed.
(d) `D` will be printed.

6.22 Given three classes `A`, `B` and `C`, where `B` is a subclass of `A` and `C` is a subclass of `B`, which one of these boolean expressions correctly identifies when an object `o` has actually been instantiated from class `B` as opposed to from `A` or `C`?

Select the one right answer.

(a) `(o instanceof B) && (!(o instanceof A))`
(b) `(o instanceof B) && (!(o instanceof C))`
(c) `!((o instanceof A) || (o instanceof B))`
(d) `(o instanceof B)`
(e) `(o instanceof B) && !((o instanceof A) || (o instanceof C))`

6.23 Which letters will be printed when the following program is run?

```
public class MyClass {
    public static void main(String args[]) {
        I x = new D();
        if (x instanceof I) System.out.println("I");
        if (x instanceof J) System.out.println("J");
        if (x instanceof C) System.out.println("C");
        if (x instanceof D) System.out.println("D");
    }
}

interface I{}
interface J{}
class C implements I {}
class D extends C implements J {}
```

Select all valid answers.

(a) `I` will be printed.
(b) `J` will be printed.
(c) `C` will be printed.
(d) `D` will be printed.

6.6 Polymorphism and Dynamic Method Lookup

Which object a reference will actually denote during runtime cannot always be determined at compile time. Polymorphism allows a reference to denote different objects in the inheritance hierarchy at different times during execution. Such a reference is a supertype reference, i.e. either a superclass reference that can denote objects of its subclasses, or an interface reference that can denote objects of classes that implement the interface.

When a method is invoked using a reference, the method definition which actually gets executed is determined both by the class of the object denoted by the reference at runtime and the method signature. Dynamic method lookup is the process of determining which method definition a method signature denotes during runtime, based on the class of the object. Polymorphism and dynamic method lookup form a powerful programming paradigm which simplifies client definitions, encourages object decoupling and supports dynamically changing relationships between objects at runtime.

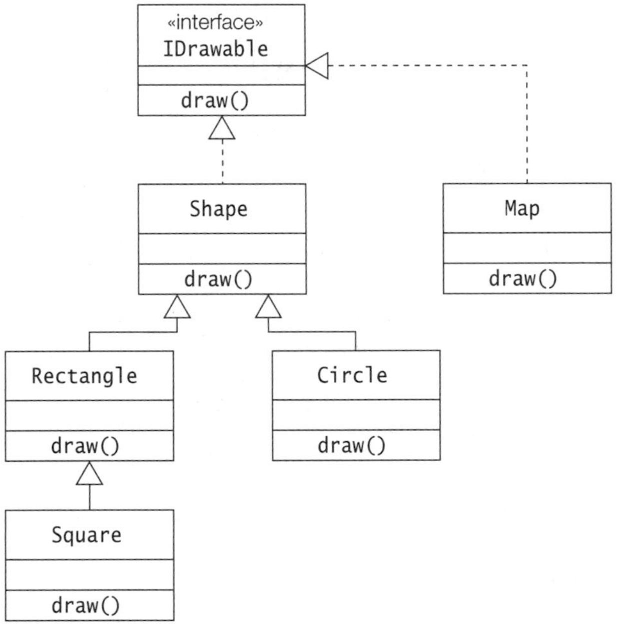

Figure 6.5 *Polymorphic Methods*

The inheritance hierarchy depicted in Figure 6.5 is implemented in Example 6.14. The implementation of the method `draw()` is overridden in all subclasses of `Shape`. The invocation of the `draw()` method in the two loops at (3) and (4) in Example 6.14 relies on the polymorphic behavior of references and dynamic method lookup. The array `shapes` holds `Shape` references denoting a `Circle`, a `Rectangle` and a `Square`, as shown at (1). At runtime, dynamic lookup determines the `draw()` implementation to execute based on the class of the object denoted by each element in the array. This is also the case for the elements of the array `drawables` at (2), which holds `IDrawable` reference elements that can be assigned any object of a class which implements the `IDrawable` interface. The first loop will still work without any change if objects of new subclasses of `Shape` are added to the array `shapes`. If they did not override the `draw()` method, then an inherited version of the method will be executed. This polymorphic behavior applies to the array `drawables`, where the subtype objects are guaranteed to have implemented the `IDrawable` interface.

Example 6.14 *Polymorphism and Dynamic Method Lookup*

```
interface IDrawable {
    void draw();
}

class Shape implements IDrawable {
    public void draw() { System.out.println("Drawing a Shape."); }
}

class Circle extends Shape {
    public void draw() { System.out.println("Drawing a Circle."); }
}

class Rectangle extends Shape {
    public void draw() { System.out.println("Drawing a Rectangle."); }
}

class Square extends Rectangle {
    public void draw() { System.out.println("Drawing a Square."); }
}

class Map implements IDrawable {
    public void draw() { System.out.println("Drawing a Map."); }
}

public class PolymorphRefs {
    public static void main(String args[]) {
        Shape[] shapes = {new Circle(), new Rectangle(), new Square()};   // (1)
        IDrawable[] drawables = {new Shape(), new Rectangle(), new Map()};// (2)

        System.out.println("Draw shapes:");
        for (int i = 0; i < shapes.length; i++)                           // (3)
            shapes[i].draw();

        System.out.println("Draw drawables:");
        for (int i = 0; i < drawables.length; i++)                        // (4)
            drawables[i].draw();
    }
}
```

Output from the program:

```
Draw shapes:
Drawing a Circle.
Drawing a Rectangle.
Drawing a Square.
Draw drawables:
Drawing a Shape.
Drawing a Rectangle.
Drawing a Map.
```

Review questions

6.24 What will be the result of attempting to compile and run the following program?

```
public class Polymorphism {
    public static void main(String args[]) {
        A ref1 = new C();
        B ref2 = (B) ref1;
        System.out.println(ref2.f());
    }
}

class A           { int f() { return 0; } }
class B extends A { int f() { return 1; } }
class C extends B { int f() { return 2; } }
```

Select the one right answer.

(a) The program will fail to compile.
(b) The program will compile without error, but will throw a `ClassCastException` when run.
(c) The program will compile without error and print `0` when run.
(d) The program will compile without error and print `1` when run.
(e) The program will compile without error and print `2` when run.

6.25 What will be the result of attempting to compile and run the following program?

```
public class Polymorphism2 {
    public static void main(String args[]) {
        A ref1 = new C();
        B ref2 = (B) ref1;
        System.out.println(ref2.g());
    }
}

class A {
    private int f() { return 0; }
    public int g() { return 3; }
}
class B extends A {
    private int f() { return 1; }
    public int g() { return f(); }
}
class C extends B {
    public int f() { return 2; }
}
```

Select the one right answer.

(a) The program will fail to compile.
(b) The program will compile without error and print `0` when run.
(c) The program will compile without error and print `1` when run.
(d) The program will compile without error and print `2` when run.
(e) The program will compile without error and print `3` when run.

6.7 Inheritance vs. Aggregation

Encapsulation

An object has properties and behaviors that are *encapsulated* inside the object. The services it offers to its clients comprises its *contract*. Only the *contract* defined by the object is available to the clients. The *implementation* of its properties and behavior is not a concern of the clients. Encapsulation helps to make clear the distinction between an object's contract and implementation. This has major consequences for program development. The implementation of an object can change without implications for the clients. Encapsulation also reduces complexity, as the internals of an object are hidden from the clients, who cannot influence its implementation.

Choosing between Inheritance and Aggregation

Figure 6.6 is a UML class diagram showing several aggregation relationships and one inheritance relationship. The class diagram shows a queue which is defined by aggregation, and a stack which is defined by inheritance. Both are based on linked lists. A linked list is defined by aggregation. The implementation of these data structures is shown in Example 6.15. The purpose of the example is to illustrate inheritance and aggregation, not industrial-strength implementation of queues and stacks. The class `Node` at (1) is straightforward, defining two instance variables, one denoting the data and the other denoting the next node in the list. The class `LinkedList` at (2) keeps track of the list by managing a head and a tail node. Nodes can be inserted in front or at the back, but deleted only from the front of the list.

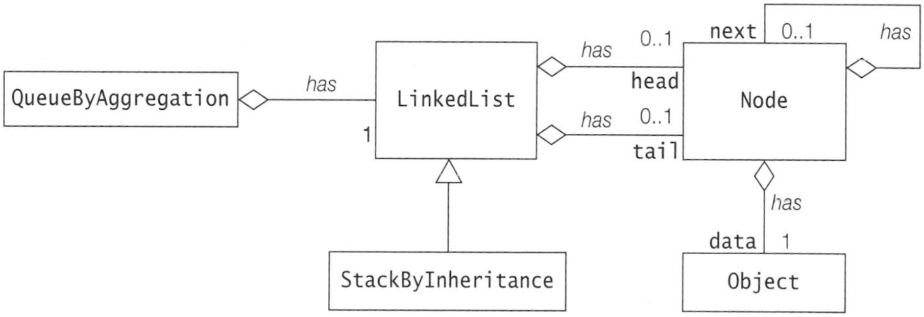

Figure 6.6 *Inheritance and Aggregation*

Example 6.15 *Inheritance and Aggregation*

```
class Node {                                          // (1)
    private Object data;    // Data
    private Node next;      // Next node
```

```
    // Constructor for initializing data and reference to the next node.
    public Node(Object obj, Node link) {
        data = obj;
        next = link;
    }

    // Accessor methods
    public void setData(Object obj) { data = obj; }
    public Object getData() { return data; }
    public void setNext(Node node) { next = node; }
    public Node getNext() { return next; }
}

class LinkedList {                                                    // (2)

    protected Node head = null;
    protected Node tail = null;
    // Modifier methods
    public void insertInFront(Object dataObj) {
        if (isEmpty()) head = tail = new Node(dataObj, null);
        else head = new Node(dataObj, head);
    }

    public void insertAtBack(Object dataObj) {
        if (isEmpty())
            head = tail = new Node(dataObj, null);
        else {
            tail.setNext(new Node(dataObj, null));
            tail = tail.getNext();
        }
    }
    public Object deleteFromFront() {
        if (isEmpty()) return null;
        Node removed = head;
        if (head == tail) head = tail = null;
        else head = head.getNext();
        return removed.getData();
    }
    // Selector method
    public boolean isEmpty() { return head == null; }
}

class QueueByAggregation {                                            // (3)
    private LinkedList qList;
    // Constructor
    public QueueByAggregation() {
        qList = new LinkedList();
    }
    // Methods
    public void enqueue(Object item) { qList.insertAtBack(item); }
    public Object dequeue() {
        if (empty()) return null;
        else return qList.deleteFromFront();
    }
```

```
    public Object peek() {
        Object obj = dequeue();
        if (obj != null) qList.insertInFront(obj);
        return obj;
    }
    public boolean empty() { return qList.isEmpty(); }
}

class StackByInheritance extends LinkedList {                     // (4)
    public void push(Object item) { insertInFront(item); }
    public Object pop() {
        if (empty()) return null;
        else return deleteFromFront();
    }
    public Object peek() {
        return (isEmpty() ? null : head.getData());
    }
    public boolean empty() { return isEmpty(); }
}

public class Client {                                              // (5)
    public static void main(String args[]) {
        String string1 = "Queues are boring to stand in!";
        int length1 = string1.length();
        QueueByAggregation queue = new QueueByAggregation();
        for (int i = 0; i<length1; i++)
            queue.enqueue(new Character(string1.charAt(i)));
        while (!queue.empty())
            System.out.print((Character) queue.dequeue());
        System.out.println();

        String string2 = "!no tis ot nuf era skcatS";
        int length2 = string2.length();
        StackByInheritance stack = new StackByInheritance();
        for (int i = 0; i<length2; i++)
            stack.push(new Character(string2.charAt(i)));
        stack.insertAtBack(new Character('!'));                     // (6)
        while (!stack.empty())
            System.out.print((Character) stack.pop());
        System.out.println();

    }
}
```

Output from the program:

```
Queues are boring to stand in!
Stacks are fun to sit on!!
```

Choosing between inheritance and aggregation to model relationships can be a crucial design decision. A good design strategy advocates that inheritance should be used only if the relationship *is-a* is unequivocally maintained throughout the lifetime of the objects involved, otherwise aggregation is the best choice. A *role* is often confused with an *is-a* relationship. For example, given the class `Employee`, it would not be a good idea to model the roles an employee can play (such as a manager or a cashier) by inheritance if these roles changed intermittently. Changing roles would involve a new object to represent the new role every time this happened.

Code reuse is also best achieved by aggregation when there is no *is-a* relationship. Enforcing an artificial *is-a* relationship which is not naturally present is usually not a good idea. This is illustrated in Example 6.15 at (6). Since the class `StackByInheritance` at (4) is a subclass of the class `LinkedList` at (2), any inherited method from the superclass can be invoked on an instance of the subclass. Also, methods which contradict the abstraction represented by the subclass can be invoked, as shown at (6). Using aggregation in such a case results in a better solution, as demonstrated by the class `QueueByAggregation` at (3). The class defines the operations of a queue by *delegating* such requests to the underlying class `LinkedList`. Clients implementing a queue in this manner do not have access to the underlying class and therefore cannot break the abstraction.

Both inheritance and aggregation promote encapsulation of *implementation*, as changes to the implementation are localized to the class. Changing the *contract* of a superclass can have consequences for the subclasses (called the *ripple effect*) and also for clients who are dependent on a particular behavior of the subclasses.

Polymorphism is achieved through inheritance and interface implementation. Code relying on polymorphic behavior will still work without any change if new subclasses or new classes implementing the interface are added. If no obvious *is-a* relationship is present, then polymorphism is best achieved by using aggregation with interface implementation.

Review questions

6.26 Given the following code, which statements are true?

```
public interface HeavenlyBody { String describe(); }

class Star {
    String starName;
    public String describe() { return "star " + starName; }
}

class Planet extends Star {
    String name;
    public String describe() {
        return "planet " + name + " orbiting star " + starName;
    }
}
```

Select all valid answers:

(a) The code will fail to compile.
(b) The use of inheritance is justified, since planet *is-a* star.
(c) The code will fail to compile if the name `starName` is replaced with the name `bodyName` throughout the `Star` class definition.

intermittently

(d) The code will fail to compile if the name `starName` is replaced with the name `name` throughout the `Star` class definition.
(e) An instance of `Planet` is a valid instance of `HeavenlyBody`.

6.27 Given the following code, which statements are true?

```
public interface HeavenlyBody { String describe(); }

class Star implements HeavenlyBody {
    String starName;
    public String describe() { return "star " + starName; }
}

class Planet {
    String name;
    Star orbiting;
    public String describe() {
        return "planet " + name + " orbiting " + orbiting.describe();
    }
}
```

Select all valid answers:

(a) The code will fail to compile.
(b) The use of aggregation is justified, since planet *has-a* star.
(c) The code will fail to compile if the name `starName` is replaced with the name `bodyName` throughout the `Star` class definition.
(d) The code will fail to compile if the name `starName` is replaced with the name `name` throughout the `Star` class definition.
(e) An instance of `Planet` is a valid instance of a `HeavenlyBody`.

Chapter summary

The following information was included in this chapter:

- Inheritance and its implications in object-oriented programming.
- Method overriding and variable shadowing.
- Method overriding vs. method overloading.
- Usage of `super` reference to access inherited members.
- Usage of `this()` and `super()` calls, including constructor chaining.
- Interfaces and multiple interface inheritance.
- Conversions due to assigning, casting and passing references.
- Identifying objects using the `instanceof` operator.
- Polymorphism and dynamic method lookup.
- Inheritance (*is-a*) vs. aggregation (*has-a*).

Programming exercises

6.1 Declare an interface called `Function` that has a method named `evaluate()` that takes an arbitrary `int` value as a parameter and returns an `int` value.

Create a class `Half` that implements `Function`. Make the implementation of the method `evaluate()` return the value obtained by dividing the `int` argument by 2.

Create a method that takes an arbitrary array of `int` values as parameter and returns an array that has the same length, but the value of an element in the new array is half that of the value in the corresponding element in the array passed as parameter. Let the implementation of this method create an instance of `Half`, and use this instance to calculate the values in the array to be returned.

6.2 Rewrite the method that operated on arrays from the previous exercise: the method should now take a `Function` reference as an argument and use this instead of creating an instance of `Half`.

Create a class called `Print` that implements `Function`, and has an implementation that simply prints the `int` value given as an argument and returns the value.

Now create a program that creates an array of the `int` values from 1 to 10 and does the following:

1. Prints the array using an instance of the `Print` class and the method described above.
2. Halves the values in the array and prints the values again, using the `Half` and `Print` classes and the method described above.

Inner Classes 7

Exam Objectives

- Write code to construct instances of any concrete class, including normal top-level classes, inner classes, static inner classes and anonymous inner classes.

Supplementary Objectives

- State the kinds of nested classes and interfaces that can be defined.
- Identify the context in which a nested class or interface can be defined.
- State which accessibility modifiers are allowed for each category of nested classes.
- State which nested classes create instances that are associated with instances of the outer context.
- State the access rules that govern accessing entities in the outer context of nested classes, and write code that uses the augmented syntax involving the `this` keyword for this purpose.
- State whether a definition of a nested class can contain static and non-static members.
- Write code to instantiate nested classes using the augmented syntax of the `new` operator.
- Write code to show how nested classes can be imported and used.
- Distinguish between the inheritance and containment hierarchy of any nested class or interface.
- Write code to implement anonymous classes by extending an existing class and by implementing an interface.

7.1 Overview of Nested Classes

An ordinary class or interface is defined at the *top level*, which is the package level. These classes and interfaces (also called *top-level package member classes or interfaces*) are grouped into packages. In addition to these top-level package member classes and interfaces, there are four categories of *nested classes* and one of *nested interfaces* defined by the context these classes and interfaces are declared in:

- Top-level Nested Classes and Interfaces
- Non-static Inner Classes
- Local Classes
- Anonymous Classes

Top-level nested classes and interfaces are also considered to be at the top level. The last three categories are collectively known as *inner classes*. These differ from top-level classes in that they can use simple non-static names from the *enclosing context*, i.e. an instance of an inner class is not limited to directly accessing only its own instance variables. In particular, an instance of an inner class may be associated with an instance of the enclosing class and may access its members.

A *top-level nested class or interface* is defined as a `static` member in a top-level (possibly nested) class or interface. Such a nested class can be instantiated like any ordinary top-level class, using its full name. No instance of the enclosing class is required to instantiate a top-level nested class. *Non-static inner classes* are defined as instance members of other classes, just like instance variable and method members are defined in a class. An instance of a non-static inner class always has an instance of the enclosing class associated with it. *Local classes* can be defined in a block of code as in a method body or a local block, just as local variables can be defined in a method body or a local block. *Anonymous classes* can be defined and instantiated "on the fly" in expressions. Local and anonymous classes can be either *static* or *non-static*, where being non-static means that an instance of such a class is associated with an instance of the enclosing class.

Table 7.1 presents a summary of various aspects relating to classes and interfaces. The Entity column lists the different kinds of classes and interfaces that can be defined. The Declaration Context column lists the lexical context in which the class or interface can be defined. The Accessibility Modifiers column indicates what accessibility can be specified for the class or interface. The Outer Instance column specifies whether an instance of the enclosing context is associated with an instance of the class. The Direct Access to Enclosing Context column lists what is directly accessible in the enclosing context from within the class. The Defines Static or Non-static Members column refers to whether the class can define static or non-static members, or both. Subsequent sections on each nested class elaborate on the summary presented in Table 7.1. (N/A in the table means not applicable.)

Nested classes can be regarded as a form of encapsulation, enforcing relationships between classes by greater proximity. Used judiciously, they can be beneficial, but unrestrained nesting can easily result in incomprehensible code.

Table 7.1 *Overview of Classes and Interfaces*

Entity	Declaration Context	Accessibility Modifiers	Outer Instance	Direct Access to Enclosing Context	Defines Static or Non-static Members
Package-level class	As package member	`public` or default	No	N/A	Both static and non-static
Top-level nested class (static)	As static class member	all	No	Static members in enclosing context	Both static and non-static
Non-static inner class	As non-static class member	all	Yes	All members in enclosing context	Only non-static
Local class (non-static)	In block with non-static context	none	Yes	All members in enclosing context + local final variables	Only non-static
Local class (static)	In block with static context	none	No	Static members in enclosing context + local final variables	Only non-static
Anonymous class (non-static)	As expression in non-static context	none	Yes	All members in enclosing context + local final variables	Only non-static
Anonymous class (static)	As expression in static context	none	No	Static members in enclosing context + local final variables	Only non-static
Interface	As package member or static class member	`public` only	N/A	N/A	Static variables + non-static method prototypes

7.2 Top-level Nested Classes and Interfaces

A *top-level nested class or interface* is similar to a top-level package member class or interface, but it is defined as a `static` member of an enclosing top-level class or interface. Top-level nested classes and interfaces can be nested to any depth, but only within other static top-level classes and interfaces.

Interfaces are implicitly static. Nested interfaces can optionally be prefixed with the keyword `static` and have any accessibility. There are no non-static inner, local or anonymous interfaces – only (possibly nested) `static` top-level interfaces.

Example 7.1 *Top-level Nested Classes and Interfaces*

```
// Filename: TopLevelClass.java
public class TopLevelClass {                                // (1)
    // ...
    static class NestedTopLevelClass {                      // (2)
        // ...

        interface NestedTopLevelInterface1 {                // (3)
            // ...
        }

        static class NestedTopLevelClass1
            implements NestedTopLevelInterface1 {           // (4)
            // ...
        }
    }
}
```

In Example 7.1, the top-level package member class `TopLevelClass` at (1) contains a nested top-level class `NestedTopLevelClass` at (2), which in turn defines a nested top-level interface `NestedTopLevelInterface1` at (3), which is implemented by the nested top-level class `NestedTopLevelClass1` at (4). Note that each nested top-level class is defined as `static`, just like `static` variables and methods in a class.

The full name of a nested top-level class or interface includes the name of the class it is defined in. For example, the full name of the nested top-level class `NestedTopLevelClass1` at (4) is `TopLevelClass.NestedTopLevelClass.NestedTopLevelClass1`. The full name of the nested top-level interface `NestedTopLevelInterface1` at (3) is `TopLevelClass.NestedTopLevelClass.NestedTopLevelInterface1`. Note that each nested top-level class or interface is uniquely identified by this naming convention, which is a generalization of the fully qualified naming scheme for package members. The full class name can be used in a program, like any other class or interface name. Note that a nested class cannot have the same name as an enclosing class or package.

If the file `TopLevelClass.java` containing the definitions in Example 7.1 is compiled, it will result in the generation of the following class files, where each file corresponds to a class or interface definition:

```
TopLevelClass$NestedTopLevelClass$NestedTopLevelClass1.class
TopLevelClass$NestedTopLevelClass$NestedTopLevelInterface1.class
TopLevelClass$NestedTopLevelClass.class
TopLevelClass.class
```

Note how the full class name corresponds to the file name (minus the extension) with the dollar sign (`$`) replaced by the dot sign (`.`).

A client can use the `import` statement to provide a shortcut for the names of nested top-level classes and interfaces. Here are some variations on usage of the `import` statement for nested top-level classes and interfaces:

```
// Filename: Client1.java
import TopLevelClass.*;                                               // (1)

public class Client {
    NestedTopLevelClass.NestedTopLevelClass1 objRef1 =
            new NestedTopLevelClass.NestedTopLevelClass1();           // (2)
}
```

```
// Filename: Client2.java
import TopLevelClass.NestedTopLevelClass.*;                           // (3)

public class Client2 {
    NestedTopLevelClass1 objRef2 = new NestedTopLevelClass1();        // (4)
}

class SomeClass implements
    TopLevelClass.NestedTopLevelClass.NestedTopLevelInterface1 {      // (5)
    /* ... */
}
```

In the file `Client1.java`, the `import` statement at (1) allows the nested top-level class `NestedTopLevelClass1` to be referenced as `NestedTopLevelClass.NestedTopLevelClass1` as at (2), whereas in the file `Client2.java`, the `import` statement at (3) will allow the same class to be referenced using the simple name as at (4). At (5), the full name of the nested top-level interface is used in an `implements` clause.

For all intents and purposes, a top-level nested class or interface is very much like any other top-level package member class or interface. Static variables and methods belong to a class, and not to instances of the class. The same is true for nested top-level classes. A (static) nested top-level class can be instantiated without any reference to any instance of the enclosing context, i.e. objects of a nested top-level class can be created without regard to its nesting. Examples of creating instances of nested top-level classes are shown above at (2) and (4) using the `new` operator.

Static methods do not have a `this` reference and can therefore only access other `static` methods and variables directly in the class. This also applies to methods in a nested top-level class. A method in a nested top-level class can only directly access static members in the enclosing class or interface, but not instance members in the enclosing context. Since nested top-level classes are static, their methods do not have any (outer) instance of the enclosing context.

Figure 7.1 is a class diagram that illustrates top-level nested classes and interfaces. These are shown as members of the enclosing context, with the {static} tag to indicate that they are static, i.e. they can be instantiated without regard to any outer object of the enclosing context. Since they are members of a class or an interface, their accessibility can be specified exactly like that of any other member of a class or interface. The classes from the diagram are implemented in Example 7.2.

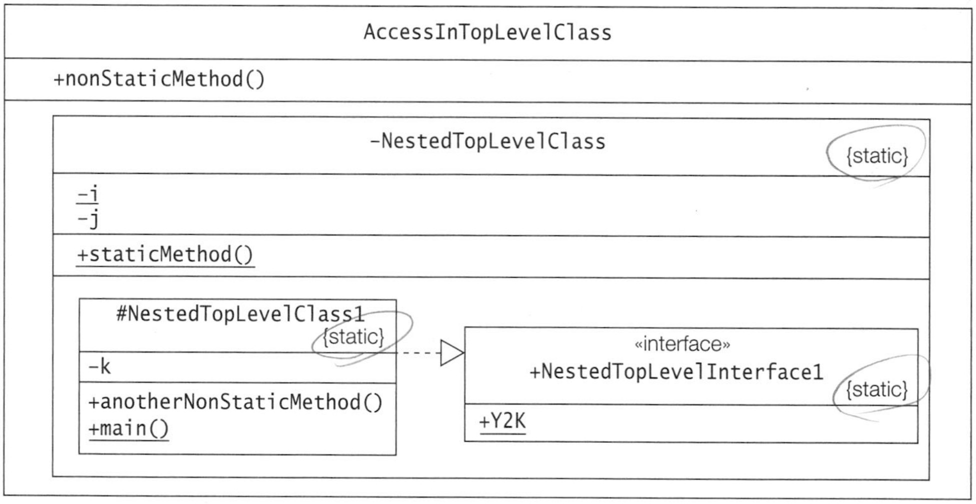

Figure 7.1 *Top-level Nested Classes and Interfaces*

Example 7.2 *Access in Top-level Nested Classes and Interfaces*

```
// Filename: AccessInTopLevelClass.java
public class AccessInTopLevelClass {                               // (1)
    public void nonStaticMethod() {                                // (2)
        System.out.println("nonstaticMethod in AccessInTopLevelClass");
    }

    private static class NestedTopLevelClass {                     // (3)
        private static int i;                                      // (4)
        private int j;                                             // (5)

        public static void staticMethod() {                        // (6)
            System.out.println("staticMethod in NestedTopLevelClass");
        }

        interface NestedTopLevelInterface1 { int Y2K = 2000; }     // (7)

        protected static class NestedTopLevelClass1
                implements NestedTopLevelInterface1 {              // (8)
            private int k = Y2K;                                   // (9)
```

```
            public void anotherNonStaticMethod() {                   // (10)
            //  int jj = j;                 // (11) Not OK.
                int ii = i;                 // (12)
                int kk = k;                 // (13)

            //  nonStaticMethod();          // (14) Not OK.
                staticMethod();             // (15)
            }

            public static void main (String args[]) {
                int ii = i;                 // (16)
            //  int kk = k;                 // (17) Not OK.
                staticMethod();             // (18)
            }
        }
    }
}
```

Output from the program:

```
staticMethod in NestedTopLevelClass
```

Example 7.2 demonstrates accessing members directly in the enclosing context of class `NestedTopLevelClass1` defined at (8). The initialization at (9) is valid, since the variable `Y2K`, defined in the outer interface `NestedTopLevelInterface1` at (7), is implicitly static. The compiler will flag an error at (11) and (14) in method `anotherNonStaticMethod()`, because direct access to non-static members in the enclosing class is not permitted by *any* method in a nested top-level class. It will also flag an error at (17) in method `main()`, because a static method cannot access directly other non-static variables in its own class. Statements at (16) and (18) only access `static` members in the enclosing context. The references in these statements can also be specified using full names:

```
int ii = AccessInTopLevelClass.NestedTopLevelClass.i;
AccessInTopLevelClass.NestedTopLevelClass.staticMethod();
```

Note that a top-level nested class can define both `static` and instance members, like any other package-level class. However, its code can only directly access `static` members in its enclosing context.

A top-level nested class, being a member of the enclosing class or interface, can have any accessibility (`public`, `protected`, package/default, `private`), like any other members of a class. The class `NestedTopLevelClass` at (3) has `private` accessibility, whereas its nested class `NestedTopLevelClass1` at (8) has `protected` accessibility. The class `NestedTopLevelClass1` defines the method `main()`, which can be executed by the command:

```
java AccessInTopLevelClass$NestedTopLevelClass$NestedTopLevelClass1
```

Note that the class `NestedTopLevelClass1` is specified using the full name of the class file, minus the extension.

7.3 Non-static Inner Classes

Non-static inner classes are defined without the keyword `static`, as members of an enclosing class, and can also be nested to any depth. Non-static inner classes are on par with other non-static members defined in a class. The following aspects about non-static inner classes should be noted:

- An instance of a non-static inner class can only exist with an instance of its enclosing class. This means that an instance of a non-static inner class must be created in the context of an instance of the enclosing class. This also means that a non-static inner class cannot have `static` members. In other words, the class does not provide any services, only instances of the class do.
- Methods of a non-static inner class can directly refer to any member (including classes) of any enclosing class, including `private` members. No explicit reference is required.
- Since a non-static inner class is a member of an enclosing class, it can have any accessibility: `public`, package/default, `protected` or `private`.

Example 7.3 *Defining Non-static Inner Classes*

```
class ToplevelClass {                                          // (1)

    private static String msg = "Shine the inner light.";      // (2)
    public NonStaticInnerClass makeInstance() {                // (3)
        return new NonStaticInnerClass();                      // (4)
    }
    public class NonStaticInnerClass {                         // (5)
    //  private static int staticVar;                          // (6) Not OK.
        private String string;                                 // (7)
        public NonStaticInnerClass() { string = msg; }         // (8)
        public void printMsg() { System.out.println(string); } // (9)
    }
}

public class Client {                                          // (10)
    public static void main(String args[]) {                   // (11)
        ToplevelClass topRef = new ToplevelClass();            // (12)
        ToplevelClass.NonStaticInnerClass innerRef1 =
                      topRef.makeInstance();                   // (13)
        innerRef1.printMsg();                                  // (14)
    //  ToplevelClass.NonStaticInnerClass innerRef2 =
    //                new ToplevelClass.NonStaticInnerClass(); // (15) Not OK.
        ToplevelClass.NonStaticInnerClass innerRef3 =
                      topRef.new NonStaticInnerClass();        // (16)
    }
}
```

Output from the program:

```
Shine the inner light.
```

In Example 7.3, the class `ToplevelClass` at (1) defines a non-static inner class at (5). Declaration of a static variable in class `NonStaticInnerClass` would be flagged as a compile time error, as a non-static inner class cannot define `static` members.

The non-static method `makeInstance()` at (3) in the class `ToplevelClass` creates an instance of the `NonStaticInnerClass` using the `new` operator, as shown at (4). This creates an instance of a non-static inner class in the context of the instance of the enclosing class on which the `makeInstance()` method is invoked. The `makeInstance()` method is called at (13). The reference to an object of the non-static inner class can then be used in the normal way to access its members, as shown at (14). An attempt to create an instance of the non-static inner class, without an outer instance, using the `new` operator with the full name of the inner class, as shown at (15), results in a compile time error. A special form of the `new` operator must be used, which is illustrated at (16):

```
topRef.new NonStaticInnerClass();           // (16)
```

The expression *<enclosing object reference>* in the syntax

<enclosing object reference>`.new`

evaluates to an instance of the enclosing class in which the designated non-static inner class is defined. It is an error to specify the full name of the inner class, as the enclosing context is already given by *<enclosing object reference>*. The reference `topRef` denotes an object of class `ToplevelClass`. After the execution of the statement at (16), the `ToplevelClass` object has two instances of the inner class `NonStaticInnerClass` associated with it. This is depicted in Figure 7.2, where the outer object (denoted by `topRef`) of class `ToplevelClass` is shown with its two associated inner objects (denoted by `innerRef1` and `innerRef3` respectively) right after the execution of the statement at (16). In other words, multiple objects of the inner classes can be associated with an object of an enclosing class at runtime.

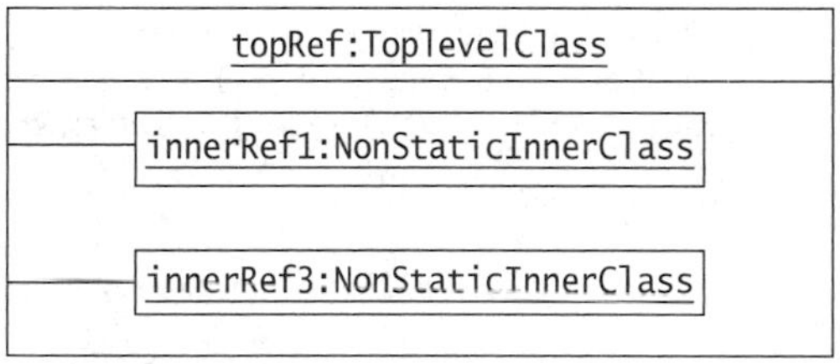

Figure 7.2 *Outer Object with Associated Inner Objects*

An implicit reference to the enclosing object is always available in every method and constructor of a non-static inner class. A method can explicitly use this reference with a special form of the `this` construct, as explained below.

From within a non-static inner class, it is possible to refer to members in the enclosing class directly. An example is shown at (8), where the instance variable `msg` from the enclosing class is accessed in the non-static inner class. It is also possible to explicitly refer to members in the enclosing class, but this requires special usage of the `this` reference. One might be tempted to define the constructor at (8) as follows:

```
public NonStaticInnerClass() { this.string = this.msg; }
```

The reference `this.string` is correct, because the instance variable `string` certainly belongs to the current object (denoted by `this`) of `NonStaticInnerClass`, but `this.msg` cannot possibly work, as the current object (indicated by `this`) of `NonStaticInnerClass` has no instance variable `msg`. The correct syntax is the following:

```
public NonStaticInnerClass() { this.string = ToplevelClass.this.msg; }
```

The expression

<enclosing class name>`.this`

evaluates to a reference that denotes the enclosing object (of class *<enclosing class name>*) of the current instance of a non-static inner class.

Accessing Shadowed Members from Non-static Inner Classes

As non-static inner classes can be nested, names of instance members in enclosing classes can become *shadowed*. The special form of the `this` syntax can be used to access members in the enclosing context.

Example 7.4 *Special Form of* `this` *and* `new` *Constructs in Non-static Inner Classes*

```
// Filename: Client2.java
class TLClassA {                                   // (1) Top-level Class
    private String msg = "TLClassA object ";
    public TLClassA(String objNo) { msg = msg + objNo; }
    public void printMessage() { System.out.println(msg); }

    class InnerB {                                 // (2) Non-static Inner Class
        private String msg = "InnerB object ";
        public InnerB(String objNo) { msg = msg + objNo; }
        public void printMessage() { System.out.println(msg); }

        class InnerC {                             // (3) Non-static Inner Class
            private String msg = "InnerC object ";
            public InnerC(String objNo) { msg = msg + objNo; }
            public void printMessage() {
                System.out.println(msg);                 // (4)
                System.out.println(this.msg);            // (5)
                System.out.println(InnerC.this.msg);     // (6)
                System.out.println(InnerB.this.msg);     // (7)
                InnerB.this.printMessage();              // (8)
                System.out.println(TLClassA.this.msg);   // (9)
                TLClassA.this.printMessage();            // (10)
            }
        }
    }
}
```

```
public class Client2 {                                                      // (11)
    public static void main(String args[]) {                                // (12)
        TLClassA a = new TLClassA("1");                                     // (13)
        TLClassA.InnerB b = a.new InnerB("1");                              // (14)
        TLClassA.InnerB.InnerC c = b.new InnerC("1");                       // (15)
        c.printMessage();                                                   // (16)
        TLClassA.InnerB bb = new TLClassA("2").new InnerB("2");// (17)
        TLClassA.InnerB.InnerC cc = bb.new InnerC("2");                     // (18)
        cc.printMessage();                                                  // (19)
        TLClassA.InnerB.InnerC ccc =
            new TLClassA("3").new InnerB("3").new InnerC("3"); // (20)
    }
}
```

Output from the program:

```
InnerC object 1
InnerC object 1
InnerC object 1
InnerB object 1
InnerB object 1
TLClassA object 1
TLClassA object 1
InnerC object 2
InnerC object 2
InnerC object 2
InnerB object 2
InnerB object 2
TLClassA object 2
TLClassA object 2
```

Example 7.4 illustrates the special form of the `this` construct to access members in the enclosing context, and also demonstrates the special form of the `new` construct to create instances of non-static inner classes. The example shows the class `InnerC`, defined at (3), which is nested in the class `InnerB` defined at (2), which in turn is nested in the top-level class `TLClassA` at (1). All three classes have a `private` non-static `String` variable `msg` and a non-static method `printMessage()`. These members are *not* overridden in the inner classes, as no inheritance is involved. Like any other class member, they have class scope.

The `main()` method at (12) uses the additional syntax of the `new` operator to create an instance of `InnerC` (denoted by `c`) at (15) in the context of an instance of class `InnerB` (denoted by `b`) at (14), which in turn is created in the context of an instance of class `TLClassA` (denoted by `a`) at (13).

The reference `c` is used at (16) to invoke the method `printMessage()` from class `InnerC`. This method uses the standard `this` reference to access members of the object on which it is invoked, as shown at (5). It also uses the special form of the `this` construct, in conjunction with the class name, to access members in (outer) objects which are associated with the current object, as shown in the statements from (6) through (10).

When the intervening references to a non-static inner class are of no interest, the `new` operator can be chained, as shown at (17), (18) and (20).

Note that the (outer) objects associated with the references `c`, `cc` and `ccc` are distinct, as evident from the program output.

Compiling and Importing Non-static Inner Classes

If the file `Client2.java` containing the definitions from Example 7.4 is compiled, it will result in the generation of the following class files, where each file corresponds to a class definition:

```
TLClassA$InnerB$InnerC.class
TLClassA$InnerB.class
TLClassA.class
Client2.class
```

Clients can use the `import` statement to provide a shortcut for the names of non-static inner classes. Example 7.5, based on Example 7.4, shows how nested classes can be imported and used. Note the specification of the class name in the `import` statement. It "imports" the *immediate* nested classes as shown at (14'). For deeply nested inner classes the intervening class names must be specified, as shown in the declarations at (15'), (18') and (20'). If the class `TLClassA` belonged to a named package, then the package name must be prepended to the class's name in the usual way in the `import` statement.

Example 7.5 *Importing Inner Classes*

```
// Filename: Client3.java
import TLClassA.*;

// Uses classes from Example 7.4.

public class Client3 {
    public static void main(String args[]) {                         // (12)
        TLClassA a = new TLClassA("1");                              // (13)
        InnerB b = a.new InnerB("1");                                // (14')
        InnerB.InnerC c = b.new InnerC("1");                         // (15')
        InnerB bb = new TLClassA("2").new InnerB("2");               // (17')
        InnerB.InnerC cc = bb.new InnerC("2");                       // (18')
        InnerB.InnerC ccc =
            new TLClassA("3").new InnerB("3").new InnerC("3"); // (20')
        ccc.printMessage();
    }
}
```

Output from the program:

```
InnerC object 3
InnerC object 3
InnerC object 3
InnerB object 3
```

```
InnerB object 3
TLClassA object 3
TLClassA object 3
```

Inheritance and Containment Hierarchy of Non-static Inner Classes

Non-static inner classes can extend other classes and can themselves be extended. Therefore both the inheritance and containment hierarchy must be considered when dealing with member access. Imagine a subclass C that is derived from superclass B, and class C is also a non-static inner class in an enclosing class A. In the absence of name conflicts there is no problem, but what if both the superclass B and the enclosing class A had a member with the name x? If a name conflict arises, the inherited member shadows the member with the same name in the enclosing class. The compiler, however, requires that explicit references be used.

In Example 7.6, the compiler would flag an error at (3) as the reference x is ambiguous. The standard form of the this reference can be used to access the inherited member, as shown at (4). The keyword super would be another alternative. To access the member from the enclosing context, the special form of the this reference together with the enclosing class name is used, as shown at (5).

Example 7.6 *Inheritance and Containment Hierarchy*

```
class B {
    protected double x = 2.17;
}

class A {                                          // (1) Top-level Class
    private double x = 3.14;

    class C extends B {                            // (2) Non-static inner Class
    //  private double w = x;                      // (3) Compile time error
        private double y = this.x;                 // (4) x from superclass
        private double z = A.this.x;               // (5) x from enclosing class
        public void printX() {                     // (6)
            System.out.println("this.x: " + y);
            System.out.println("A.this.x: " + z);
        }
    }
}

public class Client4 {                             // (7)
    public static void main(String args[]) {
        A.C ref = new A().new C();
        ref.printX();
    }
}
```

Output from the program:

```
this.x: 2.17
A.this.x: 3.14
```

Review questions

7.1 What will be the result of attempting to compile and run the following code?

```
public class MyClass {
    public static void main(String args[]) {
        Outer objRef = new Outer();
        System.out.println(objRef.createInner().getSecret());
    }
}

class Outer {
    private int secret;
    Outer() { secret = 123; }

    class Inner {
        int getSecret() { return secret; }
    }

    Inner createInner() { return new Inner(); }
}
```

Select the one right answer.

(a) The code will fail to compile, since the class Inner cannot be declared within the class Outer.
(b) The code will fail to compile, since the method createInner() cannot be allowed to pass objects of the inner class Inner to methods outside of the class Outer.
(c) The code will fail to compile, since the secret variable is not accessible from the method getSecret().
(d) The code will fail to compile, since the method getSecret() is not visible from the main() method in the class MyClass.
(e) The code will compile without error and will print 123 when run.

7.2 Which of these statements concerning nested classes are true?

Select all valid answers.

(a) An instance of a top-level nested class has an inherent outer instance.
(b) A top-level nested class can contain non-static member variables.
(c) A top-level nested interface can contain non-static member variables.
(d) A top-level nested interface has an inherent outer instance.
(e) For each instance of the outer class, there can exist many instances of a non-static inner class.

7.3 What will be the result of attempting to compile and run the following code?

```
public class MyClass {
    public static void main(String args[]) {
        State st = new State();
        System.out.println(st.getValue());
        State.Memento mem = st.memento();
        st.alterValue();
        System.out.println(st.getValue());
        mem.restore();
        System.out.println(st.getValue());
    }

    public static class State {
        protected int val = 11;

        int getValue() { return val; }
        void alterValue() { val = (val + 7) % 31; }
        Memento memento() { return new Memento(); }

        class Memento {
            int val;

            Memento() { this.val = State.this.val; }
            void restore() { ((State) this).val = this.val; }
        }
    }
}
```

Select the one right answer.

(a) The code will fail to compile, since the static `main()` method tries to create a new instance of the inner class `State`.

(b) The code will fail to compile, since the class declaration of `State.Memento` is not visible from the `main()` method.

(c) The code will fail to compile, since the inner class `Memento` declares a variable with the same name as a variable in the outer class `State`.

(d) The code will fail to compile, since the `Memento` constructor tries an invalid access through the `State.this.val` expression.

(e) The code will fail to compile, since the `Memento` method `restore()` tries an invalid access through the `((State) this).val` expression.

(f) The program compiles without errors and prints 11, 18 and 11 when run.

7.4 What will be the result of attempting to compile and run the following program?

```
public class Nesting {
    public static void main(String args[]) {
        B.C obj = new B().new C();
    }
}

class A {
    int val;
    A(int v) { val = v; }
}
```

```
class B extends A {
    int val = 1;
    B() { super(2); }

    class C extends A {
        int val = 3;
        C() {
            super(4);
            System.out.println(B.this.val);
            System.out.println(C.this.val);
            System.out.println(super.val);
        }
    }
}
```

Select all valid answers.

(a) The program will fail to compile.

(b) The program will compile without error, and print 2, 3 and 4 in that order when run.

(c) The program will compile without error, and print 1, 4 and 2 in that order when run.

(d) The program will compile without error, and print 1, 3 and 4 in that order when run.

(e) The program will compile without error, and print 3, 2 and 1 in that order when run.

7.4 Local Classes

A local class is a class that is defined in a block. This could be a method body, a constructor, a local block, a `static` initializer or an instance initializer. Such a local class is only visible within the context of the block, i.e. the name of the class is only valid in the context of the block in which it is defined. A local class cannot be specified with the keyword `static`. However, if the context is static (i.e. a static method or a static initializer) then the local class is implicitly static. Otherwise, the local class is non-static.

Like non-static inner classes, an instance of a non-static local class is passed a hidden reference designating an instance of its enclosing class in its constructors, and this gives non-static local classes much of the same capability as non-static inner classes. Some restrictions which apply to local classes are:

- Local classes cannot have `static` members, as they cannot provide class-specific services.
- Local classes cannot have any accessibility. This restriction applies to local variables, and is also enforced for local classes.

Example 7.7 *Access in Local Classes*

```
class SuperB {
    protected double x;
    protected static int n;
}

class SuperC {
    protected double y;
    protected static int m;
}

class TopLevelA extends SuperC {              // Top-level Class
    private double z;
    private static int p;

    void nonStaticMethod(final int i) {        // Non-static Method
        final int j = 10;
        int k;
        class NonStaticLocalD extends SuperB { // Non static local class
        //  static double d;    // (1) Not OK. Only non-static members allowed.
            int ii = i;         // (2) final from enclosing method.
            int jj = j;         // (3) final from enclosing method.
        //  double kk = k;      // (4) Not OK. Only finals from enclosing method.
            double zz = z;      // (5) non-static from enclosing class.
            int pp = p;         // (6) static from enclosing class.
            double yy = y;      // (7) inherited by enclosing class.
            int mm = m;         // (8) static from enclosing class.
            double xx = x;      // (9) non-static inherited from superclass
            int nn = n;         // (10) static from superclass
        }
    }

    static void staticMethod(final int i) {    // Static Method
        final int j = 10;
        int k;
        class StaticLocalE extends SuperB {    // Static local class
        //  static double d;    // (11) Not OK. Only non-static members allowed.
            int ii = i;         // (12) final from enclosing method.
            int jj = j;         // (13) final from enclosing method.
        //  double kk = k;      // (14) Not OK. Non-final from enclosing method.
        //  double zz = z;      // (15) Not OK. Non-static member.
            int pp = p;         // (16) static from enclosing class.
        //  double yy = y;      // (17) Not OK. Non-static member.
            int mm = m;         // (18) static from enclosing class.
            double xx = x;      // (19) non-static inherited from superclass
            int nn = n;         // (20) static from superclass
        }
    }
}
```

Access Rules for Local Classes

Example 7.7 illustrates the access rules for local classes, which are stated below.

- A local class can access members defined within the class. This should not come as a surprise.
- A local class can access `final` local variables, `final` method parameters and `final` catch-block parameters in the scope of the local context. Such `final` variables are also read-only in the local class. This situation is shown at (2) and (3), where the `final` parameter `i` and the `final` local variable `j` of the method `nonStaticMethod()` in the non-static local class `NonStaticLocalD` are accessed. This also applies to static local classes, as shown at (12) and (13). Access to non-final local variables is not permitted from local classes, as shown at (4) and (14).
- A non-static local class can access members defined in the enclosing class. This situation is shown at (5) and (6), where the instance variable `z` and static variable `p` defined in the enclosing class `TopLevelA` are accessed, respectively. The special form of the `this` construct can be used for *explicit* referencing of members defined in the enclosing class:

  ```
  double zz = TopLevelA.this.z;
  ```

  However, a static local class can only directly access `static` members defined in the enclosing class, as shown at (16), but not non-static members, as shown at (15).
- A non-static local class can directly access members inherited by the enclosing class. This situation is shown at (7) and (8), where the instance variable `y` and the static variable `m` are inherited by the enclosing class `TopLevelA` from the superclass `SuperC`. The special form of the `this` construct can also be used in the local class for *explicit* referencing of members inherited by the enclosing class:

  ```
  double yy = TopLevelA.this.y;
  ```

  However, a static local class can only directly access `static` members that are inherited by the enclosing class, as shown at (18), but not non-static members, as shown at (17).
- A local class can access members inherited from its superclass in the usual way. The instance variables `x` and `n` in the superclass `SuperB` are inherited by the local subclass `NonStaticLocalD`. These variables are accessed in the local class `NonStaticLocalD` as shown at (9) and (10). The standard `this` reference (or the `super` keyword) can be used for referencing members inherited by the local class:

  ```
  double xx = this.x;
  ```

  Note that this also applies for static local classes. This is shown at (19) and (20).

Instantiating Local Classes

Clients outside the context of a local class cannot create or access these classes directly, because they are after all local. A local class can be instantiated in the block in which it is defined. A method can return an instance of the local class. The local class type must then be assignable to the return type of the method. It cannot be the same as the local class type, since this type is not accessible outside of the method. Often a supertype of the local class is specified as the return type.

Example 7.8 *Instantiating Local Classes*

```
interface IDrawable {                    // (1)
    void draw();
}
class Shape implements IDrawable {       // (2)
    public void draw() { System.out.println("Drawing a Shape."); }
}

class Painter {                          // (3) Top-level Class

    public Shape createCircle(final double radius) { // (4) Non-static Method
        class Circle extends Shape {     // (5) Non-static local class
            public void draw() {
                System.out.println("Drawing a Circle of radius: " + radius);
            }
        }
        return new Circle();             // (6) Object of non-static local class
    }

    public static IDrawable createMap() {  // (7) Static Method
        class Map implements IDrawable {   // (8) Static local class
            public void draw() { System.out.println("Drawing a Map."); }
        }
        return new Map();                  // (9) Object of static local class
    }
}

public class Client {
    public static void main(String args[]) {
        IDrawable[] drawables = {        // (10)
          new Painter().createCircle(5),// (11) Object of non-static local class
          Painter.createMap(),          // (12) Object of static local class
          new Painter().createMap()     // (13) Object of static local class
        };
        for (int i = 0; i < drawables.length; i++)     // (14)
            drawables[i].draw();

        System.out.println("Local Class Names:");
        System.out.println(drawables[0].getClass());   // (15)
        System.out.println(drawables[1].getClass());   // (16)
    }
}
```

Output from the program:

```
Drawing a Circle of radius: 5.0
Drawing a Map.
Drawing a Map.
```

```
Local Class Names:
class Painter$1$Circle
class Painter$1$Map
```

Example 7.8 illustrates how clients can instantiate local classes. The non-static local class `Circle` at (5) is defined in the non-static method `createCircle()` at (4), which has the return type `Shape`. The static local class `Map` at (8) is defined in the static method `createMap()` at (7), which has the return type `IDrawable`. The inheritance hierarchy of the local classes and their supertypes `Shape` and `IDrawable` is depicted in Figure 6.5. The `main()` method creates a polymorphic array `drawables` of type `IDrawable` at (10), which is initialized with instances of the local classes:

```
IDrawable[] drawables = {              // (10)
    new Painter().createCircle(5), // (11) Object of non-static local class
    Painter.createMap(),           // (12) Object of static local class
    new Painter().createMap()      // (13) Object of static local class
};
```

Creating an instance of a non-static local class requires an instance of the enclosing class. The non-static method `createCircle()` is invoked on the instance of the enclosing class to create an instance of the non-static local class, as shown at (11). In the non-static method, the reference to the instance of the enclosing context is passed implicitly in the constructor call of the non-static local class at (6).

A static method can be invoked either through the class name or through an instance of the class. An instance of a static local class can be created in either way, by calling the `createMap()` method as shown at (12) and (13). As might be expected, no outer object is involved.

As references to a local class cannot be declared outside of the local context, the functionality of the class is only available through supertype references. The method `draw()` is invoked on objects in the array at (14). The program output indicates which objects were created. In particular, note that the `final` parameter `radius` of the method `createCircle()` at (4) is accessed by the `draw()` method of the local class `Circle` at (5). An instance of the local class `Circle` is created at (11) by a call to the method `createCircle()`. The `draw()` method is invoked on this instance of the local class `Circle` in the loop at (14). The value of the `final` parameter `radius` is still accessible to the `draw()` method invoked on this instance, although the call to the method `createCircle()`, which created the instance in the first place, has completed. Values of `final` local variables continue to be available to instances of local classes whenever these values are needed.

The output also shows the actual names of the local classes. In fact, the local class names are reflected in the class filenames.

7.5 Anonymous Classes

Classes are usually first defined and then instantiated using the `new` operator. Anonymous classes combine the process of definition and instantiation into a single step. Anonymous classes are defined at the location they are instantiated, using additional syntax with the `new` operator. As these classes do not have a name, an instance of the class can only be created together with the definition.

An anonymous class can be defined and instantiated in contexts where a reference can be used, i.e. as expressions that evaluate to a reference denoting an object. Anonymous classes are typically used for creating objects "on the fly" in contexts such as the return value of a method, or as an argument in a method call, or in initialization of variables. Anonymous classes can also be used to extend *adapter classes* (Section 14.4, p. 429).

The context determines whether the anonymous class is static, and the keyword `static` is not used explicitly. For example, an anonymous class as the return value of a static method would be static, as it would be if it was used to initialize a static member variable.

Extending an Existing Class

The following syntax can be used for defining and instantiating an anonymous class that extends an existing class specified by <*superclass name*>:

`new` <*superclass name*> `(`<*optional argument list*>`)` `{` <*class declarations*> `}`

Optional arguments can be specified, which are passed to the superclass constructor. Thus, the superclass must provide a constructor corresponding to the arguments passed. Since an anonymous class cannot define constructors (as it does not have a name), an instance initializer can be used to achieve the same effect as a constructor. No `extends` clause is used in the construct.

Example 7.9 *Defining Anonymous Classes*

```
interface IDrawable {                              // (1)
    void draw();
}
class Shape implements IDrawable {                 // (2)
    public void draw() { System.out.println("Drawing a Shape."); }
}

class Painter {                                    // (3) Top-level Class

    public Shape createShape() {                   // (4) Non-static Method
        return new Shape(){                        // (5) Extends superclass
            public void draw() { System.out.println("Drawing a new Shape."); }
        };
    }
```

```
    public static IDrawable createIDrawable() {  // (7) Static Method
        return new IDrawable(){                   // (8) Implements interface
            public void draw() {
                System.out.println("Drawing a new IDrawable.");
            }
        };
    }
}

public class Client {
    public static void main(String args[]) { // (9)
        IDrawable[] drawables = {            // (10)
            new Painter().createShape(),     // (11) non-static anonymous class
            Painter.createIDrawable(),       // (12) static anonymous class
            new Painter().createIDrawable()  // (13) static anonymous class
        };
        for (int i = 0; i < drawables.length; i++)     // (14)
            drawables[i].draw();

        System.out.println("Anonymous Class Names:");
        System.out.println(drawables[0].getClass());   // (15)
        System.out.println(drawables[1].getClass());   // (16)
    }
}
```

Output from the program:

```
Drawing a new Shape.
Drawing a new IDrawable.
Drawing a new IDrawable.
Anonymous Class Names:
class Painter$1
class Painter$2
```

Class definitions from Example 7.9, which is an adaptation of Example 7.8 to anonymous classes, are shown below. The instance method `createShape()` at (4) defines a non-static anonymous class at (5), which extends the superclass `Shape`. The anonymous class overrides the inherited method `draw()`. As references to an anonymous class cannot be declared, the functionality of the class is only available through superclass references. Usually it makes sense to either override methods from the superclass or implement abstract methods from the superclass. Any other members in the definition of an anonymous class cannot be accessed.

```
// ...
class Shape implements IDrawable {          // (2)
    public void draw() { System.out.println("Drawing a Shape."); }
}

class Painter {                              // (3) Top-level Class

    public Shape createShape() {             // (4) Non-static Method
        return new Shape(){                  // (5) Extends superclass
            public void draw() { System.out.println("Drawing a new Shape."); }
        };
```

```
    }
    // ...
}
// ...
```

Implementing an Interface

The following syntax can be used for defining and instantiating an anonymous class that implements an interface specified by <*interface name*>:

```
new <interface name> () { <class declarations> }
```

An anonymous class provides a single interface implementation, and no arguments are passed. The anonymous class implicitly extends the `Object` class. Note that no `implements` clause is used in the construct.

An anonymous class implementing an interface is shown below. Details can be found in Example 7.9. The static method `createIDrawable()` at (7) defines a `static` anonymous class at (8), which implements the interface `IDrawable` by providing an implementation of the method `draw()`. The functionality of objects of an anonymous class which implements an interface is available through references of the interface type and the `Object` type.

```
interface IDrawable {                                // (1)
    void draw();
}
// ...
class Painter {                                      // (3) Top-level Class
    // ...
    public static IDrawable createIDrawable() {      // (7) Static Method
        return new IDrawable(){                      // (8) Implements interface
            public void draw() {
                System.out.println("Drawing a new IDrawable.");
            }
        };
    }
}
// ...
```

Instantiating Anonymous Classes

The discussion on instantiating local classes (Example 7.8) is also valid for instantiating anonymous classes. The class `Client` in Example 7.9 creates one instance at (11) of the non-static anonymous class defined at (5), and two instances at (12) and (13) respectively of the static anonymous class defined at (8). The program output shows the polymorphic behavior and the runtime types of the objects. Similar to a non-static local class, an instance of a non-static anonymous class has an instance of its enclosing class at (11). An enclosing instance is not mandatory for creating objects of a static anonymous class, as shown at (12).

The names of the anonymous classes at runtime are also shown in the program output. They are also the names used to designate their respective class files. Anonymous classes are not so anonymous after all.

Access Rules for Anonymous Classes

Access rules for anonymous classes are the same as for local classes. Example 7.10 is an adaptation of Example 7.7, and illustrates the access rules for anonymous classes. Non-static anonymous classes can access all members in their enclosing context, and any `final` variables in their local scope. In fact, inside the definition of a non-static anonymous class, objects of the enclosing context can be referenced using the *<enclosing class name>*`.this` construct. As for static anonymous classes, they can only access static members in the enclosing context, and any `final` variables in their local scope.

Example 7.10 defines a non-static anonymous class (which extends the superclass `SuperB`) at (1), whose instance is assigned to the instance variable `b` when the class `TopLevelA` is instantiated. A static anonymous class (which also extends the superclass `SuperB`) is defined at (9) as the return value of the static method `staticMethod()`. The example illustrates all the significant cases involving access in anonymous classes.

Like local classes, anonymous classes cannot have `static` members, and they cannot specify any accessibility modifiers. This is shown at (2) and (10).

Example 7.10 *Access in Anonymous Classes*

```
class SuperB {
    protected double x;
    protected static int n;
}

class SuperC {
    protected double y;
    protected static int m;
}

class TopLevelA extends SuperC {   // Top-level Class
    private double z;
    private static int p;
    SuperB b = new SuperB() {     // (1) Non-static anonymous class
    //  static double d;          // (2) Not OK. Only non-static members allowed.
        double zz = TopLevelA.this.z;// (3) non-static from enclosing class.
        int pp = p;               // (4) static from enclosing class.
        double yy = y;            // (5) inherited by enclosing class.
        int mm = m;               // (6) static from enclosing class.
        double xx = this.x;       // (7) non-static inherited from superclass.
        int nn = this.n;          // (8) static from superclass.
    };
```

```
        static SuperB staticMethod(final int i) { // Static Method
            final int j = 10;
            int k;
            return new SuperB() {    // (9) Static anonymous class.
            //  static double d;     // (10) Not OK. Only non-static members allowed.
                int ii = i;          // (11) final from enclosing method.
                int jj = j;          // (12) final from enclosing method.
            //  double kk = k;       // (13) Not OK. Non-final from enclosing method.
            //  double zz = TopLevelA.this.z; // (14) Not OK. Non-static member.
                int pp = p;          // (15) static from enclosing class.
            //  double yy = y;       // (16) Not OK. Non-static member.
                int mm = m;          // (17) static from enclosing class.
                double xx = this.x;  // (18) non-static inherited from superclass.
                int nn = this.n;     // (19) static from superclass.
            };
        }
    }
```

Review questions

7.5 Which of the following statements are true?

Select all valid answers.

(a) Non-static inner classes must have either default or `public` accessibility.
(b) All nested classes can contain other top-level nested classes.
(c) Methods in all nested classes can be declared `static`.
(d) All nested classes can be declared `static`.
(e) Top-level nested classes can contain non-static methods.

7.6 Given the declaration

```
interface IntHolder { int getInt(); }
```

which of the following methods are valid?

```
//----(1)----
    IntHolder makeIntHolder(int i) {
        return new IntHolder() {
            public int getInt() { return i; }
        };
    }
//----(2)----
    IntHolder makeIntHolder(final int i) {
        return new IntHolder {
            public int getInt() { return i; }
        };
    }
//----(3)----
    IntHolder makeIntHolder(int i) {
        class MyIH implements IntHolder {
            public int getInt() { return i; }
        }
```

```
            return new MyIH();
        }
    //----(4)----
        IntHolder makeIntHolder(final int i) {
            class MyIH implements IntHolder {
                public int getInt() { return i; }
            }
            return new MyIH();
        }
    //----(5)----
        IntHolder makeIntHolder(int i) {
            return new MyIH(i);
        }
        static class MyIH implements IntHolder {
            final int j;
            MyIH(int i) { j = i; }
            public int getInt() { return j; }
        }
```

Select all valid answers.

(a) The method labeled (1)
(b) The method labeled (2)
(c) The method labeled (3)
(d) The method labeled (4)
(e) The method labeled (5)

7.7 Which of these statements are true?

Select all valid answers.

(a) You cannot declare static members within a non-static inner class.
(b) If a non-static inner class is nested within a class named `Outer`, then methods within the non-static inner class must use the prefix `Outer.this` to access the members of the class `Outer`.
(c) All member variables in any nested class must be declared `final`.
(d) Anonymous classes cannot have constructors.
(e) If `objRef` is an instance of any nested class within the class `Outer`, then `(objRef instanceof Outer)` would yield true.

7.8 Which of the following statements are true?

Select all valid answers.

(a) Package member classes can be declared `static`.
(b) Classes declared as members of top-level classes can be declared `static`.
(c) Local classes can be declared `static`.
(d) Anonymous classes can be declared `static`.
(e) No classes can be declared `static`.

Chapter summary

The following information was included in this chapter:

- Categories of nested classes: top-level nested classes and interfaces, non-static inner classes, local classes, anonymous classes.
- The following aspects pertaining to nested classes and interfaces are discussed:
  - The context in which they can be defined.
  - What accessibility modifiers are valid for such classes and interfaces.
  - Whether an instance of the outer context is associated with an instance of the nested class.
  - What entities in its outer context a nested class or interface can access.
  - Whether both static and non-static members can be defined in a nested class.
- Importing and using nested classes and interfaces.
- Accessing members in the outer context, using *<enclosing class name>*`.this` syntax.
- Instantiating instances of nested classes, using *<enclosing object reference>*`.new` syntax.
- Discussion of the inheritance and containment hierarchies of nested classes.
- Implementing anonymous classes by extending an existing class and by implementing an interface.

Programming exercise

7.1 Create a new program with a nested class named `PrintFunc` that extends the `Print` class in Exercise 6.2. In addition to just printing the value, `PrintFunc` should first apply a `Function` object on the value. The `PrintFunc` class should have a constructor that takes an instance of `Function` as a parameter. The `evaluate()` method of `PrintFunc` should use the `Function` object on its argument. The `evaluate()` method should print and return the result. The `evaluate()` method in superclass `Print` should be used to print the value.

Make the program behave just like the program in Exercise 6.2, but now using `PrintFunc` instead of `Print`.

despicable - scorn/contempt/disdain
{ considered worthless.
{ disrespect of law

8 Object Lifetime

Exam Objectives

- State the behavior that is guaranteed by the garbage collection system and write code that explicitly makes objects eligible for collection.

Supplementary Objectives

- Write code that makes proper use of the finalization mechanism to free resources before an object is garbage collected.
- Distinguish between static and instance initializer expressions and initializer blocks, and how they are used for object initialization and class initialization.
- State the phases involved in initializing the object state when an object is created using the `new` operator.

8.1 Garbage Collection

Objects occupy memory. Garbage collection is a mechanism for reclaiming memory from objects that are no longer in use, and making it available for new objects. Java provides automatic garbage collection, meaning that the runtime environment can take care of memory management concerning objects without the program having to take any special action. Objects are created using the `new` operator. Storage allocated through the `new` operator is administered by the automatic garbage collector.

The automatic garbage collection scheme guarantees that a reference to an object is always valid while the object is in use, i.e. the object will not be deleted leaving the reference "dangling". The automatic garbage collector runs as a background task, which time-critical applications need to bear in mind in case this proves detrimental to their execution.

Object Lifetime

The lifetime of an object is the time from when it is created to the time it is garbage collected. Garbage collection does not necessarily occur as soon as the object is no longer in use. An object being no longer in use means that it cannot be referenced by any "active" part of the program. Under normal circumstances, an object is *accessible* from the time when it is created to the time when it is no longer in use. Thus, the lifetime of an object can include a period when it is not accessible but is *eligible* for garbage collection. The finalization mechanism (Section 8.1, p. 252) in Java does provide a means for "resurrecting" an object after it is no longer in use and eligible for garbage collection, but the finalization mechanism is rarely used for this purpose.

Cleaning Up

The automatic garbage collector figures out which objects are not in use and therefore eligible for garbage collection. It will certainly go to work if there is a danger of running out of memory. Although the automatic garbage collector tries to run unobtrusively, certain programming practices can nevertheless help in minimizing the overhead associated with garbage collection during program execution. Automatic garbage collection should not be perceived as a license for uninhibited creation of objects and forgetting about them.

Objects that are created and accessed by local references in a method are eligible for garbage collection when the method terminates, unless references to these objects are exported out of the method. This can occur if an object reference is returned or thrown as an exception. A method, however, need not always leave objects to be garbage collected after its termination. It can facilitate garbage collection by taking suitable action. Certain objects, such as files and net connections, can tie up other resources and should be disposed of properly when they are no longer needed. The finally-block in the try-catch-finally construct (Section 5.6, p. 156) provides a convenient facility for such purposes, as it will always be executed, thereby ensuring proper disposal of any unwanted resources.

```
import java.io.*;

class WellbehavedClass {
    // ...
    void wellbehavedMethod() {

        File aFile;
        long[] bigArray = new long[20000];

        // ... uses local variables ...

        // Does cleanup after being done (before starting something extensive)
        aFile = null;                        // (1)
        bigArray = null;                     // (2)

        // Start some other extensive activity
        // ...
    }
    // ...
}
```

In the example above, the local variables are set to null after use at (1) and (2) before starting some other extensive activity. This makes the objects denoted by the local variables *eligible* for garbage collection from this point onwards, rather than after the method terminates. This optimization technique should only be used as a last resort when resources are scarce.

Object Finalization

An object can tie up other resources (files, net connections) which should be freed explicitly. Object finalization provides a last resort to an object for undertaking any action before its storage is reclaimed. The automatic garbage collector calls the finalize method in an object which is eligible for garbage collection before actually destroying the object. The finalize method is an instance method which is defined in the class Object:

```
protected void finalize() throws Throwable
```

A finalizer can be overridden in a subclass to take appropriate action before the object is destroyed. A finalizer can catch and throw exceptions like other methods (Section 5.5, p. 153). However, any exception thrown but not caught by a finalizer when invoked by the garbage collector is ignored. The finalizer is only called once on an object, regardless of being interrupted by any exception during its execution. In case of finalization failure, the object still remains eligible to be disposed of at the discretion of the garbage collector (unless it has been resurrected).

```
import java.io.*;

public class AnotherWellbehavedClass {
    // A stream for storing objects
```

```
    public Blob(int bloatedness) {                    // (4)
        fat = new int[bloatedness];
        System.out.println(blobId + ": Hello");
    }
    protected void finalize() throws Throwable {      // (5)
        System.out.println(blobId + ": Bye");
        super.finalize();
    }
}

public class Finalizers {
    public static void main(String args[]) {          // (6)
        int blobsRequired, blobSize;
        try {
            blobsRequired = Integer.parseInt(args[0]);
            blobSize      = Integer.parseInt(args[1]);
        } catch(IndexOutOfBoundsException e) {
            System.err.println("Usage: Finalizers <number of blobs> <blob size>");
            return;
        }

        for (int i=0; i<blobsRequired; ++i) {         // (7)
            new Blob(blobSize);
        }
        System.out.println(SuperBlob.population + " blobs alive"); // (8)
    }
}
```

The command

```
java Finalizers 5 500000
```

gave the following output:

```
0: Hello
1: Hello
2: Hello
0: Bye
1: Bye
2: Bye
3: Hello
4: Hello
2 blobs alive
```

Example 8.1 illustrates chaining of finalizers. It creates a given number of large objects of a particular size. The number and the size are provided through program arguments. The loop at (7) in the `main()` method creates the objects, but does not store any references to them. Objects created are instances of the class `Blob` defined at (3). The `Blob` constructor at (4) initializes the instance variable `fat` by constructing a large array. The `Blob` class extends the `SuperBlob` class which assigns each blob a unique number (`blobId`) and keeps track of the number of blobs (`population`) not yet garbage collected. Creation of each `Blob` object by the constructor at (4) prints the ID number of the object and the message `Hello`. The `finalize()` method at (5) is called before a `Blob` object is garbage collected. It prints the massage `Bye` and calls

```
        ObjectOutputStream objStorage;
        // ...
        protected void finalize() throws Throwable {              // (1)
            try {                                                 // (2)
                if (objStorage != null) objStorage.close();
            } finally {                                           // (3)
                super.finalize();                                 // (4)
            }
        }
    }
```

The finalizer at (1) will take appropriate action if called on objects of the class `AnotherWellbehavedClass` before they are garbage collected, ensuring that the I/O resources are freed.

Finalizer Chaining

Finalizers are not implicitly chained like constructors for subclasses (Section 6.3, p. 187), therefore a finalizer in a subclass should explicitly call the finalizer in its superclass as its last action, as shown at (4) in the code above. The call to the finalizer of the superclass is in a `finally` block at (3), guaranteed to be executed regardless of any exceptions thrown by the code in the `try` block at (2).

A finalize method may make the object accessible again, i.e. "resurrect" it, thus avoiding it being garbage collected. One simple technique is to assign its `this` reference to a static variable, from which it can later be retrieved. Since a finalizer is called only once on an object before being garbage collected, an object can only be resurrected once. Such measures are not recommended, as they only undermine the purpose of the finalization mechanism.

Example 8.1 *Using Finalizers*

```
class SuperBlob {                                             // (1)
    static int idCounter;
    static int population;

    protected int blobId;

    public SuperBlob() {
        blobId = idCounter++;
        ++population;
    }
    protected void finalize() throws Throwable {              // (2)
        --population;
        super.finalize();
    }
}

class Blob extends SuperBlob {                                // (3)
    int[] fat;
```

the `finalize()` method in the class `SuperBlob` at (2), which decrements the population count. The program output shows that two blobs were not garbage collected at the time the print statement at (8) was executed. It is evident from the `Bye` messages that three blobs were garbage collected before all the five blobs had been created in the loop at (7).

Invoking Garbage Collection

Java does provide facilities to invoke the garbage collection explicitly. The `System.gc()` method can be used to force garbage collection, and the `System.runFinalization()` method can be used to run the finalizers (which have not been executed before) for objects eligible for garbage collection.

Certain aspects regarding automatic garbage collection should be noted:

- There are no guarantees that the objects no longer in use will be garbage collected and their finalizers executed at all. Garbage collection might not even be run if the program execution does not warrant it. Thus, any memory allocated during program execution might remain allocated after program termination, unless reclaimed by the operating system or by other means.
- There are also no guarantees on the order in which the objects will be garbage collected, or on the order in which their finalizers will be executed. Therefore, the program should not make any decisions based on these assumptions.

Review questions

8.1 Which of these statements are true?

Select all valid answers.

(a) Objects can explicitly be destroyed using the keyword `delete`.
(b) An object will be garbage collected immediately after the last reference to the object is removed.
(c) If object `obj1` is accessible from object `obj2` and object `obj2` is accessible from `obj1`, then `obj1` and `obj2` are not eligible for garbage collection.
(d) Once an object has become eligible for garbage collection, it will remain eligible until it is destroyed.
(e) If an object `obj1` can access an object `obj2` that is eligible for garbage collection, then `obj1` is also eligible for garbage collection.

8.2 Identify the position in the following program where the object, initially referenced with `arg1`, is eligible for garbage collection.

```
public class MyClass {
    public static void main(String args[]) {
        String msg;
        String pre = "This program was called with ";
        String post = " as first argument.";
```

```
            String arg1 = new String((args.length > 0) ?
                                     "'" + args[ 0 ] + "'" :
                                     "<no argument>");
            msg = arg1;
            arg1 = null;              // (1)
            msg = pre + msg + post;   // (2)
            pre = null;               // (3)

            System.out.println(msg);

            msg = null;               // (4)
            post = null;              // (5)
            args = null;              // (6)
        }
    }
```

Select the one right answer.

(a) After the line labeled (1)
(b) After the line labeled (2)
(c) After the line labeled (3)
(d) After the line labeled (4)
(e) After the line labeled (5)
(f) After the line labeled (6)

8.3 Which of these statements are true?

Select all valid answers.

(a) If an exception is thrown during execution of the `finalize` method of an object, then the exception is ignored and the object is destroyed.
(b) All objects have a `finalize` method.
(c) Objects can be explicitly destroyed by explicitly calling the `finalize` method.
(d) The `finalize` method can be declared with any accessibility.
(e) The compiler will fail to compile code that defines an overriding `finalize` method that does not explicitly call the overridden `finalize` method inherited from the superclass.

8.4 Which of these statements are true?

Select all valid answers.

(a) The compiler will fail to compile code that explicitly tries to call the `finalize` method.
(b) The `finalize` method must be declared with `protected` accessibility.
(c) An overriding `finalize` method in any class can always throw checked exceptions.
(d) The compiler will allow code that overloads the `finalize` method name.
(e) The body of the `finalize` method can only access other objects that are eligible for garbage collection.

8.5 Which statements describe guaranteed behavior of the garbage collection and finalization mechanisms?

Select all valid answers.

(a) Objects will not be destroyed until they have no references to them.
(b) The `finalize` method will never be called more than once on an object.
(c) An object eligible for garbage collection will eventually be destroyed by the garbage collector.
(d) If object `A` became eligible for garbage collection before object `B`, then object `A` will be destroyed before object `B`.
(e) An object once eligible for garbage collection can never become accessible from an active part of the program.

8.2 Initializers

Initializers are used in initialization of objects and classes. They can also be used to define constants in interfaces. These initializers are:

- *Static and Instance Variable Initializer Expressions.*
- *Static Initializer Blocks.*
- *Instance Initializer Blocks.*

The rest of this section provides details on these initializers, concluding with a discussion on the phases involved in constructing the state of an object when the object is created.

Variable Initializer Expressions

Initialization of instance and static variables can be explicitly specified with their declaration using initializer expressions.

```
class ConstantInitializers {
    private int minAge = 12;                          // (1)
    private static double pensionPoints = 10.5;       // (2)
    // ...
}
```

Instance variables of an object are initialized with the values of initializer expressions when the object is created using the `new` operator. In the example above, the declaration at (1) will result in the instance variable `minAge` being initialized to `12` in every object of the class `ConstantInitializers` created with the `new` operator. If no explicit initializer expressions are specified, default values (Section 2.9, p. 34) are used to initialize the instance variables.

Class initialization results in static variables of a class being initialized with the values of the initializer expressions. Declaration at (2) will result in the `static` variable `pensionPoints` being initialized to `10.5` when the class is initialized. Again, if no explicit initializers are specified, default values are used to initialize the static variables.

An initializer expression for a static member variable in a class cannot refer to non-static members, for the obvious reason that only static member variables are class-specific. Instance initializer expressions can refer to all static members of a class, as the class is already initialized when an instance of the class is created.

Instance initializer expressions are executed in the order in which the instance member variables are defined in the class. The same is true for static initializer expressions. If a constant expression is used in the initialization of a member variable then all its operands must be defined before they can be used in the expression. In the example below, the initialization at (2) generates a compile time error, because the operand `WIDTH` in the constant expression has not yet been defined.

```
class ConstantInitializerOrder {
    private final int LENGTH = 10;              // (1)
    private double area = LENGTH * WIDTH;       // (2) Not Ok. Forward reference.
    private final int WIDTH = 10;               // (3)
}
```

A logical error can occur if the order of the initializer expressions is not correct. Example 8.2 shows why the order of member variable initialization can be important. The call at (2) to the method `initMaxGuests()` defined at (4) is expected to return the correct value of maximum number of guests. However, the instance variable `OCCUPANCY_PER_ROOM` at (3) will not have been explicitly initialized, therefore its default value (0) will be used in the method `initMaxGuests()`, which will return an incorrect value. The program output shows that, after object creation, the occupancy per room is correct but the maximum number of guests is wrong.

Example 8.2 *Initializer Expression Order*

```
class Hotel {

    private int NO_OF_ROOMS = 12;                       // (1)
    private int MAX_NO_OF_GUEST = initMaxGuests();      // (2) Logical error
    private int OCCUPANCY_PER_ROOM = initOccupancy(); // (3)

    public int initMaxGuests() {                        // (4)
        System.out.println("OCCUPANCY_PER_ROOM: " +
                           OCCUPANCY_PER_ROOM);
        System.out.println("MAX_NO_OF_GUEST: " +
                           NO_OF_ROOMS * OCCUPANCY_PER_ROOM);
        return NO_OF_ROOMS * OCCUPANCY_PER_ROOM;
    }
    public int getMaxGuests() {
        return MAX_NO_OF_GUEST;
    }
    public int initOccupancy() {                        // (6)
        return 2;
    }
```

```
    public int getOccupancy() {                           // (7)
        return OCCUPANCY_PER_ROOM;
    }
}

public class TestOrder {
    public static void main(String args[]) {
        Hotel objRef = new Hotel();                          // (8)
        System.out.println("After object creation: ");
        System.out.println("OCCUPANCY_PER_ROOM: " +
                           objRef.getOccupancy());           // (9)
        System.out.println("MAX_NO_OF_GUEST: " +
                           objRef.getMaxGuests());           // (10)
    }
}
```

Output from the program:

```
OCCUPANCY_PER_ROOM: 0
MAX_NO OF GUEST: 0
After object creation:
OCCUPANCY_PER_ROOM: 2
MAX_NO_OF_GUEST: 0
```

Initializer expressions cannot pass on checked exceptions, only unchecked ones (Section 5.5, p. 153). If any checked exception is thrown during execution of an initializer expression, it must be caught and handled within the initializer expression. Example 8.3 illustrates exception handling in initializer expressions. The static initializer expression at (3) calls the method `creatHotelPool()` at (4), which can catch and handle the checked `TooManyHotelsException` defined at (2). The instance initializer expression at (5) calls the method `initMaxGuests()` at (6), which can throw the unchecked `RoomOccupancyTooHighException`. If thrown, this exception will be handled by the default exception handler in the usual way. Program output confirms that the program terminated because of the uncaught unchecked exception.

Example 8.3 *Exceptions in Initializer Expressions*

```
class RoomOccupancyTooHighException
      extends RuntimeException {}                     // (1) Unchecked Exception
class TooManyHotelsException
      extends Exception {}                            // (2) Checked Exception

class Hotel {
    // Static Members
    private static int NO_OF_HOTELS = 12;
    private static Hotel[] hotelPool = creatHotelPool();  // (3)

    private static Hotel[] creatHotelPool() {             // (4)
        try {
             if (NO_OF_HOTELS > 10)
                 throw new TooManyHotelsException();
        } catch (TooManyHotelsException e) {
             NO_OF_HOTELS = 10;
```

```
                System.out.println("No. of hotels adjusted to " +
                                   NO_OF_HOTELS);
            }
            return new Hotel[NO_OF_HOTELS];
        }
        // Instance Members
        private int NO_OF_ROOMS = 215;
        private int OCCUPANCY_PER_ROOM = 5;
        private int MAX_NO_OF_GUEST = initMaxGuests();        // (5)

        private int initMaxGuests() {                         // (6)
            if (OCCUPANCY_PER_ROOM > 4)
                    throw new RoomOccupancyTooHighException();
            return NO_OF_ROOMS * OCCUPANCY_PER_ROOM;
        }
    }

    public class ExceptionsInInitializers {
        public static void main(String args[]) {
            new Hotel();
        }
    }
```

Output from the program:

```
No. of hotels adjusted to 10
Exception in thread "main" RoomOccupancyTooHighException
        at Hotel.initMaxGuests(ExceptionsInInitializers.java:29)
        at Hotel.<init>(ExceptionsInInitializers.java:25)
        at ExceptionsInInitializers.main(ExceptionsInInitializers.java:36)
```

Static Initializer Blocks

Java allows static initializer blocks to be defined in a class. Although such blocks can include arbitrary code, they are primarily used for initializing static variables. The code in a static initializer block is executed just once when the class is initialized. The syntax of a `static` initializer block consists of the keyword `static` followed by a local block that can contain arbitrary code.

```
class StaticInitializers {

    final static int ROWS = 12, COLUMNS = 10;          // (1)
    static long[][] matrix = new long[ROWS][COLUMNS];  // (2)
    // ...
    static {                                           // (3) Static Initializer
        for (int i = 0; i < matrix.length; i++)
            for (int j = 0; j < matrix[i].length; j++)
                matrix[i][j] = 2*i + j;
    }
    // ...
}
```

In the example above, first the `final static` variables at (1) are initialized and the array of arrays `matrix` of specified size created at (2), followed by the execution of the `static` block at (3) when the class `StaticInitializers` is first loaded. Note that the `static` initializer block is not contained in any method. A class can have more than one static initializer block. The static initializer expressions in the declarations and static initializer blocks are executed in the order they are specified in the class. A static block cannot make a *forward reference* to static variables that are defined after its definition. A typical use of a static initializer in a class is to load any external libraries that the class needs, for example, to execute *native* methods (Section 4.10, p. 125).

Exception handling in static initializer blocks is no different from that in static initializer expressions. Example 8.4 shows a static initializer block at (3) which throws an unchecked exception at (4) during *class initialization*. As the program output shows, this exception is handled by the default exception handler, resulting in termination of the program. Another static initializer block at (5) catches and handles a checked exception in the `try-catch` block at (6). A static block cannot pass on checked exceptions as static blocks cannot be called explicitly, and therefore there is nothing to handle the exceptions.

Example 8.4 *Static Initializer Blocks*

```
class BankrupcyException
      extends RuntimeException {}                  // (1) Unchecked Exception
class TooManyHotelsException
      extends Exception {}                         // (2) Checked Exception

class Hotel {
    // Static Members
    private static boolean BANKRUPT = true;
    private static int NO_OF_HOTELS = 11;
    private static Hotel[] hotelPool;

    static {                                       // (3) Static block
        if (BANKRUPT)
            throw new BankrupcyException();        // (4) Throws unchecked exception
    }

    static {                                       // (5) Static block
        try {                                      // (6) Handles checked exception
             if (NO_OF_HOTELS > 10)
                 throw new TooManyHotelsException();
        } catch (TooManyHotelsException e) {
             NO_OF_HOTELS = 10;
             System.out.println("No. of hotels adjusted to " +
                                    NO_OF_HOTELS);
        }
        hotelPool = new Hotel[NO_OF_HOTELS];
    }
    // ...
}

public class ExceptionInStaticInitBlocks {
    public static void main(String args[]) {
        new Hotel();
    }
}
```

Output from the program:

```
Exception in thread "main" java.lang.ExceptionInInitializerError:
BankrupcyException
        at Hotel.<clinit>(ExceptionInStaticInitBlocks.java)
```

Instance Initializer Blocks

Just as static initializer blocks can be used to initialize `static` variables in a class, Java provides the ability to initialize instance variables during object creation using instance initializer blocks. In this respect, such blocks serve the same purpose as constructors during object creation. The syntax of an instance initializer block is the same as that of a local block. The code in the local block is executed every time an instance of the class is created. Analogous to static initializer blocks, an instance initializer block cannot make a forward reference to instance variables that are defined after its definition.

```
class InstanceInitializers {

    long[] squares = new long[10];    // (1)
    // ...
    {                                 // (2) Instance Initializer
        for (int i = 0; i < squares.length; i++)
            squares[i] = i*i;
    }
    // ...
}
```

The array `squares` of specified size is created first at (1), followed by the execution of the instance initializer block at (2) every time an instance of the class `InstanceInitializers` is created. Note that the instance initializer block is not contained in any method. A class can have more than one instance initializer block, and these (and instance initializer expressions in declarations) are executed in the order they are specified in the class.

An instance initializer block can be used to factor out code which is common to all constructors of a class. Typically, initialization of `final` instance variables can be placed in an instance initializer block if these are not initialized in the declarations or in the constructors. They will be initialized as required, no matter which constructor is invoked.

A typical use of an instance initializer block is in anonymous classes (Section 7.5, p. 243), which cannot have constructors, and therefore can use instance initializer blocks to initialize instance variables. In Example 8.5, the anonymous class defined at (1) uses an instance initializer block defined at (2) to initialize its instance variables.

Example 8.5 *Instance Initializer Block in Anonymous Class*

```
class Base {
    protected int a;
    protected int b;
    void print() {
        System.out.println("a: " + a);
    }
}

class AnonClassMaker {
    Base creatAnon() {
        return new Base() {          // (1) Anonymous class
            {                        // (2) Instance initializer
                a = 5; b = 10;
            }
            void print() {
                super.print();
                System.out.println("b: " + b);
            }
        };  // end anonymous class
    }
}

public class InstanceInitBlock {
    public static void main(String args[]) {
        new AnonClassMaker().creatAnon().print();
    }
}
```

Output from the program:

```
a: 5
b: 10
```

Exception handling in instance initializer blocks is similar to that in static initializer blocks and initializer expressions. Example 8.6 shows an instance initializer block at (3) which throws an unchecked exception at (4) during *class instantiation*. The runtime system handles the exception, printing the trace of the method activation stack and terminating the program. Another instance initializer block at (5) catches and handles a checked exception in the try-catch block at (6). Exception handling in instance initializer blocks differs from that in static initializer blocks in the following respect: if an instance initializer block does not catch a checked exception that can occur during its execution, then the exception must be declared in the throws clause of *every* constructor in the class. This does not apply to static initializer blocks, which must catch and handle the checked exception in the block as no constructor is involved in class initialization. Instance initializer blocks in anonymous classes have greater freedom: they can throw any exception.

Example 8.6 *Exception Handling in Instance Initializer Blocks*

```
class RoomOccupancyTooHighException
      extends Exception {}                     // (1) Checked Exception
class BankrupcyException
      extends RuntimeException {}              // (2) Unchecked Exception

class Hotel {
    // Instance Members
    private static boolean BANKRUPT = true;
    private int NO_OF_ROOMS = 215;
    private int OCCUPANCY_PER_ROOM = 5;
    private int MAX_NO_OF_GUEST;

    {                                          // (3) Instance initializer block
        if (BANKRUPT)
            throw new BankrupcyException();    // (4) Throws unchecked exception
    }

    {                                          // (5) Instance block
        try {
             if (OCCUPANCY_PER_ROOM > 4)       // (6) Handles checked exception
                 throw new RoomOccupancyTooHighException();
        } catch (RoomOccupancyTooHighException e) {
             System.out.println("ROOM OCCUPANCY TOO HIGH: " + OCCUPANCY_PER_ROOM);
             OCCUPANCY_PER_ROOM = 4;
        }
        MAX_NO_OF_GUEST = NO_OF_ROOMS * OCCUPANCY_PER_ROOM;
    }
    // ...
}

public class ExceptionsInInstBlocks {
    public static void main(String args[]) {
        new Hotel();
    }
}
```

Output from the program:

```
Exception in thread "main" BankrupcyException
        at Hotel.<init>(ExceptionsInInstBlocks.java:15)
        at ExceptionsInInstBlocks.main(ExceptionsInInstBlocks.java:33)
```

Constructing Initial Object State

Object initialization involves constructing the initial state of an object when it is created using the `new` operator. First the instance variables are initialized to their default values (Section 2.9, p. 34), and then the constructor is invoked. This can lead to *local* chaining of constructors. The invocation of the constructor at the end of the local chain of constructor invocations results in the following actions, before the constructor's execution resumes:

- Invocation of the superclass's constructor implicitly or explicitly. Constructor chaining ensures that the inherited state of the object is constructed first (Section 6.3, p. 187).
- Initialization of the instance member variables by executing their instance initializer expressions and any instance initializer blocks in the order they are specified in the class definition.

Example 8.7 *Object State Construction*

```
class SuperclassA {
    public SuperclassA() {                              // (1)
        System.out.println("Constructor in SuperclassA");
    }
}

class SubclassB extends SuperclassA {

    public SubclassB() {                                // (2)
        this(3);
        System.out.println("Default constructor in SubclassB");
    }

    public SubclassB(int i) {                           // (3)
        System.out.println("Non-default constructor in SubclassB");
        value = i;
    }

    {                                                   // (4)
        System.out.println("Instance initializer block in SubclassB");
    //  value = 2;                                      // (5) Not Ok
    }

    private int value = initializerExpression();   // (6)

    private int initializerExpression() {          // (7)
        System.out.println("Instance initializer expression in SubclassB");
        return 1;
    }
}

public class ObjectConstruction {
    public static void main(String args[]) {
        new SubclassB();                                // (8)
    }
}
```

Output from the program:

```
Constructor in SuperclassA
Instance initializer block in SubclassB
Instance initializer expression in SubclassB
Non-default constructor in SubclassB
Default constructor in SubclassB
```

Example 8.7 illustrates object initialization. The `new` operator is used at (8) to create an object of class `SubclassB`. The default constructor `SubclassB()` at (2) uses the `this()` construct to locally chain to the non-default constructor at (3). It is this constructor that leads to an implicit call of the superclass's constructor. As can be seen from the program output, the execution of the superclass's constructor at (1) reaches completion first. This is followed by the execution of the instance initializer block at (4) and instance initializer expression at (6). Then the execution of the body of the non-default constructor at (3) is resumed. Finally the default constructor completes its execution, thereby completing the construction of the object state.

Note that the initializers are executed in the order they are specified in the class definition. As can be seen at (5), the instance variable `value` is not accessible in the instance initializer block at (4), because forward referencing of instance members is not permitted in initializers. The default value of an instance variable can be overwritten by an instance initializer expression, which in turn can be overwritten by any instance initializer block, with the first constructor invoked having the option of setting the final value.

Some care should be exercised in initializing the state of an object when it is created using the `new` operator. Example 8.8 shows a situation where use of overridden methods in *superclass* initializers and constructors can give unexpected results. The example intentionally uses the `this` reference to underline the fact that the instance methods and constructors are invoked on an object which has already been created using the `new` operator, and that the constructor call results in the initialization of the object state – at least that is its normal purpose. The program output shows that the instance variable `superValue` at (1) in class `SuperclassA` never gets initialized explicitly when an object of the `SubclassB` is created at (8). The `SuperclassA` constructor at (2) does have a call to a method called `doValue()` at (3). A method with such a name is defined in class `SuperclassA` at (4) and is overridden in `SubclassB` at (7). The program output indicates that the method `doValue()` from the `SubclassB` is called at (3) in the constructor for `SuperclassA`. The definition of the method `doValue()` at (4) never gets executed when an object of the `SubclassB` is created. Method invocation always determines the implementation of the method to be executed based on the *actual* type of the object. Keeping in mind that it is an object of `SubclassB` that is being initialized, it is not surprising that the method call at (3) results in the method from `SubclassB` being executed. This can lead to unexpected results. The overriding method `doValue()` at (7) in class `SubclassB` can access the member variable `value` declared at (5) before its initializer expression has been executed, i.e. the method invoked can access the state of the object *before* this has been completely initialized.

Example 8.8 *Initialization under Object State Construction*

```
class SuperclassA {
    protected int superValue;                                    // (1)
    public SuperclassA() {                                       // (2)
        System.out.println("Constructor in SuperclassA");
        this.doValue();                                          // (3)
```

goes to (7)

```
    }
    public void doValue() {                                  // (4)
        this.superValue = 911;
        System.out.println("superValue: " + this.superValue);
    }
}

class SubclassB extends SuperclassA {
    private int value = 800;                                 // (5)
    public SubclassB() {                                     // (6)
        System.out.println("Constructor in SubclassB");
        this.doValue();
        System.out.println("superValue: " + this.superValue);
    }
    public void doValue() {                                  // (7)
        System.out.println("value: " + this.value);
    }
}

public class ObjectInitialization {
    public static void main(String args[]) {
        new SubclassB();                                     // (8)
    }
}
```

Output from the program:

```
Constructor in SuperclassA
value: 0
Constructor in SubclassB
value: 800
superValue: 0
```

Class initialization must take place before an instance of the class can be created or a static method of the class can be invoked. A class's superclass is initialized before the class itself is initialized. Initializing a class involves initialization of the static member variables by executing their static initializer expressions, and execution of any static initializer blocks.

Initialization of an interface only involves execution of any static initializer expressions for the static variables declared in the interface.

Review questions

8.6 Given the following class, which of these static initializers are legal in the indicated context?

```
public class MyClass {
    private static int count = 5;
    static final int STEP = 10;
    boolean alive;

        // INSERT STATIC INITIALIZER HERE
}
```

Select all valid answers.

(a) `static { alive = true; count = 0; }`
(b) `static { STEP = count; }`
(c) `static { count += STEP; }`
(d) `static ;`
(e) `static {;}`
(f) `static { count = 1; }`

8.7 What will be the result of attempting to compile and run the following code?

```
public class MyClass {
    public static void main(String args[]) {
        MyClass obj = new MyClass(1);
    }

    static int i = 5;
    static int l;
    int j = 7;
    int k;

    public MyClass(int m) {
        System.out.println(i + ", " + j + ", " + k + ", " + l + ", " + m);
    }

    { j = 70; l = 20; } // Instance Initializer

    static { i = 50; } // Static Initializer
}
```

Select the one right answer.

(a) The code will fail to compile, since the instance initializer tries to assign a value to a static member.
(b) The code will fail to compile, since the member variable k will be uninitialized when it is used.
(c) The code will compile without error and will print `50, 70, 0, 20, 0` when run.
(d) The code will compile without error and will print `50, 70, 0, 20, 20` when run.
(e) The code will compile without error and will print `5, 70, 0, 20, 0` when run.
(f) The code will compile without error and will print `5, 7, 0, 20, 0` when run.

8.8 Given the following class, which of these instance initializers could be inserted at the indicated location and allow the class to compile without errors?

```
public class MyClass {
    static int gap = 10;
    double length;
    final boolean active;

    // INSERT AN INSTANCE INITIALIZER HERE
}
```

Select all valid answers.

(a) `instance { active = true; }`
(b) `MyClass { gap += 5; }`
(c) `{ gap = 5; length = (active ? 100 : 200) + gap; }`
(d) `{ ; }`
(e) `{ length = 4.2; }`
(f) `{ active = (gap > 5); length = 5.5 + gap;}`

8.9 What will be the result of attempting to compile and run the following class?

```
public class Initialization {
    private static String msg(String msg) {
        System.out.println(msg); return msg;
    }

    public Initialization() { m = msg("1"); }

    { m = msg("2"); }

    String m = msg("3");

    public static void main(String args[]) {
        Object obj = new Initialization();
    }
}
```

forward reference

Select the one right answer.

(a) The program will fail to compile.
(b) The program will compile without error and will print 1, 2 and 3 in that order when run.
(c) The program will compile without error and will print 2, 3 and 1 in that order when run.
(d) The program will compile without error and will print 3, 1 and 2 in that order when run.
(e) The program will compile without error and will print 1, 3 and 2 in that order when run.

8.10 What will be the result of attempting to compile and run the following class?

```
public class Initialization {
    private static String msg(String msg) {
        System.out.println(msg); return msg;
    }

    static String m = msg("1");

    { m = msg("2"); }

    static { m = msg("3"); }

    public static void main(String args[]) {
        Object obj = new Initialization();
    }
}
```

first this is executed (static initializer) (1)
Then " " (instance initializer) (2)

Select the one right answer.

(a) The program will fail to compile.

(b) The program will compile without error and will print `1`, `2` and `3` in that order when run.

(c) The program will compile without error and will print `2`, `3` and `1` in that order when run.

(d) The program will compile without error and will print `3`, `1` and `2` in that order when run.

(e) The program will compile without error and will print `1`, `3` and `2` in that order when run.

Chapter summary

The following information was included in this chapter:

- Discussion of automatic garbage collection, including lifetime of objects and guidelines for facilitating garbage collection.
- Discussion of object finalization and chaining as part of garbage collection.
- Discussion of static and instance initializers, both initializer expressions and initializer blocks.
- The role played by initializers in initializing objects, classes and interfaces.

Threads 9

Exam Objectives

- Write code to define, instantiate and start new threads using both `java.lang.Thread` and `java.lang.Runnable`.
- Recognize conditions that might prevent a thread from executing.
- Write code using `synchronized`, `wait()`, `notify()` and `notifyAll()` to protect against concurrent access problems and to communicate between threads. Define the interaction between threads, and between threads and object locks, when executing `synchronized` `wait()`, `notify()` or `notifyAll()`.

Supplementary Objectives

- Understand thread states and the transitions between them.

9.1 Multitasking

Multitasking allows several activities to occur concurrently on the computer. A distinction is usually made between:

- Process-based multitasking
- Thread-based multitasking

At the coarse-grain level there is *process-based* multitasking, which allows processes (i.e. programs) to run concurrently on the computer. A familiar example is running the spreadsheet program while also working with the word-processor. At the fine-grain level there is *thread-based* multitasking, which allows parts of the *same* program to run concurrently on the computer. A familiar example is a word-processor that is printing and formatting text at the same time. This is only feasible if the two tasks are performed by two independent paths of execution at runtime. The two tasks would correspond to executing parts of the program concurrently. Each such part of a program defines a separate path of execution, and is called a *thread* (*of execution*).

In a single-threaded environment only one task at a time can be performed. CPU cycles are wasted, for example, when waiting for user input. Multitasking allows idle CPU time to be put to good use.

Some advantages of thread-based multitasking as compared to process-based multitasking are:

- Threads share the same address space.
- Context switching between threads is usually inexpensive.
- Communication between threads is usually inexpensive.

Java supports thread-based multitasking and provides high-level facilities for multithreaded programming.

9.2 Threads

A thread is a path of execution within a program, that is executed separately. At runtime, threads in a program have a common memory space and can therefore share data and code, i.e. they are *lightweight*. They also share the process running the program.

Java threads make the runtime environment asynchronous, allowing different tasks to be performed concurrently. In order to take advantage of this powerful paradigm, a few central aspects of multithreaded programming in Java should be understood:

- Creation of threads, including what code gets executed by a thread (Section 9.3, p. 273).

- Since threads can share the same memory space, organized access to common data and code through synchronization is important (Section 9.4, p. 279).
- Since threads can be in different states, transitions between states should be understood (Section 9.5, p. 283).

Main Thread

The runtime environment distinguishes between *user threads* and *daemon threads*. As long as a user thread is alive, the execution does not terminate. A daemon thread is at the mercy of the runtime system: it is stopped if there are no more user threads running, thus terminating the program. Daemon threads exist only to serve user threads. When a standalone application is run, a user thread is automatically created to execute the `main()` method. This thread is called the *main thread*. If no other threads are spawned, the program terminates when the `main()` method finishes executing. All other threads, called *child* threads, are spawned from the main thread, inheriting its user-thread status. The `main()` method can then finish, but the program will keep running until all the user threads are done. A thread's status (daemon or user) can be changed by using the method `setDaemon(boolean)`, but this must be done before the thread is started. Changing the status of a thread already started throws the `IllegalThreadStateException`. Marking all threads spawned as daemon threads ensures that the application terminates when the main thread dies.

When a GUI application is started, an *AWT thread* is automatically created to monitor the user–GUI interaction (Section 15.6, p. 475). This user thread keeps the program running, even though the main thread might have died after the `main()` method has finished executing.

Using threads in applets is discussed in Section 16.3 on page 495.

9.3 Thread Creation

A thread in Java is represented by an object of the `Thread` class. Implementing threads is achieved in one of two ways:

- Implementing the `java.lang.Runnable` Interface
- Extending the `java.lang.Thread` Class

Implementing the `Runnable` Interface

The `Runnable` interface has the following specification:

```
public interface Runnable {
    public void run();
}
```

The single method run() of the Runnable interface is used to define a unit of program code. A thread created based on an object that implements the Runnable interface will execute the code defined in the run() method. In other words, the code in the run() method defines an independent path of execution and thereby the entry and the exits for the thread. The thread ends when the run() method ends.

The procedure for creating threads based on the Runnable interface is as follows:

1. A class implements the Runnable interface providing the run() method which will be executed by the thread.
2. An object of Thread class is created. An object of a class implementing the Runnable interface is passed as an argument to a constructor of the Thread class.
3. The start() method is invoked on the Thread object created in the previous step. However, the start() method returns immediately after a thread has been spawned. This method is defined in the Thread class.

Invocation of the start() method on the Thread object, which has been passed the object implementing the Runnable interface, will eventually result in the run() method being executed by the thread represented by the Thread object. This sequence of events is illustrated in Figure 9.1.

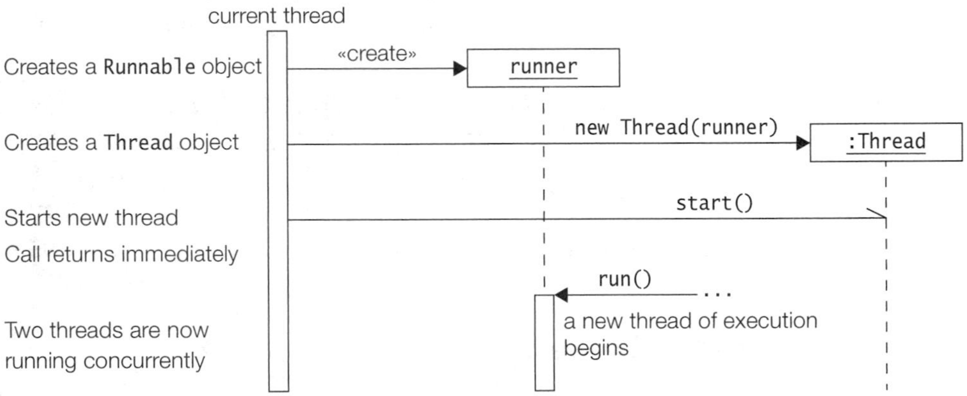

Figure 9.1 *Spawning Threads*

Various constructors are defined for the Thread class in the java.lang package. Two of these constructors are presented here:

```
Thread(Runnable threadTarget)
Thread(Runnable threadTarget, String threadName)
```

The argument threadTarget is the object whose run() method will be executed when the thread is started. The argument threadName can be specified to give an explicit name for the thread, rather than an automatically generated one. A thread's name can be retrieved by using the getName() method.

Example 9.1 *Implementing the* `Runnable` *Interface*

```
class Counter implements Runnable {

    private int currentValue;

    private Thread worker;

    public Counter(String threadName) {
        currentValue = 0;
        worker = new Thread(this, threadName);   // (1) Create a new thread
        System.out.println(worker);
        worker.start();                          // (2) Start the thread
    }

    public void run() {                          // (3) Thread entry point
        try {
            while (currentValue < 5) {
                System.out.println(worker.getName() + ": " + (currentValue++));
                Thread.sleep(500);               // (4) Current thread sleeps
            }
        } catch (InterruptedException e) {
            System.out.println(worker.getName() + " interrupted.");
        }
        System.out.println("Exit from " + worker.getName() + ".");
    }

    public int getValue() { return currentValue; }
}

public class Client {
    public static void main(String args[]) {
        Counter counterA = new Counter("Counter A"); // (5) Create a thread

        try {
            int val;
            do {
                val = counterA.getValue();       // (6) Access the counter value
                System.out.println("Main Thread: " + val);
                Thread.sleep(1000);              // (7) Current thread sleeps
            } while (val < 5);
        } catch (InterruptedException e) {
            System.out.println("Main Thread interrupted.");
        }

        System.out.println("Exit from Main Thread.");
    }
}
```

Possible output from the program:

```
Thread[Counter A,5,main]
Main Thread: 0
Counter A: 0
Counter A: 1
Main Thread: 2
Counter A: 2
Counter A: 3
```

```
Main Thread: 4
Counter A: 4
Exit from Counter A.
Main Thread: 5
Exit from Main Thread.
```

In Example 9.1, the class `Counter` implements the `Runnable` interface. The constructor for the `Counter` class ensures that each object of the `Counter` class will create a new thread by passing the `Counter` instance to the `Thread` constructor as shown at (1). In addition, the thread is enabled for execution by the call to its `start()` method as shown at (2). At (3), the class defines the `run()` method which constitutes the thread. In each iteration, after writing the current value of the counter, the currently running thread sleeps for 500 milliseconds as shown at (4). While it is sleeping, other threads may run (Section 9.5, p. 286).

The `Client` class uses the `Counter` class. It creates an object of class `Counter` at (5) and retrieves its value in a loop at (6). After each access of the value, it sleeps for 1000 milliseconds at (7), allowing other threads to proceed.

Note that the main thread executing in the `Client` class sleeps for a longer time between iterations than the `Counter` thread, giving the `Counter` thread the opportunity to be executed. The `Counter` thread is a *child* thread of the main thread. It inherits the user-thread status from the main thread. If code of the `try-catch` block in the `main()` method of the `Client` class is removed, the main thread would finish executing before the child thread. However, the program would run until the child thread completes.

Since thread scheduling is not predictable and the example above does not enforce any synchronization between the two threads in accessing the counter value, the output shown may vary.

Extending the `Thread` Class

A class can also extend the `Thread` class to create a thread. A typical procedure for doing this is as follows:

1. A class extending the `Thread` class overrides the `run()` method from the `Thread` class to define the code executed by the thread.
2. This subclass may call a `Thread` constructor explicitly in its constructors to initialize the thread.
3. The `start()` method inherited from the `Thread` class is invoked on the object of the class to make the thread eligible for running.

In Example 9.2, the `Counter` class from Example 9.1 has been modified to illustrate extending the `Thread` class. Note the call to the constructor of the superclass `Thread` at (1) and the invocation of the inherited `start()` method at (2) in the constructor of the `Counter` class. The program output shows that the `Client` class creates the thread and exits, but the program continues running until the child thread has completed.

The `Thread` class implements the `Runnable` interface, which means that this approach is not much different from implementing the `Runnable` interface directly. The only difference is that the creation of the `Runnable` object and the `Thread` object are combined in the subclass, with the implementation of the `run()` method in the subclass being invoked when the thread is run.

When creating threads, implementing the `Runnable` interface is usually preferred to extending the `Thread` class for two main reasons:

- Extending the `Thread` class means that the subclass cannot extend any other class, whereas by implementing the `Runnable` interface it has this option.
- A class might only be interested in being runnable, and therefore inheriting the full overhead of the `Thread` class would be excessive.

Example 9.2 *Extending the* `Thread` *Class*

```
class Counter extends Thread {

    private int currentValue;

    public Counter(String threadName) {
        super(threadName);                        // (1) Initialize thread
        currentValue = 0;
        System.out.println(this);
        start();                                  // (2) Start this thread
    }

    public void run() {                           // (3) Override from superclass
        try {
            while (currentValue < 5) {
                System.out.println(getName() + ": " + (currentValue++));
                Thread.sleep(500);                // (4) Current thread sleeps
            }
        } catch (InterruptedException e) {
            System.out.println(getName() + " interrupted.");
        }
        System.out.println("Exit from " + getName() + ".");
    }

    public int getValue() { return currentValue; }
}

public class Client {
    public static void main(String args[]) {
        Counter counterA = new Counter("Counter A"); // (5) Create a thread
        System.out.println("Exit from Main Thread.");
    }
}
```

Possible output from the program:

```
Thread[Counter A,5,main]
Exit from Main Thread.
```

long - 64 bits
int - 32 bits

```
Counter A: 0
Counter A: 1
Counter A: 2
Counter A: 3
Counter A: 4
Exit from Counter A.
```

Review questions

9.1 Which of the following is the correct way to start a new thread?

Select the one right answer.

(a) Just create a new thread. The thread will start automatically.
(b) Create a new thread and call the method `begin()` on the thread.
(c) Create a new thread and call the method `start()` on the thread.
(d) Create a new thread and call the method `run()` on the thread.
(e) Create a new thread and call the method `resume()` on the thread.

9.2 When extending the `Thread` class to provide a thread's behavior, which methods should be overridden?

Select all valid answers.

(a) `begin()`
(b) `start()`
(c) `run()`
(d) `resume()`
(e) `behavior()`

9.3 Which of the following statements are true?

Select all valid answers.

(a) The class `Thread` is abstract.
(b) The class `Thread` implements `Runnable`.
(c) Classes implementing the `Runnable` interface must define a method called `start()`.
(d) Calling the method `run()` on an object implementing `Runnable` will produce a new thread.
(e) Programs terminate when the last non-daemon thread ends.

9.4 What will be the result of attempting to compile and run the following program?

```
public class MyClass extends Thread {
    public MyClass(String s) { msg = s; }
    String msg;
    public void run() {
        System.out.println(msg);
    }
```

```
        public static void main(String args[]) {
            new MyClass("Hello");
            new MyClass("World");
        }
    }
```

Select the one right answer.

(a) The program will fail to compile.
(b) The program will compile correctly and will print `Hello` and `World`, in that order, every time the program is run.
(c) The program will compile correctly and will print a never-ending stream of `Hello` and `World`.
(d) The program will compile correctly and will print `Hello` and `World` when run, but the order is not predictable.
(e) The program will compile correctly and will simply terminate without any output when run.

9.4 Synchronization

Threads share the same memory space, i.e. they can share resources. However, there are critical situations where it is desirable that only one thread at a time has access to a shared resource. For instance, crediting and debiting a shared bank account concurrently amongst several users without proper discipline will jeopardize the integrity of the data. Java provides high-level concepts for *synchronization* to control access to shared resources.

Monitors

A *monitor* (a.k.a. *semaphore*) is used to synchronize access to a shared resource. A region of code, representing a shared resource, can be associated with a monitor. Threads gain access to a shared resource by first acquiring the monitor associated with the resource. At any given time, no more than one thread can own the monitor and thereby have access to the shared resource. A monitor thus implements a *mutually exclusive locking mechanism* (a.k.a. *mutex*).

The monitor mechanism enforces the following rules of synchronization:

- No other thread can *enter* a monitor if a thread has already acquired the monitor. Threads wishing to acquire the monitor will *wait* for the monitor to become available.
- When a thread *exits* a monitor, a waiting thread is given the monitor, and can proceed to access the shared resource associated with this monitor.

All Java objects have a monitor, and each object can be used as a mutually exclusive lock, providing the ability to synchronize access to shared resources.

There are two ways in which code can be synchronized:

- Synchronized Methods
- Synchronized Blocks

Synchronized Methods

If the methods of an object should only be executed by one thread at a time, then the definitions of all such methods should be modified with the keyword `synchronized`. A thread wishing to execute a `synchronized` method must first enter the object's monitor (i.e. gain ownership of the monitor). This is simply achieved by calling the method. If the monitor is already owned by another thread, the calling thread waits. No action on the part of the program is required. A thread exits a monitor simply by returning from the `synchronized` method, allowing the next waiting thread, if any, to enter.

Synchronized methods are useful in situations where methods can manipulate the state of an object in ways that can corrupt the state if executed concurrently. The class `StackImpl` below defines two methods that are synchronized, so that pushing and popping of elements is mutually exclusive. If several threads were to share a stack which was an object of class `StackImpl`, then one thread would, for example, not be able to push an element on the stack while another thread was popping off the stack. The integrity of the stack is maintained in the face of several threads accessing the same stack.

```
class StackImpl {
    private Object stackArray[];
    private int topOfStack;

    public synchronized Object pop() {            // synchronized method
        Object obj = stackArray[topOfStack];
        stackArray[topOfStack--] = null;
        return obj;
    }

    public synchronized void push(Object element)  // synchronized method
        { stackArray[++topOfStack] = element; }
    // ...
}
```

While a thread is inside a `synchronized` method of an object, all other threads that wish to execute this `synchronized` method or any other `synchronized` method of the object will have to wait. This restriction does not apply to the thread that already has the monitor and is executing a `synchronized` method of the object. Such a method can invoke other `synchronized` methods of the object without being blocked. The non-`synchronized` methods of the object can of course be called at any time by any thread.

Synchronized methods can also be `static`. Classes also have a class-specific monitor which is analogous to the object monitor. Such a monitor is actually a monitor on the `Class` object of the class. A thread acquires the class monitor before it can proceed with the execution of any `static synchronized` method in the class, blocking other threads wishing to execute any such methods in the same class. This, of course, does not apply to `static`, non-synchronized methods, which can be invoked at any time. A thread acquiring the monitor of a class to execute a `static synchronized` method has no bearing on any thread acquiring the monitor on any object of the class to execute a `synchronized` instance method. In other words, synchronization of static methods in a class is independent from the synchronization of instance methods on objects of the class.

A subclass decides whether the new definition of an inherited `synchronized` method will remain `synchronized` in the subclass.

Synchronized Blocks

Whereas `synchronized` methods of a class are synchronized on the monitor of an object of the class, the `synchronized` block allows arbitrary code to be synchronized on the monitor of an arbitrary object. The general form of the `synchronized` statement is as follows:

```
synchronized (<object reference>) { <code block> }
```

The code block is usually related to the object on which the synchronization is being done. Once a thread has entered the code block after acquiring the monitor on the specified object, no other thread will be able to execute the code block, or any other code requiring the monitor, until the monitor is released on this object. In contrast to `synchronized` methods, this mechanism allows fine-grained synchronization of code on arbitrary objects.

Object specification in the `synchronized` statement is mandatory. A class can choose to synchronize the execution of a part of a method, by using the `this` reference and putting the relevant part of the method in the `synchronized` block. The braces of the block cannot be left out, even if the code block has just one statement.

```
class SmartClient {
    BankAccount account;
    // ...
    public void updateTransaction() {
        synchronized (account) {       // (1) synchronized block
            account.update();          // (2)
        }
    }
}
```

In the above example, the code at (2) in the `synchronized` block at (1) is synchronized on the `BankAccount` object. If several threads were to concurrently execute the method `updateTransaction()` on an object of `SmartClient`, the statement at (2) would be executed by one thread at a time, only after synchronizing on the `BankAccount` object associated with this particular instance of `SmartClient`.

Inner classes can access data in their enclosing context (Section 7.1, p. 224). An inner object might need to synchronize on its associated outer object, in order to ensure integrity of data in the latter. This is illustrated in the code below, where the `synchronized` block at (5) uses the special form of the `this` reference to synchronize on the outer object associated with an object of the inner class. This setup ensures that a thread executing the method `setX()` in an inner object can only access the `private double` variable `x` at (2) in the synchronized block at (5) by first acquiring the monitor on the associated outer object. If another thread has the monitor of the associated outer object, then the thread in the inner object has to wait for the monitor to be released before it can proceed with the execution of the synchronized block at (5). However, synchronizing on an inner object and on its associated outer object are independent of each other, unless enforced explicitly, as in the code below.

```
class Outer_A {                                // (1) Top-level Class
    private double x;                          // (2)

    protected class Inner_B {                  // (3) Non-static inner Class
        public void setX() {                   // (4)
            synchronized(Outer_A.this) {       // (5) Synchronized block
                x = Math.PI;                   // (6)
            }
        }
    }
}
```

Review questions

9.5 Which of the following statements are true?

Select all valid answers.

(a) No two threads can ever simultaneously execute synchronized methods on the same object.
(b) Methods declared `synchronized` should not be recursive, since the object's monitor will not allow simultaneous invocations of the method.
(c) Synchronized methods can only call other synchronized methods directly.
(d) Inside a `synchronized` method, one can assume that no other threads are currently executing a method in the same class.

9.6 Given the following program, which one of these statements is true?

```
public class MyClass extends Thread {
    static Object lock1 = new Object();
    static Object lock2 = new Object();

    static volatile int i1, i2, j1, j2, k1, k2;

    public void run() { while (true) { doit(); check(); } }
```

```
        void doit() {
            synchronized(lock1) { i1++; }
            j1++;
            synchronized(lock2) { k1++; k2++; }
            j2++;
            synchronized(lock1) { i2++; }
        }

        void check() {
            if (i1 != i2) System.out.println("i");
            if (j1 != j2) System.out.println("j");
            if (k1 != k2) System.out.println("k");
        }

        public static void main(String args[]) {
            new MyClass().start();
            new MyClass().start();
        }
    }
```

Select the one right answer.

(a) The program will fail to compile.
(b) One cannot be certain whether any of the letters `i`, `j` and `k` will be printed during execution.
(c) One can be certain that none of the letters `i`, `j` and `k` will ever be printed during execution.
(d) One can be certain that the letters `i` and `k` will never be printed during execution.
(e) One can be certain that the letter `k` will never be printed during execution.

9.5 Thread Transitions

Thread States

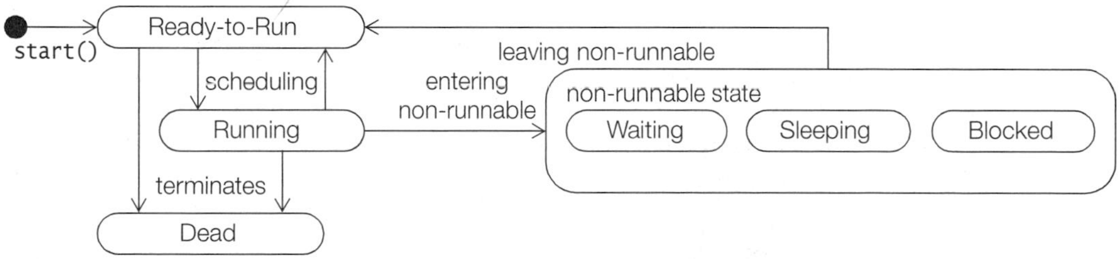

Figure 9.2 *Thread States*

Threads can exist in different states. Just because a thread's `start()` method has been called, it does not mean that the thread has access to the CPU and can start executing straight away. A thread can be in one of the following states:

- *Running state*: This means that the CPU is currently executing the thread. The *thread scheduler* decides which thread is in the Running state.
- *Non-runnable states*: A thread can go from the Running state into one of the non-runnable states, depending on the transition. A thread remains in a non-runnable state until a special transition moves it to the Ready-to-run state.
  - *Waiting* state: When in the Running state, a thread can call the `wait()` method defined in the `Object` class to put itself into the Waiting state. It must be *notified* by another thread, in order to move to the Ready-to-run state.
  - *Sleeping* state: A call to the static method `sleep()` in the `Thread` class causes the current thread in the Running state to transit to the Sleeping state. It wakes up after a specified amount of time has elapsed, and transits to the Ready-to-run state.
  - *Blocked* state: A running thread on executing a *blocking operation* requiring a resource (like a call to an I/O method) will move the thread to the Blocking state. A thread also blocks if it fails to acquire the monitor on an object. The blocking operation must complete, before the thread can proceed to the Ready-to-run state.
- *Ready-to-run* state: A thread does not go directly to the Running state from one of the waiting states. It first goes to the Ready-to-run state on transition from one of the waiting states, meaning that it is now eligible for running. A call to the static method `yield()` in the `Thread` class will cause the current running thread to move to the Ready-to-run state, thus relinquishing the CPU. In the Ready-to-run state, a thread awaits its turn to get CPU time. The thread scheduler decides which thread gets to run.
- *Dead* state: The thread can transit to the Dead state from the Runnable or the Ready-to-run states. The thread can be dead because it has completed or it has been terminated. Once in this state, the thread cannot be resurrected. A new thread of execution must be explicitly started by calling the `start()` method.

Thread Priorities

Threads are assigned priorities that the thread scheduler can use to determine how the threads will be treated. The thread scheduler can use thread priorities to determine which thread gets to run. The thread scheduler usually decides to let the thread with the highest priority in the Ready-to-run state get CPU time. This is not necessarily the thread that has been the longest time in the Ready-to-run state.

Priorities are integer values from 1 (lowest priority given by the constant `Thread.MIN_PRIORITY`) to 10 (highest priority given by the constant `Thread.MAX_PRIORITY`). If no explicit thread priority is specified for a thread, it is given the default priority of 5 (`Thread.NORM_PRIORITY`).

A thread inherits the priority of its parent thread. Priority of a thread can be set by using the `setPriority()` method and read by using the `getPriority()` method, both of which are defined in the `Thread` class. The code below sets the priority of the thread `myThread` to the minimum of two values: maximum priority and current priority incremented to the next level.

```
myThread.setPriority(Math.min(Thread.MAX_PRIORITY, myThread.getPriority()+1));
```

Thread Scheduler

Schedulers usually employ one of the two following strategies:

- Preemptive Scheduling.
  If a thread with a higher priority than the current running thread moves to the Ready-to-run state, then the current running thread can be *preempted* (moved to the Ready-to-run state) to let the higher priority thread execute.
- Time-sliced or Round-robin Scheduling.
  A running thread is allowed to execute for a fixed length of time, after which it moves to the Ready-to-run state to await its turn to run again.

It should be pointed out that thread schedulers are implementation- and platform-dependent, therefore how threads will be scheduled is unpredictable, at least from platform to platform.

Running and Yielding

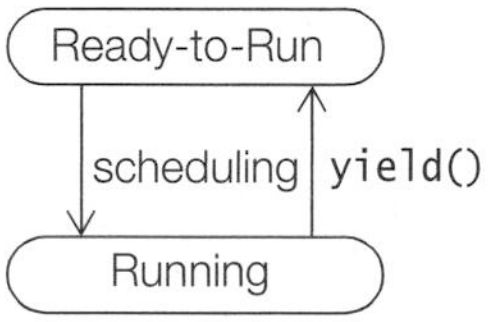

Figure 9.3 *Running and Yielding*

A call to the static method `yield()` in the `Thread` class will cause the current running thread to move to the Ready-to-run state, thus relinquishing the CPU. The thread is then at the mercy of the thread scheduler as to when it will run again. If there are no threads waiting in the Ready-to-run state, this thread continues execution. If there are other threads in the Ready-to-run state, then their priorities determine which thread gets to execute.

A running thread can call the `static` method `yield()` in the `Thread` class and move to the Ready-to-run state, in order to give other threads in this state a chance to run. A typical example where this can be useful is when a user has given some command to start a CPU-intensive computation, and has the option of canceling it by clicking on a "Cancel" button. If the computation thread hogs the CPU and the user clicks the "Cancel" button, chances are that it might take a while before the thread monitoring the user input gets a chance to run and take appropriate action to stop the computation. A thread running such a computation should do the computation in increments, yielding between increments to allow other threads to run. This is illustrated by the `run()` method below.

```
public void run() {
    try {
        while (!done()) {
            doLittleBitMore();
            Thread.yield();          // current thread yields
        }
    } catch (InterruptedException e) {
        doCleaningUp();
    }
}
```

Sleeping and Waking Up

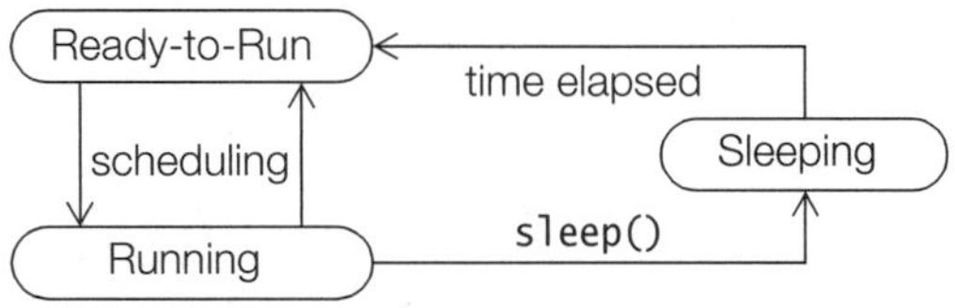

Figure 9.4 *Sleeping and Waking up*

A call to the static method `sleep()` in the `Thread` class will cause the current running thread to move to the Sleeping state, thus relinquishing the CPU. The method is overloaded, but one version is defined as follows:

> `public static void sleep (long millisec) throws InterruptedException`
>
> The thread sleeps for at least the specified amount of time before transitioning to the Ready-to-run state and taking its turn running again.

Usage of the `sleep()` methods is illustrated in Example 9.1 and Example 9.2.

Waiting and Notifying

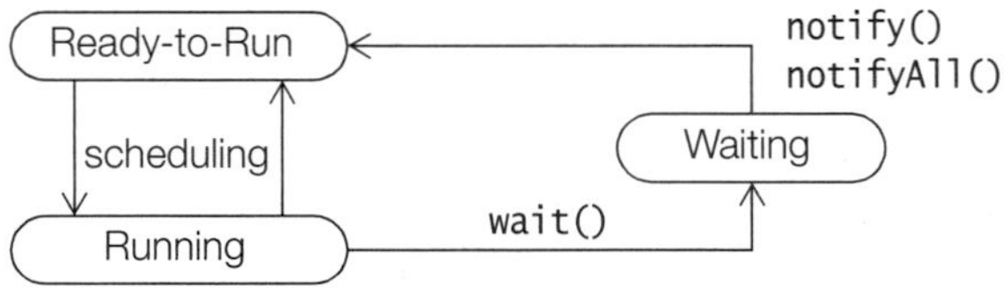

Figure 9.5 *Waiting and Notifying*

Waiting and notifying provide a means of communication between threads that *synchronize on the same object* (Section 9.4, p. 279). The following methods in the `Object` class can be used for this purpose:

```
void wait(long timeout) throws InterruptedException
void wait(long timeout, int nanos) throws InterruptedException
void wait() throws InterruptedException
void notify()
void notifyAll()
```

The overloaded `wait()` method is designed so that a thread, which is expecting some condition to occur, can leave the Running state and transit to the Waiting state to wait for this condition to occur. Usage of the `wait()` method is shown in Example 9.3 at (1). When a thread executing the `synchronized` method `pop()` on an object of class `StackImpl` finds that the stack is empty, it executes the `wait()` method, thereby leaving the Running state and entering the Waiting state. Note that threads are required to own the monitor of the object when calling the `wait()` method. While in the Waiting state, the thread relinquishes ownership of the monitor of the object. Transition to the Waiting state and relinquishing the object monitor are completed as one atomic operation. This allows other threads to run and execute synchronized code on the same object after acquiring its monitor. The `notify()` and `notifyAll()` method can be used to signal and move waiting threads to the Ready-to-Run state.

The `wait()`, `notify()` and `notifyAll()` methods must be executed in synchronized code, otherwise the call will result in an `IllegalMonitorStateException`.

Example 9.3 *Waiting and Notifying*

```
class StackImpl {
    private Object stackArray[];
    private volatile int topOfStack;

    public StackImpl (int capacity) {
        stackArray = new Object[capacity];
        topOfStack = -1;
    }

    public synchronized Object pop() {
        System.out.println(Thread.currentThread() + ": popping");
        while (isEmpty())
            try {
                System.out.println(Thread.currentThread() + ": waiting to pop");
                wait();                                  // (1)
            } catch (InterruptedException e) { }
        Object obj = stackArray[topOfStack];
        stackArray[topOfStack--] = null;
        System.out.println(Thread.currentThread() + ": notifying after pop");
        notify();                                        // (2)
        return obj;
    }

    public synchronized void push(Object element) {
        System.out.println(Thread.currentThread() + ": pushing");
```

```
        while (isFull())
            try {
                System.out.println(Thread.currentThread() + ": waiting to push");
                wait();                                   // (3)
            } catch (InterruptedException e) { }
        stackArray[++topOfStack] = element;
        System.out.println(Thread.currentThread() + ": notifying after push");
        notify();                                         // (4)
    }

    public boolean isFull() { return topOfStack == stackArray.length -1; }
    public boolean isEmpty() { return topOfStack < 0; }
}

abstract class StackUser extends Thread {             // (5) Stack user

    protected StackImpl stack;                        // (6)

    public StackUser(String threadName, StackImpl aStack) {
        super(threadName);
        stack = aStack;
        System.out.println(this);
        setDaemon(true);                              // (7) Daemon thread
        start();                                      // (8) Start this thread
    }
}

class StackPopper extends StackUser {                 // (9) Popper
    public StackPopper(String threadName, StackImpl aStack) {
        super(threadName, aStack);
    }
    public void run() { while (true) stack.pop(); }
}

class StackPusher extends StackUser {                 // (10) Pusher
    public StackPusher(String threadName, StackImpl aStack) {
        super(threadName, aStack);
    }
    public void run() { while (true) stack.push(new Integer(1)); }
}

public class WaitAndNotifyTest {
    public static void main(String args[])
           throws InterruptedException {              // (11)

        StackImpl stack = new StackImpl(5);

        new StackPusher("A", stack);
        new StackPusher("B", stack);
        new StackPopper("C", stack);
        System.out.println("Main Thread sleeping.");
        Thread.sleep(5000);
        System.out.println("Exit from Main Thread.");
    }
}
```

Possible output from the program:

```
Thread[A,5,main]
Thread[B,5,main]
Thread[C,5,main]
Main Thread sleeping.
...
Thread[A,5,main]: pushing
Thread[A,5,main]: waiting to push
Thread[B,5,main]: pushing
Thread[B,5,main]: waiting to push
Thread[C,5,main]: popping
Thread[C,5,main]: notifying after pop
Thread[A,5,main]: notifying after push
Thread[A,5,main]: pushing
Thread[A,5,main]: waiting to push
Thread[B,5,main]: waiting to push
Thread[C,5,main]: popping
Thread[C,5,main]: notifying after pop
Thread[A,5,main]: notifying after push
...
Thread[B,5,main]: notifying after push
...
Exit from Main Thread.
...
```

In Example 9.3, three threads are manipulating the same stack. Two of them are pushing an element on the stack, while the third one is popping the stack. The threads are daemon threads. Their status is set at (7). They will be terminated if they have not completed when the main user-thread dies, stopping the execution of the program. Subclasses `StackPopper` at (9) and `StackPusher` at (10) extend the superclass `StackUser` at (5). Class `StackUser`, which extends the `Thread` class, creates and starts each thread. Class `StackImpl` implements the `synchronized` methods `pop()` and `push()`. The instance variable `topOfStack` in class `StackImpl` is declared `volatile`, so that read and write operations on this variable will access the "master" value of this variable, and not any copies, during runtime (Section 4.10, p. 126).

A thread waiting as a result of calling `wait()` on an object must be notified by another thread calling `notify()` on the same object, in order for it to start running again. This is illustrated in Example 9.3. Both `synchronized` methods `pop()` and `push()` have calls to `wait()` and `notify()` methods. When a thread executing the `synchronized` method `push()` on an object of class `StackImpl` pushes an element on the stack, it calls the `notify()` method at (4). If another thread has earlier called the `wait()` method at either (1) or (3), then this thread is now enabled for running. This newly notified thread will proceed with the execution of the statement, right after the call to the `wait()` method in the code. If there were several waiting threads, all synchronized on the same object, then some arbitrary thread that executed the `wait()` call is enabled for running. A call to the `notifyAll()` method can be used to enable all such threads for running. Note that the waiting condition at (1) and (3) is executed in a loop. A waiting thread that has been notified is not guaranteed to run straight away. Before it gets to run, another thread may synchronize on the same object and empty the stack. If the notified thread was waiting to pop the stack, it would now incorrectly pop the stack, if the condition was not tested after notification. The loop ensures that the condition is always tested after notification, moving the thread back into the waiting state if the condition is not met. A similar situation occurs when a thread executing the `synchronized` method `pop()` pops an element off the stack, and calls the `notify()` method at (2).

Threads that start running again as a result of being notified will regain the monitor of the object. A call to `notify()` has no consequences if there are no threads waiting.

The behavior of each thread can be traced in the output from Example 9.3. Each push and pop operation can be traced by a sequence consisting of the name of the operation to be performed, followed by zero or more wait messages, and concluding with a notification after the operation is done. For example, thread `A` performs two pushes as shown in the output from the program:

```
Thread[A,5,main]: pushing
Thread[A,5,main]: waiting to push
...
Thread[A,5,main]: notifying after push
Thread[A,5,main]: pushing
Thread[A,5,main]: waiting to push
...
Thread[A,5,main]: notifying after push
```

Thread `B` is shown doing one push:

```
Thread[B,5,main]: pushing
Thread[B,5,main]: waiting to push
...
Thread[B,5,main]: notifying after push
```

Whereas thread `C` pops the stack twice without any waiting:

```
Thread[C,5,main]: popping
Thread[C,5,main]: notifying after pop
...
Thread[C,5,main]: popping
Thread[C,5,main]: notifying after pop
```

When the operations are interweaved, the output clearly shows that the pushers wait when the stack is full, and only push after the stack is popped.

Miscellaneous Methods in the Thread Class

`boolean isAlive()`

This method can be used to find out if a thread is alive or dead. Calling this method can be useful for a parent thread to find out whether its child threads are alive, before terminating itself. A thread being alive means that it has been started but has not terminated.

`void join() throws InterruptedException`

A call to this method invoked on a thread will wait and not return until the thread has completed. A parent thread can use this method to wait for its child thread to complete before continuing, i.e. the parent thread waits for the child thread to *join it after completion.*

In Example 9.4, the `AnotherClient` class below uses the `Counter` class which extends the `Thread` class from Example 9.2. It creates two threads and waits for them to complete. Notice how the calls to the `join()` method at (5) and (6) wait until the child threads have completed, as indicated by the output from the program. The tests at (7) and (8) show that the child threads are no longer alive.

Example 9.4 *Usage of* `isAlive()` *and* `join()` *Methods*

```
class Counter extends Thread { /* See Example 9.2. */ }

public class AnotherClient {
    public static void main(String args[]) {

        Counter cA = new Counter("Counter A");
        Counter cB = new Counter("Counter B");

        try {
            System.out.println("Wait for the child threads to finish.");
            cA.join();                                            // (5)
            cB.join();                                            // (6)

            if (!cA.isAlive())                                    // (7)
                System.out.println("Counter A not alive.");
            if (!cB.isAlive())                                    // (8)
                System.out.println("Counter B not alive.");
        } catch (InterruptedException e) {
            System.out.println("Main Thread interrupted.");
        }
        System.out.println("Exit from Main Thread.");
    }
}
```

Possible output from the program:

```
Thread[Counter A,5,main]
Thread[Counter B,5,main]
Wait for the child threads to finish.
Counter A: 0
Counter B: 0
Counter A: 1
Counter B: 1
Counter A: 2
Counter B: 2
Counter A: 3
Counter B: 3
Counter A: 4
Counter B: 4
```

```
Exit from Counter A.
Exit from Counter B.
Counter A not alive.
Counter B not alive.
Exit from Main Thread.
```

Review questions

9.7 Which of these events will cause a thread to die?

Select all valid answers.

(a) The method `sleep()` is called.
(b) The method `wait()` is called.
(c) Execution of the `start()` method ends.
(d) Execution of the `run()` method ends.
(e) Execution of the thread's constructor ends.

9.8 What can be guaranteed by calling the method `yield()`?

Select the one right answer.

(a) All lower priority threads will be granted CPU time.
(b) The current thread will sleep for some time while some other threads are doing some work.
(c) The current thread will not continue until other threads are finished with their work.
(d) The thread will sleep until it is notified.
(e) None of the above.

9.9 Where is the `notify()` method defined?

Select the one right answer.

(a) `Thread`
(b) `Object`
(c) `Applet`
(d) `Runnable`

9.10 What will calling the `notify()` method on an object implementing `Runnable` achieve?

Select the one right answer.

(a) Will cause the thread executing the `run()` method of the object to continue.
(b) Will cause a thread that called the `wait()` method while owning the monitor of the object to be enabled for running.
(c) Will cause all the threads waiting for the monitor of the object to be enabled for running.
(d) Will cause an `IllegalMonitorStateException` to be thrown.
(e) None of the above.

9.11 How can you set the priority of a thread?

Select the one right answer.

(a) Using the `setPriority()` method in the class `Thread`.
(b) Give the priority as a parameter to the constructor of the thread.
(c) Both of the above.
(d) None of the above.

9.12 What will be the result of writing a method that attempts to call `wait()` without ensuring that the current thread owns the monitor of the object?

Select the one right answer.

(a) The code will fail to compile.
(b) Nothing special will happen.
(c) An `IllegalMonitorStateException` will be thrown whenever the method is called.
(d) An `IllegalMonitorStateException` will be thrown if the method is called at a time when the current thread does not have the monitor of the object.
(e) The thread will be blocked until it gains the monitor of the object.

9.13 Which of these are plausible reasons why a thread might be alive, but still not be running?

Select all valid answers.

(a) The thread is waiting for some condition as a result of a call to `wait()`.
(b) The thread is waiting on a monitor for an object so that it may access a certain member variable of that object.
(c) The thread is not the highest priority thread and is currently not granted CPU time.
(d) The thread is sleeping as a result of a call to the `sleep()` method.

Chapter summary

The following information was included in this chapter:

- Creating threads by extending the `Thread` class and implementing the `Runnable` interface.
- Writing synchronized code using synchronized methods and synchronized blocks to achieve data sharing.
- Discussion of thread states and the transitions between them, and thread communication.

Programming exercises

9.1 Create three classes: `Storage`, `Counter` and `Printer`. The `Storage` class should store an integer. The `Counter` class should create a thread that starts counting from 0 (0, 1, 2, 3 ...) and stores each value in the `Storage` class. The `Printer` class should create a thread that keeps reading the value in the `Storage` class and printing it.

Create a program that creates an instance of the `Storage` class, and sets up a `Counter` and a `Printer` object to operate on it.

9.2 Modify the program from the previous exercise, to ensure that each number is printed exactly once, by adding suitable synchronization.

Fundamental Classes 10

Exam Objectives

- Write code using the following methods of the `java.lang.Math` class: `abs()`, `ceil()`, `floor()`, `max()`, `min()`, `random()`, `round()`, `sin()`, `cos()`, `tan()`, `sqrt()`.
- Describe the significance of the immutability of `String` objects.

Supplementary Objectives

- Understand the functionality inherited by all classes from the `Object` class, which is the root of any class hierarchy.
- Know how primitive values can be wrapped as objects using the wrapper classes, which also provide an assortment of methods for converting between primitive values and their object counterparts, including strings.
- Write code for manipulating immutable and dynamic strings, using the facilities provided by the `String` and `StringBuffer` classes respectively.

10.1 Overview of the `java.lang` package

The `java.lang` package is indispensable when programming in Java. It is automatically imported into every source file at compile time. The package contains the `Object` class which is the mother of all classes, and the wrapper classes (`Boolean`, `Character`, `Number`, `Byte`, `Short`, `Integer`, `Long`, `Float`, `Double`) used to manipulate primitive values as objects. It provides classes essential for security (`SecurityManager`), for loading classes (`ClassLoader`), for dealing with threads (`Thread`, `ThreadGroup`) and exceptions (`Throwable`). The `java.lang` package also contains classes which implement the standard streams (`System`), string handling (`String`, `StringBuffer`) and mathematical functions (`Math`).

The following important classes are discussed in detail, and their inheritance hierarchy is depicted in Figure 10.1:

- The `Object` class
- The wrapper classes (`Boolean`, `Character`, `Number`, `Byte`, `Short`, `Integer`, `Long`, `Float`, `Double`)
- The `Math` class
- The `String` class
- The `StringBuffer` class

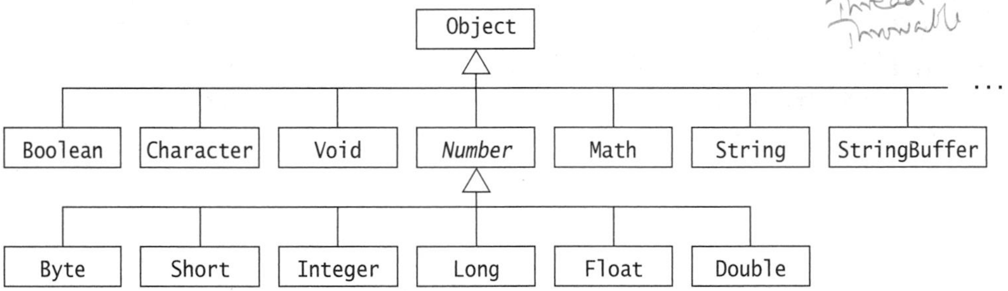

Figure 10.1 *Partial Inheritance Hierarchy in the* `java.lang` *Package*

10.2 The `Object` Class

All classes directly or indirectly extend the `Object` class. A class definition, without the `extends` clause, implicitly extends the `Object` class (Section 6.1, p. 173). Thus, the `Object` class is the root of every inheritance hierarchy. The `Object` class defines the basic functionality that all objects exhibit and which all classes inherit. Note that this also applies for arrays, since these are genuine objects in Java.

The `Object` class provides the following general utility methods for various purposes:

`int hashCode()`

When storing objects in hash tables, this method can be used to get a unique hash value for an object. This value is guaranteed to be consistent during the execution of the program.

`Class getClass()`

Returns the *runtime class* of the object, which is represented by an object of the `Class` class at runtime.

`boolean equals(Object obj)`

Object reference and value equality are discussed together with the `==` and the `!=` operators (Section 3.9, p. 59). The `equals()` method in the `Object` class returns true only if the two references compared denote the same object. The `equals()` method is usually overridden to provide the semantics of object value equality, as in the `String` class. The relationship implemented by the `equals()` method must be *reflexive* (`obj.equals(obj)` is always `true`), *symmetric* (`obj1.equals(obj2)` is `true` if and only if `obj2.equals(obj1)` is `true`), *transitive* (if both `obj1.equals(obj2)` and `obj2.equals(obj3)` are `true` then `obj1.equals(obj3)` is `true`), and *consistent* (multiple invocations of `obj1.equals(obj2)` always return the same truth-value). Finally, the expression `obj.equals(null)` is always `false`.

`protected Object clone() throws CloneNotSupportedException`

New objects that are exactly the same (i.e. have the same state) as the current object can be created by using the `clone()` method, i.e. primitive values and reference values are copied. This is called *shallow copying*. A class can implement the `Cloneable` marker interface to indicate that its objects can be safely cloned, and provide its own notion of cloning. For example, cloning an aggregate object by recursively cloning the constituent objects is called *deep copying*.

`String toString()`

If a subclass does not override this method, it returns a textual representation of the object, which has the following format:

"*<name of the class>*@*<hash code value of object>*"

The `println()` method in `PrintStream` will convert its argument to a textual representation using this method. This can be useful for debugging.

`protected void finalize() throws Throwable`

This method is discussed in connection with garbage collection (Section 8.1, p. 252). This method is called just before an object is garbage collected, so that cleanup can be done. However, the default `finalize()` method in the `Object` class does nothing.

```
// Examples
String str = new String("WhoAmI");
int objId = str.hashCode();                    // 0xfab007

Class runtimeClass = str.getClass();

boolean test = str.equals("WhoAmI");

// Given class MyClass which does not override toString() method
String classId = new MyClass().toString();  // "MyClass@fab007"
```

In addition, the `Object` class provides support for threads through the following methods which are discussed in connection with execution of synchronized code (Section 9.5, p. 286).

```
void notify()
void notifyAll()
```

These methods are used to wake up either a single thread or all threads that are waiting on this object's monitor. Only a thread which is the owner of this object's monitor can call this method. This is usually achieved by a thread executing code synchronized on this object. It throws `IllegalMonitorStateException` if the current thread is not the owner of this object's monitor.

```
void wait(long timeout) throws InterruptedException
void wait(long timeout, int nanos) throws InterruptedException
void wait() throws InterruptedException
```

These methods can be used by a thread to wait until notified by another thread that a condition has occurred on this object. A thread can choose to wait for a specified amount of time. Once notified, it regains ownership of the same object's monitor and resumes execution. These methods also throw `IllegalMonitorStateException` if the current thread is not the owner of this object's monitor. In addition, they can also throw `InterruptedException` if this thread is interrupted by another thread.

Review questions

10.1 What is the return type of the method `hashCode()` in the `Object` class?

Select the one right answer.

(a) `String`
(b) `int`
(c) `long`
(d) `Object`
(e) `Class`

10.2 Which of these statements are true?

Select all valid answers.

(a) If the references x and y denote two different objects, then the expression `x.equals(y)` is always false.
(b) If the references x and y denote two different objects, then the expression `(x.hashCode() == y.hashCode())` is always false.
(c) The `hashCode()` method in the `Object` class is declared `final`.
(d) The `equals()` method in the `Object` class is declared `final`.
(e) All array objects have a method named `clone`.

10.3 Which of these exceptions can the `wait()` method of the `Object` class throw?

Select all valid answers.

(a) `InterruptedException`
(b) `IllegalStateException`
(c) `IllegalAccessException`
(d) `IllegalThreadStateException`

10.3 The Wrapper Classes

Wrapper classes were introduced with the discussion of the primitive datatypes (Section 2.8, p. 32). Primitive values in Java are not objects. In order to manipulate these values as objects, the `java.lang` package provides a *wrapper* class for each of the primitive datatypes. The objects of all wrapper classes that can be instantiated are immutable. Note that the `Void` class is not instantiable.

Common Wrapper Class Constructors

Each wrapper class (except for the `Character` class which has only one constructor) has the following two constructors:

- A constructor that takes a primitive value and returns an object of the corresponding wrapper class.

```
Character charObj  = new Character('\n');
Boolean boolObj2   = new Boolean(true);
Integer intObj     = new Integer(2001);
Double doubleObj   = new Double(3.14);
```

- A constructor that takes a `String` object representing the primitive value, and returns an object of the corresponding wrapper class. These constructors throw `NumberFormatException` if the `String` parameter is not valid.

```
Boolean b1Obj = new Boolean("TrUe");        // case ignored: true
Boolean b2Obj = new Boolean("XX");          // false
Integer i1Obj = new Integer("2001");
Double d1Obj  = new Double("3.14");
```

Common Wrapper Class Utility Methods

Each wrapper class (except `Character`) defines a static method `valueOf(String s)` that returns the wrapper object corresponding to the primitive value represented by the `String` object passed as argument. These methods throw `NumberFormatException` if the `String` parameter is not valid.

```
Boolean boolObj1  = Boolean.valueOf("false");
Integer intObj1   = Integer.valueOf("2010");
Double doubleObj1 = Double.valueOf("3.0");
```

Each wrapper class overrides the `toString()` method from the `Object` class. The overriding method returns a `String` object representing the primitive value in the wrapper object.

```
String charStr   = charObj.toString();     // "\n"
String boolStr   = boolObj2.toString();    // "true"
String intStr    = intObj.toString();      // "2001"
String doubleStr = doubleObj.toString();   // "3.14"
```

Each wrapper class defines a *type*`Value()` method which returns the primitive value in the wrapper object. In addition, each numeric wrapper class defines *type*`Value()` methods for converting the primitive value in the wrapper object to a value of other numeric primitive datatypes.

```
char    c = charObj.charValue();           // '\n'
boolean b = boolObj2.booleanValue();       // true
int     i = intObj.intValue();             // 2001
double  d = doubleObj.doubleValue();       // 3.14
```

Each wrapper class overrides the `equals()` method from the `Object` class. The overriding method compares two wrapper objects for object value equality.

```
// Comparisons based on objects created above
Character chObj    = new Character('a');
boolean charTest   = charObj.equals(chObj);            // false
boolean boolTest   = boolObj2.equals(boolObj1);        // false
boolean intTest    = intObj.equals(intObj1);           // false
boolean doubleTest = doubleObj.equals(doubleObj1);     // false
```

Each wrapper class overrides the `hashCode()` method in the `Object` class. The overriding method returns a hash value based on the primitive value in the wrapper object.

```
int index = charObj.hashCode();
```

In addition to the methods defined for manipulating objects of primitive values, the wrapper classes also contain useful constants, variables and other conversion methods. In the discussion below, additional useful methods not covered earlier are mentioned for each wrapper class.

`Boolean` Class

The `Boolean` class defines the following objects to represent the primitive values `true` and `false` respectively:

```
Boolean.TRUE
Boolean.FALSE
```

`Character` Class

The `Character` class defines a myriad of constants, including the following which represent the minimum and the maximum value of the char type according to Unicode (Section 2.5, p. 31):

```
Character.MIN_VALUE
Character.MAX_VALUE
```

The `Character` class also defines a plethora of `static` methods for handling various attributes of a character, and case issues relating to characters, as defined by Unicode:

```
static boolean isLowerCase(char ch)
static boolean isUpperCase(char ch)
static boolean isTitleCase(char ch)
static boolean isDigit(char ch)
static boolean isLetter(char ch)
static boolean isLetterOrDigit(char ch)
static char    toUpperCase(char ch)
static char    toLowerCase(char ch)
static char    toTitleCase(char ch)
```

The following code converts a lowercase character to an uppercase character.

```
char ch = 'a';
if (Character.isLowerCase(ch)) ch = Character.toUpperCase(ch);
```

Numeric Wrapper Classes

The numeric wrapper classes `Byte`, `Short`, `Integer`, `Long`, `Float`, `Double` are all subclasses of the `abstract` class `Number`.

Each numeric wrapper class defines an assortment of constants, including the minimum and the maximum value of the corresponding primitive datatype:

```
<wrapper class name>.MIN_VALUE
<wrapper class name>.MAX_VALUE
```

The following code retrieves the minimum and maximum values of various numeric types.

```
byte minByte     = Byte.MIN_VALUE;     // -128
int maxInt       = Integer.MAX_VALUE;  // 2147483647
double maxDouble = Double.MAX_VALUE;   // 1.79769313486231570e+308
```

Each numeric wrapper class defines the following set of *type*`Value()` methods for converting the primitive value in the wrapper object to a value of any numeric primitive datatype:

```
byte   byteValue()
short  shortValue()
int    intValue()
long   longValue()
float  floatValue()
double doubleValue()
```

The following code shows converting values in wrapper objects to primitive values.

```
Byte    byteObj    = new Byte((byte) 16);       // cast mandatory
Integer intObj2    = new Integer(42030);
Double  doubleObj2 = new Double(Math.PI);

short  s = intObj2.shortValue();                // (1)
long   l = byteObj.longValue();
int    i = doubleObj2.intValue();               // (2) truncation
double d = intObj2.doubleValue();
```

Notice the potential for loss of information at (1) and (2) above, when the primitive value in a wrapper object is converted to a narrower primitive datatype.

Each numeric wrapper class defines a `static` method `parse`*Type*`(String s)`, which returns the primitive numeric value represented by the `String` object passed as argument. These methods throw `NumberFormatException` if the `String` parameter is not a valid argument.

```
byte   value1 = Byte.parseByte("16");
int    value2 = Integer.parseInt("2010");
int    value3 = Integer.parseInt("7UP");        // NumberFormatException
double value4 = Double.parseDouble("3.14");
```

`Void` Class

This class does not wrap any primitive value. It only denotes the `Class` object representing the primitive type `void`.

Review questions

10.4 Which of the following are wrapper classes?

Select all valid answers.

(a) `java.lang.Void`
(b) `java.lang.Int`
(c) `java.lang.Boolean`
(d) `java.lang.Long`
(e) `java.lang.String`

10.5 Which of the following classes do not extend the `java.lang.Number` class?

Select all valid answers.

(a) `java.lang.Float`
(b) `java.lang.Byte`
(c) `java.lang.Character`
(d) `java.lang.Boolean`
(e) `java.lang.Short`

10.6 Which of these wrapper classes produce immutable objects?

Select all valid answers.

(a) `Character`
(b) `Byte`
(c) `Short`
(d) `Boolean`

10.4 The `Math` Class

The `final` class `Math` defines a set of `static` methods to support common mathematical functions, including functions for rounding numbers, performing trigonometry, generating pseudo random numbers, finding maximum and minimum of two numbers, calculating logarithms and exponentiation.

The `final` class `Math` provides constants to represent the value of *e*, the base of the natural logarithms, and the value *pi*, the ratio of the circumference of a circle to its diameter:

```
Math.E
Math.PI
```

Miscellaneous Rounding Functions

```
static int    abs(int i)
static long   abs(long l)
static float  abs(float f)
static double abs(double d)
```

The overloaded method `abs()` returns the absolute value of the argument. For a non-negative argument, the argument is returned. For a negative argument, the negation of the argument is returned.

```
static double ceil(double d)
```

The method `ceil()` returns the smallest `double` value that is not less than the argument `d`, and is equal to a mathematical integer.

```
static double floor(double d)
```

The method `floor()` returns the largest `double` value that is not greater than the argument `d`, and is equal to a mathematical integer.

```
static int  round(float f)
static long round(double d)
```

The overloaded method `round()` returns the integer closest to the argument.

```
static int    max(int a, int b)
static long   max(long a, long b)
static float  max(float a, float b)
static double max(double a, double b)
```

The overloaded method `max()` returns the greater of the two values `a` and `b` for any numeric type.

```
static int    min(int a, int b)
static long   min(long a, long b)
static float  min(float a, float b)
static double min(double a, double b)
```

The overloaded method `min()` returns the smaller of the two values `a` and `b` for any numeric type.

The following code illustrates the use of various rounding methods from the `Math` class.

```
long   ll = Math.abs(2010L);               // 2010L
double dd = Math.abs(-Math.PI);            // 3.141592653589793

double upPI    = Math.ceil(Math.PI);       // 4.0
double downPI  = Math.floor(Math.PI);      // 3.0
long   roundPI = Math.round(Math.PI);      // 3L

long   m = Math.max(1984L, 2010L);         // 2010L
double d = Math.min(Math.PI, Math.E);      // 2.718281828459045
```

Exponential Functions

```
static double pow(double d1, double d2)
```

The method `pow()` returns the value of `d1` raised to the power of `d2`.

```
static double exp(double d)
```

The method `exp()` returns the exponential number *e* raised to the power of `d`.

```
static double log(double d)
```

The method `log()` returns the natural logarithm (base *e*) of `d`.

```
static double sqrt(double d)
```

The method `sqrt()` returns the square root of `d`. For `NaN` or negative argument, the result is a `NaN` (Section 3.4, p. 50).

```
// Examples of Exponential Functions
double r = Math.pow(2.0, 4.0);              // 16.0
double v = Math.exp(2.0);                   // 7.38905609893065
double l = Math.log(Math.E);                // 0.9999999999999981
double c = Math.sqrt(3.0*3.0 + 4.0*4.0);   // 5.0
```

9 + 16

Trigonometry Functions

```
static double sin(double d)
```

in radians

The method `sin()` returns the trigonometric sine of an angle `d` specified in radians.

```
static double cos(double d)
```

The method `cos()` returns the trigonometric cosine of an angle `d` specified in radians.

```
static double tan(double d)
```

The method `tan()` returns the trigonometric tangent of an angle `d` specified in radians.

```
// Examples of Trigonometry Functions
double r1 = Math.sin(Math.PI/2.0);  // 1.0
double r2 = Math.cos(Math.PI);      // -1.0
double r3 = Math.sin(Math.PI/4.0);  // 0.707106781186547
```

Pseudo Random Number Generator

>= 0.0 x < 1.0

```
static double random()
```

The method `random()` returns a random number greater or equal to 0.0 and less than 1.0, where the value is selected randomly from the range according to a uniform distribution.

```
// Example of Pseudorandom Number Generator
for (int i = 1; i <= 10; i++)
    System.out.println(Math.random()*i);   // between 0.0 and 10.0
```

Review questions

10.7 Given the following program, which of the lines would print exactly 11?

```
class MyClass {
    public static void main(String args[]) {
        double v = 10.5;
```

```
            System.out.println(Math.ceil(v));          // (1)
            System.out.println(Math.round(v));         // (2)
            System.out.println(Math.floor(v));         // (3)
            System.out.println((int) Math.ceil(v));    // (4)
            System.out.println((int) Math.floor(v));   // (5)
        }
    }
```

Select all valid answers.

(a) The line labeled (1)
(b) The line labeled (2)
(c) The line labeled (3)
(d) The line labeled (4)
(e) The line labeled (5)

10.8 Which of the following methods are not part of the `Math` class?

Select all valid answers.

(a) `double tan2(double)`
(b) `double cos(double)`
(c) `int abs(int a)`
(d) `double ceil(double)`
(e) `float max(float, float)`

10.9 What is the return type of the method `round(float)` from the `Math` class?

Select the one right answer.

(a) `int`
(b) `float`
(c) `double`
(d) `Integer`
(e) `Float`

10.10 What is the return type of the method `ceil(double)` from the `Math` class?

Select the one right answer.

(a) `int`
(b) `float`
(c) `double`
(d) `Integer`
(e) `Double`

10.5 The `String` Class

Handling character strings is supported through two classes: `String` and `StringBuffer`. The `String` class implements immutable character strings, which are read-only once the string has been created and initialized, whereas the `StringBuffer` class implements dynamic character strings.

Character strings implemented using these classes are genuine objects, and the characters in such a string are represented using Unicode, i.e. 16-bit characters (Section 2.1, p. 24).

This section discusses the class `String` which provides facilities for creating, initializing and manipulating character strings. The next section does the same for the `StringBuffer` class.

The `String` class provides the following functionality for handling strings:

- Creating and initializing strings.
- Reading individual characters in a string.
- Comparing strings.
- Changing the case of characters in a string.
- Concatenating strings.
- Searching for characters and substrings.
- Extracting substrings.
- Conversion of objects to strings.

Creating and Initializing Strings

The `final` class `String` has numerous `public` constructors to create and initialize `String` objects based on various types of arguments.

The easiest way of creating and initializing a `String` object is based on string literals:

```
String str1 = "You cannot touch me!";
```

A string literal is implemented as an *anonymous* `String` object. Java optimizes handling of string literals: only one anonymous `String` object is shared by all string literals with the same contents.

```
String str2 = "You cannot touch me!";
```

Both `String` references `str1` and `str2` denote the same anonymous `String` object, initialized with the character string: `"You cannot touch me!"`

Another way of creating and initializing `String` objects, based on string literals and other `String` objects, is using the following constructor:

`String(String s)`

This method creates a new `String` object, whose contents are the same as those of the `String` object passed as argument.

In the following code, the `String` object denoted by `str3` is different from the `String` object passed as argument:

```
String str3 = new String("You cannot touch me!");
```

Example 10.1 *Anonymous Strings*

```
public class AnonStrings {

    static String str1 = "You cannot touch me!";

    public static void main(String args[]) {
        String emptyStr = new String();                            // ""
        System.out.println("0: " + emptyStr);

        String str2 = "You cannot touch me!";
        String str3 = new String(str2);

        System.out.println("1: " + (str1 == str2));                // (1) true
        System.out.println("2: " + str1.equals(str2));             // (2) true

        System.out.println("3: " + (str2 == str3));                // (3) false
        System.out.println("4: " + str2.equals(str3));             // (4) true

        System.out.println("5: " + (str1 == Auxiliary.str1));      // (5) true
        System.out.println("6: " + str1.equals(Auxiliary.str1));   // (6) true
    }
}

class Auxiliary {
    static String str1 = "You cannot touch me!";
}
```

Output from the program:

```
0:
1: true
2: true
3: false
4: true
5: true
6: true
```

In Example 10.1, notice the object reference equality exhibited at (1) and (5), since the static reference `str1` in `AnonStrings`, the local reference `str2` in the `main()` method and the static reference `str1` in `Auxiliary` denote the same anonymous `String` object. Object value equality is hardly surprising at (2), (4) and (6). Using the constructor `String()` with another string object as argument creates a new `String` object. The reference `str3` denotes a `String` object that was created from the `String` object denoted by the reference `str2`. The test at (3) shows that the references are not aliases.

Constructing String objects can also be done from arrays of bytes, arrays of characters or string buffers.

```
// Example of String object creation and initialization
byte[] bytes = {97, 98, 98, 97};
char[] character = {'a', 'b', 'b', 'a'};
StringBuffer strBuf = new StringBuffer("abba");
//...
String byteStr = new String(bytes);      // Using array of bytes: "abba"
String charStr = new String(character);  // Using array of chars: "abba"
String buffStr = new String(strBuf);     // Using string buffer: "abba"
```

Reading Individual Characters in a String

`int length()`

The number of characters in a string is returned by the `length()` method. Note that arrays have a member variable called `length`, whose value is the number of elements in the array.

`char charAt(int index)`

A character at a particular index in a string can be read using the `charAt()` method. The first character is at index 0, and the last one at index one less than the number of characters in the string. If the index value is not valid, a `StringIndexOutOfBoundsException` is thrown.

Example 10.2 shows usage of method `length()` at (1) and usage of `charAt()` method at (2). The program prints the frequency of a character in a string.

Example 10.2 *Usage of* `length()` *and* `charAt()` *Methods of the* `String` *Class*

```
public class Count {

    public static void main(String args[]) {
        int[] countArray = new int [Character.MAX_VALUE];

        String str = "You cannot touch me!";

        for (int i = 0; i < str.length(); i++)                    // (1)
            try {
                countArray[str.charAt(i)]++;                      // (2)
            } catch(StringIndexOutOfBoundsException e) {
               System.out.println("Index error detected: " + i + " not in range.");
            }

        for (int i = 0; i < countArray.length; i++)
            if (countArray[i] != 0)
                System.out.println((char)i + ": " + countArray[i]);
    }
}
```

Output from the program:

```
 : 3
!: 1
Y: 1
a: 1
c: 2
e: 1
h: 1
m: 1
n: 2
o: 3
t: 2
u: 2
```

Comparing Strings

Characters are compared based on their Unicode value.

```
boolean test = 'a' < 'b';    // true since 0x61 < 0x62
```

Two strings are compared *lexicographically*, as in a dictionary or telephone directory, by comparing their corresponding characters at each position in the two strings. The string "abba" is less than "aha", since the second character 'b' in the string "abba" is less than the second character 'h' in the string "aha". The characters in the first position in each of these strings are equal.

The following public methods can be used for comparing strings:

```
boolean equals(Object obj)
boolean equalsIgnoreCase(String str2)
```

The String class overrides the equals() method from the Object class. The String class equals() method implements String object value equality as two String objects having the same sequence of characters. The equalsIgnoreCase() method does the same, but ignores the case of the characters.

```
int compareTo(String str2)
int compareTo(Object obj)
```

The first compareTo() method compares the two strings, and returns a value based on the outcome of the comparison:

- the value 0, if this string is equal to the string argument.
- a value less than 0, if this string is lexicographically less than the string argument.
- a value greater than 0, if this string is lexicographically greater than the string argument.

The second compareTo() method behaves like the first method if the argument obj is actually a String object, otherwise it throws a ClassCastException.

```
// Examples of string comparison
String strA = new String("The Case was thrown out of Court");
String strB = new String("the case was thrown out of court");

boolean b1 = strA.equals(strB);             // false
boolean b2 = strA.equalsIgnoreCase(strB);   // true

String str1 = new String("abba");
String str2 = new String("aha");

int compVal = str1.compareTo(str2);         // negative value => str1 < str2
```

Character Case in a String

```
String toUpperCase()
String toUpperCase(Locale locale)

String toLowerCase()
String toLowerCase(Locale locale)
```

Note that the original string is returned if none of the characters need their case changed, but a new `String` object is returned if any of the characters need their case changed. These methods use the corresponding methods from the `Character` class to do the case conversion.

These methods use the rules of the (default) *locale* (returned by the method `Locale.getDefault()`), which embodies the "idiosyncrasies" of a specific geographical, political or cultural region regarding number/date/currency formats, character classification, alphabet and other localizations.

```
// Example of case in strings
String strA = new String("The Case was thrown out of Court");
String strB = new String("the case was thrown out of court");

String strC = strA.toLowerCase();  // Case conversion => New String object
String strD = strB.toLowerCase();  // No case conversion => Same String object

boolean test1 = strC == strA; // false
boolean test2 = strD == strB; // true
```

Concatenation of Strings

Concatenation of two strings results in a string, which represents the first string's characters followed by the second string's characters. This operation is not commutative. The overloaded operator + for string concatenation is discussed in Section 3.5. In addition, the following method can be used to concatenate two strings:

```
String concat(String str)
```

```
// Examples of string concatenation
String motto = "Program once";                      // (1)
motto = motto + ", execute everywhere.";            // (2)
motto = motto.concat(" Don't bet on it!");          // (3)
```

Note that a new `String` object is assigned to the reference `motto` at (2) and at (3). The mechanism behind this operation is explained in the discussion on string buffers in the next section. The reference `motto` denotes a `String` object with the following contents after execution of the assignment at (3):

```
"Program once, execute everywhere. Don't bet on it!"
```

Searching for Characters and Substrings

The following overloaded methods can be used to find the index of a character, or the start index of a substring in any string. These methods search *forwards* towards the end of the string. If the search is unsuccessful, the value –1 is returned.

`int indexOf(int ch)`

Finds the index of the first occurrence of the argument character in a string.

`int indexOf(int ch, int fromIndex)`

Finds the index of the first occurrence of the argument character in a string, starting at the index specified in the second argument.

`int indexOf(String str)`

Finds the index of the first occurrence of the argument substring in a string.

`int indexOf(String str, int fromIndex)`

Finds the index of the first occurrence of the argument substring in a string, starting at the index specified in the second argument.

The `String` class also defines a set of methods that search for a character or a substring, but the search is *backwards* towards the start of the string. In other words, the index of the last occurrence of the character or substring is found.

`int lastIndexOf(int ch)`

Finds the index of the last occurrence of the argument character in a string.

`int lastIndexOf(int ch, int fromIndex)`

Finds the index of the last occurrence of the argument character in a string, starting at the index specified in the second argument.

`int lastIndexOf(String str)`

Finds the index of the last occurrence of the argument substring in a string.

`int lastIndexOf(String str, int fromIndex)`

Finds the index of the last occurrence of the argument substring in a string, starting at the index specified in the second argument.

The following method can be used to create a string in which all occurrences of a character in a string have been replaced with another character:

```
String replace(char old, char new)
```

```
// Examples of search methods
String funStr = "Java Jives";
//               0123456789

String newStr = funStr.replace('J', 'W');      // "Wava Wives"

int jInd1a = funStr.indexOf('J');              // 0
int jInd1b = funStr.indexOf('J', 1);           // 5
int jInd2a = funStr.lastIndexOf('J');          // 5
int jInd2b = funStr.lastIndexOf('J', 4);       // 0

String banner = "One man, One vote";
//               01234567890123456

int subInd1a = banner.indexOf("One");          // 0
int subInd1b = banner.indexOf("One", 3);       // 9
int subInd2a = banner.lastIndexOf("One");      // 9
int subInd2b = banner.lastIndexOf("One", 8);   // 0
```

Extracting Substrings

```
String trim()
```

This method can be used to create a string where white space (in fact all characters with values less than or equal to the space character `'\u0020'`) from the front and the end of a string has been removed.

```
String substring(int startIndex)
String substring(int startIndex, int endIndex)
```

The `String` class provides these overloaded methods to extract substrings from a string. A new `String` object, containing the substring, is created and returned. The first method extracts the string that starts at the given index `startIndex` and extends to the end of the string. The end of the substring can be specified by using a second argument `endIndex` that is the index of the first character after the substring, i.e. the last character in the substring is at index `endIndex-1`. If the index value is not valid, a `StringIndexOutOfBoundsException` is thrown.

```
// Examples of extracting substrings
String utopia = "\t\n  Java Nation \n\t  ";
utopia = utopia.trim();                          // "Java Nation"
utopia = utopia.substring(5);                    // "Nation"
String radioactive = utopia.substring(3,6);      // "ion"
```

Conversion of Objects to Strings

The `String` class overrides the `toString()` method in the `Object` class, and returns the `String` object itself. The `String` class also defines a set of static overloaded methods to convert objects and primitive values into strings.

```
static String valueOf(Object obj)
static String valueOf(char[] character)
```

These two static overloaded functions convert objects and character arrays into strings. The first one is equivalent to `obj.toString()`.

```
static String valueOf(boolean b)
static String valueOf(char c)
```

The first of these two static overloaded functions converts the boolean values `true` and `false` into the strings `"true"` and `"false"`. The second method returns a string consisting of one character which is the argument passed.

```
static String valueOf(int i)
static String valueOf(long l)
static String valueOf(float f)
static String valueOf(double d)
```

These static methods are equivalent to the `toString()` method in the corresponding wrapper class for each of the primitive data types.

```
// Examples of string conversions
String anonStr   = String.valueOf("Make me a string.");
String charStr   = String.valueOf(new char[] {'a', 'h', 'a'});
String boolTrue  = String.valueOf(true);
String doubleStr = String.valueOf(Math.PI);
```

Other miscellaneous methods exist for reading the string characters into an array of characters (`toCharArray()`), converting the string into an array of bytes (`getBytes()`), and searching for prefixes (`startsWith()`) and suffixes (`endsWith()`) of the string. The method `hashCode()` can be used to compute a hash value based on the characters in the string.

Review questions

10.11 Which of the following operators cannot be used in conjunction with a `String` object?

Select all valid answers.

(a) `+`
(b) `-`
(c) `+=`
(d) `.`
(e) `&`

10.12 Which one of these expressions will obtain the substring `"kap"` from a string defined by `String str = "kakapo"`?

Select the one right answer.

(a) `str.substring(2, 2)`
(b) `str.substring(2, 3)`
(c) `str.substring(2, 4)`
(d) `str.substring(2, 5)`
(e) `str.substring(3, 3)`

10.13 What will be the result of attempting to compile and run the following code?

```
class MyClass {
    public static void main(String args[]) {
        String str1 = "str1";
        String str2 = "str2";
        String str3 = "str3";

        str1.concat(str2);
        System.out.println(str3.concat(str1));
    }
}
```

Select the one right answer.

(a) The code will fail to compile, since `str3.concat(str1)` is not a printable expression.
(b) The program will print `str3str1str2` when run.
(c) The program will print `str3` when run.
(d) The program will print `str3str1` when run.
(e) The program will print `str3str2` when run.

10.14 What function does the `trim()` method of the `String` class perform?

Select the one right answer.

(a) It returns a string where the leading white space of the original string has been removed.
(b) It returns a string where the trailing white space of the original string has been removed.
(c) It returns a string where both the leading and trailing white space of the original string has been removed.
(d) It returns a string where all the white space of the original string has been removed.
(e) None of the above.

10.15 Which of the following statements are true?

Select all valid answers.

(a) For any reference `obj`, the expression `(obj instanceof obj)` will yield `true`.
(b) You can make mutable subclasses of the `String` class.
(c) All wrapper classes are declared `final`.
(d) All objects have a `public` method named `clone()`.
(e) You can change the contents of a `String` object by using a `StringBuffer` object.

10.16 Which of these expressions are legal?

Select all valid answers.

(a) `"house".concat("boat")`
(b) `("house" + "boat")`
(c) `(new String("house") + "boat")`
(d) `("house" + new String("boat"))`

10.17 Which of these parameter lists have a corresponding constructor in the `String` class?

Select all valid answers.

(a) `()`
(b) `(int capacity)`
(c) `(char[] data)`
(d) `(String str)`

10.18 Which of these methods are not part of the `String` class?

Select all valid answers.

(a) `trim()`
(b) `length()`
(c) `concat(String)`
(d) `hashCode()`
(e) `reverse()`

10.19 Which of these statements concerning the `charAt()` method of the `String` class are true?

Select all valid answers.

(a) The `charAt()` method takes a `char` value as an argument.
(b) The `charAt()` method returns a `Character` object.
(c) The expression `("abcdef").charAt(3)` is illegal.
(d) The expression `"abcdef".charAt(3)` evaluates to the character `'d'`.
(e) The index of the first character is 1.

10.20 Which of these expressions will evaluate to `true`?

Select all valid answers.

(a) `"hello: there!".equals("hello there")`
(b) `"HELLO THERE".equals("hello there")`
(c) `("hello".concat("there")).equals("hello there")`
(d) `"Hello There".compareTo("hello there") == 0`
(e) `"Hello there".toLowerCase().equals("hello there")`

10.6 The `StringBuffer` Class

In contrast to the `String` class which implements immutable character strings, the `StringBuffer` class implements mutable character strings. Not only can the character string in a string buffer be changed, but the string buffer's capacity can also change dynamically. The *capacity* of a string buffer is the maximum number of characters that a string buffer can accommodate, before its size is automatically augmented.

Although there is a close relationship between objects of the `String` and `StringBuffer` classes, these are two independent `final` classes, both directly extending the `Object` class. Both `String` and `StringBuffer` are thread-safe.

The `StringBuffer` class provides various facilities for manipulating string buffers:

- Constructing string buffers.
- Changing, deleting and reading characters in string buffers.
- Constructing strings from string buffers.
- Appending, inserting and deleting in string buffers.
- Controlling string buffer capacity.

Constructing String Buffers

The `final` class `StringBuffer` provides three constructors which create, initialize and set the initial capacity of `StringBuffer` objects.

`StringBuffer(String s)`

This creates a new `StringBuffer` object, whose contents are the same as the contents of the `String` object passed as argument. The initial capacity of the string buffer is set to the length of the argument string, plus room for 16 more characters.

`StringBuffer(int length)`

This creates a new `StringBuffer` object with no content. The initial capacity of the string buffer is set to the value of the argument length, which cannot be less than 0.

`StringBuffer()`

This creates a new `StringBuffer` object with no content. The initial capacity of the string buffer is set for 16 characters.

```
// Examples: StringBuffer object creation and initialization
StringBuffer strBuf1 = new StringBuffer("Javv");      // "Javv", capacity 20
StringBuffer strBuf2 = new StringBuffer(10);          // "", capacity 10
StringBuffer strBuf3 = new StringBuffer();            // "", capacity 16
```

Changing and Reading Characters in String Buffers

`int length()`

Returns the number of characters in the string buffer.

```
char charAt(int index)
void setCharAt(int index, char ch)
```

These methods read and change the character at a specified index in the string buffer respectively. The first character is at index 0 and the last one at index one less than the number of characters in the string buffer. A `StringIndexOutOfBoundsException` is thrown if the index is not valid.

```
// Example of reading and changing string buffer contents.
StringBuffer strBuf1 = new StringBuffer("Javv");          // "Javv", capacity 20
strBuf1.setCharAt(strBuf1.length()-1, strBuf1.charAt(1)); // "Java"
```

Constructing Strings from String Buffers

The `StringBuffer` class overrides the `toString()` method from the `Object` class. It returns the contents of a string buffer in a `String` object.

```
String fromBuf = strBuf1.toString();     // "Java"
```

Appending, Inserting and Deleting Characters in String Buffers

Appending, inserting and deleting characters automatically results in adjustment of the string buffer's capacity, if necessary. The indices passed as arguments in the methods must be equal to or greater than 0, and a `StringIndexOutOfBoundsException` is thrown if an index is not valid.

The overloaded method `append()` can be used to append at the end of a string buffer.

`StringBuffer append(Object obj)`

The `obj` argument is converted to a string as if by applying the method `String.valueOf()`, and then appending the string to the string buffer.

```
StringBuffer append(String str)
StringBuffer append(char[] str)
StringBuffer append(char[] str, int offset, int len)
StringBuffer append(char c)
```

The following methods also convert the primitive value of the argument to a string by applying the method `String.valueOf()` to the argument, before appending the result to the string buffer:

```
StringBuffer append(boolean b)
StringBuffer append(int i)
StringBuffer append(long l)
StringBuffer append(float f)
StringBuffer append(double d)
```

The overloaded method `insert()` can be used to insert characters at a given position in a string buffer.

```
StringBuffer insert(int offset, Object obj)
StringBuffer insert(int offset, String str)
StringBuffer insert(int offset, char[] str)
StringBuffer insert(int offset, char c)
StringBuffer insert(int offset, boolean b)
StringBuffer insert(int offset, int i)
StringBuffer insert(int offset, long l)
StringBuffer insert(int offset, float f)
StringBuffer insert(int offset, double d)
```

The argument is converted if necessary, by applying the method `String.valueOf()`. The `offset` argument specifies where the characters are to be inserted, and must be greater than or equal to 0.

The following methods can be used to delete characters from specific positions in a string buffer.

```
StringBuffer deleteCharAt(int index)
StringBuffer delete(int start, int end)
```

The first method deletes a character at a specified index in the string buffer, contracting the string buffer by one character. The second method deletes a substring, which is specified by the (inclusive) `start` index and the (exclusive) `end` index.

The contents of a string buffer can be reversed using the following method:

```
StringBuffer reverse()
```

```
// Examples of appending, inserting and deleting in string buffers
StringBuffer buffer = new StringBuffer("banana split");   // "banana split"
buffer.delete(4,12);                                      // "bana"
buffer.append(42);                                        // "bana42"
buffer.insert(4,"na");                                    // "banana42"
buffer.setCharAt(0,'s');                                  // "sanana42"
buffer.reverse();                                         // "24ananas"
```

The compiler uses string buffers to implement the string concatenation operator `+`. The following example code of string concatenation

```
String str1 = 4 + "U" + "Only";                               // (1) "4UOnly"
```

is equivalent to the following code using a string buffer:

```
String str2 = new StringBuffer().
                  append(4).append("U").append("Only").toString(); // (2)
```

The code at (2) does not create any temporary `String` objects when concatenating several strings, where a single `StringBuffer` object is modified and finally converted to a string.

Controlling String Buffer Capacity

`int capacity()`

The method returns the current capacity of the string buffer, i.e. the total number of characters the buffer can accommodate.

`void ensureCapacity(int minCapacity)`

It ensures that there is room for at least `minCapacity` number of characters. It expands the string buffer depending on the current capacity of the buffer.

`void setLength(int newLength)`

This method ensures that the actual number of characters, i.e. length of the string buffer, is exactly equal to the value of the `newLength` argument which must be greater than or equal to 0. This operation can result in the string being truncated, or padded with null characters (`"\u0000"`).

This method does not affect the capacity of the string buffer. One use of this method is to reset the string buffer:

```
buffer.setLength(0);      // Empty the buffer.
```

Review questions

10.21 What will be the result of attempting to compile and run the following program?

```
public class MyClass {
    public static void main(String args[]) {
        String s = "hello";
        StringBuffer sb = new StringBuffer(s);
        sb.reverse();
        if (s == sb) System.out.println("a");
        if (s.equals(sb)) System.out.println("b");
        if (sb.equals(s)) System.out.println("c");
    }
}
```

Select the one right answer.

(a) The code will fail to compile, since the constructor of the `String` class is not properly called.
(b) The code will fail to compile, since `(s == sb)` is an illegal expression.
(c) The code will fail to compile, since the expression `(s.equals(sb))` is illegal.
(d) The program will print `c` when run.
(e) The program will throw a `ClassCastException` when run.

10.22 What will be the result of attempting to compile and run the following program?

```
public class MyClass {
    public static void main(String args[]) {
        StringBuffer sb = new StringBuffer("have a nice day");
        sb.setLength(6);
        System.out.println(sb);
    }
}
```

Select the one right answer.

(a) The code will fail to compile, since there is no method named `setLength()` in the `StringBuffer` class.
(b) The code will fail to compile, since `sb` is a `StringBuffer` reference, not a `String` reference, and cannot be printed.
(c) The program will throw a `StringIndexOutOfBoundsException` when run.
(d) The program will print `have a nice day` when run.
(e) The program will print `have a` when run.
(f) The program will print `ce day` when run.

10.23 Which of these parameter lists have a corresponding constructor in the `StringBuffer` class?

Select all valid answers.

(a) `()`
(b) `(int capacity)`
(c) `(char[] data)`
(d) `(String str)`

10.24 Which of these methods are not part of the `StringBuffer` class?

Select all valid answers.

(a) `trim()`
(b) `length()`
(c) `append(String)`
(d) `reverse()`
(e) `setLength(int)`

Chapter summary

The following information was included in this chapter:

- Discussion of the `Object` class, which is the fundamental class in Java.
- Discussion of the wrapper classes, which not only allow primitive values to be treated as objects, but contain useful methods for converting values.

- Discussion of the `Math` class, which provides an assortment of mathematical functions.
- Discussion of the `String` class, showing how read-only strings are created and used.
- Discussion of the `StringBuffer` class, showing how dynamic string buffers are created and manipulated.

Programming exercises

10.1 Create a class name `Pair` which aggregates two arbitrary objects. Implement the `equals()` and `hashCode()` methods in such a way that a `Pair` object is identical to another `Pair` object if, and only if, the pair of objects they aggregate are identical. Make the `toString()` implementation return the textual representation of both aggregated objects. Objects of the `Pair` class should be immutable.

10.2 A palindrome is a text phrase that reads the same backwards and forwards. The word *redivider* is a palindrome, since the word would read the same even if the character sequence were reversed. Write a program that takes a word as an argument and reports whether the word is a palindrome.

Collections 11

Exam Objectives

- Make appropriate selection of collection classes/interfaces to suit specified behavior requirements.

Supplementary Objectives

- Identify the core collection interfaces and their inheritance relationship: `Collection`, `Set`, `SortedSet`, `List`, `Map`, `SortedMap`.
- Understand the differences between collections and maps.
- State the major algorithms provided by the `Collections` class.
- Understand the operations performed by the `addAll()`, `removeAll()` and `retainAll()` methods in the `Collection` interface.
- Recognize destructive and non-destructive collection operations.
- Understand how data can be passed between collections.
- Identify the implementations of the core collection interfaces and state their usage: `HashSet`, `TreeSet`, `ArrayList`, `Vector`, `LinkedList`, `HashMap`, `Hashtable`, `TreeMap`.
- Write code to create views on collections.
- Use an iterator to iterate through all the elements of a collection.
- Distinguish between sorted and unsorted collections.
- Understand the natural ordering on elements provided by the `Comparable` class and the role of a comparator.
- State the conditions under which an `UnsupportedOperationException` may occur.
- Identify the methods in the `Collections` class that can be used to produce immutable and thread-safe versions of various types of collections.
- Write code to pass data between arrays and collections.

11.1 Collections Framework

A *collection* allows a group of objects to be treated as a single unit. Arbitrary objects can be stored, retrieved and manipulated as *elements* of collections.

Program design often requires handling of groups of objects. The collections framework presents a set of standard utility classes to manage such collections. This framework is provided in the `java.util` package and comprises three main parts:

- The core *interfaces* which allow collections to be manipulated independent of their implementation (Figure 11.1). These interfaces define the common functionality exhibited by collections, and facilitate data exchange between collections.
- A small set of *implementations* which are concrete implementations of the core interfaces (Table 11.2), providing data structures that a program can use.
- An assortment of *algorithms* which can be used to perform various operations on collections, such as sorting and searching.

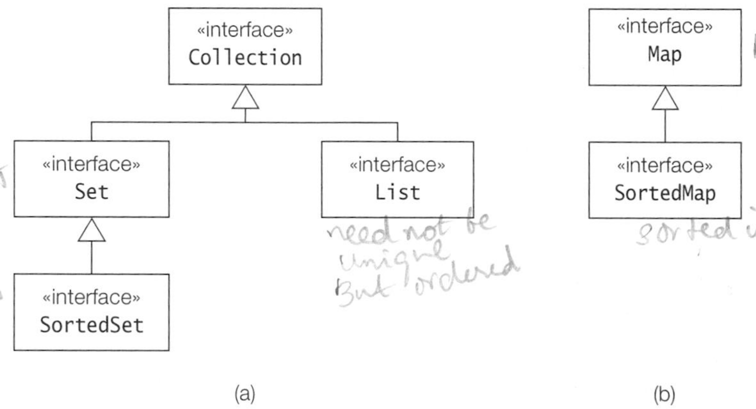

Figure 11.1 *The Core Interfaces*

Core interfaces

The `Collection` interface factors out the commonality of maintaining collections, and forms the root of the interface inheritance hierarchy for collections shown in Figure 11.1a. These interfaces are summarized in Table 11.1. The `Set` interface augments the `Collection` interface to represent its mathematical namesake: a *set* of unique elements. The `SortedSet` interface extends the `Set` interface to provide the required functionality for maintaining a set in which the elements are ordered.

The `List` interface extends the `Collection` interface to maintain a *sequence* of elements which need not be unique. The elements can be accessed according to their position in the list.

As can be seen from Figure 11.1b, the `Map` interface does not extend the `Collection` interface. This is because conceptually a map is not a collection. A map does not contain elements. It contains *mappings* from a set of *key* objects to a set of *value* objects. As the name implies, the `SortedMap` interface augments the `Map` interface to maintain its mappings sorted in *key order*.

Table 11.1 *Core Interfaces in the Collections Framework*

Interface	Description
`Collection`	A basic interface that defines the operations that all the classes that maintain collections of objects typically implement.
`Set`	Extends the `Collection` interface for sets that maintain unique elements.
`SortedSet`	Augments the `Set` interface for sets that maintain their elements in a sorted order.
`List`	Extends the `Collection` interface for lists that maintain their elements in a sequence, i.e. the elements are in order.
`Map`	A basic interface that defines operations that classes that represent mappings of keys to values typically implement.
`SortedMap`	Extends the `Map` interface for maps that maintain their mappings in key order.

Implementations

The `java.util` package provides implementations of a selection of well-known data structures, based on the core interfaces (Table 11.2). Figure 11.2 shows the inheritance relationship between the core interfaces and the corresponding implementations. Note that the sorted implementations, `TreeSet` and `TreeMap`, implement `SortedSet` and `SortedMap` respectively, and thereby also the corresponding super-interfaces `Set` and `Map` respectively.

Table 11.2 *Implementations of the Core Interfaces*

	Interfaces				
Data structures	`Set`	`SortedSet`	`List`	`Map`	`SortedMap`
Hash table	`HashSet`			`HashMap` `Hashtable`	
Resizable array			`ArrayList` `Vector`		
Balanced tree		`TreeSet`			`TreeMap`
Linked list			`LinkedList`		

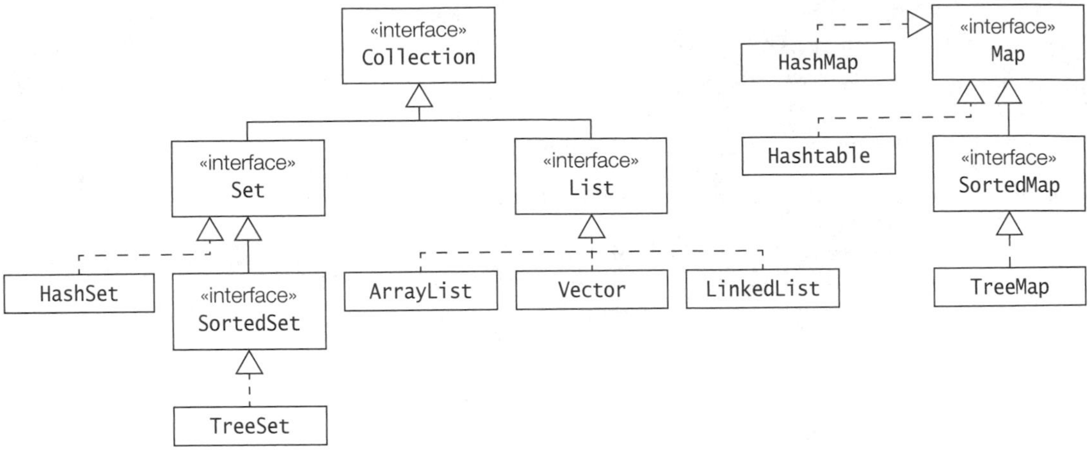

Figure 11.2 *The Core Interfaces and their Implementations*

There is no direct implementation of the `Collection` interface. The `Collection` interface is a superinterface which allows data to be passed from one collection to another. By convention, each of the collection implementation classes provides a constructor to create a collection based on the elements in the `Collection` object passed as argument. This allows the implementation of a collection to be changed by merely passing the collection to the constructor of the desired implementation. This interchangeability is also true between `Map` implementations. But collections and maps are not interchangeable.

Algorithms

The class `java.util.Collections` (not to be confused with the `Collection` interface) provides static methods which implement *polymorphic algorithms* for various operations on collections, including sorting, searching and shuffling elements. These methods operate on the collection passed as the first argument of the method. Most methods accept a `List` object, while a few operate on arbitrary `Collection` objects. A few of these methods are listed below:

```
static int binarySearch(List list, Object key)
```

Uses binary search to find the index of the `key` element in the list.

```
static void fill(List list, Object o)
```

Replaces all of the elements of the list with the specified element.

```
static void shuffle(List list)
```

Randomly permutes the list, i.e. "shuffles" the elements.

```
static void sort(List list)
```

Sorts the elements in the list into ascending order, according to their *natural order* (Section 11.6, p. 341).

The `Collections` class has useful *factory methods* for creating collection instances, which are discussed in Section 11.7.

The collections framework is *interface-based*, meaning that collections are manipulated according to their interface types, rather than by the implementation types. By using these interfaces whenever collections of objects need to be handled, interoperability can be achieved. Also, since collections are defined in terms of interfaces, various implementations of collections can be used interchangeably. Through usage of interfaces to provide interoperability and interchangeability, collections encourage code reuse.

Each core interface and its corresponding implementation are discussed in the following sections.

11.2 Collections

The `Collection` interface specifies the contract that all collections should implement. Some of the operations in the interface are *optional*, meaning that a collection may choose not to provide a proper implementation of such an operation. In such a case, an `UnsupportedOperationException` is thrown when the optional operation is invoked. The implementations of collections from the `java.util` package, shown in Table 11.2, support all the optional operations in the `Collection` interface. Many of the methods return a `boolean` value to indicate whether the collection was changed as a result of the operation.

Basic Operations

The basic operations are used to query a collection about its contents, and add and remove elements.

```
int size();
boolean isEmpty();
boolean contains(Object element);
boolean add(Object element);         // Optional
boolean remove(Object element);      // Optional
```

The `add()` and `remove()` methods return `true` if the collection was modified as a result of the operation. The `contains()` method checks for membership.

Bulk Operations

These operations perform on a collection as a single unit.

```
boolean containsAll(Collection c);
boolean addAll(Collection c);        // Optional
boolean removeAll(Collection c);     // Optional
boolean retainAll(Collection c);     // Optional
void clear();                        // Optional
```

These bulk operations can be used to perform the equivalent of set logic on *arbitrary collections* (not just on sets). The `containsAll()` method returns `true` if all elements of the specified collection are also contained in the current collection.

The operations performed by the `addAll()`, `removeAll()` and `retainAll()` methods are visualized by Venn diagrams in Figure 11.3. Note that the `addAll()`, `removeAll()` and `retainAll()` methods are *destructive* in the sense that the collection on which they are invoked can be modified.

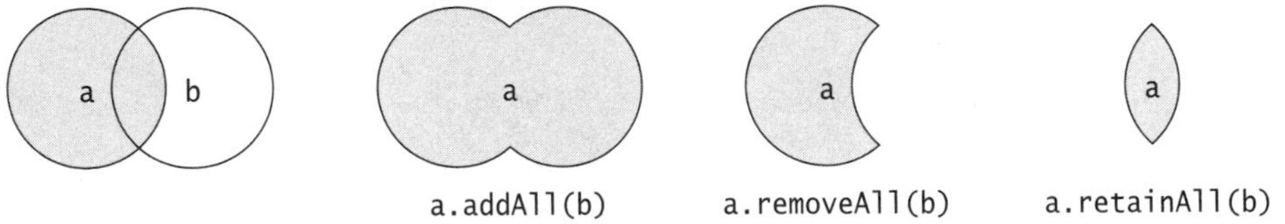

Figure 11.3 *Bulk Operations on Collections*

Array Operations

These operations allow conversion of collections to arrays.

```
Object[] toArray();
Object[] toArray(Object a[]);
```

The first `toArray()` method fills an array with the elements of the collection and returns an array. The second variant of the method can be used to specify the type of the array into which the elements of this collection are to be stored. If this array is big enough, the elements are stored in this array. If there is room to spare in the array, i.e. the length of the array is greater than the number of elements in the collection, the spare room is filled with `null` before the array is returned. If the array is not big enough, a new array of the same runtime type and appropriate size is created.

Iterators

An iterator allows serial access to the elements of a collection.

```
Iterator iterator();
```

Returns an object which implements the `Iterator` interface:

```
interface Iterator {
    boolean hasNext();
    Object next();
    void remove();    // Optional
}
```

Given a `Collection c`, the following loop iterates through the elements of a collection:

```
Iterator iter = c.iterator();
while (iter.hasNext()) {
    Object currentElement = iter.next();      // handle on the current element
    // ...
    iter.remove();    // removes the last element returned by next()
    // ...
}
```

The code above works for any collection. The `remove()` method is the only recommended way to remove elements from a collection during iteration.

Review questions

11.1 Which of these are core interfaces in the collections framework?

Select all valid answers.

(a) `Set`
(b) `Bag`
(c) `LinkedList`
(d) `Collection`
(e) `Map`

11.2 Which of these implementations are provided by the `java.util` package?

Select all valid answers.

(a) `HashList`
(b) `HashMap`
(c) `ArraySet`
(d) `ArrayMap`
(e) `TreeMap`

11.3 What is the name of the interface used to represent collections that maintain non-unique elements in order?

Select all valid answers.

(a) `Collection`
(b) `Set`
(c) `SortedSet`
(d) `List`
(e) `Sequence`

11.3 Sets

Unlike other implementations of `Collection`, implementations of `Set` will not allow duplicate elements. The `Set` interface does not define any new methods, but adds the restriction that duplicates are prohibited. A `Set` models a mathematical set (Table 11.3).

Table 11.3 *Bulk Operations and Set Logic*

Set Methods (a and b are sets)	Corresponding Mathematical Operations
`a.containsAll(b)`	$b \subseteq a$? (subset)
`a.addAll(b)`	$a = a \cup b$ (union)
`a.removeAll(b)`	$a = a - b$ (difference)
`a.retainAll(b)`	$a = a \cap b$ (intersection)
`a.clear()`	$a = \emptyset$ (empty set)

Implementations acting as *multisets* (a.k.a. *bags*) that allow duplicate elements cannot be implemented using the `Set` interface, since elements must be unique in a set.

HashSet

The primary implementation of the `Set` interface is `HashSet`, which offers near constant time performance for most operations, but does not guarantee ordering of elements. The sorted counterpart is `TreeSet`, which implements the `SortedSet` interface and has logarithmic time complexity (Section 11.6, p. 341).

A `HashSet` can be created based on an existing collection. The initial *capacity* (i.e. number of buckets in the hash table) and its *load factor* (the ratio of number of elements stored to its current capacity) can be tuned when the set is created, but in most cases the default values provide acceptable performance. The constructors for the `HashSet` class are summarized below.

`HashSet()`

Constructs a new, empty set.

`HashSet(Collection c)`

Constructs a new set containing the elements in the specified collection. The new set will not contain any duplicates.

`HashSet(int initialCapacity)`

Constructs a new, empty set with the specified initial capacity.

`HashSet(int initialCapacity, float loadFactor)`

Constructs a new, empty set with the specified initial capacity and the specified load factor.

Example 11.1 *Using Sets*

```
import java.util.*;

public class CharacterSets {
    public static void main(String args[]) {
        int nArgs = args.length;

        // A set keeping track of all characters previously encountered.
        Set encountered = new HashSet();                                // (1)

        // For each command line argument...
        for (int i=0; i<nArgs; i++) {
            String argument = args[i];

            // Convert string to a set of characters.
            Set characters = new HashSet();                             // (2)
            int size = argument.length();

            // For each character in the argument...
            for (int j=0; j<size; j++)
                // append character.
                characters.add(new Character(argument.charAt(j)));     // (3)

            // Determine if there exists a common subset.                  (4)
            Set commonSubset = new HashSet(encountered);
            commonSubset.retainAll(characters);
            boolean areDisjunct = commonSubset.size()==0;

            if (areDisjunct)
                System.out.println(characters + " and " + encountered +
                    " are disjunct.");
            else {
                // Determine superset and subset relations.                (5)
                boolean isSubset = encountered.containsAll(characters);
                boolean isSuperset = characters.containsAll(encountered);
                if (isSubset && isSuperset)
                    System.out.println(characters + " is equivalent to " +
                        encountered);
                else if (isSubset)
                    System.out.println(characters + " is a subset of " +
                        encountered);
                else if (isSuperset)
                    System.out.println(characters + " is a superset of " +
                        encountered);
                else
                    System.out.println(characters + " and " +
                        encountered + " have " + commonSubset + " in common.");
            }

            // Remember the characters encountered.
            encountered.addAll(characters);                             // (6)
        }
    }
}
```

Running the program with the following arguments:

```
java CharacterSets i said i am maids
```

results in the following output:

```
[i] and [] are disjunct.
[d, a, s, i] is a superset of [i]
[i] is a subset of [d, a, s, i]
[a, m] and [d, a, s, i] have [a] in common.
[d, a, s, m, i] is equivalent to [d, a, s, m, i]
```

Example 11.1 demonstrates set operations. It determines a relationship between two sets, in the following order:

- whether they are disjunct.
- whether they have the same elements, i.e. are equivalent.
- whether one is a subset of the other.
- whether one is a superset of the other.
- whether they have a common subset.

Given a list of words as program arguments, each argument is turned into a set of characters and compared with the set containing all the characters encountered prior to the current argument in the argument list.

The set keeping track of all the characters encountered is called `encountered`, and is created at (1). For each argument, a set is created, as shown at (2). This set, called `characters`, is populated with the characters of the current argument, as shown at (3). The program first determines if there is a common subset between the two sets, as shown at (4).

```
// Determine if there exists a common subset.                (4)
Set commonSubset = new HashSet(encountered);
commonSubset.retainAll(characters);
boolean areDisjunct = commonSubset.size()==0;
```

Note that the `retainAll()` operation is destructive. The code above does not affect the `encountered` and the `characters` sets. If the size of the common subset is zero, then the sets are disjunct, otherwise the relationship must be narrowed down. The subset and superset relations are determined at (5), using the `containsAll()` method.

```
// Determine superset and subset relations.                 (5)
boolean isSubset = encountered.containsAll(characters);
boolean isSuperset = characters.containsAll(encountered);
```

The sets are equivalent if both the above relations are true. If they are both false, i.e. no subset or superset relationship exists, then they only have the common subset between them. The current set of characters is added to the set of all encountered characters, by using the `addAll()` method as shown at (6).

```
encountered.addAll(characters);                              // (6)
```

Textual representation of a set is supplied by the overriding method `toString()` in the *abstract implementation* on which the `HashSet` implementation is based (Section 11.7, p. 345).

11.4 Lists

Lists are collections which maintain their elements *in order* (also called a *sequence*), and can contain duplicates. In addition to the operations inherited from the `Collection` interface, the `List` interface also defines operations that operate specifically on lists: access by numerical position, search in list, customized iterators, operations on parts of a list (called *open range-view* operations). This additional functionality is provided by the following methods:

```
// Element Access by Index
Object get(int index);
Object set(int index, Object element);          // Optional
void add(int index, Object element);            // Optional
Object remove(int index);                       // Optional
boolean addAll(int index, Collection c);        // Optional
```

In a non-empty list, the first element is at index `0` and the last element is at `size()-1`. As might be expected, an illegal index throws an `IndexOutOfBoundsException`.

The `get()` method returns the element at the specified index. The `set()` method replaces the element at the specified index with the specified element. The `add()` method inserts the specified element at the specified index, displacing the previous element and any other elements necessary one position towards the end of the list. The inherited method `add(Object obj)` from the `Collection` interface will append the specified element to the end of the list. The `remove()` method deletes and returns the element at the specified index, contracting the list accordingly. The inherited method `remove(Object element)` from the `Collection` interface will remove the first occurrence of the element from the list.

The `addAll()` method inserts the elements from the specified collection at the specified index, using the specified collection's iterator.

```
// Element Search
int indexOf(Object o);
int lastIndexOf(Object o);
```

These methods respectively return the index of the first and the last occurrence of the element in the list if the element is found, otherwise the value –1 is returned.

```
// List Iterators
ListIterator listIterator();
ListIterator listIterator(int index);
```

The iterator from the first method returns the elements consecutively, starting with the first element, whereas the iterator from the second method starts iterating from the element indicated by the index.

```
interface ListIterator extends Iterator {
    boolean hasNext();
    boolean hasPrevious();

    Object next();           // Element after the cursor
    Object previous();       // Element before the cursor

    int nextIndex();         // Index of element after the cursor
    int previousIndex();     // Index of element before the cursor

    void remove();           // Optional
    void set(Object o);      // Optional
    void add(Object o);      // Optional
}
```

The `ListIterator` interface is a customized iterator for lists. It augments the `Iterator` interface, and allows the list to be iterated in either direction. When traversing lists, it can be helpful to imagine a *cursor* between the elements, which moves forwards or backwards, depending on the call to the `next()` or `previous()` method respectively.

```
// Open Range-View
List subList(int fromIndex, int toIndex);
```

This method returns a *view* of the list, which consists of a sublist of the elements from the index `fromIndex`, inclusive, to the index `toIndex`, exclusive. A view allows the range it represents in the underlying list to be manipulated. Any changes in the view are reflected in the underlying list. Views facilitate range operations on lists.

ArrayList, Vector and LinkedList

Three implementations of the `List` interface are provided in the `java.util` package: `ArrayList`, `Vector` and `LinkedList`. The `ArrayList` class provides the primary implementation of the `List` interface. All three classes provide a standard constructor which creates a new empty list, and a constructor which creates a list based on an existing collection. The `ArrayList` and the `Vector` classes also allow creating a new empty list with an initial capacity.

The `Vector` and `ArrayList` classes implement dynamically resizable arrays. Unlike the `ArrayList` class, the `Vector` class is thread-safe, meaning that concurrent calls to the vector will not compromise its integrity.

`ArrayList` and `Vector` offer comparable performance, but `ArrayList` offers slightly better performance as it has no synchronization. Positional access has constant time performance in `ArrayList` and `Vector`, but linear time in `LinkedList`. In most cases the primary implementation `ArrayList` is the best choice for implementing lists. Where frequent insertions and deletions occur inside a list, a `LinkedList` can be worth considering.

Example 11.2 *Using Lists*

```java
import java.util.*;

public class TakeAGuess {
    final static int N_DIGITS = 5;

    public static void main(String args[]) {
        // Sanity check on the given data.
        if (args.length != N_DIGITS) {
            System.err.println("Guess " + N_DIGITS + " digits.");
            return;
        }

        /* Initializes the solution list. This program has a fixed solution. */
        List secretSolution = new ArrayList();                        // (1)
        secretSolution.add("5");
        secretSolution.add("3");
        secretSolution.add("2");
        secretSolution.add("7");
        secretSolution.add("2");

        // Converts the user's guess from string array to list.         (2)
        List guess = new ArrayList();
        for (int i=0; i<N_DIGITS; i++)
            guess.add(args[i]);

        // Find the number of digits that were correctly included.      (3)
        List duplicate = new ArrayList(secretSolution);
        int nIncluded = 0;
        for (int i=0; i<N_DIGITS; i++)
            if (duplicate.remove(guess.get(i))) ++nIncluded;

        /* Find the number of correctly placed digits by comparing the two
           lists, element for element, counting each correct placement. */
        int nPlaced = 0;
        // Need two iterators to iterate through guess and solution.    (4)
        ListIterator correct = secretSolution.listIterator();
        ListIterator attempt = guess.listIterator();
        while (correct.hasNext())
            if (correct.next().equals(attempt.next())) nPlaced++;

        // Print results.
        System.out.println(nIncluded + " digit(s) correctly included.");
        System.out.println(nPlaced +   " digit(s) correctly placed.");
    }
}
```

Running the program with the following arguments:

```
java TakeAGuess 3 2 2 2 7
```

gives the following output:

```
4 digit(s) correctly included.
1 digit(s) correctly placed.
```

Example 11.2 illustrates some basic operations on lists. The user gets one shot to guess a five-digit code. The solution is hard-wired in the example as a list of five elements, where each element represents a digit as a `String` object. The `secretSolution` list is created at (1) and populated using the `add()` method. The guess specified at the command line is placed in a separate list (`guess`) at (2).

The number of digits which are correct is determined at (3). The solution is first duplicated, and each digit in the guess is removed from the duplicated solution. The number of deletions corresponds to the number of correct digits in the guess. A digit at a particular index in the guess list is returned by the `get()` method. The `remove()` method returns `true` if the duplicate list was modified, i.e. the digit from the guess was found and removed from the duplicated solution.

```
// Find the number of digits that were correctly included.     (3)
List duplicate = new ArrayList(secretSolution);
int nIncluded = 0;
for (int i=0; i<N_DIGITS; i++)
    if (duplicate.remove(guess.get(i))) ++nIncluded;
```

Finding the number of digits that are correctly placed is achieved by two list iterators, which allow digits in the same position in the `guess` and the `secretSolution` list to be compared:

```
// Need two iterators to iterate through guess and solution.    (4)
ListIterator correct = secretSolution.listIterator();
ListIterator attempt = guess.listIterator();
while (correct.hasNext())
    if (correct.next().equals(attempt.next())) nPlaced++;
```

Review questions

11.4 Which of these statements concerning the use of collection operations are true?

Select all valid answers.

(a) Some operations may throw an `UnsupportedOperationException`.
(b) Methods using some operations must either catch `UnsupportedOperationException` or declare that they throw such exceptions.
(c) Collection classes implementing `List` can have duplicate elements.
(d) `ArrayList` can only accommodate a fixed number of elements.
(e) The `Collection` interface contains a method named `get`.

11.5 What will be the result of attempting to compile and run the following program?

```
import java.util.*;

public class Sets {
    public static void main(String args[]) {
        HashSet set1 = new HashSet();
        addRange(set1, 1);
        ArrayList list1 = new ArrayList();
        addRange(list1, 2);
```

```
            TreeSet set2 = new TreeSet();
            addRange(set2, 3);
            LinkedList list2 = new LinkedList();
            addRange(list2, 5);

            set1.removeAll(list1);
            list1.addAll(set2);
            list2.addAll(list1);
            set1.removeAll(list2);

            System.out.println(set1);
        }

        static void addRange(Collection col, int step) {
            for (int i = step*2; i<=25; i+=step)
                col.add(new Integer(i));
        }
    }
```

Select the one right answer.

(a) The program will fail to compile, since operations are performed on mismatching collection implementations.

(b) The program will fail to compile, since the `TreeSet` instance has not been given a `Comparator` to use when sorting its elements.

(c) The program will compile without error, but will throw an `UnsupportedOperationException` when run.

(d) The program will compile without error, and will print all primes below 25 when run.

(e) The program will compile without error, and will print some other sequence of numbers when run.

11.6 Which of these methods are defined in the `Collection` interface?

Select all valid answers.

(a) `add(Object o)`

(b) `retainAll(Collection c)`

(c) `get(int index)`

(d) `iterator()`

(e) `indexOf(Object o)`

11.7 Which of these methods from the `Collection` interface return the value `true` if the collection object was modified during the operation?

Select all valid answers.

(a) `contains()`

(b) `add()`

(c) `containsAll()`

(d) `retainAll()`

(e) `clear()`

11.5 Maps

A `Map` defines mappings from keys to values. A map does not allow duplicate keys, in other words the keys are unique, and each key maps to at most one value, implementing what are called *single-valued maps*.

A map is not a collection and the `Map` interface does not extend the `Collection` interface. However, the mappings can be viewed as a collection in various ways: a key set, a value collection or a *<key, value>* set. These collection views are the only means to iterate over a map.

Maps also have optional methods: implementations throw an `UnsupportedOperationException` if they do not support the operation. The implementations of maps from the `java.util` package, shown in Table 11.2, support all the optional operations of the `Map` interface.

Basic Operations

These operations constitute the basic functionality provided by a map.

```
Object put(Object key, Object value);     // Optional
Object get(Object key);
Object remove(Object key);                // Optional
boolean containsKey(Object key);
boolean containsValue(Object value);
int size();
boolean isEmpty();
```

The `put()` method inserts a mapping, i.e. a *<key, value>* pair, also called an *entry*. The `get()` method returns the value to which the specified key is mapped, or `null` if no mapping is found. The `remove()` method deletes the entry for the specified key. The `containsKey()` method returns `true` if the specified key is mapped to a value in the map. The `containsValue()` returns `true` if there exists one or more keys that are mapped to the specified value. The methods `size()` and `isEmpty()` return the number of entries and whether the map is empty or not, respectively.

Bulk Operations

```
void putAll(Map t);  // Optional
void clear();        // Optional
```

The first method copies all entries from the specified map and the second method deletes all the entries from a map.

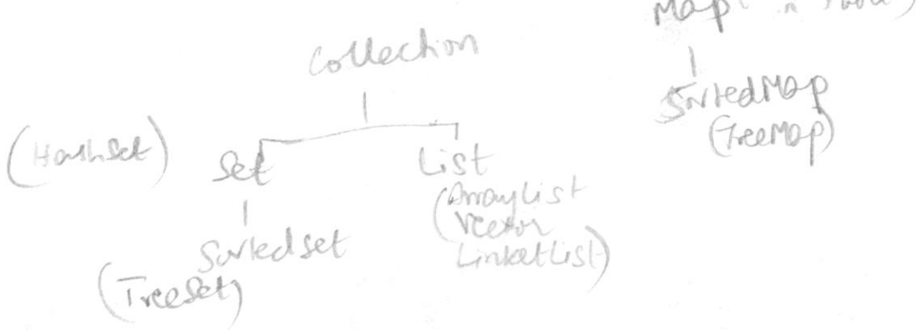

Collection Views

```
Set keySet();
Collection values();
Set entrySet();
```

These methods provide different views on a map. Changes in the map are reflected in the view, and vice versa. These methods respectively return a set view of keys, a collection view of values and a set view of <*key, value*> entries. Note that the `Collection` returned by the `values()` method is not a `Set`, as several keys can map to the same value, i.e. duplicate values can be included in the returned collection. Each <*key, value*> entry in the set view is represented by an object implementing the `Map.Entry` interface. An entry in the entry set view can be manipulated by methods defined in this interface:

```
interface Entry {
    Object getKey();
    Object getValue();
    Object setValue(Object value);
}
```

HashMap and Hashtable

There are two implementations of the `Map` interface in the `java.util` package: `HashMap` and `Hashtable`. The `HashMap` class provides the primary implementation of the `Map` interface. As was the case with collections, implementation classes provide a standard constructor which creates a new empty map, and a constructor which creates a new map based on an existing one. These classes also allow creating a new empty map with an initial capacity and/or load factor.

While the `HashMap` class is not thread-safe, the `Hashtable` class is.

Example 11.3 *Using Maps*

```
import java.util.*;

public class WeightGroups {
    public static void main(String args[]) {

        // Create a map to store the frequency for each group.
        Map groupFreqCount = new HashMap();

        int nArgs = args.length;
        for (int i=0; i<nArgs; i++) {
            // Get the value from argument and group into intervals of 5     (1)
            double weight = Double.parseDouble(args[i]);
            Integer weightGroup = new Integer((int) Math.round(weight/5)*5);

            // Increment count, set to 1 if it's the first value of group.  (2)
            Integer oldCount = (Integer) groupFreqCount.get(weightGroup);
            Integer newCount = (oldCount==null) ?
                new Integer(1) :
                new Integer(oldCount.intValue()+1);
            groupFreqCount.put(weightGroup, newCount);                     // (3)
        }
```

```
            /* Now print by iterating over a sorted list of groups (keys)
               and extracting count (values) from the groupFreqCount map. */
            List keys = new ArrayList(groupFreqCount.keySet());          // (4)

            // Use the sort algorithm from the Collections class to sort the keys.
            Collections.sort(keys);                                      // (5)

            /* Create an iterator on the sorted keys. Iterate over the keys,
               looking up the frequency from the frequency map. */
            ListIterator keyIterator = keys.listIterator();              // (6)
            while (keyIterator.hasNext()) {
                // Current key (group).                                     (7)
                Integer group = (Integer) keyIterator.next();
                // Extract count (value) from the map.
                Integer count = (Integer) groupFreqCount.get(group);     // (8)
                int intCount = count.intValue();

                /* Use the fill() method from the Arrays class to create a
                   string consisting of intCount number of '*'. */
                char[] bar = new char[intCount];
                Arrays.fill(bar, '*');                                   // (9)

                System.out.println(group + ":\t" + new String(bar));
            }
        }
    }
```

Running the program with the following arguments:

```
java WeightGroups 74 75 93 75 93 82 61 92 10 185
```

gives the following output:

```
10:     *
60:     *
75:     ***
80:     *
90:     *
95:     **
185:    *
```

Example 11.3 outputs a textual histogram for the frequency of weight measurements in a weight group, where a weight group is defined as an interval of 5 units. The weight measurements are supplied as program arguments. The example illustrates using maps, creating key views, and using a list iterator to iterate over a map. The program proceeds as follows:

1. It reads the program arguments, converting each weight to its corresponding weight group and updating the frequency of the weight group:
    - The weight group is determined at (1).
    - The count is incremented, if necessary, as shown at (2) and registered for the group as shown at (3). Since keys are unique in a map, any previous mapping is overwritten.

```
// Increment count, set to 1 if it's the first value of group.      (2)
Integer oldCount = (Integer) groupFreqCount.get(weightGroup);
Integer newCount = (oldCount==null) ?
new Integer(1) :
new Integer(oldCount.intValue()+1);
groupFreqCount.put(weightGroup, newCount);                         // (3)
```

2. It creates a list of keys (which are weight groups) from the `groupFreqCount` map and sorts them. The `keySet()` method returns a set view of keys, which is converted to a list as shown at (4). The key list is sorted by the algorithm `sort()` from the `Collections` class, as shown at (5).

```
List keys = new ArrayList(groupFreqCount.keySet());          // (4)
Collections.sort(keys);                                       // (5)
```

3. It uses an iterator to iterate over the keys, looking up the frequency in the `groupFreqCount` map. A map can only be iterated through one of its views.

   - The list iterator is created at (6).

   ```
   ListIterator keyIterator = keys.listIterator();           // (6)
   ```

   - For each key, the corresponding value (i.e. frequency count) is retrieved, as shown at (7) and (8).

   ```
   // Current key (group).                                    (7)
   Integer group = (Integer) keyIterator.next();
   // Extract count (value) from the map.
   Integer count = (Integer) groupFreqCount.get(group);      // (8)
   ```

   - A "bar" for each frequency is created using the `fill()` method from the `Arrays` class, as shown at (9).

11.6 Sorted Sets and Sorted Maps

Sets and maps have special interfaces, called `SortedSet` and `SortedMap` (Figure 11.2), for implementations that sort their elements in a specific order. Objects can specify their *natural order* by implementing the `Comparable` interface, or be dictated a *total order* by a comparator which implements the `Comparator` interface.

The Comparator Interface

Specific `Comparator` implementations can be constructed to order elements according to some custom order, or the default comparator which uses the natural order of the elements can be used (see `Comparable` interface below). All comparators implement the `Comparator` interface, which has the following single method:

```
int compare(Object o1, Object o2)
```

The `compare()` method returns a negative integer, zero or a positive integer if the first object is less than, equal to or greater than the second object, according to the total order. Since this method tests for equality, it is recommended that its implementation does not contradict the semantics of the `equals()` method.

The Comparable Interface

A class can define the natural order of its instances by implementing the `Comparable` interface. Many of the standard classes in the Java API, such as the wrapper classes, `String`, `Date` and `File`, implement this interface. The `java.lang.Comparable` interface specifies a single method:

```
int compareTo(Object o)
```

This method returns a negative integer, zero or a positive integer if the current object is less than, equal to or greater than the specified object according to the natural order.

A *natural comparator* exists, which queries objects implementing `Comparable` about their natural order, using this interface. Objects implementing this interface can be used:

- as elements in a sorted set.
- as keys in a sorted map.
- in lists which can be sorted automatically by the `Collections.sort()` method.

This natural order of `Comparable` objects can be overruled by passing a `Comparator` to the constructor when the sorted set or map is created.

SortedSet Interface

The `SortedSet` interface extends the `Set` interface to provide the functionality for handling sorted sets.

```
// Range-view operations
SortedSet headSet(Object toElement);
SortedSet tailSet(Object fromElement);
SortedSet subSet(Object fromElement, Object toElement);
```

The `headSet()` method returns a view of a portion of this sorted set, whose elements are strictly less than the specified element. Similarly, the `tailSet()` method returns a view of the portion of this sorted set, whose elements are greater than or equal to the specified element. The `subSet()` method returns a view of the portion of this sorted set, whose elements range from `fromElement`, inclusive, to `toElement`, exclusive. Note that the views present the elements sorted in the same order as the underlying sorted map.

```
// Min-max points
Object first();
Object last();
```

The `first()` method returns the first (minimum) element currently in this sorted set, and the `last()` method returns the last (maximum) element currently in this sorted set.

```
// Comparator access
Comparator comparator();
```

This method returns the comparator associated with this sorted set, or `null` if it uses the natural ordering of its elements. This comparator, if defined, is used by default when a sorted set is constructed, and also used when copying elements into new sorted sets.

SortedMap Interface

The `SortedMap` interface extends the `Map` interface to provide the functionality for implementing maps with *sorted keys*. Its operations are analogous to those of the `SortedSet` interface, applying to maps and keys rather than to sets and elements.

```
// Range-view operations
SortedMap headMap(Object toKey);
SortedMap tailMap(Object fromKey);
SortedMap subMap(Object fromKey, Object toKey);
// Min-max points
Object firstKey();
Object lastKey();
// Comparator access
Comparator comparator();
```

TreeSet and TreeMap

The `TreeSet` and `TreeMap` classes implement the `SortedSet` and `SortedMap` interfaces, respectively. Each class provides four constructors:

```
TreeSet()
TreeMap()
```

A standard constructor to create a new empty sorted set or map, according to the elements' or the keys' natural order.

```
TreeSet(Comparator c)
TreeMap(Comparator c)
```

A constructor which takes an explicit comparator for ordering the elements or the keys.

```
TreeSet(Collection c)
TreeMap(Map m)
```

A constructor that can create a sorted set or a sorted map based on a (unsorted) collection or a (unsorted) map respectively, according to the elements or the keys' natural order.

```
TreeSet(SortedSet s)
TreeMap(SortedMap m)
```

A constructor which creates a new set or map containing the same elements or mappings as the specified sorted set or sorted map, sorted according to the same ordering.

Example 11.4 *Using SortedMaps*

```
import java.util.*;

public class WeightGroups2 {
    public static void main(String args[]) {

        // Create a map to store the frequency for each group.
        Map groupFreqCount = new HashMap();

        int nArgs = args.length;
        for (int i=0; i<nArgs; i++) {
            // Get the value from argument and group into intervals of 5     (1)
            double weight = Double.parseDouble(args[i]);
            Integer weightGroup = new Integer((int) Math.round(weight/5)*5);

            // Increment count, set to 1 if it's the first value of group.  (2)
            Integer oldCount = (Integer) groupFreqCount.get(weightGroup);
            Integer newCount = (oldCount==null) ?
                new Integer(1) :
                new Integer(oldCount.intValue()+1);
            groupFreqCount.put(weightGroup, newCount);                    // (3)
        }

        /* Only histogram for the weight groups between 50 and 150
           is of interest. Print frequency for these groups in a sorted order. */

        // Migrate the data to a sorted map.
        SortedMap groupSortedCount = new TreeMap(groupFreqCount);         // (4)

        // Select the interesting sub-map.
        SortedMap intervalCount =                                         // (5)
            groupSortedCount.subMap(new Integer(50), new Integer(150));

        /** Print by iterating over the sorted entries of weight
            groups (key) and count (value). */
        Iterator entryIterator = intervalCount.entrySet().iterator();     // (6)
        while (entryIterator.hasNext()) {
            Map.Entry entry = (Map.Entry) entryIterator.next();           // (7)

            // Extract groups (key) and count (value) from entry.            (8)
            Integer group = (Integer) entry.getKey();
            Integer count = (Integer) entry.getValue();
            int intCount = count.intValue();

            /* Use the fill() method from the Arrays class to create a
               string consisting of intCount number of '*'. */
            char[] bar = new char[intCount];
            Arrays.fill(bar, '*');                                        // (9)

            System.out.println(group + ":\t" + new String(bar));
        }
    }
}
```

Running the program with the following argument:

```
java WeightGroups2 74 75 93 75 93 82 61 92 10 185
```

gives the following output:

```
60:     *
75:     ***
80:     *
90:     *
95:     **
```

Example 11.4 illustrates sorted maps. It also outputs a textual histogram like the one in Example 11.3, but now the histogram is limited to a range of weight groups. The program defines the following steps:

1. Reading the program arguments, converting each weight to its corresponding weight group and updating the frequency of the weight group. This is the same step as in Example 11.3.
2. Migrating the data to a sorted map, as shown at (4).

```
SortedMap groupSortedCount = new TreeMap(groupFreqCount);         // (4)
```

3. Creating a sorted submap view of the required range of weight groups, as shown at (5).

```
SortedMap intervalCount =
    groupSortedCount.subMap(new Integer(50), new Integer(150));  // (5)
```

4. Setting up an iterator on a set view of mappings (i.e. entries) in the submap, as shown at (6). First a set view of the entries is created using the `entrySet()` method. The elements (i.e. mappings) in this set view will be sorted, since the underlying submap is sorted. An iterator is then created on this set.

```
Iterator entryIterator = intervalCount.entrySet().iterator();    // (6)
```

5. Using the iterator to iterate over the underlying set. Each element in this set is a mapping, i.e. an entry, in the underlying sorted submap. Each entry conforms to the `Map.Entry` interface, which allows the key and the value to be extracted as shown at (8).

```
// Extract groups (key) and count (value) from entry.            (8)
Integer group = (Integer) entry.getKey();
Integer count = (Integer) entry.getValue();
int intCount = count.intValue();
```

11.7 Customizing Collections

The functionality of the collection implementations can be customized with regard to two important aspects:

- thread-safety
- data immutability

The collection implementations, except for `Vector` and `Hashtable`, are not thread-safe, i.e their integrity is jeopardized by concurrent access. A situation might demand that the collection is immutable. Java provides a solution to these two requirements through *decorators*. A decorator object "wraps around" a collection, modifying the collection's behavior.

Instead of providing public decorator classes, Java provides *static factory methods* which return appropriately decorated collection instances. In this regard, such decorators are known as *anonymous implementations*. The `Collections` class, in addition to being a repository of useful algorithms, provides decorators for thread-safety and data immutability.

for Thread-safety

Synchronized Collection Decorators

The following static factory methods from the `Collections` class can be utilized to create decorators that provide thread-safety for collections:

```
Collection synchronizedCollection(Collection c)
List       synchronizedList(List list)
Map        synchronizedMap(Map m)
Set        synchronizedSet(Set s)
SortedMap  synchronizedSortedMap(SortedMap m)
SortedSet  synchronizedSortedSet(SortedSet s)
```

All threads must access the underlying collection through the synchronized view, otherwise serial access is not guaranteed.

```
// Create a synchronized decorator.
Collection syncDecorator = Collections.synchronizedCollection(someCollection);
```

For iterating over a synchronized collection, in addition, the iteration code must be synchronized on the decorator:

```
// Each thread must iterate when synchronized on the decorator.
synchronized(syncDecorator) {
    for (Iterator iter = syncDecorator.iterator(); iter.hasNext();)
        doSomething(iter.next());
}
```

For Data Immutability

Unmodifiable Collection Decorators

The following static factory methods from the `Collections` class can be utilized to create *views* that provide read-only access to the underlying collection:

```
Collection unmodifiableCollection(Collection c)
List       unmodifiableList(List list)
Map        unmodifiableMap(Map m)
Set        unmodifiableSet(Set s)
SortedMap  unmodifiableSortedMap(SortedMap m)
SortedSet  unmodifiableSortedSet(SortedSet s)
```

The view intercepts all operations that can modify the underlying collection. Any attempt to call such an operation on the view results in an `UnsupportedOperationException`.

Other Collection Views

The `subList()` method in the `List` interface provides a view of a portion of a list (Section 11.4, p. 333). The `nCopies()` method in the `Collections` class creates an immutable list where each element denotes the specified object:

```
List nCopies(int n, Object o)
```

The following code conjures up a list initialized with 99 `null` elements :

```
List itemsList = new ArrayList(Collections.nCopies(99, null));
```

A *singleton set* (i.e. a set containing one element) can be created by calling the static factory method `Collections.singleton(Object obj)`. Removing an element from a set can be done utilizing an immutable singleton set:

```
// Create a singleton set with the element to remove.
Set fishBone = Collections.singleton(bone);      // bone is a fish part
// Remove the element
fish.removeAll(fishBone);                         // fish is a set of fish parts.
```

The empty set and the empty list are designated by the following two constants:

```
Collections.EMPTY_SET
Collections.EMPTY_LIST
```

These constants come in handy when a collection that need not be populated is required.

Collection Adapters

The class `Arrays` provides useful algorithms that operate on arrays. It also provides the static `asList()` method, which can be used to create `List` views of arrays. Changes to the `List` view reflect in the array, and vice versa. The `List` size is equal to the array length and cannot be changed. The `asList()` method in the `Arrays` class and the `toArray()` method in the `Collection` interface provide the bridge between arrays and collections.

```
Set jiveSet = new HashSet(Arrays.asList(jiveArray));
String[] uniqueJiveArray = (String[]) jiveSet.toArray(new String[0]);
```

In the above code, the final array will also be devoid of duplicates.

Abstract Implementations

A look at the API for the collection implementations (Figure 11.2) in the `java.util` package will quickly reveal that they are based on other *abstract implementations*. For example, the `HashSet` implementation is based on the `AbstractSet` implementation, which in turn extends the `AbstractCollection` implementation. These abstract classes already provide most of the heavy machinery by implementing the relevant collection interfaces, and are excellent starting points for implementing customized collections.

Review questions

11.8 Which of these collection implementations are thread-safe?

Select all valid answers.

(a) `ArrayList`
(b) `HashSet`
(c) `Vector`
(d) `TreeSet`
(e) `LinkedList`

11.9 Which of these methods can be called on objects implementing the `Map` interface?

Select all valid answers.

(a) `contains(Object o)`
(b) `addAll(Collection c)`
(c) `remove(Object o)`
(d) `values()`
(e) `toArray()`

11.10 Which of these statements concerning maps are true?

Select all valid answers.

(a) The return type of the `values()` method is `Set`.
(b) Changes made in the set view returned by `keySet()` will be reflected in the original map.
(c) The `Map` interface extends the `Collection` interfaces.
(d) All keys in a map are unique.
(e) All `Map` implementations keep the keys sorted.

11.11 Which sequence of digits will the following program print?

```
import java.util.*;
public class Lists {
    public static void main(String args[]) {
        List list = new ArrayList();
        list.add("1");
        list.add("2");
        list.add(1, "3");
        List list2 = new LinkedList(list);
        list.addAll(list2);
        list2 = list.subList(2, 5);
        list2.clear();
        System.out.println(list);
    }
}
```

Select the one right answer.

(a) The sequence `1, 3, 2` is printed.
(b) The sequence `1, 3, 3, 2` is printed.
(c) The sequence `1, 3, 2, 1, 3, 2` is printed.
(d) The sequence `3, 1, 2` is printed.
(e) The sequence `3, 1, 1, 2` is printed.
(f) None of the above.

11.12 Which of these classes has a `comparator()` method?

Select all valid answers.

(a) `ArrayList`
(b) `HashMap`
(c) `TreeSet`
(d) `HashSet`
(e) `TreeMap`

Chapter summary

The following information was included in this chapter:

- An overview of the collections framework: core interfaces, implementations and algorithms.
- Discussion of the functionality specified by the `Collection` interface and its role in the collections framework.
- Discussion of sets, how their functionality is defined by the `Set` interface and implemented by `HashSet`.
- Discussion of lists, how their functionality is defined by the `List` interface and implemented by `ArrayList`, `Vector` and `LinkedList`.
- Discussion of maps, how their functionality is defined by the `Map` interface and implemented by `HashMap` and `Hashtable`.
- The role of the `Comparator` and `Comparable` interfaces for providing ordering of elements.
- Discussion of sorted sets and sorted maps, how their functionality is defined by the `SortedSet` and `SortedMap` interfaces and implemented by `TreeSet` and `TreeMap`.
- Customizing collections using anonymous implementations to achieve synchronization and data immutability.

Programming exercise

11.1 Create a class with a method that takes a string and returns the number of characters that only occur once in the string. It is expected that the method will be called repeatedly with the same strings. Since the counting operation can be time consuming, the method should cache the results so that when the method is given a string previously encountered, it will simply retrieve the stored result. Use collections wherever appropriate.

AWT Components

12

Supplementary Objectives

- State the inheritance hierarchy of components and containers: `Component`, `Container`, `Panel`, `Window`, `Frame`, `Dialog`.
- Write code to demonstrate the use of the following methods of the `java.awt.Component` class: `setVisible(boolean)`, `setEnabled(boolean)`, `getSize()`, `setForeground()` and `setBackground()`.
- Write code using the GUI control components: `Button`, `Canvas`, `Checkbox`, `Choice`, `Label`, `List`, `Scrollbar`, `TextField`, `TextArea`.
- State the significance of a "column" where one of the text components is using a proportional (variable) pitch font or a fixed pitch font.
- State the inheritance hierarchy of the menu-related components: `MenuComponent`, `MenuBar`, `MenuItem`, `Menu`, `CheckboxMenuItem`, `PopupMenu`.

12.1 Overview of the `java.awt` package

The *Java Foundation Classes* (JFC) provide two frameworks for building GUI-based applications. The *Abstract Windowing Toolkit* (AWT) relies on the underlying windowing system on a specific platform to present its GUI components. The other GUI toolkit in the JFC, called *Swing*, implements a new set of *lightweight* GUI components that are written in Java and have a pluggable look and feel. They are lightweight because they are not dependent on the underlying windowing system. Swing relies on the same event handling model as AWT, and provides lightweight counterparts to the components found in the AWT. Swing is discussed in Chapter 17.

The package `java.awt` provides the primary facilities of the AWT:

- Managing the *layout* of components within container objects (Chapter 13).
- Support for *event handling* that is essential for user interaction in GUI-based systems (Chapter 14).
- Rendering *graphics* in GUI components using color, fonts, images and polygons (Chapter 15).

This chapter provides an overview of major *containers* and *components* found in the AWT, and summarizes the functionality they provide.

12.2 Components and Containers

The partial class hierarchy in Figure 12.1 depicts the principal *container* classes that provide the underlying functionality for building GUI-based applications. A

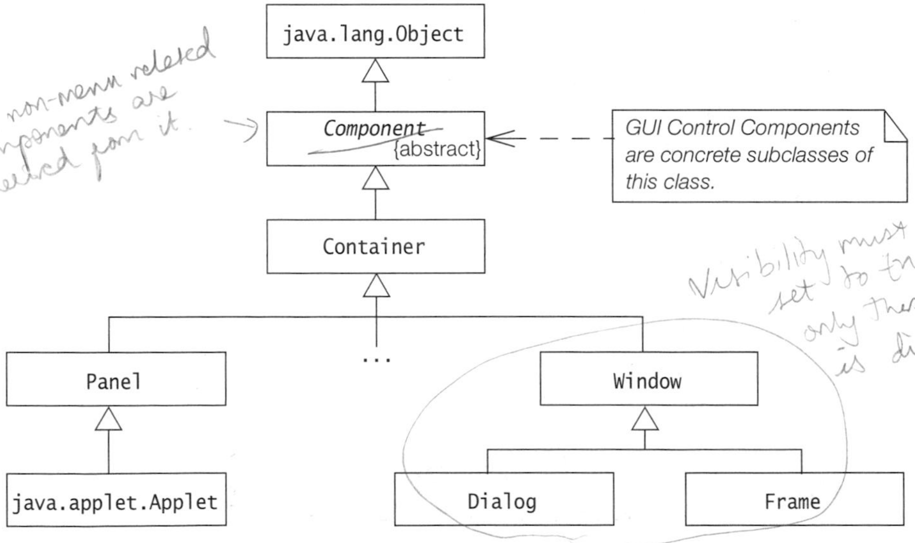

Figure 12.1 *Partial Inheritance Hierarchy of Components and Containers in AWT*

Table 12.1 *Components and Containers in AWT*

`Component`	The superclass of all non-menu-related components that provides basic support for handling of events, changing of component size, controlling of fonts and colors, and drawing of components and their contents.
`Container`	A container is a component that can accommodate other components and also other containers. Containers provide the support for building complex hierarchical graphical user interfaces.
`Panel`	A panel is a container ideal for packing other components and panels to build component hierarchies.
`Applet`	An applet is a specialized panel that can be used to develop programs that run in a web browser (Chapter 16).
`Window`	The `Window` class represents a top-level window that has no title, menus or borders.
`Frame`	A frame is an optionally user resizable and movable top-level window that can have a title-bar, an icon, and menus.
`Dialog`	The `Dialog` class defines an independent, optionally user resizable window that can only have a title-bar and a border. A `Dialog` window can be modal, meaning that all input is directed to this window until it is dismissed.

summary of these GUI containers is given in Table 12.1. The objects of these classes can be populated with *GUI control components* like buttons, checkboxes, lists and text fields to provide the right interface and interaction with the user. A summary of these GUI control components is given in Table 12.2 on page 360.

`Component` Class

All non-menu-related elements that comprise a graphical user interface are derived from the abstract class `Component`. The menu-related components are derived from the abstract class `MenuComponent`, which is discussed in Section 12.4.

The `Component` class specifies a large assortment of methods for handling events, changing window bounds, controlling fonts and colors, and drawing components and their contents. A component uses the visual properties (font face, background color, foreground color, etc.) of its parent container, unless set explicitly for the component.

The following common utility methods are provided by the `Component` class and its subclasses:

```
Dimension getSize()
void setSize(int width, int height)
void setSize(Dimension d)
```

The `getSize()` method can be used to get the size of a component in pixels. The return object is of type `Dimension`, which has two `public` data members `width` and `height`. The `setSize()` methods can be used to set the size of a component in pixels.

```
Point getLocation()
void setLocation(int x, int y)
void setLocation(Point p)
```

The `getLocation()` method returns the coordinates of the top-left corner of the component. The return object is of type `Point`, which has two `public` data members `x` and `y`. The `setLocation()` methods can be used to move the component to the specified coordinates.

```
Rectangle getBounds()
void setBounds(int x, int y, int width, int height)
void setBounds(Rectangle r)
```

The `getBounds()` method can be used to get the bounds of a component, i.e. both size and location. The return object is of type `Rectangle`, which has four `public` data members: `x`, `y`, `width` and `height`. The `setBounds()` methods can be used to set the bounds of a component.

```
void setForeground(Color c)
void setBackground(Color c)
```

The `setForeground()` method can be used to set the foreground color of a component. The `setBackground()` method can be used to set the background color of a component. The argument passed to both methods is a single object of the class `Color` (Section 15.2, p. 454). Normally the background color is used to fill the area occupied by the component, and text is rendered in the component's area using the foreground color.

A label can have blue as its background color and black as its foreground color, resulting in a blue label with black text. If foreground and background colors are not explicitly specified for a component, the corresponding values from this component's immediate container are used.

```
Font getFont()
void setFont(Font f)
```

The `getFont()` method returns the font used for rendering text in a component. The `setFont()` method can be used to set a particular font. Fonts are discussed in Section 15.3 on page 458.

```
void setEnabled(boolean b)
```

If the argument of this method is `true`, the component acts as normal, i.e. it is *enabled*, and can respond to user input and generate events. If the argument is `false`, then the component appears grayed out and does not respond to external stimuli. All components are initially enabled.

`void setVisible(boolean b)`

A component is either shown on the screen (i.e. visible) or hidden, depending on the argument to this method being either `true` or `false` respectively. It influences the visibility of the child components. Default visibility is `true` for all components except for `Window`, `Frame` and `Dialog` classes, whose instances must explicitly be made visible by this method.

Examples of usage of these methods can be found throughout this chapter. Several methods of the `Component` class are overridden by its concrete subclasses and are discussed where appropriate. Note that objects of *concrete* subclasses of the abstract `Component` class must be used to define a GUI.

`Container` Class

The class `Container` is a subclass of the abstract class `Component`. It defines methods for nesting components in a container; i.e. a container is a component that can accommodate other components, and thereby other containers, since a container is also a component by virtue of inheritance.

Containers provide the functionality for building complex hierarchical graphical user interfaces. They define a component hierarchy, in contrast to the inheritance hierarchy defined by classes. Containers provide the overloaded method `add()` to include components in a container. A container uses a layout manager to position its components, usually based on constraints given when components are added. These aspects are covered in Chapter 13.

`Panel` Class

The `Panel` class is a subclass of the `Container` class. It provides an intermediate level for GUI organization. A panel is a recursively nested container that is *not* a top-level window. It also does not have a title, menus or borders. It is therefore ideal for packing other components and panels to build component hierarchies using the inherited `add()` method.

`Applet` Class

The `Applet` class belongs to the `java.applet` package. It is a subclass of the `Panel` class and thus inherits its functionality. An applet is a specialized panel used to develop programs that run in a web browser. Applets are discussed in Chapter 16.

`Window` Class

The `Window` class represents a top-level window that is without a title, menus or borders. A top-level window cannot be incorporated into other components. The `Window` class is seldom used directly; instead, its two subclasses `Frame` and `Dialog` are used to provide independent top-level windows. The following methods should be noted:

`void pack()`

This method initiates the layout management of the subcomponents of the window, leading to the window size being set to match the preferred size of its subcomponents. The method is usually called after the component hierarchy has been constructed to facilitate the layout of the subcomponents in the window.

`void show()`

After the layout of the subcomponents in a window has been determined, the method `show()` can be used to make the window actually visible and bring it to the front of any other windows. Unlike other components, windows are initially hidden. Note that the `setVisible()` method from the `Component` class can be used to make a window visible, without bringing it to the front.

`void dispose()`

When a window is no longer needed, this method should be called to free the windowing resources. Although this does not actually delete the window object, the window object should not be used after a call to this method.

`Frame` Class

The `Frame` class is a subclass of the `Window` class. It is used to create what we usually mean by a GUI-application window. A frame is an optionally user resizable and movable top-level window that can have a title-bar, an icon, and menus. A `Frame` object is usually the starting point of a GUI application, and serves as the root of the component hierarchy. A `Frame` object can contain several panels which in turn can hold other GUI control components and other nested panels.

The `Frame` class defines two constructors:

```
Frame()
Frame(String title)
```

Both constructors create an initially invisible frame. The argument in the second constructor specifies the frame title.

A typical scenario for building the GUI is the following:

1. Create the frame:

   ```
   Frame guiFrame = new Frame("My Frame");
   ```

2. Construct the component hierarchy by adding panels and other GUI control components.

   ```
   guiFrame.add(new Button("OK"));
   ```

3. Set the size of the frame by using the inherited `setSize()` method.

   ```
   guiFrame.setSize(200, 300);
   ```

4. Pack the frame by calling the `pack()` method:

```
guiFrame.pack();
```

5. Make the frame (and its constituents) visible by calling the `setVisible()` method:

```
guiFrame.setVisible(true);
```

Examples of GUI building using the AWT are provided in Chapter 13 and Chapter 14.

`Dialog` Class

The `Dialog` class is a subclass of the `Window` class. The class defines an optionally user resizable and movable top-level window with a title-bar. Unlike a `Frame`, a dialog window does not have an icon or a menu-bar. Such a window is usually called a *dialog box*. Like a frame, a dialog box serves as a container and can be the root of a component hierarchy.

A `Dialog` window can be *modal*, meaning that all input is directed to its window until it is dismissed. A non-modal `Dialog` window, on the other hand, allows input to other windows to be accepted while it is still visible.

The `Dialog` class defines several constructors:

```
Dialog(Frame parent)
Dialog(Frame parent, boolean modal)
Dialog(Frame parent, String title)
Dialog(Frame parent, String title, boolean modal)
```

All constructors create an initially invisible dialog box. Note that a dialog box is created as a child component of a `Frame` object. Some constructors allow the title of the dialog box to be specified, and some also allow the modality to be specified. A `Dialog` box is non-modal by default.

Usage of a dialog box is similar to that of a frame, but it is normally used as a temporary window to obtain input from the user.

Review questions

12.1 Which of these methods can be used to manipulate the bounds of a `Component` object?

Select all valid answers.

(a) `setSize()`
(b) `setDimensions()`
(c) `setBounds()`
(d) `setLocation()`
(e) `setPosition()`

12.2 In which class is the method `setVisible()` first defined?

Select the one right answer.

(a) `Component`
(b) `Container`
(c) `Window`
(d) `Dialog`
(e) `Frame`

12.3 Which of the labeled lines can be omitted from the following code without affecting the program?

```
import java.awt.*;

public class MyClass extends Frame {
    Button button = new Button("Button");

    MyClass() {
        super("Test button");
        add(button, BorderLayout.CENTER);
        button.setVisible(true);          // (1)
        pack();                           // (2)
        setVisible(true);                 // (3)
    }

    public static void main(String[] args) {
        new MyClass();
    }
}
```

Select the one right answer.

(a) The line labeled (1).
(b) The line labeled (2).
(c) The line labeled (3).
(d) The lines labeled (1) and (3).
(e) None of the lines can be omitted.

12.4 In which class is the method `pack()` first defined?

Select the one right answer.

(a) `Component`
(b) `Container`
(c) `Window`
(d) `Dialog`
(e) `Frame`

12.5 What will be the result of attempting to compile and run the following program?

See Answer

```
import java.awt.*;

public class DialogTest {
    public static void main(String args[]) {
```

```
        Dialog dialog = new Dialog("Hello");
        dialog.pack();
        dialog.setVisible(true);
    }
}
```

Select the one right answer.

(a) The program will fail to compile, since the `Dialog` class does not have an appropriate constructor.
(b) The program will fail to compile, since the `Dialog` class does not have a method named `setVisible(true)`.
(c) The program will compile without error, but will throw an exception during execution since no owner has been set for the `Dialog`.
(d) The program will compile without error, but might show a dialog with an erratic size.
(e) The program will compile without error, and will show a dialog with the size of 200 by 200 pixels.

12.6 Which one of the following classes represents a top-level window with a title and border decorations?

Select the one right answer.

(a) `Container`
(b) `Panel`
(c) `Window`
(d) `Frame`

12.3 GUI Control Components

GUI control components are the primary elements of a graphical user interface that enable interaction with the user. They are all concrete subclasses of the `Component` class, and are summarized in Table 12.2.

GUI control components for constructing menus are derived from the abstract class `MenuComponent` and are discussed in Section 12.4.

The following three steps are essential in making use of a GUI control component:

1. A GUI control component is created by calling the appropriate constructor.

   ```
   Button guiComponent = new Button("OK");
   ```

2. The GUI control component is added to a container using a layout manager. This usually involves invoking the overloaded method `add()` on a container with the GUI control component as the argument:

   ```
   guiFrame.add(guiComponent);
   ```

   Details of constructing component hierarchies can be found with the discussion on layout management in Chapter 13.

3. *Listeners* are registered with the GUI component, so that they can receive events when these occur. GUI components generate particular events in response to user actions. The event model is discussed in Chapter 14.

Table 12.2 *GUI Control Components in AWT*

`Button`	A button with a textual label, designed to invoke an action when pushed, called a push button.
`Canvas`	A generic component for drawing and designing new GUI components.
`Checkbox`	A checkbox with a textual label that can be toggled on and off. Checkboxes can be grouped to represent radio buttons.
`Choice`	A component that provides a pop-up menu of choices. Only the current choice is visible in the `Choice` component.
`Label`	A label is a component that displays a single line of read-only, non-selectable text.
`List`	A component that defines a scrollable list of text items.
`Scrollbar`	A slider to denote a position or a value.
`TextField`	A component that implements a single line of optionally editable text.
`TextArea`	A component that implements multiple lines of optionally editable text.

Running the Examples

Each GUI control component is described below. Discussion on layout management and event handling for components is deferred to Chapter 13 and Chapter 14, respectively. The emphasis here is on functionality and graphical representation of components. The appearance of a component is dependent on the native windowing system, but is nevertheless easily identifiable.

Since these control component classes are subclasses of the `Component` class, they all generate keyboard and mouse events. However, in the discussion below, only events specific to each component are mentioned.

Examples of GUI components, presented in the subsequent sections, are written as applets. Details on applets can be found in Chapter 16. An applet overrides the `init()` method, which is executed when the applet is started, and the `paint()` method which is invoked when the screen needs updating. The `add()` method is used to add components to the applet. The following generic HTML file can be modified to run the examples in a web browser or using an applet viewer. Only the appropriate class name (here `AppletClassName`) for the applet needs to be changed.

```
<!-- HTML file to run an applet -->
<!-- Change AppletClassName as appropriate. -->

<title>GUI Control Component</title>
<hr>
<applet code="AppletClassName.class" width=200 height=200> </applet>
<hr>
```

Button

The `Button` class demonstrates a push-button that can only have a textual label.

```
Button()
Button(String label)
```

These constructors are used for creating buttons.

```
String getLabel()
void setLabel(String label)
```

These methods can be used to get and set the textual label.

Example 12.1 implements a push button which is shown in Figure 12.2.

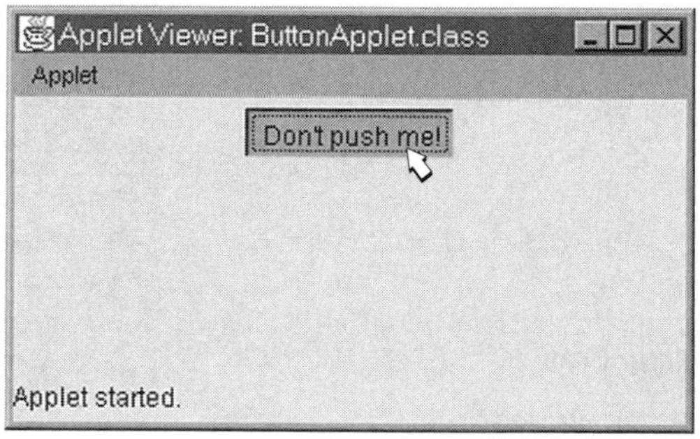

Figure 12.2 *Button*

Example 12.1 *Illustrating Button*

```
import java.awt.*;
import java.applet.*;

public class ButtonApplet extends Applet {
    public void init() {
        Button button = new Button("Don't push me!");
        add(button);
    }
}
```

Canvas

A Canvas class provides the ability to construct generic GUI components. The class does not have any default graphical representation, or any event handlers of its own. It inherits these capabilities from its superclass Component. The Canvas class is usually subclassed to construct customized GUI components consisting of drawings or images, and can handle user input events relating to mouse and keyboard actions. Its paint() method is usually overridden to render graphics in the component.

Example 12.2 demonstrates a rectangular drawing region on a canvas, which is shown in Figure 12.3.

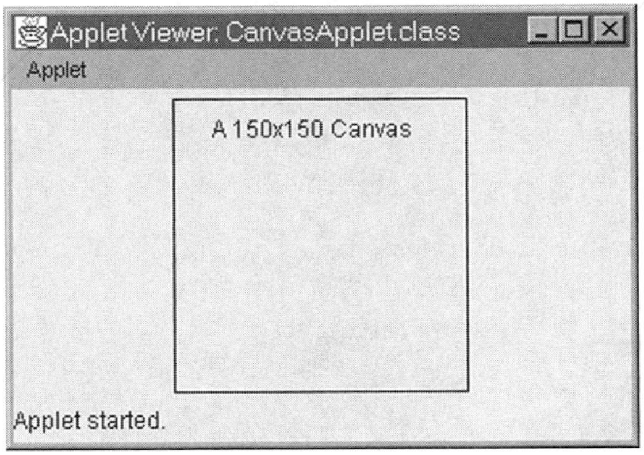

Figure 12.3 *Canvas*

Example 12.2 *Illustrating Canvas*

```
import java.awt.*;
import java.applet.*;

public class CanvasApplet extends Applet {
    public void init() {
        DrawingRegion region = new DrawingRegion();
        add(region);
    }
}

class DrawingRegion extends Canvas {
    public DrawingRegion() {
        setSize(150,150);
    }
    public void paint(Graphics g) {
        g.drawRect(0,0,149,149);                     // draw border around region
        g.drawString("A 150x150 Canvas", 20,20);  // draw a string
    }
}
```

Checkbox **and** CheckboxGroup

The `Checkbox` class implements a GUI checkbox with a textual label. A `Checkbox` object can be in one of two states:

- `true` – meaning that it is checked.
- `false` – meaning that it is unchecked.

The `Checkbox` class has the following constructors:

```
Checkbox()
Checkbox(String label)
Checkbox(String label, boolean state)
Checkbox(String label, boolean state, CheckboxGroup group)
```

If the state is not explicitly specified in the appropriate constructor, the initial state is unchecked. The state of the checkbox can be toggled by clicking on the checkbox.

A checkbox can be incorporated in a `CheckboxGroup` to implement radio buttons, as explained below. Unless the `CheckboxGroup` is specified in the appropriate constructor, the checkbox is not part of any `CheckboxGroup`.

Example 12.3 demonstrates usage of a checkbox as illustrated in Figure 12.4.

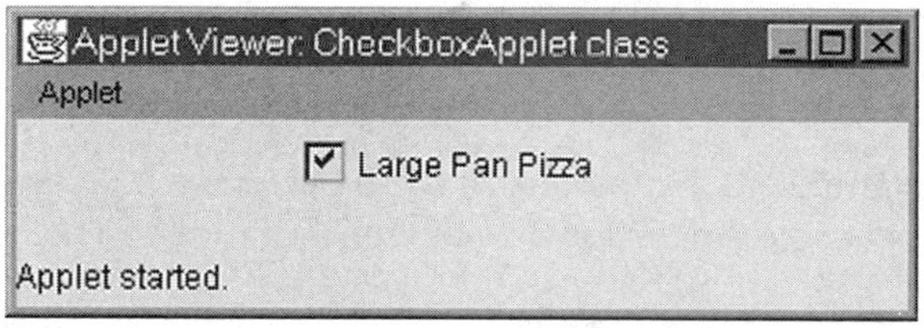

Figure 12.4 *Checkbox*

Example 12.3 *Illustrating Checkbox*

```
import java.awt.*;
import java.applet.*;

public class CheckboxApplet extends Applet {
    public void init() {
        Checkbox option = new Checkbox("Large Pan Pizza");
        option.setState(true);
        add(option);
    }
}
```

```
boolean getState()
void setState(boolean state)
```

These methods read and change the state of a checkbox.

```
String getLabel()
void setLabel(String label)
```

These methods read and change the textual label of a checkbox.

```
CheckboxGroup getCheckboxGroup()
void setCheckboxGroup(CheckboxGroup g)
```

These methods read and change the `CheckboxGroup` of a checkbox.

The class `java.awt.CheckboxGroup` can be used to control the behavior of a group of checkboxes. Such a group only allows a single selection (meaning only one checkbox is checked at any given time). Clicking on a different checkbox in a group automatically unchecks the previous checkbox. Such mutually exclusive checkboxes are often called radio buttons. Membership in a `CheckboxGroup` is usually specified when the `Checkbox` is created.

The following methods return the currently selected checkbox and set a particular checkbox as the current selection in a `CheckboxGroup`:

```
Checkbox getSelectedCheckbox()
void setSelectedCheckbox(Checkbox box)
```

Note that a `CheckboxGroup` object does not have a graphical representation, and is not a subclass of `Component`. The `CheckboxGroup` is just a class to implement mutual exclusion among a set of checkboxes. A recommended practice is to set one of the checkboxes in a checkbox group, to provide a default selection.

Example 12.4 implements radio buttons which are shown in Figure 12.5. Only one checkbox can be checked at any given time in a checkbox group.

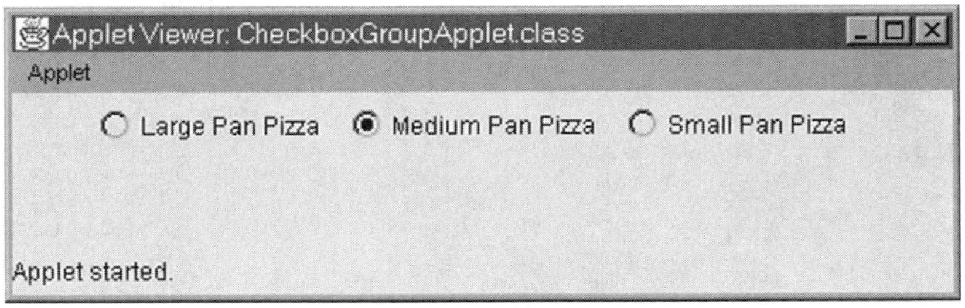

Figure 12.5 *Radio Buttons*

Example 12.4 *Illustrating Radio Buttons*

```
import java.awt.*;
import java.applet.*;

public class CheckboxGroupApplet extends Applet {
    public void init() {
        // create a radio button controller
        CheckboxGroup pizzaGroup = new CheckboxGroup();
```

```
            // create the individual checkboxes
            Checkbox cbLarge  = new Checkbox("Large Pan Pizza", pizzaGroup, false);
            Checkbox cbMedium = new Checkbox("Medium Pan Pizza", true, pizzaGroup);
            Checkbox cbSmall  = new Checkbox("Small Pan Pizza" , false);
            cbSmall.setCheckboxGroup(pizzaGroup);
            // Add the checkboxes to the applet.
            add(cbLarge);
            add(cbMedium);
            add(cbSmall);
        }
    }
```

Choice

The Choice class implements a pop-up menu of choices. Only the current choice is visible in a Choice component. The choice can be changed by "popping-up" the list of choices by clicking on the menu and selecting another item on the choice list.

Constructing a pop-up menu of choices involves the following steps:

1. Creating a Choice object using the single default constructor provided.
2. Adding the items using the add() method. Note that the items in the pop-up menu are strings.

```
void add(String item)
```

Various accessor methods are defined for pop-up menus:

`int getItemCount()`

Returns the number of items in the pop-up menu.

`String getItem(int index)`

Returns the item at a particular index in the pop-up menu. Start index is 0.

`String getSelectedItem()`

Returns the currently selected item in the pop-up menu.

`int getSelectedIndex()`

Returns the index of the currently selected item in the pop-up menu.

`void select(int pos)`

Makes the item at the given position in the pop-up menu the current choice.

`void select(String str)`

Makes the item with the argument string in the pop-up menu the current choice.

The `Choice` class also defines methods for inserting and removing items from the pop-up menu.

Example 12.5 demonstrates a choice, i.e. a pop-up menu, which is shown "popped up" in Figure 12.6.

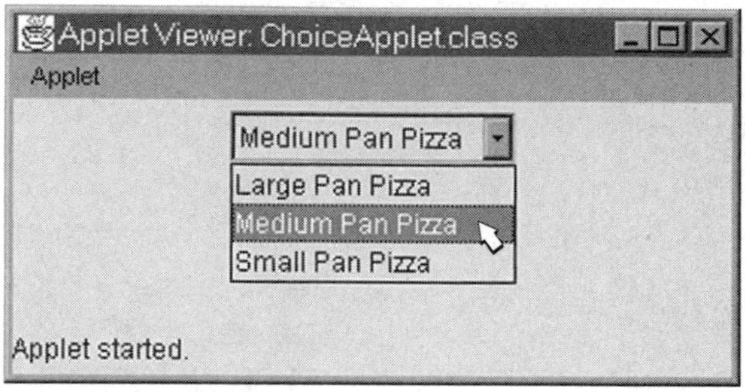

Figure 12.6 *Choice*

Example 12.5 *Illustrating Choice*

```
import java.awt.*;
import java.applet.*;

public class ChoiceApplet extends Applet {
    public void init() {
        Choice pizzaChoice = new Choice();
        pizzaChoice.add("Large Pan Pizza");
        pizzaChoice.add("Medium Pan Pizza");
        pizzaChoice.add("Small Pan Pizza");
        add(pizzaChoice);
        pizzaChoice.select("Medium Pan Pizza");
    }
}
```

Label

A label is a component that displays a single line of read-only, non-selectable text. It does not generate any special events. The `Label` class defines three constructors for creating labels:

```
Label()
Label(String text)
Label(String text, int alignment)
```

The alignment of the label in a container can be specified by the following constants of the `Label` class. The default alignment is left.

```
public static final int LEFT
public static final int CENTER
public static final int RIGHT
```

The `Label` class defines accessor methods for reading the current text and changing the text in a label:

```
String getText()
void setText(String text)
```

There are also accessor methods for reading the current alignment and setting a particular alignment for a label:

```
int getAlignment()
void setAlignment(int alignment)
```

Example 12.6 demonstrate two labels, one with default (left) alignment and another centered, both shown in Figure 12.7. A `GridLayout` manager is used to place the components (Section 13.4, p. 389).

Figure 12.7 *Labels*

Example 12.6 *Illustrating Labels*

```
import java.awt.*;
import java.applet.*;

public class LabelApplet extends Applet {
    public void init() {
        setLayout(new GridLayout(2,1));                         // 2 rows, 1 column
        add(new Label("A sticky label"));                       // top row
        // center next label
        add(new Label("One more sticky label", Label.CENTER)); // bottom row
    }
}
```

List

The `List` class implements a scrollable list of text items. Since the list is scrollable, the number of items that can be visible in the list box is defined as the number of rows in the list. The list can of course have any number of text items, and a scrollbar appears when necessary to scroll the list.

Clicking on an item toggles selection and deselection of the item. A list can be constructed to allow either a single selection or multiple selections.

A `List` object can be created using one of the following constructors, with options for specifying the number of rows (the number of visible items or lines as opposed to the total number of items) and multiple selection mode.

```
List()
List(int rows)
List(int rows, boolean multipleMode)
```

Constructing a list involves the following steps:

1. Creating a `List` object, optionally specifying the number of rows and multiple selection mode.
2. Adding the items using the `add()` method. The items added are strings.

```
void add(String item)
void add(String item, int index)
```

Various accessor methods are defined for scrollable lists:

`int getRows()`

Returns the number of rows in the list.

`boolean isMultipleMode()`

Returns `true` if multiple selections are allowed in the list.

`int getItemCount()`

Returns the number of items (as opposed to rows) in the list.

`String getItem(int index)`

Returns the item at a particular index in the list.

`String[] getItems()`

Returns the items in the list.

`String getSelectedItem()`

Returns the selected item if one is selected, otherwise returns the `null` value.

`String[] getSelectedItems()`

Returns the selected items if any, otherwise returns the `null` value.

`int getSelectedIndex()`

Returns the index of the selected item if one is selected, otherwise returns the value -1.

`void select(int index)`

Selects the item at the given index in the list.

`void select(String str)`
Selects the item that matches the argument string in the list.

`void deselect(int index)`
Deselects the item at the given index in the list.

The `List` class also defines methods for changing, inserting and removing items.

Example 12.7 demonstrates a list with three rows, shown in Figure 12.8. A scrollbar appears automatically when there are more items in the list than the number of rows.

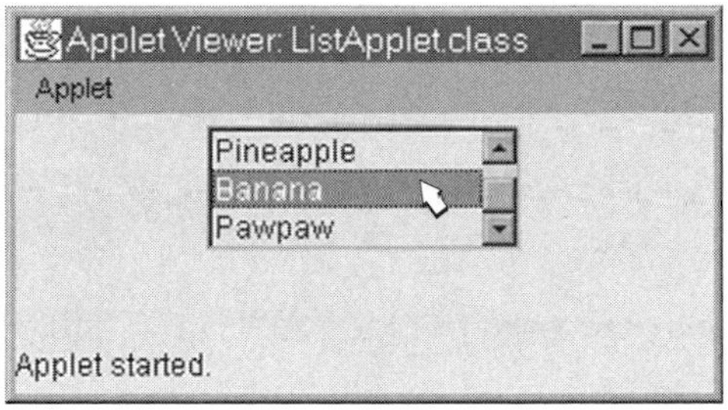

Figure 12.8 *List*

Example 12.7 *Illustrating List*

```
import java.awt.*;
import java.applet.*;

public class ListApplet extends Applet {
    public void init() {
        String[] fruit = {"Mango", "Pineapple", "Banana", "Pawpaw"};
        List fruitList = new List(fruit.length -1, true);
        for (int i=0; i<fruit.length; i++) {
            fruitList.add(fruit[i]);
        }
        add(fruitList);
    }
}
```

Scrollbar

A document window in a text processor usually has two scrollbars. A vertical scrollbar to scroll up (making visible contents towards the top of the document) and down (making visible contents towards the end of the document). A horizontal scrollbar similarly scrolls the document left and right. A scrollbar thus indicates the relative position of the visible contents in relation to the whole document. This is one typical use of scrollbars. A scrollbar can also be used as a controller to specify a value from a given interval. Note that most GUI control components (for example, `List, TextArea`) that need scrollbars create them when necessary.

The following features of scrollbars should be noted:

- A scrollbar has an orientation that can be either horizontal or vertical. Vertical orientation is the default.
- A scrollbar has a *slider* that, by its position, indicates the current value in the range represented by the scrollbar. The slider can be moved on the scrollbar.
- A scrollbar has two gadgets (usually arrowheads at the ends of the scrollbar). Clicking on such an arrowhead scrolls one unit. The default unit size is 1.
- Clicking on the area between an arrowhead and the slider scrolls by one block. The default block size is 10 units.

The `Scrollbar` class provides two constants to indicate orientation:

```
public static final int HORIZONTAL
public static final int VERTICAL
```

Three constructors provide various ways to create scrollbars:

```
Scrollbar()
Scrollbar(int orientation)
Scrollbar(int orientation, int value, int visible,
          int minimum, int maximum)
```

The `visible` argument is used to determine the visible width of the slider. The `value` argument specifies the initial position of the slider in the scrollbar. The arguments `minimum` and `maximum` specify the interval represented by the scrollbar, i.e. the values at the ends.

The class `Scrollbar` defines an assortment of accessor methods:

```
int getValue()
```

Returns the current value of the scrollbar.

```
void setValue(int newValue)
```

Sets the value of the scrollbar to the argument value.

```
int getMinimum()
```

Returns the minimum value of the scrollbar.

```
void setMinimum(int newMinimum)
```

Sets the minimum value for the scrollbar.

```
int getMaximum()
```

Returns the maximum value of the scrollbar.

```
void setMaximum(int newMaximum)
```

Sets the maximum value for the scrollbar.

`int getVisibleAmount()`

Returns the visible amount of the scrollbar.

`void setVisibleAmount(int newAmount)`

Sets the visible amount of the scrollbar, that is, the range of values represented by the width of the scrollbar's slider.

`int getUnitIncrement()`

Returns the unit increment for the scrollbar.

`void setUnitIncrement(int v)`

Sets the unit increment for the scrollbar.

`int getBlockIncrement()`

Gets the block increment for the scrollbar.

`void setBlockIncrement(int v)`

Sets the block increment for the scrollbar.

Example 12.8 implements a scrollbar. Figure 12.9 illustrates the parts of a scrollbar.

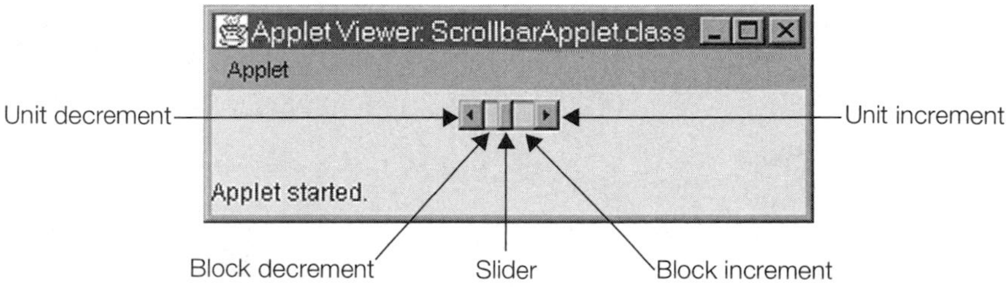

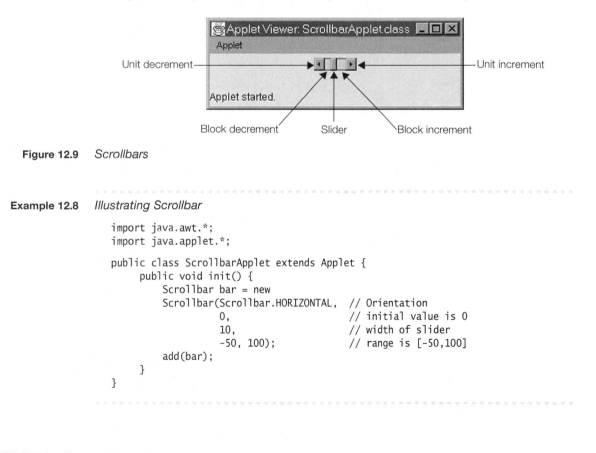

Figure 12.9 *Scrollbars*

Example 12.8 *Illustrating Scrollbar*

```
import java.awt.*;
import java.applet.*;

public class ScrollbarApplet extends Applet {
     public void init() {
         Scrollbar bar = new
         Scrollbar(Scrollbar.HORIZONTAL,  // Orientation
                   0,                     // initial value is 0
                   10,                    // width of slider
                   -50, 100);             // range is [-50,100]
         add(bar);
     }
}
```

`TextField` and `TextArea`

The class `TextComponent` provides the functionality for selecting and editing text. Its two subclasses `TextField` and `TextArea` inherit this functionality to implement a single line of text or multiple lines of text, respectively. The text in the component can be read-only or editable.

The `TextField` class implements a single line of optionally editable text. The size of the text field is measured in *columns*. Some initial text and a preferred size can be specified when a text field is created.

```
TextField()
TextField(String text)
TextField(int columns)
TextField(String text, int columns)
```

Example 12.9 demonstrates a text field with column length 18, in which the text is rendered in 12 pt Serif plain font. Figure 12.10 shows the text field with its initial contents.

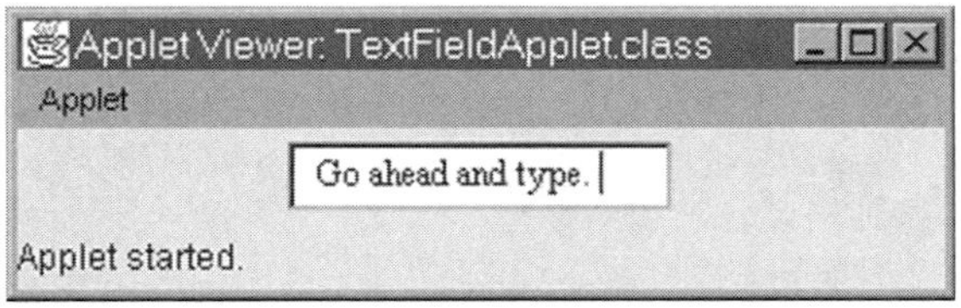

Figure 12.10 *Text Field*

Example 12.9 *Illustrating Text Field*

```
import java.awt.*;
import java.applet.*;

public class TextFieldApplet extends Applet {
    public void init() {
        TextField entryField = new TextField(18);
        entryField.setFont(new Font("Serif", Font.PLAIN, 12));
        entryField.setText("Go ahead and type.");
        add(entryField);
    }
}
```

The `TextArea` class implements multiple lines of optionally editable text. These lines are separated by the `'\n'` (newline) character. The size of the text area is measured in columns and rows. When creating text areas, the initial text and the preferred size of the component can be specified. Constructors provide various ways of creating a text area.

```
TextArea()
TextArea(String text)
TextArea(int rows, int columns)
TextArea(String text, int rows, int columns)
TextArea(String text, int rows, int columns, int scrollbars)
```

```
public static final int SCROLLBARS_BOTH
public static final int SCROLLBARS_VERTICAL_ONLY
public static final int SCROLLBARS_HORIZONTAL_ONLY
public static final int SCROLLBARS_NONE
```

The value of the `scrollbars` argument can be any of the above constants defined in the `TextArea` class.

Both `TextField` and `TextArea` provide the following two methods:

```
int getColumns()
void setColumns(int columns)
```

These accessor methods read and set the number of columns in a text field or a text area.

The `TextComponent` class does not provide any `public` constructors and is therefore uninstantiable. Its two subclasses `TextField` and `TextArea` inherit the following methods:

```
String getText()
void setText(String t)
```

These accessor methods read and set the text in a text field or a text area.

```
String getSelectedText()
```

This method returns the selected portion of the text in a text field or a text area.

```
boolean isEditable()
void setEditable(boolean b)
```

The first method returns whether the text is editable or not, and the second method sets the text to be editable depending on the value of its argument.

Example 12.10 demonstrates a text area with ten rows and six columns, in which the text is rendered in 12 pt monospaced plain font. Figure 12.11 shows the text area with its initial contents. In this example, the text cannot be edited, but it can be selected.

Example 12.10 *Illustrating Text Area*

```
import java.awt.*;
import java.applet.*;

public class TextAreaApplet extends Applet {
    public void init() {
        TextArea display = new TextArea(10, 6);  // rows, columns
        display.setFont(new Font("Monospaced", Font.PLAIN, 12));
```

```
            display.setText("Mono\n123456\nBanana\n");
            display.setEditable(false);
            add(display);
        }
    }
```

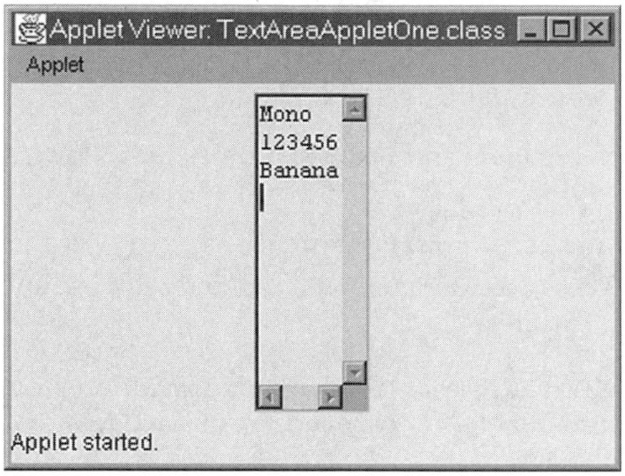

Figure 12.11 *Text Area*

The number of columns is a measure of the size of the text line according to the particular font used for rendering the text. A 30-column text line rendered in a small font size could appear narrow, while a 5-column text line in a large font could be quite wide.

For fixed pitch fonts, the number of columns is equal to the number of characters in the text line. For proportional (variable) pitch fonts, the column width is taken to be the average character width of the font used for rendering the text. It is always advisable to make the size a few columns larger than the expected number of characters in the text area.

The size that is specified for a text field and a text area is not the absolute size of the component. The component might allow longer strings to be typed than the line size specified. For a text area, it might additionally allow more lines than the specified rows. The arrow keys can be used to move the cursor in a text component, and the text will scroll to keep the cursor visible.

Example 12.11 implements a GUI with three text areas, each with four rows and six columns, in which the text is rendered in 18 pt plain font. The first text area uses a fixed-pitch font, while the remaining two use variable pitch fonts. As can be seen in Figure 12.12, the actual length of the same text lines (i.e. columns) varies depending on the kind of font used, and scrollbars automatically appear if necessary.

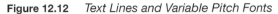

Figure 12.12 *Text Lines and Variable Pitch Fonts*

Example 12.11 *Illustrating Text Lines and Variable Pitch Fonts*

```
import java.awt.*;
import java.applet.*;

public class TextAreaAppletTwo extends Applet {
    public void init() {
        TextArea display1 = new TextArea(4, 6);      // rows, columns
        display1.setFont(new Font("Monospaced", Font.PLAIN, 18));
        display1.setText("Mono\n123456\nBanana\n");

        TextArea display2 = new TextArea(4, 6);      // rows, columns
        display2.setFont(new Font("Serif", Font.PLAIN, 18));
        display2.setText("Serif\n123456\nBanana\n");

        TextArea display3 = new TextArea(4, 6);      // rows, columns
        display3.setFont(new Font("SansSerif", Font.PLAIN, 18));
        display3.setText("Sans\n123456\nBanana\n");

        add(display1);
        add(display2);
        add(display3);
    }
}
```

Review questions

12.7 Which of the following classes are subclasses of the `Component` class?

Select all valid answers.

(a) `List`
(b) `Applet`
(c) `CheckboxGroup`
(d) `MenuItem`
(e) `Container`

12.8 What is the name of the method that should be used to change the color of the text in a `Label` component?

Select the one right answer.

(a) `setBackground()`
(b) `setForeground()`
(c) `setText()`
(d) `setColor()`
(e) `setFont()`

12.9 How can the number of columns to display in a `TextArea` component be specified?

Select all valid answers.

(a) Call a `setLine()` method on the `TextArea` component.
(b) Call a `setWidth()` method on the `TextArea` component.
(c) Call a `setColumns()` method on the `TextArea` component.
(d) Specify the number of columns as an argument to the constructor of `TextArea`.
(e) Specifying the number of columns to display in a `TextArea` component is not possible unless you subclass the `TextArea` class.

12.10 How can the number of items that should be visible in a `List` component be specified?

Select all valid answers.

(a) Call a `setLines()` method on the `List` component.
(b) Call a `setRows()` method on the `List` component.
(c) Specify the number of items as an argument to the constructor of `List`.
(d) Specifying the number of items to display in a `List` component is not possible unless you subclass the `List` class.

12.11 Which checkboxes will initially be selected when the following program is run?

```
import java.awt.*;

public class MyClass extends Frame {
    MyClass() {
        CheckboxGroup cbGroup1 = new CheckboxGroup(),
                      cbGroup2 = new CheckboxGroup();
        CheckboxGroup[] groups = { cbGroup1, cbGroup1, cbGroup2, cbGroup2, null };
        setLayout(new FlowLayout());
        for (int i=0; i<groups.length; i++) add(
            new Checkbox("box"+i, true, groups[i])
        );

        pack();
        setVisible(true);
    }
```

```
        public static void main(String[] args) {
            new MyClass();
        }
    }
```

Select the one right answer.

(a) All checkboxes.
(b) None of the checkboxes.
(c) Only the checkbox labeled `box0`.
(d) The checkboxes labeled `box0`, `box2` and `box4`.
(e) The checkboxes labeled `box1`, `box3` and `box4`.

12.12 How can it be specified that a `TextArea` should only have a vertical scrollbar?

Select all valid answers.

(a) Send an instance of a scrollbar with vertical orientation as an argument to the constructor of `TextArea`.
(b) Send `TextArea.SCROLLBARS_VERTICAL_ONLY` as an argument to the constructor of `TextArea`.
(c) Call `setScrollbarVisibility(TextArea.SCROLLBARS_VERTICAL_ONLY)` on the `TextArea` instance.
(d) None of the methods above will work.

12.13 Which of the following approaches for selecting an item in a `Choice` component will work?

Select all valid answers.

(a) Calling a method `setSelected()` on the `Choice` component.
(b) Calling a method `select()` on the `Choice` component.
(c) Calling a method `selected()` on the `Choice` component.
(d) Retrieving an item object using a method name called `getItem` on the `Choice` component, and then calling a method named `select` on the item object.
(e) Passing an argument to the constructor of `Choice`, telling it which item should be selected.

12.4 Menu Components

The abstract class `MenuComponent` is the superclass of all menu-related classes.

The `MenuBar` class implements a menu-bar that can contain pull-down menus. The pull-down menus are `Menu` objects. The `add()` method can be used to add menus to a menu-bar, and the `remove()` method can be used to remove menus from a menu-bar. A menu-bar can be attached to a `Frame` object. Note that an applet is not a subclass of the `Frame` class, and therefore cannot have a menu-bar.

The `MenuItem` class defines a menu item that has a textual label. A keyboard shortcut can also be defined for a menu item.

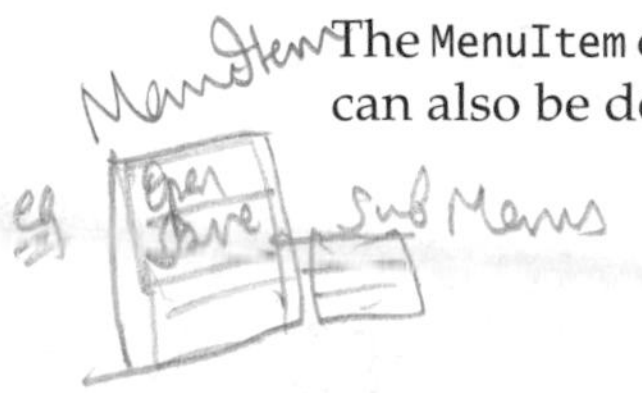

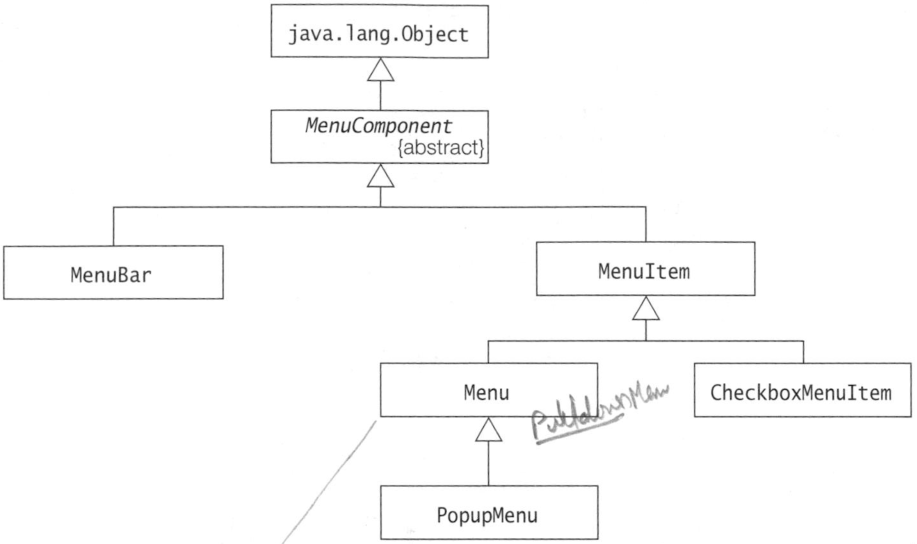

Figure 12.13 *Inheritance Hierarchy of Menu Components and Containers in AWT*

The `Menu` class implements a pull-down menu that can appear in a menu-bar. A `Menu` is a container of `MenuItem` objects. Since a `Menu` is also a `MenuItem`, menus can be nested to create submenus. The `Menu` class defines methods for inserting and removing items from a menu. A menu item can be added using the `add()` method. A separator (i.e. a visible horizontal mark for organizing menu items into sections) can be added using the `addSeparator()` method.

The `PopupMenu` class represents a pop-up menu that can be popped up at a specified position within a component, as opposed to a pull-down menu represented by its superclass `Menu`. A pop-up menu can be added to a component using the `add(PopupMenu popup)` method defined in the `Component` class. Since they are pop-up menus, they cannot be contained in a menu-bar.

The `CheckboxMenuItem` class implements a checkbox with a textual label that can appear in a menu. The menu checkbox toggles its state when clicked, just like an ordinary checkbox.

The following steps can be followed to create a menu-bar for a frame:

1. Create a menu-bar.

   ```
   MenuBar foodBar = new MenuBar();
   ```

2. Create a menu.

   ```
   Menu pizzaMenu = new Menu("Pizza Menu");
   ```

3. Create menu items and add them to the menu. The menu items appear from top to bottom in the menu, according to the order in which they are added to the menu. The following elements can be added to a menu:

- `MenuItem` objects, such as `CheckboxMenuItem` objects and `Menu` objects (i.e. submenus)
- Separators

```
pizzaMenu.add(new MenuItem("Large Pan Pizza"));
pizzaMenu.addSeparator();
pizzaMenu.add(new MenuItem("Medium Pan Pizza"));
pizzaMenu.addSeparator();
pizzaMenu.add(new CheckboxMenuItem("Small Pan Pizza"));
```

4. Add each menu to the menu-bar. The menus appear from left to right in the menu-bar, according to the order in which they are added to the menu-bar.

```
foodBar.add(pizzaMenu);
```

5. Add the menu-bar to the frame.

```
Frame fastFood = new Frame("Fast Food");
fastFood.setMenuBar(foodBar);
```

Example 12.12 illustrates the steps given above for constructing menus. The GUI is shown in Figure 12.14, with the menu opened from the menu-bar.

Steps
1) MenuItems added to Menus
2) Menus added to MenuBar
3) MenuBar added to Frames

Figure 12.14 *Menus*

Example 12.12 *Illustrating Menus*

```
import java.awt.*;
import java.applet.*;

public class MenuDemo {
    public static void main(String args[]) {
        MenuBar foodBar = new MenuBar();                          // (1)
        Menu pizzaMenu = new Menu("Pizza Menu");                  // (2)
        pizzaMenu.add(new MenuItem("Large Pan Pizza"));           // (3)
        pizzaMenu.addSeparator();
        pizzaMenu.add(new MenuItem("Medium Pan Pizza"));
        pizzaMenu.addSeparator();
        pizzaMenu.add(new CheckboxMenuItem("Small Pan Pizza"));
        foodBar.add(pizzaMenu);                                   // (4)
```

```
            Frame fastFood = new Frame("Fast Food");                // (5)
            fastFood.setMenuBar(foodBar);
            fastFood.pack();
            fastFood.setVisible(true);
        }
    }
```

Review questions

12.14 Which of these classes can have instances that can be added to a `Panel` component?

Select all valid answers.

(a) `Button`
(b) `Panel`
(c) `MenuBar`
(d) `PopupMenu`
(e) `Window`

12.15 Which of these classes can have instances that can be added to a `Canvas` component?

Select all valid answers.

(a) `Button`
(b) `Panel`
(c) `MenuBar`
(d) `PopupMenu`

12.16 Which of these classes can have instances that can be added to a `Menu` instance?

Select all valid answers.

(a) `MenuItem`
(b) `Menu`
(c) `Checkbox`
(d) `CheckboxMenuItem`
(e) `MenuBar`

12.17 What types of parameters can be given to `add()` methods in the `Component` class?

Select all valid answers.

(a) `Component`
(b) `MenuComponent`
(c) `Menu`
(d) `MenuItem`
(e) `PopupMenu`

12.18 Which one of these classes is used to create submenus in pull-down menus?

Select the one right answer.

(a) `MenuBar`
(b) `Menu`
(c) `MenuItem`
(d) `SubMenu`
(e) `PopupMenu`

Chapter summary

The following information was included in this chapter:

- Discussion of the `Component` class and of the GUI *container* classes (`Container`, `Panel`, `Window`, `Frame`, `Dialog`) in the `java.awt` package.
- Discussion of the GUI *non-menu-related control components* in the `java.awt` package: `Button`, `Canvas`, `Checkbox`, `Choice`, `Label`, `List`, `Scrollbar`, `TextField`, `TextArea`.
- Discussion of the GUI *menu-related components* in the `java.awt` package: `MenuComponent`, `MenuBar`, `MenuItem`, `Menu`, `CheckboxMenuItem`, `PopupMenu`.
- Emphasis has been on graphical representation of GUI components.

Programming exercise

12.1 Create a program that shows the text from this exercise in a text area. Make the size of the frame containing the text area 200 by 200 pixels. The text area should not have any scrollbars and the text should not be editable. Make the text appear as yellow lettering on a black background.

13 Layout Management

Exam Objectives

- Write code using component, container and layout manager classes of the `java.awt` package to present a GUI with specified appearance and resize behavior, and distinguish the responsibilities of layout managers from those of containers.
  - *For components and containers, see Chapter 12.*

Supplementary Objectives

- Demonstrate the use of the methods `add(Component)` and `add(Component, Object)` of the `java.awt.Container` class and recognize which classes in the `java.awt` package are valid arguments to these methods.
- Write code to use `FlowLayout`, `BorderLayout`, `GridLayout`, `CardLayout` and `GridBagLayout` to build component hierarchies.

13.1 Layout Management Policies

When designing a GUI application, attention must be paid to the location and size of the interface components. Another important issue is how to update the interface when the user resizes a window. Constructing a GUI by defining absolute locations and size of components is a tedious business, not to mention the bookkeeping required when the graphical interface needs updating. This practice is not encouraged in Java. It defeats the purpose of creating platform-independent applications, since component size varies from platform to platform. This is most likely to cause visual glitches if the absolute placement layout tuned for one platform is subsequently used on another.

Layout Managers

A layout manager implements a *layout policy* that defines spatial relationships between components in a container. These relationships or constraints specify the placement and sizes of components, and come into play when the container is resized. The placement and sizing of components, including resizing of the GUI, is taken care of by layout managers in Java. A layout manager works in conjunction with a container holding the components.

A component can be a container, with other components embedded in it. Containers and components are discussed in Chapter 12. An example of building a GUI is given in the last section of this chapter. Event handling is covered in Chapter 14.

The Java AWT provides five layout managers. They all implement the `LayoutManager` interface. These layout managers are summarized in Table 13.1.

Table 13.1 *Overview of Layout Managers*

Manager	Description
`FlowLayout`	Lays out the components in row-major order: in rows growing from left to right, and rows placed top to bottom in the container. This is the default layout manager for the `Panel` and `Applet` classes.
`GridLayout`	Lays out the components in a specified rectangular grid, from left to right in each row, and filling rows from top to bottom in the container.
`BorderLayout`	Up to five components can be placed in a container in locations specified by the following directions: north, south, west, east and center. This is the default layout manager for `Window` and its subclasses (`Frame` and `Dialog`).
`CardLayout`	Components are handled as a stack of indexed cards with only the top component being visible in the container.
`GridBagLayout`	Customizable and flexible layout manager that lays out the components in a rectangular grid. A component can occupy multiple cells in the grid.

Common Methods for Designing a Layout

A layout manager is registered with a container. The following methods of the `Container` class can be used for getting and setting a layout manager for a container:

```
LayoutManager getLayout()
void setLayout(LayoutManager mgr)
```

Components are added to a container. The following overloaded `add()` methods of the `Container` class can be used for adding components to a container:

```
Component add(Component comp)
Component add(Component comp, int index)
void add(Component comp, Object constraints)
void add(Component comp, Object constraints, int index)
```

The order in which the components are added, and the layout manager used, influences the placement of the component in the container.

The `index` argument can be used to specify a position where the component should be inserted (in the ordering of the components already added). The value of –1 inserts the component at the end, which is the default placement.

The `constraints` argument specifies properties that are used by the layout manager to place the components in the container. These properties are specific to the layout manager used.

Components can also be removed from a container. The following methods of the `Container` class can be used for removing components from a container:

```
void remove(int index)
void remove(Component comp)
void removeAll()
```

The component at a specified `index` can be removed, a particular component can be removed, or all the components can be removed.

Examples illustrating the usage of these methods can be found in the discussion on the individual layout managers.

Communication between Container and Layout Manager

Once a layout manager is registered with a container, and components have been added to the container, the layout manager is responsible for the placement and sizing of components whenever this becomes necessary. Applications usually never call the methods of the layout manager directly. Since a layout manager is registered with a container, the container calls the appropriate methods in the layout manager when necessary. Table 13.2 shows which methods in the `Container` class call which methods in the `LayoutManager` interface that is implemented by a layout manager.

Table 13.2 *Layout Operations*

Methods of the Container Class:	Methods of the LayoutManager Interface:
`add()`	`addLayoutComponent()`
`doLayout()`	`layoutContainer()`
`getMinimumSize()`	`minimumLayoutSize()`
`getPreferredSize()`	`preferredLayoutSize()`
`remove` or `removeAll()`	`removeLayoutComponent()`

A typical scenario for updating the layout, when the container size changes, is as follows:

1. The container's `invalidate()` method is invoked. This marks the container and the parents above it in the component hierarchy as needing layout updating.
2. The container's `validate()` method is called. This invocation leads to the following chain of events, resulting in the layout of the container and its parents being updated:
   - The `validate()` method invokes the container's `doLayout()` method.
   - The `doLayout()` method delegates the job to its layout manager, by calling the layout manager's `layoutContainer()` method and passing itself as the argument.

A component added to a container can itself be a container that can hold other components, and have its own specific layout manager. This provides the basis for building complex GUIs. It is also important to distinguish between the following types of containers:

- Containers that must be attached to a parent container. They cannot exist on their own. Objects of the `Panel` class and its subclass `Applet` are typical examples of such containers. An applet panel is attached to the applet context provided by the web browser. This is in contrast to a non-applet panel, which is frequently stuffed with other components, and then attached to another container when building GUIs.
- Containers that can exist independently and cannot be put in other containers. They are sometimes called *top-level* windows. They denote the root of a component hierarchy. The `Window` class and its subclasses `Frame` and `Dialog` are such containers.

Layout and Preferred Size

A layout manager enforces a layout policy (i.e. placement of components). Although a component can request a certain size, it is not certain that the layout manager will honor it. In other words, the size specified by a component is interpreted as its *preferred* size and not as its absolute size. Given the size of the container, the layout manager arbitrates between placement of components in the container and their size. Layout managers in the AWT always give precedence to placement if honoring the preferred size would violate the layout policy. However, it is possible to write custom layout managers where this might not be the case (Section 13.8, p. 407).

Review questions

13.1 Which of these methods are not available in an instance of the `Container` class?

Select all valid answers.

(a) `Component add(Component comp)`
(b) `Component add(Component comp, int index)`
(c) `void add(Object constraints, Component comp)`
(d) `void add(Component comp, Object constraints, int index)`
(e) `void add(PopupMenu popup)`

13.2 Which of these layout managers would make it impossible to lay out two buttons side by side?

Select all valid answers.

(a) `BorderLayout`
(b) `CardLayout`
(c) `FlowLayout`
(d) `GridBagLayout`
(e) `GridLayout`

13.3 Which of these layout managers can only accommodate a limited number of components?

Select all valid answers.

(a) `BorderLayout`
(b) `CardLayout`
(c) `FlowLayout`
(d) `GridBagLayout`
(e) `GridLayout`

13.2 Running the Example Code

The example code given below for each layout manager is written as an applet, which can be compiled and run using the applet viewer. This allows experimenting to see the effect of resizing on the component layout in the applet window. Emphasis is on the layout policies of the layout managers. The applets override the `init()` method, which is executed when the applet is started, and the `start()` method, which is invoked every time the applet page is made visible. Details on applets can be found in Chapter 16. The following HTML file can be used to load the applet. Only the appropriate class name (here `AppletClassName`) for the applet needs to be changed for each example.

```
<!-- HTML file to run an applet -->
<!-- Change AppletClassName as appropriate. -->

<title>Layout Manager</title>
<hr>
<applet code="AppletClassName.class" width=250 height=250> </applet>
<hr>
```

13.3 FlowLayout Manager

The layout policy employed by the flow layout manager associated with a container is quite straightforward: components added to the container are placed in rows that grow from left to right. The rows are constructed from top to bottom in the container. This is sometimes called *row-major allocation*. Components towards the end of a row spill over to the next row if there is not enough space in the current row.

Resizing the container can cause the width of the rows to change, and thereby affect the components' placement, resulting in a different layout on the screen (Figure 13.1).

A flow layout manager honors the preferred size of the components. The size of the components never changes, regardless of the size of the container. If the container is too small, the rendering of the component appears cropped.

The `FlowLayout` manager is the default layout manager for `Panel`, and hence, `Applet` classes.

The `FlowLayout` class provides constructors which allow the alignment and the horizontal and vertical gaps for the layout to be specified.

```
FlowLayout()
FlowLayout(int alignment)
FlowLayout(int alignment, int horizontalgap, int verticalgap)
public static final int LEFT
public static final int CENTER
public static final int RIGHT
```

The alignment of the components in the rows, and the gap between components (horizontally between columns and vertically between rows), can be specified in the appropriate constructors. The alignment and gap properties apply to *all* the components in the container. The default alignment is centered rows, and the default gap is five pixels both vertically and horizontally between components. The constants in the `FlowLayout` class specify the different alignments.

Example 13.1 *Demonstrating Flow Layout*

```
import java.awt.*;
import java.applet.*;

public class FlowLayoutApplet extends Applet {

    public void init() {
        // Create a checkboxgroup
        CheckboxGroup sizeOptions = new CheckboxGroup();

        // Create 3 checkboxes and add them to the checkboxgroup.
        Checkbox cb1 = new Checkbox("Large",  sizeOptions, true);
        Checkbox cb2 = new Checkbox("Medium", sizeOptions, false);
        Checkbox cb3 = new Checkbox("Small",  sizeOptions, false);

        // Add the checkboxes
        add(cb1);
        add(cb2);
        add(cb3);
    }
}
```

The `FlowLayoutApplet` class in Example 13.1 creates three checkboxes that are placed in rows. Each row of components is centered. The number of rows is dependent on the width of the window. If this applet is run in the applet viewer, resizing the applet window will not change the actual size of the checkboxes. However, it can result in a different arrangement of the checkboxes depending on the size of the applet window, as shown in Figure 13.1.

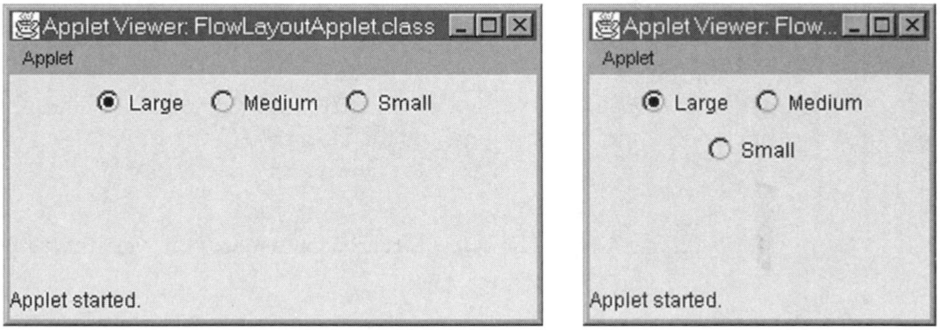

Figure 13.1 *Flow Layout*

Review questions

13.4 What policy does `FlowLayout` use to determine the number of components in each row?

Select the one right answer.

(a) All components will be placed in a single row.
(b) The number of components in a row is predetermined.
(c) It will place as few components as possible in each row, creating as many rows as the height of the container will allow.
(d) It will place components into as few rows as the width of the container will allow, while ensuring the bounds of components are within the container.
(e) The policy is customizable.

13.5 How do you specify the primary direction of layout when using `FlowLayout`?

Select the one right answer.

(a) Specify the primary direction in the constructor of the `FlowLayout` class.
(b) Specify the primary direction by calling a method named `setOrientation` on an instance of `FlowLayout`.
(c) Specify the direction as a constraint parameter when calling the `add()` method on the container, to add the component.
(d) Specifying primary layout direction is not possible. The primary layout direction is always from left to right.
(e) Specifying primary layout direction is not possible. The primary layout direction is always from top to bottom.

13.6 How can each row of components be aligned horizontally in the middle of the container using `FlowLayout` manager?

Select the one right answer.

(a) Pass the value 0.5 as an argument to the constructor of `FlowLayout`.
(b) Pass the string `"Center"` as an argument to the constructor of `FlowLayout`.
(c) Pass `FlowLayout.CENTER` as an argument to the constructor of `FlowLayout`.
(d) Pass `FlowLayout.MIDDLE` as an argument to the constructor of `FlowLayout`.
(e) Specifying the horizontal alignment is not possible. The components in each row are always aligned to the left.

13.4 `GridLayout` Manager

A `GridLayout` manager divides the region of a container into a rectangular grid. Each component is then placed in a cell in this grid, and its position uniquely identified by the row and column number. Only one component can be placed in each cell. All the cells in the grid have the same size, i.e. same width and height. The cell size is dependent on the number of components to be placed in the container and the container's size. A component is resized to fill the cell. A common practice to avoid components being stretched is to first stick the component in a panel, and then add the panel to the container. Components in the panel do not stretch when the `FlowLayout` manager is used. In contrast to a `FlowLayout` manager, a `GridLayout` manager ignores a component's preferred size.

After a GridLayout has been constructed and registered with a container, components are added left to right and top to bottom (i.e. row-major) in the container.

The GridLayout class provides the following constructors:

```
GridLayout()
GridLayout(int rows, int columns)
```

Creates a rows × columns grid layout.

```
GridLayout(int rows, int columns, int horizontalgap, int verticalgap)
```

Creates a rows × columns grid layout, with the specified horizontal and vertical gaps. Either rows or columns can be zero, but not both. The geometry of the grid is then determined by the non-zero value and the number of components added. The first constructor is equivalent to GridLayout(1,0), i.e. one row with any number of components added. The default gap between components is zero pixels, both horizontally and vertically.

Example 13.2 *Demonstrating Grid Layout*

```
import java.awt.*;
import java.applet.*;

public class GridLayoutApplet extends Applet {

    public void init() {
        // Create 2 labels and 2 text fields
        Label xLabel = new Label("X Coordinate:");
        Label yLabel = new Label("Y Coordinate:");
        TextField xInput = new TextField(5);
        TextField yInput = new TextField(5);

        // Create and set a GridLayout with 2 x 2 grid
        setLayout(new GridLayout(2,2));

        // Add the components
        add(xLabel); // [1,1]
        add(xInput); // [1,2]
        add(yLabel); // [2,1]
        add(yInput); // [2,2]
    }
}
```

The GridLayoutApplet class in Example 13.2 creates two rows with two components in each. Each row depicts a label together with a text field. Note that the cells have the same size, as shown in Figure 13.2. Each component is stretched to fill the cell. This is also true for labels, even though it might not appear so, since the text is not stretched.

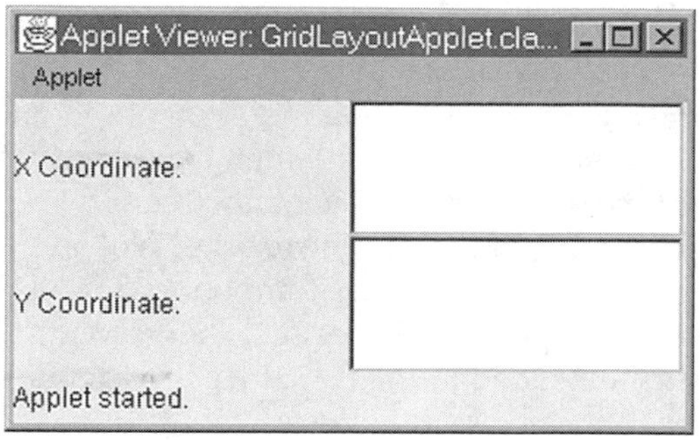

Figure 13.2 *Grid Layout*

Review questions

13.7 How will the following program lay out its buttons?

```
import java.awt.*;

public class MyClass {
    public static void main(String args[]) {
       String[] labels = { "A", "B", "C", "D", "E", "F" };

       Window grid = new Frame();
       grid.setLayout(new GridLayout(0, 1, 2, 3));
       for (int i=0; i<labels.length; i++)
           grid.add(new Button(labels[i]));
       grid.pack();
       grid.setVisible(true);
    }
}
```

Select the one right answer.

(a) The program will not show any buttons at all.
(b) It will place all buttons in one row: `A B C D E F`.
(c) It will place all buttons in one column, i.e. each button in a separate row: `A`, `B`, `C`, `D`, `E` and `F`.
(d) It will place pairs of buttons in three separate rows: `A B`, `C D` and `E F`.
(e) It will place pairs of buttons in three separate columns: `A B`, `C D` and `E F`.
(f) It will place triples of buttons in two separate rows: `A B C` and `D E F`.

13.8 Which of these statements are true?

Select all valid answers.

(a) A grid made by `GridLayout` must have an equal number of rows and columns.
(b) All components in a `GridLayout` will be square. Their width will be equal to their height.
(c) All components in a `GridLayout` will have the same height.
(d) All components in a `GridLayout` will have the same width.
(e) All components within a row of a `GridLayout` will have the same height.

13.5 `BorderLayout` Manager

A `BorderLayout` manager allows one component to be placed in each of the four compass directions in a container. Any space left over can be used for a fifth component in the center of the container, as shown in Figure 13.3. A component can be explicitly added to one of the regions. Not all the regions need to be occupied with a component. Only the last component added to a region is shown. Adding more than one component to a region is not recommended. The order in which the components are added to the container is irrelevant.

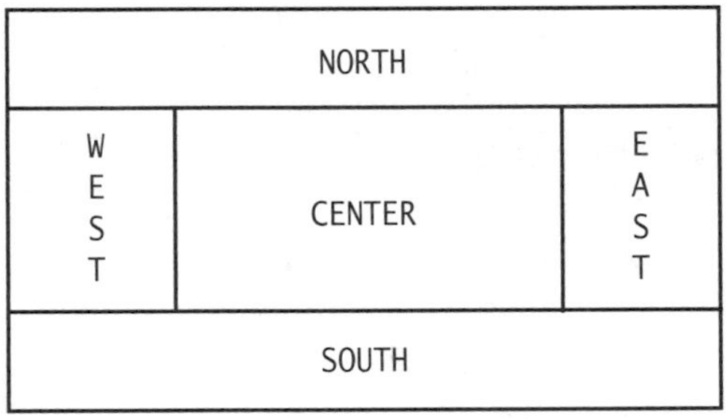

Figure 13.3 *Locations in Border Layout*

The `BorderLayout` class defines the following constructors:

```
BorderLayout()
BorderLayout(int horizontalgap, int verticalgap)
```

The gaps between the components, both horizontal and vertical, can be specified. The default gap in either direction is zero pixels.

A component can be added to a container by using the `add()` method from the `Container` class. The region is specified as an argument to the `add()` method.

```
Component add(Component comp)
void add(Component comp, Object constraints)
public static final String NORTH
public static final String SOUTH
public static final String EAST
public static final String WEST
public static final String CENTER
```

The default region is the center region. The region can be explicitly specified using the `constraints` argument. The constraint is a `String` object defined by the constants from the `BorderLayout` class. As might be expected, these constants correspond to the strings `"North"`, `"South"`, `"East"`, `"West"` and `"Center"` respectively, and are case-sensitive.

If a north or a south component exists, it will stretch horizontally across the width of the container. The `BorderLayout` manager will attempt to honor the preferred

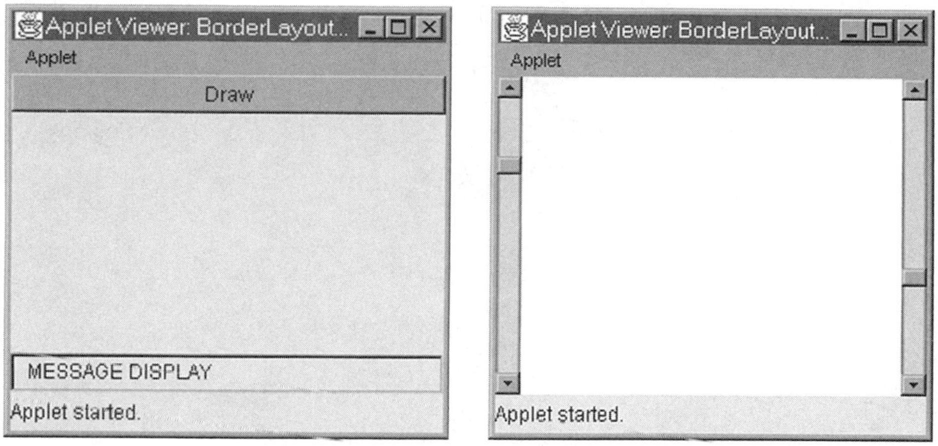

a) Horizontal Stretching b) Vertical Stretching

Figure 13.4 *Horizontal and Vertical Stretching*

height of the components in the north and south regions (Example 13.3, Figure 13.4a).

Example 13.3 *Demonstrating Border Layout – Only North and South Regions*

```
import java.awt.*;
import java.applet.*;

/**
    Demonstrate Border Layout: Only North and South
*/
public class BorderLayoutApplet extends Applet {

    public void init() {

        // Create a text field
        TextField msg = new TextField("MESSAGE DISPLAY");
        msg.setEditable(false);

        // Create a button
        Button drawButton = new Button("Draw");

        // Create and set border layout
        setLayout(new BorderLayout());

        // Add the components
        add(drawButton, BorderLayout.NORTH);
        add(msg, BorderLayout.SOUTH);
    }
}
```

A west or east component is sandwiched between any north or south component, otherwise it stretches vertically along the height of the container. The `BorderLayout` manager will attempt to honor the preferred *width* of the components in the west and east regions (Example 13.4, Figure 13.4b).

Example 13.4 *Demonstrating Border Layout – Only East, West and Center Regions*

```
import java.awt.*;
import java.applet.*;

/**
    Demonstrate Border Layout: Only East, West and Center
*/
public class BorderLayoutApplet extends Applet {

    public void init() {

        // Create a canvas
        Canvas drawRegion = new Canvas();
        drawRegion.setSize(150,150);
        drawRegion.setBackground(Color.white);

        // Create 2 vertical scrollbars
        Scrollbar sb1 = new Scrollbar(Scrollbar.VERTICAL, 0, 10, -50, 100);
        Scrollbar sb2 = new Scrollbar(Scrollbar.VERTICAL, 0, 10, -50, 100);
        // Create and set border layout
        setLayout(new BorderLayout());

        // Add the components
        add(drawRegion, BorderLayout.CENTER);
        add(sb1, BorderLayout.WEST);
        add(sb2, BorderLayout.EAST);
    }
}
```

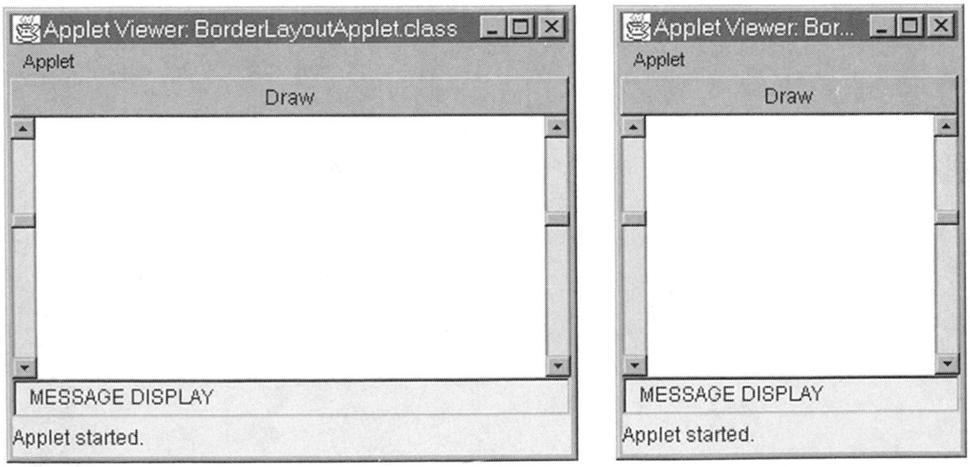

Figure 13.5 *Regions in Border Layout*

The center component takes up whatever space is left and not used by the compass regions in the container. The center component can be stretched both horizontally and vertically, as evident in Figure 13.4 and Figure 13.5.

Border layout keeps the same spatial relationship between the components in the face of the container being resized (Example 13.5, Figure 13.5). This layout policy is useful for keeping components at the top and bottom of a container.

The `BorderLayout` manager is the default layout manager for the `Window` class and its subclasses (`Frame` and `Dialog`).

Example 13.5 *Demonstrating Border Layout – North, South, East, West and Center*

```
import java.awt.*;
import java.applet.*;

/**
    Demonstrate Border Layout: North, South, East, West and Center
*/
public class BorderLayoutApplet extends Applet {

    public void init() {

        // Create a text field
        TextField msg = new TextField("MESSAGE DISPLAY");
        msg.setEditable(false);

        // Create a button
        Button drawButton = new Button("Draw");

        // Create a canvas
        Canvas drawRegion = new Canvas();
        drawRegion.setSize(150,150);
        drawRegion.setBackground(Color.white);

        // Create 2 vertical scrollbars
        Scrollbar sb1 = new Scrollbar(Scrollbar.VERTICAL,0, 10,-50,100);
        Scrollbar sb2 = new Scrollbar(Scrollbar.VERTICAL,0, 10,-50,100);

        // Create and set border layout
        setLayout(new BorderLayout());

        // Add the components in designated regions
        add(drawButton, BorderLayout.NORTH);
        add(msg, BorderLayout.SOUTH);
        add(drawRegion, BorderLayout.CENTER);
        add(sb1, BorderLayout.WEST);
        add(sb2, BorderLayout.EAST);
    }
}
```

Review questions

13.9 Which of the following is a valid placement constraint when using `BorderLayout`?

Select all valid answers.

(a) The string `"NORTH"`
(b) `BorderLayout.MIDDLE`
(c) `BorderLayout.CENTER`
(d) `BorderLayout.EAST`
(e) The string `"south"`

13.10 Given the following code, name the buttons that will occupy the top left and bottom right corners of the container when the program is run.

```
import java.awt.*;

public class MyClass {
    public static void main(String args[]) {

    Window compass = new Frame();

    String[] names = {
        "North", "South", "East", "West", "Center"
    };
    for (int i=0; i<names.length; i++)
        compass.add(new Button(names[i]), names[i]);
    compass.pack();
    compass.setVisible(true);
    }
}
```

Select all valid answers.

(a) Button `North` will occupy the top left corner.
(b) Button `West` will occupy the top left corner.
(c) Button `South` will occupy the bottom right corner.
(d) Button `East` will occupy the bottom right corner.
(e) Buttons will overlap.

13.6 `CardLayout` Manager

The card layout policy handles the components in a container like a *stack of indexed cards*. Only the top component is visible, and it fills the whole region of the container. The card layout does not give any visual clue that the container consists of a stack of components. Neither does it provide any interface gadgetry that allows the user to switch between the cards.

The `CardLayout` class defines the following constructors:

```
CardLayout()
CardLayout(int horizontalgap, int verticalgap)
```

Both horizontal and vertical gaps between the edges of a component and the borders of the container can be specified. The default gap in either direction is zero pixels.

Individual components can be added to a container by using the `add()` methods from the `Container` class. The `constraints` argument in the `add()` methods is a `String` object which can be associated with the component, and later used to make this particular component visible using the `show()` method in the `CardLayout` class.

The `CardLayout` class defines methods to handle the components in a specified container that uses this policy:

```
void first(Container parent)
void next(Container parent)
void previous(Container parent)
void last(Container parent)
```

The parent argument is the container associated with the card layout manager. These methods can be used to choose which card should be shown. Note that the methods are invoked on a `CardLayout` object and not on the parent container.

```
void show(Container parent, String name)
```

Shows the specified component `name` in the specified container.

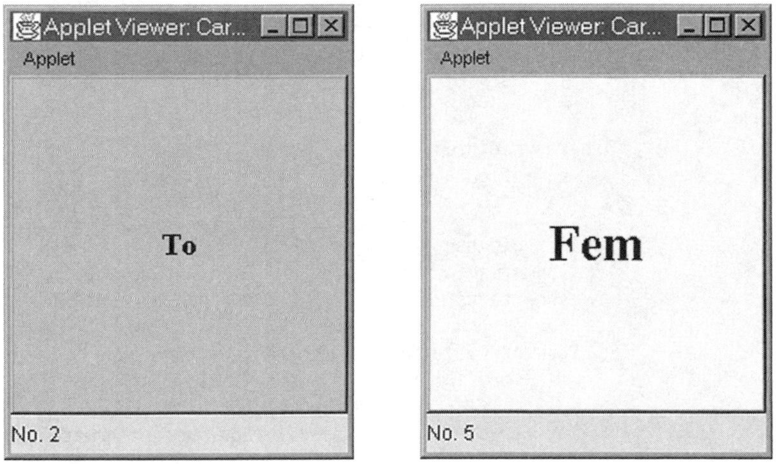

Figure 13.6 *Card Layout*

Example 13.6 *Demonstrating Card Layout*

```
import java.awt.*;
import java.applet.*;

public class CardLayoutApplet extends Applet implements Runnable {
```

```
    // Arrays of card names and their corresponding color.
    String[] cardNames = {"En", "To", "Tre", "Fire", "Fem"};
    Color[]  colors    = {Color.green, Color.pink, Color.white,
                          Color.blue, Color.yellow};

    // Create a CardLayout object
    CardLayout layout = new CardLayout();                            // (1)

    public void init() {                                             // (2)

        // Set the CardLayout as the layout manager
        setLayout(layout);

        // Add buttons to the container
        for (int i = 0; i < cardNames.length; i++) {

            // Create a new button with name
            Button displayButton = new Button(cardNames[i]);

            // Set the background color and (increasing) font size
            displayButton.setBackground(colors[i]);
            displayButton.setFont(new Font("Serif", Font.BOLD, 14 + (4*i)));

            // Add button with its identification name
            add(displayButton, cardNames[i]);                        // (3)
        }
    }

    Thread animation;
    public void start() {                                            // (4)
        // Create and start a thread if none present.
        if (animation == null) {
            animation = new Thread(this);
            animation.start();
        }
    }

    public void stop() {                                             // (5)
        animation = null;
    }

    public void run() {                                              // (6)
        layout.show(this, cardNames[0]); // Show card "En"              (7)
        showStatus("No. 1"); // Let the applet context show the string.
        try {
            // Cycle through the rest of the cards
            for (int i = 1; i < cardNames.length; i++) {
                Thread.sleep(1000);
                if (animation != Thread.currentThread()) break;

                layout.next(this);                                   // (8)
                showStatus("No. " + (i+1));
            }
        } catch(InterruptedException e) {}
    }
}
```

The applet in Example 13.6 defines five buttons that are displayed in consecutive order every time the applet is started. Each button has a specific name, background color and font size. A `CardLayout` object is created at (1). It is registered with the applet. The `init()` method at (2) adds each button, together with its identifying name, to the applet at (3). Note that the button label need not be the same as the name used to identify the button in the container. The cards are animated in a separate thread (Section 16.4, p. 497). Each time a thread executes the `run()` method at (6), the first "card" labeled `"En"` is made visible by calling the `show()` method on the `CardLayout` object at (7). The `show()` method takes the container, i.e. the applet, and the name of the card as argument. Each consecutive card is shown by calling the `next()` method on the `CardLayout` object with the applet as the argument at (8). The thread sleeps between swapping cards.

Review questions

13.11 Which of these are methods in the `CardLayout` class?

Select all valid answers.

(a) `first()`
(b) `last()`
(c) `end()`
(d) `previous()`
(e) `top()`

13.12 How do you show the next component (card) when using the `CardLayout` manager?

Select all valid answers.

(a) Call `setVisible(true)` on the component in question.
(b) Call `next()` without any arguments on the container of the component.
(c) Call `next()` without any arguments on the `CardLayout` instance used.
(d) Call `next(comp)` on the `CardLayout` instance used, where `comp` is the component (card) to be shown.
(e) Call `next(cont)` on the `CardLayout` instance used, where `cont` is the container using the `CardLayout` instance.

13.7 `GridBagLayout` Manager

The grid bag layout policy also uses a rectangular grid but, unlike the grid layout manager, a component can occupy multiple cells in the grid, and the width and the height of the cells need not be uniform. This means that a component can span several rows and columns, but the region it occupies is always rectangular. The components in the container can have different sizes. The grid bag layout manager allows different size components to be aligned in the container.

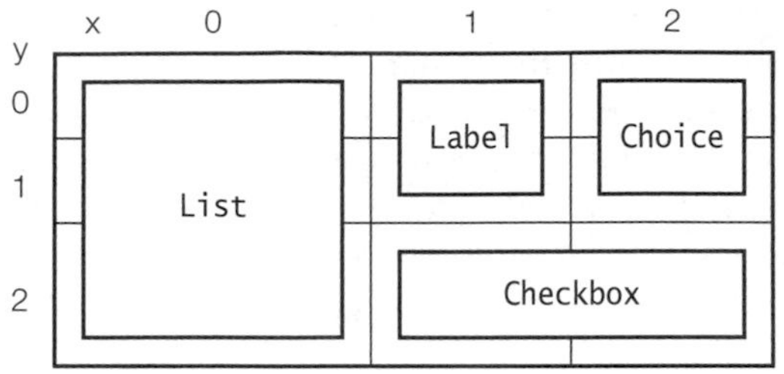

Figure 13.7 *Alignment of Different Size Components in Grid Bag Layout*

As can be seen from Figure 13.7, the container is a 3×3 grid, but all the components occupy multiple cells. The grid bag layout manager assists in aligning such components, as shown in the diagram. The following steps describe how to construct such a layout:

1. Create an object of the class `GridBagLayout`.

   ```
   GridBagLayout gbl = new GridBagLayout();
   ```

   Note that the dimensions of the grid are not specified. That information will be deduced when the components are added.

2. Set the layout manager for the container.

   ```
   container.setLayout(gbl);
   ```

3. Create an object of the class `GridBagConstraints`. This object is used to specify the layout information.

   ```
   GridBagConstraints gbc = new GridBagConstraints();
   ```

4. For each component to be added, do the following:
   - Fill in the layout information in the `GridBagConstraints` object, as shown below.
   - Add the component supplying the `GridBagConstraints` object.

     ```
     container.add(new Checkbox("Fill", false), gbc);
     ```

The key to using the grid bag layout is to understand how the `GridBagConstraints` object affects the layout. Note that the same `GridBagConstraints` object can be reused for adding other components. In the discussion below, *x*-direction indicates horizontal direction from left to right, and *y*-direction indicates vertical direction from top to bottom. Constraints can be specified using the public data members of the `GridBagConstraints` class, which are explained below. A `GridBagConstraints` object can be constructed using the following constructors:

```
GridBagConstraints()
GridBagConstraints(int gridx, int gridy, int gridwidth, int gridheight,
                   double weightx, double weighty, int anchor, int fill,
                   Insets insets, int ipadx, int ipady)
```

The first constructor sets all the members in the `GridBagConstraints` object to their default values, whereas the second one sets them to the specified values.

Location

```
int gridx
int gridy
```

The values of `gridx` and `gridy` define the *column* and *row* positions of the upper left corner of the component in the grid.

Both values can also be set to the constant `GridBagConstraints.RELATIVE`. The components are then added in relation to the previous component. The dimension (`gridwidth`, `gridheight` explained below) then indicates the last component in each row and column.

The default value in both directions is `GridBagConstraints.RELATIVE`.

Dimension

```
int gridwidth
int gridheight
```

The values of `gridwidth` and `gridheight` specify the number of cells occupied by the component horizontally and vertically in the grid.

The values of `gridwidth` and `gridheight` can be set to either `GridBagConstraints.RELATIVE` or `GridBagConstraints.REMAINDER`. The value `GridBagConstraints.REMAINDER` indicates that the component extends to the end of the row or column. In other words, it is the *last* component in the row or column. The value `GridBagConstraints.RELATIVE` should be used to specify that the component is *next-to-last* in its row (for `gridwidth`) or column (for `gridheight`).

The default value in both directions is one cell.

Growth Factor

```
double weightx
double weighty
```

These values define the portion of the "slack" that should be allocated to the area occupied by the component. A certain amount of trial and error is usually necessary to set these values to get the layout just right.

The default value for `weightx` and `weighty` is zero, meaning that the area allocated to the component does not grow beyond the preferred size of the component, in the horizontal and vertical directions respectively.

Anchoring

```
int anchor
public static final int CENTER
public static final int NORTH
public static final int NORTHEAST
public static final int EAST
public static final int SOUTHEAST
public static final int SOUTH
```

```
public static final int SOUTHWEST
public static final int WEST
public static final int NORTHWEST
```

Anchoring specifies where a component should be placed within its display area (Figure 13.8). If the component does not fill its allocated area, it can be anchored by specifying one of the constants defined in the `GridBagConstraints` class. The default value is `GridBagConstraints.CENTER`.

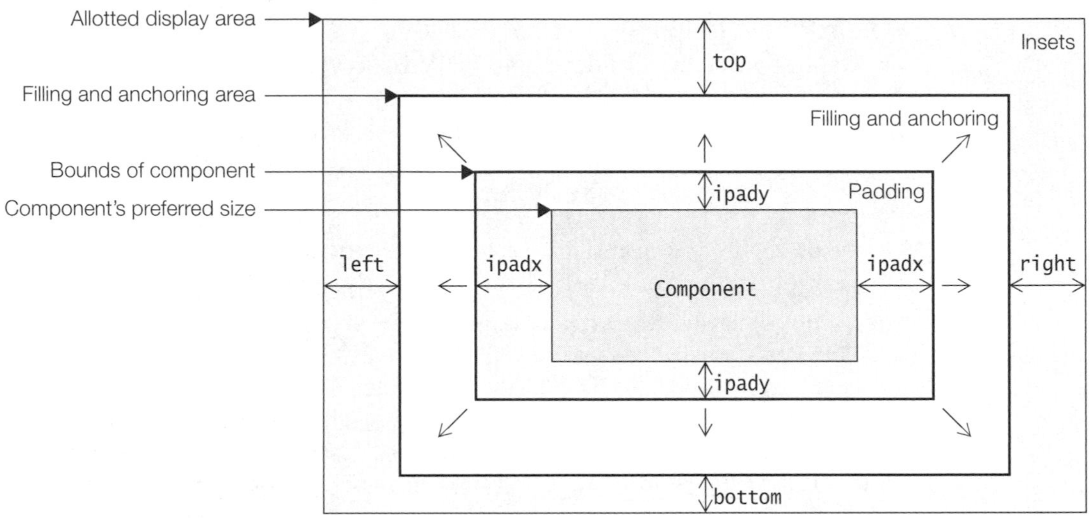

Figure 13.8 *Layout Constraints*

Filling

```
int fill
public static final int NONE
public static final int BOTH
public static final int HORIZONTAL
public static final int VERTICAL
```

How the component is to stretch and fill its display area is given by the `fill` value, which can be set to one of the constants defined in the `GridBagConstraints` class (Figure 13.8). The default value is `GridBagConstraints.NONE`.

Padding

```
int ipadx
int ipady
```

Specifies the padding that will be added internally to each side of the component. The dimension of the component will be padded in the horizontal (2 × `ipadx`) and the vertical (2 × `ipady`) direction. The default value is zero pixels in either direction. Padding is illustrated in Figure 13.8.

External padding

Insets

`Insets insets`

The `insets` variable defines the external padding (border) around the component in its display area. The default value is `(0,0,0,0)` specifying top, left, bottom and right insets. Insets are illustrated in Figure 13.8.

Example 13.7 *Demonstrating Grid Bag Layout*

```
import java.awt.*;
import java.applet.*;

public class GridBagLayoutApplet extends Applet {

    public void init() {

        // Create a list of colors
        String[] colors = {"Black", "Blue", "Green", "Red", "Yellow"};
        List colorList = new List(colors.length -2, false);
        for (int i=0; i<colors.length; i++)
            colorList.add(colors[i]);

        // Create a label
        Label shape = new Label("Shape:");
        shape.setFont(new Font("Serif", Font.BOLD, 14));

        // Create a choice list
        Choice shapeChoice = new Choice();
        shapeChoice.add("Square");
        shapeChoice.add("Circle");
        shapeChoice.add("Ellipse");

        // Create a checkbox
        Checkbox cbFill = new Checkbox("Fill", false);
        cbFill.setFont(new Font("Serif", Font.BOLD, 14));

        // Create and set the GridBagLayout
        setLayout(new GridBagLayout());

        // Create a GridBagConstraints object
        GridBagConstraints gbc = new GridBagConstraints();        // (1)

        /*
           Set the "global" constraints.                           (2)
           Each component will not fill and is anchored in the top left corner.
           The area allocated to each component will grow in the horizontal
           direction, but not in the vertical direction.
        */
        gbc.fill    = GridBagConstraints.NONE;
        gbc.anchor  = GridBagConstraints.NORTHWEST;
        gbc.weightx = 1;
        gbc.weighty = 0;
```

```
        // Add the components using the constraints                    // (3)
        addUsingGBL(colorList,   gbc, 0, 0, 1, 3);
        addUsingGBL(shape,       gbc, 1, 0, 1, 2);
        addUsingGBL(shapeChoice, gbc, 2, 0, 1, 2);
        addUsingGBL(cbFill,      gbc, 1, 2, 2, 1);
    }

    void addUsingGBL(Component component, GridBagConstraints gbc,
                     int x, int y, int w, int h) {                     // (4)
        gbc.gridx      = x;
        gbc.gridy      = y;
        gbc.gridwidth  = w;
        gbc.gridheight = h;
        add(component, gbc);                                           // (5)
    }
}
```

The applet in Example 13.7 demonstrates the grid bag layout. It implements the layout shown in Figure 13.7. Table 13.3 shows the four components that are laid out from left to right and top to bottom, together with each component's location (`gridx`, `gridy`) and number of cells occupied (`gridwidth`, `gridheight`) as depicted in Figure 13.7. This information is utilized at (3) in Example 13.7. For example, the upper left corner of the choice is in cell (2, 0) and occupies one column but two rows, as evident from Figure 13.7.

Table 13.3 *Components in Grid Bag Layout*

Component	Column (`gridx`)	Row (`gridy`)	No. of Columns (`gridwidth`)	No. of Rows (`gridheight`)
A list of five colors	0	0	1	3
A label with the value "`Shape`"	1	0	1	2
A choice of three shapes	2	0	1	2
A checkbox with the name "`Fill`"	1	2	2	1

A `GridBagConstraints` object is created to specify the constraints at (1). All components will not stretch to fill their display area, and each component will be anchored in the top left corner of its allocated area (`GridBagConstraints.NORTHWEST`). The growth factor in the vertical direction (`weighty`) is set to zero for all components, so that the components will not grow beyond their initial size in the vertical direction. These constraints are set in the `GridBagConstraints` object at (2).

An auxiliary method, `addUsingGBL()` defined at (4), is used to set the other constraints for each component. A single `GridBagConstraints` object is used to set the constraints for all the components at (3). The state of the `GridBagConstraints` object

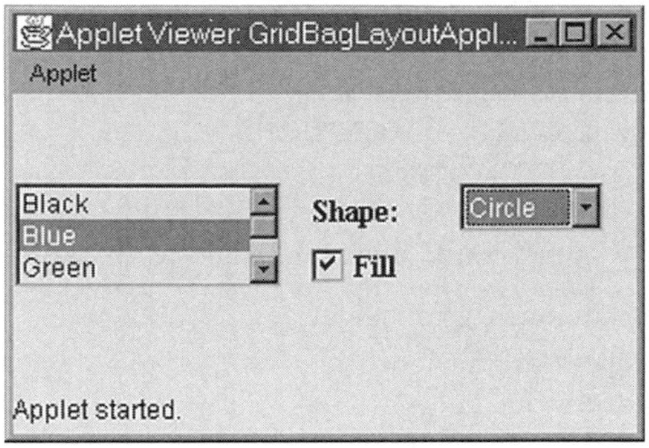

Figure 13.9 *Grid Bag Layout*

is modified in the `addUsingGBL()` method before adding the component to the container, using the constraints object, as shown at (5). The applet is shown in Figure 13.9.

Review questions

13.13 What will the following program show when run?

```
import java.awt.*;

public class MyClass {
    public static void main(String args[]) {

        Window window = new Frame();
        window.setLayout(new GridBagLayout());
        GridBagConstraints gbc = new GridBagConstraints();
        window.add(new Button("A"), gbc);
        window.add(new Button("B"), gbc);

        window.setSize(400, 400);
        window.setVisible(true);
    }
}
```

Select the one right answer.

(a) An empty window.
(b) Two buttons side by side, covering the whole window.
(c) Two small buttons side by side in the center of the window.
(d) Two small buttons side by side placed in the top left area of the window.
(e) None of the above.

13.14 What is the default anchoring of `GridBagConstraints`?

Select the one right answer.

(a) `GridBagConstraints.CENTER`
(b) `GridBagConstraints.NORTH`
(c) `GridBagConstraints.WEST`
(d) `GridBagConstraints.NORTHWEST`
(e) None of the above.

13.15 What is the default layout manager for instances of the `Frame` class?

Select the one right answer.

(a) `BorderLayout`
(b) `CardLayout`
(c) `GridBagLayout`
(d) `GridLayout`
(e) `FlowLayout`

13.16 What is the default layout manager for instances of the `Panel` class?

Select the one right answer.

(a) `BorderLayout`
(b) `CardLayout`
(c) `GridBagLayout`
(d) `GridLayout`
(e) `FlowLayout`

13.8 Customized Layout

Two options are outlined, that allow explicit control over the layout.

No Layout Manager

For absolute positioning of components in a container at fixed locations, one can proceed as follows:

1. Do not define a layout manager for the container.

```
guiPanel.setLayout(null);
```

2. Add the components in the standard way using the `add()` method.

```
Checkbox cb = new Checkbox("Large Font");
guiPanel.add(cb);
```

3. Set the absolute position and required size for the component, using the `setBounds()` method.

```
cb.setBounds(5,   // x coordinate along horizontal axis
             5,   // y coordinate along vertical axis
             10,  // width along horizontal axis
             20); // height along vertical axis
```

Note that not using any layout manager also places the responsibility of updating the layout on the application. Using absolute positioning can easily defeat the purpose of platform independence, because native windowing systems are notoriously eccentric regarding layout of GUI components.

Custom Layout Manager

It is also possible to design a custom layout manager. This requires implementing either the `LayoutManager` or its subinterface `LayoutManager2`. Implementing one of the interfaces defines the layout policy. Using a layout manager frees the application from the responsibility of handling the updating of the layout.

13.9 Building Component Hierarchies

For simple applications, the components can be put directly into an applet or a single frame. An example is shown here, where a GUI can be programmed from the ground up using the capabilities in Java. The main concept is that components can be placed into containers, which in turn can be put into other containers, resulting in a *component hierarchy*. However, this should not be confused with inheritance hierarchy. The main container for a GUI is usually an applet, a frame or a dialog box. This container denotes the *root* of the component hierarchy. Note that not all containers (like the panels) have a visual representation on the screen. However, they are ideal for nesting other components and containers. Subdividing the GUI into regions, identifying the components and the containers, is an essential part of designing a GUI.

In the GUI shown in Figure 13.10 the user can draw different shapes by interacting through the GUI. The user can pick a shape, enter the coordinates where the shape will be placed in a drawing region, indicate the size, and choose whether the shape

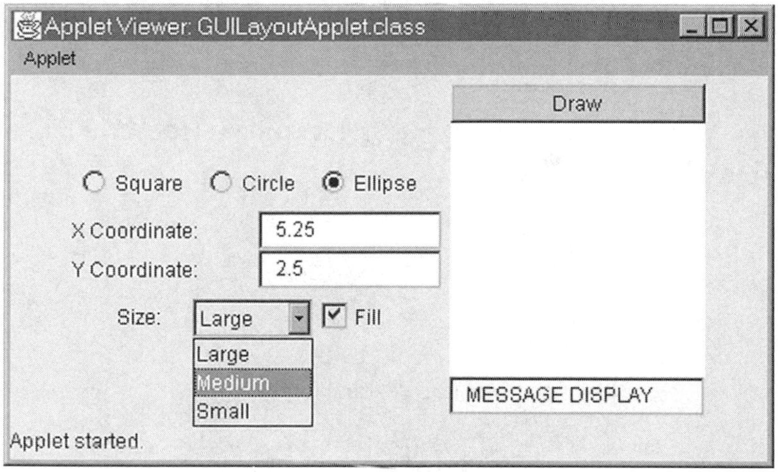

Figure 13.10 *GUI*

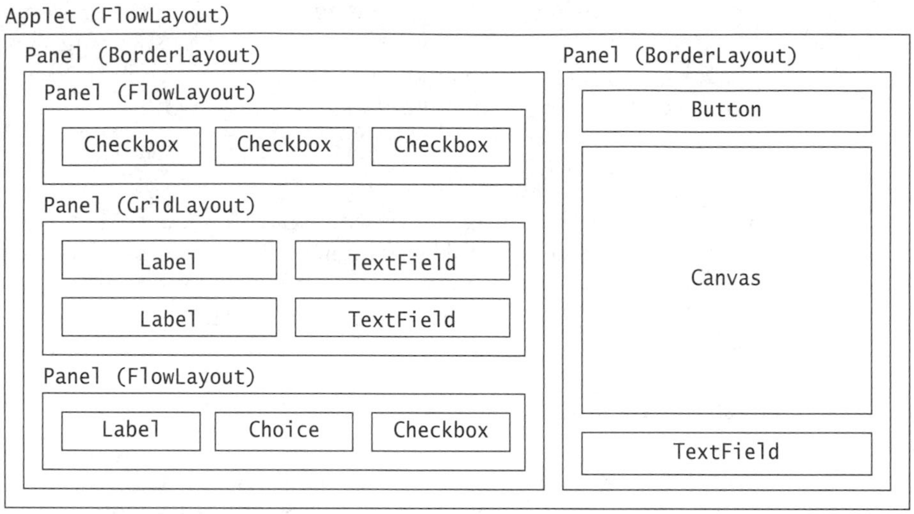

Figure 13.11 *Component Hierarchy*

should be filled or not. A text field is used for messages to the user. Figure 13.11 identifies the components and the containers for the GUI. The layout managers used by a container are also indicated in Figure 13.11.

In Example 13.8, the source code for this applet systematically constructs the component hierarchy. It is worth the effort to identify the components shown in the GUI with their position in the component hierarchy, and see their implementation in the source code. The following procedure is used in building each panel used in the source code:

1. Create the panel.
2. Register a layout manager with the panel.
3. Add the components to the panel.
4. Add the panel to its parent container.

In Chapter 14, this applet is augmented with event handling to provide the user interaction.

Example 13.8 *Demonstrating Component Hierarchy*

```
import java.awt.*;
import java.applet.*;

/**
    Demo of Component Hierarchy
*/
public class GUILayoutApplet extends Applet {
    // Panel for shape
    Panel shapePanel;
```

```
CheckboxGroup shapeCBG;
Checkbox      squareCB;
Checkbox      circleCB;
Checkbox      ellipseCB;

// Panel for x,y coordinates
Panel     xyPanel;
Label     xLabel;
TextField xInput;
Label     yLabel;
TextField yInput;

// Panel for size and fill
Panel    sizePanel;
Label    sizeLabel;
Choice   sizeChoice;
Checkbox fillCB;

// Panel for shape, coordinates, size and fill
Panel leftPanel;

// Panel for Message display, draw button and canvas
Panel     rightPanel;
Button    drawButton;
Canvas    drawRegion;
TextField msg;

public void init() {
    makeShapePanel();
    makeXYPanel();
    makeSizePanel();
    makeLeftPanel();
    makeRightPanel();

    add(leftPanel);
    add(rightPanel);
}

// Panel for shape
private void makeShapePanel() {
    shapePanel = new Panel();

    shapeCBG   = new CheckboxGroup();

    squareCB   = new Checkbox("Square",  shapeCBG, true);
    circleCB   = new Checkbox("Circle",  shapeCBG, false);
    ellipseCB  = new Checkbox("Ellipse", shapeCBG, false);

    shapePanel.setLayout(new FlowLayout());
    shapePanel.add(squareCB);
    shapePanel.add(circleCB);
    shapePanel.add(ellipseCB);
}

// Panel for x,y coordinates
private void makeXYPanel() {
    xyPanel = new Panel();

    xLabel  = new Label("X Coordinate:");
    yLabel  = new Label("Y Coordinate:");
```

```
        xInput  = new TextField(5);
        yInput  = new TextField(5);

        xyPanel.setLayout(new GridLayout(2,2));
        xyPanel.add(xLabel);
        xyPanel.add(xInput);
        xyPanel.add(yLabel);
        xyPanel.add(yInput);
    }

    // Panel for size and fill
    private void makeSizePanel() {
        sizePanel   = new Panel();

        sizeLabel   = new Label("Size:");

        sizeChoice = new Choice();
        sizeChoice.add("Large");
        sizeChoice.add("Medium");
        sizeChoice.add("Small");

        fillCB = new Checkbox("Fill", false);

        sizePanel.setLayout(new FlowLayout());
        sizePanel.add(sizeLabel);
        sizePanel.add(sizeChoice);
        sizePanel.add(fillCB);
    }

    // Panel for shape, coordinates, size and fill
    private void makeLeftPanel() {
        leftPanel = new Panel();

        leftPanel.setLayout(new BorderLayout());
        leftPanel.add(shapePanel, BorderLayout.NORTH);
        leftPanel.add(xyPanel,    BorderLayout.CENTER);
        leftPanel.add(sizePanel,  BorderLayout.SOUTH);
    }

    // Panel for Message display, draw button, and canvas
    private void makeRightPanel() {
        rightPanel = new Panel();

        msg = new TextField("MESSAGE DISPLAY");
        msg.setEditable(false);
        msg.setBackground(Color.yellow);

        drawButton = new Button("Draw");
        drawButton.setBackground(Color.lightGray);

        drawRegion = new Canvas();
        drawRegion.setSize(150,150);
        drawRegion.setBackground(Color.white);

        rightPanel.setLayout(new BorderLayout());
        rightPanel.add(drawButton, BorderLayout.NORTH);
        rightPanel.add(msg,        BorderLayout.SOUTH);
        rightPanel.add(drawRegion, BorderLayout.CENTER);
    }
}
```

Chapter summary

The following information was included in this chapter:

- What a layout policy is, and how a container and its layout manager together implement this policy for the components inside the container.
- The five layout managers in the AWT API: `FlowLayout` manager, `GridLayout` manager, `BorderLayout` manager, `CardLayout` manager, `GridBagLayout` manager.
- Building component hierarchies.

Programming exercises

13.1 Create a program that displays a button at the top of a framed window. The button should cover the whole width of the window, but should be given its preferred height whenever possible. The rest of the area of the window should be covered by two text areas placed side by side, sharing the remaining area of the window equally between them (Figure 13.12).

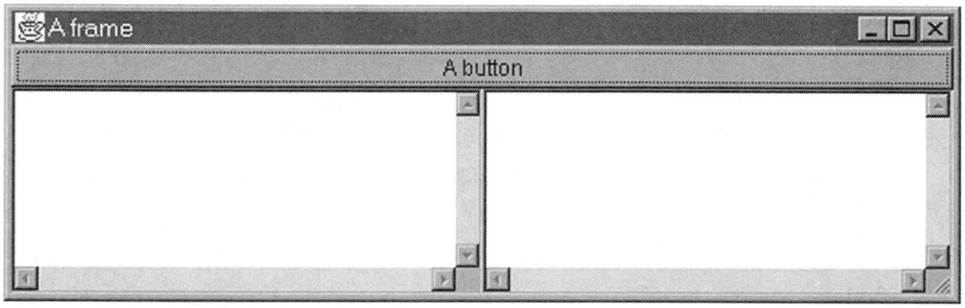

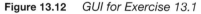

Figure 13.12 *GUI for Exercise 13.1*

13.2 Create a program that displays a small button in each corner of a framed window. The buttons should have their preferred size whenever possible. Leave the remainder of the window blank (Figure 13.13).

Figure 13.13 *GUI for Exercise 13.2*

14 Event Handling

Exam Objectives

- Write code to implement listener classes and methods, and in listener methods extract information from the event to determine the affected component, mouse position, nature and time of the event. State the event class name for any specified event listener interface in the `java.awt.event` package.

Supplementary Objectives

- Demonstrate event handling in AWT by implementing appropriate listeners.
- Illustrate the usage of event adapters.
- Write code that takes advantage of low-level event processing.

14.1 Overview of Event Handling

GUI applications are *event-driven*. User interaction with the GUI results in *events* being generated to inform the application of user actions. Clicking a button, closing a window, or hitting a key results in an appropriate event being sent to the application. Note that since the user actions can take place in any arbitrary order, the events are also occurring in arbitrary order and the application must be able to handle them when they occur.

Event handling in Java is based on the *event delegation model*. Its principal elements are:

- Event classes that can encapsulate information about different types of user interaction.
- Event source objects that inform *event listeners* about events when these occur and supply the necessary information about these events.
- Event listener objects that are informed by an event source when designated events occur, so that they can take appropriate action.

Handling events in a GUI application, using the event delegation model, can be divided into the following two tasks when building the application:

- Setting up the propagation of events from event sources to event listeners.
- Providing the appropriate actions in event listeners to deal with the events received.

This chapter discusses the event delegation model and the facilities provided in Java for event handling. It provides examples to illustrate the different techniques for organizing the delivery of events from event sources to event listeners.

14.2 The Event Hierarchy

Events are represented by objects in Java. Each such object encapsulates all the pertinent information about an event. The superclass of all events is `java.util.EventObject`. A partial inheritance hierarchy of event classes is shown in Figure 14.1. The `EventObject` class provides a method that returns the object that generated the event:

```
Object getSource()
```

Returns the object that originated the event.

The class `java.util.EventObject` has a subclass `java.awt.AWTEvent` which is the superclass of all AWT-related event classes. These AWT event classes all reside in the `java.awt.event` package and represent *categories of events*. Objects of these event classes encapsulate additional information that identifies the exact nature of the event. For example, the `MouseEvent` class categorizes events relating to a mouse

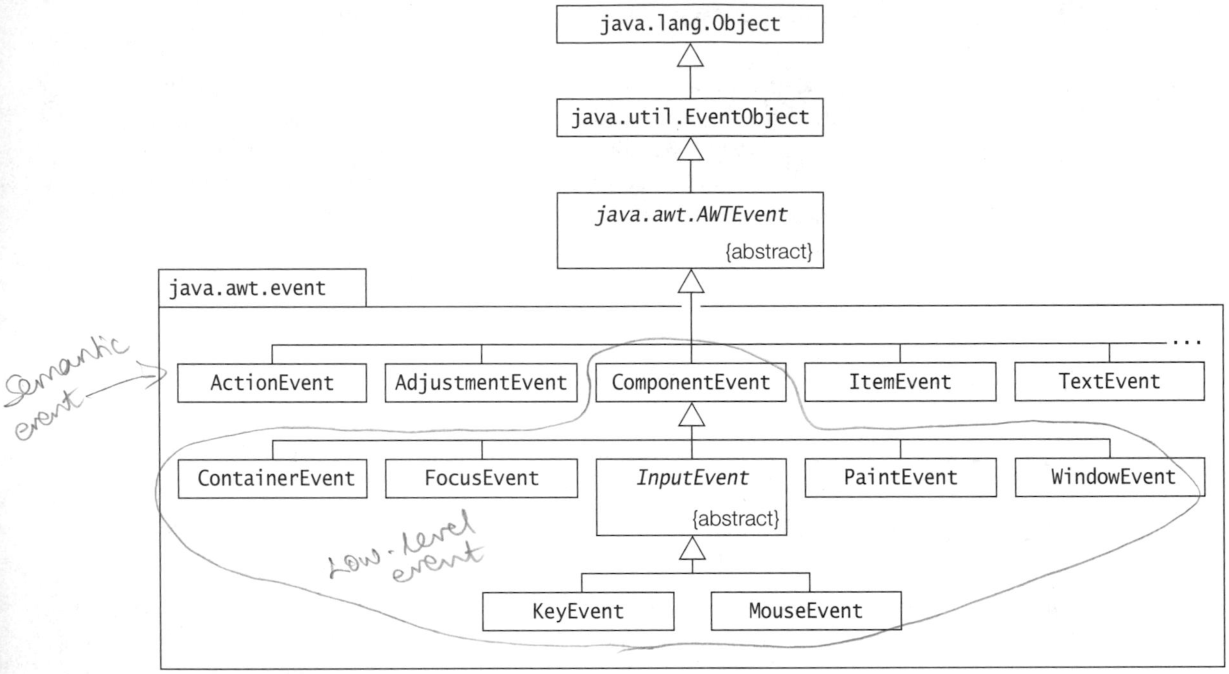

Figure 14.1 *Partial Inheritance Hierarchy of Event Classes*

button being clicked (`MouseEvent.MOUSE_CLICKED`), the mouse being dragged (`MouseEvent.MOUSE_DRAGGED`) and so on for other mouse-related events. These values (`MouseEvent.MOUSE_CLICKED`, `MouseEvent.MOUSE_DRAGGED`) constitute an ID for the event. The class `java.awt.AWTEvent` provides a method that returns an event's ID:

```
int getID()
```

Returns an ID in the form of an integer value that identifies the type of event.

`AWTEvent` Classes

It is useful to divide the subclasses of the `AWTEvent` class further into two groups:

1. Semantic Events
2. Low-level Events

```
ActionEvent
AdjustmentEvent
ItemEvent
TextEvent
```

These classes are used for high-level semantic events, to represent user interaction with a GUI component. For example, clicking a button, selecting a menu item, selecting a checkbox, scrolling, and changing text in a text field or text area all result in individual semantic events.

```
ComponentEvent
ContainerEvent
FocusEvent
KeyEvent
MouseEvent
PaintEvent
WindowEvent
```

These classes are used to represent low-level input or window operations. Several low-level events can constitute a single semantic event. For example, clicking on a button is actually a sequence of mouse movements to position the cursor followed by pressing and releasing a mouse button.

Semantic Event Classes

This section describes each of the semantic event classes.

ActionEvent

This event is generated by an action performed on a GUI component.

The GUI components that generate this event are:

- `Button` – when a button is clicked.
- `List` – when a list item is double-clicked.
- `MenuItem` – when a menu item is selected.
- `TextField` – when the ENTER key is hit in the text field.

The `ActionEvent` class provides the following useful methods:

```
String getActionCommand()
```

Returns the command name associated with this action. The command name is a button label, a list-item name, a menu-item name or text, depending on whether the component is a `Button`, `List`, `MenuItem` or `TextField` object.

```
int getModifiers()
```

```
public static final int SHIFT_MASK
public static final int CTRL_MASK
public static final int META_MASK
public static final int ALT_MASK
```

Returns the sum of the modifier constants corresponding to the keyboard modifiers held down during this action. This could be a combination of the *shift*, *control*, *meta* or *alt* keys used during this action.

AdjustmentEvent

This event is generated when adjustments are made to an adjustable component like a scrollbar.

The GUI component that generates the adjustment event is:

- `Scrollbar` – when any adjustment is made to the scrollbar.

The `AdjustmentEvent` class provides the following method:

> `int getValue()`
>
> Returns the current value designated by the adjustable component.

ItemEvent

This event is generated when an item is selected or deselected in an `ItemSelectable` component.

GUI components that generate this event are:

- `Checkbox` – when the state of a checkbox changes.
- `CheckboxMenuItem` – when the state of a checkbox associated with a menu item changes.
- `Choice` – when an item is selected or deselected in a choice-list.
- `List` – when an item is selected or deselected from a list.

The `ItemEvent` class provides the following useful methods:

> `Object getItem()`
>
> Returns the object that was selected or deselected. The label of the `Checkbox` or the `CheckboxMenuItem`, or the label of the item in a choice or a list, is returned as a `String` object.
>
> ```
> int getStateChange()
> public static final int SELECTED
> public static final int DESELECTED
> ```
>
> The returned value indicates whether it was a selection or a deselection that took place, given by the two constants from the `ItemEvent` class.

TextEvent

This event is generated whenever the content of a text component is changed.

GUI components that generate these events are subclasses of the `TextComponent` class:

- `TextArea`
- `TextField`

Low-level Events

This section describes each of the low-level events.

ComponentEvent

This event is generated when a component is hidden, shown, moved, or resized. These events are handled internally by the AWT, and are normally not directly dealt with by the application.

These events are generated by the `Component` class and its subclasses.

The `ComponentEvent` class provides the following useful method:

> `Component getComponent()`
>
> Returns a reference to the same object as `getSource()` method, but the returned reference is of type `Component`.

ContainerEvent

This event is generated when a component is added or removed from a container. These events are handled internally by the AWT, and are normally not directly dealt with by the application.

FocusEvent

This event is generated when a component gains or loses focus. Having the focus means that the component can receive keystrokes.

A component usually provides a visual clue to indicate that the component currently has the focus. For example, a text field can have a blinking caret, and a button can have a rectangle around its border when it has the focus.

The inherited method `getComponent()` from the superclass `ComponentEvent` can be used to determine the component that lost or gained focus.

The inherited method `getID()` from its superclass `AWTEvent` can be used to determine whether the focus was lost or gained (`FocusEvent.FOCUS_LOST`, `FocusEvent.FOCUS_GAINED`). Focus can be lost either permanently or temporarily, and this can be determined by calling the method `isTemporary()` in the `FocusEvent` class.

> `boolean isTemporary()`
>
> Determines whether the loss of focus is permanent or temporary.

KeyEvent

This class is a subclass of the abstract `InputEvent` class.

This event is generated when the user presses or releases a key, or does both (i.e. types a character). These situations are characterized by the following constants in the `KeyEvent` class:

`public static final int KEY_PRESSED`

This event is delivered when a key is pressed.

`public static final int KEY_RELEASED`

This event is delivered when a key is released.

`public static final int KEY_TYPED`

This event is delivered when a character has been typed on the keyboard, i.e. a key has been pressed (`KEY_PRESSED`) and then released (`KEY_RELEASED`) to signify typing a character.

The inherited `getID()` method returns the specific type of event denoted by one of the constants given above. In addition, the inherited method `getWhen()` from the parent class `InputEvent` can be used to get the time when the event took place.

These events are generated by the `Component` class and its subclasses.

The `KeyEvent` class provides the following useful methods:

`int getKeyCode()`

For `KEY_PRESSED` or `KEY_RELEASED` events, this method can be used to get the integer key-code associated with the key. The key-codes are defined as constants in `KeyEvent`.

`char getKeyChar()`

For `KEY_TYPED` events, the method can be used to get the Unicode character that resulted from hitting a key.

MouseEvent

This class is a subclass of the abstract `InputEvent` class.

This event is generated when the user moves the mouse or presses a mouse button. The exact action is identified by the following constants in the `MouseEvent` class:

`public static final int MOUSE_PRESSED`

This event is delivered when a mouse button is pressed.

`public static final int MOUSE_RELEASED`

This event is delivered when a mouse button is released.

`public static final int MOUSE_CLICKED`

This event is delivered when a mouse button is pressed and released without any intervening mouse dragging.

`public static final int MOUSE_DRAGGED`

This event is delivered when the mouse is dragged, i.e. moved while a mouse button is pressed.

`public static final int MOUSE_MOVED`

This event is delivered when the mouse is moved without any mouse button being pressed.

`public static final int MOUSE_ENTERED`

This event is delivered when the mouse crosses the boundary of a component and enters it.

`public static final int MOUSE_EXITED`

This event is delivered when the mouse crosses the boundary of a component and exits it.

The inherited `getID()` method returns the specific type of event denoted by one of the constants given above. The inherited method `getWhen()` can also be used here to get the time when the event took place.

Mouse events are generated by the `Component` class and its subclasses.

The `MouseEvent` class provides the following useful methods:

```
int getX()
int getY()
Point getPoint()
```

These methods can be used to get the x- and/or y-position of the event relative to the source component.

`void translatePoint(int dx, int dy)`

Translates the coordinate position of the event by (`dx`, `dy`). This affects the values returned by `getX()`, `getY()` and `getPoint()` methods.

`int getClickCount()`

Returns the number of mouse clicks associated with the event. This is useful for detecting such events as double clicks.

PaintEvent

This event is generated when a component should have its `paint()`/`update()` methods invoked (Section 15.1, p. 451). These events are handled internally by the AWT, and should not directly be dealt with by the application.

WindowEvent

This event is generated when an important operation is performed on a window. These operations are identified by the following constants in the `WindowEvent` class:

`public static final int WINDOW_OPENED`

This event is delivered only once for a window when it is created, opened and made visible the first time.

`public static final int WINDOW_CLOSING`

This event is delivered when the user action dictates that the window should be closed. The application should explicitly call either `setVisible(false)` or `dispose()` on the window as a response to this event.

`public static final int WINDOW_CLOSED`

This event is delivered after the window has been closed as the result of a call to `setVisible(false)` or `dispose()`.

`public static final int WINDOW_ICONIFIED`

This event is delivered when the window is iconified.

`public static final int WINDOW_DEICONIFIED`

This event is delivered when the window is de-iconified.

`public static final int WINDOW_ACTIVATED`

This event is delivered when the window is activated, i.e. keyboard events will be delivered to the window or its subcomponents.

`public static final int WINDOW_DEACTIVATED`

This event is delivered when the window is deactivated, i.e. keyboard events will no longer be delivered to the window or its subcomponents.

The inherited `getID()` method returns the specific type of the event, denoted by one of the constants given above.

Window events are generated by the `Window` class and its subclasses.

The `WindowEvent` class provides the following useful method:

`Window getWindow()`

This method returns the `Window` object that caused the event to be generated.

Review questions

14.1 Which of these classes do not generate item events?

Select all valid answers.

(a) `Checkbox`
(b) `CheckboxMenuItem`
(c) `MenuItem`
(d) `Choice`
(e) `List`

14.2 Which of these are not AWT event classes?

Select all valid answers.

(a) `MouseEvent`
(b) `MouseMotionEvent`
(c) `ItemEvent`
(d) `WindowEvent`
(e) `AdjustmentEvent`

14.3 In which of these situations does a `Checkbox` component generate an `ItemEvent`?

Select all valid answers.

(a) When being selected.
(b) When being deselected.
(c) When double-clicked.
(d) When it gains focus.
(e) When the mouse pointer enters the bounds of the component.

14.4 Which of the these AWT classes are sources for action events?

Select all valid answers.

(a) `Choice`
(b) `MenuItem`
(c) `List`
(d) `TextField`
(e) `Checkbox`

14.5 What does gaining focus entail?

Select all valid answers.

(a) The component will receive all mouse events.
(b) The component will receive all keyboard events.
(c) All other components do not respond to input.

14.3 The Event Delegation Model

AWT events are represented by the subclasses of the `java.awt.AWTEvent` class. The source of an event can be identified by calling the `getSource()` method, and the event's type value determined by calling the `getID()` method. Several sources can generate the same types of events. For example, an `ActionEvent` can be generated by objects of the `Button`, `List`, `MenuItem` and `TextField` classes.

The event delegation model is employed by the Java Foundation Classes (JFC) which encompass the AWT and Swing component sets. In the event delegation model, an event source informs event listeners about events when these occur, and supplies the necessary information about these events. In other words, an event listener, which is interested in receiving events, is informed by an event source when certain types of events occur, so that it can take appropriate action.

An event source can generate one or more types of events, and maintains a list of event listeners for each type of event. Table 14.1 and Table 14.2 summarize the event sources of each event type. As can be seen from Table 14.1, a `Button` object can generate an `ActionEvent` when the button is clicked. Since a `Button` object is also a `Component`, it can generate all the events for the `Component` class as well: `ComponentEvent`, `FocusEvent`, `KeyEvent`, `MouseEvent` (Table 14.2). Subclasses of a source can generate the same events that the source can.

How is the association between the source and the listener established? Each event source defines methods for registering (`add`*X*`Listener()`) and removing (`remove`*X*`Listener()`) listeners, which implement a particular *listener interface* (*X*`Listener`). The significance of the listener interface is explained below. Each *X*`Listener` interface defines methods which accept a specific event type as argument. Event types, event sources, listener registration and removal methods in event sources, and corresponding listener interfaces are listed in Table 14.1 and Table 14.2. The methods in each listener interface are listed in Table 14.3 and Table 14.4, showing which event types are passed as arguments. As an example of listener registration, a potential listener object `cmd` interested in being informed when a particular `Button` object `button` is pushed (which generates an `ActionEvent`) can be added as a listener to this button by using the `addActionListener()` method in the `Button` class:

```
button.addActionListener(cmd);
```

Table 14.1 *Semantic Event Handling*

Event Type	Event Source	Listener Registration and Removal Methods provided by the source	Event Listener Interface implemented by a listener

`ActionEvent`	`Button`
	`List`
	`MenuItem`
	`TextField`
		`addActionListener`
		`removeActionListener`
			`ActionListener`

`AdjustmentEvent`	`Scrollbar`	`addAdjustmentListener` `removeAdjustmentListener`	`AdjustmentListener`

`ItemEvent`	`Choice`
	`Checkbox`
	`CheckboxMenuItem`
	`List`
		`addItemListener`
		`removeItemListener`
			`ItemListener`

`TextEvent`	`TextArea` `TextField`	`addTextListener` `removeTextListener`	`TextListener`

Table 14.2 *Low-Level Event Handling*

Event Type	Event Source	Listener Registration and Removal Methods provided by the source	Event Listener Interface implemented by a listener
`ComponentEvent`	`Component`	`addComponentListener` `removeComponentListener`	`ComponentListener`
`ContainerEvent`	`Container`	`addContainerListener` `removeContainerListener`	`ContainerListener`
`FocusEvent`	`Component`	`addFocusListener` `removeFocusListener`	`FocusListener`
`KeyEvent`	`Component`	`addKeyListener` `removeKeyListener`	`KeyListener`
`MouseEvent`	`Component`	`addMouseListener` `removeMouseListener`	`MouseListener`
		`addMouseMotionListener` `removeMouseMotionListener`	`MouseMotionListener`
`WindowEvent`	`Window`	`addWindowListener` `removeWindowListener`	`WindowListener`

How does the event source inform the event listener that a particular event that it is interested in has occurred? It calls a particular method in the listener. To ensure that the listener really does provide the relevant method that can be called by the event source, the listener must implement a listener interface *X*`Listener` (Table 14.3, Table 14.4). Each registration and removal method in an event source takes as argument the corresponding *X*`Listener` interface. At compile time, it is therefore possible to ensure that any listener added or removed implements the required interface. Any listener of a `Button` object, that wants to be informed of an `Action Event`, must implement the corresponding `ActionListener` interface. This interface specifies only one method: `actionPerformed(ActionEvent evt)`. This method will be invoked on the listener, with the information about the event supplied in the `ActionEvent` argument, when the button is clicked. The listener can take appropriate action to handle the event in its implementation of the `actionPerformed(ActionEvent evt)` method.

Table 14.3 *Semantic Event Listener Interfaces and Their Methods*

Event Listener Interface	Event Listener Methods
`ActionListener`	`actionPerformed(ActionEvent evt)`
`AdjustmentListener`	`adjustmentValueChanged(AdjustmentEvent evt)`
`ItemListener`	`itemStateChanged(ItemEvent evt)`
`TextListener`	`textValueChanged(TextEvent evt)`

Table 14.4 *Low-level Event Listener Interfaces and Their Methods*

Event Listener Interface	Event Listener Methods
`ComponentListener`	`componentHidden(ComponentEvent evt)`
	`componentMoved(ComponentEvent evt)`
	`componentResized(ComponentEvent evt)`
	`componentShown(ComponentEvent evt)`
`ContainerListener`	`componentAdded(ContainerEvent evt)`
	`componentRemoved(ContainerEvent evt)`
`FocusListener`	`focusGained(FocusEvent evt)`
	`focusLost(FocusEvent evt)`
`KeyListener`	`keyPressed(KeyEvent evt)`
	`keyReleased(KeyEvent evt)`
	`keyTyped(KeyEvent evt)`
`MouseListener`	`mouseClicked(MouseEvent evt)`
	`mouseEntered(MouseEvent evt)`
	`mouseExited(MouseEvent evt)`
	`mousePressed(MouseEvent evt)`
	`mouseReleased(MouseEvent evt)`
`MouseMotionListener`	`mouseDragged(MouseEvent evt)`
	`mouseMoved(MouseEvent evt)`
`WindowListener`	`windowActivated(WindowEvent evt)`
	`windowClosed(WindowEvent evt)`
	`windowClosing(WindowEvent evt)`
	`windowDeactivated(WindowEvent evt)`
	`windowDeiconified(WindowEvent evt)`
	`windowIconified(WindowEvent evt)`
	`windowOpened(WindowEvent evt)`

Other points to note about the event delegation model:

- The events generated by an event source are independent of any enclosing component. In other words, an event source transmits the same events regardless of its location in the component hierarchy of a GUI.
- Note that events generated by an event source component are also generated by subclasses of the source component, unless explicitly inhibited.
- An event listener interface can contain more than one method. This is true for all the low-level event classes. For example, the `KeyEvent` class represents different key events, and the appropriate method in the listeners (`KeyListener`) is called for each type of key event.

- `MouseEvent` has *two* listener interfaces: `MouseListener` and `MouseMotionListener` (Table 14.1). A source that generates a `MouseEvent` provides two sets of registration and removal methods corresponding to the two listener interfaces, and can dispatch the `MouseEvent` to the appropriate listeners, based on the interface these listeners implement.
- All listeners of a particular event are notified, but the order in which they are notified is not necessarily the same as the order in which they were added as listeners.
- Notification of all listeners is not guaranteed to occur in the same thread. Access to any data shared between the listeners should be synchronized.
- Each listener interface extends the `java.util.EventListener` interface.

Figure 14.2 *Handling Events*

Example 14.1 *Illustrating Event Delegation Model*

```
/** A simple application to demonstrate the Event Delegation Model */
import java.awt.*;
import java.awt.event.*;

public class SimpleWindow extends Frame {

    Button quitButton;                      // The source
    QuitHandler quitHandler;                // The listener

    public SimpleWindow() {

        // Create a window
        super("SimpleWindow");

        // Create one button
        quitButton = new Button("Quit");

        // Set a layout manager, and add the button to the window.
        setLayout(new FlowLayout(FlowLayout.CENTER));
        add(quitButton);

        // Create and add the listener to the button
        quitHandler = new QuitHandler(this);                     // (1)
        quitButton.addActionListener(quitHandler);               // (2)

        // Pack the window and pop it up.
        pack();
        setVisible(true);
    }
```

```
    /** Create an instance of the application */
    public static void main(String args[]) { new SimpleWindow(); }

}

// Definition of the Listener
class QuitHandler implements ActionListener {                    // (3)

    private SimpleWindow application;    // The associated application

    public QuitHandler(SimpleWindow window) {
        application = window;
    }

    // Invoked when the user clicks the quit button.
    public void actionPerformed(ActionEvent evt) {               // (4)
        if (evt.getSource() == application.quitButton) {         // (5)
            System.out.println("Quitting the application.");
            application.dispose();                               // (6)
            System.exit(0);                                      // (7)
        }
    }
}
```

The application in Example 14.1 sets up a single window with a "Quit"-button, shown in Figure 14.2. Clicking the button terminates the application. The class diagram in Figure 14.3 shows the relationship between a client (`SimpleWindow`), an event source (`Button`) and an event listener (`QuitHandler`). The sequence diagram in Figure 14.4 illustrates how events are delivered from the source to the listener.

After the GUI has been created, the following steps can be used to set up the delegation of events from the source (in this case, a button) to a listener (in this case, an external class):

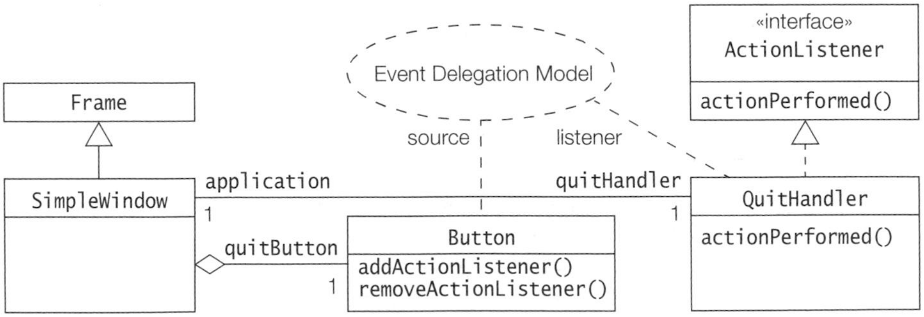

Figure 14.3 *Event Delegation*

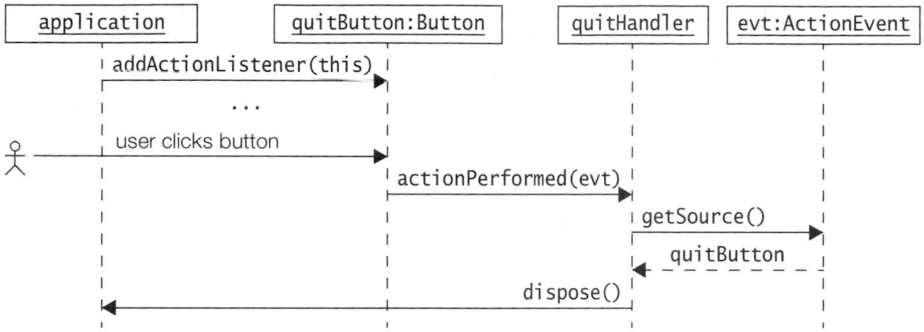

Figure 14.4 *Delegating Events*

1. Create a listener in the application.

```
quitHandler = new QuitHandler(this);                    // (1)
```

   Note that in this particular example, a reference to the application is passed in the constructor for the listener. This allows the listener access to the application in order to handle the event.

2. Add the listener to the source.

```
quitButton.addActionListener(quitHandler);              // (2)
```

   The button, which is the event source, generates `ActionEvent` objects when it is clicked, therefore the `addActionListener()` method from the `Button` class is used to add the listener.

The above procedure can be repeated for all listeners. The same listener can of course be added to several event sources, if required. In this particular case the listener will handle `ActionEvent` objects, so it must implement the `ActionListener` interface, as shown at (3). This interface contains only one method called `actionPerformed(ActionEvent evt)`, which is implemented at (4). Although not strictly necessary in this case, the `actionPerformed()` method checks to see that it was the Quit-button that was clicked, by comparing the reference of the event source with that of the button object at (5). The `actionPerformed()` method calls the application to dispose of its resources at (6), and invokes the `System.exit()` method with status 0 to terminate execution at (7). These two last steps are usually employed in terminating a GUI application.

Review questions

14.6 What is the principle of the event delegation model?

Select the one right answer.

(a) Authority for event handling is delegated by subclassing the AWT component classes to provide implementations that do the event handling.

(b) Authority for event handling is delegated by subclassing the AWT event classes to provide implementations that do the event handling.
(c) Authority for event handling is delegated by implementing event listener interfaces to provide implementations that do the event handling.

14.7 Which of these are AWT event listener interfaces?

Select all valid answers.

(a) `ActionListener`
(b) `WindowListener`
(c) `ItemListener`
(d) `ButtonListener`
(e) `MotionListener`

14.8 Given a reference `listener` that denotes an object that implements `ActionListener`, how do you make the listener listen to events originating from an event source component referenced by `source`?

Select the one right answer.

(a) `listener.setSource(source);`
(b) `listener.addSource(source);`
(c) `source.setListener(listener);`
(d) `source.addListener(listener);`
(e) `source.addActionListener(listener);`

14.9 Which of these event classes are never handled in the event listener model?

Select all valid answers.

(a) `ComponentEvent`
(b) `ContainerEvent`
(c) `FocusEvent`
(d) `PaintEvent`
(e) `WindowEvent`

14.10 Which interface should be implemented if the program should respond to menu selections?

Select the one right answer.

(a) `ActionListener`
(b) `MenuItemListener`
(c) `TextListener`
(d) `MouseListener`
(e) `WindowListener`

14.11 Which of these methods are part of the `java.awt.Component` class?

Select all valid answers.

(a) `addMouseListener()`
(b) `addMouseMotionListener()`
(c) `addActionListener()`
(d) `addKeyListener()`
(e) `addItemListener()`

14.12 What will happen if you register more than one `ActionListener` in a button component?

Select the one right answer.

(a) The program will fail to compile.
(b) The program will issue a runtime exception during execution.
(c) All the registered action listeners will be notified when the button is clicked.
(d) The last registered action listener will be notified when the button is clicked.
(e) The first registered action listener will be notified when the button is clicked.

14.4 Event Adapters

Event adapters facilitate implementing listener interfaces. The Quit-button application from Example 14.1 will be extended, first without and then with the use of event adapters.

In these examples, when the user closes the window by clicking its close-box, the application terminates. Clicking the close-box results in the event source (which is a `Window` or a subclass of `Window`) calling the `windowClosing(WindowEvent evt)` method of the `WindowListener` interface.

Example 14.2 *Implementing Listener Interfaces*

```
/* SimpleWindowTwo: A simple setup for Event Delegation Model */
import java.awt.*;
import java.awt.event.*;

/** A simple application to demonstrate the Event Delegation Model */
public class SimpleWindowTwo extends Frame {

    Button quitButton;                     // The source
    QuitHandler quitHandler;               // The listener

    public SimpleWindowTwo() {

        // Create a window
        super("SimpleWindow");

        // Create one button
        quitButton = new Button("Quit");
```

```
        // Set a layout manager, and add the button to the window.
        setLayout(new FlowLayout(FlowLayout.CENTER));
        add(quitButton);

        // Create and add the listener to the button
        quitHandler = new QuitHandler(this);                       // (1)
        quitButton.addActionListener(quitHandler);                 // (2)

        // Add the listener to the window
        addWindowListener(quitHandler);                            // (3)

        // Pack the window and pop it up.
        pack();
        setVisible(true);
    }

    /** Create an instance of the application */
    public static void main(String args[]) { new SimpleWindowTwo(); }

}

// Definition of the Listener
class QuitHandler implements ActionListener, WindowListener {   // (4)

    private SimpleWindowTwo application; // The associated application

    public QuitHandler(SimpleWindowTwo window) {
        application = window;
    }

    // Terminate the application.
    private void terminate() {                                     // (5)
        System.out.println("Quitting the application.");
        application.dispose();
        System.exit(0);
    }

    // Invoked when the user clicks the quit button.
    public void actionPerformed(ActionEvent evt) {
        if (evt.getSource() == application.quitButton) {
            terminate();
        }
    }

    // Invoked when the user clicks the close-box
    public void windowClosing(WindowEvent evt) {                  // (6)
        terminate();
    }

    // Unused methods of the WindowListener interface.               (7)
    public void windowOpened(WindowEvent evt) {}
    public void windowIconified(WindowEvent evt) {}
    public void windowDeiconified(WindowEvent evt) {}
    public void windowDeactivated(WindowEvent evt) {}
    public void windowClosed(WindowEvent evt) {}
    public void windowActivated(WindowEvent evt) {}
}
```

Instead of these you can extend WindowAdapter & override only the reqd method (in this case: windowClosing())

The application in Example 14.2 uses the `QuitHandler` class from Example 14.1 to handle the window-closing event:

```
        addWindowListener(quitHandler);                      // (3)
```

The listener is registered with the application window, and the `QuitHandler` implements the `WindowListener` interface which consists of seven methods. Note that the `QuitHandler` class only provides a proper implementation for the `windowClosing()` method of this interface, as shown at (6). The other methods of the `WindowListener` interface are not of interest, but they still have to be implemented as stubs, i.e. methods with empty bodies, as shown at (7).

To facilitate the implementation of listener interfaces, the `java.awt.event` package defines an *adapter* class corresponding to each low-level listener interface (Table 14.5). An event adapter implements stubs for all the methods of the corresponding interface. A listener can subclass the adapter and override only stub-methods for handling events of interest. It makes sense to define such adapters for low-level event listener interfaces, as only these interfaces have more than one method in their specification. The `QuitHandler` class in Example 14.3 extends the `WindowAdapter` class, as shown at (4), and overrides the `windowClosing(WindowEvent evt)` method from the superclass, as shown at (6).

Table 14.5 *Low-Level Event Listener Interfaces and Their Adapters*

Low-Level Event Listener Interface	Low-Level Event Listener Adapter
`ComponentListener`	`ComponentAdapter`
`ContainerListener`	`ContainerAdapter`
`FocusListener`	`FocusAdapter`
`KeyListener`	`KeyAdapter`
`MouseListener`	`MouseAdapter`
`MouseMotionListener`	`MouseMotionAdapter`
`WindowListener`	`WindowAdapter`

Example 14.3 *Using Event Adapters*

```
/* SimpleWindowTwo: A simple setup for Event Delegation Model */
import java.awt.*;
import java.awt.event.*;

/** A simple application to demonstrate the Event Delegation Model */
public class SimpleWindowTwo extends Frame { /* See Example 14.2 */ }

// Definition of the Listener
class QuitHandler extends WindowAdapter implements ActionListener { // (4)

    private SimpleWindowTwo application;    // The associated application

    public QuitHandler(SimpleWindowTwo window) {
        application = window;
    }
```

```
        // Terminate the application.
        private void terminate() {                                    // (5)
            System.out.println("Quitting the application.");
            application.dispose();
            System.exit(0);
        }

        // Invoked when the user clicks the quit button.
        public void actionPerformed(ActionEvent evt) {
            if (evt.getSource() == application.quitButton) {
                terminate();
            }
        }

        // Invoked when the user clicks the close-box
        public void windowClosing(WindowEvent evt) {                  // (6)
            terminate();
        }
    }
```

A listener can be any object, as long as it implements the relevant listener interface. In the previous examples, the client could have registered itself as a listener by passing itself to the source, and implementing the appropriate listener interfaces. For low-level events, a listener can decide to extend the relevant listener adapter.

Event Listeners as Anonymous Inner Classes

Anonymous classes (Section 7.5, p. 243) provide an elegant solution for creating listeners and adding them to event sources. Yet another version of the Quit-button application is shown in Example 14.4. The listener that handles clicking of the Quit-button is created and added at (1). This listener is an anonymous class. It *implements* the `ActionListener` interface by providing the implementation of the `actionPerformed(ActionEvent evt)` method.

The listener that handles the closing of the window when the close-box is clicked is shown at (3). The anonymous class implementing this listener *extends* the `WindowAdapter` by overriding the `windowClosing(WindowEvent evt)` method.

Notice the convenience of accessing the enclosing context from an anonymous class. For example, the call to the `private` method `terminate()` in the enclosing class from the anonymous classes at (2) and (4). To explicitly access a member in the enclosing context, the special syntax of the `this` construct must be used. For example, the call to the `terminate()` method could be written as: `SimpleWindowThree.this.terminate()`.

Example 14.4 *Listeners as Anonymous Classes*

```
/*
   SimpleWindowThree: A simple setup for Event Delegation Model
   using Anonymous Classes.
 */
```

```
import java.awt.*;
import java.awt.event.*;

public class SimpleWindowThree extends Frame {

    Button quitButton;

    public SimpleWindowThree() {

        // Create a window
        super("SimpleWindowThree");

        // Create one button
        quitButton = new Button("Quit");

        // Set a layout manager, and add the button to the window.
        setLayout(new FlowLayout(FlowLayout.CENTER));
        add(quitButton);

        // Create and add the listener to the button
        quitButton.addActionListener(new ActionListener() {      // (1)
            // Invoked when the user clicks the quit button.
            public void actionPerformed(ActionEvent evt) {
                terminate();                                      // (2)
            }
        });

        // Create and add the listener to the window
        addWindowListener(new WindowAdapter() {                   // (3)
            // Invoked when the user clicks the close-box.
            public void windowClosing(WindowEvent evt) {
                terminate();                                      // (4)
            }
        });

        // Pack the window and pop it up.
        pack();
        setVisible(true);
    }

    private void terminate() {
        System.out.println("Quitting the application.");
        dispose();
        System.exit(0);
    }

    /** Create an instance of the application */
    public static void main(String args[]) { new SimpleWindowThree(); }

}
```

14.5 Building GUI-based Applications

A complete GUI-based application is presented in this section. The component hierarchy of the GUI for this application was built in the discussion on component hierarchies (Section 13.9, p. 407). In this section, the emphasis will be on adding the event handling to the GUI which is discussed in Example 13.8.

Example 14.5 *GUI + Event Handling*

```
/* DemoApplet: Demonstrating GUI + EVENT HANDLING */

import java.awt.*;
import java.awt.event.*;
import java.applet.*;

interface IGeometryConstants {
    int SQUARE  = 0;
    int CIRCLE  = 1;
    int ELLIPSE = 2;
    String[] shapeNames = {"Square", "Circle", "Ellipse"};

    int SMALL  = 0;
    int MEDIUM = 1;
    int LARGE  = 2;
    String[] sizeNames = {"Small", "Medium", "Large"};
}

public class DemoApplet extends Applet implements IGeometryConstants {

    // Panel for shape
    Panel         shapePanel;
    CheckboxGroup shapeCBG;
    Checkbox      squareCB;
    Checkbox      circleCB;
    Checkbox      ellipseCB;

    // Panel for x,y coordinates
    Panel     xyPanel;
    Label     xLabel;
    TextField xInput;
    Label     yLabel;
    TextField yInput;

    // Panel for size and fill
    Panel    sizePanel;
    Label    sizeLabel;
    Choice   sizeChoices;
    Checkbox fillCB;

    // Panel for shape, coordinates, size and fill
    Panel leftPanel;

    // Panel for Message display, draw button and canvas
    Panel      rightPanel;
    Button     drawButton;
    DrawRegion drawRegion;
    TextField  messageDisplay;

    public void init() {

        makeShapePanel();
        makeXYPanel();
        makeSizePanel();
```

```
        makeLeftPanel();
        makeRightPanel();

        addListeners();

        add(leftPanel);
        add(rightPanel);

    }

    // Panel for shape
    void makeShapePanel() {
        shapePanel = new Panel();

        shapeCBG   = new CheckboxGroup();

        squareCB   = new Checkbox(shapeNames[SQUARE],  shapeCBG, true);
        circleCB   = new Checkbox(shapeNames[CIRCLE],  shapeCBG, false);
        ellipseCB  = new Checkbox(shapeNames[ELLIPSE], shapeCBG, false);

        shapePanel.setLayout(new FlowLayout());
        shapePanel.add(squareCB);
        shapePanel.add(circleCB);
        shapePanel.add(ellipseCB);
    }

    // Panel for x,y coordinates
    void makeXYPanel() {
        xyPanel = new Panel();

        xLabel  = new Label("X Coordinate:");
        yLabel  = new Label("Y Coordinate:");

        xInput  = new TextField(5);
        yInput  = new TextField(5);

        xyPanel.setLayout(new GridLayout(2,2));
        xyPanel.add(xLabel);
        xyPanel.add(xInput);
        xyPanel.add(yLabel);
        xyPanel.add(yInput);
    }

    // Panel for size and fill
    void makeSizePanel() {

        sizePanel   = new Panel();

        sizeLabel   = new Label("Size:");

        sizeChoices = new Choice();
        sizeChoices.add(sizeNames[0]);
        sizeChoices.add(sizeNames[1]);
        sizeChoices.add(sizeNames[2]);

        fillCB = new Checkbox("Fill", false);

        sizePanel.setLayout(new FlowLayout());
        sizePanel.add(sizeLabel);
        sizePanel.add(sizeChoices);
        sizePanel.add(fillCB);

    }
```

```
// Panel for shape, coordinates, size and fill
void makeLeftPanel() {
    leftPanel = new Panel();

    leftPanel.setLayout(new BorderLayout());
    leftPanel.add(shapePanel, "North");
    leftPanel.add(xyPanel,    "Center");
    leftPanel.add(sizePanel,  "South");
}

// Panel for Message display, draw button, and canvas
void makeRightPanel() {
    rightPanel = new Panel();

    messageDisplay = new TextField("MESSAGE DISPLAY");
    messageDisplay.setEditable(false);
    messageDisplay.setBackground(Color.yellow);

    drawButton = new Button("Draw");
    drawButton.setBackground(Color.lightGray);

    drawRegion = new DrawRegion();
    drawRegion.setSize(150,150);
    drawRegion.setBackground(Color.white);

    rightPanel.setLayout(new BorderLayout());
    rightPanel.add(drawButton,     BorderLayout.NORTH);
    rightPanel.add(messageDisplay, BorderLayout.SOUTH);
    rightPanel.add(drawRegion,     BorderLayout.CENTER);
}

// Add the listeners.
void addListeners() {

    drawButton.addActionListener(new ActionListener() {         // (1)
        public void actionPerformed(ActionEvent evt) {          // (2)

            int shape, xCoord, yCoord, width;

            messageDisplay.setText("");

            // Get the shape                                        (3)
            if (squareCB.getState())
                shape = SQUARE;
            else if (circleCB.getState())
                shape = CIRCLE;
            else if (ellipseCB.getState())
                shape = ELLIPSE;
            else {
                messageDisplay.setText("Unknown shape.");
                return;
            }

            // Get the coordinates                                  (4)
            try {
                xCoord = Integer.parseInt(xInput.getText());
                yCoord = Integer.parseInt(yInput.getText());
```

```
                } catch (NumberFormatException e) {
                    messageDisplay.setText("Illegal coordinates.");
                    return;
                }

                // Get the size                                           (5)
                switch (sizeChoices.getSelectedIndex()) {
                    case SMALL:  width = 30;  break;
                    case MEDIUM: width = 60;  break;
                    case LARGE:  width = 120; break;
                    default: messageDisplay.setText("Unknown size."); return;
                }

                messageDisplay.setText("Drawing" + shapeNames[shape]);
                drawRegion.doDraw(                                     // (6)
                        shape,
                        xCoord, yCoord,
                        fillCB.getState(),
                        width
                );
            }
        });

        xInput.addTextListener(new TextListener() {                    // (7)
            public void textValueChanged(TextEvent evt) {
                checkTF(xInput);
            }
        });

        yInput.addTextListener(new TextListener() {                    // (8)
            public void textValueChanged(TextEvent evt) {
                checkTF(yInput);
            }
        });
    }

    // Check for legal integer value in the text field
    void checkTF(TextField tf) {                                       // (9)

        messageDisplay.setText("");
        try {
            Integer.parseInt(tf.getText());                            // (10)

        } catch (NumberFormatException e) {
            messageDisplay.setText("Illegal coordinate.");
        }
    }
}

/** Canvas for doing the drawing */
class DrawRegion extends Canvas implements IGeometryConstants {    // (11)

    // Values needed for drawing the shape
    private int     shape;
    private int     xCoord;
    private int     yCoord;
    private boolean fillFlag;
    private int     width;
```

```
    public DrawRegion() {
        setSize(150,150);
        setBackground(Color.white);
    }

    // Set the values and repaint the drawing region.
    public void doDraw(int shape,                                    // (12)
                       int xCoord, int yCoord,
                       boolean fillFlag, int width) {

        this.shape    = shape;
        this.xCoord   = xCoord;
        this.yCoord   = yCoord;
        this.fillFlag = fillFlag;
        this.width    = width;

        repaint();                                                   // (13)
    }

    // Do the drawing of the shape
    public void paint(Graphics g) {                                  // (14)

        switch (shape) {
            case SQUARE:
                if (fillFlag) g.fillRect(xCoord, yCoord, width, width);
                else g.drawRect(xCoord, yCoord, width, width);
                break;
            case CIRCLE:
                if (fillFlag) g.fillOval(xCoord, yCoord, width, width);
                else g.drawOval(xCoord, yCoord, width, width);
                break;
            case ELLIPSE:
                if (fillFlag) g.fillOval(xCoord, yCoord, width, width/2);
                else g.drawOval(xCoord, yCoord, width, width/2);
        }
    }
}
```

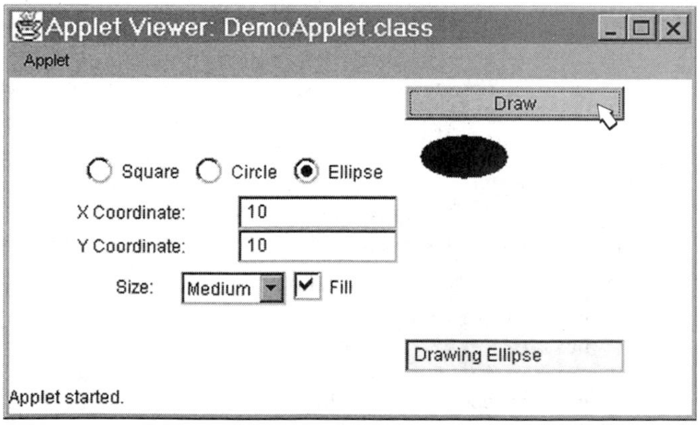

Figure 14.5 *GUI + Event Handling*

In Example 14.5, the user can specify the shape, size, fill and coordinates for a drawing. Clicking the draw button renders the shape according to the specifications indicated by the user. The user interface is shown in Figure 14.5.

The drawing region is implemented by the class `DrawRegion` which extends the `Canvas` class, as shown at (11). The class `DrawRegion` defines a method called `doDraw()` that sets up the values needed for drawing a shape, and calls the `repaint()` method, as shown as (12). The `repaint()` method eventually results in the `paint()` method of the `DrawRegion` class being called to actually render the shape, as shown at (13). Details on rendering graphics can be found in Section 15.7.

The application uses three listeners implemented as anonymous classes at (1), (7) and (8). The listener at (1) is added to the draw button and is called when the draw button is clicked. The `actionPerformed()` method of the listener at (2) determines the shape at (3), parses the coordinates at (4), sets the size at (5), and at (6) sends all the specifications for drawing a shape to the `doDraw()` method of the `DrawRegion` class.

The listener at (7) is added to the x-coordinate text field, so that any changes made to the text results in this listener being notified. The listener calls the method `checkTF(TextField tf)` at (9) to check whether the text in the text field is a valid integer. If an illegal character is typed, so that the text cannot be parsed to a valid integer at (10), a message is immediately displayed. An analogous listener for the y-coordinate text field is implemented, as shown at (8). A `TextEvent` is generated to signal any change in the contents of a text component. The event source, in this case a `TextField`, calls the method `textValueChanged(TextEvent evt)` of the `TextListener` interface. This method is implemented by the event listeners which, in this case, are anonymous classes defined at (7) and (8).

Review questions

14.13 Which one of these interfaces does the `java.awt.event.MouseMotionAdapter` class implement?

Select the one right answer.

(a) `MouseAdapter`
(b) `MouseEvent`
(c) `MouseMotionEvent`
(d) `MouseListener`
(e) `MouseMotionListener`

14.14 What will be the result of attempting to compile and run the following program?

```
import java.awt.*;
import java.awt.event.*;

public class MyClass {
    public static void main(String args[]) {
```

```
        Window window = new Frame("Test");
        Button button = new Button("Hello");
        window.add(button, BorderLayout.CENTER);
        button.addMouseListener(new MyListener());
        window.pack();
        window.setVisible(true);
    }
}

class MyListener extends MouseAdapter implements ActionListener {
    public void mouseClicked(MouseEvent evt) { System.out.println("A"); }

    public void mousePressed(MouseEvent evt) { System.out.println("B"); }

    public void mouseReleased(MouseEvent evt) { System.out.println("C"); }

    public void actionPerformed(ActionEvent evt) { System.out.println("D"); }
}
```

Select the one right answer.

(a) It will fail to compile, since `MyListener` cannot be two types of listener at the same time.
(b) It will fail to compile, since `MyListener` fails to provide implementations for the `mouseEntered()` and `mouseExited()` methods.
(c) It will compile and run without error and will print `B`, `D`, `A`, `C`, in that order, when the user clicks the button.
(d) It will compile and run without error and will print `B`, `C`, `D`, `A`, in that order, when the user clicks the button.
(e) It will compile and run without error and will print `B`, `C`, `A`, in that order, when the user clicks the button.

14.15 Which of these is not an event listener adapter defined in the `java.awt.event` package?

Select all valid answers.

(a) `ActionAdapter`
(b) `MouseAdapter`
(c) `MouseMotionAdapter`
(d) `WindowAdapter`
(e) `FocusAdapter`

14.16 What will be the result of attempting to compile and run the following program?

```
import java.awt.*;
import java.awt.event.*;

public class MyClass {
    public static void main(String args[]) {
        Window window = new Frame("Test");
        Button button = new Button("Hello");
        window.add(button, BorderLayout.CENTER);
        window.addMouseListener(new MyListener("A"));
```

```
            button.addMouseListener(new MyListener("B"));
            window.pack();
            window.setVisible(true);
        }
    }

    class MyListener extends MouseAdapter {
        String messageDisplay;

        MyListener(String str) {
            messageDisplay = str;
        }

        public void mouseClicked(MouseEvent evt) {
            System.out.println(messageDisplay);
        }
    }
```

Select the one right answer.

(a) It will fail to compile.
(b) It will compile and run without error and will print nothing when the user clicks the button.
(c) It will compile and run without error and will print `A` when the user clicks the button.
(d) It will compile and run without error and will print `B` when the user clicks the button.
(e) It will compile and run without error and will print `A`, `B`, in that order, when the user clicks the button.
(f) It will compile and run without error and will print `B`, `A`, in that order, when the user clicks the button.

14.17 Which of these listener interfaces have a corresponding adapter class?

Select all valid answers.

(a) `ActionListener`
(b) `AdjustmentListener`
(c) `FocusListener`
(d) `ItemListener`
(e) `TextListener`

14.6 Low-Level Event Processing

The event delegation model works well for building GUIs from predefined components. Components receive events that they dispatch to event listeners. The AWT delivers `AWTEvent`s to a component by calling the `processEvent(AWTEvent evt)` method of the component. This method is at the core of low-level event processing. Its default implementation calls an event-specific method in the component. If the component received an `ActionEvent`, the `processEvent()` method calls the `processActionEvent()` method of the component. In other words, when an *X*`Event` is received by a component, it is dispatched by the `processEvent()` method to a corresponding `processXEvent()` method of the component. It is the `processXEvent()` method that is responsible for invoking the appropriate method in all registered listeners of this event. Each `processXEvent()` method corresponds to an `XListener` interface. An `ActionEvent` received via the `processEvent()` method will be dispatched to the `processActionEvent()` method, which in turn calls the `actionPerformed()` method of the `ActionListener` interface implemented by the event listener.

If a component is customized by subclassing another component, it has the opportunity to implement its own low-level event processing. This can be done in one of two ways:

- The subclass component can keep the default behavior of the `processEvent()` method, but provide its own implementations of the `processXEvent()` methods which override the default versions of these methods.
- The subclass component can override the `processEvent()` method and thereby bypass the default behavior of the `processXEvent()` methods.

In order for either scheme to work, one additional requirement must be met. The subclass component must explicitly enable all events of interest. This is done by calling the `enableEvents()` method of the component. This method is passed a bit mask formed from OR'ing `EVENT_MASK` constants defined in the `java.awt.AWTEvent` class, and shown in Table 14.6.

Table 14.6 *Event Masks and Event Processing Methods*

Enabling `EVENT_MASK`	Corresponding Event Processing Method
AWTEvent.COMPONENT_EVENT_MASK	processComponentEvent()
AWTEvent.CONTAINER_EVENT_MASK	processContainerEvent()
AWTEvent.FOCUS_EVENT_MASK	processFocusEvent()
AWTEvent.KEY_EVENT_MASK	processKeyEvent()
AWTEvent.MOUSE_EVENT_MASK	processMouseEvent()
AWTEvent.MOUSE_MOTION_EVENT_MASK	processMouseMotionEvent()
AWTEvent.WINDOW_EVENT_MASK	processWindowEvent()
AWTEvent.ACTION_EVENT_MASK	processActionEvent()
AWTEvent.ADJUSTMENT_EVENT_MASK	processAdjustmentEvent()
AWTEvent.ITEM_EVENT_MASK	processItemEvent()
AWTEvent.TEXT_EVENT_MASK	processTextEvent()

Example 14.6 *Low-level Event Processing I*

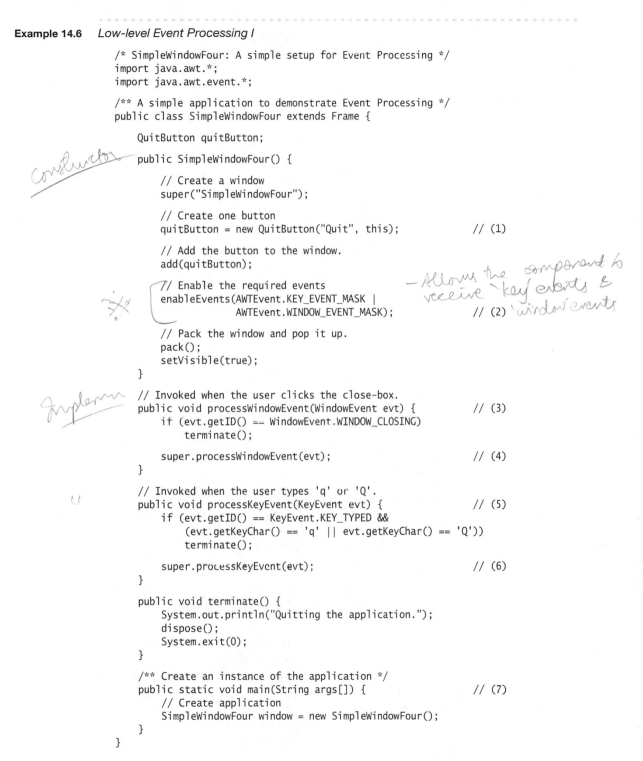

```
/* SimpleWindowFour: A simple setup for Event Processing */
import java.awt.*;
import java.awt.event.*;

/** A simple application to demonstrate Event Processing */
public class SimpleWindowFour extends Frame {

    QuitButton quitButton;

    public SimpleWindowFour() {

        // Create a window
        super("SimpleWindowFour");

        // Create one button
        quitButton = new QuitButton("Quit", this);                // (1)

        // Add the button to the window.
        add(quitButton);

        // Enable the required events
        enableEvents(AWTEvent.KEY_EVENT_MASK |
                     AWTEvent.WINDOW_EVENT_MASK);                 // (2)

        // Pack the window and pop it up.
        pack();
        setVisible(true);
    }

    // Invoked when the user clicks the close-box.
    public void processWindowEvent(WindowEvent evt) {             // (3)
        if (evt.getID() == WindowEvent.WINDOW_CLOSING)
            terminate();

        super.processWindowEvent(evt);                            // (4)
    }

    // Invoked when the user types 'q' or 'Q'.
    public void processKeyEvent(KeyEvent evt) {                   // (5)
        if (evt.getID() == KeyEvent.KEY_TYPED &&
            (evt.getKeyChar() == 'q' || evt.getKeyChar() == 'Q'))
            terminate();

        super.processKeyEvent(evt);                               // (6)
    }

    public void terminate() {
        System.out.println("Quitting the application.");
        dispose();
        System.exit(0);
    }

    /** Create an instance of the application */
    public static void main(String args[]) {                      // (7)
        // Create application
        SimpleWindowFour window = new SimpleWindowFour();
    }
}
```

```
class QuitButton extends Button {

    private SimpleWindowFour application;

    public QuitButton(String name, SimpleWindowFour window) {  // (8)
        super(name);
        application = window;
        enableEvents(AWTEvent.ACTION_EVENT_MASK |
                     AWTEvent.KEY_EVENT_MASK);                 // (9)
    }

    // Invoked when the user clicks the quit button.
    public void processActionEvent(ActionEvent evt) {          // (10)
        if (evt.getSource() == this)
           application.terminate();

        super.processActionEvent(evt);                         // (11)
    }

    // Invoked when the user types 'q' or 'Q'.
    public void processKeyEvent(KeyEvent evt) {                // (12)
        if (evt.getID() == KeyEvent.KEY_TYPED &&
            (evt.getKeyChar() == 'q' || evt.getKeyChar() == 'Q'))
            application.terminate();

        super.processKeyEvent(evt);                            // (13)
    }
}
```

Steps for explicit event handling can be summarized as follows:

1. Define a subclass of the component.
2. Enable the events by making the subclass constructor call the `enableEvents()` method with the appropriate bit mask formed from `AWTEvent.`*X*`_EVENT_MASK` constants.
3. Choose one of two strategies to intercept the events in the subclass:
   - For each `AWTEvent.`*X*`_EVENT_MASK` constant, the subclass can provide an implementation of the corresponding `process`*X*`Event()` method.
   - The subclass can override the `processEvent()` method by providing an implementation to handle the events explicitly.

No matter which strategy is chosen, each event processing method must call the overridden version in the superclass before returning. This ensures that any registered listeners will also be notified.

The `SimpleWindowFour` application in Example 14.6 follows the first strategy for handling events. The class `SimpleWindowFour` uses the `QuitButton` class. The `QuitButton` constructor is passed the `this` reference at (1), allowing the button access to information in the application. The `SimpleWindowFour` constructor also enables the component to receive `KeyEvent`s and `WindowEvent`s at (2). The `SimpleWindowFour` class implements the corresponding `processKeyEvent()` and `processWindowEvent()` methods, as shown at (3) and (5). The `processWindowEvent()` method terminates the application if the event had the ID of `WindowEvent.WINDOW_CLOSING`, otherwise the overridden version from the superclass is called at (4). The `processWindowEvent()` method at (5) checks to see if a character was typed, and if this character was either `'q'` or `'Q'`, the application is terminated, otherwise the overridden version of the method from the superclass is called, as shown at (6).

The subclass `QuitButton` extends the `Button` class. Its constructor at (8) enables it for receiving `ActionEvent` and `KeyEvent` objects, as shown at (9). The subclass implements the corresponding methods `processActionEvent()` and `processKeyEvent()` at (10) and (12), respectively.

This simple application can be terminated in several ways: by clicking on the close-box, by clicking on the Quit button, and by typing either 'Q' or 'q' when the focus is on the button or on the window (Figure 14.6).

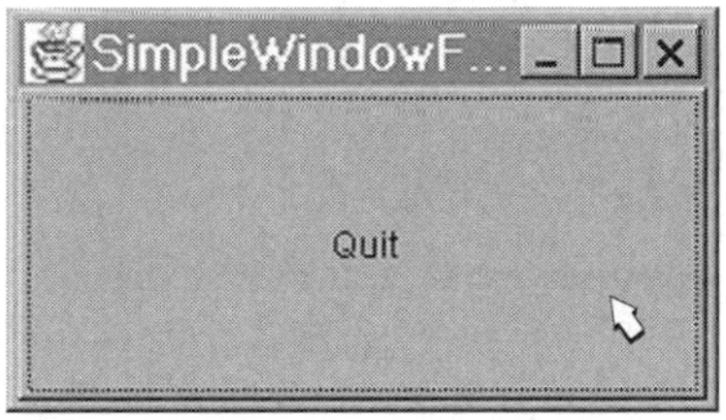

Figure 14.6 *Low-level Event Processing*

The `SimpleWindowFive` application in Example 14.7 follows the second strategy. The main difference between the `SimpleWindowFour` and `SimpleWindowFive` applications is that the latter does all the event processing in the `processEvent()` method at (1). The `processEvent()` method in the `SimpleWindowFive` class processes both `WindowEvents` and `KeyEvents`. It terminates the application if the event had the ID of `Window Event.WINDOW_CLOSING`. It checks to see if a character was typed, and if this character was either `'q'` or `'Q'`, the application is terminated. If the application is not terminated, then the overridden version of the `processEvent()` method from the superclass is executed.

The class `QuitButton` also implements its own `processEvent()` method to process `ActionEvent` and `KeyEvent` objects, as shown at (2).

Example 14.7 *Low-level Event Processing II*

```
/* SimpleWindowFive: A simple setup for Event Processing */
import java.awt.*;
import java.awt.event.*;

/** A simple application to demonstrate Event Processing */
public class SimpleWindowFive extends Frame {

    QuitButton quitButton;

    public SimpleWindowFive() {
```

```
        // Create a window
        super("SimpleWindowFive");

        // Create one button
        quitButton = new QuitButton("Quit", this);

        // Add the button to the window.
        add(quitButton);

        // Enable the required events
        enableEvents(AWTEvent.KEY_EVENT_MASK |
                     AWTEvent.WINDOW_EVENT_MASK);

        // Pack the window and pop it up.
        pack();
        setVisible(true);
    }

    // Event processing
    public void processEvent(AWTEvent evt) {                    // (1)
        // Invoked when the user clicks the close-box.
        if (evt.getID() == WindowEvent.WINDOW_CLOSING)
            terminate();

        // Invoked when the user types 'q' or 'Q'.
        if (evt.getID() == KeyEvent.KEY_TYPED &&
            (((KeyEvent) evt).getKeyChar() == 'q' ||
            ((KeyEvent) evt).getKeyChar() == 'Q'))
            terminate();

        super.processEvent(evt);
    }

    public void terminate() {
        System.out.println("Quitting the application.");
        dispose();
        System.exit(0);
    }

    /** Create an instance of the application */
    public static void main(String args[]) {

        SimpleWindowFive window = new SimpleWindowFive();
    }

}

class QuitButton extends Button {

    private SimpleWindowFive application;

    public QuitButton(String name, SimpleWindowFive window) {
        super(name);
        application = window;
        enableEvents(AWTEvent.ACTION_EVENT_MASK |
                     AWTEvent.KEY_EVENT_MASK);
    }
```

```
        // Event processing
        public void processEvent(AWTEvent evt) {                    // (2)
            // Invoked when the user clicks the quit button.
            if ((evt instanceof ActionEvent) &&
                ((ActionEvent) evt).getSource() == this)
                application.terminate();

            // Invoked when the user types 'q' or 'Q'.
            if (evt.getID() == KeyEvent.KEY_TYPED &&
                (((KeyEvent) evt).getKeyChar() == 'q' ||
                ((KeyEvent) evt).getKeyChar() == 'Q'))
                 application.terminate();

            super.processEvent(evt);
        }
    }
```

Review questions

14.18 What would be the effect of calling `enableEvent(AWTEvent.KEY_EVENT_MASK)` on a component?

Select the one right answer.

(a) It would enable event delivery of key events to the component.
(b) It would enable event delivery of key events and disable delivery of all other events to the component.
(c) It would disable event delivery of key events to the component.
(d) It would disable event delivery of key events and enable delivery of all other events to the component.
(e) None of the above.

14.19 Are there any events that can be handled using low-level event processing, that otherwise could not be handled using the event listener model?

Select the one right answer.

(a) Yes, container events.
(b) Yes, key events.
(c) Yes, component and container events.
(d) Yes, adjustment events.
(e) No.

14.20 Which of these methods exist in the `java.awt.Component` class?

Select all valid answers.

(a) `processEvent()`
(b) `processMouseEvent()`
(c) `processMouseMotionEvent()`
(d) `processPaintEvent()`

Chapter summary

The following information was included in this chapter:

- A discussion of the `AWTEvent` class hierarchy.
- Discussion of the low-level and semantic events, including specific constants and methods.
- Discussion of the event delegation model which is based on event sources and event listeners.
- Identification of which events are generated by which components.
- Identification of listener interfaces and their methods that listeners must implement for receiving particular events.
- Identification and use of event adapter classes for low-level events.
- Use of anonymous classes for implementing event listeners.
- Strategies for low-level event processing when components are subclassed, either by overriding the `processEvent()` method or by overriding the `process`*X*`Event()` methods.

Programming exercises

14.1 Create a program that can be used to scribble down temporary notes. A sample GUI is shown in Exercise 14.7. The program should present the user with a window consisting of the following:

- A row of command buttons at the top of the window.
- A text area for writing notes.
- A status line at the bottom of the window.
- The row of buttons should provide the following commands:
  - Clear – This button should clear the text area.
  - Remember – This button should store away the current contents of the text area.
  - Recall – This button should replace the text in the text area with the text last remembered.

The status line should change whenever the mouse pointer moves over one of the command buttons, to provide a small description of the command.

The status line should also change to notify the user whenever a command has been executed.

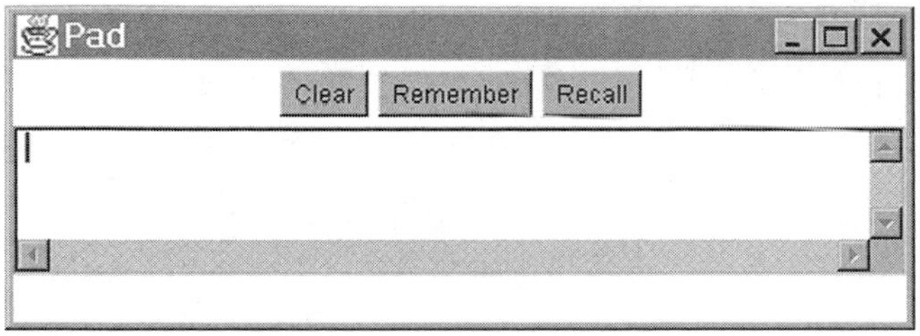

Figure 14.7 *GUI for Exercise 14.1*

14.2 Create a program that presents the user with a simple window with only one button. Whenever the mouse pointer moves into the vicinity of the button, the program should move the button to a new random location in the window, thus making it hard for the user to actually push the button. Initially the button should have the taunting label "Click me". If the user actually manages to press the button, the label should change to "Congratulations!"

15 Painting

Supplementary Objectives

- Identify the sequence of `Component` methods involved in redrawing areas of an AWT GUI under exposure and programmed redraw conditions.
- Write code to implement the `paint()` method of a `java.awt.Component`.
- Write code to use color in graphics rendering operations.
- Write code to render text and make use of fonts.
- Identify the following as methods of the `Graphics` class: `drawString()`, `drawLine()`, `drawRect()`, `drawImage()`, `drawPolygon()`, `drawArc()`, `fillRect()`, `fillPolygon()`, `fillArc()`.
- Write code to organize painting and event handling for components.
- Understand clipping, and how it affects graphics operations.
- Distinguish between methods invoked by the user thread and those normally invoked by an AWT thread.
- Write code to set the painting modes for graphics operations.
- Write code to obtain a suitable `Graphics` object from an `Image`.
- Distinguish between situations that require the use of an `Image` object and those that require the use of a `Graphics` object.

15.1 Rendering Graphics

The abstract class `java.awt.Graphics` provides a *device-independent interface* for rendering graphics. Specific subclasses of the `Graphics` class have been implemented for different platforms and graphics output devices. An instance of the `Graphics` class or its subclasses cannot be created directly using a constructor. How a graphics instance is obtained is explained below. Such an instance constitutes a *graphics context* in which graphics operations are performed.

Graphics Context

The graphics context encapsulates the following state information:

- The *target* of the graphics context.
- The *color* in which drawing is done.
- The *font* in which text is rendered.
- The *clip region* that defines the area in which drawing is done.
- The *translation origin* relative to which all drawing coordinates are interpreted.
- The *paint mode* for rendering graphics.
- The color of the *XOR paint mode* toggle.

The graphics context provides a variety of methods for both changing its state information and for rendering graphics. Among the capabilities provided for rendering graphics are:

- Drawing lines, (filled) rectangles, (filled) ovals and (filled) polygons.
- Rendering text strings using different fonts.
- Displaying, scaling, cropping, and flipping images.

The Java AWT provides graphics contexts that can render graphics on the following *targets*:

- Components
- Images
- Printers (not covered here)

Drawing Components

It is important to understand the chain of operations involved when a component is drawn for the first time or subsequently redrawn. A component may need to be redrawn for a variety of reasons: its size might have changed, it might have been covered but now has become uncovered, user interaction may initiate a redraw of the component.

The following methods defined in the `Component` class are involved in drawing components:

```
void repaint()
void update(Graphics g)
void paint(Graphics g)
```

The code for drawing the component is usually implemented in the overriding method `paint()` defined by a concrete component. This method is passed an object of the `Graphics` class that provides the graphics context for drawing the component. The AWT will automatically call `paint()` when the size of the component has changed or the component has been uncovered. The `paint()` method is seldom called directly by the component, instead the following procedure is relied upon to change its appearance:

- The `repaint()` method is usually called by the application for screen updating.
- The call to the `repaint()` method eventually leads to invocation of the `update()` method. By default, this method does the following:
  - It clears the component's screen-area by filling it with the current component background color.
  - It sets the current drawing color to the foreground color of the component.
  - It invokes the `paint()` method, passing it the same `Graphics` object that it received.

In the AWT, most GUI control components (buttons, text fields, checkboxes) are drawn using the underlying windowing system, and therefore their graphics contexts should not be used by an application to draw on them. In other words, an application should not override the `paint()` method of these components, but rely instead on the default implementation of this method to display them on the screen. Components that lend themselves to graphics rendering by the application are those that do not have any default external graphical representation:

- `Canvas` class.
- Subclasses of the `Component` class that are not part of the AWT.
- `Container` class and its subclasses: `Window`, `Frame`, `Dialog`, `Panel`, `Applet`.

A subclass of these components can override the `paint()` method, and use the graphics context passed to this method to render graphics onto the component.

The user thread (i.e. the application) usually relies on the indirect calls to the `update()` method through the `repaint()` method to update components. However, the AWT thread (i.e. the AWT event handler) calls the `paint()` method directly on a component if the component needs refreshing (for example, when the component is resized). The `paint()` method should draw the desired visuals using the graphics context given in the argument. The `paint()` method is called upon to do screen updating whenever this becomes necessary. Note that the graphics context passed to the `paint()` method by the AWT need not be the same every time this method is called. However, any drawing done using a graphics context will appear in the associated component, subject to the state of the graphics context.

The examples of this chapter override the component updating methods `paint()` and `update()`, and use the graphics context passed as parameter for rendering graphics onto the component.

The `Graphics` Class

A graphics context cannot be created directly by calling a constructor, because the `Graphics` class is abstract. Inside the `paint()` method this is not a problem, as the method is passed such a context via a `Graphics` reference. This context is associated with the component of the `paint()` method, and only this context should be used to render graphics in the component. In other situations, a graphics context can be obtained in one of the following two ways:

- An existing `Graphics` object can be used to create a new one, by invoking the `create()` method in the `Graphics` class.
- Since every component has an associated graphics context, this can be explicitly obtained by calling the `getGraphics()` method of the `Component` class.

The creator of a graphics context should ensure that the `dispose()` method is called to free the resources it uses when the graphics context is no longer needed.

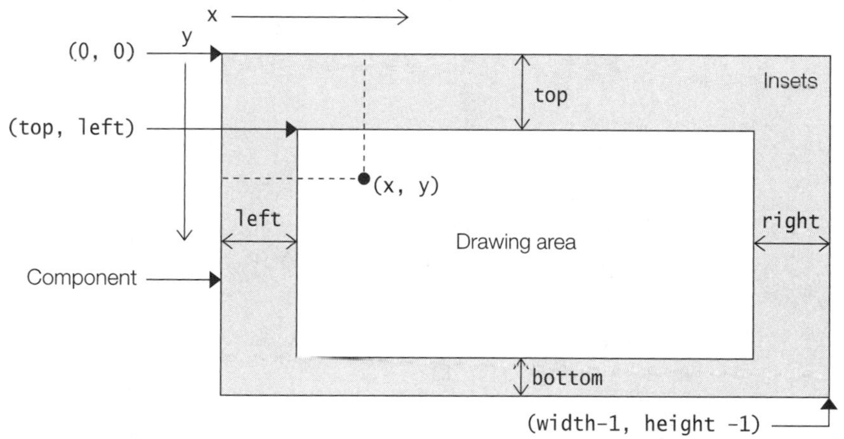

Figure 15.1 *Coordinates of a Component*

The top left-hand corner of the component is defined as the origin (0,0) of the coordinate system used for rendering graphics. The (horizontal) x-coordinate increases towards the right and the (vertical) y-coordinate increases downwards. The coordinates are measured in *pixels* and supplied as integer values to the many drawing methods of the `Graphics` class.

The drawing area in a component is not necessarily the same size as the component. The size of the component is returned by the following method of the `Component` class:

```
Dimension getSize() // (width, height)
```

However, the size returned includes the borders (and any title-bar in the case of a frame). The insets (i.e. size of the borders) of the component, shown in Figure 15.1, are given by the following method of the `Container` class:

```
Insets getInsets() // (top, bottom, left, right)
```

The size of the drawing region in a component can be calculated as follows:

```
Dimension size = getSize();
Insets insets = getInsets();
int drawHeight = size.height - insets.top - insets.bottom;
int drawWidth = size.width - insets.left - insets.right;
```

The origin of the drawing region in a component is given by (`getInsets().top`, `getInsets().left`). The method `translate(int x, int y)` of the `Graphics` class can be used to set the *translation origin* of the graphics context. All coordinate arguments to the methods of the `Graphics` object are then considered relative to this origin in subsequent operations.

All drawing or text rendering is done using the current color, the current paint mode, and the current font, inside the current clip region. Note that changes to the state of a graphics context take effect in *subsequent* operations involving the context.

15.2 Using Color

The following methods of the `Graphics` class can be used to get the current color or to set a color in the graphics context. Any change of color applies to all subsequent operations.

```
Color getColor()
void setColor(Color c)
```

The following methods of the `Component` class can be used to set the background or foreground color, or to get the current background or foreground color of a component respectively:

```
Color getBackground()
Color getForeground()
void setBackground(Color c)
void setForeground(Color c)
```

It is customary to express the basic colors used in the rendering operations of a component using the foreground and the background color properties of the component. Text in the component appears in the foreground color on top of the background color of the component.

There are 13 predefined colors designated by constants in the `Color` class:

```
Color.black
Color.blue
Color.cyan
Color.darkGray
Color.gray
Color.green
Color.lightGray
Color.magenta
Color.orange
Color.pink
Color.red
Color.white
Color.yellow
```

The `Color` class defines constructors that can be used to define different colors in various ways.

`Color(int r, int g, int b)`

Creates a color using the separate red, green, and blue (RGB) values for the color in the range (0–255).

`Color(int rgb)`

Creates a color with the specified combined RGB value consisting of the red component in bits 16–23, the green component in bits 8–15, and the blue component in bits 0–7.

`Color(float r, float g, float b)`

Creates a color with the specified red, green, and blue (RGB) values in the range (0.0–1.0).

The applet in Example 15.1 writes the text in blue (foreground color of the applet) on aquamarine (background color of the applet).

Figure 15.2 *Foreground and Background Color*

The class `SystemColor` provides the desktop color scheme for the current platform. Constants are provided for properties such as the background color of the desktop (`SystemColor.desktop`), background color for the controls (`SystemColor.control`) and text color for menus (`SystemColor.menuText`). These color properties can be used to provide a look which is consistent with that of the host platform.

Example 15.1 *Color*

```
// Color Demo
import java.applet.*;
import java.awt.*;

public class ColorApplet extends Applet {

    public void init() {
        setForeground(Color.blue);
        setBackground(new Color(127, 255, 212));  // aquamarine
    }

    public void paint(Graphics g) {
        g.drawString("Paint me blue!", 75, 50);
    }
}
```

Review questions

15.1 Which of the following properties are not encapsulated by the `Graphics` class?

Select all valid answers.

(a) Drawing color
(b) Background color
(c) Font
(d) Clip region
(e) Paint mode

15.2 Which of these classes is least suited for providing a customized `paint()` method?

Select the one right answer.

(a) `Component`
(b) `Canvas`
(c) `Label`
(d) `Panel`
(e) `Window`

15.3 Which of these procedures for acquiring a `Graphics` instance will work?

Select all valid answers.

(a) `new Graphics()`
(b) Given another graphics instance `gfx`: `gfx.create()`
(c) Given another graphics instance `gfx`: `new Graphics(gfx)`
(d) Given a visible component `comp`: `comp.getGraphics()`
(e) Override the `paint()` method of a component and receive a graphics instance as an argument.

15.4 Which `Graphics` objects are not used properly in the following code?

```
import java.awt.*;

public class MyClass extends Frame {
    public static void main(String args[]) {
        Window win = new MyClass();
        win.setSize(400, 300);
        win.setVisible(true);
    }

    public void paint(Graphics gfx1) {
        Graphics gfx2 = gfx1.create();
        Graphics gfx3 = getGraphics();

        gfx1.drawLine(50, 50, 100, 50);
        gfx2.drawLine(50, 60, 100, 60);
        gfx3.drawLine(50, 70, 100, 70);

        gfx1.dispose();
        gfx2.dispose();
        gfx3.dispose();
    }
}
```

Select the one right answer.

(a) None.
(b) The `Graphics` object referenced by `gfx1` is not used correctly.
(c) The `Graphics` object referenced by `gfx2` is not used correctly.
(d) The `Graphics` object referenced by `gfx3` is not used correctly.
(e) Both `Graphics` objects referenced by `gfx2` and `gfx3` are not used correctly.

15.5 Which of these are names of colors defined in the `Color` class?

Select all valid answers.

(a) `lightBlue`
(b) `DARK_GREEN`
(c) `LIGHTGRAY`
(d) `darkGray`
(e) `Black`

15.3 Rendering Text and Working with Fonts

Like color, the font can be set for a graphics context and for a component. Subsequent text rendering with the same graphics context will be displayed in the new font.

Text rendering in a component is done using the following methods of the `Graphics` class:

```
void drawString(String str, int x, int y)
```

The string is drawn with the baseline of the first character at the specified coordinates, using the current font and color.

```
void drawChars(char[] data, int offset, int length, int x, int y)
```

Starting at the `offset` argument, `length` characters from the character array are drawn with the baseline of the first character at the specified coordinates, using the current font and color.

```
void drawBytes(byte[] data, int offset, int length, int x, int y)
```

Starting at the `offset` argument, `length` bytes from the byte array are drawn with the baseline of the first character (given by the byte array) at the specified coordinates, using the current font and color.

The following methods of the `Graphics` class can be used to get the font property or set a font in the graphics context. Methods with the same signatures are also defined in the `Component` class to obtain the current font or set a font for a component.

```
Font getFont()
void setFont(Font f)
```

The `Font` class defines a constructor that can be used to obtain available fonts:

```
Font(String name, int style, int size)
```

The following font names (called *logical font names*) are standard on all platforms and are mapped to actual fonts on a particular platform:

- `"Serif"` which is a variable pitch font with serifs.
- `"SansSerif"` which is a variable pitch font without serifs.
- `"Monospaced"` which is a fixed pitch font.
- `"Dialog"` which is a font for dialogs.
- `"DialogInput"` which is a font for dialog input.
- `"Symbol"` which is mapped to the Symbol font.

Font style can be specified using constants from the `Font` class:

```
Font.BOLD
Font.ITALIC
Font.PLAIN
(Font.BOLD | Font.ITALIC) // both bold and italic
```

Font size is specified in typographic *points* (1 point ≈ 1/72 inch).

Figure 15.3 *Standard Fonts (Windows Platform)*

Example 15.2 *Standard Font Names*

```
// Font Demo
import java.applet.*;
import java.awt.*;

public class FontApplet extends Applet {

    public void init() {
        setBackground(Color.white);
        setForeground(Color.black);
    }

    public void paint(Graphics g) {
        g.setFont(new Font("Serif", Font.BOLD, 20));
        g.drawString("Serif", 50, 50);
        g.setFont(new Font("SansSerif", Font.ITALIC, 20));
        g.drawString("SansSerif", 50, 75);
        g.setFont(new Font("Monospaced", Font.PLAIN, 20));
        g.drawString("Monospaced", 50, 100);
        g.setFont(new Font("Dialog", Font.BOLD | Font.ITALIC, 20));
        g.drawString("Dialog", 50, 125);
        g.setFont(new Font("DialogInput", Font.BOLD, 20));
        g.drawString("DialogInput", 50, 150);
        g.setFont(new Font("Symbol", Font.PLAIN, 20));
        g.drawString("\u03A4\u03A6\u03C4", 50, 175);
    }
}
```

The `paint()` method in the applet of Example 15.2 shows examples of how a font, its style and its size can be set in a graphics context. The applet uses all the standard fonts which are shown in Figure 15.3.

Font availability is platform-dependent. The glyphs which make up a font are also platform-dependent. The `boolean` method `canDisplay(char c)` in the `Font` class can be used to find out if a font has a glyph for a specific character. The `GraphicsEnvironment` class provides access to platform-specific information about fonts. The local `GraphicsEnvironment` can be used to get a list of names for the available fonts:

```
GraphicsEnvironment ge = GraphicsEnvironment.getLocalGraphicsEnvironment();
String[] fontNames = ge.getAvailableFontFamilyNames();
```

Figure 15.4 *Font Measurements*

In Example 15.2, the y-coordinate specified in the calls to the `drawstring()` methods indicates the *baseline* of the font, which together with the x-coordinate value, specifies the pixel marked with × in Figure 15.4. In rendering text with the `drawString()` method, properties of the font must be taken into consideration to ensure proper rendering of text. Properties of a font are accessed by using a *font metrics* (represented by objects of the `FontMetrics` class) associated with the font. The font metrics can be queried for *vertical measurements* (ascent, descent, height, leading) of the font and for *horizontal measurements* (single character width, string width) for glyphs in the font. All font measurements are in pixels.

```
int getAscent()
int getDescent()
int getMaxDescent()
int getMaxAscent()
```

The first two methods return the typical ascent and descent for the font associated with the metrics, respectively. This value might not be large enough for some characters in the font. The last two methods return the maximum ascent or descent, taking into consideration all the characters in the font. See Figure 15.4.

```
int getLeading()
```

Returns the standard leading value, a.k.a. *interline spacing*, which is the amount of space between the descent of one line of text and the ascent of the next line.

`int getHeight()`

Returns the standard height of a line of text in the font associated with the metrics. Font height is the distance between the baseline of adjacent lines of text. It is the sum of the leading + ascent + descent of the font.

`int getMaxAdvance()`

Returns the maximum advance of any character in this font. This is defined as the maximum distance between one character to the next, in a line of text.

`int charWidth(int ch)`
`int charWidth(char ch)`

Returns the advance width of the specified character.

`int stringWidth(String str)`

Returns the advance width of the characters in the specified string.

A font metrics can be obtained in one of the following ways:

- A component can be used to get a font metrics for a font:

```
Font font12 = new Font("Dialog", Font.ITALIC, 12);
FontMetrics metrics2 = component.getFontMetrics(font12);
```

- A graphics context can be used to get a font metrics for a font:

```
FontMetrics metrics3 = graphicsContext.getFontMetrics(); // current font
FontMetrics metrics4 = graphicsContext.getFontMetrics(font18);
```

Example 15.3 queries a font metrics to obtain information about a font. The applet's `init()` method at (1) sets the foreground color, which will be used to render the text. The `paint()` method at (2) first creates and sets a font at (3), and then translates the origin at (4) so that the coordinates for the component are interpreted according to the actual drawing area (Figure 15.1). It then draws the string at (5). At (6), the applet obtains a font metrics from the graphics context. This font metrics is associated with the current font set in the graphics context. The font metrics is queried to obtain the maximum ascent and descent of the font. It is also used to find the number of pixels required to render the text string. These measurements are used to put a box around the text. The result is shown in Figure 15.5.

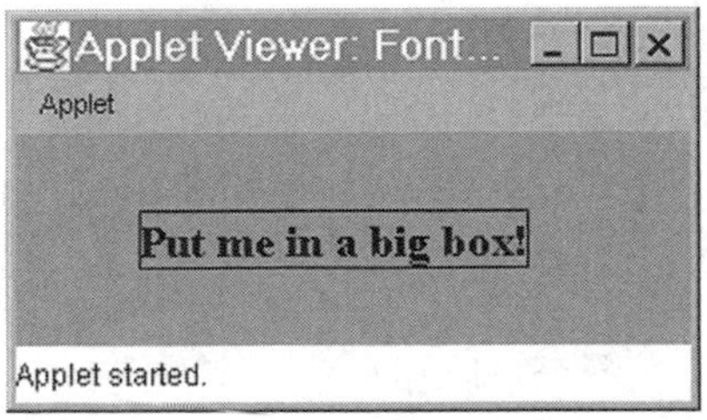

Figure 15.5 *Rendering Text*

Example 15.3 *Rendering Text*

```
// Font Metrics Demo: Box round a string
import java.applet.*;
import java.awt.*;

public class FontMetricsApplet extends Applet {

    public void init() {                                           // (1)
        setForeground(Color.black);
        setBackground(new Color(0.444f, 0.502f, 1.0f));
    }

    public void paint(Graphics g) {                                // (2)
        // Create and set the font                                    (3)
        Font font = new Font("Serif", Font.BOLD, 18);
        g.setFont(font);

        // Translate the origin                                       (4)
        g.translate(getInsets().left, getInsets().top);

        // Draw a string                                              (5)
        String str = "Put me in a big box!";
        g.drawString(str, 50, 50);

        // Get the font metrics for the font                          (6)
        FontMetrics metrics = g.getFontMetrics(font);
        // Find the maximum ascent for all characters in the font.
        int maxAscent = metrics.getMaxAscent();
        // Find the maximum descent for all characters in the font.
        int maxDescent = metrics.getMaxDescent();
        // Find the width of the string
        int stringWidth = metrics.stringWidth(str);
        // Draw box round the string
        g.drawRect(50, 50- maxAscent,                  // top left-hand corner
                   stringWidth,                        // width of the box
                   maxAscent + maxDescent);            // height of the box
    }
}
```

15.4 Drawing Shapes

The Graphics class provides methods for drawing lines, rectangles, ovals, arcs and polygons. The Graphics class also provides methods that can draw *filled* shapes.

Drawing Lines

The Graphics class provides the following method for drawing lines:

```
void drawLine(
        int x1, int y1,       // from point
        int x2, int y2        // to point
)
```

The line is drawn from point (x1, y1) to point (x2, y2) using the current color.

Example 15.4 draws a letter using lines having different colors. The letter is shown in Figure 15.6.

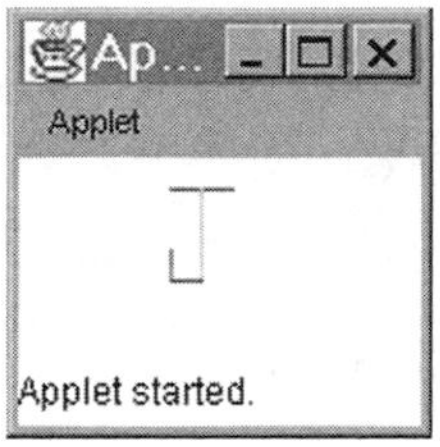

Figure 15.6 *Drawing Lines*

Example 15.4 *Drawing Lines*

```
// Lines
import java.applet.*;
import java.awt.*;

public class LineApplet extends Applet {

    public void paint(Graphics g) {
        Color[] colors = { Color.blue, Color.green, Color.red, Color.darkGray };
        int[][] coordinates = {
        //     x1  y1  x2  y2
            { 50, 10, 70, 10 },
            { 60, 10, 60, 40 },
            { 50, 30, 50, 40 },
            { 50, 40, 60, 40 }
        };
        // Draw the letter 'J'
        for (int i = 0; i<colors.length; i++) {
            g.setColor(colors[i]);
            g.drawLine(coordinates[i][0], coordinates[i][1],    // from (x1, y1)
                       coordinates[i][2], coordinates[i][3]);   // to   (x2, y2)
        }
    }
}
```

Drawing Rectangles

The `Graphics` class provides methods for drawing outlines of rectangles. Methods are also provided to fill the rectangle with the current color. The rectangle is specified by giving the coordinates of the top left corner of the rectangle, and the width and the height of the rectangle. For methods that draw the outline of a rectangle, the resulting rectangle will cover an area of (width + 1) × (height + 1) pixels. For methods that fill a rectangle, the resulting rectangle will cover an area of width × height pixels.

```
void drawRect(
        int x, int y,              // top left corner
        int width, int height      // of rectangle
)
```

The outline of the specified rectangle is drawn using the current color. The resulting rectangle will cover an area `(width + 1)` × `(height + 1)` pixels.

```
void fillRect(
        int x, int y,              // top left corner
        int width, int height      // of rectangle
)
```

The method fills the specified rectangle with the current color.

```
void drawRoundRect(
        int x, int y,              // top left corner
        int width, int height,     // of rectangle
        int arcWidth, int arcHeight
)
```

Draws the outline of the specified rectangle with rounded corners, using the current color. The parameters `arcWidth` and `arcHeight` specify the horizontal and the vertical diameters of the arc at the four corners.

```
void fillRoundRect(
        int x, int y,              // top left corner
        int width, int height,     // of rectangle
        int arcWidth, int arcHeight
)
```

Fills the specified rectangle with rounded corners, using the current color.

```
void draw3DRect(
        int x, int y,              // top left corner
        int width, int height,     // of rectangle
        boolean raised
)
```

Draws a 3-D highlighted outline of the specified rectangle. The edges of the rectangle will be highlighted, so that it appears as if the edges were beveled and lit from the upper left corner. The colors used for the highlighting effect will be determined from the current color. The `raised` argument determines whether the rectangle appears to be raised above or sunk into the drawing surface.

```
void fill3DRect(
        int x, int y,              // top left corner
        int width, int height,     // of rectangle
        boolean raised
)
```

Paints a 3-D highlighted rectangle filled with the current color.

```
void clearRect(
        int x, int y,              // top left corner
        int width, int height      // of rectangle
)
```

Clears the specified rectangle by filling it with the background color of the current drawing surface.

The applet in Example 15.5 uses the methods mentioned above to draw different rectangles, shown in Figure 15.7.

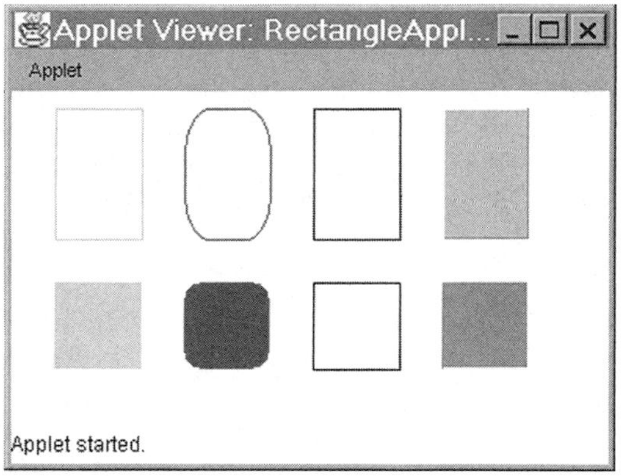

Figure 15.7 *Drawing Rectangles*

Example 15.5 *Drawing Rectangles*

```
// Rectangles
import java.applet.*;
import java.awt.*;

public class RectangleApplet extends Applet {

    public void paint(Graphics g) {
        // Rectangle and filled square
        g.setColor(Color.orange);
        g.drawRect(25, 10, 50, 75);
        g.fillRect(25, 110, 50, 50);

        // Rounded: rectangle and filled square
        g.setColor(Color.blue);
        g.drawRoundRect(100, 10, 50, 75, 30, 50);
        g.fillRoundRect(100, 110, 50, 50, 20, 20);

        // 3D: rectangle and square
        g.setColor(Color.black);
        g.draw3DRect(175, 10, 50, 75, true);
        g.draw3DRect(175, 110, 50, 50, false);
```

```
        // 3D: filled rectangle and square
        g.setColor(Color.lightGray);
        g.fill3DRect(250, 10, 50, 75, true);
        g.fill3DRect(250, 110, 50, 50, false);
    }
}
```

Drawing Ovals

The `Graphics` class provides a method for drawing *ovals* (for example, ellipses). A method is also provided to fill the oval with the current color. The oval is bounded by an invisible rectangle. The bounding rectangle is specified by giving the coordinates of the top left corner, and the width and the height of the rectangle (Figure 15.8). The two diameters of the oval are equal to the width and the height of the bounding rectangle.

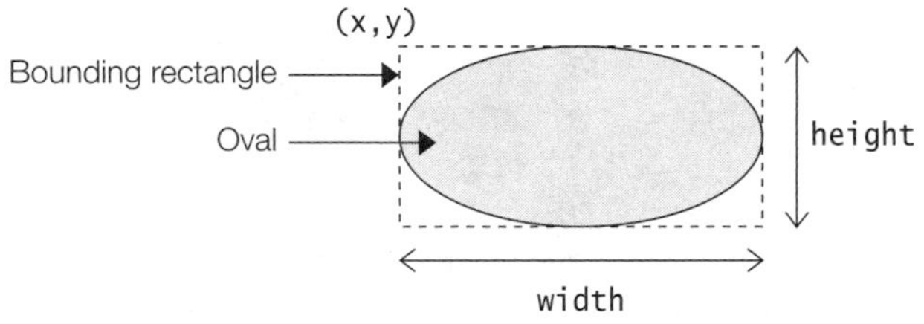

Figure 15.8 *Bounding Rectangle for Ovals*

```
void drawOval(
        int x, int y,                 // top left corner
        int width, int height         // bounding rectangle
)
```

Draws the outline of an oval bounded by the specified rectangle, using the current color.

```
void fillOval(
        int x, int y,                 // top left corner
        int width, int height         // bounding rectangle
)
```

Fills an oval bounded by the specified rectangle with the current color.

Example 15.6 illustrates drawing ellipses and circles, which are shown in Figure 15.9.

Example 15.6 *Drawing Ovals*

```
// Ovals
import java.applet.*;
import java.awt.*;
```

```
public class OvalApplet extends Applet {

    public void paint(Graphics g) {

        // Ellipses
        g.setColor(Color.blue);
        g.drawOval(60, 10, 50, 75);
        g.fillOval(60, 95, 50, 75);

        // Circles
        g.setColor(Color.green);
        g.drawOval(130, 10, 75, 75);
        g.fillOval(130, 95, 75, 75);
    }
}
```

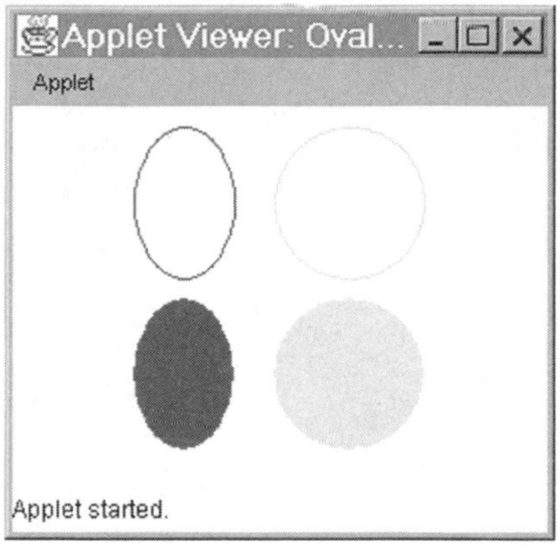

Figure 15.9 *Drawing Ovals*

Drawing Arcs

The `Graphics` class provides a method for drawing arcs. These arcs can be circular or elliptical. The starting point of the arc is given by a starting angle, and the ending point is given by the angle swept by the arc. Angles are measured in degrees. All positive angles are measured in a counterclockwise direction with the 0 degrees given by the three-o'clock position. Negative angles are measured in a clockwise direction from the 0 degrees position. The arc is *bounded* by a rectangle. The center of the arc coincides with the center of the bounding rectangle. The bounding rectangle is specified by giving the coordinates of the top left corner, and the width and the height of the rectangle. A method is also provided to fill the area bounded by the arc and its two radii with the current color, resulting in a pie segment. See Figure 15.10.

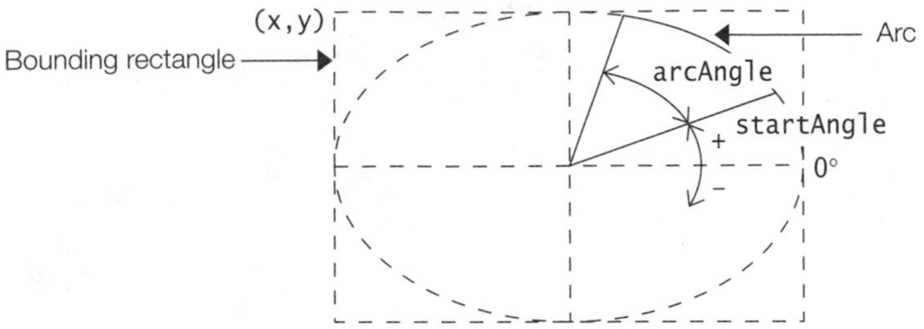

Figure 15.10 *Measurements for Drawing Arcs*

```
void drawArc(
        int x, int y,                // top left corner
        int width, int height,       // bounding rectangle
        int startAngle,
        int arcAngle
)
```

Draws the outline of an arc bounded by the specified rectangle, starting at `startAngle` and extending for `arcAngle` degrees, using the current color.

```
void fillArc(
        int x, int y,                // top left corner
        int width, int height,       // bounding rectangle
        int startAngle,
        int arcAngle
)
```

Fills the area bounded by the arc and its two radii (pie-segment) with the current color.

Example 15.7 illustrates drawing arcs, which are shown in Figure 15.11. Notice the bounding rectangles that the example draws to show the relationship between the arcs and the associated bounds.

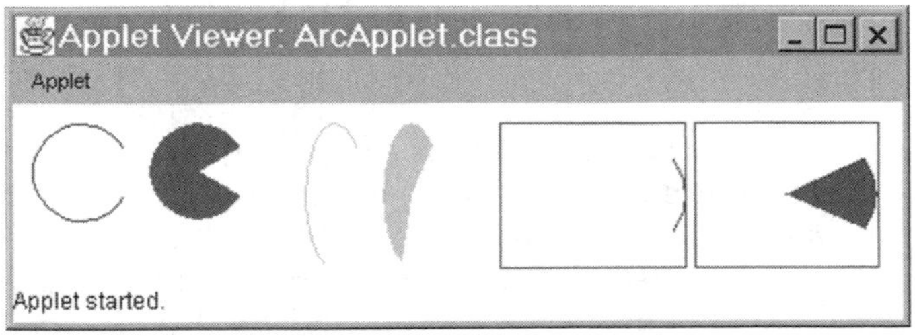

Figure 15.11 *Drawing Arcs*

Example 15.7 *Drawing Arcs*

```
// Arcs
import java.applet.*;
import java.awt.*;

public class ArcApplet extends Applet {

    public void paint(Graphics g) {
        // Pac-man
        g.setColor(Color.blue);
        g.drawArc(10, 10, 50, 50, 30, 300);
        g.fillArc(70, 10, 50, 50, 30, 300);

        // Elliptical arc
        g.setColor(Color.lightGray);
        g.drawArc(150, 10, 30, 75, 40, 210);
        g.fillArc(190, 10, 30, 75, 40, 210);

        // Pie-segment
        g.setColor(Color.darkGray);
        g.drawRect(250, 10, 95, 75);  // Draw bounding rectangle
        g.drawArc(250, 10, 95, 75, -30, 60);
        g.drawRect(350, 10, 95, 75);  // Draw bounding rectangle
        g.fillArc(350, 10, 95, 75, -30, 60);
    }
}
```

Drawing Polygons

A polygon is a closed sequence of line segments. Given a sequence of points (called *vertices*), line segments connect one vertex to the next in the sequence, finishing with the last vertex being connected with the first one.

The vertices of a polygon can be specified as arrays of `int` or as a `Polygon` object. The `Polygon` class has the following constructors:

```
Polygon(int[] xpoints, int[] ypoints, int npoints)
```

The `Graphics` class provides two methods for drawing polygons:

```
void drawPolygon(int[] xPoints, int[] yPoints, int nPoints)
```

Draws the outline of a polygon, defined by arrays of *x-coordinates* and *y-coordinates*, using the current color. Each point `(xPoints[i], yPoints[i])` defines a vertex. The figure is automatically closed by drawing a line segment between the first vertex and the last one if they are different. Note that the total number of vertices is given by the `nPoints` argument.

```
void drawPolygon(Polygon p)
```

Draws the outline of a polygon, defined by the specified `Polygon` object, using the current color. Before using this method a `Polygon` object must be created and populated with the vertices.

The Graphics class also defines two methods that draw and fill a polygon with the current color:

```
void fillPolygon(int[] xPoints, int[] yPoints, int nPoints)
void fillPolygon(Polygon p)
```

A *polyline* is an open figure, similar to a polygon, where the last vertex is not connected to the first one. The method has the following signature, where the arguments have the same meaning as the arguments for the corresponding drawPolygon() method:

```
void drawPolyline(int[] xPoints, int[] yPoints, int nPoints)
```

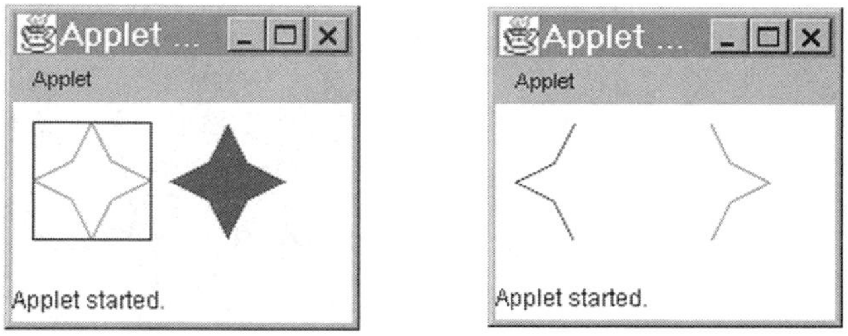

(a) Polygons (b) Polylines

Figure 15.12 *Drawing Polygons and Polylines*

Example 15.8 and Example 15.9 illustrate polygons and polylines, respectively. The corresponding applets are shown in Figure 15.12a and Figure 15.12b.

Example 15.8 *Drawing Polygons*

```
// Polygons
import java.applet.*;
import java.awt.*;

public class PolygonApplet extends Applet {

    public void paint (Graphics g) {

        // Create the vertices
        int[] xPoints = {10, 30, 40, 50, 70, 50, 40, 30};
        int[] yPoints = {40, 30, 10, 30, 40, 50, 70, 50};
        int nPoints = xPoints.length;

        // Create a polygon and draw it
        Polygon starShape = new Polygon(xPoints, yPoints, nPoints);
        g.setColor(Color.red);
        g.drawPolygon(starShape);

        // Put a box around it.
        g.setColor(Color.black);
        Rectangle bounds = starShape.getBounds();
        g.drawRect(bounds.x, bounds.y, bounds.width, bounds.height);
```

```
        // Fill a polygon given by two anonymous arrays
        g.setColor(Color.darkGray);
        g.fillPolygon(
            new int[] {80, 100, 110, 120, 140, 120, 110, 100},
            new int[] {40, 30, 10, 30, 40, 50, 70, 50},
            8);
    }
}
```

Example 15.9 *Drawing Polylines*

```
// Polylines
import java.applet.*;
import java.awt.*;

public class PolylineApplet extends Applet {

    public void paint (Graphics g) {

        // Create the vertices
        int[] xPoints = {40, 30, 10, 30, 40};
        int[] yPoints = {10, 30, 40, 50, 70};
        int nPoints = xPoints.length;

        // Draw the polyline (left half of a star)
        g.setColor(Color.darkGray);
        g.drawPolyline(xPoints, yPoints, nPoints);

        // Draw a polyline (right half of a star)
        // given by two anonymous arrays
        g.setColor(Color.red);
        g.drawPolyline(new int[] {110,120, 140, 120, 110},
                       new int[] {10, 30, 40, 50, 70},
                       5);
    }
}
```

15.5 Clipping

A `Graphics` object maintains a *clip region*. The clip region of a graphics context defines the area in which all drawing will be done. In other words, the clip region defines the actual drawing area used for rendering operations. This region can be all or part of the associated component. Rendering operations have no effect outside the clip region. Only pixels that lie within the clip region can be modified.

Clipping also comes into play when a part of a component is damaged or when a window is resized and needs updating. The clip region is already set in the graphics context passed as argument to the `paint()` method.

The `Graphics` class defines the following methods for the clip region:

```
Rectangle getClipBounds()
Shape getClip()
void setClip(int x, int y, int width, int height)
void setClip(Shape clip)
```

The clip region can be rectangular or any arbitrary shape. See `Shape` interface in the API documentation.

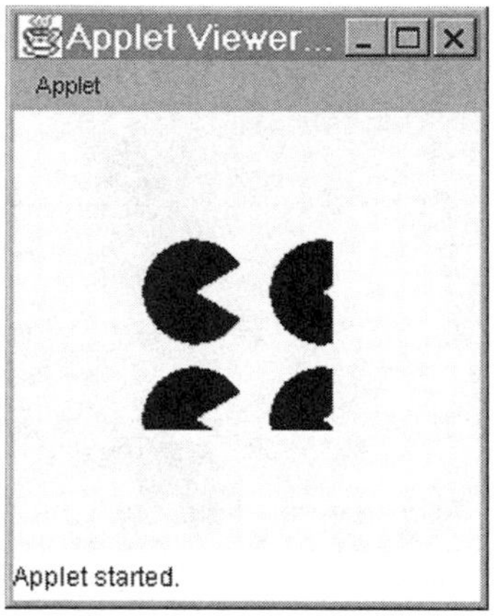

Figure 15.13 *Clipping Region*

The applet in Example 15.10 sets a clip region of 100 × 100 pixels at coordinates (50, 50). It draws Pac-man figures in an area of 300 × 300 pixels which contains the clip region. The rendering operations are only effective in the clip region, as evident from Figure 15.13.

Example 15.10 *Clipping Region*

```
// Clipping Demo
import java.applet.*;
import java.awt.*;

public class ClippingApplet extends Applet {

    public void init () {
        setForeground(Color.black);
        setBackground(Color.yellow);
    }

    public void paint (Graphics g) {
        g.translate(getInsets().left, getInsets().top);

        // Set clipping region
        g.setClip(50,50,100,100);
```

```
            // Draw Pac-man in a 300 x 300 area
            for (int i = 0; i < 300; i += 60)
                for (int j = 0; j < 300; j += 60)
                    g.fillArc(i, j,          // top left-hand corner
                              50, 50,        // width, height
                              30, 300);      // start angle, sweep angle
        }
    }
```

Review questions

15.6 Which of the following statements will draw the string "Hello", using a Graphics object referenced by a variable named gfx?

Select all valid answers.

(a) `gfx.paintString("Hello")`
(b) `gfx.fillString(30, 30, "Hello")`
(c) `gfx.drawString(30, 30, "Hello")`
(d) `gfx.fillString("Hello", 30, 30)`
(e) `gfx.drawString("Hello", 30, 30)`

15.7 What do the coordinates (x,y) given to the text rendering methods of the Graphics class describe?

Select the one right answer.

(a) The top left coordinates of the area covered by the text rendered.
(b) The bottom left coordinates of the area covered by the text rendered.
(c) The center coordinates of the left edge of the area covered by the text rendered.
(d) The start coordinates of the baseline of the rendered text.
(e) The center coordinates of the baseline of the rendered text.
(f) The end coordinates of the baseline of the rendered text.

15.8 What size is the area affected by the following code?

```
public void paint(Graphics gfx) {
    gfx.fillRect(10, 10, 30, 30);
}
```

Select the one right answer.

(a) The area affected is 19×19 pixels.
(b) The area affected is 20×20 pixels.
(c) The area affected is 21×21 pixels.
(d) The area affected is 29×29 pixels.
(e) The area affected is 30×30 pixels.
(f) The area affected is 31×31 pixels.

15.9 What size is the area affected by the following code?

```
public void paint(Graphics gfx) {
    gfx.draw3DRect(10, 10, 30, 30, false);
}
```

Select the one right answer.

(a) The area affected is 19×19 pixels.
(b) The area affected is 20×20 pixels.
(c) The area affected is 21×21 pixels.
(d) The area affected is 29×29 pixels.
(e) The area affected is 30×30 pixels.
(f) The area affected is 31×31 pixels.

15.10 What parameters are given to the `drawOval()` method in the `Graphics` class?

Select all valid answers.

(a) Center coordinates
(b) Top left coordinates
(c) Bottom right coordinates
(d) Horizontal and vertical radii
(e) Horizontal and vertical diameters

15.11 The following program draws two unfilled rectangles. How much of the rectangles painted by the following program will be displayed?

```
import java.awt.*;

public class MyClass extends Frame {

    public static void main(String args[]) {
        Window win = new MyClass();
        win.setSize(400, 300);
        win.setVisible(true);
    }

    static final int PAD = 10;

    public void paint(Graphics gfx) {
        Insets insets = getInsets();
        Dimension size = getSize();

        size.width -= insets.left + insets.right + PAD*2;
        size.height -= insets.top + insets.bottom + PAD*2;

        gfx.translate(insets.left + PAD, insets.top + PAD);
        gfx.setClip(0, 0, size.width, size.height);

        gfx.setColor(Color.red);
        gfx.drawRect(0, 0, size.width, size.height);
        gfx.setColor(Color.green);
        gfx.drawRect(1, 1, size.width-2, size.height-2);
    }
}
```

Select the one right answer.

(a) The entire red rectangle and the entire green rectangle will be shown.
(b) Nothing of the red rectangle will be shown, but the entire green rectangle will be shown.
(c) The bottom and right edges of both rectangles will not be shown.
(d) The bottom and right edges of the red rectangle will not be shown, but the entire green rectangle will be shown.
(e) Nothing of either rectangle will be shown.

15.6 The AWT Thread

Every GUI application has an *AWT thread* that monitors the user inputs and delivers events to components. (This is why a GUI application does not terminate when the call to the `main()` method returns after setting up the GUI.) The AWT thread updates the GUI when components need refreshing. The application must organize its screen painting code such that painting initiated by the AWT thread and by the application re-creates the screen faithfully.

The `AWTApplet` in Example 15.11 illustrates painting which is initiated by the AWT thread (and not by the application). The `AWTApplet` has two panels: each one of them fills its area with a rectangle of a certain color. The calls to the `paint()` method of the panels toggle between two colors when filling the rectangle. The size of the rectangle is always equal to the size of the panel. The applet itself never takes any direct action to update the screen.

Example 15.11 *Screen Updating*

```
import java.applet.*;
import java.awt.*;

public class AWTApplet extends Applet {

    public void init () {
        Panel panelOne = new SubPanel(Color.lightGray, Color.white);
        Panel panelTwo = new SubPanel(Color.yellow, Color.black);
        setLayout(new GridLayout(0,1));
        add(panelOne);
        add(panelTwo);
    }
}

class SubPanel extends Panel {

    private boolean toggle = false;
    private Color color1;
    private Color color2;

    public SubPanel(Color c1, Color c2) {
        color1 = c1;
        color2 = c2;
    }
```

```
    public void paint(Graphics g) {
        if (toggle)
            g.setColor(color1);
        else
            g.setColor(color2);
        Rectangle bounds = getBounds();
        g.fillRect(0, 0, bounds.width, bounds.height);
        toggle = !toggle;
    }
}
```

The AWTApplet in Example 15.11 demonstrates screen updating. The AWT thread calls the paint() method of *each* component inside a component hierarchy that needs updating, whenever this becomes necessary. The AWT thread sets the appropriate size of the clip region for each component that needs updating.

When the AWT calls the paint() method, a graphics context is passed as parameter. The size of the clip region in this graphics context is set according to the damaged area of the component that needs updating. If a component is not damaged at all, the paint() method of the component is not called.

The paint() method of the panel in Example 15.11 always fills the whole panel with a rectangle equal to its size. However, the effects of this operation are only visible in the clip region set by the AWT.

When the applet window in Figure 15.14a is exposed, the whole panel is not refreshed (by filling it with a rectangle), only the part that is re-exposed. This is evident by each panel showing two different colors, as shown in Figure 15.14b.

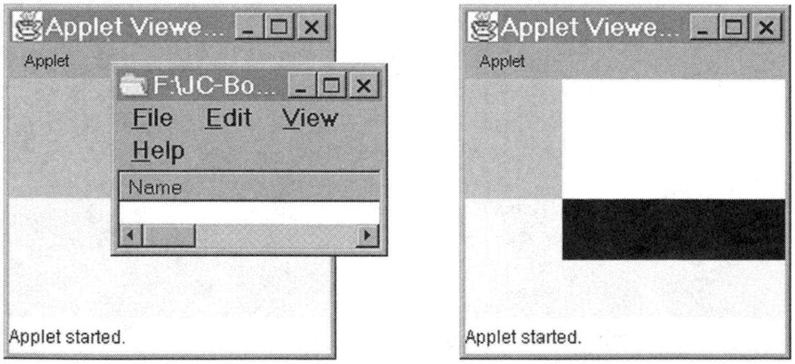

(a) Before (b) After exposure

Figure 15.14 *Clip Region set by AWT*

15.7 Organizing Painting and Event Handling

Event handlers in an application should not deal directly with painting. One reason is that they are not handed any graphics context to do the painting. They should also refrain from calling the `paint()` (or the `update()`) method directly, as this would also require a graphics context. If event handlers need the component to be repainted to reflect a change in the component state, they should instead call the `repaint()` method. The AWT thread will then eventually call the `update()` method with a graphics context. The `update()` method then calls the `paint()` method to do the actual painting. Components are usually designed so that event handlers set state information in member variables of the component and call the `repaint()` method. The `paint()` method, when called, can consult the state information to refresh the component. This way the screen is rendered correctly, regardless of how the painting is initiated. It is also usual for a component to override the `update()` method in situations where the previous contents of the component should not be erased, since the `update()` method fills the component with the background color every time this method is called. Overriding the `update()` can reduce *flickering* due to constant erasing of the component visuals by filling with the background color, when frequent updates are made to the component.

If event handlers were bombarded by events and they in turn kept demanding screen updating, the application could get bogged down in painting. The component refreshing mechanism described above ensures that this does not happen. The `repaint()` method actually *schedules* calls to the `update()` method, meaning that the `update()` method gets called at regular intervals and any intervening calls for update are merged. This gives the `paint()` method the chance to complete its job. This also means that the main concern of the `paint()` method should be to update the GUI.

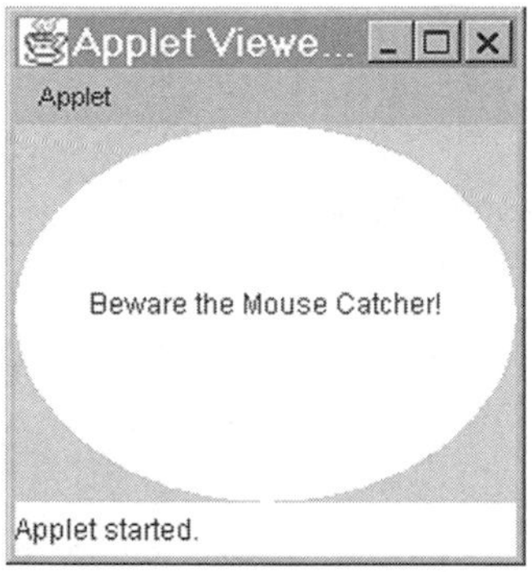

(a)

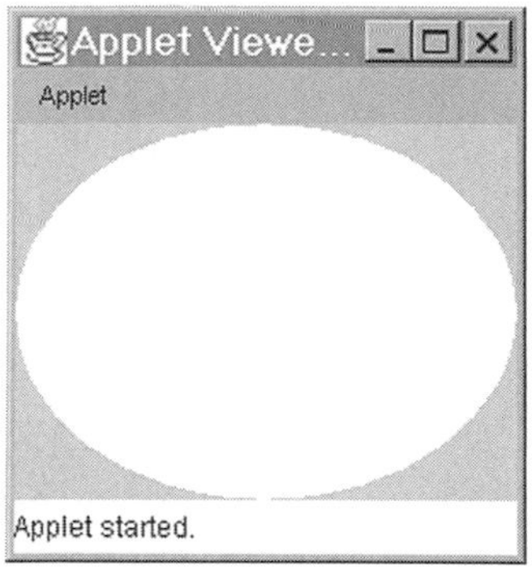

(b)

Figure 15.15 *Painting and Event Handling*

Example 15.12 *Organizing Painting and Event Handling*

```
// Demo for Painting and Event handling
import java.applet.*;
import java.awt.*;
import java.awt.event.*;

public class PaintingApplet extends Applet {

    // Global toggle which the event listener sets and paint() uses.
    private boolean toggle;

    public void init () {
        setForeground(Color.white);
        setBackground(Color.lightGray);

        // Add event listener
        addMouseListener(new MouseAdapter() {                  // (1)
            public void mouseClicked(MouseEvent e) {
                // Toggle to change the text color
                toggle = !toggle;                              // (2)
                // Update the screen
                repaint();                                     // (3)
            }
        });
    }

    public void paint (Graphics g) {                           // (4)
        // Translate the origin
        g.translate(getInsets().left, getInsets().top);
        // Draw oval in foreground color of the applet
        g.fillOval(0, 0, getBounds().width, getBounds().height);

        // Info that is governed by the event handler.
        // Only changed if toggled by the event handler.
        if (toggle) {
            // Set the color and draw the string.
            g.setColor(Color.black);
            String str = "Beware the Mouse Catcher!";
            FontMetrics metrics = g.getFontMetrics();
            int stringWidth = metrics.stringWidth(str);
            g.drawString(str,                  // Center the string
                         Math.max(0,(getBounds().width - stringWidth))/2,
                         getBounds().height/2);
        }
    }

    // Override update() to reduce flickering
    public void update(Graphics g) {                           // (5)
        // Do the painting
        paint(g);
    }
}
```

The `PaintingApplet` in Example 15.12 illustrates organizing painting and event handling. The applet displays a string in the middle of a circle. The appearance of the string is controlled by an event listener at (1) when the user clicks the mouse (Figure 15.15). Every other mouse click will make the text visible, because the text is drawn only when the toggle is true. The graphics context is set to the foreground color (white in this case) of the applet every time the `paint()` method is called. The event listener does not do the string drawing itself. It sets a "global" toggle at (2) every time the mouse is clicked, and calls the `repaint()` method at (3) to request painting. The `paint()` method at (4) does the painting in all situations, taking into consideration the toggle set by the event handler. With this organization, the current view of the applet is reflected on the screen at all times when screen updating is done, regardless of whether the event handler or the AWT thread initiated the painting. The applet also overrides the `update()` method at (5) to remove flickering caused by the whole area being cleared and then the oval being repainted. It is instructive to run the applet both with the `update()` method overridden and when it is not.

Painting Modes

The default paint mode is to *overwrite* pixels in the drawing region. The AWT offers another rendering mode called the *XOR paint mode*. The following methods of the `Graphics` class can be used to switch between overwrite and XOR paint modes:

`void setPaintMode()`

Sets the mode to overwrite paint mode. All subsequent rendering operations will overwrite the destination with the current color.

`void setXORMode(Color c1)`

Sets the mode to XOR paint mode, which alternates pixels between the current color and a new specified XOR alternation color.

In the XOR paint mode, painting is done by applying a reversible graphical operation on the existing pixel colors. By performing the same operation again, the original pixel colors can be restored. The current color and the alternation color will influence the exact result of the XOR operation. It is guaranteed that when the XOR operation is applied on pixels with the alternation color, the color changes to the current color, and vice versa. Pixels in other colors will be changed in some undetermined way. The important point is that the XOR paint mode is a *toggle*, so that doing the same rendering operation any even number of times leaves the drawing area unchanged.

Example 15.13 *Painting Modes*

```
// XOR Demo
import java.applet.*;
import java.awt.*;
```

```
public class XORApplet extends Applet {

    public void paint(Graphics g) {
        // Set background color to yellow
        setBackground(Color.yellow);

        // Set current color to blue. Draw the top left square.
        g.setColor(Color.blue);
        g.fillRect(50, 10, 50, 50);

        // Set current color to cyan. Draw the bottom right square.
        g.setColor(Color.cyan);
        g.fillRect(110, 60, 50, 50);

        // Set XOR color to blue
        g.setXORMode(Color.blue);

        // Use current color to cyan. Draw the middle square.
        g.fillRect(75, 35, 50, 50);

        // Same operation again leaves screen unchanged
        // g.fillRect(75, 35, 50, 50);
    }
}
```

In Example 15.13, first the top left square is drawn in blue. Next, the bottom right square is drawn in cyan. The XOR alternation color is set to blue and the middle square is drawn. The intersection of the middle square with the other two squares illustrates XOR paint mode in Figure 15.16. Pixels in the XOR alternation color (blue) changed to the current color (cyan), as can be seen by the intersection of the middle square with the top left square. Pixels in the current color (cyan) changed to the XOR alternation color (blue), as can be seen by the intersection of the middle square with the bottom right square.

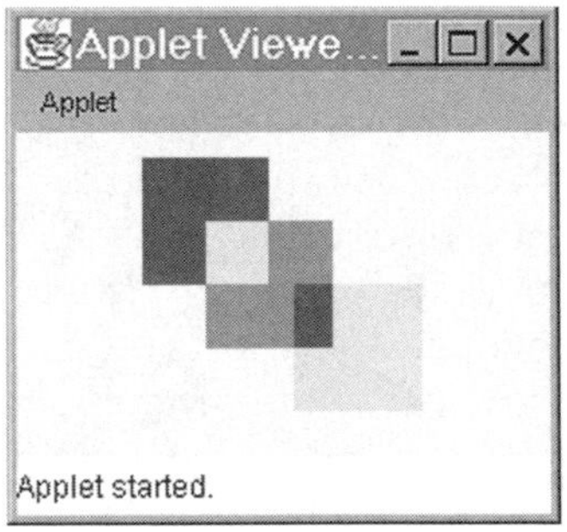

Figure 15.16 *Painting Modes*

15.8 Handling Images

Rendering pixel-based images onto components using a graphics context can degrade performance. The `Image` class provides a platform-independent interface to handle images off-screen. An image that is to be displayed must first either be loaded from an external source or created from scratch.

The following procedure can be used to initialize an `Image` object from an existing image stored locally or on the net. The `Toolkit` class provides methods for loading images. The current toolkit can be used to read the graphics file (GIF or JPEG formats) into an `Image` object.

```
Toolkit currentTK = Toolkit.getDefaultToolkit();
Image image1 = currentTK.getImage("Cover.gif");
```

For a graphics file on the net, a URL must be supplied:

```
URL url = new URL("http://www.example.com/Cover.gif");
Image image2 = currentTK.getImage(url);
```

The `Applet` class also provides `getImage()` methods for reading graphics files:

```
Image getImage(URL url)
Image getImage(URL url, String name)
```

The `url` argument must specify an absolute URL. The `name` argument is the name of the file, interpreted relative to the URL. These methods return immediately. Image data first starts loading when the applet attempts to draw the image. Example 15.14 illustrates the mechanism for loading and showing images.

An image can be displayed using a graphics context associated with a component. The `Graphics` class defines a variety of `drawImage()` methods which can scale and fit the image. The simplest form of the `drawImage()` method is shown here:

```
boolean drawImage(Image img,
                  int x, int y,
                  ImageObserver observer)
```

The method paints as much of the image as is available and returns. If the process of loading the image has not completed, the value `false` is returned. The `observer` object is notified when more of the image becomes available. It is the responsibility of the `observer` object to initiate repainting when notified. Image drawing is thus asynchronous and incremental. The `Component` class implements the `ImageObserver` interface. Example 15.14 illustrates the mechanism for loading and showing images.

Example 15.14 *Displaying Images*

```
// Reading and displaying an Image
import java.applet.*;
import java.awt.*;
```

```
public class ImageApplet extends Applet {
    Image image;

    public void init() {                                              // (1)
        // Read in the image from same directory as the applet page
        image = getImage(getDocumentBase(), "Cover.gif");
    }
    public void paint(Graphics g) {                                   // (2)
        // Display the image, passing itself as the ImageObserver.
        g.drawImage(image, 10, 10, this);
    }
}
```

Figure 15.17 *Displaying Images*

The image loading process is asynchronous and incremental, as demonstrated by the `ImageApplet` in Example 15.14, and is illustrated in Figure 15.18. The process of actually loading the image commences when the first call to the method `drawImage()` is made in the `paint()` method at (2). The `drawImage()` method draws as much of the image as is available and returns (and thereby the `paint()` method returns). If the loading is not yet complete, the `ImageObserver` object is notified when more of the image becomes available. In this particular case this object is the applet (the `this` argument in the `drawImage()` call). The `ImageObserver` defines a method named `imageUpdate()`, which is invoked in the observer if the loading process is not complete. The default implementation of this method, which the applet inherits, is called in this case. It calls the `repaint()` method, which eventually results in a call to the `paint()` method to do some more drawing of the image. Thus the `paint()` method gets called repeatedly, until the loading process is completed.

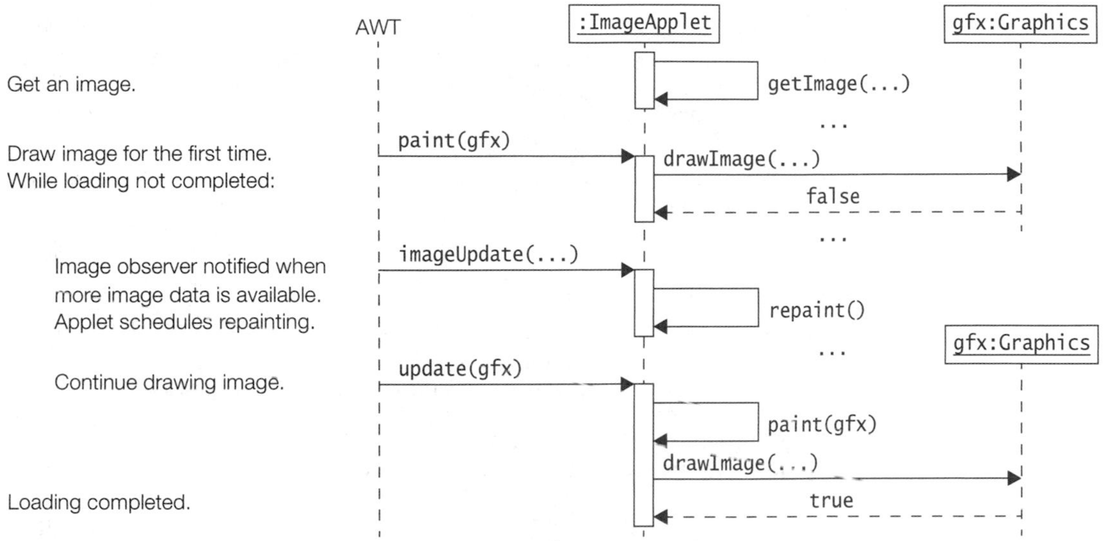

Figure 15.18 *Incremental Image Drawing*

Another use for images is to implement *image buffering*. The `BufferingApplet` in Example 15.15 illustrates this technique using images. The applet shows a Pac-man figure with the text `"Come and play!"` underneath it. The figure and the text swap colors if the screen needs updating, as shown in Figure 15.19.

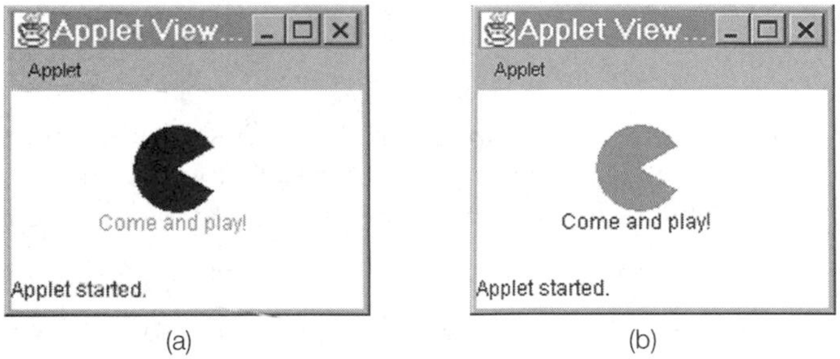

Figure 15.19 *Image Buffering*

Example 15.15 *Image Buffering*

```
import java.applet.*;
import java.awt.*;

public class BufferingApplet extends Applet {

    private Image bufferImage;
    private Graphics imageGfx;

    private Color color1 = Color.gray;
    private Color color2 = Color.black;
```

```
    public void init() {
        // Create an image                                                  (1)
        bufferImage = createImage(getSize().width, getSize().height);
        // Get the graphics context associated with the image
        imageGfx = bufferImage.getGraphics();                            // (2)
    }

    public void paint(Graphics gfx) {                                    // (3)
        // Swap colors
        Color temp = color2;
        color2 = color1;
        color1 = temp;

        // Clear buffer image                                               (4)
        imageGfx.setColor(getBackground());
        imageGfx.fillRect(0,0, getSize().width, getSize().height);
        // Render graphics in the buffer image
        imageGfx.setColor(color1);
        imageGfx.fillArc(20, 0,       // top left-hand corner               (5)
                         50, 50,      // width, height
                         30, 300);    // start angle, sweep angle
        imageGfx.setColor(color2);
        imageGfx.drawString("Come and play!", 0, 60);
        // Display the buffer image, passing applet as the ImageObserver.
        gfx.drawImage(bufferImage, 50, 20, this);                       // (6)
    }

    // Override update to reduce flickering
    public void update(Graphics gfx) {                                   // (7)
        paint(gfx);
    }
}
```

The `BufferingApplet` in Example 15.15 shows how an image can also be created from scratch, using the `createImage()` method of the `Component` class. An empty `Image` object is created that is equal in size to that of the applet shown at (1):

```
bufferImage = createImage(getSize().width, getSize().height);
```

Each `Image` object has a graphics context associated with it. In the `BufferingApplet`, this graphics context is obtained as shown at (2):

```
imageGfx = bufferImage.getGraphics();                          // (2)
```

Rendering operations can be carried out on the image by using the graphics context associated with it, before the image is displayed on the screen. This can also be done with images that have been read in. This provides the means of creating complex images off-screen and allowing them to be displayed on the screen when appropriate. Note that the graphics context for rendering operations on the image is not the same as the one used to display it on the screen.

In the `BufferingApplet`, the `paint()` method at (3) does the rendering in the buffer image, using the buffer image's graphics context, and displays it on the screen using the `drawImage()` method on the applet's graphics context. Screen updating will always result in rendering graphics in the buffer image first, and then displaying the buffer image in the component.

The `update()` method at (7) is overridden to reduce flickering, as filling the buffer image with the background color of the component, as shown at (4), does the same job when the image is displayed.

An image can be drawn once into a buffer, and later copied to the screen whenever necessary. If the image does not change, time-consuming drawing operations can be avoided by simply copying from the buffer.

Review questions

15.12 Which method should the application call when it wants to redraw the visuals of a component?

Select the one right answer.

(a) `paint()`
(b) `repaint()`
(c) `update()`
(d) `layout()`
(e) None of the above.

15.13 When does a call to the method `repaint()` of the `Component` class end?

Select the one right answer.

(a) Immediately, i.e. repainting is done asynchronously.
(b) When the AWT thread responds by calling the `update()` method.
(c) When the call to the `update()` method by the AWT thread ends.
(d) When the AWT thread goes idle.
(e) None of the above.

15.14 How do you change a `Graphics` instance from XOR paint mode to (normal overwrite) paint mode?

Select all valid answers.

(a) `gfx.setXORMode()`
(b) `gfx.setXORMode(false)`
(c) `gfx.setPaintMode()`
(d) `gfx.setPaintMode(true)`
(e) Changing from XOR mode to paint mode is not possible.

15.15 How do you obtain a `Graphics` object suitable for painting in an `Image` object?

Select all valid answers.

(a) Pass the `Image` object as an argument to the constructor of `Graphics`.
(b) Call method named `create()` on the `Image` object.
(c) Call method named `getGraphics()` on the `Image` object.
(d) Call method named `getGraphics()` on the component that was used to obtain the `Image` object.

Chapter summary

The following information was included in this chapter:

- A discussion of the `Graphics` class, with emphasis on the functionality it provides for rendering graphics.
- The role of the `repaint()`, `update()` and `paint()` methods in painting and updating components on the screen.
- Usage of color in text and graphics.
- Usage of fonts and basics of rendering text.
- Drawing of shapes, including lines, rectangles, ovals, arcs, polygons and polylines.
- Setting of a clip region in a graphics context.
- Organizing painting and event handling in an application.
- Discussion of the painting modes (overwrite and XOR) provided by the graphics context.
- Retrieving and displaying images.

Programming exercise

15.1 Panels are useful for grouping components together in a GUI. Often one wants to provide some visual cue that the components within a panel are actually grouped together. The standard `Panel` class does not provide such a clue. Create a subclass of `Panel` that features an appropriate border surrounding the components grouped inside it. The class should be usable as a drop-in replacement for the `Panel` class.

Pay attention to the following:

- Be sure to accommodate any insets the superclass (`Panel`) may have.
- Be sure to supply constructors that match the constructors of the `Panel` class.
- Make sure that the components inside the panel will not be placed on top of the border.

Applets 16

Supplementary Objectives

- Write code to create applets by subclassing the `Applet` class.
- Specify information in the HTML `Applet` element in order to run applets, including the passing of parameters to the applet.
- State the methods that govern the life cycle of an applet.
- Write code to run an applet in its own thread.
- Write code to use images and sound in applets.
- Understand why JAR files are useful and how to create them.
- State the main restrictions placed on applets because of security reasons.

16.1 Creating Applets

An *applet* is a special kind of Java program that is run when embedded in another application (usually a *Java-enabled web browser,* or a specialized tool such as the *applet viewer*). The `java.applet.Applet` class provides a standard framework for developing applets. The applet's environment can use the facilities provided by this framework to control the running of the applet. An *applet context* is the environment the applet runs in. The applet can access certain facilities (for example, a status message area) in its environment through the applet context.

The following differences between applets and standalone Java applications should be noted:

- In order to run an applet, an HTML (*HyperText Markup Language*) file with the appropriate information about the applet's class file must be provided.
- The `main()` method, which is necessary for executing standalone applications, is not necessary for running applets.
- There are restrictions on what an applet is allowed to do.

The `java.applet.Applet` class provides the base implementation of the contract between an applet and the applet context. An applet is implemented by creating a subclass of the `Applet` class and overriding the appropriate methods to customize the running of the applet. As can be seen from the inheritance hierarchy in Figure 12.1, the `Applet` class is an AWT component (but it is in the `java.applet` package and not in the `java.awt` package). Applets therefore provide the following functionality:

- GUI components and containers can be embedded in an applet to build a GUI for the applet.

  The default layout manager for applets is the `FlowLayout` manager, but other layout managers can also be used. Event handling in applets is no different from that of standalone applications.
- Rendering operations can be performed onto an applet by overriding the `paint()` method.

In addition, the `Applet` class provides facilities for dealing with images and sounds.

16.2 Running Applets

In order to run an applet, an HTML file with the appropriate information about the applet's class file must be provided. In versions prior to HTML 4.0, an `APPLET` element was used for specifying information about an applet. In HTML 4.0, the `APPLET` element has been deprecated in favor of the `OBJECT` element. Since not all browsers yet support the `OBJECT` element, both elements are discussed in this section.

The APPLET element specification below shows the minimum information that must always be provided in the APPLET element:

- the name of the applet class file (code attribute)
- the size of the applet in pixels (width and height attributes)

```
<APPLET code="AppletName.class" width=w height=h>
</APPLET>
```

An equivalent version of the same information using the OBJECT element is the following HTML code, where the value of the classid attribute specifies the name of the applet class file:

```
<OBJECT classid="AppletName.class" width=w height=h>
</OBJECT>
```

The web browser or the applet viewer uses the applet HTML file to load and run the applet. In a web browser, the applet is loaded when the HTML page containing the APPLET or OBJECT element is read. Inside a web browser, the applet can be viewed by specifying the HTML file location. The location, given as a URL (*Universal Resource Locator*), specifies a local or a remote HTML file.

```
file:///local-path/AppletName.html
http://www.example.com/local-path/AppletName.html
```

An applet can be run from the command line using the applet viewer and by specifying the path of the HTML file:

```
appletviewer AppletName.html
```

Note that the HTML file with the applet information can contain other HTML content (including other applets) that can be displayed by the web browser. The applet viewer only interprets the APPLET and OBJECT elements, and ignores any other HTML content.

Depending on the web client used, if the source code of the applet is changed and recompiled, then simply reloading the applet HTML file may not reload the applet *class* file. In some cases, you must restart the web browser. This situation does not arise when using the default applet viewer distributed with the JDK (Java Development Kit), as the applet view reloads the class files each time it is started.

The HTML file with the applet information need not have the applet class name in its file name.

HTML APPLET Element

The APPLET element in HTML provides information that the web browser uses to lay out and run the applet in a web page. An HTML page can include other useful information about the applet, not just the APPLET element:

```
<HTML>
    <HEAD>
        <TITLE>The Applet Name</TITLE>
    </HEAD>
    <BODY>
        <P>Text explaining what this applet is all about.</P>
        <APPLET code="AppletName.class" width=w height=h></APPLET>
    </BODY>
</HTML>
```

Note that several APPLET elements (<APPLET>-</APPLET> tag pairs – one for each applet) can appear within the BODY element (<BODY>-</BODY> tag pair) defining the body of the HTML page. An HTML reference should be consulted for details about creating HTML pages.

The general syntax of the APPLET element is as follows:

```
<APPLET
    CODE= class file
    WIDTH= width of applet in pixels
    HEIGHT= height of applet in pixels
    [ CODEBASE= URL directory ]
    [ ARCHIVE= names of the JAR files ]
    [ OBJECT= alternative serialized applet file ]
    [ NAME= name for identification by other applets on this HTML page ]
    [ ALIGN= alignment on HTML page ]
    [ HSPACE= horizontal spacing in pixels ]
    [ VSPACE= vertical spacing in pixels ]
    [ ALT= alternate text message in case applet is not loaded ]
>
[ <PARAM NAME= paramName_1 [VALUE= paramValue_1]> ]
[ <PARAM NAME= paramName_2 [VALUE= paramValue_2]> ]
...
[ <PARAM NAME= paramName_n [VALUE= paramValue_n]> ]
[ Alternate HTML text interpreted by Java-illiterate browsers only. ]
</APPLET>
```

An attribute or element in square brackets ([]) is optional. The values of the attributes are specified as *strings*. These values are case-sensitive in most cases (file names, parameter names and parameter values). The order in which the attributes are specified is irrelevant. Note that the PARAM elements can only appear between the <APPLET>-</APPLET> tag pair, whereas all the other attributes are inside the <APPLET> tag.

The attributes for applet specification can roughly be divided into these two categories:

- Attributes that concern the *code* for the applet.
- Attributes that concern the *layout* of the applet.

The PARAM element is discussed in the section on passing parameters to applets (Section 16.6, p. 501).

HTML OBJECT Element

The OBJECT element in HTML is very similar in syntax to the APPLET element. An HTML page could use the OBJECT element as shown in this example:

```
<HTML>
    <HEAD>
        <TITLE>The Applet Name</TITLE>
    </HEAD>
    <BODY>
        <P>Text explaining what this applet is all about.</P>
        <OBJECT classid="AppletName.class" width=w height=h></OBJECT>
    </BODY>
</HTML>
```

The main difference is that the OBJECT element uses the CLASSID attribute to specify the code to execute, whereas the APPLET element uses the CODE attribute. The salient features of the OBJECT element for running applets are specified by the following syntax:

```
<OBJECT
    CLASSID= class file
    WIDTH= width of applet in pixels
    HEIGHT= height of applet in pixels
    [ CODEBASE= URL directory ]
    [ ARCHIVE= names of the JAR files ]
    [ NAME= name for identification by other applets on this HTML page ]
    [ ALIGN= alignment on HTML page ]
    [ HSPACE= horizontal spacing in pixels ]
    [ VSPACE= vertical spacing in pixels ]
>
[ <PARAM NAME=paramName_1 [VALUE=paramValue_1]> ]
[ <PARAM NAME=paramName_2 [VALUE=paramValue_2]> ]
...
[ <PARAM NAME=paramName_n [VALUE=paramValue_n]> ]
[ Alternate HTML text interpreted by Java-illiterate browsers only. ]
</OBJECT>
```

The attributes are discussed below. The discussion applies to both APPLET and OBJECT elements, unless explicitly indicated.

Applet Layout Management Specification

All attributes that concern visual alignment and presentation have been deprecated in favor of *style sheets* in HTML 4.0. Style sheets are used to describe the visual appearance of documents. Few web browsers currently provide adequate support for them.

WIDTH and HEIGHT

These attributes are mandatory and they specify the width and height of the applet in pixels. In web browsers, the applet cannot be resized – only the HTML page window can be resized, but that does not change the applet size. However, the applet viewers allow the user to change the applet size when the applet is running. An applet can find its size by calling the `getSize()` method inherited from the `Component` class.

ALIGN

This optional attribute affects the alignment of the applet in the HTML page. Valid values for the `ALIGN` attribute are given below, and illustrated in Figure 16.1.

`LEFT` or `RIGHT`

The `LEFT` and `RIGHT` values make the text flow around the left or the right side of the applet, respectively.

`BOTTOM`

The `BOTTOM` value aligns the *bottom* of the applet vertically with the current baseline. This is the default value.

`MIDDLE`

The `MIDDLE` value aligns the *center* of the applet vertically with the current baseline.

`TOP`

The `TOP` value aligns the *top* of the applet vertically with the top of the current line.

The following alignment specification will align the applet with the top of the current line.

```
<APPLET code="VIPApplet.class" width=100 height=100 align=TOP>
</APPLET>
```

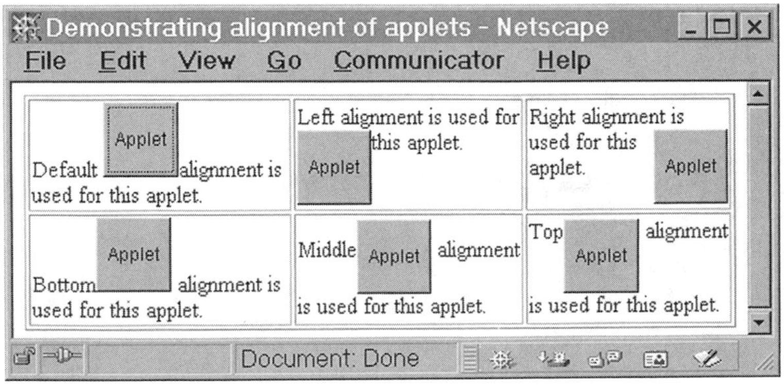

Figure 16.1 *Alignment of Applets*

HSPACE and VSPACE

The optional HSPACE attribute specifies the horizontal spacing in pixels to the left and right of the applet. The optional VSPACE attribute specifies the vertical spacing in pixels above and below the applet.

```
<APPLET code="VIPApplet.class" width=100 height=100
        hspace=10 vspace=15>
</APPLET>
```

Applet Code Specification

CODE (APPLET element only) / CLASSID (OBJECT element only)

This attribute is used to specify the name of the applet class file. The file name is interpreted relative to the directory of its *applet HTML page* (called the *document base*) if no CODEBASE attribute is specified. If the CODEBASE attribute is specified, the file name is interpreted relative to the directory given by the CODEBASE attribute.

The following HTML content specifies the class file in an APPLET element:

```
<APPLET code="VIPApplet.class" width=100 height=100>
</APPLET>
```

The following HTML content specifies the class file in an OBJECT element:

```
<OBJECT classid="VIPApplet.class" width=100 height=100>
</OBJECT>
```

The VIPApplet.class file is then interpreted as having the path ./VIPApplet.class.

Note that the CODE attribute is not specified if the OBJECT attribute (explained below) is specified in the APPLET element, and vice versa.

An applet can obtain its document base (a URL) by calling the getDocumentBase() method.

CODEBASE

This optional attribute can be used to specify the URL of the *directory* (called the *code base*) in which the class files and other resources for the applet are located. The CODE attribute is then interpreted relative to this directory.

```
<APPLET codebase="project/applets" code="VIPApplet.class"
        width=100 height=100>
</APPLET>
```

The VIPApplet.class file is then interpreted as having the path ./project/applets/VIPApplet.class.

An applet can obtain its code base (a URL) by calling the getCodeBase() method.

ARCHIVE

All classes and resources that are needed by an applet can be put in JAR files (Section 16.8, p. 505) that can be specified using the optional ARCHIVE attribute. Note that it is possible to name several JAR files in a comma-separated list as the value of the ARCHIVE attribute.

```
<APPLET archive="VIPArchive.jar" code="VIPApplet.class"
        width=100 height=100>
</APPLET>
```

OBJECT (APPLET element only)

Objects in Java can be *serialized*, i.e. an object can be written out to a stream and read back with its state information intact (Section 18.6, p. 587). An applet that has been serialized can be read in (i.e. deserialized) by specifying its serialized file in the OBJECT attribute.

The following HTML content specifies the serialized file of the applet in an APPLET element:

```
<APPLET object= "VIPApplet.obj" width=100 height=100>
</APPLET>
```

Note that the OBJECT attribute is not specified if the CODE attribute is specified in an APPLET element, and vice versa.

NAME

This optional attribute can be used to specify the name of the applet within an HTML page. This name can be used by applets to identify each other for inter-applet communication.

```
<APPLET code="VIPApplet.class" width=100 height=100
        name="VIP">
</APPLET>
```

ALT (APPLET element only)

The text string specified with this optional attribute is only displayed by a Java-enabled browser if for some reason the Java runtime environment is deactivated, otherwise it is ignored.

```
<APPLET code="VIPApplet.class" width=100 height=100
        alt="JVM seems to be deactivated.">
</APPLET>
```

Alternate Text

A Java-illiterate browser will always display the optional alternative HTML text specified inside the <APPLET> and the <OBJECT> elements, and this text will be ignored by a Java-enabled browser.

```
<APPLET code="VIPApplet.class" width=100 height=100>
Sorry. I am a Java-illiterate browser.
</APPLET>
```

16.3 Applet Life Cycle

The applet context calls methods in the applet at the appropriate times during the life of the applet for specific purposes:

- Initialize the applet.
- Start the applet.
- Stop the applet.
- Destroy the applet.

The initializing and destroying occur only once, but starting and stopping the applet occur every time the user returns to or leaves the applet page.

The methods of the `Applet` class responsible for these actions are discussed below. Note that the default implementation of these methods does nothing, and that normally these methods are not called directly by the applet, but by the applet context to control the applet. The applet has to override these methods to implement the required behavior. Examples in the rest of the chapter demonstrate usage of these applet methods.

`void init()`

This method is called once by the applet context to inform the applet that it has been loaded into the system. This is always followed by calls to the `start()` and the `paint()` methods. This call sequence gives the applet the opportunity to initialize, start up and display itself on the screen.

The `init()` method serves the same purpose as a constructor, and an applet should override this method to perform any initialization. For example, an applet with threads would use the `init()` method to create the threads, or construct the GUI, or process the `PARAM` values from the `APPLET` element.

Although subclasses of the `Applet` class can provide a default constructor for initialization purposes, this is usually done in the `init()` method of the applet.

`void start()`

The applet context calls this method for the first time after calling the `init()` method, and thereafter every time the applet page is made visible. This gives the applet the opportunity to start or continue its execution. The applet must override this method if it wants any operations performed each time the applet page is visited. For example, an applet doing animation would use the `start()` method to ensure that a thread was present to do the animation.

`void stop()`

The applet context calls this method when it wants the applet to stop executing. This method is called when the applet is no longer visible. This might happen if another HTML page replaces the applet page, or if the applet is scrolled out of the browser window. This method is also called just before the applet is to be destroyed. The applet must override this method if it wants any operations performed each time the applet becomes invisible. For example, an applet doing animation would override the `stop()` method to signal that the thread doing the animation should desist, or to stop the playing of an audio file temporarily, or any other CPU-intensive computation that need not continue once the applet is not on the screen.

`void destroy()`

The applet context calls this method to inform the applet that it should relinquish any system resources that it has allocated. The applet context calls the `stop()` method prior to calling the `destroy()` method. All resources are destroyed when the browser terminates.

Review questions

16.1 Which element should be used to embed an applet into an HTML document according to the official HTML standard?

Select the one right answer.

(a) An `Applet` element
(b) An `Embed` element
(c) An `Object` element
(d) An `Applet` or `Object` element, depending on the version of the HTML specification.

16.2 Which attribute in the `Applet` element is used to specify the base URL for the applet?

Select the one right answer.

(a) The `Archive` attribute
(b) The `Classid` attribute
(c) The `Code` attribute
(d) The `Codebase` attribute
(e) The `Object` attribute

16.3 When an applet is run, which one of the these methods is executed first?

Select the one right answer.

(a) `destroy()`
(b) `init()`
(c) `main()`
(d) `start()`
(e) `stop()`

16.4 Which of the following methods are never run by the applet context?

Select all valid answers.

(a) `destroy()`
(b) `init()`
(c) `main()`
(d) `start()`
(e) `stop()`

16.5 Which of these methods can be executed more than once on the same `Applet` object by the applet context?

Select all valid answers.

(a) `destroy()`
(b) `init()`
(c) `main()`
(d) `start()`
(e) `stop()`

16.6 Which one of these methods must a subclass of `Applet` implement?

Select the one right answer.

(a) `destroy()`
(b) `init()`
(c) `run()`
(d) `start()`
(e) None of the above.

16.4 Applets and Threads

If an applet is going to do any computation-intensive work, then it should do so in its own thread, rather than impede the AWT thread employed by the web browser.

The `ThreadApplet` in Example 16.1 demonstrates threads, event handling and screen updating in applets. For exposition purposes, the applet only draws a "Pac-man" figure in two alternating colors continuously in its own thread, but it can be stopped and restarted by clicking the mouse (Figure 16.2). The `init()` method at (1) sets up the mouse listener (as an anonymous class) at (2) to handle the mouse clicks. The `start()` method at (3) creates and starts a thread if none is present, every time the applet page is revisited. The `stop()` method at (4) sets the thread reference to null, so that the run() method at (5) can terminate (and thereby the thread terminates) when the applet goes out of sight. The run() method implements the code executed by the thread. It constantly changes the foreground color (and thereby the rendering color) of the applet and calls for the repainting of the applet, while in between taking a short break by calling the sleep() method at (7). On waking up, it tests to see if the painting has been stopped. If that is the case, it decides to wait by calling the wait() method at (10). Note that the wait() method is called in the loop at (9). Another thread can thus notify the applet thread to restart the painting when the wait condition at (9) becomes true. Note that the mouse clicking is not registered by the applet thread, but by the AWT thread.

The paint() method at (11) just draws the figure in the current color, every time it is called.

The toggleAnimation() method at (12) is called by the mouse listener at (2) when it receives a mouse click. The toggleAnimation() method checks to see if the applet thread is alive. If that is the case, it toggles the painting status at (13). If it is time to restart the painting, it notifies, at (14), the applet thread that might be waiting. Note that the call to notify occurs in synchronized code, since the toggleAnimation() method is synchronized. The thread executing this method will have the monitor of the applet, and can notify any thread waiting on a condition on the same object. If the applet thread is not alive to begin with, the start() method is called to create and start a new thread to run the applet, as shown at (15).

Example 16.1 also demonstrates the usage of the wait and notify mechanism (Section 9.5, p. 286) to pause and restart the applet thread. The example also shows the typical setup for running applets in threads. The recommended practice is to override the start() and the stop() methods as shown. The thread should be terminated by a condition similar to the one in the loop of the run() method. The thread should do screen updating by calling the repaint() method, and the applet should customize its graphical presentation by overriding the paint() method.

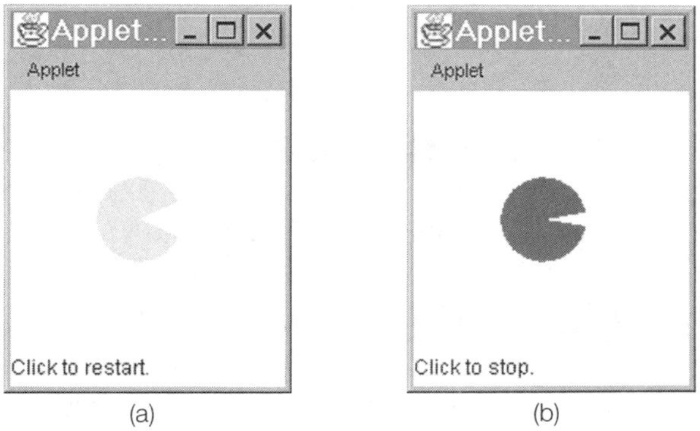

Figure 16.2 *Threads in Applets*

Example 16.1 *Using Threads in Applets*

```
// Demo for usage of standard methods in an applet.
// Runs in its own thread, continuously drawing a Pac-man figure
// in two alternating colors.

import java.awt.*;
import java.awt.event.*;
import java.applet.*;

public class ThreadApplet extends Applet implements Runnable {

    private Thread appletThread = null;
    private boolean stopped = false;
    private int mouthGap = 0;

    public void init() {                                        // (1)
        // Set the foreground color
        setForeground(Color.green);

        // Alternate mouse clicks will stop or restart the painting.
        addMouseListener(new MouseAdapter() {                   // (2)
            public void mouseClicked(MouseEvent e) {
                toggleAnimation();
            }
        });
    }

    public void start() {                                       // (3)
        // Create and start a thread if none present.
        if (appletThread == null) {
            appletThread = new Thread(this);
            appletThread.start();
        }
    }

    public void stop() {                                        // (4)
        appletThread = null;
    }

    public void run() {                                         // (5)
        Thread thisThread = Thread.currentThread();
        while (thisThread == appletThread) {                    // (6)
            // Change foreground color while running.
            // Painting color will change accordingly.
            if(getForeground().equals(Color.green))
                setForeground(Color.blue);
            else
                setForeground(Color.green);

            // Update mouth gap
            mouthGap = (mouthGap+5) % 60;

            // Update the screen
            repaint();
            showStatus("Click to stop.");
```

```
            // Take a break between painting
            try {
                Thread.sleep(100);                            // (7)
                // If drawing is stopped, then wait.
                synchronized(this) {                          // (8)
                    while (stopped) {                         // (9)
                        showStatus("Click to restart.");
                        wait();                               // (10)
                    }
                }
            } catch (InterruptedException e) {}
        }
    }

    public void paint(Graphics gfx) {                         // (11)
        // Draw a "Pac-man" in the current color
        int angle = Math.abs(mouthGap-30) + 5;  // Set mouth angle
        gfx.fillArc (50, 50, 50, 50, angle, 360 - angle*2);
    }

    private synchronized void toggleAnimation() {             // (12)
        // Check if the thread is present.
        if (appletThread != null && appletThread.isAlive()) {

            // Toggle between stopping and resuming the painting
            stopped = !stopped;                               // (13)

            // If drawing should restart, then notify.
            if (!stopped) {
                notify();                                     // (14)
            }
        } else { // No thread. Create one and start it.          (15)
            stopped = false;
            start();
        }
    }
}
```

16.5 Other Useful Methods of the Applet Class

Apart from the methods that allow the applet context to run the applet, the `Applet` class defines a number of other useful methods.

`URL getDocumentBase()`

Returns the *document* URL, i.e. the URL of the *HTML file* in which the applet is embedded. See Example 16.3 for usage of this method.

`URL getCodeBase()`

Returns the *base* URL, i.e. the URL of the *applet class file* that contains the applet.

`void showStatus(String msg)`

The applet can request that the applet context display the argument string in its "status window". See Example 16.3 for usage of this method.

`String getAppletInfo()`

The applet context can use this method to get information from the applet about itself. An applet usually overrides this method to return a `String` containing information about the author, version, and copyright of the applet. This information can be made available to the user by the applet context.

See Example 16.2 for usage of this method.

`String getParameter(String parameterName)`

Returns the string value (given by the `VALUE` attribute) of the named parameter (specified by the `PARAM` element) in the `APPLET` element contained in the applet HTML file.

The `parameterName` argument is case-insensitive, but the string value returned is always case-sensitive.

See Example 16.2 and Example 16.3 for usage of this method.

`String[][] getParameterInfo()`

The applet context can use this method to get information from the applet about the parameters it uses. An applet should override this method to return an array of strings describing these parameters. See the `PARAM` element (Section 16.2, p. 489).

Each element of the array should be a set of three strings containing the parameter name, the type, and a description.

See Example 16.2 for usage of this method.

`AppletContext getAppletContext()`

This method returns the applet context of the applet. The applet context provides methods to find other applets in the context, and load other web pages.

16.6 Supplying Applet Parameters

Information can be supplied to an applet using `PARAM` elements in the applet HTML file:

```
<APPLET code="AppletName.class" width=w height=h ... >
<PARAM NAME="name_1" [VALUE="value_1"]>
<PARAM NAME="name_2" [VALUE="value_2"]>
...
<PARAM NAME="name_n" [VALUE="value_n"]>
</APPLET>
```

For each parameter, the `NAME` attribute must be specified, but the `VALUE` attribute is optional. Note that these parameter names and any values specified are *strings*, whether or not they are quoted. An applet should always check that a valid string is returned as the parameter value. It should also check that the conversion of the returned string to the required value type is valid. The applet should supply a default value if no valid value is supplied.

As an example, the following applet HTML file specifies two parameters and their corresponding values for an applet called `AppletParams`:

```
<APPLET code="AppletParams.class" width=200 height=200>
<PARAM NAME="background" VALUE="DDFFBB">
<PARAM NAME="foreground" VALUE="880000">
</APPLET>
```

The `AppletParams` applet in Example 16.2 accesses this information using `getParameter()` as shown at (1), and converts it to the right type as shown at (2). The applet also implements the methods `getAppletInfo()` and `getParameterInfo()`, which the applet context can use to obtain information about the applet and its parameters, as shown at (3) and (4) respectively. The result of this GUI customization is shown in Figure 16.3.

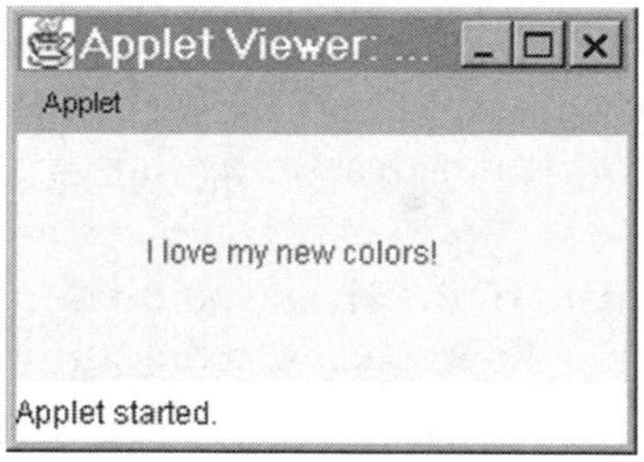

Figure 16.3 *Using Applet Parameters*

Example 16.2 *Applet Parameters*

```
// Demo for Applet Parameters
import java.applet.*;
import java.awt.*;

public class AppletParams extends Applet {

    public void init() {
        // Read two color parameters
        Color foreground = getColorParam("foreground");
        Color background = getColorParam("background");
        // Set the colors.
        if (foreground != null) setForeground(foreground);
        if (background != null) setBackground(background);
    }
```

```
    private Color getColorParam(String paramName) {
        // Read parameter value as string
        String paramValue = getParameter(paramName);              // (1)

        try { // Convert to hex integer value
            return new Color(Integer.parseInt(paramValue, 16));   // (2)
        } catch (NumberFormatException e) { return null; }
    }

    public void paint(Graphics gfx) {
        gfx.translate(getInsets().left, getInsets().top);
        gfx.drawString("I love my new colors!", 50, 50);
    }

    // Provide info for display in a dialog box
    public String getAppletInfo() {                                // (3)
        return "AppletParams 1.0 written by KAM";
    }

    // Provide info about applet parameters
    public String[][] getParameterInfo() { return paramInfo; }    // (4)

    private String[][] paramInfo = {
        // Parameter name, Parameter type, Parameter description
        {"foreground", "Hex RGB color value", "Foreground color"},
        {"background", "Hex RGB color value", "Background color"}
    };
}
```

16.7 Using Images and Sound in Applets

Applets can handle images (GIF and JPEG formats) and audio files (AU, AIFF, WAV, and MIDI files). Retrieving, manipulating and displaying images in applets and standalone applications is discussed in Section 15.8.

Audio clips are handled by an interface called `AudioClip` which all audio clips implement. The following methods from the `AudioClip` interface can be invoked on an audio clip once it has been retrieved:

```
void loop()
void play()
void stop()
```

The `loop()` method plays the audio clip continuously. The `play()` method plays it only once, and if the audio clip is playing, it can be stopped by calling the `stop()` method.

The `Applet` class provides `getAudioClip()` methods for retrieving sound files specified by a URL:

```
AudioClip getAudioClip(URL url)
AudioClip getAudioClip(URL url, String fileName)
```

The `url` argument must specify an absolute local or remote URL. The `fileName` argument specifies the name of the file relative to the base location given by the URL.

The `Applet` class also provides two overloaded `play()` methods, which can retrieve and play an audio clip:

```
void play(URL url)
void play(URL url, String fileName)
```

The `url` argument must specify an absolute local or remote URL. The `fileName` argument specifies the name of the file relative to the base location given by the URL.

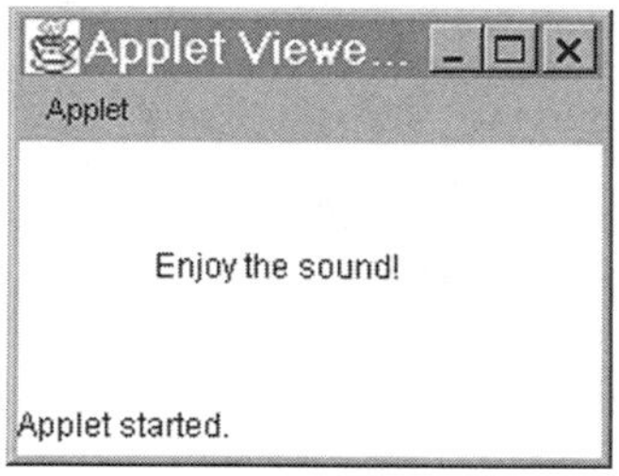

Figure 16.4 *GUI for the SoundApplet*

Example 16.3 *Playing Sounds*

```
// Retrieving and playing sound
import java.applet.*;
import java.awt.*;

public class SoundApplet extends Applet {

    AudioClip audioClip;
    String msg = "Enjoy the sound!";

    public void init() {
        // Read the file name
        String audioFile = getParameter("audiofile");                  // (1)

        if (audioFile != null) {
            audioClip = getAudioClip(getDocumentBase(), audioFile);   // (2)
            msg = "Enjoy the sound!";
        } else {
            showStatus("Audio file cannot be found.");
            msg = "Enjoy the silence!";
        }
    }
```

```
    public void start() {
        // Start the music.
        if (audioClip != null) audioClip.loop();                 // (3)
    }

    public void stop() {      // Stop the music.
        if (audioClip != null) audioClip.stop();                 // (4)
    }

    public void destroy() {  // Clean up.
        audioClip = null;                                        // (5)
    }

    public void paint(Graphics gfx) {
        gfx.translate(getInsets().left, getInsets().top);

        // Display the message.
        gfx.drawString(msg, 50, 50);
    }
}
```

The `SoundApplet` in Example 16.3 plays an audio file continuously, but stops the playing when the applet page is in any way concealed, and starts the playing when the applet page is revisited. The applet reads the parameter specifying the name of the audio file from the HTML file containing the applet, as shown at (1), using the `getParameter()` method. The audio clip is retrieved, as shown at (2), using the `getAudioClip()` method. The `start()` method of the applet uses the `loop()` method to play the audio clip continuously, as shown at (3). The `stop()` method of the applet stops the playing of the audio clip, as shown at (4). The `destroy()` method of the applet relinquishes the audio clip when the applet terminates, as shown at (5). The simple GUI for the applet is shown in Figure 16.4. HTML content that can be used to run the applet is given below, where the name of the audio file should be changed as appropriate.

```
<title>SoundApplet</title>
<hr>
<applet archive="JavaClasses.jar" code="SoundApplet.class" width=200 height=200>
<PARAM NAME="audiofile" VALUE="music.au">
</applet>
<hr>
```

16.8 JAR Files

The web browser makes a net connection to load the applet class file specified in the applet HTML file. The *class loader* of the Java Virtual Machine used by the web browser then resolves any other classes needed by the applet. The web browser may make a new net connection for each class file required to run the applet. This process is obviously time-consuming if many files have to be downloaded. In order to alleviate this process, all the files (including class files and other files for images, sounds, etc.) that comprise the applet can be put into a Java Archive (JAR) file. The JAR file is specified using the ARCHIVE attribute in the APPLET element in the applet HTML file:

```
<APPLET archive="appletbundle.jar" code="AppletName.class" width=w height=h>
<APPLET>
```

The web browser can download the JAR file by making a single net connection. It searches the JAR files first to find any files needed by the applet, before attempting to retrieve the file over the net. JAR files are compressed to make them even faster to download.

JAR files can be made by using the `jar` tool. A typical command for making a compressed JAR file (for example, with the name `appletbundle.jar`) has the following syntax:

```
jar cf appletbundle.jar *.class image*.gif audio*.au ...
```

The `jar` command has many options (akin to the Unix `tar` command). The options `cf` create a JAR file whose name is specified after the options. Files to be included are listed on the command line after the JAR file name.

16.9 Applet Security

Because an applet can be transported and run anywhere on the net, some obvious restrictions are placed on applets. Usually applets loaded over the net are more restricted than applets loaded from a local file, because local applets are deemed more trustworthy.

The following limitations are quite common on applets running in a web browser:

- Reading, writing or deleting files on the local host is not allowed.
- Running other applications from within the applet is prohibited.
- Calling the `System.exit()` method to terminate the applet is not allowed.
- Accessing user, file and system information, other than locale-specific information like Java version, OS name and version, text-encoding standard, file-path (`'/', '\'`) and line-separators (`'\n', '\r', "\r\n"`), is prohibited.
- Connecting to hosts other than the one from which the applet was loaded is not permitted.
- Top-level windows that an applet creates have a warning message for applets loaded over the net.

Applet viewers are usually more liberal, but they will not allow deletion of files.

Java provides *signed applets* that carry a secure *signature* that the web browser can use to authenticate the applet and set its level of security. However, this subject is beyond the scope of this book.

Review questions

16.7 From within an applet, which of the following expressions will return the value of a parameter named `color`?

Select the one right answer.

(a) `getParameter("color")`
(b) `getParameterInfo("color")`
(c) `getParameterInfo().getParameter("color")`
(d) `getAppletContext().getParameter("color")`
(e) None of the above.

16.8 Which method can the applet context use to get information about the parameters that an applet will accept?

Select the one right answer.

(a) `getParameter()`
(b) `getParameterInfo()`
(c) `getAppletContext()`
(d) `getAppletInfo()`
(e) None of the above.

16.9 Which method can the applet context use to get a textual description of an applet?

Select the one right answer.

(a) `getParameter()`
(b) `getParameterInfo()`
(c) `getAppletContext()`
(d) `getAppletInfo()`
(e) None of the above.

16.10 Which of the following methods must a subclass of `Applet` implement?

Select all valid answers.

(a) `getParameter()`
(b) `getParameterInfo()`
(c) `getAppletContext()`
(d) `getAppletInfo()`
(e) None of the above.

Chapter summary

The following information was included in this chapter:

- Creating and running applets.
- The components of the `APPLET` element in HTML.
- Discussion of the applet life cycle, and the functionality provided by the `Applet` class.
- Discussion of running applets in threads.
- Passing parameters to applets.
- Using images and sounds in applets.
- Creating and using JAR files.
- Overview of applet security.

Programming exercises

16.1 Create an applet that takes a string as parameter and displays that string within the applet area. Make the applet provide information about itself and its parameters, using the standard facilities available for applets.

16.2 Create an HTML document conforming to any HTML specification of your choice, to display the applet created in the previous exercise. Make the applet display the string `"An applet a day keeps the browser awake"`.

Swing 17

Supplementary Objectives

- Recognize the inheritance dependencies between AWT and Swing classes.
- Understand how the content pane of the root component is used to hold the component hierarchy.
- Identify the basic steps in constructing a Swing program that uses a particular look and feel.
- Use `BoxLayout` to achieve the required dynamic resizing behavior of a component.
- Write code that implements and uses action objects.

17.1 Swing Overview

Like the AWT, Swing is a framework for building GUI-based applications, provided in the JFC (Java Foundation Classes). Swing is far too comprehensive a topic to be covered completely in a single chapter. This chapter only gives an introduction to the components and facilities provided by Swing. Details on the AWT can be found in Chapter 12.

Swing provides features not present in the AWT:

- More dynamic components.
  Through the use of *delegation* objects, new functionality can easily be added to Swing components.
- More complex components.
  New complex components (such as `JTree`, `JTable`, `JFileChooser`) that have no AWT counterparts.
- New *containment model* for root containers.
  Root containers like `JFrame`, `JDialog` and `JApplet` use a containment model to maintain their component hierarchy.
- Extensive support through auxiliary APIs.
  Interfaces and classes that provide support for Swing components, and facilities useful for implementing Swing-based applications.
- A new layout manager.
  A box layout manager and a convenience container (called `Box`) for using the `BoxLayout` manager.
- Pluggable look and feel.
  Swing has the ability to masquerade as native component sets of a range of platforms, and allows new look & feel schemes to be designed. The look and feel can be changed dynamically.
- Accessibility
  Swing has been designed to support hardware and software designed for people with special needs.

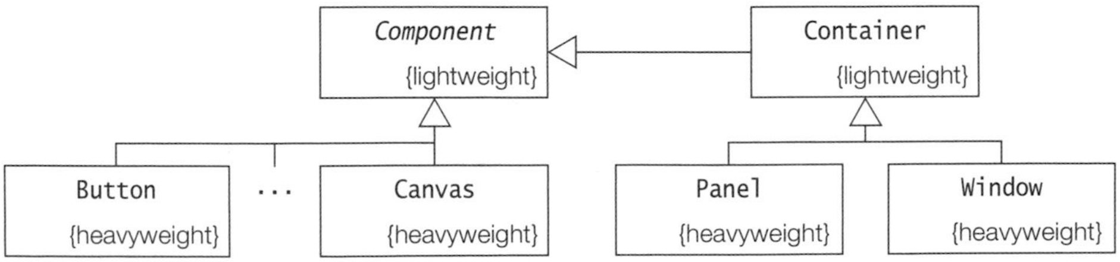

Figure 17.1 *Lightweight and Heavyweight Components in AWT*

Heavyweight and Lightweight Components

The AWT control components use native *peer* components to provide their graphical representation. These control components are *heavyweight*. For example, a `Button` object is associated with a native button peer when it is displayed on the screen. The peer will actually be responsible for the look and feel of that particular component.

Lightweight components are not directly backed by a native peer. The lightweight and heavyweight components in the AWT are shown in Figure 17.1. Note that `Component` and `Container` classes do not have native peers, and are lightweight.

Using the AWT, it is possible to create new components by subclassing any of these classes: `Component`, `Container`, `Canvas` and `Panel`. Since `Canvas` and `Panel` are heavyweight, extending these creates new heavyweight components. However, `Component` and `Container` are lightweight, and directly subclassing these creates new lightweight components.

Swing and the AWT

Swing has a set of lightweight components. Swing is partly meant as an alternative to existing heavyweight components in the AWT, and partly meant to provide more advanced components than those available in the AWT.

The Swing components avoid some of the drawbacks associated with AWT components:

- The use of native heavyweight components can entail significant overhead when the number of components becomes high.
- The application will not have a consistent look and feel across platforms. However, the components will be consistent with other applications running on the same platform, given that the platform in question has a standardized set of GUI components.
- The AWT control components represent the common subset of components usually found on all platforms. As such, more complex components popular on some platforms are not represented in the AWT. Also, interfaces for the components that are present address only the common functionality supported by the native component sets of each platform.

From an architectural standpoint, Swing is not a replacement for the AWT, but rather an extension that contains alternative lightweight components for many of the native heavyweight components in the AWT. Swing uses many of the same concepts as the AWT. It uses the same event model and the same layout managers. Many Swing and AWT components share the `Component`, `Container` and `Window` classes as common superclasses. Thus, to a large degree, both Swing and AWT applications make use of the methods found in these classes in a similar way.

Swing Packages

All the classes directly related to Swing are contained within the `javax.swing` package. Importing from both packages `javax.swing` and `java.awt` is quite common in an application, since Swing still relies heavily on the common framework shared with the AWT components. Table 17.1 summarizes the packages comprising Swing.

Table 17.1 *Swing Packages*

Package	Description
`javax.swing`	The parent package of all Swing-related packages. The package contains the most important Swing interfaces and classes, including the set of lightweight components provided by Swing.
`javax.swing.event`	Provides interfaces and classes for specialized events generated by Swing components.
`javax.swing.border`	Provides an interface and a set of classes for drawing various kinds of borders around Swing components.
`javax.swing.plaf`	Provides the pluggable look and feel (L&F) support. Concrete L&Fs are implemented in subpackages. This package contains abstract classes providing the framework for pluggable L&F.
`javax.swing.undo`	Provides support for creating undo and redo functionality in applications.
`javax.swing.colorchooser`	Contains support for the `JColorChooser` component.
`javax.swing.filechooser`	Contains support for the `JFileChooser` component.
`javax.swing.table`	Contains support for the `JTable` component.
`javax.swing.tree`	Contains support for the `JTree` component.
`javax.swing.text`	Contains support for the text components in Swing.

17.2 The Root Pane Container Model

Building applications using Swing requires understanding of the *root pane container model*. The `JFrame` class and other *root component* classes, such as `JDialog`, `JWindow` and `JApplet`, use the containment model illustrated in Figure 17.2.

The `JRootPane` class implements the containment model (Figure 17.3), and provides the following facilities:

- A *content pane* which constitutes the main area of the root component. The pane acts like a traditional container for which a layout manager can be registered and components can be added. In Swing, the content pane of a root component must be used to add new components, rather than calling the `add()` method on the root component directly.

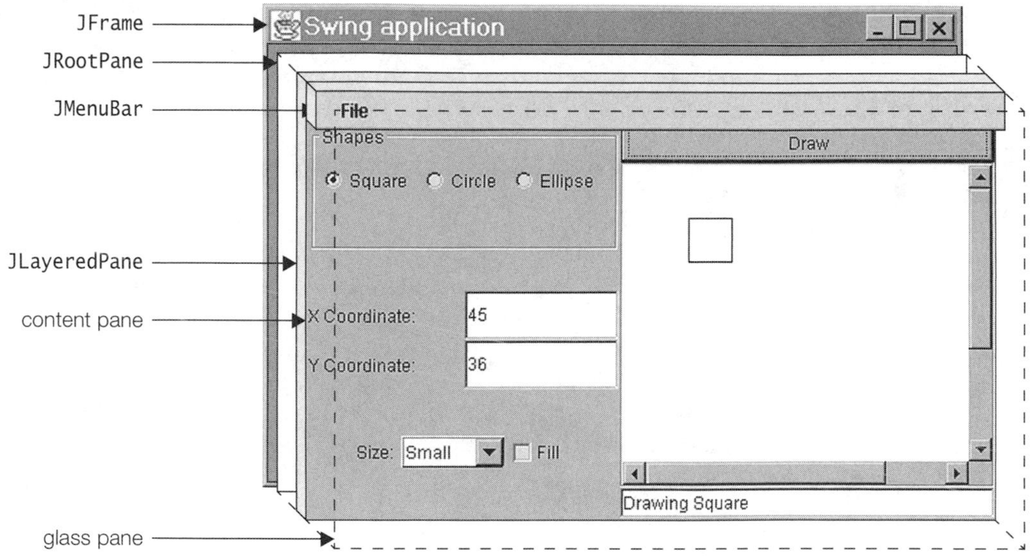

Figure 17.2 *Containment Model*

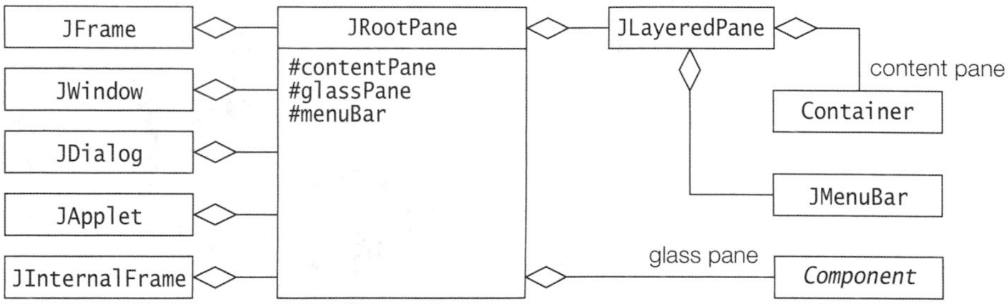

Figure 17.3 *Containment Model for Root Components*

- A *layered pane* for placing components in layers. The `JRootPane` class uses the `JLayeredPane` class to provide facilities for placing components in different layers, thereby extending the spatial relations between components to three dimensions. The content pane and the optional menu-bar described above reside in separate layers within the layered pane. The layered pane is seldom manipulated directly.
- A *glass pane*, which provides an easy way of intercepting mouse events and drawing visuals that should lie on top of all the components within the root component.
- An optional menu-bar. Menu-bars in Swing are represented by the lightweight component `JMenuBar`.

The root components `JFrame`, `JDialog`, `JWindow` and `JApplet`, and the lightweight container `JInternalFrame` use the containment model provided by the `JRootPane` class. These root component classes contain convenience methods that forward requests to the `JRootPane` component. These methods are defined by the `RootPaneContainer` interface:

```
Container getContentPane()
Component getGlassPane()
JLayeredPane getLayeredPane()
```

Returns the content pane, glass pane and layered pane respectively.

```
JRootPane getRootPane()
```

Returns the whole root pane component. The root pane component is the only *real child* of containers using the root pane containment model. All other contents are located within the root pane component.

```
void setContentPane(Container contentPane)
void setGlassPane(Component glassPane)
void setLayeredPane(JLayeredPane layeredPane)
```

Sets the content pane, glass pane and layered pane respectively.

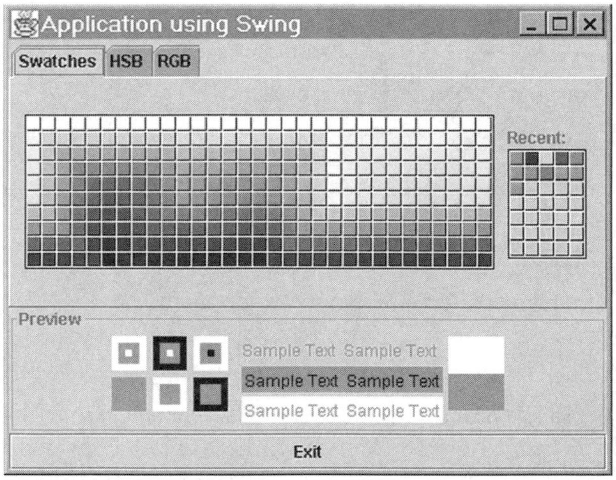

Figure 17.4 *Simple Swing Application*

Example 17.1 *A Simple Swing Application*

```
import javax.swing.*;      // Importing the Swing component set.          (1)
import java.awt.*;         // Still use parts of the AWT.
import java.awt.event.*;   // Swing uses the same event model as the AWT.

public class SwingApp {
```

```
    public static void main(String args[]) {
        final JFrame appWin = new JFrame("Application using Swing");    // (2)
        // appWin.add( ... ); // Will not work

        // Get the content pane of the root component.
        Container frameContent = appWin.getContentPane();               // (3)

        frameContent.setLayout(new BorderLayout());  // Not needed         (4)

        JButton exitButton = new JButton("Exit");  // Mirrors AWT          (5)
        frameContent.add(exitButton, BorderLayout.SOUTH);

        JComponent complexComponent = new JColorChooser();  // New complex (6)
        frameContent.add(complexComponent, BorderLayout.CENTER);

        // Simple event handling                                           (7)
        exitButton.addActionListener(new ActionListener() {
            public void actionPerformed(ActionEvent aEvt) {
                System.exit(0);
            }
        });
        appWin.addWindowListener(new WindowAdapter() {
            public void windowClosing(WindowEvent wEvt) {
                System.exit(0);
            }
        });

        appWin.pack(); // Same as for the AWT                             (8)
        appWin.setVisible(true);
    }
}
```

Operations, such as setting a layout manager, and adding and removing components, must be done on the content pane when working with root components in Swing. Setting the layout manager is shown at (4) in Example 17.1. Note that setting the layout manager in this example is not really necessary, since `BorderLayout` is the default layout manager of the content pane.

The content pane component can be obtained by first retrieving the root pane component and then extracting the content pane, which is located inside the layered pane.

```
JRootPane framePane = appWin.getRootPane();
JLayeredPane frameLayers = framePane.getLayeredPane();
// ...the content pane can be retrieved from the layered pane, but that is awkward

// Get the content pane from the JRootPane object
Container frameContent = framePane.getContentPane();
```

The simplest way to obtain the content pane is through the convenience method in the root component, as shown at (3). Quite often the code is written like this:

```
JFrame window = new JFrame("Swing Dance Styles");
window.getContentPane().setLayout(new FlowLayout());
window.getContentPane().add(new JButton("Arthur Murray Shag"));
window.getContentPane().add(new JButton("Belboa"));
```

Other Swing containers, such as `JPanel`, are not root components and use the traditional containment model:

```
JPanel panel = new JPanel();
panel.setLayout(new BorderLayout());
panel.add(new JButton("Beach Bop"), BorderLayout.NORTH);
panel.add(new JButton("Boogie Woogie"), BorderLayout.SOUTH);
```

Example 17.1 shows at (5) how Swing provides alternatives for existing heavyweight components in the AWT, and at (6) how it provides more advanced components than those available in the AWT. Figure 17.4 shows how these Swing components look when the example is run.

Swing relies heavily on the common framework shared with the AWT component set. At (1), the program imports from both Swing and AWT components. The similarities between Swing and AWT layout management and event handling are shown at (4) and (7), respectively. At (8), the `pack()` method from `Window` and the `setVisible()` method from `Component` are used on a Swing component, showing how the usage of many methods is the same for both Swing and the AWT.

17.3 Swing Components

Swing components are highly dynamic. They use *delegates* to draw the visual representation of the components, and these delegates can be replaced to support multiple look & feel schemes. They also reuse common functionality by delegating the responsibility of maintaining models and rendering visual items to other objects. The following delegations are commonly used:

- Data model.
  Many components use a delegate object to maintain their data model. Various models are used by different components. All the text-related components use a document model. Components that contain multiple items, such as lists, tables and trees, use special data models to represent the items in the component. The component does not itself keep track of the items, but queries the data model on demand. This allows the data model to have different representations. The default data models usually act as containers and allow items to be added and removed. It is also possible to create models that generate the items on the fly or models that are backed by more complex models, such as databases.
- Rendering.
  Components that use content models to represent the items in the component often also use a rendering delegate to provide a visual representation of the items.
- Selection model.
  Components that contain multiple items and components that are grouped often allow the user to select one or more of the items or components. Swing

components allow selection policies to be dictated by selection models. Swing provides models that allow one or no item to be selected, and models that allow multiple items to be selected.

- Forwarding requests to other components.
  Many Swing components are implemented by forwarding requests to other component objects. For instance, all menus that can contain menu items are implemented by using the `JPopupMenu` class. The root containers are examples of containers that forward their requests to a common container implementation, and masquerade as the container by installing it as their only child.

The contract between the components and the delegate objects is specified through interfaces that define the facilities provided by the delegates. This means that anyone can create a class that implements these interfaces to expand the functionality of the Swing components.

Event handling in Swing uses the same model as the AWT. Objects that wish to receive notification implement predefined interfaces and register themselves with event sources. For basic event handling, Swing uses the same listener interfaces and the same event classes as the AWT. Complex Swing components define new listener interfaces and new event classes that are adapted to their particular model. These events originate from the model objects associated with the components, and listeners are often registered directly with the model object, instead of the component.

Root Containers

Root components represent the root of component hierarchies. All root components in Swing use the containment model `RootPane`. Root components `JComponent`, `JWindow`, `JFrame`, `JDialog` and `JApplet` all extend their respective native AWT components, as shown in Figure 17.5. As such, these components are heavyweight, in contrast to `JInternalFrame`, which is a lightweight component without any corresponding AWT component. Table 17.2 gives an overview of the root containers in Swing. The top-level root containers use the same `WindowListener` interface as the native AWT containers. The `JInternalFrame` container is not a top-level container and does not use the `WindowListener` interface.

JInternalFrame

`JInternalFrame` is a special lightweight root container that mimics native top-level frames. Internal frames can be dragged, resized, iconified and closed, just like normal frames. These `JInternalFrame` containers are not actual top-level frames and are usually placed inside a `JDesktopPane` container. The `JDesktopPane` container emulates the look and feel of native desktop managers, providing a multiple document interface or a virtual desktop.

A specialized `InternalFrameListener` interface is used to listen to internal frames. The `InternalFrameListener` is functionally equivalent to `WindowListener`, but uses `InternalFrameEvent` objects instead of `WindowEvent` objects.

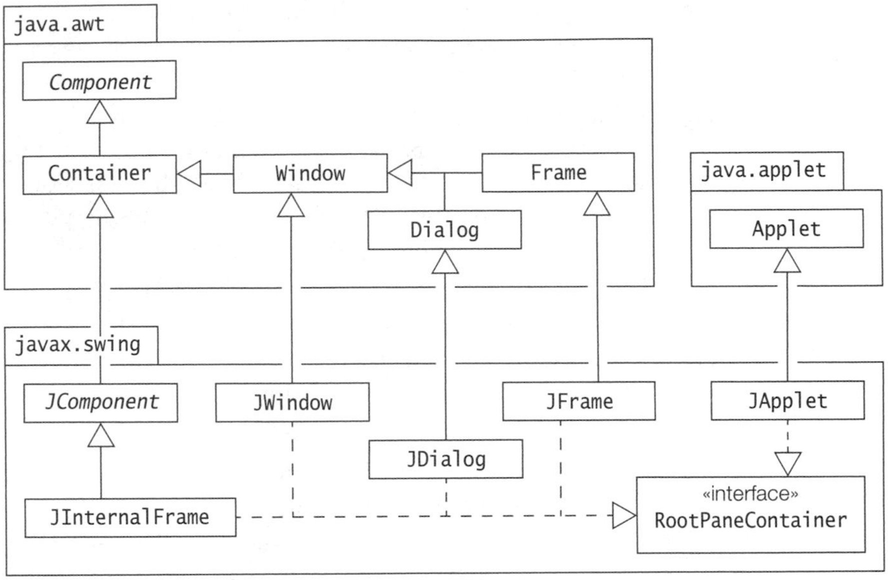

Figure 17.5 *Root Containers*

Table 17.2 *Swing Root Containers*

Swing Root Container	Description
`JWindow`	A top-level container without any window decorations such as borders, title-bar or window management functions.
`JFrame`	A top-level container with window decorations. Normally used as application windows.
`JDialog`	A top-level window with decorations. Normally used as a temporary window to take input from the user.
`JApplet`	A container meant to be embedded inside another application, such as a web browser.
`JInternalFrame`	A lightweight container that emulates the features of a native frame.

`JComponent`

All lightweight Swing components inherit from the `JComponent` class, which extends the `java.awt.Container` class. For each native AWT component there exists a corresponding Swing component.

The abstract `JComponent` class defines common functionality that is shared by all lightweight Swing components:

```
Border getBorder()
void setBorder(Border border)
```

Each component can be surrounded by a border. Borders are specified using border objects that implement the `javax.swing.border.Border` interface. The `javax.swing.border` package contains many implementations of borders that can be used to decorate Swing components. In addition to decorating components, borders can be used to specify margins and padding for components.

```
boolean isDoubleBuffered()
void setDoubleBuffered(boolean aFlag)
```

By default, Swing components are double buffered, meaning that updating is done in an off-screen buffer and only copied to the screen when all rendering is done. This aids the appearance of components that are complex to draw. The double buffering can also be turned off.

```
void setToolTipText(String text)
```

Sets a text to be displayed in a tool tip associated with the component. Tool tips are small informative windows that pop up near the component, to inform the user about the role of the component.

Labels and Buttons

The inheritance hierarchy of the Swing components does not directly mirror the inheritance hierarchy of the AWT components. For instance, the common functionality of all button-like components has been factored out into the `AbstractButton` class, as shown in Figure 17.6.

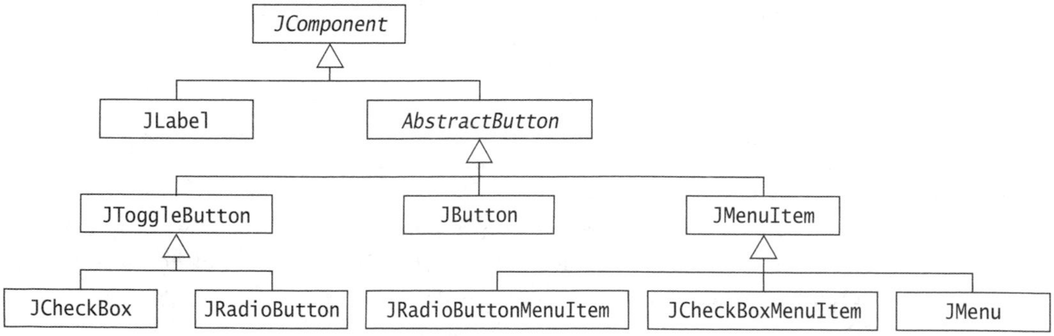

Figure 17.6 *Label and Button Components*

In the AWT, labels and buttons can only contain a short text string. In Swing, buttons and labels can contain a short text string or an image, or both. The following methods are implemented by both the `JLabel` and `AbstractButton` classes:

```
Icon getIcon()
String getText()
void setIcon(Icon defaultIcon)
void setText(String text)
```

Get and set the icon and text of a label or a button.

In addition, many of the components in Table 17.3 can have any combination of an icon and a text string as arguments to their constructors.

Table 17.3 *Label and Button Components*

Swing Component	Corresponding AWT Component	Description of Swing Component
`JLabel`	`Label`	A small area containing a visual cue that can be used to label other components. (Example 17.3)
`AbstractButton`	*none*	Provides common functionality for all button-like components.
`JButton`	`Button`	A push button. (Example 17.1)
`JToggleButton`	*none*	Provides the common functionality for all two-state buttons.
`JCheckBox`	`Checkbox` without `CheckboxGroup`	A two-state checkbox item that can be optionally selected. (Example 17.5)
`JRadioButton`	`Checkbox` with `CheckboxGroup`	A two-state radio button item that can be used with a `ButtonGroup` item to implement mutually exclusive items. (Example 17.5)
`JMenuItem`	`MenuItem`	An item within a menu.
`JMenu`	`Menu`	A menu. (Example 17.4)
`JCheckBoxMenuItem`	`CheckboxMenuItem`	A checkbox within a menu.
`JRadioButtonMenuItem`	*none*	A radio button within a menu.

The model of the button-like components is represented by an object implementing the `ButtonModel` interface. The `AbstractButton` class defines some methods that can be used on any button-like component:

```
void doClick()
void doClick(int pressTime)
```

Programmatically do a *click* on the button. The result will be exactly the same as if the user had clicked the button. The `pressTime` argument specifies how long the button will remain pressed.

```
int getMnemonic()
void setMnemonic(char mnemonic)
```

Get and set the mnemonic (a.k.a. *hot-key*) of a button. The mnemonic specifies a character that can be typed on the keyboard, as a functionally equivalent alternative to clicking the button. The use of mnemonics is encouraged, since it makes using the GUI without a mouse easier.

```
ButtonModel getModel()
void setModel(ButtonModel newModel)
```

Get and set the objects used as models for button-like components.

The `ButtonModel` interface provides methods to register listeners to the button models. Implementations of `ActionListener` can listen to `ActionEvent` objects fired off when the button is pushed. The `ActionListener` interface and the `ActionEvent` are defined in the `java.awt.event` package, and apply equally to buttons in Swing. Swing also defines the `ChangeListener` interface and a `ChangeEvent` class in `javax.swing.event` that can be used to listen to general changes in some models of Swing components. Implementations of `ChangeListener` can listen to `ChangeEvent` objects fired off each time the state of the button changes. As a convenience, listeners can also be registered directly with the component.

Button Groups

The `Checkbox` components in the AWT are registered with `CheckboxGroup` objects to form component groups with radio button behavior. Swing uses the `ButtonGroup` class to provide the semantics of the multiple-exclusion mechanism. Swing has a `JRadioButton` class that provides the visual appearance of a radio button, but in fact any button component can be registered in a button group. All Swing button components implement the same `ItemSelectable` interface as the `Checkbox` component in the AWT. This interface can be used to listen to changes in selections within a group of components.

Basic Components

All the components in Table 17.4 are lightweight components that inherit from `JComponent`. Unlike the menu components in the AWT, the menu components in Swing are part of the main inheritance hierarchy.

JPanel

The `JPanel` class provides a generic container that uses the traditional containment model, just like `Panel` in the AWT. A layout manager can be registered with the container, and children can be added and removed. A `JPanel` is not a root component and does not use the containment model provided by `JRootPane`.

Table 17.4 *General Lightweight Swing Components*

Lightweight Swing Component	Corresponding AWT Component	Description of Lightweight Swing Component
`JPanel`	`Panel`	A general purpose container.
`JMenuBar`	`MenuBar`	A menu-bar that can contain `JMenu` components. (Example 17.4)
`JToolBar`	*none*	A container that typically lets the user invoke commonly used actions. (Example 17.4)
`JScrollBar`	`Scrollbar`	A scrollbar often used with scroll panes.
`JSlider`	`Scrollbar`	A component that lets a user select a value by sliding a knob. (Example 17.4)
`JProgressBar`	*none*	A component that tracks the progress of some process by displaying the degree of completion. (Example 17.4)
`JList`	`List`	A list of items that the user can select from.
`JComboBox`	similar to `Choice`	An editable text field with an associated pop-up list of predefined choices. (Example 17.5)
`JSeparator`	*none*	A simple component to provide a visual separator line between components. (Example 17.3)

JMenuBar

A `JMenuBar` component can contain `JMenu` components, and presents them as a horizontal bar of pull-down menus. A `JMenuBar` component is usually attached to a root component using the `setJMenuBar()` method in `JRootPane`.

JToolBar

These tool-bar components are usually placed in one of the compass directions of a container using `BorderLayout`. The tool-bar can be undocked by users and left floating as a top-level window. The usual `add()` methods of the container can be used on a tool-bar to place any kind of component into the tool-bar. The tool-bar also has an `add()` method that takes a special `Action` object and inserts a `JButton` that will activate this action. This is illustrated in Example 17.4.

Bounded Range Model

The components `JScrollBar`, `JSlider` and `JProgressBar` revolve around tracking a value within certain bounds. These components delegate the implementation of this model, and provide these methods:

```
BoundedRangeModel getModel()
void setModel(BoundedRangeModel newModel)
```

Set and get the objects used as a model for the components `JScrollBar`, `JSlider` and `JProgressBar`.

Any object implementing the `BoundedRangeModel` interface can be used as a model. The bounded range model represents a changeable integer interval (a value and an extent) within a bounded range. When the user manipulates the scrollbar for example, or the slider, the model is updated. The same `ChangeListener` interface used to listen to the state changes in button components can be used to listen to the changes in the bounded range models. Each time the values in the model change, a `ChangeEvent` object is fired off to all the listeners registered with the model object.

JList

The content of the list is dictated by an object implementing the `ListModel` interface, the items in the list are rendered using an object implementing the `ListCellRenderer` interface, and the selection model is defined by an object implementing the `ListSelectionModel` interface. The default list model is a `DefaultListModel`, which allows elements to be added and removed freely. The default cell renderer is `DefaultListCellRenderer`, which renders a text representation of the item. The default selection model allows, at most, one item to be selected at a time.

The `JList` class provides methods to get and set the various delegate objects that should be used. The model interfaces provide methods to register listeners to the models used. The `ListDataListener` objects can listen to `ListDataEvent` objects fired off by `ListModel` objects, and the `ListSelectionListener` objects can listen to `ListSelectionEvent` objects fired off by `ListSelectionModel` objects.

The list does not provide scrolling facilities. To make the list scrollable for the user, it should be decorated with a `JScrollPane`.

Text Components

As shown in Figure 17.7, the inheritance hierarchy of `JTextComponent`, `JTextField` and `JTextArea` has the same structure as the inheritance hierarchy of `TextComponent`, `TextField` and `TextArea` in the AWT. The Swing text components are to some degree source compatible with their AWT counterparts.

All text components listed in Table 17.5 use an object implementing the `Document` interface to represent the text in the component, and they all inherit common functionality defined in the abstract `JTextComponent` class. Both the `Document` interface and the `JTextComponent` class reside in the `javax.swing.text` package. Some methods defined in the `JTextComponent` class are:

```
Document getDocument()
void setDocument(Document doc)
```

Get and set the model representing the text inside the component.

```
String getText()
String getText(int offs, int len)
void setText(String t)
```

Get and set text in the component. These methods correspond to the methods with the same name in the `TextField` class in the AWT. These methods are actually convenience methods that will retrieve information from the associated `Document` object.

```
void setEditable(boolean b)
boolean isEditable()
```

Set and check whether the text component can edit the document. These methods also correspond to the methods in the `TextField` class in the AWT.

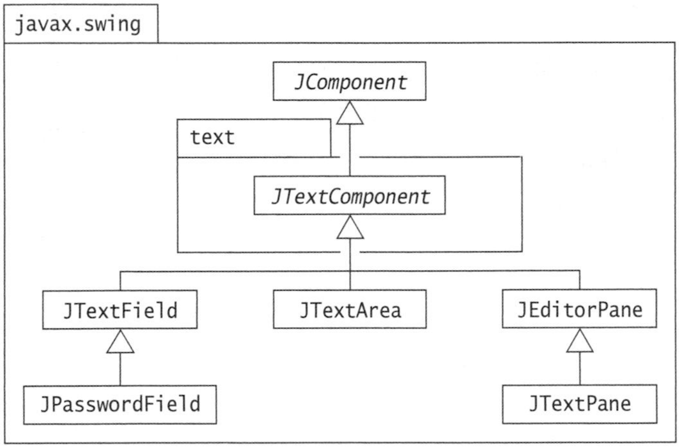

Figure 17.7 *Text Component Hierarchy*

Table 17.5 *Swing Text Components*

Swing text Component	Corresponding AWT Component	Description of Swing Text Component
`JTextComponent`	`TextComponent`	An abstract component class that is the base class for all text components.
`JTextField`	`TextField`	A single line of editable text. (Example 17.4)
`JPasswordField`	`TextField` with echo char set.	A single line of editable but unreadable text.
`JTextArea`	`TextArea`	Multiple lines of editable text.
`JEditorPane`	*none*	A text component that can be used to edit various kinds of content.
`JTextPane`	*none*	A text component that can be used to edit text that can be styled in various ways.

Swing defines a `DocumentListener` interface and a `DocumentEvent` class in the `javax.swing.event` package that can be used to listen to changes in the document model. Each time a change is made to the document, a `DocumentEvent` object is fired off to all the listeners registered with the document object.

A `TextField` in the AWT provided the ability to show a placeholder as the echo character, instead of the actual text typed. This functionality has been factored out into the class `JPasswordField` in Swing.

Space-saving Components

Swing has components which are useful when large GUIs need to be presented in a compact form. All the components listed in Table 17.6 help to save space in some way. Only `JScrollPane` has a corresponding AWT component.

Table 17.6 *Space-saving Components*

Swing Component	Corresponding AWT Component	Description
`JScrollPane`	`ScrollPane`	Lets the user scroll a large component behind a view port. (Example 17.2)
`JTabbedPane`	*none*	Lets the user select between multiple pages of content using tabs. (Figure 17.4)
`JSplitPane`	*none*	A user-adjustable divider between two components. (Example 17.2)

JTabbedPane

A tabbed pane allows the user to select one of several "cards", where each card can contain unique content. The tabbed pane, unlike the card layout manager, presents the user with graphical gadgetry that can be used to switch between the cards, usually in the form of tabs with a title and/or an icon. Components can be added and removed using the normal `add()` and `remove()` methods inherited from the `Container` class. Components can also be added using the specialized `addTab()`, `insertTab()` and `removeTabAt()` methods, which accept positions and labels for the tabs. A tabbed pane is shown in Figure 17.4.

JSplitPane

A component that divides two components, and lets the user adjust the size of each component. The split can be either vertical or horizontal.

JScrollPane

A component that displays a larger component through a view port, and has scroll-bars which allow the user to adjust which portion of the large component should be visible in the view port. The ability to view a portion of a larger component is provided by the JViewPort class. A JScrollPane simply decorates a JViewPort component with scrollbars, and allows the user to adjust the portion of the larger component viewed using these scrollbars. Each JViewPort component can have only one component, which is the large component that should be scrolled. Any component can be used within a JViewPort, but components like JList, which generally rely on JScrollPane to provide scrolling functionality, usually implement the Scrollable interface. This interface allows components to communicate with the view port and state their preferences with regard to scrolling.

Components with Complex Models

The JList component and all the text components in Swing rely on delegate objects to represent their data models, thus making the components more flexible than their AWT counterparts. In addition, Swing has some other components with complex models that do not have any counterparts in the AWT. These components are listed in Table 17.7. Common to these components is that they depend quite extensively on other objects to implement their functionality.

Table 17.7 *Components with Complex Models*

Component	Description
JTable	Represents data in a two-dimensional table. (Example 17.2)
JTree	Represents a set of hierarchical data as a collapsible outline. (Example 17.2)

JTable

The JTable component presents rows of data, separated into columns. All the support interfaces and classes reside in the javax.swing.table package. JTable uses the following delegates:

- A data model.
  The model of the data presented in the table is represented by an object implementing the TableModel interface. Implementations of TableModelListener can be registered using this interface, in order to receive TableModelEvent notification whenever the data in the model changes.
- A column model.
  The model of the columns in the table is represented by an object implementing the TableColumnModel interface. The column model further delegates the selection of columns to an object implementing the ListSelectionModel interface. Implementations of TableColumnModelListener can be registered using this interface, in order to receive TableColumnModelEvent, ChangeEvent and ListSelection Event notifications whenever columns, column margins and selection of columns change, respectively.

- Row selection model.
  The model managing the selected rows in the table is represented by an object implementing the `ListSelectionModel` interface. This is not the same object that handles the selection of columns. The selection model in `JTable` can be used in the same manner as the selection model from `JList`.
- Table header component.
  The `JTableHeader` class extends `JComponent` and implements the column headers of a table. The user can manipulate the columns in the table using this component. The `JTableHeader` uses and manipulates the same column model as the main `JTable` component.
- Table cell renderers.
  Just like `JList`, tables rely on renderers to render the items within the component. `JTable` uses an object implementing the `TableCellRenderer` interface to render cells in each column of the table. By default, the contents of cells are rendered as the text representation of the cell object as drawn by `JLabel`.
- Table cell editors.
  Table cell editors are objects that implement the `TableCellEditor` interface, which provides facilities for editing table cells when the user wishes to change the value of a table entry.

In addition, tables use a `JScrollPane` to provide scrolling.

JTree

The `JTree` component presents hierarchical data as tree nodes that can be collapsed and expanded, to hide or show sub-nodes. `JTree` uses the following delegates:

- Tree model.
  The model of the elements presented in the tree is represented by an object implementing the `TreeModel` interface. Implementations of the `TreeModelListener` interface can be registered using this interface, in order to receive `TreeModelEvent` objects whenever the tree structure changes.
- Tree selection model.
  The tree will keep track of the selected node(s), using an object that implements the `TreeSelectionModel` interface. Implementations of `PropertyChangeListener` can be registered with the selection model, to receive notification when the selection changes. The `PropertyChangeListener` interface and the `PropertyChangeEvent` class are defined in the `java.beans` package.
- Tree cell renderers.
  A `JTree` uses an object implementing the `TreeCellRenderer` interface to render cells in each column of the table. By default, the elements of the tree are rendered as textual representation of the node object, and by an icon indicating whether the node is a *leaf*, or whether it is an open or a closed *branch*.

- Tree cell editors.
  Tree cell editors are objects that implement the `TreeCellEditor` interface, which allows editing of tree nodes.

Figure 17.8 shows `JTree` and `JTable`. The GUI in the figure is implemented in Example 17.2. The data displayed in the tree and the table is defined at (1). The default tree model (`DefaultTreeModel`) of `JTree` uses `DefaultMutableTreeNode` to represent tree nodes. At (2), the tree structure is constructed from instances of `DefaultMutableTreeNode`. The GUI is assembled and shown at (3).

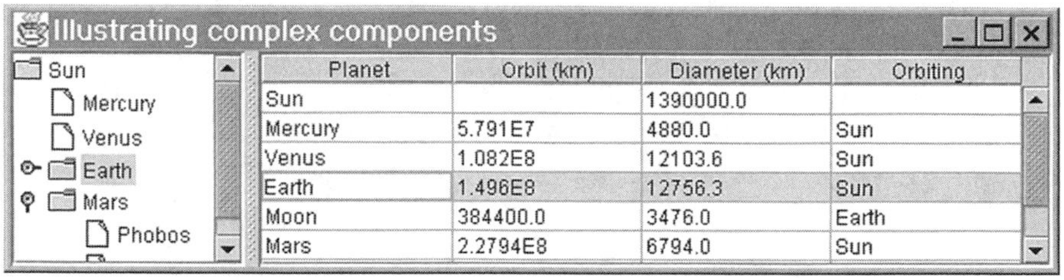

Figure 17.8 *Illustrating Complex Components*

Example 17.2 *Using Complex Components*

```
import javax.swing.*;
import javax.swing.tree.DefaultMutableTreeNode;     // Used as nodes in JTree.
import java.util.*;                              // Map used while creating tree.

public class SolarSystem {
    public static void main(String args[]) {

        // Data to initialize the components:                               (1)
        final int NAME     = 0;    // Index constants for accessing
        final int ORBITING = 3;    // data in the following arrays.
        Object[] columnNames =
            {"Planet", "Orbit (km)",           "Diameter (km)",    "Orbiting"};
        Object[][] planetaryData = {
            {"Sun",     null,                  new Float(1390000), null    },
            {"Mercury", new Float(57910000),   new Float(4880),    "Sun"   },
            {"Venus",   new Float(108200000),  new Float(12103.6), "Sun"   },
            {"Earth",   new Float(149600000),  new Float(12756.3), "Sun"   },
            {"Moon",    new Float(384400),     new Float(3476),    "Earth"},
            {"Mars",    new Float(227940000),  new Float(6794),    "Sun"   },
            {"Phobos",  new Float(9378),       new Float(22.2),    "Mars"  },
            {"Deimos",  new Float(23459),      new Float(12.6),    "Mars"  },
        };  // The last column indicates a parent-child relationship.

        // Build tree nodes based on data.                                  (2)
        Map namesToNodes = new HashMap();  // mapping names to nodes.

        for (int i=0; i<planetaryData.length; i++) {     // For all planets...
            Object[] planetProfile = planetaryData[i];        // lookup data

            DefaultMutableTreeNode newNode =                  // make new node
                new DefaultMutableTreeNode(planetProfile[NAME]);
```

```
                namesToNodes.put(planetProfile[NAME], newNode);  // store node

                DefaultMutableTreeNode parent = (DefaultMutableTreeNode)
                    namesToNodes.get(planetProfile[ORBITING]);   // find parent

                if (parent != null) parent.add(newNode);         // add to parent
            }

            // Find node for "Sun", which will be used as the root of the JTree
            DefaultMutableTreeNode rootNode = (DefaultMutableTreeNode)
                namesToNodes.get("Sun");

            // Construct and display the GUI:                              (3)
            JTree tree = new JTree(rootNode);
            JTable table = new JTable(planetaryData, columnNames);

            JScrollPane scrollableTree  = new JScrollPane(tree);
            JScrollPane scrollableTable = new JScrollPane(table);

            JSplitPane windowContents = new           // Split window contents
                JSplitPane(JSplitPane.HORIZONTAL_SPLIT, // horizontally,
                           scrollableTree,              // place tree left,
                           scrollableTable);            // place table right.

            JFrame mainWindow = new JFrame("Illustrating complex components");
            mainWindow.setContentPane(windowContents);

            mainWindow.pack();
            mainWindow.setVisible(true);
        }
    }
```

Large Compound Components

Compound components are components that are built using other components, to produce large modular pieces of GUI. Three such components are listed in Table 17.8. The support interfaces and classes for color chooser and file chooser are located in the `javax.swing.colorchooser` and `javax.swing.filechooser` packages, respectively.

Table 17.8 *Large Compound Components*

Compound Swing Component	Corresponding AWT Component	Description
`JFileChooser`	`FileDialog`	Allows the user to select one or more files or directories.
`JColorChooser`	*none*	Allows the user to select a color, using one of several color models. (Example 17.1)
`JOptionPane`	*none*	Presents a list of options for the user. Can be used to create a dialog box which asks the user to make a choice.

Review questions

17.1 Given a `JDialog` component referenced by `dialog` and a layout manager object referenced by `layout`, which of the following are legal ways of making the component use the layout manager?

Select all valid answers.

(a) `dialog.setLayout(layout)`
(b) `dialog.getRootPane().setLayout(layout)`
(c) `dialog.getContentPane().setLayout(layout)`
(d) `dialog.getRootPane().getContentPane().setLayout(layout)`
(e) `dialog.getContentPane().getRootPane().setLayout(layout)`

17.2 Which of these methods can be called on a `JLabel` object?

Select all valid answers.

(a) `setIcon()`
(b) `getText()`
(c) `setLabel()`
(d) `setBorder()`
(e) `getMnemonic()`

17.3 Which of these component classes use implementations of the `BoundedRangeModel` as the data model of the component?

Select all valid answers.

(a) `JButton`
(b) `JScrollBar`
(c) `JSplitPane`
(d) `JProgressBar`
(e) `JToolBar`

17.4 Which of these interfaces are used by implementations of models for `JTable`?

Select all valid answers.

(a) `TableModel`
(b) `TableColumnModel`
(c) `TableSelectionModel`
(d) `ListModel`
(e) `ListSelectionModel`

17.5 Which of these components are lightweight?

Select all valid answers.

(a) `Canvas`
(b) `Component`
(c) `Container`
(d) `Panel`
(e) `JComponent`

17.6 Given the following code, which of these statements are true?

```
import javax.swing.*;

public class UsingContentModel {
    public static void main(String args[]) {
        JPanel panel = new JPanel();
        JFrame frame = new JFrame();

        frame.setContentPane(panel);                       // (1)
        panel.getContentPane().add(new JLabel("Some"));    // (2)
        frame.add(new JLabel("random"));                   // (3)
        panel.add(new JLabel("text"));                     // (4)

        frame.pack();
        frame.setVisible(true);
    }
}
```

Select all valid answers.

(a) The program will fail to compile.
(b) Line (1) does not use the content model of `JFrame` correctly.
(c) Line (2) does not use the content model of `JPanel` correctly.
(d) Line (3) does not use the content model of `JFrame` correctly.
(e) Line (4) does not use the content model of `JPanel` correctly.

17.4 Other Swing Topics

`BoxLayout`

The box layout manager places the components either horizontally in a row or vertically in a column. The row or the column does not wrap, regardless of resizing the window. When a box layout manager is created, its *major axis* is specified in the constructor. Components, when added, are inserted at the end of the row (or bottom of the column).

`BoxLayout(Container target, int axis)`

The `axis` argument specifies the major axis, which can either be `BoxLayout.X_AXIS` for laying out the components from left to right in a row, or `BoxLayout.Y_AXIS` for laying out the components from top to bottom in a column.

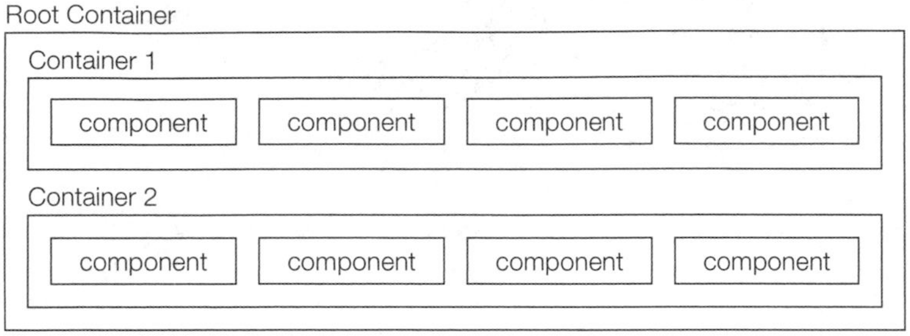

Figure 17.9 *Layout to demonstrate Box Layout*

The layout shown in Figure 17.9 can be constructed using box layout. The layout of `Container 1` and `Container 2` can be constructed by laying out the components horizontally using box layout. The two containers can be arranged vertically in a column in the root container, also using box layout. Example 17.3 implements the layout shown in Figure 17.9.

When using a horizontal box layout, if all components do not have the same height, an attempt is made to make all components as high as the highest component. If this is not possible for some components, then their *alignment* determines how they will be placed. Similar considerations apply when using vertical box layout.

Swing also defines a container named `Box` that facilitates using the `BoxLayout` manager. The `Box` class also facilitates the creation of invisible separator components, which can be placed in between components in a box layout to improve the placement of components. There are two types of separators:

- Slack consumers.
  Called *glue*, these components will not take any space when space is scarce, but will take an equal share of any left-over slack.
- Fixed size separators.
  These are *struts* and *rigid areas* that consume a fixed amount of space, and can be useful for creating fixed size gaps between components.

```
static Component createHorizontalGlue()
static Component createVerticalGlue()
```

Creates a glue component that consumes either horizontal or vertical slack.

```
static Component createHorizontalStrut(int width)
static Component createVerticalStrut(int height)
```

Creates a strut which occupies a fixed amount of space in the horizontal or the vertical direction.

```
static Component createRigidArea(Dimension d)
```

Creates a rigid area of the specified size.

The box layout will allocate space to the components according to their preferred sizes; any space left over is distributed equally between the components, including glue components. Struts and rigid areas will always keep their fixed size.

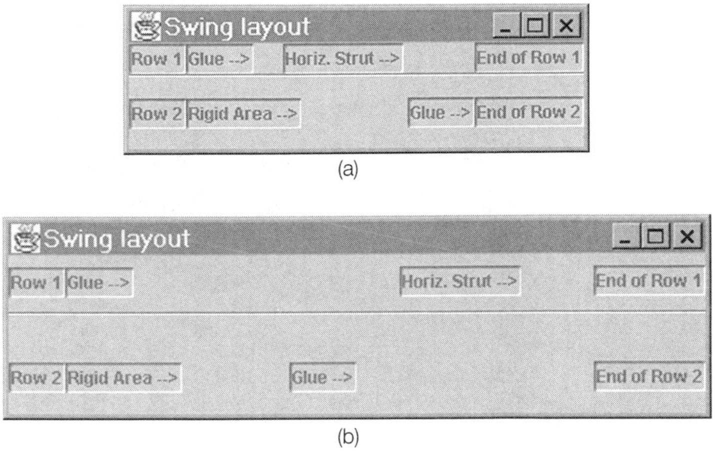

Figure 17.10 *Demonstrating Box Layout*

Example 17.3 *Using Box Layout*

```
import javax.swing.*;
import javax.swing.border.*;
import java.awt.*;
import java.awt.event.*;

public class SwingBoxLayout {
    public static void main(String args[]) {

        // Create the first row using a box.                          (1)
        Container row1 = new Box(BoxLayout.X_AXIS);
        row1.add(createLabel("Row 1"));
        row1.add(createLabel("Glue -->"));
        row1.add(Box.createHorizontalGlue());
        row1.add(createLabel("Horiz. Strut -->"));
        row1.add(Box.createHorizontalStrut(50));
        row1.add(createLabel("End of Row 1"));

        // Create the second row using a box layout manager.          (2)
        Container row2 = new JPanel();
        row2.setLayout(new BoxLayout(row2, BoxLayout.X_AXIS));
        row2.add(createLabel("Row 2"));
        row2.add(createLabel("Rigid Area -->"));
        row2.add(Box.createRigidArea(new Dimension(75, 50)));
        row2.add(createLabel("Glue -->"));
        row2.add(Box.createHorizontalGlue());
        row2.add(createLabel("End of Row 2"));
```

```
            // Create the root component and compose its content pane.      (3)
            JFrame window = new JFrame("Swing layout");
            Container content = window.getContentPane();
            LayoutManager lm = new BoxLayout(content, BoxLayout.Y_AXIS);
            content.setLayout(lm);
            content.add(row1);
            content.add(new JSeparator(JSeparator.HORIZONTAL));
            content.add(row2);

            window.addWindowListener(new WindowAdapter() {
                public void windowClosing(WindowEvent wEvt) {
                    System.exit(0);
                }
            });

            window.pack();
            window.setVisible(true);
        }

        private static Component createLabel(String text) {
            JComponent label = new JLabel(text, SwingConstants.CENTER);
            label.setBorder(new SoftBevelBorder(SoftBevelBorder.LOWERED));
            return label;
        }
    }
```

Example 17.3 illustrates how box layout works. It implements the layout shown in Figure 17.9. The resulting GUI is shown in Figure 17.10. The first row is implemented using a `Box` component created at (1). A `Box` implicitly uses a `BoxLayout`, and the argument given to the constructor tells the box to lay out the components horizontally. The second row is a `JPanel`, which uses a `BoxLayout` created explicitly at (2) also to lay out the components horizontally. The two rows are added to the content pane of the root container at (3), using a `BoxLayout` manager which lays them out vertically. All (visible) components added are instances of the `JLabel` class. Glue, struts and rigid area are added between certain components in the two rows. When the window is resized (going from Figure 17.10a to Figure 17.10b) the glue changes size in the two rows, but the size of the strut in row one and the rigid area in row two remains fixed.

Look and Feel

In Swing, one can select one of several look & feel (L&F) schemes for a GUI. Each look and feel is represented by a factory class that will create L&F delegates for components on demand.

The various look & feel schemes are represented by objects of the `LookAndFeel` class. Methods from the `UIManager` class can be used to control the look & feel for Swing components:

```
static String getSystemLookAndFeelClassName()
```

Get the name of the native L&F factory class. On platforms running MS Windows, this returns the MS Windows L&F. On platforms running the X11 Window system, this usually returns the CDE/Motif L&F.

```
static LookAndFeel getLookAndFeel()
static void setLookAndFeel(LookAndFeel newLookAndFeel)
        throws UnsupportedLookAndFeelException
static void setLookAndFeel(String className)
        throws ClassNotFoundException, InstantiationException,
        IllegalAccessException, UnsupportedLookAndFeelException
```

Set the given look and feel. New components created will use this look and feel.

By default, the program uses a platform-neutral Java look & feel. The look & feel is usually set using code similar to the following:

```
try {
    UIManager.setLookAndFeel(
        // "com.sun.java.swing.plaf.motif.MotifLookAndFeel"    // specific
        UIManager.getSystemLookAndFeelClassName());           // native platform
} catch (Exception e) {
    System.err.println("Could not use the native platform look and feel: " + e);
}
```

To update a component which has already been created, the `updateUI()` method from `JComponent` can be used. To update a whole GUI after changing the look & feel, use the static method `updateComponentTreeUI()` from the `SwingUtilities` class. An example of setting the L&F and using the `updateComponentTreeUI()` method is shown later, in Example 17.5.

Alternatives to Traditional Event Handling

In the AWT, events could be handled in one of two ways. Either the component could be extended to implement event handling, or listener objects could be registered with the component. Swing introduces a few more options.

Actions

Special action objects can be created as an extension of traditional event handling. These action objects can be attached to various components, such as buttons, to represent an action that should be executed when the button is pressed.

The `Action` interface from the `javax.swing` package extends the `ActionListener` interface from the `java.awt.event` package. The extended interface represents actual actions that will be performed when an action event is fired at the listener. It also allows information such as a name, a description and a small icon to be attached to the event.

Actions can then be added to components, such as menu-bars, and automatically be represented by buttons, using the information associated with the action. When the user invokes the action, the `Action` object is notified using the traditional `ActionListener` interface.

To facilitate creation of action objects, the `AbstractAction` class can be used. Action implementations can be created by extending this class and providing an implementation for the `actionPerformed()` method.

Implementing Models

Swing components make extensive use of model objects to represent the state or data of the component. Changes in these model objects can be monitored, since the models generally allow various kinds of listeners to be registered. However, there is an alternative. By implementing the model used by the components, rather than just listening to them, greater control can be achieved. Not only is the model informed about changes initiated by the user through the components, but new behavior can be given to the model. It is also possible to make components share the same models, and thereby automatically have them update each other.

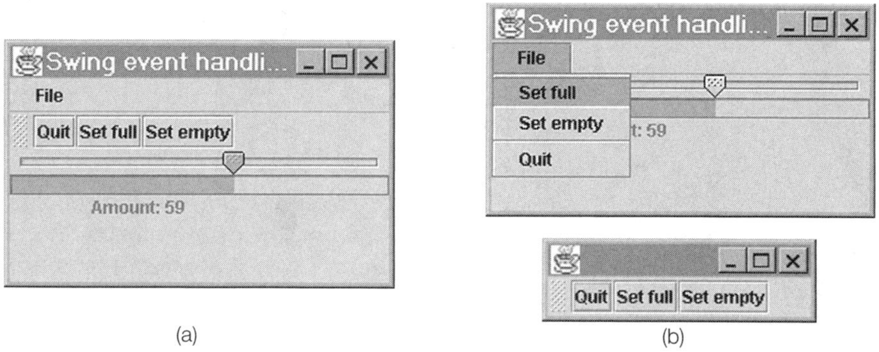

Figure 17.11 *Demonstrating Actions*

Example 17.4 *Using Actions and Implementing Models*

```
import javax.swing.*;
import java.awt.*;
import java.awt.event.*;

public class SwingActions {
    public static void main(String args[]) {
        final JLabel amountLabel = new JLabel("Amount: 0");

        // Create a bounded range model                                   (1)
        final BoundedRangeModel amountModel =
            new DefaultBoundedRangeModel(0, 0, 0, 100) {
                public void setValue(int n) {
                    super.setValue(n);
                    amountLabel.setText("Amount: " + n);
                }
            };
```

```
        // Create actions that the user can activate                       (2)
        Action quitOperation = new AbstractAction("Quit") {
            public void actionPerformed(ActionEvent evt) { System.exit(0); }
        };
        Action fullOperation = new AbstractAction("Set full") {
            public void actionPerformed(ActionEvent evt) {
                amountModel.setValue(amountModel.getMaximum());
            }
        };
        Action emptyOperation = new AbstractAction("Set empty") {
            public void actionPerformed(ActionEvent evt) {
                amountModel.setValue(amountModel.getMinimum());
            }
        };

        // Create the toolbar and add the actions                          (3)
        JToolBar toolbar = new JToolBar();
        toolbar.add(quitOperation);
        toolbar.add(fullOperation);
        toolbar.add(emptyOperation);

        // Create the menu and add the actions                             (4)
        JMenu menu = new JMenu("File");
        menu.add(fullOperation);
        menu.add(emptyOperation);
        menu.addSeparator();
        menu.add(quitOperation);

        // Put the menu in the menu bar
        JMenuBar menubar = new JMenuBar();
        menubar.add(menu);

        // Share the model between a slider and a progress bar             (5)
        JSlider amountSlider = new JSlider(amountModel);
        JProgressBar progressBar = new JProgressBar(amountModel);

        // Pack components in a vertical box
        Box box = new Box(BoxLayout.Y_AXIS);
        box.add(amountSlider);
        box.add(progressBar);
        box.add(amountLabel);

        // Create the root component and compose its content pane
        JFrame window = new JFrame("Swing event handling");
        window.getContentPane().add(toolbar, BorderLayout.NORTH);
        window.getContentPane().add(box);
        window.getRootPane().setJMenuBar(menubar);

        window.addWindowListener(new WindowAdapter() {
            public void windowClosing(WindowEvent wEvt) {
                System.exit(0);
            }
        });
        window.pack();
        window.setVisible(true);
    }
}
```

Example 17.4 shows how models can be implemented or extended as an alternative to event handling, and how models can be shared by several components. A bounded range model is created at (1) by extending the default model. Three action objects are created at (2), where two of them use this model. These actions in turn are shared by a tool-bar and a menu at (3) and (4), respectively. The model is also shared between a slider and a progress bar, as shown at (5). Figure 17.11 shows the GUI. Figure 17.11b shows the menu pulled down and the tool-bar "torn off" into a separate window.

The Single-Thread Rule

The methods of the AWT components were thread-safe, meaning that concurrent method invocations on the components would not harm the internal state of the component.

Thread safety was abandoned in Swing in favor of efficiency. Extra care should be exercised when using Swing components from multiple threads. The recommended practice regarding threads and Swing can be summarized by the Single Thread Rule:

> Once a Swing component is ready to receive events, all code that might affect or depend on the state of that component should be executed in the event-dispatching thread.

Some of the Swing methods, such as `repaint()`, `revalidate()`, `invalidate()` and methods that modify listener lists, are still thread-safe.

Methods in the `SwingUtilities` class can be invoked to execute code using the event-dispatching thread:

```
static void invokeAndWait(Runnable doRun)
static void invokeLater(Runnable doRun)
```

Execute the method `run()` in the `doRun` object using the AWT event dispatching thread. The `invokeAndWait()` version will block until the `run()` method has been executed, the `invokeLater()` version will return immediately.

Review questions

17.7 Which of the these containers use `JRootPane` to implement their containment model?

Select all valid answers.

(a) `Box`
(b) `JApplet`
(c) `JComponent`
(d) `JFrame`
(e) `JPanel`

17.8 Which of these statements are true?

Select all valid answers.

(a) `JToggleButton` is a subclass of `JButton`.
(b) `BoxLayout` places components in a grid.
(c) `JComponent` is a lightweight component.
(d) `JMenuItem` inherits from `JComponent`.

17.9 Given the following program, which one of these statements is true?

```
import javax.swing.*;

public class BoxStacker {
    public static void main(String args[]) {
        Box componentRow = new Box(BoxLayout.X_AXIS);

        componentRow.add(Box.createHorizontalGlue());
        componentRow.add(new JButton("Button"));
        componentRow.add(Box.createVerticalGlue());

        JFrame displayWindow = new JFrame();
        displayWindow.getContentPane().add(componentRow);
        displayWindow.setSize(400, 400);
        displayWindow.setVisible(true);
    }
}
```

Select the one right answer.

(a) The button will be aligned with the left edge of the window.
(b) The button will be aligned with the right edge of the window.
(c) The button will be horizontally centered in the window.
(d) The button will be stretched to cover the whole width of the window.

17.10 Which of these statements are true?

Select all valid answers.

(a) None of the containers using the root pane container model are lightweight.
(b) `JSeparator` is an invisible component.
(c) `JMenu` inherits from `AbstractButton`.
(d) The method `getCrossPlatformLookAndFeelClassName()` returns the name of the class that implements the look and feel of the native system.
(e) A `JScrollBar` uses a `BoundedRangeModel` as its model.

17.11 What is the default layout manager used in association with `JApplet` components?

Select the one right answer.

(a) `FlowLayout`
(b) `BorderLayout`
(c) `BoxLayout`
(d) `GridLayout`
(e) `LayeredLayout`

17.5 Building a GUI with Swing

This section provides an example of building an applet using Swing.

Example 17.5 is the Swing version of the application from Example 14.5. Two different L&Fs (Windows and Motif) for the application are shown in Figure 17.12 and Figure 17.13, respectively. The user can draw different shapes by specifying the shape, its size, whether it is filled or not, and the coordinates where it should be placed in the drawing region.

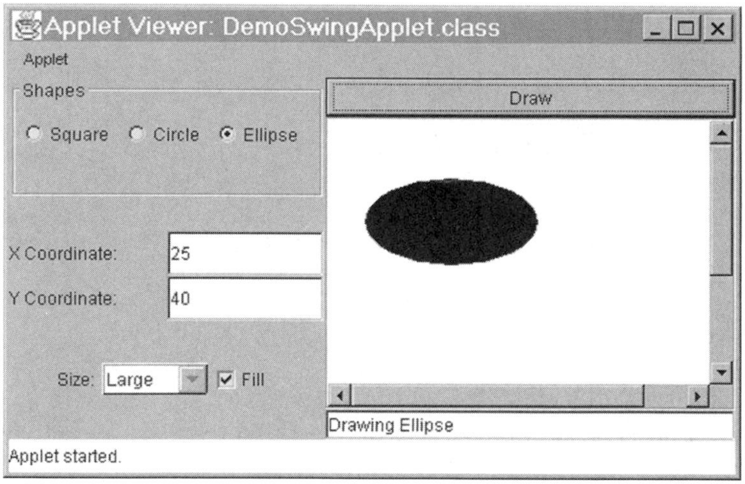

Figure 17.12 *GUI with Windows Look and Feel*

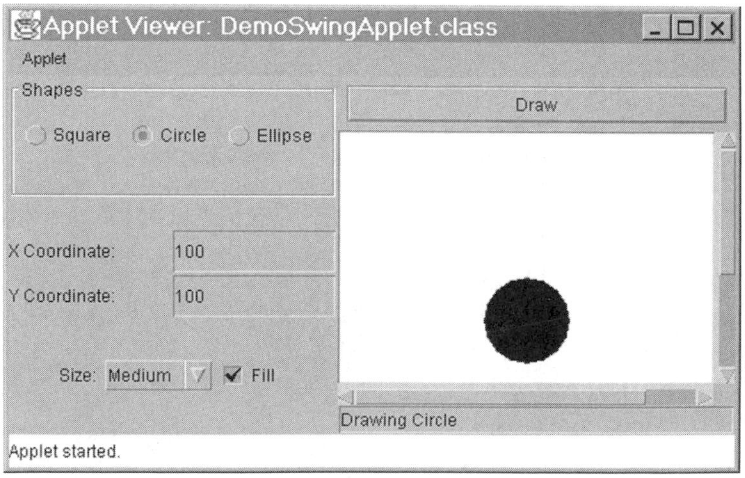

Figure 17.13 *GUI with Motif Look and Feel*

Example 17.5 *Building GUI with Swing*

```
/* DemoSwingApplet: Demonstrating GUI + Event Handling in Swing */

import javax.swing.*;
import javax.swing.border.*;
import java.awt.*;
import java.awt.event.*;
import java.applet.*;

interface IGeometryConstants {                                          // (1)
    int SQUARE  = 0;
    int CIRCLE  = 1;
    int ELLIPSE = 2;
    String[] shapeNames = {"Square", "Circle", "Ellipse"};

    int SMALL  = 0;
    int MEDIUM = 1;
    int LARGE  = 2;
    String[] sizeNames = {"Small", "Medium", "Large"};
}

public class DemoSwingApplet extends JApplet implements IGeometryConstants {

    // Panel for shape                                                     (2)
    JPanel       shapePanel;
    ButtonGroup  shapeGroup;
    JRadioButton squareRB;
    JRadioButton circleRB;
    JRadioButton ellipseRB;

    // Panel for x, y coordinates
    JPanel     xyPanel;
    JLabel     xLabel;
    JTextField xInput;
    JLabel     yLabel;
    JTextField yInput;

    // Panel for size and fill
    JPanel    sizePanel;
    JLabel    sizeLabel;
    JComboBox sizeChoices;
    JCheckBox fillCB;

    // Box for shape, coordinates, size and fill
    Box leftBox;

    // Panel for draw button, drawing region and message display.
    JPanel      rightPanel;
    JButton     drawButton;
    JScrollPane scrollPane;
    DrawRegion  drawRegion;
    JTextField  messageDisplay;

    // Top container
    Container topContainer;
```

```
    public void init() {                                        // (3)
        makeShapePanel();
        makeXYPanel();
        makeSizePanel();
        makeLeftBox();
        makeRightPanel();

        addListeners();                                         // (4)

        topContainer = getContentPane();                        // (5)
        topContainer.add(leftBox,    BorderLayout.WEST);
        topContainer.add(rightPanel, BorderLayout.CENTER);

        try {                                                   // (6)
            UIManager.setLookAndFeel(
                UIManager.getSystemLookAndFeelClassName()
//              "com.sun.java.swing.plaf.motif.MotifLookAndFeel"
//              "com.sun.java.swing.plaf.windows.WindowsLookAndFeel"
//              "javax.swing.plaf.mac.MacLookAndFeel"
            );
        } catch (Exception e) { messageDisplay.setText(e.toString()); }
        SwingUtilities.updateComponentTreeUI(this);             // (7)
    }

    // Panel for shape                                             (8)
    void makeShapePanel() {
        squareRB  = new JRadioButton(shapeNames[SQUARE],  true);
        circleRB  = new JRadioButton(shapeNames[CIRCLE],  false);
        ellipseRB = new JRadioButton(shapeNames[ELLIPSE], false);

        shapeGroup = new ButtonGroup();
        shapeGroup.add(squareRB);
        shapeGroup.add(circleRB);
        shapeGroup.add(ellipseRB);

        shapePanel = new JPanel();
        shapePanel.setLayout(new FlowLayout());
        shapePanel.add(squareRB);
        shapePanel.add(circleRB);
        shapePanel.add(ellipseRB);
        shapePanel.setBorder(new TitledBorder("Shapes"));
    }

    // Panel for x,y coordinates                                   (9)
    void makeXYPanel() {
        xyPanel = new JPanel();

        xLabel  = new JLabel("X Coordinate:");
        yLabel  = new JLabel("Y Coordinate:");

        xInput  = new JTextField(5);
        yInput  = new JTextField(5);

        xyPanel.setLayout(new GridLayout(2,2));
        xyPanel.add(xLabel);
        xyPanel.add(xInput);
        xyPanel.add(yLabel);
        xyPanel.add(yInput);
    }
```

```
// Panel for size and fill                                        (10)
void makeSizePanel() {

    sizePanel   = new JPanel();

    sizeLabel   = new JLabel("Size:");

    sizeChoices = new JComboBox(sizeNames);
    sizeChoices.setSelectedIndex(0);

    fillCB = new JCheckBox("Fill", false);

    sizePanel.setLayout(new FlowLayout());
    sizePanel.add(sizeLabel);
    sizePanel.add(sizeChoices);
    sizePanel.add(fillCB);
}

// Box for shape, coordinates, size and fill                      (11)
void makeLeftBox() {
    leftBox = new Box(BoxLayout.Y_AXIS);

    leftBox.add(shapePanel);
    leftBox.add(Box.createGlue());
    leftBox.add(xyPanel);
    leftBox.add(Box.createGlue());
    leftBox.add(sizePanel);
}

// Panel for message display, draw button, and drawing region    (12)
void makeRightPanel() {
    rightPanel = new JPanel();

    messageDisplay = new JTextField("MESSAGE DISPLAY");
    messageDisplay.setEditable(false);

    drawButton = new JButton("Draw");

    drawRegion = new DrawRegion();
    scrollPane = new JScrollPane(drawRegion);

    rightPanel.setLayout(new BorderLayout());
    rightPanel.add(drawButton, BorderLayout.NORTH);
    rightPanel.add(messageDisplay, BorderLayout.SOUTH);
    rightPanel.add(scrollPane, BorderLayout.CENTER);
}

// Add the listeners.
void addListeners() {

    drawButton.addActionListener(new ActionListener() {       // (13)
        public void actionPerformed(ActionEvent evt) {

            int shape, xCoord, yCoord, width;

            messageDisplay.setText("");
            // Get the shape                                      (14)
            if (squareRB.isSelected())
                shape = SQUARE;
            else if (circleRB.isSelected())
                shape = CIRCLE;
```

```
                else if (ellipseRB.isSelected())
                    shape = ELLIPSE;
                else {
                    messageDisplay.setText("Unknown shape.");
                    return;
                }

                // Get the coordinates                               (15)
                try {
                    xCoord = Integer.parseInt(xInput.getText());
                    yCoord = Integer.parseInt(yInput.getText());
                } catch (NumberFormatException e) {
                    messageDisplay.setText("Illegal coordinates.");
                    return;
                }

                // Get the size                                      (16)
                switch (sizeChoices.getSelectedIndex()) {
                    case SMALL:  width = 30;  break;
                    case MEDIUM: width = 60;  break;
                    case LARGE:  width = 120; break;
                    default: messageDisplay.setText("Unknown size."); return;
                }

                messageDisplay.setText("Drawing " + shapeNames[shape]);
                drawRegion.doDraw(                                // (17)
                        shape,
                        xCoord, yCoord,
                        fillCB.isSelected(),
                        width
                );
            }
        });
    }
}

class DrawRegion extends JPanel implements IGeometryConstants {   // (18)

    // Values needed for drawing the shape
    private int     shape;
    private int     xCoord;
    private int     yCoord;
    private boolean fillFlag;
    private int     width;

    // Default constructor
    public DrawRegion() {
        setSize(300,300);
        setBackground(Color.white);
    }

    // Overridden to always keep the same size
    public Dimension getPreferredSize() {
        return getSize();
    }

    // Set the values and repaint the drawing region.               (19)
    public void doDraw(int shape,
```

```
                          int xCoord, int yCoord,
                          boolean fillFlag, int width) {

        this.shape    = shape;
        this.xCoord   = xCoord;
        this.yCoord   = yCoord;
        this.fillFlag = fillFlag;
        this.width    = width;

        repaint();                                              // (20)
    }

    // Do the drawing of the shape                                 (21)
    public void paintComponent (Graphics g) {
        super.paintComponent(g);
        switch (shape) {
            case SQUARE:
                if (fillFlag) g.fillRect(xCoord, yCoord, width, width);
                else g.drawRect(xCoord, yCoord, width, width);
                break;
            case CIRCLE:
                if (fillFlag) g.fillOval(xCoord, yCoord, width, width);
                else g.drawOval(xCoord, yCoord, width, width);
                break;
            case ELLIPSE:
                if (fillFlag) g.fillOval(xCoord, yCoord, width, width/2);
                else g.drawOval(xCoord, yCoord, width, width/2);
                break;
        }
    }
}
```

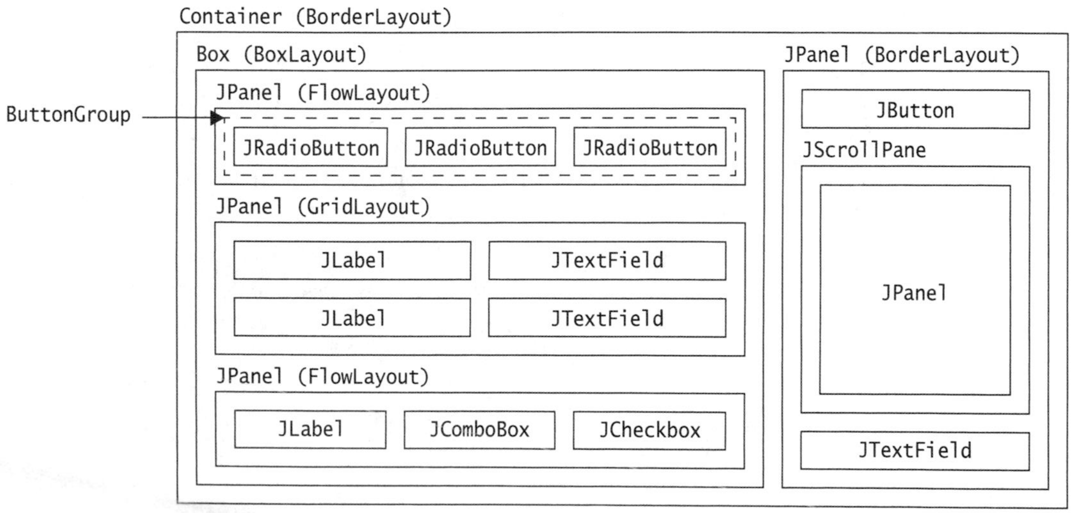

Figure 17.14 *Component Hierarchy*

Figure 17.14 presents the component hierarchy identifying the Swing components that comprise the GUI. It is based on its AWT counterpart in Figure 13.11. The following differences should be noted:

- The root of the component hierarchy is a `Container`, which is the content pane of the applet implemented using a `JApplet`.
- A `Box` container is used as one of the main panels of the GUI. It uses the `Box Layout` manager.
- Radio buttons for the different shapes are implemented using a `ButtonGroup`, as opposed to a `CheckBoxGroup` in Figure 13.11.
- The drawing region in Figure 13.11 was based on a `Canvas`. In Figure 17.14, it is based on a `JPanel` (which is placed in a `JScrollPane` to provide the scrollbars).
- The list of shape sizes in Figure 13.11 was implemented using a `Choice` list. In Figure 17.14, it is implemented using a `JComboBox`.

In building the GUI for Figure 17.14, the same procedure is used as the one advocated in Section 13.9:

1. Create the panel.
2. Register a layout manager with the panel.
3. Add the components to the panel.
4. Add the panel to its parent container.

Interface `IGeometryConstants`, at (1) in Example 17.5, defines constants that are used by the other classes in the application. The `DemoSwingApplet` class declares all the components and containers, starting at (2). The `init()` method at (3) of this class systematically builds the GUI, by calling the various auxiliary methods which create the different components and panels. It adds the listeners at (4), and populates the top content pane at (5). The pluggable L&F is set by the code at (6) and (7).

In the `makeShapePanel()` method at (8), the radio buttons are first added to the `ButtonGroup` to provide the semantics of radio buttons, and then to the `shapePanel`. A border is also set explicitly for the `shapePanel`.

In the `makeSizePanel()` method at (10), a list of choices is created, using a `JComboBox` initialized with the `sizeNames` array.

In the `makeLeftBox()` method at (11), vertical orientation is specified for the components in the box, and components are added with some glue in between them.

In the `makeRightPanel()` method at (12), scrollbars are added to a `JPanel`, using a `JScrollPane`.

The only event handling that takes place is when the user clicks the draw button. The same event delegation model as in the AWT is also used in Swing. The action listener is added at (13). It successively collects all the information required to do the drawing: the kind of shape at (14), the coordinates at (15) and the size at (16). It uses this information to initiate drawing at (17).

The drawing region at (18) is a subclass of `JPanel`. Its `doDraw()` method at (19) sets the information for drawing, and calls the `repaint()` method at (20) to update the screen. This eventually results in the `paintComponent()` method of the class being called, as shown at (21). This method calls the corresponding overridden method from the superclass, to ensure that the component `JPanel` component is painted correctly. Afterwards, the overriding method renders the specified shape in the drawing region. Overriding the `paintComponent()` method can be done, to implement customized components with a particular graphical representation.

Chapter summary

The following information was included in this chapter:

- An overview of the Swing packages.
- Similarities and differences between Swing and the AWT.
- Description of the root pane container model for root components.
- Overview of the different models (data, rendering, selection) employed by Swing components.
- Overview of Swing components: root containers, basic GUI components, text components, space-saving components, complex-model components, large compound components.
- Introduction to miscellaneous Swing topics: Box layout, look & feel, actions, model implementation, thread safety.
- A complete application demonstrating GUI building in Swing.

Programming exercise

17.1 Implement a Swing application with the same functionality as the application described in Exercise 14.1. The implementation should use the appropriate Swing components, rather than AWT components. Encapsulate the actions that the user can initiate in `Action` objects. Let the actions be available both from a menu and from a tool-bar. Do not create a status line.

18 Files and Streams

Supplementary Objectives

- Write code that uses objects of the `File` class to navigate the file system.
- Distinguish between byte and character streams, and identify the roots of their inheritance hierarchies.
- Select valid constructor arguments for `FilterInputStream` and `FilterOutputStream` subclasses from a list of classes in the `java.io` package.
- Write appropriate code to read, write and update files using `FileInputStream`, `FileOutputStream` and `RandomAccessFile` objects.
- Write code that uses the classes `DataOutputStream` and `DataInputStream` for writing and reading Java primitive values.
- Write code that uses objects of the classes `InputStreamReader` and `OutputStreamWriter` to translate between Unicode and either platform default or other character encodings.
- Write code to set up (buffered) readers and writers for text files.
- Write code that uses the classes `ObjectOutputStream` and `ObjectInputStream` for writing and reading objects.

18.1 Input and Output

The `java.io` package provides an extensive library of classes for dealing with input and output. Java provides *streams* as a general mechanism for dealing with data I/O. Streams implement *sequential access* of data. There are two kinds of streams: *byte streams* and *character streams*. An *input stream* is an object that an application can use to read a sequence of data, and an *output stream* is an object that an application can use to write a sequence of data. An *input stream* acts as a *source* of data, and an *output stream* acts as a *destination* of data. The following entities can act as both input and output streams:

- an array of bytes or characters
- a file
- a *pipe*
- a network connection

Streams can be *chained* with *filters* to provide new functionality. In addition to dealing with bytes and characters, streams are provided for input and output of Java primitive values and objects. The `java.io` package also provides support for *random access* of files, and a general interface to interact with the file system of the host platform.

18.2 `File` Class

The `File` class provides a general machine-independent interface to the file system of the underlying platform. A `File` object represents the pathname of a file or directory in the host file system. An application can use the functionality provided by the `File` class for handling files and directories in the file system. The `File` class is *not meant* for handling the contents of files. For that purpose, there are the `FileInputStream`, `FileOutputStream` and `RandomAccessFile` classes, which are discussed later in this chapter.

The pathname for a file or directory is specified using the naming conventions of the host system. However, the `File` class defines platform-dependent constants that can be used to handle file and directory names in a platform-independent way:

```
public static final char separatorChar
public static final String separator
```

Defines the character or string that separates the directory and the file components in a pathname. This separator is `'/'`, `'\'` or `':'` for Unix, Windows and Macintosh, respectively.

```
public static final char pathSeparatorChar
public static final String pathSeparator
```

Defines the character or string that separates the file or directory names in a "path list". This character is `':'` or `';'` for Unix and Windows, respectively.

Some examples of pathnames are:

`/book/chapter1`	on Unix
`C:\book\chapter1`	on Windows
`HD:book:chapter1`	on Macintosh

Some examples of path lists are:

`/book:/manual:/draft`	on Unix
`C:\book;D:\manual;A:\draft`	on Windows

Files and directories can be referenced using both absolute and relative pathnames, but the pathname must follow the conventions of the host platform. On Unix platforms, a pathname is absolute if its first character is the separator character. On Windows platforms, a path is absolute if the ASCII `'\'` is the first character, or follows the volume name (e.g., `C:`), in a pathname. On the Macintosh, a pathname is absolute if it begins with a name followed by a colon. Java programs should not rely on system-specific pathname conventions. The `File` class provides facilities to construct pathnames in a platform-independent way.

The `File` class has various constructors for assigning a file or a directory to an object of the `File` class. Creating a `File` object does not mean creation of any file or directory based on the pathname specified. A `File` instance, called the *abstract pathname,* is a representation of the pathname of a file and directory. The pathname cannot be changed once the `File` object is created.

`File(String pathname)`

The pathname (of a file or a directory) can be an absolute pathname or a pathname relative to the current directory. An empty string as argument results in an abstract pathname for the current directory.

```
// "/book/chapter1" - absolute pathname of a file
File chap1 = new File(File.separator + "book" +
                      File.separator + "chapter1");
// "draft/chapters" - relative pathname of a directory
File draftChapters = new File("draft" + File.separator + "chapters");
```

`File(String directoryPathname, String filename)`

This creates a `File` object whose pathname is as follows: `directoryPathname` + `separator` + `filename`.

```
// "/book/chapter1" - absolute pathname of a file
File updatedChap1 = new File(File.separator + "book", "chapter1");
```

`File(File directory, String filename)`

If the `directory` argument is `null`, the resulting `File` object represents a file in the current directory. If the `directory` argument is not `null`, it creates a `File` object that represents a file in the given directory. The pathname of the file is then the pathname of the `directory` `File` object + separator + `filename`.

```
// "chapter13" - relative pathname of a file
File parent = null;
File chap13 = new File(parent, "chapter13");

// "draft/chapters/chapter13" - relative pathname of a file
File draftChapters = new File("draft" + File.separator + "chapters");
File updatedChap13 = new File(draftChapters, "chapter13");
```

An object of the `File` class provides a handle to a file or directory in the file system, and can be used to create, rename, and delete the entry.

A `File` object can also be used to query the file system for information about a file or directory:

- whether the entry exists
- whether the `File` object represents a file or directory
- whether the entry has read or write access
- get pathname information about the file or directory
- list all entries under a directory in the file system

Many methods of the `File` class throw a `SecurityException` in the case of a security violation, for example if read or write access is denied. Some also return a boolean value to indicate whether the operation was successful.

Querying the File System

The `File` class provides a number of methods for obtaining the platform-dependent representation of a pathname and its components.

`String getName()`

Returns the name of the file entry, excluding the specification of the directory in which it resides.

On Unix, the name part of `"/book/chapters/one"` is `"one"`.

On Windows platforms, the name part of `"c:\java\bin\javac"` is `"javac"`.

On the Macintosh, the name part of `"HD:java-tools:javac"` is `"javac"`.

`String getPath()`

The method returns the (absolute or relative) pathname of the file represented by the `File` object.

`String getAbsolutePath()`

If the `File` object represents an absolute pathname then this pathname is returned, otherwise the returned pathname is constructed by concatenating the current directory pathname, the separator character and the pathname of the `File` object.

`String getCanonicalPath() throws IOException`

Also platform-dependent, the canonical path usually specifies a pathname in which all relative references have been completely resolved.

For example, if the `File` object represented the absolute pathname `"c:\book\chapter1"` on Windows, then this pathname would be returned by these methods. On the other hand, if the `File` object represented the relative pathname `"..\book\chapter1"` and the current directory had the absolute pathname `"c:\documents"`, the pathname returned by the `getPath()`, `getAbsolutePath()` and `getCanonicalPath()` methods would be `"..\book\chapter1"`, `"c:\documents\..\book\chapter1"` and `"c:\book\chapter1"`, respectively.

`String getParent()`

The parent part of the pathname of this `File` object is returned if one exists, otherwise the `null` value is returned. The parent part is generally the prefix obtained from the pathname after deleting the file or directory name component found after the last occurrence of the separator character. However, this is not true for all platforms.

On Unix, the parent part of `"/book/chapter1"` is `"/book"`, whose parent part is `"/"`, which in turn has no parent.

On Windows platforms, the parent part of `"c:\java-tools"` is `"c:\"`, which in turn has no parent.

On the Macintosh, the parent part of `"HD:java-tools"` is `"HD:"`, which in turn has no parent.

`boolean isAbsolute()`

Whether a `File` object represents an absolute pathname can be determined using this method.

The following three methods can be used to query the file system about the modification time of a file or directory, determine the size (in bytes) of a file, and ascertain whether two pathnames are identical.

`long lastModified()`

The modification time returned is encoded as a `long` value, and should only be compared with other values returned by this method.

`long length()`

Returns the size (in bytes) of the file represented by the `File` object.

`boolean equals(Object obj)`

This method only compares the pathnames of the `File` objects, and returns `true` if they are identical.

File or Directory Existence

A `File` object is created using a pathname. Whether this pathname denotes an entry that actually exists in the file system can be checked using the `exists()` method:

```
boolean exists()
```

Since a `File` object can represent a file or a directory, the following methods can be used to distinguish whether a given `File` object represents a file or a directory respectively:

```
boolean isFile()
boolean isDirectory()
```

Read and Write Access

To check whether the specified file has write and read access, the following methods can be used. They throw a `SecurityException` if general access is not allowed, i.e. the application is not even allowed to check whether it can read or write a file.

```
boolean canWrite()
boolean canRead()
```

Listing Directory Entries

The entries in a specified directory can be obtained as a table of file names or abstract pathnames, using the following `list()` methods. The current directory and the parent directory are excluded from the list.

```
String[] list()
String[] list(FilenameFilter filter)
File[]   listFiles()
File[]   listFiles(FilenameFilter filter)
File[]   listFiles(FileFilter filter)
```

The `filter` argument can be used to specify a *filter* that determines whether an entry should be included in the list. These methods return `null` if the abstract pathname does not denote a directory, or if an I/O error occurs. A filter is an object of a class that implements either of these two interfaces:

```
interface FilenameFilter {
    boolean accept(File currentDirectory, String entryName);
}
interface FileFilter {
    boolean accept(File pathname);
}
```

The `list()` methods call the `accept()` methods of the filter for each entry, to determine whether the entry should be included in the list.

Creating New Files and Directories

The `File` class can be used to create files and directories. A file can be created whose pathname is specified in a `File` object using the following method:

```
boolean createNewFile() throws IOException
```

It creates a new, empty file named by the abstract pathname if, and only if, a file with this name does not already exist. The returned value is `true` if the file was successfully created, `false` if the file already exists. Any I/O error results in an `IOException`.

A directory whose pathname is specified in a `File` object can be created using the following methods:

```
boolean mkdir()
boolean mkdirs()
```

The `mkdirs()` method creates any intervening parent directories in the pathname of the directory to be created.

Renaming Files and Directories

A file or a directory can be renamed, using the following method which takes the new pathname from its argument:

```
boolean renameTo(File dest)
```

Deleting Files and Directories

A file or a directory can be deleted using the following method. In the case of a directory, it must be empty before it can be deleted.

```
boolean delete()
```

Example 18.1 *Listing Files Under a Directory*

```
import java.io.*;

public class DirectoryLister {
    public static void main(String args[]) {
        File entry;
        if (args.length == 0) {                // (1)
            System.err.println("Please specify a directory name.");
            return;
        }
        entry = new File(args[0]);             // (2) user specified

        listDirectory(entry);
    }
```

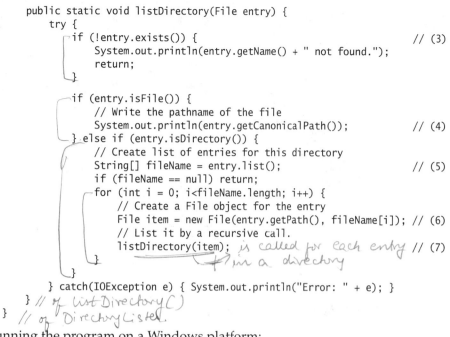

```
    public static void listDirectory(File entry) {
        try {
            if (!entry.exists()) {                                      // (3)
                System.out.println(entry.getName() + " not found.");
                return;
            }

            if (entry.isFile()) {
                // Write the pathname of the file
                System.out.println(entry.getCanonicalPath());           // (4)
            } else if (entry.isDirectory()) {
                // Create list of entries for this directory
                String[] fileName = entry.list();                       // (5)
                if (fileName == null) return;
                for (int i = 0; i<fileName.length; i++) {
                    // Create a File object for the entry
                    File item = new File(entry.getPath(), fileName[i]); // (6)
                    // List it by a recursive call.
                    listDirectory(item);                                // (7)
                }
            }
        } catch(IOException e) { System.out.println("Error: " + e); }
    }
}
```

Running the program on a Windows platform:

```
java DirectoryLister D:\docs\JC-Book\special
```

produces the following output:

```
D:\docs\JC-Book\special\book19990308\JC-14-applets.fm
D:\docs\JC-Book\special\book19990308\JC-16-swing.fm
D:\docs\JC-Book\special\JC-11-awtlayout.fm
```

The class `DirectoryLister` in Example 18.1 lists all entries in a directory specified in the command line. If no directory is given, an error message is written. This is shown at (1) and (2). In the method `listDirectory()`, each entry is tested to see if it exists, as shown at (3). The entry could be an alias (*symbolic link* in Unix or *shortcut* in Windows terminology) and its destination might not exist. The method determines whether the entry is a file, in which case the absolute pathname is listed, as shown at (4). In the case of a directory, an array of entry names is created, as shown at (5). For each entry in the directory, a `File` object is created, as shown at (6). The method `listDirectory()` is called recursively for each entry, as shown at (7).

18.3 Byte Streams: Input Streams and Output Streams

The abstract classes `InputStream` and `OutputStream` are the root of the inheritance hierarchies for handling the reading and writing of *bytes* (Figure 18.1). Their subclasses, implementing different kinds of input and output streams, override the

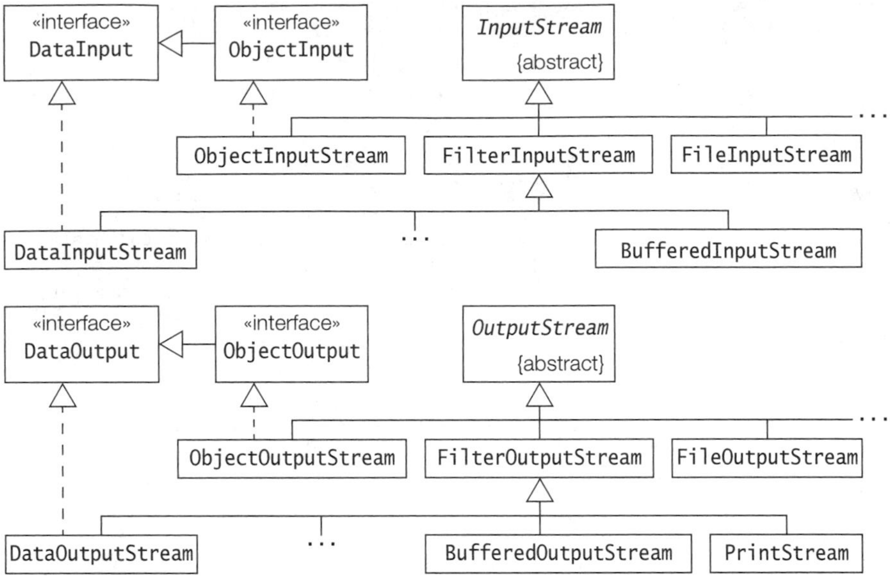

Figure 18.1 *Byte Stream Inheritance Hierarchies*

following methods from the `InputStream` and `OutputStream` classes to customize the reading and writing of bytes, respectively:

```
int read() throws IOException
int read(byte[] b) throws IOException
int read(byte[] b, int off, int len) throws IOException
void write(int b) throws IOException
void write(byte[] b) throws IOException
void write(byte[] b, int off, int len) throws IOException
```

Note that the first `read()` method read a byte, but returns an `int` value. The byte read resides in the eight least significant bits of the `int`, while the remaining bits in the `int` are zeroed out. The `read()` methods return the value –1 when the end of stream is reached. The first `write()` method takes an `int` as argument, but truncates it down to the eight least significant bits before writing it out as a byte.

A stream should be closed when no longer needed, to free system resources:

```
void close() throws IOException
void flush() throws IOException
```

Closing an output stream automatically *flushes* the stream, meaning that any data in its internal buffer is written out. An output stream can also be manually flushed by calling the second method.

Read and write operations on streams are synchronous (*blocking*) operations, i.e. a call to a read or write method does not return before a byte has been read or written.

Many methods in the classes contained in the `java.io` package throw an `IOException`. A calling method must either catch the exception explicitly, or specify it in a `throws` clause.

Table 18.1 and Table 18.2 give an overview of the byte streams.

Table 18.1 *Input Streams*

`ByteArrayInputStream`	Data is read from a byte array that must be specified.
`FileInputStream`	Data is read as bytes from a file. The file acting as the input stream can be specified by a `File` object, a `FileDescriptor` or a `String` file name.
`FilterInputStream`	Superclass of all input stream filters. An input filter must be chained to an underlying input stream.
`BufferedInputStream`	A filter that buffers the bytes read from an underlying input stream. The underlying input stream must be specified, and an optional buffer size can be included.
`DataInputStream`	A filter that allows the binary representation of Java primitive values to be read from an underlying input stream. The underlying input stream must be specified.
`PushbackInputStream`	A filter that allows bytes to be "unread" from an underlying input stream. The number of bytes to be unread can optionally be specified.
`ObjectInputStream`	Allows binary representations of Java objects and Java primitive values to be read from a specified input stream.
`PipedInputStream`	Reads bytes from a `PipedOutputStream` to which it must be connected. The `PipedOutputStream` can optionally be specified when creating the `PipedInputStream`.
`SequenceInputStream`	Allows bytes to be read sequentially from two or more input streams consecutively. This should be regarded as concatenating the contents of several input streams into a single continuous input stream.

Table 18.2 *Output Streams*

`ByteArrayOutputStream`	Data is written to a byte array. The size of the byte array created can be specified.
`FileOutputStream`	Data is written as bytes to a file. The file acting as the output stream can be specified by a `File` object, a `FileDescriptor` or a `String` file name.
`FilterOutputStream`	Superclass of all output stream filters. An output filter must be chained to an underlying output stream.
`BufferedOutputStream`	A filter that buffers the bytes written to an underlying output stream. The underlying output stream must be specified, and an optional buffer size can be given.

Table 18.2 *Output Streams (continued)*

`DataOutputStream`	A filter that allows the binary representation of Java primitive values to be written to an underlying output stream. The underlying output stream must be specified.
`ObjectOutputStream`	Allows the binary representation of Java objects and Java primitive values to be written to a specified underlying output stream.
`PipedOutputStream`	Writes bytes to a `PipedInputStream` to which it must be connected. The `PipedInputStream` can optionally be specified when creating the `PipedOutputStream`.

File Streams

The classes `FileInputStream` and `FileOutputStream` define byte input and output streams that are connected to files. Data can only be read or written as a sequence of bytes.

An input stream for reading bytes can be created using the following constructors:

```
FileInputStream(String name) throws FileNotFoundException
FileInputStream(File file) throws FileNotFoundException
FileInputStream(FileDescriptor fdObj)
```

The file can be specified by its name, through a `File` or a `FileDescriptor` object.

If the file does not exist, a `FileNotFoundException` is thrown. If it exists, it is set to be read from the beginning. A `SecurityException` is thrown if the file does not have read access.

An output stream for writing bytes can be created using the following constructors:

```
FileOutputStream(String name) throws FileNotFoundException
FileOutputStream(String name, boolean append) throws FileNotFoundException
FileOutputStream(File file) throws IOException
FileOutputStream(FileDescriptor fdObj)
```

The file can be specified by its name, through a `File` object or using a `FileDescriptor` object.

If the file does not exist, it is created. If it exists, its contents are reset, unless the appropriate constructor is used to indicate that output should be appended to the file. A `SecurityException` is thrown if the file does not have write access or it cannot be created.

The `FileInputStream` class provides an implementation for the `read()` methods in its superclass `InputStream`. Similarly, the `FileOutputStream` class provides an implementation for the `write()` methods in its superclass `OutputStream`.

Example 18.2 demonstrates usage of writing and reading bytes to and from file streams. It copies the contents of one file to another file. The input and the output file names are specified on the command line. The streams are created as shown at (1) and (2). The input file is read a byte at a time and written straight to the output file, as shown in the try block at (3). The streams are explicitly closed, as shown at (4). Note that most of the code consists of try-catch constructs to handle the various exceptions. The example could be optimized by using buffering, and reading and writing several bytes at a time.

Example 18.2 *Copy a File*

```
/* Copy a file.
   Command syntax: java CopyFile <from-file> <to-file>
*/

import java.io.*;

class CopyFile {
    public static void main(String args[]) {
        FileInputStream fromFile;
        FileOutputStream toFile;

        // Assign the files
        try {
            fromFile = new FileInputStream(args[0]);      // (1)
            toFile = new FileOutputStream(args[1]);       // (2)
        } catch(FileNotFoundException e) {
            System.err.println("File could not be copied: " + e);
            return;
        } catch(IOException e) {
            System.err.println("File could not be copied: " + e);
            return;
        } catch(ArrayIndexOutOfBoundsException e) {
            System.err.println("Usage: CopyFile <from-file> <to-file>");
            return;
        }

        // Copy bytes
        try {                                             // (3)
            int i = fromFile.read();
            while (i != -1) { // check end of file
                toFile.write(i);
                i = fromFile.read();
            }
        } catch(IOException e) {
            System.err.println("Error reading/writing.");
        }

        // Close the files
        try {                                             // (4)
            fromFile.close();
            toFile.close();
```

```
            } catch(IOException e) {
                System.err.println("Error closing file.");
            }
        }
    }
```

Filter Streams

A *filter* is a high-level stream that provides additional functionality to an underlying stream to which it is chained. The data from the underlying stream is manipulated in some way by the filter. The `FilterInputStream` and `FilterOutputStream` classes, together with their subclasses, define input and output filter streams. Subclasses `BufferedInputStream` and `BufferedOutputStream` implement filters that respectively buffer input from, and output to, the underlying stream. Subclasses `DataInputStream` and `DataOutputStream` implement filters that allow Java primitive values to be read and written respectively to and from an underlying stream.

I/O of Java Primitive Values

The `java.io` package contains two interfaces: `DataInput` and `DataOutput`, that streams can implement to allow reading and writing of binary representations of Java primitive values (`boolean`, `char`, `byte`, `short`, `int`, `long`, `float`, `double`). Methods for writing binary representations of Java primitive values are named `write`*X*`()`, where *X* is any Java primitive datatype. Methods for reading binary representations of Java primitive values are similarly named `read`*X*`()`. Table 18.3 gives an overview of the `read`*X*`()` and `write`*X*`()` methods found in these two interfaces. Note the methods provided for reading and writing strings. Whereas the methods `readChar()` and `writeChar()` handle a single character, the methods `readLine()` and `writeChars()` handle a string of characters. The methods `readUTF()` and `writeUTF()` also read and write a string of characters, but use the UTF-8 character encoding (see Table 18.7 on page 570).

The filter streams `DataOutputStream` and `DataInputStream` implement `DataOutput` and `DataInput` interfaces respectively, and can be used to write and read binary representations of Java primitive values to and from an underlying stream. Both the `write`*X*`()` and `read`*X*`()` methods throw an `IOException` in the event of an I/O error. Bytes can also be skipped from a `DataInput` stream, using the `skipBytes(int n)` method which skips `n` bytes. The following constructors can be used to set up filters for reading and writing Java primitive values respectively from an underlying stream:

```
DataInputStream(InputStream in)
DataOutputStream(OutputStream out)
```

For handling character streams, Java provides special streams called *readers* and *writers* which are discussed in Section 18.4.

Table 18.3 `DataInput` ***and*** `DataOutput` ***Interfaces***

Type	Methods in *DataInput*	Methods in *DataOutput*
`boolean`	`readBoolean()`	`writeBoolean(boolean v)`
`char`	`readChar()`	`writeChar(int v)`
`byte`	`readByte()`	`writeByte(int v)`
`short`	`readShort()`	`writeShort(int v)`
`int`	`readInt()`	`writeInt(int v)`
`long`	`readLong()`	`writeLong(long v)`
`float`	`readFloat()`	`writeFloat(float v)`
`double`	`readDouble()`	`writeDouble(double v)`
`String`	`readLine()`	`writeChars(String s)`
`String`	`readUTF()`	`writeUTF(String s)`

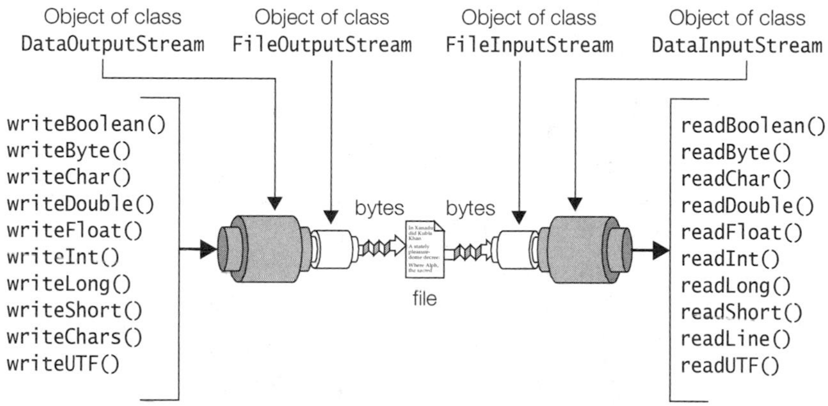

Figure 18.2 *Stream Chaining*

To write the binary representation of Java primitive values to a *file*, the following procedure can be used, which is also depicted in Figure 18.2.

1. Create a `FileOutputStream`:

```
FileOutputStream outputFile = new FileOutputStream("primitives.data");
```

2. Create a `DataOutputStream` which is chained to the `FileOutputStream`:

```
DataOutputStream outputStream = new DataOutputStream(outputFile);
```

3. Write Java primitive values using relevant `writeX()` methods:

```
outputStream.writeBoolean(true);
outputStream.writeChar('A');                // int written as Unicode char
outputStream.writeByte(Byte.MAX_VALUE);     // int written as 8-bits byte
outputStream.writeShort(Short.MIN_VALUE);   // int written as 16-bits short
outputStream.writeInt(Integer.MAX_VALUE);
```

```
outputStream.writeLong(Long.MIN_VALUE);
outputStream.writeFloat(Float.MAX_VALUE);
outputStream.writeDouble(Math.PI);
```

Note that in the case of `char`, `byte` and `short` datatypes, the `int` argument to the `writeX()` method is converted to the corresponding type, before it is written.

4. Close the filter stream, which also closes the underlying stream:

```
outputStream.close();
```

To read the binary representation of Java primitive values from a *file* the following procedure can be used, which is also depicted in Figure 18.2.

1. Create a `FileInputStream`:

```
FileInputStream inputFile = new FileInputStream("primitives.data");
```

2. Create a `DataInputStream` which is chained to the `FileInputStream`:

```
DataInputStream inputStream = new DataInputStream(inputFile);
```

3. Read Java primitive values in the same order they were written out, using relevant `readX()` methods :

```
boolean v = inputStream.readBoolean();
char    c = inputStream.readChar();
byte    b = inputStream.readByte();
short   s = inputStream.readShort();
int     i = inputStream.readInt();
long    l = inputStream.readLong();
float   f = inputStream.readFloat();
double  d = inputStream.readDouble();
```

4. Close the filter stream, which also closes the underlying stream:

```
inputStream.close();
```

Example 18.3 uses both the procedures described above: first to write and then to read some Java primitive values to and from a file. The values are also written to the terminal.

Example 18.3 *Reading and Writing Java Primitive Values*

```
import java.io.*;

public class JavaPrimitiveValues {
    public static void main(String args[]) throws IOException {
        // Create a FileOutputStream.
        FileOutputStream outputFile =
                new FileOutputStream("primitives.data");

        // Create a DataOutputStream which is chained to the FileOutputStream.
        DataOutputStream outputStream = new DataOutputStream(outputFile);

        // Write Java primitive values.
        outputStream.writeBoolean(true);
        outputStream.writeChar('A');              // int written as Unicode char
        outputStream.writeByte(Byte.MAX_VALUE);   // int written as 8-bits byte
```

```
            outputStream.writeShort(Short.MIN_VALUE);  // int written as 16-bits short
            outputStream.writeInt(Integer.MAX_VALUE);
            outputStream.writeLong(Long.MIN_VALUE);
            outputStream.writeFloat(Float.MAX_VALUE);
            outputStream.writeDouble(Math.PI);

            // Close the output stream, which also closes the underlying stream.
            outputStream.close();

            // Create a FileInputStream.
            FileInputStream inputFile = new FileInputStream("primitives.data");

            // Create a DataInputStream which is chained to the FileInputStream.
            DataInputStream inputStream = new DataInputStream(inputFile);

            // Read Java primitive values in the same order they were written out.
            boolean v = inputStream.readBoolean();
            char    c = inputStream.readChar();
            byte    b = inputStream.readByte();
            short   s = inputStream.readShort();
            int     i = inputStream.readInt();
            long    l = inputStream.readLong();
            float   f = inputStream.readFloat();
            double  d = inputStream.readDouble();

            // Close the input stream, which also closes the underlying stream.
            inputStream.close();

            // Write the values read on the terminal
            System.out.println(v);
            System.out.println(c);
            System.out.println(b);
            System.out.println(s);
            System.out.println(i);
            System.out.println(l);
            System.out.println(f);
            System.out.println(d);
        }
    }
```

Output from the program:

```
true
A
127
-32768
2147483647
-9223372036854775808
3.4028235E38
3.141592653589793
```

Buffered Byte Streams

The filter classes `BufferedInputStream` and `BufferedOutputStream` implement *buffering of bytes* for input and output streams, respectively. Data is read and written in *blocks of bytes*, rather than a single byte at a time. Buffering can enhance performance significantly. These filter classes only provide methods for reading and writing bytes. A buffering filter must be chained to an underlying stream:

```
BufferedInputStream(InputStream in)
BufferedOutputStream(OutputStream out)
```

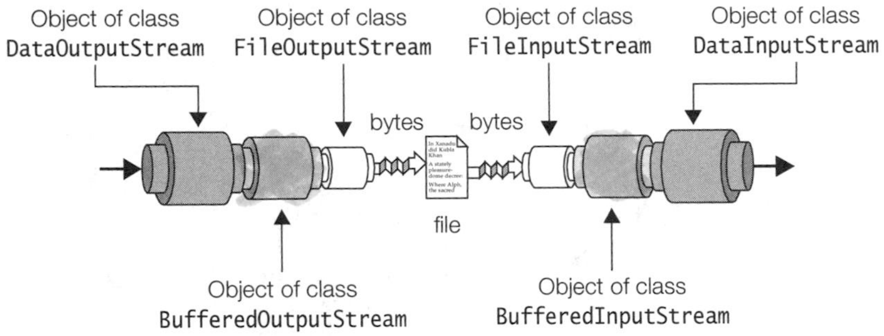

Figure 18.3 *Buffering Byte Streams*

Other filters can be chained to byte buffering filters to provide buffering of data. For example, during the writing of binary representations of Java primitive values to a file, bytes can be buffered (see Figure 18.3):

```
FileOutputStream outputFile = new FileOutputStream("primitives.data");
BufferedOutputStream bufferedOutput = new BufferedOutputStream(outputFile);
DataOutputStream outputStream = new DataOutputStream(bufferedOutput);
```

Values are now written using the `DataOutputStream` `outputStream`, with the buffering of bytes being provided by the `BufferedOutputStream` `bufferedOutput`.

Likewise, during the reading of binary representations of Java primitive values from a file, bytes can be buffered (see Figure 18.3):

```
FileInputStream inputFile = new FileInputStream("primitives.data");
BufferedInputStream bufferedInput = new BufferedInputStream(inputFile);
DataInputStream inputStream = new DataInputStream(bufferedInput);
```

Values are now read using the `DataInputStream` `inputStream`, with the buffering of bytes being provided by the `BufferedInputStream` `bufferedInput`.

Comparison of Byte Output Streams and Input Streams

Usually an output stream has a corresponding input stream of the same type. The table below shows the correspondence between byte output and input streams. Note that not all classes have a corresponding counterpart.

Table 18.4 *Comparing Output Streams and Input Streams*

OutputStreams	InputStreams
`ByteArrayOutputStream`	`ByteArrayInputStream`
`FileOutputStream`	`FileInputStream`
`FilterOutputStream`	`FilterInputStream`
`BufferedOutputStream`	`BufferedInputStream`
`DataOutputStream`	`DataInputStream`
No counterpart	`PushbackInputStream`
`ObjectOutputStream`	`ObjectInputStream`
`PipedOutputStream`	`PipedInputStream`
No counterpart	`SequenceInputStream`

Review questions

18.1 Which of these can act both as an input stream and as an output stream, based on the classes provided by the `java.io` package?

Select all valid answers.

(a) A file
(b) A network connection
(c) A pipe
(d) A string
(e) An array of chars

18.2 Which of these statements about the constant named `separator` of the `File` class are true?

Select all valid answers.

(a) The variable is of type `char`.
(b) The variable is of type `String`.
(c) It can be assumed that the value of the variable always is the character `'/'`.
(d) It can be assumed that the value of the variable always is one of `'/'`, `'\'` or `':'`.
(e) The separator can consist of more than one character.

18.3 Which one of these methods in the `File` class will return the name of the entry, excluding the specification of the directory in which it resides?

Select the one right answer.

(a) `getAbsolutePath()`
(b) `getName()`
(c) `getParent()`
(d) `getPath()`
(e) None of the above.

18.4 What will the method `length()` in the class `File` return?

Select the one right answer.

(a) The number of characters in the file.
(b) The number of kilobytes in the file.
(c) The number of lines in the file.
(d) The number of words in the file.
(e) None of the above.

18.5 A file is readable but not writable on the file system of the host. What will be the result of calling the method `canWrite()` on a `File` object representing this file?

Select the one right answer.

(a) A `SecurityException` is thrown.
(b) The boolean value `false` is returned.
(c) The boolean value `true` is returned.
(d) The file is modified from being unwritable to being writable.
(e) None of the above.

18.6 What is the type of the parameter given to the method `renameTo()` in the class `File`?

Select the one right answer.

(a) `File`
(b) `FileDescriptor`
(c) `FileNameFilter`
(d) `String`
(e) `char[]`

18.7 If `write(0x01234567)` is called on an instance of `OutputStream`, what will be written to the destination of the stream?

Select the one right answer.

(a) The bytes `0x01`, `0x23`, `0x34`, `0x45` and `0x67`, in that order.
(b) The bytes `0x67`, `0x45`, `0x34`, `0x23` and `0x01`, in that order.
(c) The byte `0x01`.
(d) The byte `0x67`.
(e) None of the above.

18.8 Given the following code, under which circumstances will the method return `false`?

```
public static boolean test(InputStream is) throws IOException {
    int value = is.read();
    return value == (value & 0xff);
}
```

Select all valid answers.

(a) A character of more than 8 bits was read from the stream.
(b) An I/O error occurred.
(c) Never.
(d) The end of the input was reached in the input stream.

18.9 Which of these classes provides methods for writing binary representations of primitive Java types?

Select all valid answers.

(a) `DataOutputStream`
(b) `FileOutputStream`
(c) `ObjectOutputStream`
(d) `PrintStream`
(e) `BufferedOutputStream`

18.4 Character Streams: Readers and Writers

A *character encoding* is a scheme for representing characters. Java programs represent characters internally in the 16-bit Unicode character encoding, but the host platform might use another character encoding to represent characters externally. For example, the ASCII (American Standard Code for Information Interchange) character encoding is widely used to represent characters on many platforms. However, it is only one small subset of the Unicode standard.

The abstract classes `Reader` and `Writer` are the roots of the inheritance hierarchies for streams that read and write *Unicode characters* using a specific character encoding.

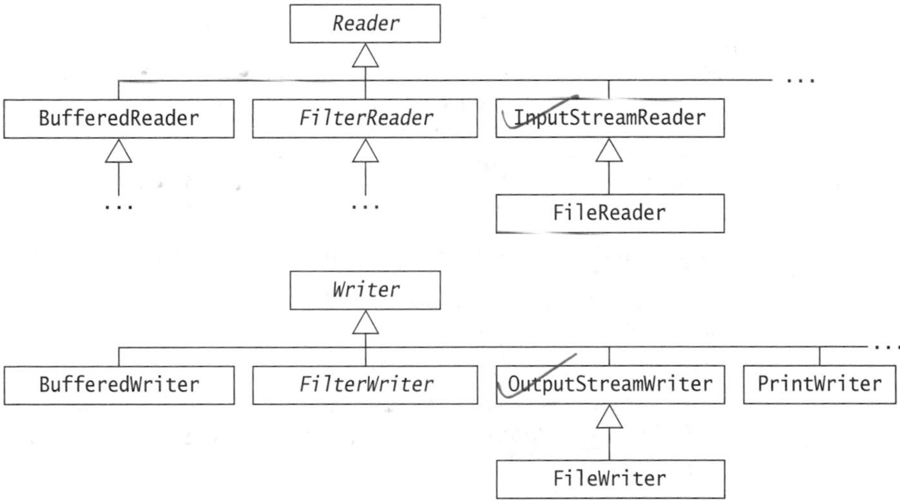

Figure 18.4 *Character Stream Inheritance Hierarchies*

A *reader* is an input character stream that reads a sequence of Unicode characters, and a *writer* is an output character stream that writes a sequence of Unicode characters. Character encodings are used by readers and writers to convert between external encoding and internal Unicode characters. Table 18.5 and Table 18.6 give an overview of the character streams found in the `java.io` package.

Table 18.5 *Readers*

`BufferedReader`	A reader that buffers the characters read from an underlying reader. The underlying reader must be specified, and an optional buffer size can be given.
`LineNumberReader`	A buffered reader that reads characters from an underlying reader while keeping track of the number of *lines* read. The underlying reader must be specified, and an optional buffer size can be given.
`CharArrayReader`	Characters are read from a character array that must be specified.
`FilterReader`	Abstract superclass of all character input stream *filters*. A `FilterReader` must be chained to an underlying reader which must be specified.
`PushbackReader`	A filter that allows characters to be "unread" from a character input stream. A `PushbackReader` must be chained to an underlying reader which must be specified. The number of characters to be unread can optionally be specified.
`InputStreamReader`	Characters are read from a byte input stream which must be specified. The default character encoding is used if no character encoding is explicitly specified.
`FileReader`	Reads characters from a file using the default character encoding. The file can be specified by a `File` object, a `FileDescriptor`, or a `String` file name. It automatically creates a `FileInputStream` for the file.
`PipedReader`	Reads characters from a `PipedWriter` to which it must be connected. The `PipedWriter` can optionally be specified when creating the `PipedReader`.
`StringReader`	Characters are read from a `String` which must be specified.

Readers use the following methods for reading Unicode characters:

```
int read() throws IOException
int read(char cbuf[]) throws IOException
int read(char cbuf[], int off, int len) throws IOException
```

Note that the `read()` methods read an `int` in the range 0 to 65535 (0x0000–0xFFFF), i.e. a Unicode character. The value –1 is returned if the end of file has been reached.

```
long skip(long n) throws IOException
```

A reader can skip over characters using the `skip()` method.

Table 18.6 *Writers*

`BufferedWriter`	A writer that buffers the characters before writing them to an underlying writer. The underlying writer must be specified, and an optional buffer size can be specified.
`CharArrayWriter`	Characters are written to a character array that grows dynamically. The size of the character array initially created can be specified.
`FilterWriter`	Abstract superclass of all character output stream filters. The `java.io` package does not have any concrete character output stream filters.
`OutputStreamWriter`	Characters are written to a byte output stream which must be specified. The default character encoding is used if no explicit character encoding is specified.
`FileWriter`	Writes characters to a file, using the default character encoding. The file can be specified by a `File` object, a `FileDescriptor`, or a `String` file name. It automatically creates a `FileOutputStream` for the file.
`PipedWriter`	Writes characters to a `PipedReader`, to which it must be connected. The `PipedReader` can optionally be specified when creating the `PipedWriter`.
`PrintWriter`	A filter that allows *textual* representations of Java objects and Java primitive values to be written to an underlying output stream or writer. The underlying output stream or writer must be specified.
`StringWriter`	Characters are written to a `StringBuffer`. The initial size of the `StringBuffer` created can be specified.

Writers use the following methods for writing Unicode characters:

```
void write(int c) throws IOException
```

The `write()` method takes an `int` as argument, but only writes out the least significant 16 bits.

```
void write(char[] cbuf) throws IOException
void write(String str) throws IOException
void write(char[] cbuf, int off, int len) throws IOException
void write(String str, int off, int len) throws IOException
```

These methods write the characters from an array of characters or a string.

```
void close() throws IOException
void flush() throws IOException
```

Like byte streams, a character stream should be closed when no longer needed, to free system resources. Closing a character output stream automatically *flushes* the stream, and a character output stream can also be manually flushed.

Like byte streams, many methods of the character stream classes throw an `IOException` that a calling method must either catch explicitly, or specify in a `throws` clause.

Character Encodings

Every platform has a *default* character encoding that can be used by readers and writers to convert between external encodings and internal Unicode characters. Readers and writers can also explicitly specify which encoding schemes to use for reading and writing. Some common encoding schemes are given in Table 18.7.

Table 18.7 *Encoding Schemes*

Encoding Name	Character Set Name
`8859_1`	ISO Latin-1 (subsumes ASCII)
`8859_2`	ISO Latin-2
`8859_3`	ISO Latin-3
`8859_4`	ISO Latin/Cyrillic
`UTF8`	Standard UTF-8 (UCS Transformation Format; UCS stands for Universal Character Set) (subsumes ASCII)

Not all Unicode characters can be represented in other encoding schemes. In that case, the `'?'` character is usually used to denote any such character in the resulting output, during translation from Unicode.

The raw 16-bit Unicode is not particularly space efficient for storing characters derived from the Latin alphabet, because the majority of the characters can be represented by one byte (same as ASCII), making the higher byte in the 16-bit Unicode superfluous. For this reason, Unicode characters are usually encoded externally, using the UTF8 encoding which has a multi-byte encoding format. It represents ASCII characters as one-byte characters but uses multiple bytes for others. The readers and writers can correctly and efficiently translate between UTF8 and Unicode.

The class `OutputStreamWriter` implements writers that can translate Unicode characters into bytes, using a character encoding which can be either the default encoding of the host platform or an encoding that is explicitly specified, and write the resulting bytes to a byte output stream:

```
OutputStreamWriter(OutputStream out)
```

This creates a writer that uses the default character encoding.

```
OutputStreamWriter(OutputStream out, String encodingName)
        throws UnsupportedEncodingException
```

This creates a writer that uses the specified character encoding.

The class `InputStreamReader` implements readers that can read bytes in the default character encoding or a particular character encoding from an input stream, and translate them to Unicode characters:

```
InputStreamReader(InputStream in)
```

This creates a reader that reads bytes in the default character encoding.

```
InputStreamReader(InputStream in, String encodingName)
       throws UnsupportedEncodingException
```

This creates a reader that reads bytes in the specified character encoding.

An `InputStreamReader` or an `OutputStreamWriter` can be queried about the encoding scheme it uses:

```
String getEncoding()
```

The `OutputStreamWriter` and the `InputStreamReader` classes provide methods for writing and reading individual characters and arrays of characters to and from byte streams. The `OutputStreamWriter` class in addition provides a method for writing strings to byte output streams.

The rest of this section provides examples that illustrate readers and writers for handling text files, including textual representation of Java primitive values and objects, and usage of character encodings.

Print Writers

The capabilities of the `OutputStreamWriter` and the `InputStreamReader` classes are limited, as they primarily write and read characters.

In order to write textual representation of Java primitive values and objects, a `PrintWriter` should be chained to either a writer or a byte output stream, using one of the following constructors:

```
PrintWriter(Writer out)
PrintWriter(Writer out, boolean autoFlush)
PrintWriter(OutputStream out)
PrintWriter(OutputStream out, boolean autoFlush)
```

The `autoFlush` argument specifies whether the `PrintWriter` should be flushed when any `println()` method of the `PrintWriter` class is called.

When the underlying writer is specified, the character encoding supplied by the underlying writer is used. However, an `OutputStream` has no notion of any character encoding, so the necessary intermediate `OutputStreamWriter` is automatically created, which will convert characters into bytes, using the default character encoding.

The `PrintWriter` class provides the following methods for writing textual representation of Java primitive values and objects:

Table 18.8 *Print Methods of the* `PrintWriter` ***Class***

`print()`-**methods**	`println`-**methods**
	`println()`
`print(boolean b)`	`println(boolean b)`
`print(char c)`	`println(char c)`
`print(int i)`	`println(int i)`
`print(long l)`	`println(long l)`
`print(float f)`	`println(float f)`
`print(double d)`	`println(double d)`
`print(char[] s)`	`println(char[] s)`
`print(String s)`	`println(String s)`
`print(Object obj)`	`println(Object obj)`

The `println()` methods write the text representation of their argument to the underlying stream, and then append a *line-separator*. The `println()` methods use the correct platform-dependent line-separator. For example, on Unix platforms the line-separator is `'\n'` (linefeed), while on Windows platforms it is `"\r\n"` (carriage return + linefeed) and on the Macintosh it is `'\r'` (carriage return).

The `print()` methods create a textual representation of an object by calling the `toString()` method on the object. The `print()` methods do not throw any `IOException`. Instead, the `checkError()` method of the `PrintWriter` class must be called to check for errors.

Writing Text Files

When writing text to a file using the default character encoding, the following three procedures for setting up a `PrintWriter` are equivalent.

Setting up a `PrintWriter` based on an `OutputStreamWriter` which is chained to a `FileOutputStream` (Figure 18.5a):

1. Create a `FileOutputStream`:

   ```
   FileOutputStream outputFile = new FileOutputStream("info.txt");
   ```

2. Create an `OutputStreamWriter` which is chained to the `FileOutputStream`:

   ```
   OutputStreamWriter outputStream = new OutputStreamWriter(outputFile);
   ```

   The `OutputStreamWriter` uses the default character encoding for writing the characters to the file.

3. Create a `PrintWriter` which is chained to the `OutputStreamWriter`:

   ```
   PrintWriter printWriter1 = new PrintWriter(outputStream, true);
   ```

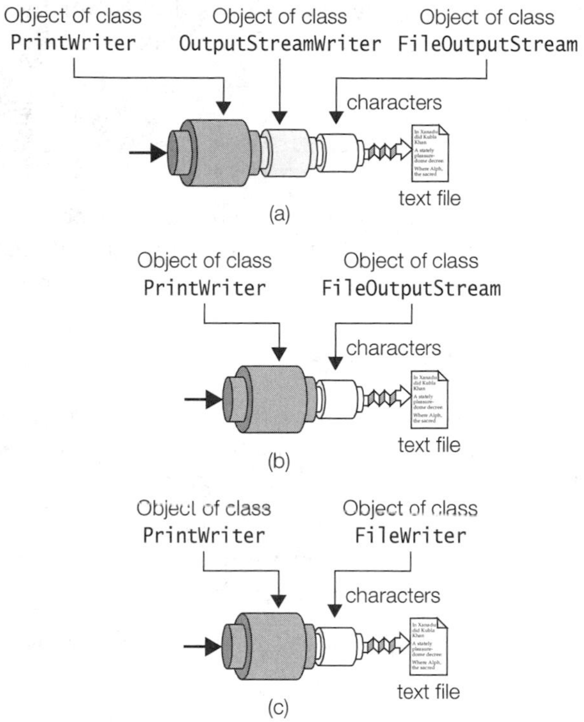

Figure 18.5 *Setting up a Print Writer*

Setting up a `PrintWriter` based on a `FileOutputStream` (Figure 18.5b):

1. Create a `FileOutputStream`:

```
FileOutputStream outputFile = new FileOutputStream("info.txt");
```

2. Create a `PrintWriter` which is chained to the `FileOutputStream`:

```
PrintWriter printWriter2 = new PrintWriter(outputFile, true);
```

   The intermediate `OutputStreamWriter` to convert the characters using the default encoding is automatically supplied.

Setting up a `PrintWriter` based on a `FileWriter` (Figure 18.5c):

1. Create a `FileWriter` which is a subclass of `OutputStreamWriter`:

```
FileWriter fileWriter = new FileWriter("info.txt");
```

   This is equivalent to having an `OutputStreamWriter` chained to a `FileOutputStream` for writing the characters to the file, as shown in Figure 18.5a.

2. Create a `PrintWriter` which is chained to the `FileWriter`:

```
PrintWriter printWriter3 = new PrintWriter(fileWriter, true);
```

If a specific character encoding is desired for the writer, then the first procedure (Figure 18.5a) must be used, the encoding being specified for the `OutputStreamWriter`:

```
FileOutputStream   outputFile   = new FileOutputStream("info.txt");
OutputStreamWriter outputStream = new OutputStreamWriter(outputFile, "8859_1");
PrintWriter        printWriter4 = new PrintWriter(outputStream, true);
```

This writer will use the 8859_1 character encoding to write the characters to the file. A `BufferedWriter` can be used to improve the efficiency of writing to the underlying stream.

Reading Text Files

Java primitive values and objects cannot be read directly from their textual representation. Characters must be read and converted to the relevant values explicitly. One common strategy is to write *lines of text* and tokenize the characters as they are read, a line at a time.

When reading characters from a file using the default character encoding, the following two procedures for setting up an `InputStreamReader` are equivalent.

Set up an `InputStreamReader` which is chained to a `FileInputStream` (Figure 18.6a):

1. Create a `FileInputStream`:

   ```
   FileInputStream inputFile = new FileInputStream("info.txt");
   ```

2. Create an `InputStreamReader` which is chained to the `FileInputStream`:

   ```
   InputStreamReader reader = new InputStreamReader(inputFile);
   ```

   The `InputStreamReader` uses the default character encoding for reading the characters from the file.

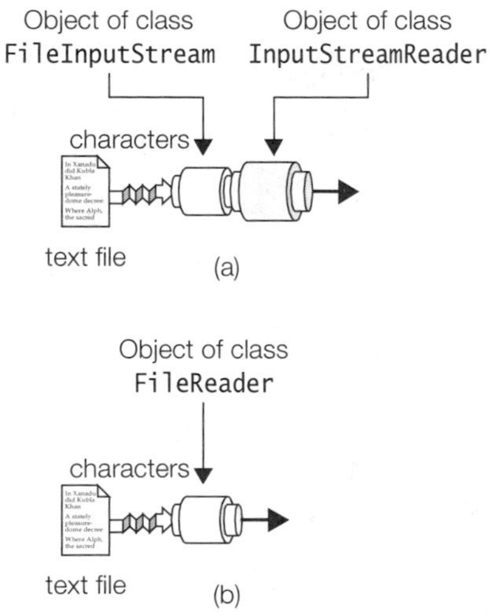

Figure 18.6 *Setting up Readers*

Set up a `FileReader` which is a subclass of `InputStreamReader` (Figure 18.6b):

1. Create a `FileReader`:

```
FileReader fileReader = new FileReader("info.txt");
```

   This is equivalent to having an `InputStreamReader` chained to a `FileInputStream` for reading the characters from the file, using the default character encoding.

If a specific character encoding is desired for the reader, then the first procedure must be used (Figure 18.6a), the encoding being specified for the `InputStreamReader`:

```
FileInputStream inputFile = new FileInputStream("info.txt");
InputStreamReader reader = new InputStreamReader(inputFile, "8859_1");
```

This reader will use the 8859_1 character encoding to read the characters from the file.

Buffered Character Streams

To improve the efficiency of I/O operations, readers and writers can buffer their input and output. For this purpose, a `BufferedWriter` or a `BufferedReader` can be chained to the underlying writer or reader, respectively:

```
BufferedWriter(Writer out)
BufferedWriter(Writer out, int size)
BufferedReader(Reader in)
BufferedReader(Reader in, int size)
```

The default buffer size is used, unless the buffer size is explicitly specified.

The `BufferedReader` class provides the method `readLine()` to read a line of text from the underlying reader:

```
String readLine() throws IOException
```

The `null` value is returned when the end of input is reached. The returned string must explicitly be converted to other values.

The `BufferedWriter` class provides the method `newLine()` for writing the platform-dependent line-separator.

Using Buffered Writers

The following code creates a `PrintWriter` whose output is buffered, and the characters are written using the 8859_1 character encoding (Figure 18.7a):

```
FileOutputStream   outputFile      = new FileOutputStream("info.txt");
OutputStreamWriter outputStream    = new OutputStreamWriter(outputFile, "8859_1");
BufferedWriter     bufferedWriter1 = new BufferedWriter(outputStream);
PrintWriter        printWriter1    = new PrintWriter(bufferedWriter1, true);
```

The following code creates a `PrintWriter` whose output is buffered, and the characters are written using the default character encoding (Figure 18.7b):

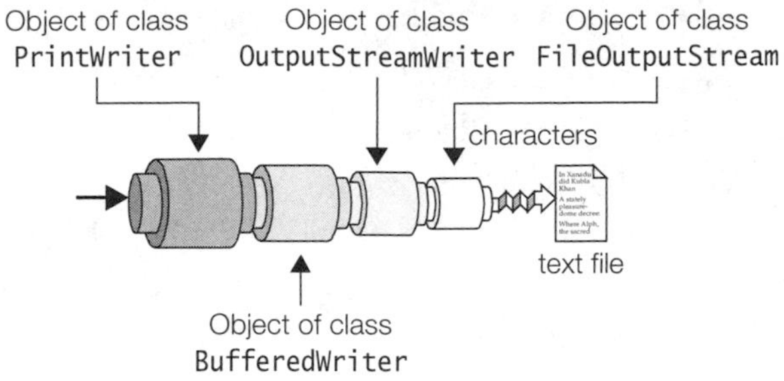

(a)

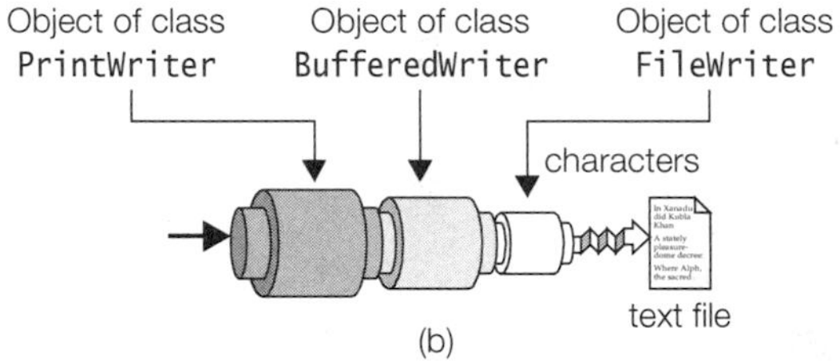

(b)

Figure 18.7 *Buffered Writers*

```
FileWriter     fileWriter      = new FileWriter("info.txt");
BufferedWriter bufferedWriter2 = new BufferedWriter(fileWriter);
PrintWriter    printWriter2    = new PrintWriter(bufferedWriter2, true);
```

Note that in both cases the `PrintWriter` is used to write the characters. The `BufferedWriter` is sandwiched between the `PrintWriter` and the underlying `OutputStreamWriter`.

Using Buffered Readers

The following code creates a `BufferedReader` that can be used to read text lines from a file, using the 8859_1 character encoding (Figure 18.8a):

```
FileInputStream   inputFile       = new FileInputStream("info.txt");
InputStreamReader reader          = new InputStreamReader(inputFile, "8859_1");
BufferedReader    bufferedReader1 = new BufferedReader(reader);
```

The following code creates a `BufferedReader` that can be used to read text lines from a file, using the default character encoding (Figure 18.8b):

```
FileReader     fileReader      = new FileReader("lines.txt");
BufferedReader bufferedReader2 = new BufferedReader(fileReader);
```

Note that in both cases the `BufferedReader` object is used to read the text lines.

In contrast to Example 18.3, which demonstrated the reading and writing of binary representations of primitive data values, Example 18.4 shows the reading and writing of textual representations of primitive data values.

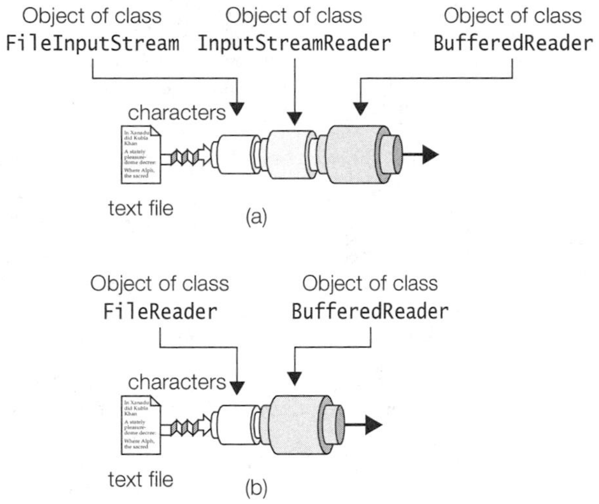

Figure 18.8 *Buffered Readers*

The `CharEncodingDemo` class in Example 18.4 writes textual representations of Java primitive values, using the 8859_1 character encoding (Figure 18.7a). The `PrintWriter` is buffered. Its underlying writer uses the specified encoding, as shown at (1). Values are written out with one value on each line, as shown at (2), and the writer is closed, as shown at (3). The example uses the same character encoding to read the values. A `BufferedReader` is created (Figure 18.8a). Its underlying reader uses the specified encoding, as shown at (4). The values are read in the same order they were written out, one value per line. The line is explicitly converted to an appropriate value, as shown at (5). The `BufferedReader` is closed, as shown at (6), and the values are echoed on the terminal, as shown at (7). Note the exceptions that are specified in the `throws` clause of the `main()` method.

Example 18.4 *Demonstrating Readers and Writers, and Character Encoding*

```
import java.io.*;

public class CharEncodingDemo {

    public static void main(String args[])
                    throws IOException, NumberFormatException {
        // character encoding.                                          (1)
        FileOutputStream outputFile = new FileOutputStream("info.txt");
        OutputStreamWriter writer = new OutputStreamWriter(outputFile, "8859_1");
        BufferedWriter bufferedWriter1 = new BufferedWriter(writer);
        PrintWriter printWriter = new PrintWriter(bufferedWriter1, true);
        System.out.println("Writing using encoding: " + writer.getEncoding());

        // Print Java primitive values, one on each line.               (2)
        printWriter.println(true);
        printWriter.println('A');
        printWriter.println(Byte.MAX_VALUE);
```

```
            printWriter.println(Short.MIN_VALUE);
            printWriter.println(Integer.MAX_VALUE);
            printWriter.println(Long.MIN_VALUE);
            printWriter.println(Float.MAX_VALUE);
            printWriter.println(Math.PI);

            // Close the writer, which also closes the underlying stream      (3)
            printWriter.close();

            // Create a BufferedReader which uses 8859_1 character encoding   (4)
            FileInputStream inputFile = new FileInputStream("info.txt");
            InputStreamReader reader = new InputStreamReader(inputFile, "8859_1");
            BufferedReader bufferedReader = new BufferedReader(reader);
            System.out.println("Reading using encoding: " + reader.getEncoding());

            // Read Java primitive values in the same order they              (5)
            // were written out, one on each line
            boolean v = bufferedReader.readLine().equals("true")? true : false;
            char    c = bufferedReader.readLine().charAt(0);
            byte    b = (byte) Integer.parseInt(bufferedReader.readLine());
            short   s = (short) Integer.parseInt(bufferedReader.readLine());
            int     i = Integer.parseInt(bufferedReader.readLine());
            long    l = Long.parseLong(bufferedReader.readLine());
            float   f = Float.parseFloat(bufferedReader.readLine());
            double  d = Double.parseDouble(bufferedReader.readLine());

            // Close the reader, which also closes the underlying stream      (6)
            bufferedReader.close();

            // Write the values read on the terminal                          (7)
            System.out.println("Values:");
            System.out.println(v);
            System.out.println(c);
            System.out.println(b);
            System.out.println(s);
            System.out.println(i);
            System.out.println(l);
            System.out.println(f);
            System.out.println(d);
        }
    }
```

Output from the program:

```
Writing using encoding: ISO8859_1
Reading using encoding: ISO8859_1
Values:
true
A
127
-32768
2147483647
-9223372036854775808
3.4028235E38
3.141592653589793
```

I/p stream } are all PrintStream
O/p stream } objects
Error stream }

Terminal I/O

The *standard output* stream (usually the screen) is represented by the `PrintStream` object `System.out`. The *standard input* stream (usually the keyboard) is represented by the `InputStream` object `System.in`. In other words, it is a byte input stream. The *standard error* stream (also usually the screen) is represented by `System.err` which is another object of the `PrintStream` class. The `PrintStream` class is now mostly deprecated, but its `print()` methods, which act as corresponding `print()` methods from the `PrintWriter` class, can still be used to write output to `System.out` and `System.err`. In other words, both `System.out` and `System.err` act like `PrintWriter`, but in addition they have `write()` methods for writing bytes.

In order to read and translate characters correctly and efficiently, `System.in` should be chained to an `InputStreamReader` that in turn should be buffered:

```
InputStreamReader inStream = new InputStreamReader(System.in);
BufferedReader stdInStream = new BufferedReader(inStream);
```

In this case, the default character encoding is used to translate the characters.

In Example 18.5, a `BufferedReader` is chained to an `InputStreamReader` that in turn is chained to `System.in`, as shown at (1). This allows the characters from the standard input stream to be buffered and read using the default character encoding. The `BufferedReader` in the example always reads a whole line at a time from the terminal. If a line of text is requested, the whole line read is returned, as shown at (3). If an `int` is to be read, the line is parsed to an `int`, as shown at (5). If a `double` is to be read, the line is parsed to a `double`, as shown at (7). Note the exception handling that is necessary to read a line of characters and ensure that it contains a valid numerical value.

Parsed

The Java class libraries provide a class named `java.text.NumberFormat` that can be used to format numeric values according to a specified locale. At (8), the example uses a `NumberFormat` object created to format values according to the locale `java.util.Locale.US`.

Example 18.5 *Demonstrating Terminal I/O*

```
import java.io.*;
import java.text.*;
import java.util.*;

public final class Stdin {

    // A BufferedReader chained to an InputStreamReader chained to an InputStream.
    private static BufferedReader reader = new BufferedReader(         // (1)
            new InputStreamReader(System.in)
    );

    // Read one line of text from the terminal and return it as a string.
    public static String readLine() {                                  // (2)
        while (true) try {
            return reader.readLine();                                  // (3)
```

```
        } catch(IOException ioe) {
            reportError(ioe);
        }
    }

    // Read one integer value from the terminal.
    public static int readInteger() {                                      // (4)
        while (true) try {
            return Integer.parseInt(reader.readLine());                     // (5)
        } catch (IOException ioe) {
            reportError(ioe);
        } catch(NumberFormatException nfe) {
            reportError(nfe);
        }
    }

    // Read one double value from the terminal.
    public static double readDouble() {                                    // (6)
        while (true) try {
            return Double.parseDouble(reader.readLine());                   // (7)
        } catch(IOException ioe) {
            reportError(ioe);
        } catch(NumberFormatException nfe) {
            reportError(nfe);
        }
    }

    private static void reportError(Exception e) {
        System.err.println("Error in input: " + e);
        System.err.println("Please re-enter data.");
    }

    public static void main(String args[]) {
        System.out.println("Input a string:");
        String str = Stdin.readLine();
        System.out.println("Input an integer:");
        int i = Stdin.readInteger();
        System.out.println("Input a double:");
        double d = Stdin.readDouble();

        NumberFormat formatter = NumberFormat.getInstance(Locale.US);   // (8)
        System.out.println("Data read:");
        System.out.println(str);
        System.out.println(formatter.format(i));
        System.out.println(formatter.format(d));
    }
}
```

Output from the program:

```
Input a string:
Habari
Input an integer:
0201596148
Input a double:
47.584152
```

```
Data read:
Habari
201,596,148
47.584
```

Comparison of Character Writers and Readers

Usually a writer has a corresponding reader. Table 18.9 shows the correspondence between character output and character input streams. Note that not all classes have a corresponding counterpart.

Table 18.9 *Correspondence between Writers and Readers*

Writers	Readers
`BufferedWriter`	`BufferedReader`
No counterpart	`LineNumberReader`
`CharArrayWriter`	`CharArrayReader`
`FilterWriter`	`FilterReader`
No counterpart	`PushbackReader`
`OutputStreamWriter`	`InputStreamReader`
`FileWriter`	`FileReader`
`PipedWriter`	`PipedReader`
`PrintWriter`	*No counterpart*
`StringWriter`	`StringReader`

Comparison of Byte Streams and Character Streams

It is instructive to see which byte streams correspond to which character streams. Table 18.10 shows the correspondence between byte and character streams. Note that not all classes have a corresponding counterpart.

Table 18.10 *Correspondence between Byte Streams and Character Streams*

Byte Streams	Character Streams
`OutputStream`	`Writer`
`InputStream`	`Reader`
`ByteArrayOutputStream`	`CharArrayWriter`
`ByteArrayInputStream`	`CharArrayReader`
No counterpart	`OutputStreamWriter`
No counterpart	`InputStreamReader`

Table 18.10 *Correspondence between Byte Streams and Character Streams (continued)*

Byte Streams	Character Streams
`FileOutputStream`	`FileWriter`
`FileInputStream`	`FileReader`
`FilterOutputStream`	`FilterWriter`
`FilterInputStream`	`FilterReader`
`BufferedOutputStream`	`BufferedWriter`
`BufferedInputStream`	`BufferedReader`
`PrintStream`	`PrintWriter`
`DataOutputStream`	*No counterpart*
`DataInputStream`	*No counterpart*
`ObjectOutputStream`	*No counterpart*
`ObjectInputStream`	*No counterpart*
`PipedOutputStream`	`PipedWriter`
`PipedInputStream`	`PipedReader`
No counterpart	`StringWriter`
No counterpart	`StringReader`
No counterpart	`LineNumberReader`
`PushbackInputStream`	`PushbackReader`
`SequenceInputStream`	*No counterpart*

Review questions

18.10 Which of these are valid parameter types for the `write()` methods of the `Writer` class?

Select all valid answers.

(a) Type `String`
(b) Type `char`
(c) Type `char[]`
(d) Type `int`

18.11 What is the default encoding for an `OutputStreamWriter`?

Select the one right answer.

(a) 8859_1
(b) UTF8
(c) Unicode
(d) The default is system-dependent.
(e) The default is not system-dependent, but is none of the above.

18.12 Which of these integer types do not have their own `print()` method in the `PrintWriter` class?

Select all valid answers.

(a) `byte`
(b) `char`
(c) `int`
(d) `long`
(e) All have their own `print()` method.

18.13 How can one access the standard error stream?

Select all valid answers.

(a) It is accessed as a member of the class `System.err`.
(b) It is accessed as a static variable named `out` in the class `System`.
(c) It is accessed as a static variable named `err` in the class `System`.
(d) It is accessed as a static variable named `err` in the class `Runtime`.
(e) It is returned by a method in the class `System`.

18.5 Random Access for Files

The `RandomAccessFile` class implements *direct access for files*, i.e. bytes can be read from or written to any specified location in a file. The `RandomAccessFile` class inherits directly from the `Object` class. It implements both the `DataInput` and `DataOutput` interfaces, meaning that Java primitive values can be written and read from a random access file. However, note that objects of the `RandomAccessFile` class cannot be chained with streams.

A random access file must be created and assigned to a file, before it can be used.

```
RandomAccessFile(String name, String mode) throws IOException
RandomAccessFile(File file, String mode) throws IOException
```

The file is specified by a file name or by a `File` object. The mode argument must be equal to either `"r"` (for reading) or `"rw"` (for both reading and writing), otherwise an `IllegalArgumentException` is thrown. Note that opening the file for writing does not reset the contents of the file. The file should have the access specified in the constructor.

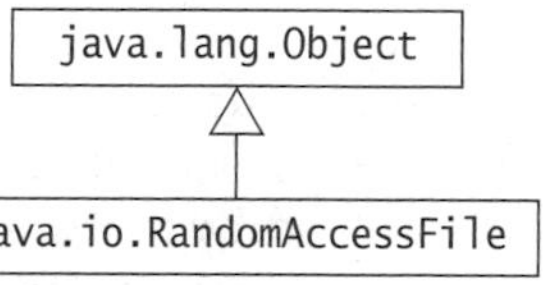

Figure 18.9 *Random Access File Inheritance Hierarchy*

An `IOException` is thrown if an I/O error occurs, most notably when the mode is `"r"` and the file does not exist. However, if the mode is `"rw"` and the file does not exist, a new empty file is created. Regardless of the mode, if the file does exist, its file pointer is set to the beginning of the file.

A `SecurityException` is thrown if the application does not have the necessary access rights.

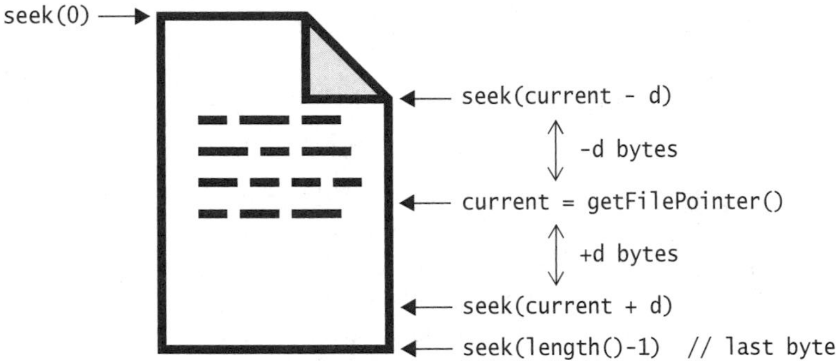

Figure 18.10 *Positioning the File Pointer for Direct File Access*

A *file pointer* indicates the next location in the file where bytes can be read from or written to. The current position of the file pointer can be obtained by using the `getFilePointer()` method:

```
long getFilePointer() throws IOException
```

The number of bytes in the file can be obtained by using the `length()` method:

```
long length() throws IOException
```

The file pointer can be positioned using the `seek()` method:

```
void seek(long offset) throws IOException
```

The `offset` argument specifies the position from the beginning of the file, the first byte being at position 0. The position will be the target of the next read or write operation. See Figure 18.10.

When a random access file is no longer needed, it should be closed, to free the resources:

```
void close() throws IOException
```

Example 18.6 illustrates usage of random access files. The program creates a file and writes the byte representation of the squares of numbers from 0 to 9. It then reads the squares of odd numbers back from the file, using direct access. The squares are represented as `int` values. The file is then extended with the squares of numbers from 10 to 19, and again the squares of odd numbers are read from the file. In the method `createFile()`, the initial file is created using a `RandomAccessFile` object with "rw" mode. The squares of odd numbers are read in the method readFile() using a RandomAccessFile object with "r" mode, which opens the file for direct read access. The numbers are read after the current file pointer value is incremented with the size of an int value, thereby reading every other integer from the file, as shown at (1).

The file is extended in the method extendFile(). The file is opened for direct read and write access. The file pointer is first positioned at the end of the file, before writing the new numbers as shown at (2).

The output from the program shows that only squares of odd numbers were read from the file.

Example 18.6 *Random Access File*

```
import java.io.*;

public class RandomAccessDemo {
    static String fileName = "new-numbers.data";

    final static int INT_SIZE = 4;

    public static void main(String args[]) {
        try {
            RandomAccessDemo random = new RandomAccessDemo();
            random.createFile();
            random.readFile();
            random.extendFile();
            random.readFile();
        } catch (IOException ex) {
            System.err.println(ex);
        }
    }

    // Create a file with squares of numbers from 0 to 9.
    public void createFile() throws IOException {
        File dataFile = new File(fileName);
        RandomAccessFile outputFile = new RandomAccessFile(dataFile, "rw");
        for (int i = 0; i < 10; i++)
            outputFile.writeInt(i*i);
        outputFile.close();
    }

    // Read every other number from the file i.e. the squares of odd numbers
    public void readFile() throws IOException {
        File dataFile = new File(fileName);
        RandomAccessFile inputFile = new RandomAccessFile(dataFile, "r");
        System.out.println("Squares of odd numbers from the file:");
        long length = inputFile.length();
        for (int i = INT_SIZE; i < length; i += 2 * INT_SIZE) {
            inputFile.seek(i);                                          // (1)
            System.out.println(inputFile.readInt());
        }
        inputFile.close();
    }
```

```
    // Extend the file with squares from 10 to 19.
    public void extendFile() throws IOException {
        RandomAccessFile outputFile = new RandomAccessFile(fileName, "rw");
        outputFile.seek(outputFile.length());                          // (2)
        for (int i = 10; i < 20; i++)
            outputFile.writeInt(i*i);
        outputFile.close();
    }
}
```

Output from the program:

```
Squares of odd numbers from the file:
1
9
25
49
81
Squares of odd numbers from the file:
1
9
25
49
81
121
169
225
289
361
```

Review questions

18.14 Which of the these are valid access mode specifiers for a constructor of the `RandomAccessFile` class?

Select all valid answers.

(a) `""`
(b) `"r"`
(c) `"rw"`
(d) `"w"`
(e) `"wr"`
(f) `null`

18.15 Which of the following method calls would, if executed on a `RandomAccessFile` object, position the file pointer so that reading the last byte of the file could be done with a single call to `read()`?

Select the one right answer.

(a) `seek(length())`
(b) `seek(length()+1)`

(c) `seek(length()+2)`
(d) `seek(length()-1)`
(e) `seek(length()-2)`

18.6 Object Serialization

Object serialization allows an object to be transformed into a sequence of bytes that can later be re-created (*deserialized*) into the original object. After deserialization the object has the same state as it had when it was serialized, barring any data members that were not serializable. Java provides this facility through the `ObjectInput` and `ObjectOutput` interfaces, which allow the reading and writing of objects from and to streams. These interfaces extend the `DataInput` and `DataOutput` interfaces respectively.

The `ObjectOutputStream` class implements the `ObjectOutput` interface. This means that the `ObjectOutputStream` class provides methods to write objects as well as bytes, text and Java primitive values. Similarly `ObjectInputStream` class implements the `ObjectInput` interface. This means that the `ObjectInputStream` class provides methods to read objects as well as bytes, text and Java primitive values. Figure 18.11 gives an overview of how these classes can be chained and the methods they provide.

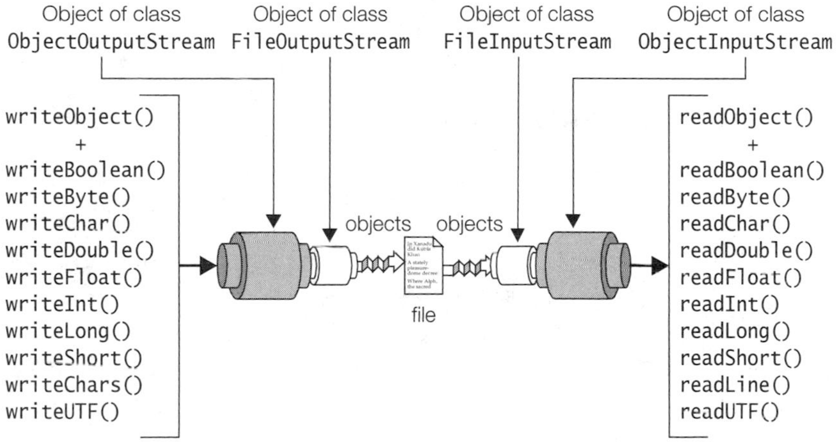

Figure 18.11 *Object Stream Chaining*

`ObjectOutputStream` Class

The class `ObjectOutputStream` can write objects to any stream that is a subclass of the `OutputStream`, for example to a file or a network connection (socket). An `ObjectOutputStream` must be chained to an `OutputStream`, using the following constructor:

```
ObjectOutputStream(OutputStream out) throws IOException
```

For example, in order to store objects in a file and thus provide persistent storage for objects, an `ObjectOutputStream` can be chained to a `FileOutputStream`:

```
FileOutputStream outputFile = new FileOutputStream("obj-storage.dat");
ObjectOutputStream outputStream = new ObjectOutputStream(outputFile);
```

Objects can be written to the stream, using the `writeObject()` method of the `ObjectOutputStream` class:

```
final void writeObject(Object obj) throws IOException
```

The `writeObject()` method can be used to write *any* object to a stream, including strings and arrays, as long as the object supports the `java.io.Serializable` interface, which is a marker interface with no methods. The `String` class and all array types implement the `Serializable` interface. A serializable object can be any compound object containing references to other objects, and all constituent objects that are serializable are serialized recursively when the compound object is written out. Each object is written out once during serialization. The following information is included when an object is serialized:

- the class information needed to reconstruct the object.
- the values of all serializable non-transient and non-static members, including those that are inherited.

`ObjectInputStream` Class

An `ObjectInputStream` is used to restore (*deserialize*) objects that have previously been serialized using an `ObjectOutputStream`. An `ObjectInputStream` must be chained to an `InputStream`, using the following constructor:

```
ObjectInputStream(InputStream in)
        throws IOException, StreamCorruptedException
```

For example, in order to restore objects from a file, an `ObjectInputStream` can be chained to a `FileInputStream`:

```
FileInputStream inputFile = new FileInputStream("obj-storage.dat");
ObjectInputStream inputStream = new ObjectInputStream(inputFile);
```

The method `readObject()` of the `ObjectInputStream` class is used to read an object from the stream:

```
final Object readObject()
        throws OptionalDataException, ClassNotFoundException, IOException
```

Note that the reference returned is of type `Object` regardless of the actual type of the retrieved object, and can be cast to the desired type. Objects and values must be read in the same order as when they were serialized.

Serializable, non-transient data members of an object, including those data members that are inherited, are restored to the values they had at the time of serialization. For compound objects containing references to other objects, the constituent objects are read to re-create the whole object structure. In order to deserialize objects, the appropriate classes must be available at runtime. Note that new objects are created during deserialization, so that no existing objects are overwritten.

The class `ObjectSerializationDemo` in Example 18.7 serializes some objects in the `writeData()` method at (1), and then deserializes them in the `readData()` method at (2). The `readData()` method also writes the data to the standard output stream.

The `writeData()` method writes the following: an array of strings (`strArray`), a `long` value (`num`), an array of `int` values (`intArray`), and lastly a `String` object (`commonStr`) which is shared with the array of strings, `strArray`. However, this shared `String` object is actually only serialized once. Duplication is automatically avoided when the same object is serialized several times. Note that the array elements and the characters in a `String` object are not written out explicitly one by one. It is enough to specify the object reference in the `writeObject()` method. The method also recursively goes through the array of strings, `strArray`, serializing each `String` object in the array.

The method `readData()` deserializes the data in the order in which it was written. An explicit cast is needed to convert the reference of a deserialized object to the right type. Note that new objects are created by the `readObject()` method, and that an object created during the deserialization process has the same state as the object that was serialized.

Example 18.7 *Object Serialization*

```
// Reading and Writing Objects
import java.io.*;

public class ObjectSerializationDemo {

    void writeData() {                                      // (1)
        try {
            // Setup the Output stream
            FileOutputStream outputFile = new FileOutputStream("obj-storage.dat");
            ObjectOutputStream outputStream = new ObjectOutputStream(outputFile);

            // Write data
            String[] strArray = {"Seven", "Eight", "Six"};
            long num = 2001;
            int[] intArray = {1, 3, 1949};
            String commonStr = strArray[2];

            outputStream.writeObject(strArray);
            outputStream.writeLong(num);
            outputStream.writeObject(intArray);
            outputStream.writeObject(commonStr);
```

```
            // Close the stream
            outputStream.flush();
            outputStream.close();
        } catch (IOException ex) {
            System.err.println(ex);
        }
    }

    void readData() {                                          // (2)
        try {
            // Setup the Input stream
            FileInputStream inputFile = new FileInputStream("obj-storage.dat");
            ObjectInputStream inputStream = new ObjectInputStream(inputFile);

            // Read data
            String[] strArray = (String[]) inputStream.readObject();
            long num = inputStream.readLong();
            int[] intArray = (int[]) inputStream.readObject();
            String commonStr = (String) inputStream.readObject();

            // Write data on standard output stream
            for (int i = 0; i < strArray.length; i++) {
                System.out.print(strArray[i] + "\t");
            }
            System.out.println();
            System.out.println(num);
            for (int i = 0; i < intArray.length; i++) {
                System.out.print(intArray[i] + "\t");
            }
            System.out.println();
            System.out.println(commonStr);

            // Close the stream
            inputStream.close();
        } catch (Exception ex) {
            System.err.println(ex);
        }
    }

    public static void main(String args[]) {
        ObjectSerializationDemo demo = new ObjectSerializationDemo();
        demo.writeData();
        demo.readData();
    }
}
```

Output from the program:

```
Seven   Eight   Six
2001
1       3       1949
Six
```

Review questions

18.16 How many methods are defined in the `Serializable` interface?

Select the one right answer.

(a) None
(b) One
(c) Two
(d) Three
(e) None of the above.

18.17 Which of the following best describes the data an `ObjectOutputStream` can write?

Select the one right answer.

(a) Bytes and other primitive Java types.
(b) Object hierarchies.
(c) Object hierarchies and primitive Java types.
(d) Single objects.
(e) Single objects and primitive Java types.

Chapter summary

The following information was included in this chapter:

- Discussion of the `File` class, which provides an interface to the host file system.
- Byte streams, as represented by the `InputStream` and `OutputStream` classes.
- File streams, as represented by the `FileInputStream` and `FileOutputStream` classes.
- Reading and writing Java primitive values using the `DataInputStream` and `DataOutputStream` classes.
- Buffering byte streams for improved efficiency, using the `BufferedInputStream` and `BufferedOutputStream` classes.
- Character streams, as represented by the `Reader` and `Writer` classes.
- Usage of character encodings, including Unicode and UTF8, by the `InputStreamReader` and `OutputStreamWriter` classes.
- Reading and writing text files.
- Buffered character streams, as represented by the `BufferedReader` and `BufferedWriter` classes.
- Terminal I/O using `System.in`, `System.out` and `System.err`.
- Random access files for direct access I/O.
- Object serialization: reading and writing objects.

Programming exercise

18.1 Write a program that reads text from a source using one encoding, and writes the text to a destination using another encoding. The program should have four optional arguments:

- First argument, if present, should specify the encoding of the source. The default source encoding should be `"8859_1"`.
- Second argument, if present, should specify the encoding of the destination. The default destination encoding should be `"UTF8"`.
- Third argument, if present, should specify a source file. If no argument is given, the standard input should be used.
- Fourth argument, if present, should specify a destination file. If no argument is given, the standard output should be used.

Use buffering, and read and write 512 bytes at a time to make the program efficient.

Errors should be written to the standard error stream.

Javadoc Facility 19

Supplementary Objectives

- State which Javadoc tags can be employed for classes, interfaces and members in a Java source file.
- State which options can be used with the `javadoc` tool to extract different content from the Java source files.

19.1 Javadoc Facility

A *documentation comment* is a special purpose comment which, when placed at appropriate places in the source code, can be extracted and used by the `javadoc` utility to generate HTML documentation for the program. A documentation comment starts with "/**" and ends with "*/". It can span several lines, and contain special Javadoc and HTML tags for formatting the generated documentation. A single documentation comment may be placed *immediately preceding* the following constructs:

- Class definitions and interface declarations.
- Member method definitions, including constructors.
- Member variable definitions.

Such a comment will be treated as a regular comment, if placed elsewhere. Information contained in the documentation comment and the construct declaration are used by the `javadoc` utility to generate documentation akin to the API documentation for the JDK, and as such can be read using a web browser. In order for the `javadoc` tool to be able to generate the documentation, each interface and class must be placed in their own compilation unit, i.e. a separate source file.

Here is an example of a documentation comment:

```
/**
 *  This class implements a <i>generic stack</i>. The stack is
 *  implemented using an array.
 *  @author K.A.M.
 *  @version 1.0
 */
public class Stack { /* class definition */ }
```

Inside a documentation comment, white space at the beginning of each line, followed by an optional sequence of asterisks ('*'), are all ignored by the `javadoc` utility. The first sentence in the comment is used as a summary for the construct in the generated documentation. The Javadoc facility recognizes the end of the first sentence as period ('.') followed by white space. Text in the comment, including the summary sentence, can be formatted, and hyperlinks to other documents can be specified using HTML tags. The first line that begins with the character `@` ends the general description, and starts a section containing special *Javadoc tags.*

Example 19.1 *Using Javadoc Tags*

```
// Filename: Stack.java
package com.example.extras.util;

/**
 *  This class implements a <i>generic stack</i>. An array is
 *  used to implement the stack.
 *  @author K.A.M.
 *  @version 1.1
 */
```

```
public class Stack {

    /** The array that implements the stack. */
    private Object[] stackArray;

    /** The top of the stack. */
    private int topOfStack;

    /**
     *  Initialize the stack.
     *  @param capacity Length of the stack.
     */
    public Stack (int capacity) {
        stackArray = new Object[capacity];
        topOfStack = -1;
    }

    /**
     *  Push a value on the stack.
     *  @param element The object to push on the stack.
     *  @exception FullStackException The stack is full.
     *  @see #pop()
     */
    public synchronized void push(Object element) throws FullStackException {
        if (isFull()) throw new FullStackException();
        stackArray[++topOfStack] = element;
    }

    /**
     *  Insert a value on the stack.
     *  @param element The object to insert on the stack.
     *  @exception FullStackException The stack is full.
     *  @deprecated As of version 1.1,
     *  replaced by the {@link #push(Object) <i>push</i>} method. The insert name
     *  was misleading.
     */
    public synchronized void insert(Object element) throws FullStackException {
        push(element);
    }

    /**
     *  Pop the value from top of the stack.
     *  @return The object on top of the stack.
     *  @exception EmptyStackException The stack is empty.
     *  @see #push(Object)
     */
    public synchronized Object pop() throws EmptyStackException {
        if (isEmpty()) throw new EmptyStackException();
        Object obj = stackArray[topOfStack];
        stackArray[topOfStack] = null;
        topOfStack--;
        return obj;
    }

    /**
     *  Peek at the object on top of the stack. The stack is
     *  not popped.
     *  @return The object on top of the stack.
```

```
     *  @exception EmptyStackException The stack is empty.
     */
    public synchronized Object peek() throws EmptyStackException {
        if (isEmpty()) throw new EmptyStackException();
        return stackArray[topOfStack];
    }

    /**
     *  Check if the stack is empty.
     *  @return <code>true</code>, if stack is empty.
     */
    public boolean isEmpty() { return topOfStack < 0; }

    /**
     *  Check if the stack is full.
     *  @return <code>true</code>, if stack is full.
     */
    public boolean isFull() {return topOfStack == stackArray.length - 1; }
}
```

```
// Filename: EmptyStackException.java
package com.example.extras.util;
/**
 *  This exception indicates that the stack is empty.
 */
public class EmptyStackException extends Exception {
    public EmptyStackException() {
        super("Empty Stack");
    }
}
```

```
// Filename: FullStackException.java
package com.example.extras.util;
/**
 *  This exception indicates that the stack is full.
 */
public class FullStackException extends Exception {
    public FullStackException() {
        super("Full Stack");
    }
}
```

19.2 Using Tags

Following the description inside a documentation comment, groups of special Javadoc tags can be used to provide additional information that can be extracted by the javadoc utility. All Javadoc tags have the following general syntax:

@*<tag-name>* *<text>*

A Javadoc tag starts at a new line in the comment, and ends at the next Javadoc tag or at the end of the comment. Tags with the same name must be grouped together inside the comment. Some tags also have pre-assigned formatting for the first argument of the tag (for example, `@exception`, `@throws` and `@param`). Details of Javadoc tags for documenting different constructs are given below.

The text in the comment can be formatted using HTML tags. For example, the HTML tag pairs `<b>-</b>` (bold), `<i>-</i>` (italics), and `<code>-</code>` (code style) can be used without conflicting with the document structure generated by the `javadoc` utility. However, HTML tags like `<h1>` and `<h2>` should be avoided. Paragraphs can be created by using the `<p>` element pairs in the comment.

Example 19.1 is used in this section to illustrate Javadoc tags.

Table 19.1 *Common Javadoc Tags*

Tag Name	Used with:	Tag Description
`@author`	Class, Interface	Specifies an author of the class or interface.
`@deprecated`	Class, Interface, Method, Member Variable	Specifies that the declaration has been deprecated.
`@exception`	Method	Specifies the exception thrown by the method.
`{@link}`	Class, Interface, Method, Member Variable	Creates an inline hyperlink.
`@param`	Method	Specifies a formal parameter of the method.
`@return`	Method	Specifies the value returned by the method.
`@see`	Class, Interface, Method, Member Variable	Creates a hyperlink.
`@since`	Class, Interface, Method, Member Variable	States the version of the code in which the declaration was first introduced.
`@throws`	Method	Specifies an exception thrown by the method. Same as `@exception` tag.
`@version`	Class, Interface	States the version of the class or interface.

Javadoc Tags for Classes, Interfaces and Members

The following tags may be used in documentation comments for classes, interfaces, methods and member variables:

```
@see
{@link}
@deprecated
@since
```

Specifying Hyperlinks to Classes and Interfaces

```
@see <class-name or interface-name> <label>
@see <full class-name or interface-name> <label>
@see <full package-name> <label>
{@link <class-name or interface-name> <label>}
{@link <full class-name or interface-name> <label>}
{@link <full package-name> <label>}
```

A *hyperlink* to the specified class or interface is created in the generated document. If the optional label is specified, it is used as the link's visible link. The class or interface is in the current package, if the full class or interface name is not specified.

```
@see Stack
@see com.example.extras.util.Stack Stack
@see java.util

See also this {@link java.util.Stack Stack} class.
For information on extra utilities, try {@link com.example.extras.util here}.
See {@link java.util Collections}.
```

Specifying Hyperlinks to Members

```
@see #<member-name> <label>
@see <full class-name>#<member-name> <label>
@see <full class-name>#<method-signature> <label>
{@link #<member-name> <label>}
{@link <full class-name>#<member-name> <label>}
{@link <full class-name>#<method-signature> <label>}
```

The `@see` and `{@link}` tags create a *hyperlink* to the specified member in the generated documentation. Whereas the link created by the `@see` tag is placed in a "`See Also`" section, the `{@link}` generates an inline link in the text where this tag appears. If the optional label is specified, it is used as the link's visible label. The member is in the current class or interface if no class or interface is specified.

```
@see #topOfStack
@see #peek()
@see com.example.extras.util.Stack#topOfStack
@see com.example.extras.util.Stack#peek() here
@see com.example.extras.util.Stack#push(Object) push

Use the {@link com.example.extras.util.Stack#push(Object) push method}.
For more information, click {@link com.example.extras.util.Stack#peek() here}.
```

Specifying Hyperlinks to Other Documentation

```
@see <a href="URL#value">label</a>
```

In the documentation, a `See Also` entry is added as the specified *hyperlink*.

```
@see <a href="Stack.html#peek">Usage Restrictions</a>
```

Marking Features as Deprecated

@deprecated <*explanation*>

This tag allows entities to be marked as *deprecated*, meaning that their continued usage is discouraged. The Java compiler reads these tags and issues a warning if a deprecated feature is used by a program. The javadoc utility generates a Deprecated entry in the documentation, together with the explanation. All members in a class or interface are marked deprecated if the class or interface is marked deprecated.

```
@deprecated As of version 1.1, replaced by this {@link #push() push} method.
```

Dating Features

@since <*version*>

This tag allows a specific *version* for a feature to be recorded in the documentation. The intended usage of this tag is to indicate when the feature was added.

```
@since Version 1.1
```

Documenting Classes and Interfaces

The following tags may only be placed in documentation comments for classes and interfaces.

@author
@version

Documenting the Author of a Class or Interface

@author <*author-name*>

In the documentation, an Author entry is created with the specified author name. Several authors can be specified, using a separate @author tag for each author. The command-line option -author must be given to the javadoc utility to generate this entry.

```
@author A. Writer
@author N. Scribble
@author unascribed
```

Documenting the Version of a Class or Interface

@version <*text*>

In the documentation, a Version entry is created with the specified text. The command-line option -version must be given to the javadoc utility to generate this entry.

```
@version 1.1.2a, 1-March-1999
```

Documenting Methods

The following tags may only be placed in documentation comments for methods (and constructors).

```
@param
@return
@exception
@throws
```

Documenting the Parameters of a Method

`@param` *<parameter-name> <description>*

The specified parameter and its description are added to the `Parameters` section of the documentation pertaining to the current method. Each parameter should be specified using a separate `@param` tag.

```
@param element The element to push on the stack
```

Documenting the Return Value of a Method

`@return` *<description>*

The description of the returned value is added to the `Returns` section of the documentation pertaining to the current method. This tag is omitted if the return type is `void`.

```
@return The value on top of the stack
```

Documenting the Exceptions of a Method

`@exception` *<exception-class-name> <explanation>*
`@throws` *<exception-class-name> <explanation>*

These two tags are synonyms. The specified class name of the exception and its explanation are added to the `Throws` section of the documentation pertaining to the current method. Each exception should be specified using a separate tag.

```
@exception EmptyStackException Tried to pop the stack when its empty.
@throws java.io.IOException Read operation failed.
```

Documenting Member Variables

There are no specific Javadoc tags for documenting member variables. The documentation comment together with the common Javadoc tags `@see`, `{@link}`, `@deprecated` and `@since` suffice for document variables.

Some Documentation Conventions

The CODE element of HTML is typically used for formatting Java keywords, and for formatting package, class, interface, method and variable names, and also for code in the documentation comment.

```
@return <code>true</code>, if stack is empty.
```

The parameter list is not specified with a method name, except when a particular method *signature* is desired.

```
@see com.example.extras.util.Stack#push
@see com.example.extras.util.Stack#push(Object)
```

The tag order is usually: `@author`, `@version`, `@param`, `@return`, `@exception`, `@throws`, `@see`, `@since` and `@deprecated`, with the `{@link}` tag being used for inline hyperlinks where necessary.

Table 19.2 *Common Options for the* `javadoc` *Utility*

`-sourcepath <path>` `-classpath <path>`	List of directories and files containing the source files. List-separator is platform-dependent: `':'` for Unix, `';'` for Windows.
`-d <directory>`	Destination directory for the output files generated by the `javadoc` utility. The default is the current directory.
`-public`	Documentation is generated for public classes, interfaces and members only.
`-protected`	Documentation is generated for protected/public classes, interfaces and members. This is the default action.
`-package`	Documentation is generated for package/protected/public classes and interfaces and members.
`-private`	Documentation is generated for all classes, interfaces and members.
`-author`	`@author` paragraphs are only included if this option is specified.
`-version`	`@version` paragraphs are only included if this option is specified.
`-nodeprecated`	`@deprecated` paragraphs are excluded if this option is specified.

19.3 Running `javadoc`

The `javadoc` utility takes as input either a list of *packages* or a list of Java source files specified on the command line:

```
javadoc gui.2d.components db.queries.sql
javadoc FancyFrame.java DBConnentInterface.java
```

Note that the *package names* are specified using the dot-notation (.), not by their directory location. For the individual classes and interfaces, the *filenames* must be specified. If the `javadoc` utility cannot find the specified input sources, their location may be specified on the command line, using either the `-sourcepath` or `-classpath` option.

The generated files comprising the HTML documentation are placed under the current directory, unless a destination directory is specified using the `-d` option.

```
javadoc -d doc/gui gui.2d.components db.queries.sql
```

Options are provided to tailor the generated documentation according to the accessibility modifier of the class, interface or member. The default action of the `javadoc` utility is to generate documentation for classes, interfaces and members that have `protected` or `public` accessibility. This corresponds to the `-protected` option. Documentation can be restricted to `public` declarations, using the `-public` option. The `-package` option can be used to expand the documentation to include classes and interfaces that have package or `public` accessibility, and members that are non-private. The `-private` option can be used to generate documentation for all classes, interfaces and members.

A simple way to generate documentation for one or more packages is to issue the `javadoc` command in the *root directory* of the package hierarchy, and specify the names of the relevant packages. For example, if the fully qualified name of the package is `com.example.extras.util` and it is in a directory called `dev/com/example/extras/util`, then the following command can be given in the `dev` directory:

```
javadoc -private com.example.extras.util
```

One way to generate documentation for one or more classes is to issue the `javadoc` command in the directory containing the source files. For example, if the source files are in a directory `dev/com/example/extras/util`, then the following command can be given in the `util` directory:

```
javadoc -private *.java
```

The author and version information are not included, unless the options `-author` and `-version` are specified. Information about deprecated features is normally included, unless `-nodeprecated` option is specified.

```
javadoc -author -version -private com.example.extras.util
```

The generated file named `index.html` is the starting point for navigating the generated documentation. For each class and interface, the (default) generated documentation includes:

- Class hierarchy diagram for the class or interface.
- Links to inherited members.
- Variable, constructor and method *summary* sections.
- Variable, constructor and method *detail* sections.

It is instructive to run the source code of Example 19.1 through `javadoc`, and navigate its HTML documentation. Figure 19.1 shows a screenshot of this documentation.

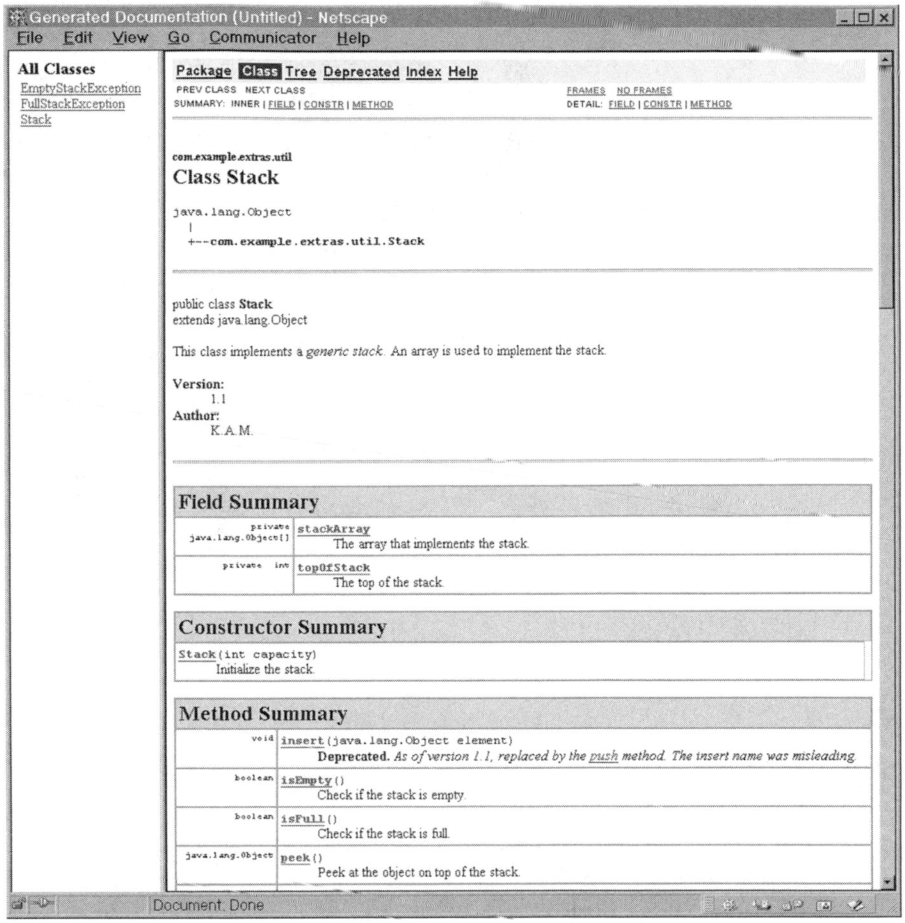

Figure 19.1 *Javadoc Document*

In summary, a single documentation comment may be placed in front of classes, interfaces and members. The general syntax of a documentation comment is as follows:

```
/**
 *  A summary sentence.
 *  Followed by any additional explanation.
 *  Followed by any Javadoc tags, grouped by name, with each one starting
 *  on a new line.
 */
```

The summary sentence, the additional explanation and the Javadoc tags can span several lines, and HTML tags can be used to format the contents of a document comment.

Common Pitfalls when Using Javadoc

- Trying to generate documentation for the source code in incremental steps. Documentation for all the classes must be generated in one go.
- Trying to generate documentation for incomplete code. If the compiler fails to compile the source code, then `javadoc` is likely to fail in generating the documentation.
- Trying to generate documentation for classes that have package or `private` accessibility, without specifying the option `-package` or `-private`.

Review questions

19.1 Preceding which of these constructs would a document comment be recognized?

Select all valid answers.

(a) Class definition
(b) Interface declaration
(c) Local variable declaration
(d) Member method definition
(e) Member variable definition

19.2 How many asterisks (*) would the document generated by the following comment contain?

```
/**
 ** * *Hello
 */
```

Select the one right answer.

(a) None
(b) One
(c) Two
(d) Three
(e) Four

19.3 Which segment of the following comment would be considered the first sentence of the comment?

```
/**
 * com.foo.bar was invented by prof. Freddy T. Baz.<!-- -->© 1998.
 */
```

Select the one right answer.

(a) `com.`
(b) `com.foo.bar`
(c) `com.foo.bar was invented by prof..`

(d) com.foo.bar was invented by prof. Freddy T.
(e) com.foo.bar was invented by prof. Freddy T. Baz.
(f) com.foo.bar was invented by prof. Freddy T. Baz.<!-- -->© 1998.

19.4 Given the task of writing a document comment for a member of a class named Bar in a package called com.foo, which ways of referring to a method named doIt() with no parameters, which is located in the same class, are valid?

Select all valid answers.

(a) #doIt
(b) #doIt()
(c) Bar#doIt()
(d) com.foo.Bar#doIt()

19.5 Which of these are Javadoc tags?

Select all valid answers.

(a) @seealso
(b) @deprecated
(c) @exception
(d) @returns
(e) @since

19.6 Which of these statements concerning the options of the javadoc tool are true?

Select all valid answers.

(a) Using only the -public option generates documentation for public classes and members only.
(b) Using only the -protected option generates documentation for protected classes and members only.
(c) Using only the -package option generates documentation for package classes and members only.
(d) Using only the -private option generates documentation for private classes and members only.

19.7 Which of these are options of the javadoc tool?

Select all valid answers.

(a) -private
(b) -noprivate
(c) -deprecated
(d) -nodeprecated
(e) -noversion

19.8 Which of these Javadoc tags are applicable to a member variable?
Select all valid answers.

(a) `@author`
(b) `@deprecated`
(c) `@see`
(d) `@since`

Chapter summary

The following information was included in this chapter:

- Usage of the Javadoc tags to document Java source files.
- Running the `javadoc` tool to generate HTML documentation.

Programming exercise

19.1 Document the code from Example 17.5 to generate appropriate HTML documentation using the `javadoc` tool.

Appendix A

Taking the SCPJ2 Exam

Preparing for the programmer exam

Sun Educational Services offers three types of certification exams for Java:

- Programmer exam
  Basically a multiple choice examination, testing the candidate's knowledge of the Java language and its usage.
- Developer exam
  Comprising a programming assignment and an essay exam testing comprehension of advanced Java features.
- Technology Architect exam
  Basically a multiple choice examination, dealing with the large-scale issues of deploying Java technology. This exam tests the candidate's knowledge regarding Java-related technologies and products, and also the planning and designing involved in Java projects.

Passing the Sun Certified Programmer for the Java 2 Platform (SCPJ2) exam is a prerequisite for taking the Sun Certified Developer for the Java Platform exam. The focus of this book is on the programmer exam.

The goal of the programmer exam is to test practical knowledge of the Java language. The exam tests for thorough understanding of both the syntax and the semantics of the Java programming language.

The exam covers a wide variety of topics, as defined in the objectives for the programmer exam (see page 616). It covers everything from the basic syntax of the language to detailed knowledge of the core APIs such as the `java.lang` package, the AWT layout managment and the collections framework.

The need for real-world experience for this exam cannot be stressed enough. It is next to impossible to pass the test without having some actual experience programming in Java. Simply reading straight through this book is not recommended. Readers should take time to try out what they have learned along every step of the way. Readers are encouraged to gauge their newly acquired knowledge using the review questions provided after every major topic.

Experimenting with the examples and working through the programming exercises in the book will serve to give the reader a much better chance of passing the test. The exam is considered to be hard, and requires a fair amount of studying on the part of the candidate.

When the reader feels ready for the exam, he or she should test his or her skills on the sample exam that is provided in the back of the book (page 698). This will give an indication of how well the reader is prepared for the exam, and which topics need further study. The structure of the book should make it easy for the reader to focus on single topics, if necessary.

Even seasoned Java programmers should invest some time in preparing for the exam. Simply having real-world experience is not enough to pass the exam.

Registering for the exam

The exam is administered through a company called *Sylvan Prometric*. They provide computer-based testing services for a wide variety of clients. Sylvan Prometric has more than 1,300 testing centers located around the world. The test is paid for through the purchase of vouchers. An exam voucher must be obtained before signing up for the test at a local testing center.

Obtaining an exam voucher

Exam vouchers are sold by Sun Educational Services. Some testing centers may be able to help in obtaining a voucher for the exam. If not, Sun Educational Services can be called to purchase one. The main number for Sun Educational Services within the USA is 1-800-422-8020.

The correct voucher for the programmer exam should be obtained. The test number for the Sun Certified Programmer for the Java 2 Platform is *310-025*. Sun will need credit card information to arrange payment. A voucher for the programmer exam for Java 2 costs $150.

Sun will send the voucher as soon as the credit information has been verified. The voucher is sent by FedEx and will normally arrive within one business day.

It is important to take good care of the voucher, as it is needed when signing up for the test at Sylvan Prometric. Note that your voucher has an expiration date, usually of 6 to 12 months. Neither Sun nor Sylvan Prometric will replace lost or expired vouchers, nor will they offer refunds for unused vouchers.

Signing up for the test

After obtaining the exam voucher, Sylvan Prometric can be called to sign up for the test by making an appointment at one of the local testing centers. The main number for signing up at Sylvan Prometric within the USA is 1-800-795-3926.

Contact information

Both Sun and Sylvan Prometric have offices world wide that can be contacted to purchase a voucher or sign up for the test.

Sun has both offices and associates around the world that can be contacted for information about the exam or to purchase vouchers.

The web site of Sun Educational Services maintains an up-to-date list with detailed contact information for each of the offices. See the following web site:

<URL:`http://suned.sun.com/usa/cert_reg.html?content=globalcontacts`>

Local test centers can be found using a search facility on the Sylvan Prometric web site.

Contact information for some of the major locations is listed below. These locations can provide information and sell vouchers for the exam.

United States

Sun Service Division
Educational Services
2550 Garcia Avenue, MIL02-34
Mountain View, CA 94043-1100
Tel: 1-800-422-8020
Fax: 1-408-263-9367
<URL:`http://suned.sun.com/suned/`>

Authorized Prometric Testing Center:
Tel: 1-800-795-3926 (toll free)
<URL:`http://www.sylvanprometric.com/`>

Test no.: 310-025
Exam voucher price: $150.

Great Britain

Sun Educational Services
Training Administration
Watchmoor Park
Riverside Way
Camberley, GU15 3YL
Surrey
ENGLAND
Tel: +44 1 276 416520
Fax: +44 1 276 681546

This office is also the contact for Alderney, Faroe Islands, Gibraltar, Guernsey, Ireland, Isle of Man and Jersey.

Authorized Prometric Testing Center:
Tel: 0800-592-873 (toll free)

Germany

Sun Microsystems GmbH
Trainingszentrum München
Richard-Reitzner-Allee 8
85540 Haar
GERMANY
Tel: +49 89 46008 788
Fax: +49 89 46008 789

This office is also the contact for Austria.

Authorized Prometric Testing Center:
Tel: 0130-83-97-08 (toll free)

France

Sun Microsystems
143 bis, avenue de Verdun
92442 Issy les Moulineaux Cedex
FRANCE
Tel: +33 1 41 33 17 12
Fax: +33 1 41 33 17 20

This office is also the contact for French Guiana, French Polynesia, Guadeloupe, Martinique, Monaco, New Caledonia, Reunion Island and Tahiti.

Authorized Prometric Testing Center:
Tel: +33 1 42 89 31 22

Australia

Sun Microsystems
Level 5
60 Albert Road
South Melbourne Vic 3205
AUSTRALIA
Tel: +61 3 9679 6234
Fax: +61 3 9686 5098

This office is also the contact for Equatorial Guinea, Fiji, Guinea, Papua New Guinea, Solomon Island, Tuvalu and Vanuatu.

Authorized Prometric Testing Center:
Tel: 1-800-806-944 (toll free)

After taking the exam

Those passing the exam will immediately receive a temporary certificate. Sylvan Prometric will inform Sun Educational Services about the passing of the exam, and Sun will send a permanent certificate by mail which should arrive within a few weeks.

Moving on to the developer exam

Those passing the programmer exam may want to go on to take the Sun Certified Developer for the Java Platform exam. This exam tests the ability to put together real-world applications using Java. This book does not focus on the developer exam. The developer exam usually requires writing a working client/server application with an advanced graphical user interface. The exam comprises a programming assignment and five to ten essay questions regarding the assignment. Unlike the programmer exam, this exam will be graded by a person rather than a program.

The objectives for the developer exam include the following topics:

- TCP/IP networking
- I/O streams
- GUI construction using standard AWT components
- JDK 1.1 event model
- Object serialization
- Javadoc
- Printing
- Packages
- Threads
- Implementing interfaces

Except for TCP/IP networking and printing, all the above topics are discussed in this book.

The programming assignment can be downloaded from the web site of Sun Educational Services by those who have passed the programmer exam.

Submitting the completed programming assignment costs $250, and the essay exam will cost another $150. More information about the developer exam can be obtained by contacting Sun, by using the same numbers as the ones listed for the programmer exam or by checking their web site.

How the examination is conducted

The testing locations

When a candidate shows up at the local testing center at the appointed time, he or she will be escorted to his or her own little cubicle with a desktop computer. The test will be conducted in this cubicle, using a testing program on the computer. The program will ask questions, record answers and tabulate scores.

Candidates will not be allowed to bring personal belongings or food with them to the cubicle. During the exam, candidates will be allowed to make notes on a single piece of paper, but they will not be allowed to take these notes with them after the exam. Quite often the exam area is fitted with security cameras.

Utilizing the allotted time

The exam consists of 59 questions, which must be answered within 2 hours. The questions vary in difficulty. Some are easy and some are hard. With about 2 minutes on average to answer each question, the candidate cannot afford to get stuck on the hard questions. If the answer does not become apparent within a reasonable time, it is advisable to move on to the next question. Time permitting, it is possible to return to the unanswered questions later.

An experienced Java programmer who is good at taking exams should be able to complete the exam well within the allotted time. Any remaining time is best used reviewing the answers.

The exam program

The computer program used to conduct the exam will select a set of questions at random, and present them through a graphical user interface. The interface is designed in such a way that candidates are able to move back and forth through the questions for reviewing purposes. Questions can be temporarily left unanswered, and the candidate can return to them later. Before the exam starts, the candidate is allowed a test run with the computer program. A demo test that has nothing to do with the Java exam is used. Its sole purpose is to allow the candidate to get acquainted with the program being used to conduct the exam.

Immediately after the exam is over, the program will present the candidate with the following information:

- An indication of whether the candidate passed or failed. A score of 71% or more correct answers is needed to pass the exam.
- The total score. All the questions are weighted equally, and the score is calculated based on the percentage of correct answers. No credit is given for partially correct answers.

- Indications on how well the candidate did on each of the categories of the objectives. Candidates who fail the exam should pay close attention to this information. If the candidate is planning to retake the exam, it may give a good indication of which topics need closer attention.

The program will, however, not divulge which questions were answered correctly.

The questions

The questions in the exam come in a variety of forms. The questions can be classified using three basic factors:

- The form of answer that is expected.
- The form of question.
- The topic covered by the question.

Forms of answers expected

The majority of the questions expect the answer to be given in one of the following forms:

- Multiple choice, select the one right answer.
- Multiple choice, select all appropriate responses. All of the appropriate and none of the inappropriate choices must be selected, for the question as a whole to be considered correctly answered.

A rarer form of question expects the candidate to type in short answers manually.

There should be no problem identifying which form of answer each question requires. The wording of the questions will indicate this, and the software used will present the candidate with an input method corresponding to the form of answer expected.

For multiple choice questions, the program will ask the candidate to select a specific number of answers from a list. Where a single correct answer is expected, radio buttons will only allow the selection of one of the answers. The most appropriate response should be selected here.

In questions where all appropriate responses should be selected, checkboxes will allow the selection of each response individually. In this case, all choices should be considered on their own merit. They should not be weighed against each other. It can be helpful to think of each of the choices for the question as an individual true–false question.

Care should be exercised when answering a question requiring all appropriate responses to be selected. A common mistake is to select only one of the appropriate responses, as a result of assuming the question only has one right answer.

For short-answer type-in questions, the program will present a text field in which the answer should be typed. The exam usually contains three to four questions of this type. As with the other forms of answer, these fill-in answers will be judged by the computer. It is therefore a common concern that basically correct answers can be rejected because of minute differences from the correct answer that the program holds. These concerns are usually unfounded. The program allows the candidate a certain amount of flexibility, and will most often accept several variations of an answer. Answers should, however, be typed in with extra care. Attention should be paid to correct spelling and capitalization. Some questions describe the exact format of the answer expected.

Forms of questions

Most of the questions follow some common form that requires candidates to apply their knowledge in a special way.

- Analyzing program code.
  The question provides a source code snippet, and asks a specific question pertaining to the snippet. Will running the program provide the expected result? What will be written to the standard output when the program is run? Will the code compile?
- Identifying true or false statements.
- Naming specific classes or members.

When analyzing program code, it is useful to try to apply the same rules a compiler uses: examining the exact syntax used, rather than making assumptions on what the code tries to accomplish.

The wording of the questions is precise, and expects the responses selected in multiple choice questions to be precise. This often causes the test to be perceived as fastidious. Close attention should be paid to the wording of the responses in a multiple choice question.

None of the questions are intentionally meant to be trick questions. Exam questions have been reviewed by both Java experts and language experts, to remove as much ambiguity from the wording of the questions as possible.

Since the program used in the exam will select and present the questions in a random fashion, there is no point in trying to guess the form of the questions. The order of the answers in multiple choice questions has been randomized and thus has no significance.

Topics covered by the questions

Topics covered by the exam are basically derived from the set of objectives for the programmer exam defined by Sun. These objectives are included in a separate appendix, together with study notes that highlight important topics to study for the exam. All the major topics are covered extensively in the relevant chapters of the book.

The ultimate goal of the exam is to differentiate experienced Java programmers from the rest. Some of the questions are therefore aimed at topics that new Java programmers usually find difficult. Such topics include:

- Casting and conversion
- Polymorphism, overriding and overloading
- Exceptions and `try-catch-finally` block
- Thread control
- GUI layout
- Event model
- I/O
- Nested/inner classes

Knowledge obtained from studying other languages such as C++ should be used with care. Some of the questions often seem to lead astray C++ programmers who have not grasped the many differences between C++ and Java. Those with a C++ background should pay special attention to the following Java topics:

- Use `null`, not `NULL`
- Use `true` and `false`, not `1` and `0`.
- Signed and unsigned shifts
- Widening conversions
- Conditional and boolean logic operators
- Labeled statements
- Accessibility rules
- How polymorphism works
- Applets

Some of the questions may require intimate knowledge of the APIs. This book covers the most important classes and methods of the API, but it does not go as far as listing every member of every class. There are API references readily available from many sources. The Java API reference documentation is usually shipped with the JDK. It is essential that readers familiarize themselves with the relevant parts of API documentation.

Appendix B

Objectives for the SCPJ2 Exam

The objectives for the Sun Certified Programmer for Java 2 Platform exam are defined by Sun, and can be found at:

<URL:`http://suned.sun.com/USA/certification/progobj.html#java2`>

The objectives (Copyright 1998, 1999 Sun MicroSystems Inc.) are organized in sections, and each section is *reproduced verbatim* in this appendix. For each section, we have provided study notes, which highlight related topics that are essential for the exam. Each section title provides a reference to the main chapter that covers the topics in the section.

Section 1: Declarations and Access Control (Chapter 4)

- Write code that declares, constructs, and initializes arrays of any base type using any of the permitted forms both for declaration and for initialization.
- Declare classes, inner classes, methods, instance variables, static variables, and automatic (method local) variables making appropriate use of all permitted modifiers (such as public, final, static, abstract, and so forth). State the significance of each of these modifiers both singly and in combination, and state the effect of package relationships on declared items qualified by these modifiers.
- For a given class determine if a default constructor will be created and if so state the prototype of that constructor.
- State the legal return types for any method given the declarations of all related methods in this or parent classes.

Study notes

Arrays are objects. They contain a fixed number of elements of a specific type. The index of the first element is 0. The index of the last element is one less than the length of the array. Note how arrays are declared and constructed. Array size is not specified in the declaration, but is given when the array object is created. Multidimensional arrays are implemented as arrays of arrays.

Modifiers affect classes, methods and variables and each modifier has a specific significance. Accessibility modifiers specify where classes and methods can be accessed and used. Knowing which modifiers are applicable in a given context is important.

Constructors are not normal methods and must have the same name as the class. Constructors do not declare a return value. Implicit default constructors come into play when no constructors are specified. Calls to other constructors from within a constructor must be done as the first statement in the constructor body.

Section 2: Flow Control and Exception Handling (Chapter 5)

- Write code using if and switch statements and identify legal argument types for these statements.
- Write code using all forms of loops including labeled and unlabeled use of break and continue and state the values taken by loop control variables during and after loop execution.
- Write code that makes proper use of exceptions and exception handling clauses (try, catch, finally) and declares methods and overriding methods that throw exceptions.

Study notes

The `if` statement affects control flow based on a boolean expression. The `switch` statement affects control flow based on an integral expression. The `break` statement exits the loop or `switch` statement, and the `continue` statement skips the rest of the current iteration in a loop. Transfer of control using labeled `break` and `continue` statements should be understood.

Exceptions are objects in Java. An exception is either checked or unchecked. Methods must explicitly declare any checked exceptions they throw. Declaration of `try`, `catch` and `finally` blocks must follow certain rules. There are three basic flow control scenarios that may occur in conjunction with exceptions. The control flow for each of these scenarios should be understood:

1. When no exception is generated.
2. When an exception is thrown within a `try`-block, and a `catch`-block handles the exception.
3. When an exception is thrown within a `try`-block, and no `catch`-block handles the exception.

The `finally` block is always executed.

Section 3: Garbage Collection (Chapter 8)

- State the behavior that is guaranteed by the garbage collection system and write code that explicitly makes objects eligible for collection.

Study notes

There is no guarantee that any object will ever be garbage collected. Objects become eligible for garbage collection when they are no longer accessible through any references. Objects may override the `finalize()` method, which is called just before the object is deleted.

Section 4: Language Fundamentals (Chapter 2)

- Identify correctly constructed source files, package declarations, import statements, class declarations (of all forms including inner classes), interface declarations and implementations (for java.lang.Runnable or other interface described in the test), method declarations (including the main method that is used to start execution of a class), variable declarations and identifiers.
- State the correspondence between index values in the argument array passed to a main method and command line arguments.
- Identify all Java programming language keywords and correctly constructed identifiers.
- State the effect of using a variable or array element of any kind when no explicit assignment has been made to it.
- State the range of all primitive data types and declare literal values for String and all primitive types using all permitted formats, bases, and representations.

Study notes

The structure of a Java source file, containing declarations of package and import statements, interfaces and classes, follows certain rules. Classes, interfaces, methods and variables can be defined within several contexts, and the contexts influence the meaning of the declaration and the modifiers applicable. The modifiers used also influence the restrictions that apply for the implementation of methods. Certain rules of consistency must be observed when extending classes, and when extending or implementing interfaces. Variables can be shadowed by extending classes, methods can be overridden by extending classes. Methods are distinguished from each other at compile time, based on the method signature.

A method with the signature `public static void main(String args[])` serves as the entry point for executing applications. The parameter in the `main()` method corresponds to the program arguments given on the command line.

It is important to know all the keywords in the Java language, and to be able to identify valid identifiers.

Each primitive data type has a range of valid values and has a default value. Depending on the context of the declaration, some variables are either initialized to a default value or remain uninitialized, until first assigned a value. Code that tries to access uninitialized variables is illegal. Elements of array objects are always initialized. Various notations are used to specify literals.

Section 5: Operators and Assignments (Chapter 3)

- Determine the result of applying any operator, including assignment operators and instanceof, to operands of any type, class, scope, or accessibility, or any combination of these.
- Determine the result of applying the boolean equals(Object) method to objects of any combination of the classes java.lang.String, java.lang.Boolean, and java.lang.Object.
- In an expression involving the operators &, |, &&, | |, and variables of known values state which operands are evaluated and the value of the expression.
- Determine the effect upon objects and primitive values of passing variables into methods and performing assignments or other modifying operations in that method.

Study notes

Operators require operands of certain types. The operands used with an operator influence which conversions can occur, and determine the type of the resulting expression. Some operators, such as +, can be applied to non-numeric values. Some operators are related, such as >> and >>>, | and ||, and & and &&, but their behavior is different.

There are several forms of conversions, and all except for casts happen implicitly depending on the context. The key to casting and conversion is to know the rules for widening numeric promotion, narrowing conversion, and conversion of references up and down the inheritance hierarchy (up and down conversions). The `instanceof` operator returns `true` if an object can be cast to the given class type.

In addition to the == operator, objects have the `equals()` method which can be used to compare objects. The == operator and the default `equals()` method consider every object to be unique. Classes can provide implementations of the `equals()` method that are less discriminatory.

Some operators exhibit short-circuit behavior, which means that some operands may never be evaluated.

Parameters are passed by value. Methods get their own copy of the argument values. This holds for values of primitive data types, as well as for reference values denoting objects. Objects themselves are not passed as arguments.

Section 6: Overloading Overriding Runtime Type and Object Orientation (Chapter 6)

- State the benefits of encapsulation in object oriented design and write code that implements tightly encapsulated classes and the relationships "is a" and "has a".
- Write code to invoke overridden or overloaded methods and parental or overloaded constructors; and describe the effect of invoking these methods.

- Write code to construct instances of any concrete class including normal top level classes, inner classes, static inner classes, and anonymous inner classes.

Study notes

Is-a relationships are implemented through inheritance; *has-a* relationships are implemented through aggregation. Subclass instances may take on the role of superclass instances, but not vice versa. Encapsulation in object-oriented design places the focus on an object's contract, and safely hides its implementation from clients.

Pay attention to which casts are allowed between superclasses and subclasses at compile time, and the effect of casts at runtime. Polymorphism is the result of dynamic method binding of overridden methods at runtime, and the binding is based on the actual type of the object, not the type of the reference. It is illegal for overriding methods to contradict the declaration of the overridden methods. Overloaded methods are distinct methods not subject to dynamic method binding. The ability to overload method names is purely a result of methods being identified by the full signature, rather than just by the method name.

Special language constructs allow explicit access to variables and methods in superclasses and in enclosing contexts. Shadowed variables can be accessed, and overriding methods may call the overridden versions of the methods.

Interface and class definitions can be nested. The exact nature of such definitions and the restrictions placed on the definitions depend on the declaration context. Instances of some nested classes are associated with an outer instance. It is important to understand the correlation between an instance of an inner class and the outer class, and what can be accessed from within an inner class and how. There are several ways of declaring nested classes, and this affects the correlation between an instance of an inner class and its outer class.

Section 7: Threads (Chapter 9)

- Write code to define, instantiate, and start new threads using both java.lang. Thread and java.lang.Runnable.
- Recognize conditions that might prevent a thread from executing.
- Write code using synchronized, wait, notify, and notifyAll to protect against concurrent access problems and to communicate between threads. Define the interaction between threads and between threads and object locks when executing synchronized wait notify or notifyAll.

Study notes

Both `java.lang.Thread` and `java.lang.Runnable` can be used to create new threads. A thread can exist in one of several states. Various method calls and events may cause a thread to go from one state to another. Several conditions may prevent a thread from executing.

Most questions related to thread control concern using and implementing threads (through the `Thread` class or `Runnable` interface) and the use of the `notify()` and `wait()` methods. A good understanding of monitors and synchronized code is required. Note the difference between the `notify()` and `notifyAll()` methods.

Section 8: The java.awt package – Layout (Chapter 13)

- Write code using component, container, and layout manager classes of the java.awt package to present a GUI with specified appearance and resize behavior, and distinguish the responsibilities of layout managers from those of containers.
- Write code to implement listener classes and methods, and in listener methods, extract information from the event to determine the affected component, mouse position, nature, and time of the event. State the event classname for any specified event listener interface in the `java.awt.event` package.

Study notes

The JFC, including AWT and Swing, use the event delegation model. Classes wishing to receive notification of events implement listener interfaces and are registered with event sources. The event sources notify the listeners through the methods defined by the listener interfaces. The `java.awt.event` package contains event classes and corresponding listener interfaces that are used by both the AWT and Swing component sets.

AWT- and Swing-based applications can use layout managers associated with containers to create GUIs with specific component layout and resizing behavior. Pay attention to which kinds of layout constraints the layout managers such as `GridBagLayout` use, and how layout managers affect the size of components in a container when the container is resized.

Section 9: The java.lang package (Chapter 10)

- Write code using the following methods of the java.lang.Math class: abs, ceil, floor, max, min, random, round, sin, cos, tan, sqrt.
- Describe the significance of the immutability of String objects.

Study notes

The `java.lang.Math` class defines many useful mathematical functions, whose purpose should be understood. Argument type, result type, and the effect of applying each of these functions should be known.

Strings are immutable objects, i.e. their contents cannot be changed in any way. String manipulation operations in the `String` class return new `String` objects as the result of the operation. The indexing of characters used by string operations is important.

`StringBuffer` implements a mutable sequence of characters. Most string buffer operations manipulate the character sequence directly. There is no inheritance relationship between the classes `String` and `StringBuffer`, and objects of these classes cannot be compared directly.

Section 10: The java.util package (Chapter 11)

- Make appropriate selection of collection classes/interfaces to suit specified behavior requirements.

Study notes

The collections framework consists of various interfaces, concrete implementations of collections and utility classes. Familiarity with the methods defined by the interfaces is required. Some collection interfaces are better suited for certain types of information. Knowledge of which collection implementation is best suited for a particular situation is important.

Section 11: The java.io package (Chapter 18)

- Write code that uses objects of the `File` class to navigate a file system.
- Write code that uses objects of the classes `InputStreamReader` and `OutputStreamWriter` to translate between Unicode and either platform default or ISO 8859-1 character encodings.
- Distinguish between conditions under which platform default encoding conversion should be used and conditions under which a specific conversion should be used.
- Select valid constructor arguments for `FilterInputStream` and `FilterOutputStream` subclasses from a list of classes in the `java.io` package.
- Write appropriate code to read, write and update files using `FileInputStream`, `FileOutputStream`, and `RandomAccessFile` objects.
- Describe the permanent effects on the file system of constructing and using `FileInputStream`, `FileOutputStream`, and `RandomAccessFile` objects.

Study notes

Navigation in the file system is done using the `File` class. The concept of a stream is central to dealing with input and output.

Input and output streams are provided for reading and writing bytes and characters. Classes `FileInputStream` and `FileOutputStream` are streams for dealing with the file content. Class `RandomAccessFile` allows direct access to the file content as opposed to sequential access provided by `FileInputStream` and `FileOutputStream`. Readers and writers are provided for reading from and writing characters to streams. Classes `InputStreamReader` and `OutputStreamWriter` can be used to specify a character encoding when reading from and writing characters to a stream. Streams can be chained to filters (subclasses of `FilterInputStream` and `FilterOutputStream`) to provide additional functionality (for example buffering of data, reading and writing Java primitive values).

Appendix C

Annotated Answers to Review Questions

1 Basics of Java programming

1.1 *(d)*

A method is an operation defining the behavior for a particular abstraction. Java implements abstractions using classes that have properties and behavior. Behavior is dictated by the operations of the abstraction. In Java the operations are defined in classes using methods.

1.2 *(b)*

An object is an instance of a class. Objects are created from class definitions that implement abstractions. The objects that are created are concrete realizations of those abstractions.

1.3 *(b)*

The code marked with (2) is a constructor. A constructor in Java is declared like a method, except that the name is identical to the class name and it does not specify a return value.

1.4 *(b) and (f)*

Two objects and three reference variables are created by the code. Objects are typically created by using the `new` operator. A declared reference variable exists regardless of whether a reference value (i.e. an object handle) has been assigned to it or not.

1.5 *(d)*

An instance member belongs to a single instance, not the class as a whole. An instance member is a member variable or a member method that belongs to a specific object instance. All non-static members are instance members.

1.6 *(c)*

An object can pass a message to another object by calling an instance method of the other object.

1.7 *(d)*

Class B is a subclass of class A. Given the declaration "class B extends A" we can conclude that class B extends class A, class A is the superclass of class B, class B is a subclass of class A, and class B inherits from class A, which means that objects of class B also have all the members that objects of class A have.

1.8 *(d)*

The compiler supplied with the JDK is named javac. It requires the names of the source files that should be compiled.

1.9 *(a)*

Java programs need a runtime environment to run. In the JDK, the command java provides this runtime environment. The command java will start the program by calling the main() method of a given class. The command java requires the name of a class that has a valid main() method as an argument. The exact name of the class should be given, not the name of the class file.

2 Language Fundamentals

2.1 *(c)*

52pickup is not a legal identifier. The first character of an identifier cannot be a digit.

2.2 *(e)*

In Java delete, thrown, exit, unsigned and next are not keywords. Java has a goto keyword, but it is reserved and not currently used.

2.3 *(b)*

It is a completely valid comment. Comments do not nest. Everything from the start marker of a comment block (/*) until the first occurrence of the end marker of the comment block (*/) is ignored by the compiler.

2.4 *(a) and (d)*

String is a class, and "hello" and "t" denote String objects. Java has only the following primitive data types: boolean, byte, short, char, int, long, float and double.

2.5 *(a), (b) and (c)*

All are valid declarations. The \u*xxxx* notation can be used anywhere in the source to represent Unicode characters.

2.6 *(c)*

The bit representation of int is 32 bits wide and can hold values in the range -2^{31} through $2^{31}-1$.

2.7 *(c)*

Variable a is declared but not initialized. The first line of code declares the variables a and b. The second line of code initializes the variable b. Variable a remains uninitialized.

2.8 *(c)*

The local float variable will remain uninitialized. Instance variables and static variables receive a default value unless explicitly initialized. Local variables remain uninitialized unless explicitly initialized. The type of the variable does not affect whether a variable is initialized or not.

2.9 *(c)*

The class will fail to compile, since the package declaration can never occur after an import statement. The package and import statements, if present, must always precede any class definitions. If a file contains both import statements and a package statement, then the package statement must occur before the import statements.

2.10 *yes*

Although nonsensical, an empty file is a valid source file. A source file can contain an optional package declaration, any number of import statements and any number of class and interface definitions.

2.11 *(d)*

A valid declaration of the main() method must be public and static, have void as return type and take a single array of String objects as arguments. The order of the static and public keywords is irrelevant. Also, declaring the method final does not affect the method's potential to be used as a main() method.

3 Operators and Assignments

3.1 *(a)*

A value of type char can be assigned directly to a variable of type int. An implicit widening conversion will convert the value to int.

3.2 *(d)*

An assignment statement is also an expression. The value of the expression is the value being assigned. The statement "a = b = c = 20;" states that the value 20 should be assigned to variable c, then the same value should be assigned to variable b and finally to variable a. The program will compile correctly and display 20 when run.

3.3 *(c)*

Strings are objects. The variables a, b and c contain references that can denote such objects. Assigning to a reference only changes the reference value, not the object pointed to by the previous reference value. In other words, assignment to references only affects which object the reference denotes, not the contents of the object. The reference value to the "cat" object is first assigned to variable a, then the reference value is copied to variable b and later to variable c. The string "cat" is printed using the reference value in variable c.

3.4 *(d)*

0x10 is a hexadecimal literal equivalent to the decimal value 16. 10 is a decimal literal. 010 is an octal literal equivalent to the decimal value 8. The println() method will print the sum of these values, which is 34, in decimal form.

3.5 *(b)*

The expression evaluates to –6. The sub-expressions are grouped as (- -1) - (3*10/5) - 1 according to the precedence rules, and the whole expression is parsed as ((-(-1)) - ((3 * 10) / 5)) - 1 according to the associativity rules.

3.6 *(a), (c) and (d)*

The left associativity of the + operator makes the evaluation of (1 + 2 + "3") proceed as follows: (1 + 2) + "3" → 3 + "3" → "33". Evaluation of the expression ("1" + 2 + 3), however, will proceed as follows: ("1" + 2) + 3 → "12" + 3 → "123". (4 + 1.0f) evaluates as 4.0f + 1.0f → 5.0f and (10/9) performs integer division, resulting in the value 1. Both operands in the expression ('a' + 1) will be promoted to int and the resulting value will be of type int.

3.7 *(d)*

The expression "++k + k++ + + k" is parsed as ((++k) + (k++)) + (+k) → ((2) + (2) + (3)), therefore the program prints 7 when run.

3.8 *(d)*

The types char and int are both integral. A char value can be assigned to an int variable, since the int type is wider than the char type and an implicit widening conversion will be done. An int type cannot be assigned to a char variable since the char type is narrower than the int type. The compiler will therefore report an error on the line labeled (4).

3.9 *(b)*

Variables of type byte can store values in the range –128 to 127. The right side expression of the first assignment is the constant value –128 of type int. Since the value is a constant and the constant value will fit in the byte variable, an implicit narrowing conversion will be done during assignment. The variable b now contains the value –128. The right side of the next assignment is of type byte, while the target variable on the left side is of type int. Since int is wider than byte, an implicit widening conversion is done on assignment. The variable i now contains the value –128. Since all the assignments are valid, the program will compile correctly and will print –128 when run.

3.10 *(a), (b), (d) and (e)*

The expression (a) is valid, since an implicit narrowing conversion converts the constant `int` value of 12 to the corresponding `short` value upon assignment. The expressions (b), (d) and (e) are valid, since the type being assigned is narrower than the target type and an implicit widening conversion will be applied. The expression (c) is not valid. Values of type `boolean` cannot be converted to other types.

3.11 *(b) and (f)*

The method `test()` will print out its second argument if the results of performing a signed and an unsigned 1-bit right shift on its first argument differ. The only difference between these operations is that when performing a signed shift, the leftmost bit of the bit representation of the value will retain its state, rather than being assigned bit value 0. The operational difference will therefore only be apparent when applied on values where the bit value of the leftmost bit of the bit representation is 1. Of the values being fed to the test method, only `1<<31` and `-1` have the leftmost bit set.

3.12 *(b)*

Java has the operators >> and >>> to perform signed and unsigned right shifts. For left shifts there is no difference between shifting signed and unsigned values. Java therefore only has one left shift operator, which is <<. <<< is not an operator in Java.

3.13 *(c) and (e)*

The modulus operator is not limited to integer values, but can also be used on floating point operands. Identifiers in Java are case-sensitive. Operators *, / and % have the same level of precedence. `(+15)` is a legal expression using the unary + operator.

3.14 *(b), (c), (d) and (e)*

All the expressions will return the same result. All expressions will accommodate negative values, and `x` can be any value of type `int`. However, expression (a) will not assign the result back to the variable `x`.

3.15 *(b), (c) and (e)*

All the values of the expressions on the right-hand side of the assignments are implicitly promoted to type `int`. For expression (b) this works, since the target type is also `int`. The extended assignment operators in expressions (c) and (e) ensure that an implicit narrowing conversion makes the result fit back in the target variable. Expressions (a) and (d) are simply invalid, since the type of expression on the right side of the assignment operator is not compatible with the type of the target variable on the left side.

3.16 *(b)*

The element referenced by `a[i]` is determined based on the current value of `i`, which is zero, i.e. the element `a[0]`. The expression `i = 9` will evaluate to the value

9, which will be assigned to the variable `i`. The value 9 is also assigned to the array element `a[0]`. After the execution of the statement, the variable `i` will contain the value 9, and the array `a` will contain the values 9 and 6. The program will print `9 9 6` when run.

3.17 *(c) and (d)*

Unlike the `&` and `|` operators, the `&&` and `||` operators short-circuit the evaluation of their operands if the result of the operation can be determined just based on the value of the first operand. The second operand of the `||` operator in the program is never evaluated because of short-circuiting. All the other operands in the program are evaluated. Variable `i` ends up with a value of 3 which is the first digit printed, and `j` ends up with a value of 1 which is the second digit printed.

3.18 *(d)*

The variables `a` and `b` are local variables that contain primitive values. When these variables are given as parameters to another method, the method receives copies of the primitive values of the variables. The original variables are unaffected by operations performed on the copies of the primitive values within the other method. The variable `bArr` contains a value which is a reference to an array object containing primitive values. When the variable is given as a parameter to another method, the method receives a copy of the reference value. Using this reference value, the method can manipulate the object that the reference value denotes. This allows the elements within the array object referenced by `bArr` to be affected by a call to `inc(bArr)`.

3.19 *(d)*

The length of the array passed to `main()` corresponds exactly to the number of command-line arguments given to the program. Unlike with some other languages, the element at index 0 does not contain the name of the program. The first argument given is retrieved using `args[0]`, and the last argument given is retrieved using `args[args.length-1]`.

4 Declarations and Access Control

4.1 *(d)*

Arrays in Java are objects. Each array object has a member variable named `length` that contains the size of the array.

4.2 *(a)*

Java allows arrays of length zero to be created. A common natural occurrence of an array of length zero is the array given as an argument to the `main()` method when a Java program is run without any program arguments.

4.3 *(c)*

The `[]` notation can be placed both before and after the variable name in an array declaration. Multidimensional arrays are created by creating arrays that can contain references to other arrays. The statement `new int[4][]` will create an array of length 4, which can contain references to arrays of `int` values. The statement `new int[4][4]` will create the same array, but will also create four arrays, each containing four `int` values. References to each of these arrays are stored in the first array. The statement `int[][4]` will not work, because the dimensions must be created from left to right.

4.4 *(b) and (e)*

The size of the array cannot be specified as in (b) and (e). The size of the array is given implicitly by the initialization code. The size of the array is never given during the declaration of an array reference. The size of an array is always associated with the array instance, not the array reference.

4.5 *(e)*

The array declaration is valid and will declare and initialize an array of length 20 containing `int` values. All the values of the array are initialized to their default value of 0. The `for` loop will print all the values of the array, i.e. it will print `0` twenty times.

4.6 *(e)*

The program will type "`no arguments`" and "`four arguments`" when called with 0 and 3 arguments respectively. When the program is called with no arguments, the `args` array will be of length zero. The program will in this case type "`no arguments`". When the program is called with three arguments, the `args` array will have length 3. Using the index 3 on the `numbers` array will retrieve the string `"four"`, because the start index is 0.

4.7 *(d)*

The program will print "`0 false 0 null`" when run. All the variables, including the array element, will be initialized to their default values. When concatenated with a string, the values are converted to their string representation. Notice that the `null` pointer is converted to the string `"null"` rather than throwing a `NullPointerException`.

4.8 *(b)*

Only the code labeled (2) is a valid method declaration. Methods need to specify a return type. If the method does not want to return a value, it should specify `void`. This excludes (4) and (5) from being valid method declarations. Methods need a list of zero or more comma-separated parameters delimited by `( )`. The keyword `void` is not a valid type for a parameter. This excludes (1) and (3) from being valid method declarations.

4.9 *(a), (b) and (e)*

Non-static methods have an implicit `this` object reference. The `this` reference is not a normal reference variable that can be changed in the way attempted by statement (c). The `this` reference can be used to refer to both object and class members within the current context. However, it cannot be used to refer to local variables in the way attempted by statement (d).

4.10 *(a) and (d)*

The first and third pairs of methods will compile correctly. The second pair of methods will not compile correctly, since their method signatures do not differ and the compiler has therefore no way of differentiating between the two methods. Note that return type and the names of the parameters are not a part of the method signatures. Both methods in the first pair are named `fly` and therefore overload this method name. The methods in pair three do not overload the method name `glide`, since only one method has that name. The method named `Glide` is distinct from the method named `glide`, as identifiers in Java are case-sensitive.

4.11 *(a)*

A constructor does not declare any return type, not even `void`. A constructor cannot be `final`, `static` or `abstract`.

4.12 *(b) and (e)*

A constructor can be declared `private`, but this means that this constructor can only be used directly within the class. Constructors need not initialize all the member variables of the class. A member variable will be assigned a default value if not explicitly initialized. A constructor is non-static, and as such it can access directly both the static and non-static members of the class.

4.13 *(c)*

A compilation error will be encountered at (3), since the class does not have a constructor accepting a single argument of type `int`. The declaration at (1) declares a method, not a constructor, since it has a return value. The method happens to have the same name as the class, but that is irrelevant. The class has an implicit default constructor since the class contains no constructor declarations. This allows the instantiation at (2) to work.

4.14 *(c) and (d)*

A class or interface name can be referred to by using either its fully qualified name or its simple name. Using the fully qualified name will always work, but in order to use the simple name it has to be imported. By importing `net.basemaster.*` all the type names from the package `net.basemaster` will be imported and can now be referred to using simple names. Importing `net.*` will not import the subpackage `basemaster`.

4.15 *(c)*

A class is uninstantiable if the class is declared `abstract`. The declaration of an abstract method cannot provide an implementation. The declaration of a non-abstract method must provide an implementation. If any method in a class is declared `abstract`, then the whole class must be declared `abstract`. Definition (d) is not valid, since it omits the `class` keyword.

4.16 *(e)*

A class can be extended unless it is declared `final`. While declaring a method `static` usually implies that it is also `final`, this is not true for classes. An inner class can be declared `static` and still be extended. Notice the distinction. For classes, `final` means it cannot be extended, while for methods, `final` means it cannot be overridden in a subclass. The `native` keyword can only be used on methods, not on classes and instance variables.

4.17 *(b) and (d)*

Member `j` is accessible to any class outside the package, and member `k` is accessible to subclasses of `MyClass` outside the package.

Variable `i` has package accessibility and is only accessible by classes inside the package. Variable `j` has public accessibility and is accessible from anywhere. Variable `k` has protected accessibility and is only accessible from subclasses. Whether the subclasses are within the same package is irrelevant. Variable `l` has private accessibility and is only accessible within its own class.

4.18 *(c)*

The default accessibility is more restrictive than protected, but less restrictive than private. Members with default accessibility are only accessible within the class itself and from classes in the same package. Protected members are in addition accessible from subclasses. Members with private accessibility are only accessible within the class itself.

4.19 *(b)*

A private member is only accessible by code from within the class of the member. A member has default accessibility, also known as package accessibility, if no access modifier has been given. The keyword `default` is not an access modifier, and its only use is as a label in a `switch` statement. Members with package accessibility are only accessible from classes in the same package. Subclasses outside the package cannot access members with default accessibility.

4.20 *(b) and (e)*

You cannot specify visibility of local variables. They are accessible only within the block in which they are declared.

Objects themselves do not have any visibility, only the references to the object. If no visibility modifier (`public`, `protected` or `private`) is given in the member declaration of a class, the member is only accessible to classes in the same package. A class does not have access to members of a superclass with default accessibility, unless both classes are in the same package. Inheritance has no consequence with respect to accessing members with default accessibility. Local variables cannot be declared `static` and cannot be given an accessibility modifier.

4.21 *(c)*

The line "`void k() { i++; }`" can be reinserted without introducing errors. Reinserting line (1) will cause the compilation to fail, since `MyOtherClass` will try to override a final method. Reinserting line (2) will fail since `MyOtherClass` will no longer have a default constructor. The `main()` method needs a constructor that takes zero arguments. Reinserting line (3) will work without any problems, but reinserting line (4) will fail, since the method will try to access a private member of the superclass.

4.22 *(f)*

An object reference is needed to access non-static members. Static methods do not have any implicit object reference `this` and must always supply an explicit object reference when referring to non-static members. The static method `main()` refers legally to the non-static method `func()` using the reference variable `ref`. Static members are accessible both from static and non-static methods without needing to supply an object reference.

4.23 *(c)*

Local variables can have the same name as member variables. The local variables will simply shadow the member variables with the same names. Declaration (4) defines a static method that tries to access a variable named a which is not locally declared. Since the method is static, this access will only be valid if variable `a` is declared `static` within the class. Therefore declarations (1) and (4) cannot occur in the same class definition, while declarations (2) and (4) can.

4.24 *(b)*

The keyword `this` can only be used in non-static methods. Only one instance of each static member variable of a class is created. This instance is shared among all the objects of the class. Local variables are only accessible within the local scope, regardless of whether the local scope is defined within a static method.

4.25 *(c)*

The variable `k` cannot be declared synchronized. Only methods can be declared synchronized.

4.26 *(c)*

The declaration "`abstract int t;`" is not legal. Keywords `static` and `final` are valid modifiers for both variable and method declarations within a class. The `transient` modifier is only valid for variables, and the modifiers `abstract` and `native` are only valid for methods.

4.27 *(a) and (c)*

Abstract classes can contain both final methods and non-abstract methods. Non-abstract classes cannot, however, contain abstract methods. Nor can abstract classes be final. Only methods can be declared `native`.

4.28 *(a)*

The `transient` keyword signifies that the variables should not be stored when objects are serialized. Constructors cannot be declared `abstract`. Elements in an uninitialized array object get the default value corresponding to the type of the elements. Whether the reference variable pointing to the array object is a local or a member variable does not matter. Abstract methods from a superclass need not be implemented by abstract subclasses.

5 Flow Control and Exception Handling

5.1 *(d)*

The program will display the letter `b` when run.The second `if`-statement is evaluated, since the boolean expression of the first `if`-statement is true. The `else`-block belongs to the second `if`-statement. Since the boolean expression of the second `if`-statement is false, the `if`-clause is skipped and the `else`-clause is executed.

5.2 *(a), (b) and (e)*

The boolean expression of an `if`-statement can contain anything, including method calls, as long as it evaluates to a value of type `boolean`. The expression `(a = b)` does not compare the variables `a` and `b`, but rather assigns the value of `b` to the variable `a`. The result of the expression is the value being assigned. Since `a` and `b` are `boolean` variables, the value returned by the expression is also `boolean`. This allows the expression to be used as the condition for an `if`-statement. An `if`-statement must always have an `if`-clause, but the `else`-clause is optional. The expression `if (false) ; else ;` is legal. In this case, both the `if`-clause and the `else`-clause are simply the empty statement.

5.3 *(f)*

There is nothing wrong with the code. The `case` and `default` labels do not need to be specified in any specific order. The use of the `break` keyword is not mandatory, and without it the control flow will simply fall through the labels of the `switch` statement.

5.4 *(a)*

The type of the `switch` expression must be either `byte`, `char`, `short` or `int`. This excludes (b) and (e). The type of the `case` labels must be assignable to the type of the `switch` expression. This excludes (c) and (d).

5.5 *(e)*

The loop body is executed twice and the program will print `3`. The first time the loop is executed, the variable `i` changes from 1 to 2 and the variable `b` changes from `false` to `true`. Then the loop condition is evaluated. Since `b` is `true`, the loop body is executed again. This time the variable `i` changes from 2 to 3 and the variable `b` changes from `true` to `false`. The loop condition is now evaluated again. Since `b` is now false, the loop terminates and the current value of `i` is printed.

5.6 *(b) and (e)*

Both the first and the second number printed will be `10`. Both the loop body and the increment expression will be executed exactly 10 times. Each execution of the loop body will be directly followed by an execution of the increment expression. Afterwards, the condition `j<10` is evaluated to see whether the loop body should be executed again.

5.7 *(c)*

Only (c) contains a valid `for` loop. The initializer in a `for` statement can contain either declarations or a list of statements, but not both as attempted in (a). The loop condition must be of type `boolean`. (b) tries to use an assignment (notice the use of `=` rather than `==`) as a loop condition, and is therefore not valid. The condition expression in the `for` loop (d) tries to use the uninitialized variable `i`, and the `for` loop in (e) is simply syntactically invalid.

5.8 *(f)*

The code will compile without error, but will never terminate when run. All the sections in the `for` header are optional and can be left blank. A blank condition expression is interpreted as always being `true`. Thus a `for` loop with a blank condition expression will never terminate, unless a `break` is encountered. The program will enter an infinite loop at (4).

5.9 *(b), (d) and (e)*

The condition expression in a `while` header is not optional. It is not possible to break out of an `if` statement. Notice that if the `if` statement had been placed within a labeled block, a `switch` statement or a loop construct, the usage of `break` would be valid.

5.10 *(a) and (d)*

"`i=1, j=0`" and "`i=2, j=1`" are part of the output. The variable `i` iterates through the values 0, 1 and 2 in the outer loop, while `j` toggles between the values 0 and 1 in the inner loop. If the values of `i` and `j` are equal, the printing of the values is skipped and the execution continues with the next iteration of the outer loop. The following can be deduced when the program is run: Variables `i` and `j` are both 0 and the execution continues with the next iteration of the outer loop. "`i=1, j=0`" is printed and the next iteration of the inner loop starts. Variables `i` and `j` are both 1 and the execution continues with the next iteration of the outer loop. "`i=2, j=0`" is printed and the next iteration of the inner loop starts. "`i=2, j=1`" is printed, `j` is incremented, `j < 2` fails and the inner loop ends. Variable `i` is incremented, `i < 3` fails and the outer loop ends.

5.11 *(b)*

The code will fail to compile, since the condition expression of the `if`-statement is not of type `boolean`. The condition expression of an `if`-statement must be of type `boolean`. The variable `i` is of type `int`. There is no implicit conversion from `int` to `boolean`.

5.12 *(d)*

Implementation (4) will correctly return the largest value. The `if` statement does not return any value and therefore cannot be used as in implementations (1) and (2). Implementation (3) is invalid, since neither the `switch` expression nor the `case` label values can be of type `boolean`.

5.13 *(c)*

As it stands, the program will compile correctly and will print "`3, 2`" when run. If the `break` is replaced with `continue`, the loop will perform all four iterations and will print "`4, 3`". If the `break` is replaced with `return`, the whole method will end when `i` equals 2, before anything is printed. If the `break` is simply removed, leaving the empty ; statement, the loop will complete all four iterations and will print "`4, 4`".

5.14 *(a) and (c)*

The block construct `{}` is a compound statement. The compound statement can contain zero or more arbitrary statements. Thus, `{{}}`, which is a compound statement containing one statement which is a compound statement containing no statement, is legal. `{ continue; }` by itself is not valid, since the `continue` statement cannot be used outside the context of a loop. (c) is a valid example of breaking out of a labeled block. (d) is not valid for the same reasons (b) was not valid. The statement at (e) is not true, since the `break` keyword can also be used to break out of labeled blocks, as illustrated by (c).

5.15 *(d)*

The program will print `1`, `4` and `5`, in that order. The expression `5/k` will throw an `ArithmeticExecption`, since `k` equals 0. Control is transferred to the first `catch` block, since it is the first block that can handle arithmetic exceptions. This exception handler simply prints `1`. The exception has now been caught and normal execution can resume. Before leaving the `try` statement, the `finally` block is executed. This block prints `4`. The last statement of the `main()` method prints `5`.

5.16 *(b) and (e)*

If run with one argument, the program will print the given argument followed by "The end". The `finally` block will always be executed, no matter how control leaves the `try` block.

5.17 *(d)*

The program will compile without error, but will throw a `java.lang.NullPointerException` when run. The `throw` statement can only throw throwable objects. A `NullPointerException` will be thrown if the expression given to the `throw` statement results in a `null` pointer.

5.18 *(c) and (d)*

Normal execution will not resume if an exception is uncaught by a method. The exception will propagate up the invocation stack until some method handles it. An overriding method need only declare that it can throw a subset of the exceptions the overridden method can throw. The `main()` method can declare that it throws checked exceptions just like any other method. The `finally` block will always be executed, no matter how control leaves the `try` block.

5.19 *(b)*

The program will print `1` and `4`, in that order. The `InterruptedException` is handled in the first `catch` block. Inside this block a new `RuntimeException` is thrown. This exception was not thrown inside the `try` block and will not be handled by the `catch` blocks, but will rather be sent to the caller of `main()`. Before this happens, the `finally` block is executed. The code printing `5` is never reached, since the `RuntimeException` remains uncaught after the execution of the `finally` block.

5.20 *(a)*

The program will print `2` and throw `InterruptedException`. An `InterruptedException` is thrown in the `try` block. No `catch` block will handle the exception, but it will rather be sent to the caller of `main()`. Before this happens, the `finally` block is executed. The code printing `3` is never reached.

5.21 *(b)*

The only thing that is wrong with the code is the ordering of the `catch` and `finally` blocks. If present, the `finally` block must always appear last in a `try-catch-finally` statement.

5.22 *(a)*

The overriding method `f()` does not have to specify any exception classes. Overriding methods only need to specify a subset of the exception classes the overridden method declares it can throw. A set of no classes is a valid subset of the classes `ArithmeticException` and `InterruptedException`.

5.23 *(c)*

The overriding `f()` method in `MyClass` is not allowed to throw `InterruptedException`, since the `f()` method in class `A` is not allowed to throw this exception. To avoid compilation errors, either the overriding `f()` must not throw `InterruptedException` or the overridden `f()` must declare that it can throw `InterruptedException`.

6 Object-oriented Programming

6.1 *(a), (b) and (c)*

The `extends` clause is used to specify that a class extends another class and thereby inherits all members of that class. A subclass can be declared `abstract` regardless of whether the superclass was declared `abstract`. A class cannot be declared both `abstract` and `final`, since `abstract` classes need to be subclasses to be useful and `final` forbids subclasses. The visibility of the class is not limited by the visibility of its members. A class with all the members declared `private` can still be declared `public`.

6.2 *(b) and (e)*

Inheritance defines an *is-a* relation. Aggregation defines a *has-a* relation. All Java objects have the class `Object` as a superclass, since `Object` is always at the root of the inheritance hierarchy. When a class is extended, all its members are inherited by the subclass. This means that every Java object has the members of the `Object` class. The `Object` class has a method named `equals()`, but does not have a method named `length()`. In Java, classes can only extend a single class, but there is no limit to how many classes can extend the same class.

6.3 *(b) and (c)*

Subclasses inherit all the members of the superclass and do not have to redefine all the methods that the superclass defines. It is possible for a subclass to define a member that will shadow a member defined in a superclass. The process of defining a method with the same signature and same return type as a method in a superclass is generally called method overriding.

6.4 *(a), (b) and (d)*

`Bar` is a legal subclass of `Foo` that overrides the method `g()`. The statement `a.j = 5` is not legal, since the member `j` in class `Bar` cannot be accessed through a `Foo` reference. The statement `b.i = 3` is not legal either, since the `private` member `i` cannot be accessed from outside of the class `Foo`.

6.5 *(a)*

A method can be overridden by defining a method with the same signature (i.e. name and parameter list) and return type as the method in a superclass. Only methods that are accessible can be overridden. A `private` method cannot therefore be overridden in subclasses, but the subclasses are allowed to define a new method with exactly the same signature. A `final` method cannot be overridden. An overriding method cannot exhibit behavior that contradicts the declaration of the original method. An overriding method therefore cannot return a different type or throw a wider spectrum of exceptions than the original method in the superclass.

6.6 *(g)*

It is not possible to invoke the `doIt()` method in `A` from an instance method in class `C`. The method in `C` needs to call a method in a superclass two levels up. The `super.super.doIt()` strategy will not work, since `super` is a keyword, not an attribute. If the member to be accessed had been an instance variable, the solution would be to cast the `this` reference to the class of the desired member and use the resulting reference to access the variable. Variable access is determined by the declared type of the reference, whereas the method to execute is determined by the actual type of the object denoted by the reference.

6.7 *(e)*

The code will compile without errors. None of the calls to a `max()` method are ambiguous. When the program is run, the `main()` method will call the `max()` method in `C` with the parameters `13` and `29`. This method will call the `max()` method in `B` with the parameters `23` and `39`. The `max()` method in `B` will in turn call the `max()` method in `A` with the parameters `39` and `23`. The `max()` method in `A` will return `39` to the `max()` method in `B`. The `max()` method in `B` will return `29` to the `max()` method in `C`. The `max()` method in `C` will return `29` to the `main()` method.

6.8 *(c)*

The simplest way to find and print the message text would be to use `System.out.println(msg.text)`. The `main()` method creates an instance of `MyClass` and calls `print()` on it. The instance has a member `msg` which is inherited from the superclass and can be accessed directly.

6.9 *(e)*

The class `MySuper` does not have a default constructor. This means that constructors in subclasses must explicitly call the superclass constructor to provide the required parameters. The existing constructor accomplishes this by calling `super(num)` in its first statement. Additional constructors can accomplish this either by calling the superclass constructor directly, or by calling another constructor in the same class which in turn will call the superclass constructor. (a) and (b) are not valid, since they fail to do either. (d) fails since the `super()` must always be the first statement in the constructor body. (f) fails since the `super()` and `this()` statements cannot be combined.

6.10 *(b)*

In a subclass without any declared constructors, the implicit default constructor will call `super()`. The use of the `super()` and `this()` statements are not mandatory as long as the superclass has a default constructor. If neither `super()` nor `this()` is declared as the first statement in the body of a constructor, then `super()` will implicitly be the first statement. A constructor body cannot have both a `super()` and a `this()` statement. Calling `super()` will not always work, since a superclass might not have only a default constructor.

6.11 *(d)*

The program will print 12 followed by Test. When the main() method is executed, it will create a new instance of B by giving "Test" as an argument. This results in a call to the constructor of class B that has one String parameter. The constructor does not explicitly call any superclass constructor, but instead the default constructor of the superclass A is called implicitly. The default constructor of class A calls the constructor in A that has two String parameters, giving it the arguments "1", "2". This constructor calls the constructor with one String parameter, passing the argument "12". This constructor prints the argument. Now the execution reaches the end of all the constructors in A, and control flow continues in the constructor in B. This constructor now prints the original argument "Test" and returns to the main() method.

6.12 *(b) and (c)*

Interfaces do not contain any implementations and only permit multiple interface inheritance. An interface can extend any number of other interfaces and can be extended by any number of other interfaces. Variables in interfaces are always static and method prototypes in interfaces can never be static.

6.13 *(a), (b), (c), (d) and (e)*

All the declarations are equivalent. Interfaces cannot have instance variables, since they do not define a concrete class. Interfaces can, however, define constants by defining variables that are final and static. All variables in interfaces are therefore implicitly static and final. In addition, all declarations in interfaces are implicitly public.

6.14 *(a) and (d)*

The keyword implements is used when a class inherits method prototypes from an interface. The keyword extends is used when an interface inherits from another interface, or a class inherits from another class.

6.15 *(e)*

The code will compile without errors. The class MyClass declares that it implements the interfaces Interface1 and Interface2. Since the class is declared abstract it does not need to supply implementations for all the method prototypes defined in those interfaces. Any non-abstract subclasses of MyClass must supply the missing method implementations. The two interfaces share a common method prototype void g(). MyClass provides an implementation for this prototype that satisfies both Interface1 and Interface2. Both interfaces provide declarations of constants named VAL_B. This leads to an ambiguity when simply referring to VAL_B from MyClass. The ambiguity can be avoided by using fully qualified names: Interface1.VAL_B and Interface2.VAL_B.

6.16 *(c)*

The program will throw a `java.lang.ClassCastException` at the line labeled (3) when run. The line labeled (1) will be allowed during compilation, since assignment is done from a subclass reference to a superclass reference. The line labeled (2) convinces the compiler that `arrA` will refer to an object that can be referenced by `arrB`, and this will work when run, since `arrA` will refer to an object of type `B[]`. The line labeled (3) also convinces the compiler that `arrA` will refer to an object that can be referenced by `arrB`. This will not work when run, since `arrA` will refer to an object of type `A[]`.

6.17 *(d)*

Line (4) will fail, since it attempts to assign a reference value of a supertype to a reference of a subtype. The type of the source reference value is `MyClass` and the type of the destination reference variable is `MySubclass`. Lines (1) and (2) will work, since the reference is assigned a reference value of the same type. Line (3) will work, since the reference is assigned a reference value of a subtype.

6.18 *(e)*

Only the assignment `I1 b = obj3` is valid. The assignment is allowed since `C3` extends `C1` which implements `I1`. Assignment `obj2 = obj1` is not legal, since `C1` is not a subclass of `C2`. Assignments `obj3 = obj1` and `obj3 = obj2` are not legal, since neither `C1` nor `C2` is a subclass of `C3`. Assignment `I1 a = obj2` is not legal, since `C2` does not implement `I1`. Assignment `I2 c = obj1` is not legal, since `C1` does not implement `I2`.

6.19 *(b)*

The statement would be legal at compile time, since the reference in `x` might actually refer to an object of type `Sub`. The cast tells the compiler to go ahead and allow the assignment. At runtime the reference `x` may turn out to denote an object of type `Super` instead. If this happens, the assignment will be aborted and a `ClassCastException` will be thrown.

6.20 *(c)*

Only `A a = d` is legal. The reference value in `d` can be assigned to `a`, since `D` implements `A`. The statements `c = d` and `d = c` are illegal, since neither of the classes `C` and `D` is a subclass of the other. Even though a cast is provided, the statement `d = (D) c` is illegal. The object referred to by `c` cannot possibly be of type `D`, since `D` is not a subclass of `C`. The statement `c = b` is illegal, since assigning a reference value from a reference of type `B` to a reference of type `C` requires a cast.

6.21 *(a), (b) and (c)*

The program will print `A`, `B` and `C` when run. The object denoted by reference `a` is of type `C`. The object is also an instance of `A` and `B`, since `C` is a subclass of `B` and `B` is a subclass of `A`. The object is not an instance of `D`.

6.22 *(b)*

The expression `(o instanceof B)` will return `true` if the object referred to by `o` is of type `B` or a subtype of `B`. The expression `(!(o instance of C))` will return `true` unless the object referred to by `o` is of type `C` or a subtype of `C`. Thus, the expression `(o instanceof B) && (!(o instanceof C))` will only return `true` if the object is of type `B` or a subtype of `B` that is not `C` or a subtype of `C`. Given objects of classes `A`, `B` and `C`, this expression will only return true for objects of class `B`.

6.23 *(a), (b), (c) and (d)*

The program will print all of `I`, `J`, `C` and `D` when run. The object referred to by reference `x` is of class `D`. Class `D` extends class `C` and class `C` implements interface `I`. This makes `I`, `J` and `C` supertypes of class `D`. A reference of type `D` can be cast to any of its supertypes, and is therefore an `instanceof` these types.

6.24 *(e)*

The program will print `2` when `System.out.println(ref2.f())` is executed. The object referenced by `ref2` is of class `C`, but the reference is of type `B`. Since `B` contains a method `f()`, the method call will be allowed at compile time. During execution it is determined that the object is of class `C`, and dynamic method lookup will cause `C`'s version of the overridden method to be executed.

6.25 *(c)*

The program will print `1` when run. The `f()` methods in `A` and `B` are `private` and are not accessible by the subclasses. Because of this, the subclasses cannot overload or override these methods, but simply define new methods with the same signature. The object being called is of class `C`. The reference used to access the object is of type `B`. Since `B` contains a method `g()`, the method call will be allowed at compile time. During execution it is determined that the object is of class `C`, and dynamic method lookup will cause `B`'s version of the overridden method to be called. This method calls a method named `f()`. It can be determined during compilation that this can only refer to the `f()` method in `B`, since the method is `private` and cannot be overridden.

6.26 *(c) and (d)*

The code as it stands will compile without error. The use of inheritance in this code is not justifiable, since conceptually, a planet *is-not-a* star. The code will fail if the name of the member `starName` is changed in the `Star` class, since the class `Planet` tries to access it using the name `starName`. An instance of `Planet` is not an instance of `HeavenlyBody`; neither `Planet` nor `Star` implements `HeavenlyBody`.

6.27 *(b)*

The code will compile without error. The use of aggregation in this code is justifiable. The code will not fail if the name of the member `starName` is changed in the `Star` class, since the `Planet` class does not try to access the member by name, but rather uses the public interface. An instance of `Planet` is not an instance of

HeavenlyBody, since it does not implement HeavenlyBody, nor does it extend a class that implements HeavenlyBody.

7 Inner Classes

7.1 *(e)*

The code will compile without error and will print 123 when run. An instance of Outer will be created and the variable secret will be initialized to 123. A call to createInner() will return a reference to a newly created Inner instance. This object is an instance of a non-static inner class and is associated with the outer instance. This means that an object of an inner class has access to the members within the outer instance. Since the inner class is within the class containing the member secret, the member will be accessible to the inner instance, even though secret is declared private.

7.2 *(b) and (e)*

A top-level nested class is in most respects, aside from the nesting, the same as a package member class, and can contain non-static member variables. Instances of non-static inner classes are created in the context of an outer instance. The outer instance is inherently associated with the inner instance. Several inner class instances can be created and associated with the same outer instance. Static classes do not have any inherent outer instance. A top-level nested interface, just like package member interfaces, cannot contain non-static member variables. Nested interfaces are always static. A non-static nested interface does not exist.

7.3 *(e)*

The code will fail to compile, since the Memento method restore() tries an invalid access through the ((State) this).val expression. The correct way to access the member val in State, which is shadowed by the val member in Memento, is to use the expression State.this.val. Other than that, there are no problems with the code.

7.4 *(d)*

The program will compile without error, and will print 1, 3, 4 in that order when run. The expression B.this.val will access the 1 stored in the variable from the outer instance of obj. The expression C.this.val will access the 3 stored in the variable defined in class C from obj. The expression super.val will access the variable from A, the superclass of C.

7.5 *(e)*

Non-static inner classes, unlike normal package members, can have any type of accessibility. Inner classes can only contain non-static members and therefore cannot contain top-level nested classes and static methods. Only top-level nested classes can be declared static. Declaring a class static only means that instances of the class are created without having an outer instance. It does not put any limits on whether the members of the class can be static or not.

7.6 *(d) and (e)*

The (1) and (3) methods will fail, since the non-final parameter `i` is not accessible from within the inner class. The syntax in (2) is illegal, since the parameter list for the anonymous class is missing.

7.7 *(a) and (d)*

Non-static inner classes cannot contain static members. Anonymous classes cannot have constructors, since they have no names. Members in outer instances are directly accessible using simple names. There is no restriction that member variables in inner classes must be `final`. Nested classes define distinct types from the enclosing class, and the `instanceof` operator does not take the type of the outer instance into consideration.

7.8 *(b)*

Only classes declared as members of top-level classes can be declared `static`. Such a member is a top-level nested class if it is declared `static`, otherwise it is a non-static inner class. Package member classes, local classes and anonymous classes cannot be declared `static`.

8 Object Lifetime

8.1 *(e)*

An object is only eligible for garbage collection if the only references to the object are from other objects that are also eligible for garbage collection. Therefore, if an object `obj2` is eligible for garbage collection and object `obj1` contains a reference to it, then object obj1 must also be eligible for garbage collection. Java does not have a keyword named `delete`. An object will not necessarily be garbage collected immediately after the last reference to the object has been removed. The object will, however, be eligible for garbage collection. Circular references do not prevent objects from being garbage collected. An object is not eligible for garbage collection as long as the object can be reached from the active part of the program. An object that has been eligible for garbage collection may stop being eligible and return to normal life. This occurs if the call to the `finalize()` method re-establishes a reference from the active part of the program to the object.

8.2 *(b)*

Before (1) the string initially referenced with `arg1` is denoted by both `msg` and `arg1`. After (1) the string is only denoted by `msg`. At (2), reference `msg` is assigned a new reference value. The new reference value is denoting a `String` object created by concatenating several other `String` objects. After (2) there are no references to the string initially referenced with `arg1`. The `String` object is now eligible for garbage collection.

8.3 *(b)*

The `Object` class contains a `finalize()` method. All classes inherit from `Object`, thus all objects have a `finalize()` method. Classes can override the `finalize()` method and, as with all overriding, the new method must not reduce the accessibility. The `finalize()` method is called by the garbage collector to allow an object to clean up, before destroying it. Normal exception handling occurs when an exception is encountered during execution of the `finalize()` method, i.e. exceptions are not simply ignored. When the garbage collector calls the `finalize()` method, it will catch and ignore any exceptions thrown by the method. Calling the `finalize()` method in itself does not destroy the object. Chaining of the `finalize()` methods is not enforced by the compiler and it is not mandatory to call the overridden `finalize()` method.

8.4 *(d)*

The `finalize()` method is like any other method, it can be called by anyone as long as it is accessible. However, the intended purpose of the method is to be called by the garbage collector in order to clean up before an object is destroyed. Overloading the `finalize()` method name is allowed, but only the method with the original `finalize()` signature will be called by the garbage collector. The new declaration cannot contradict the old declaration. The `finalize()` method in `Object` is protected. This means that overriding methods can be either `protected` or `public`. The `finalize()` method in `Object` can throw any throwable `Object`. Overriding methods can limit the range of throwable to unchecked exceptions. Further overridden definitions of this method in subclasses will not be able to throw checked exceptions.

8.5 *(b)*

The `finalize()` method will never be called more than once on an object, even if the `finalize()` method resurrects the object. An object can be eligible for garbage collection even if there are references pointing to the object, as long as the objects with the references are also eligible for garbage collection. There is no guarantee that the garbage collector will destroy an eligible object before the program ends. The order in which the objects are destroyed is not guaranteed. The `finalize()` method can make an object that has been eligible for garbage collection become accessible again from the active part of the program.

8.6 *(c), (e) and (f)*

Static initializers (a) and (b) are not legal, since members `alive` and `STEP` are non-static and `final`, respectively. (d) is not legal, since a static initializer must consist of a block.

8.7 *(c)*

The program will compile without error and will print `50, 70, 0, 20, 0` when run. All member variables are initialized to default values unless they are explicitly initialized. Member `i` is assigned the value 50 in a static initializer which is executed the first time the class is used. This assignment will override the explicit initialization of the variable. Members `j` and `l` are assigned values in an instance initializer which is executed immediately before the constructor body is executed. When the `main()` method is executed, the variable `i` is 50 and variable `l` is 0. There are no `j` and `k` variables, since these are instance members and no instances of the class have been created. The value 0 is passed to the constructor. Before the body of the constructor is executed, the instance initializer is executed and assigns values 70 and 20 to variables `j` and `l`, respectively.

8.8 *(f)*

This class has a final blank `boolean` variable `active`. This variable must be initialized when an instance is constructed, or else the code will fail to compile. The keyword `static` is used to signify that a block is a static initializer. No keyword is used to signify that a block is an instance initializer. (a) and (b) are not instance initializers, and (c), (d) and (e) fail to initialize the final blank variable `active`.

8.9 *(a)*

The code will fail to compile, since an instance initializer cannot make forward references to member variables declared after the initializer.

8.10 *(e)*

The program will compile without error and will print `1`, `3` and `2`, in that order. First the static initializers are executed when the class is initialized, printing `1` and `3`. When the object is created and initialized, the instance initializer is executed, printing `2`.

9 Threads

9.1 *(c)*

Create a new thread and call the method `start()` on it. The call to `start()` will return immediately, and the thread will start executing the `run()` method asynchronously.

9.2 *(c)*

The `run()` method should be overridden to provide the code executed by the thread, when extending the `Thread` class. This is analogous to implementing the `run()` method of the `Runnable` interface.

9.3 *(b) and (e)*

The `Thread` class implements the `Runnable` interface and is not abstract. A program terminates when the last non-daemon thread ends. The `Runnable` interface has a method prototype named `run()`, but the interface does not dictate that implementations must define a method called `start()`. `Runnable` is just an interface, and `run()` is just a method. Calling `run()` will not produce a new thread. Instances of the `Thread` class must be created to spawn new threads.

9.4 *(e)*

The program will compile correctly and will simply terminate without any output when run. Two thread objects will be created, but they will never be started. The `start()` method must be called on the thread objects to make the threads execute the `run()` method asynchronously.

9.5 *(a)*

No two threads can ever simultaneously execute synchronized methods on the same object. This does not prevent one thread from executing a non-synchronized method while another thread executes a synchronized method on the same object. Java's synchronization mechanism acts like recursive semaphores, which means that during the time a thread owns the monitor it may enter and re-enter all regions of code requiring the monitor.

9.6 *(b)*

One cannot be certain whether any of the letters `i`, `j` and `k` will be printed during execution. For each invocation of `doit()`, each variable pair is incremented and their values are always equal when the method returns. The only way a letter could be printed would be if the method `check()` was executed between the time the first and the second variable was incremented. Since the `check()` method does not depend on owning any monitor, it can be executed at any time, and the method `doit()` cannot protect the atomic nature of its operations by acquiring monitors.

9.7 *(d)*

A thread dies when the `run()` method, invoked asynchronously by a call to `start()`, ends. The call to `start()` returns immediately. Calling the `sleep()` or `wait()` methods will only block the thread temporarily.

9.8 *(e)*

The exact behavior of the scheduler is not defined. There is no guarantee that a call to the `yield()` method will grant other threads use of the CPU.

9.9 *(b)*

The `notify()` method is defined in the `Object` class.

9.10 *(b)*

Calling the `notify()` method on an object implementing `Runnable` will cause a thread that called the `wait()` method while owning the monitor of the object to be enabled for running. At most one thread is enabled for running. The fact that the object implements `Runnable` is inconsequential. The `notifyAll()` method will enable all such threads for running.

9.11 *(a)*

The priority of a thread is set by calling the `setPriority()` method in the `Thread` class. No `Thread` constructor accepts a priority level as an argument.

9.12 *(d)*

An `IllegalMonitorStateException` will be thrown if the current thread does not have the monitor of the object. Since the method itself does not ensure that the thread owns the monitor, an `IllegalMonitorStateException` will be thrown, if the current thread does not own the monitor before the method is called.

9.13 *(a), (b), (c) and (d)*

Note that only methods and code blocks can be specified as synchronized. Variables cannot be declared as synchronized. Code blocks can be synchronized on any object.

10 Fundamental Classes

10.1 *(b)*

The method `hashCode()` in the `Object` class returns a hash code value of type `int`.

10.2 *(e)*

All array objects are genuine objects and have all the methods defined in the `Object` class, including the `clone()` method. Neither of the methods `hashCode()` and `equals()` is declared `final` in the `Object()` class, and it cannot be guaranteed that implementations of these methods will discriminate between all objects.

10.3 *(a)*

The `wait()` method of the `Object` class will throw `InterruptedException` if it is interrupted by another thread.

10.4 *(a), (c) and (d)*

There is no class named `java.lang.Int`, but there is a wrapper class named `java.lang.Integer`. A class named `java.lang.String` also exists, but it is not a wrapper class since all strings in Java are objects.

10.5 *(c) and (d)*

Classes `Character` and `Boolean` are non-numeric wrapper classes and they do not extend the `Number` class. Classes `Float`, `Byte` and `Short` are numeric wrapper classes and they do extend the `Number` class.

10.6 *(a), (b), (c) and (d)*

All instances of wrapper classes are immutable.

10.7 *(b) and (d)*

The lines labeled (2) and (4) will print exactly `11`, since their expressions return the value 11 as an integral type. The expression `Math.ceil(v)` will also return the value 11, but it will be printed as `11.0` since it is of type `double`. The other lines will round the value down to 10.

10.8 *(a)*

The `Math` class does not have a method named `tan2`. However, it does have a method named `atan2`, which converts rectangular coordinates to polar coordinates.

10.9 *(a)*

The method `round(float)` will return a value of type `int`. A `round(double)` method also exists, which returns a value of type `long`.

10.10 *(c)*

The rounding function `ceil()` will return a value of type `double`. This is in contrast to the `round()` methods which will return values of integral type.

10.11 *(b) and (e)*

The operators `-` and `&` cannot be used in conjunction with a `String` object. The operators `+` and `+=` perform concatenation on strings, and the dot operator accesses members of the `String` object.

10.12 *(d)*

The expression `str.substring(2, 5)` will obtain the substring `"kap"`. The method extracts the characters from index 2 to index 4, inclusive.

10.13 *(d)*

The program will print `str3str1` when run. The `concat()` method will create and return a new `String` object, which is the concatenation of the current `String` object and the `String` object given as an argument. The statement `str1.concat(str2)` creates a new `String` object, but its reference is not stored anywhere.

10.14 *(c)*

The `trim()` method of the `String` class returns a string where both the leading and trailing white space of the original string have been removed.

10.15 *(c)*

The `String` class and all wrapper classes are declared `final` and cannot have subclasses. The `instanceof` operator does not accept objects as right-side operands. The method `clone()` is declared protected in `Object`. `String` objects are immutable and cannot be changed in any way.

10.16 *(a), (b), (c) and (d)*

All the expressions are legal. String literals are `String` objects and can be used just like any other object.

10.17 *(a), (c) and (d)*

The `String` class does not have a constructor that takes a single `int` as a parameter.

10.18 *(e)*

The `String` class has no `reverse()` method.

10.19 *(d)*

The expression `"abcdef".charAt(3)` evaluates to the character `'d'`. The `charAt()` method takes an `int` value as an argument and returns a `char` value. The index of the first character in a string is 0.

10.20 *(e)*

The expression `"Hello there".toLowerCase().equals("hello there")` will evaluate to `true`. The `equals()` method in `String` will only return `true` if the two strings have the same sequence of characters.

10.21 *(b)*

The code will fail to compile since `(s == sb)` is an illegal expression. The expression tries to compare two references and will fail, since neither `String` nor `StringBuffer` is a superclass of the other.

10.22 *(e)*

The program will compile without error and will print `have a` when run. The rest of the string buffer has been truncated.

10.23 *(a), (b) and (d)*

The `StringBuffer` class does not have a constructor that takes an array of `char` as a parameter.

10.24 *(a)*

The `StringBuffer` class has no `trim()` method.

11 Collections

11.1 *(a), (d) and (e)*

`Set`, `Collection` and `Map` are core interfaces in the collections framework. `LinkedList` is a class that implements the `List` interface. There is no class or interface named `Bag`.

11.2 *(b) and (e)*

The `java.util` package provides map implementations named `HashMap` and `TreeMap`. It does not provide any implementations named `HashList`, `ArraySet` and `ArrayMap`.

11.3 *(d)*

The `List` interface is implemented by collections that maintain sequences of possibly non-unique elements. Elements retain their ordering in the sequence. Collection classes implementing `SortedSet` maintain their elements sorted in the set.

11.4 *(a) and (c)*

Some operations may throw an `UnsupportedOperationException`. This exception type is unchecked, and code calling these operations is not required to explicitly handle exceptions of this type. The contract of the `List` interface allows duplicate elements. `ArrayList` is a resizable array implementation. The capacity of the array will be increased when needed. The `List` interface defines a `get()` method, but there is no method by that name in the `Collection` interface.

11.5 *(d)*

The program will compile without error and will print all primes below 25 when run. All the collection implementations used implement the `Collection` interface. The implementation instances are interchangeable when used through `Collection` references. None of the operations performed on the implementations will result in an `UnsupportedOperationException` being thrown. The program finds the primes below 25 by removing all values divisible by 2, 3 and 5 from the set of values from 2 through 25.

11.6 *(a), (b) and (d)*

The methods `add()`, `retainAll()` and `iterator()` are defined in the `Collection` interface. The `get()` and `indexOf()` methods are defined in the `List` interface.

11.7 *(b) and (d)*

The methods `add()` and `retainAll()` return the value `true` if the collection object was modified during the operation. The `contains()` and `containsAll()` methods return a `boolean` value, but these test operations never modify the collection, and the return value is the result of the test. The `clear()` method does not have a return value.

11.8 *(c)*

Of all the collection classes of the `java.util` package, only `Vector` and `HashTable` are thread-safe. The `Collections` class contains a `synchronizedCollection()` method that creates thread-safe instances based on collections which are not.

11.9 *(c) and (d)*

The `Map` interface defines the methods `remove()` and `values()`. It does not define methods `contains()`, `addAll()` and `toArray()`. Methods with these names are defined in the `Collection` interface, but `Map` does not inherit from `Collection`.

11.10 *(b) and (d)*

While all the keys in a map must be unique, multiple identical values may exist. Since values are not unique, the `values()` method returns a `Collection` instance and not a `Set` instance. The collection objects returned by the `keySet()`, `entrySet()` and `values()` methods are backed by the original `Map` object. This means that changes made in one are reflected in the other. While implementations of `SortedMap` keep the entries sorted, this is not a requirement for classes that implement `Map`. For instance, the `HashMap` implementation does not keep its entries sorted.

11.11 *(a)*

The sequence `1, 3, 2` is printed. First, `"1"` and `"2"` are appended to an empty list. Next, `"3"` is wedged between `"1"` and `"2"`, and then the list is duplicated and the original is concatenated with the copy. The sequence of elements in the list is now `"1", "3", "2", "1", "3", "2"`. Then a sublist view allowing access to elements from index 2 to index 5 (exclusive) is created (the elements `"2", "1", "3"`). The sublist is cleared, thus removing the elements. This is reflected in the original list and the sequence of elements is now `"1", "3", "2"`.

11.12 *(c) and (e)*

The implementations `TreeSet` and `TreeMap` implement the `comparator()` method. The `comparator()` method is defined in the `SortedSet` and `SortedMap` interfaces, and the `TreeSet` and `TreeMap` classes implement these interfaces.

12 AWT Components

12.1 *(a), (c) and (d)*

The bounds of a component are comprised of the location and dimensions of the component. The `Component` class does not have any methods named `setDimensions()` or `setPosition()`.

12.2 *(a)*

The method `setVisible()` is defined in the class `Component`, which means that all component classes have this method.

12.3 *(a)*

The line labeled (1) could have been omitted from the code without changing the effect of the program. The line is unnecessary, since only top-level components need to have their visibility set explicitly.

12.4 *(c)*

The `pack()` method is defined in the `Window` class. This means that subclasses such as `Dialog` and `Frame` have this method.

12.5 *(a)*

The program will fail to compile, since the `Dialog` class does not have an appropriate constructor. All constructors in `Dialog` require an *owner* parameter that is either a `Frame` or another `Dialog` object.

12.6 *(d)*

The class `Frame` represents a top-level window with border decorations which can include borders, a title, an icon and a menu-bar. The class `Window` is the superclass of `Frame`, and represents a top-level window without border decorations.

12.7 *(a), (b) and (e)*

The classes `List`, `Applet` and `Container` are subclasses of the `Component` class. `CheckboxGroup` is a direct subclass of `Object`, and `MenuItem` is a direct subclass of `MenuComponent`. `MenuComponent` is not a subclass of `Component`.

12.8 *(b)*

The `setForeground()` method should be used to change the color of the text in a `Label` component. The text of labels is painted using the foreground color of the component.

12.9 *(c) and (d)*

The number of columns to display in a `TextArea` component can be specified either by giving the number of columns as an argument to the constructor or with the `setColumns()` method.

12.10 *(c)*

The number of items that should be visible in a `List` component can be specified by giving the number of items as an argument to the constructor. `List` has no other method to specify the number of items that should be visible.

12.11 *(e)*

Boxes 0 through 3 will act like radio buttons, since they were assigned a `Checkbox Group`. Box 4 will be a normal checkbox. During construction all checkboxes are set to be selected. Checkbox groups only allow one box to be selected at a time. The most recent selection overrides any previous selection in the group. Boxes 0 and 1 share the same checkbox group. Only `box1` will remain selected. Boxes 2 and 3 also share a checkbox group. Only `box3` will remain selected. Box 4 is a normal checkbox and will remain selected.

12.12 *(b)*

It can be specified that a `TextArea` should have a vertical scrollbar by sending `TextArea.SCROLLBARS_VERTICAL_ONLY` as an argument to the constructor of `TextArea`. `TextArea.SCROLLBARS_VERTICAL_ONLY` is one of several constants defined as members of the `TextArea` class, and can be passed to the constructor to specify the visibility of the scrollbars of the text area.

12.13 *(b)*

The Choice component has two methods named select(), which can be used to programmatically select an item from a Choice component.

12.14 *(a), (b) and (d)*

Instances of the classes Button, Panel and PopupMenu can be added to a Panel component. The class PopupMenu is not a subclass of Component, but instances can be added to the panel as a pop-up menu associated with the component. The class MenuBar is not a subclass of Component and instances cannot be added to a Panel. Window is a subclass of Component, but it represents top-level windows which cannot be nested within containers such as a Panel.

12.15 *(d)*

Instances of PopupMenu can be added to a Canvas. The Canvas class is not a subclass of Container, and instances of Canvas cannot nest other components. The class PopupMenu is not a subclass of Component, but instances of PopupMenu can be added to a Canvas, since a pop-up menu can be associated with any component.

12.16 *(a), (b) and (d)*

Instances of MenuItem, Menu and CheckboxMenuItem can be added to a Menu instance. The class Menu is not a subclass of Component and cannot nest components. It can only nest MenuItem and subclasses such as CheckboxMenuItem and Menu. MenuBar is not a subclass of MenuItem, but a direct subclass of MenuComponent.

12.17 *(e)*

The Component class has only one add() method and it takes a PopupMenu as a parameter. The Container class defines numerous add() methods which take Component as a parameter, but these methods are not available in Component.

12.18 *(b)*

The class Menu is used to create submenus in pull-down menus. Instances of the Menu class can either be a pull-down menu or a submenu of another Menu object.

13 Layout Managment

13.1 *(c)*

There is no add() method in Container that takes an Object and a Component, in that order, as parameters. There is an add() method which takes the parameters in the reverse order. Methods (a), (b) and (d) are defined in Container, method (e) is inherited from Component.

13.2 *(b)*

The layout managers BorderLayout, FlowLayout, GridBagLayout and GridLayout all allow components to be arranged so that two components are laid out side by side.

The layout manager `CardLayout` stacks the components on top of each other, allowing only one component to be visible at a time.

13.3 *(a)*

The layout manager `BorderLayout` has only 5 predefined slots where components can be placed. The layout managers `CardLayout`, `FlowLayout`, `GridBagLayout` and `GridLayout` can all accommodate any number of components.

13.4 *(d)*

The layout manager `FlowLayout` will place components into as few rows as the width of the container will allow, while ensuring that the bounds of components are within the container.

13.5 *(d)*

Specifying the primary layout direction for `FlowLayout` is not possible. The components are always laid out from left to right.

13.6 *(c)*

The argument `FlowLayout.CENTER` can be passed to the constructor of `FlowLayout` to specify that each row of components be aligned horizontally in the middle of the container.

13.7 *(c)*

The program will place all buttons in one column. Each button will occupy one row. The first and second parameters of the constructor specify the number of rows and columns, respectively. The value `0` means any number of rows or columns. The grid was constructed to have any number of rows, but only one column.

13.8 *(c), (d) and (e)*

The available width and height of a grid is shared equally between the components. All the components in a `GridLayout` will have the same dimensions. A grid does not need to be square or have the same number of rows and columns.

13.9 *(c) and (d)*

The constants `BorderLayout.CENTER` and `BorderLayout.EAST` are valid placement constraints when using `BorderLayout`. The strings `"NORTH"` and `"south"` are not valid, since the case of the strings is wrong. There is no constant named `MIDDLE` in `BorderLayout`. Constants from `FlowLayout` cannot be used for `BorderLayout`.

13.10 *(a) and (c)*

The `North` button will stretch over the top region of the container, occupying the top left corner of the container. The `South` button will stretch over the bottom region of the container, occupying the bottom right corner. None of the buttons will overlap.

1 *(a), (b) and (d)*

The `CardLayout` class has methods named `first()`, `last()` and `previous()`. It does not have methods named `end()` and `top()`.

13.12 *(e)*

Call `next(cont)` on the `CardLayout` instance is used to show the next component in a stack of components inside a container referenced by `cont`.

13.13 *(c)*

The program will show two small buttons side by side in the center of the window. The default weights of a `GridBagConstraints` object is 0, which means that none of the left-over space will be allotted to the components. Since no components claim the left-over space, it will be distributed to the area around the components.

13.14 *(a)*

The default anchoring of `GridBagConstraints` is `GridBagConstraints.CENTER`.

13.15 *(a)*

`BorderLayout` is the default layout manager for instances of the `Frame` class. The `Window` class defines `BorderLayout` to be the default layout manager. Subclasses such as `Frame` and `Dialog` inherit this setting.

13.16 *(e)*

`FlowLayout` is the default layout manager for instances of the `Panel` class.

14 Event Handling

14.1 *(c)*

The `MenuItem` class does not generate item events. The classes `Ch`
`MenuItem`, `Choice` and `List` all deliver `ItemEvent` objects to item eve

14.2 *(b)*

There is no event class named `MouseMotionEvent`. There are li
`MouseListener` and `MouseMotionListener`, but they both use

14.3 *(a) and (b)*

The `Checkbox` component generates an `ItemEvent` v
deselected, i.e. the state of the checkbox change

14.4 *(b), (c) and (d)*

The `MenuItem`, `List` and `TextField` classes a
and `Checkbox` components do not genera

14.5 *(b)*

A component that has gained focus will receive

14.6 *(c)*

In the event delegation model, the event handling is de
of event listener interfaces that are registered with the ev

14.7 *(a), (b) and (c)*

`ActionListener`, `WindowListener` and `ItemListener` are event listen
AWT. There are no event listener interfaces named `ButtonLis`
`Listener`. There are listener interfaces named `MouseMotionListen`
`Listener`, whose implementations can be registered with `Button` comp

14.8 *(e)*

The methods used to add listeners to event sources are named after the l
interfaces. The method `addActionListener()` is used to register listeners that in
ment the `ActionListener` interface.

14.9 *(d)*

The paint event, represented by the `PaintEvent` class, is not intended for public use in the event listener model. There is no listener interface for handling this event. The `paint()` method of the component should be overridden to receive notification that the component needs painting.

14.10 *(a)*

Code wishing to respond to menu selections should implement the `ActionListener` interface. There is no listener interface named `MenuItemListener`. The listener interfaces `TextListener`, `MouseListener` and `WindowListener` exist, but they do not deal with menu selections.

14.11 *(a), (b) and (d)*

The `java.awt.Component` class contains the methods `addMouseListener()`, `addMouseMotionListener()` and `addKeyListener()`. The `addActionListener()` and `addItemListener()` methods are not defined in the `java.awt.Component` class.

14.12 *(c)*

All action listeners registered with a button will be notified when the button is clicked. The `Button` component does not put any limitations on the number of action listeners that can be registered.

13 *(e)*

The `java.awt.event.MouseMotionAdapter` class implements the `MouseMotionListener` interface.

14.14 *(e)*

The program will compile without error and will print `B`, `C`, `A`, in that order, when the user clicks the button. A click on a button consists of pressing down the button and releasing it. The `mousePressed()` method is called when the button is pressed down. The `mouseReleased()` method is called when the button is released. The `actionPerformed()` method is never called: the `MyListener` object is not registered with the button as an `ActionListener` using the `addActionListener()` method.

14.15 *(a)*

There is no event listener adapter named `ActionAdapter` defined in the `java.awt.event` package. There is no need for an `ActionAdapter`, since the `Action Listener` interface only declares one method.

14.16 *(d)*

The program will compile and run without error and will print `B` when the user clicks the button. The event is handled by the `MyListener` instance registered with the `Button` component. The `MyListener` instance registered with the `Frame` object will not receive an event when the user clicks on the button.

14.17 *(c)*

The `FocusListener` interface has a corresponding `FocusAdapter` class. All the other listed listener interfaces only have one method, therefore there is no need for an adapter class.

14.18 *(a)*

Calling `enableEvent(AWTEvent.KEY_EVENT_MASK)` on a component will enable event delivery of key events to the component. No existing delivery events will be disabled as a result of calling the `enableEvent()` method.

14.19 *(e)*

There are no events that can be handled using low-level event processing that cannot be handled using the event listener model.

14.20 *(a), (b) and (c)*

The methods `processEvent()`, `processMouseEvent()` and `processMouseMotionEvent()` all exist in the `Component` class. There is no method named `processPaintEvent()` in the `Component` class. There is, however, a method named `paint()`.

15 Painting

15.1 *(b)*

The `Graphics` class does not encapsulate any background color property. Components do, however, have a background color property, and this color can be assigned to the `Graphics` object.

15.2 *(c)*

The `Label` component relies on the native platform to display itself. The visual representation of the component is generally not rendered using the `paint()` method, but uses native support for its rendering. Therefore, overriding the `paint()` method of such a component is not particularly useful.

15.3 *(b), (d) and (e)*

A `Graphics` instance can be acquired by calling `create()` on another `Graphics` instance, by calling `getGraphics()` on a component, or by overriding the `paint()` method. The `Graphics` class has a `Graphics()` constructor with no parameters, but this constructor is not publicly available. The `Graphics` class has no constructor taking another `Graphics` instance as an argument.

15.4 *(b)*

The program incorrectly disposes of the graphics object referenced by `gfx1`. A `Graphics` object should be disposed of when it is no longer in use. The `Graphics` object passed as argument to the `paint()` method is only temporarily made available, and should not be disposed of.

15.5 *(d)*

The `Color` class defines the constant color `darkGray`. The `Color` class does not define any colors named `lightBlue`, `DARK_GREEN`, `LIGHTGRAY` or `Black`. It does, however, define colors named `blue`, `green`, `lightGray` and `black`.

15.6 *(e)*

The statement `gfx.drawString("Hello", 30, 30)` will draw the string `"Hello"`. The prototype of the method used is `void drawString(String str, int x, int y)`.

15.7 *(d)*

The coordinates given to the text rendering methods specify the start coordinates of the baseline of the rendered text.

15.8 *(e)*

The rectangular area of pixels affected will be the exact width and height given as arguments to the `fillRectangle()` method. The last two parameters of the method specify the width and the height, not the bottom right coordinates of the rectangle.

15.9 *(f)*

The rectangular area of pixels affected will be one pixel wider and taller than the width and height given as arguments to the `draw3DRect()` method. The same rectangular area is affected when the `drawRect()` method is employed.

15.10 *(b) and (e)*

The `drawOval()` method of the `Graphics` class has top left coordinates and horizontal and vertical diameters as parameters. The horizontal and vertical diameters correspond to the width and height of the bounding rectangle.

15.11 *(d)*

Due to clipping, the bottom and right edges of the red rectangle will not be shown, but the entire green rectangle will be shown. The red rectangle will extend exactly one pixel to the right and one pixel at the bottom in relation to the clip region. The right and bottom edges will be clipped away during rendering. The right and bottom edges of the green rectangle will exactly border the corresponding edges of the clip region.

15.12 *(b)*

The application should call the `repaint()` method when it wants the visuals of a component to be repainted. This will schedule a repainting of the component, and the `update()` method will eventually be called by the AWT thread.

15.13 *(a)*

The call to the `repaint()` method ends immediately. The call to the `repaint()` method only schedules a repainting of the component. The AWT thread will eventually call the `update()` method to perform the actual repainting of the component.

15.14 *(c)*

A `Graphics` object can be changed from XOR paint mode to normal paint mode by calling the `setPaintMode()` method on the `Graphics` object. The `setPaintMode()` method has no parameters.

15.15 *(c)*

The method `getGraphics()` can be called on an `Image` object, to obtain a `Graphics` object suitable for rendering in the image.

16 Applets

16.1 *(d)*

The official HTML standard allows the use of either an `Applet` or an `Object` element to embed an applet in a document. The `Applet` element is deprecated in the current version of HTML. However, not all web browsers support the `Object` element.

16.2 *(d)*

The base URL for applets can be specified using the `Codebase` attribute.

16.3 *(b)*

When an applet is run, the method `init()` is executed first. Applets usually do not have any `main()` method, as the applet context never calls this method.

16.4 *(c)*

There is no method named `main()` in the `Applet` class. No `main()` method is thus part of the contract between applets and their applet context. A `main()` method is used as the main entry point for applications only.

16.5 *(d) and (e)*

The methods `start()` and `stop()` may be called by the applet context several times during the lifetime of an `Applet` object.

16.6 *(e)*

Classes extending the `Applet` class do not need to implement any of these methods. In fact, none of the methods of the `Applet` class are abstract.

16.7 *(a)*

The expression `getParameter("color")` will return the value of the parameter named `color`, specified in the `PARAM` element.

16.8 *(b)*

The method `getParameterInfo()` can be used to query an applet about the parameters it will accept. Some applet contexts can use this information to allow the user to specify parameter values for the applet. The applet in question must override this method for this mechanism to work.

16.9 *(d)*

The method `getAppletInfo()` can be used to get a textual description of the applet. Some applet contexts can present this information to the user. The applet must override this method for this mechanism to work.

16.10 *(e)*

Classes extending the `Applet` class do not need to implement any of these methods. In fact, none of the methods of the `Applet` class are abstract.

17 Swing

17.1 *(c) and (d)*

Each `JDialog` uses a `JRootPane` to implement its containment model. The root pane object can be accessed using the `getRootPane()` method in `JDialog`. Each `JRootPane` contains a `JLayeredPane`, containing the content pane of the dialog box. The content pane can be accessed using the `getContentPane()` method in either `JDialog` or `JRootPane`.

17.2 *(a), (b) and (d)*

The methods `setIcon()`, `getText()` and `setBorder()` can be called on a `JLabel` object. The `setBorder()` method is defined in the `JComponent` superclass. The `setIcon()` and `getText()` methods are defined in `JLabel`. There are no `setLabel()` or `getMnemonic()` methods defined for `JLabel` components.

17.3 *(b) and (d)*

`JScrollBar` and `JProgressBar` use implementations of `BoundedRangeModel` as data models for the components.

17.4 *(a), (b) and (e)*

The objects used as models by `JTable` implement the `TableModel`, `TableColumnModel` and `ListSelectionModel` interfaces. `TableModel` represents the data in the table. `TableColumnModel` represents the columns of the table. `ListSelectionModel` is used to keep track of which rows and columns are selected.

17.5 *(b), (c) and (e)*

`Component`, `Container` and `JComponent` are not backed by any native peers, and are lightweight. `Canvas` and `Panel` are backed by native peers and are heavyweight.

17.6 *(a), (c) and (d)*

The code will fail to compile, since line (2) tries to use a method `getContentPane()` that does not exist in `JPanel`. The lines (2) and (3) do not use the content model of their respective containers correctly. The `JFrame` uses the root pane containment model, while `JPanel` uses the traditional containment model.

17.7 *(b) and (d)*

`JApplet` and `JFrame` use `JRootPane` to implement their containment model. This means that child components cannot be added directly by using the `add()` method of the component.

17.8 *(c) and (d)*

`JComponent` extends `Component` and is a lightweight component. `JMenuItem` extends `AbstractButton`, which is a subclass of `JComponent`. `JToggleButton` is not a subclass of `JButton`. `JToggleButton` and `JButton` both extend `AbstractButton`.

17.9 *(b)*

The button will appear in the top right corner of the window. The horizontal glue added before the button will consume as much space as possible between the left edge of the window and the left edge of the button. The vertical glue added after the button will not consume any horizontal space on the right side of the button. The button will therefore be aligned with the right edge of the window.

17.10 *(c) and (e)*

JMenu extends JMenuItem, which is a subclass of AbstractButton. A JScrollBar uses an object implementing BoundedRangeModel as its model. The container JInternalFrame is a lightweight component that uses the root pane container model. The method getCrossPlatformLookAndFeelClassName() returns the name of the look and feel class that implements the default cross-platform Java look and feel.

17.11 *(b)*

The default layout manager associated with JApplet components is BorderLayout. The JApplet component uses JRootPane to implement its content model. The content pane managed by the root pane is the main region of the JApplet. The default layout manager for the content pane is BorderLayout. This is in contrast to the Applet container from the java.applet package, which has FlowLayout as its default layout manager.

18 Files and Streams

18.1 *(a), (b), (c) and (e)*

A file, a network connection, a pipe and an array of chars can all act as input and output streams by using the classes provided by the java.io package. A string cannot act as a stream using these classes.

18.2 *(b) and (e)*

The separator constant is of type String and contains the sequence of characters used as path separators on the native platform. The most common platforms only use a single character as a path separator, but there is no such restriction.

18.3 *(b)*

The method getName() can be used on a File object to return the name of the entry. The name excludes the specification of the directory in which the entry resides.

18.4 *(e)*

The length() method can be used on a File object to return the number of bytes in the file. Note that bytes are not the same as characters, and the size of characters in a file depends on the encoding scheme used.

18.5 *(b)*

The boolean value false is returned when the method canWrite() is called on a File object representing a file that is not writable in the file system.

18.6 *(a)*

The parameter of the renameTo() method is of type File. The current file will be renamed to the file name represented by the File object. Note that the File object given does not need to represent an actual entry in the file system. It only represents a valid pathname.

18.7 *(d)*

The `write()` method only writes bytes. When given an `int`, it will only write the 8 least significant bits.

18.8 *(d)*

The `read()` method will return –1 when the end of the input has been reached. Normally a single 8-bit integer value is returned. I/O errors result in exceptions being thrown.

18.9 *(a) and (c)*

Classes that implement the `DataOutput` interface, such as `DataOutputStream` and `ObjectOutputStream`, provide methods for writing binary representations of primitive Java types. The output stream classes `FileOutputStream`, `PrintStream` and `BufferedOutputStream` do not provide these methods.

18.10 *(a), (c) and (d)*

The `Writer` class has no `write()` method with a parameter of type `char`. It has methods with parameters of types `String`, `int` and `char[]`.

18.11 *(d)*

The default encoding for `OutputStreamWriter` is the default encoding of the host system.

18.12 *(a)*

The type `byte` does not have its own `print()` method in the `PrintWriter` class. There is no natural textual representation of a `byte`.

18.13 *(c)*

The standard error stream is accessed as a static variable named `err` in the `System` class.

18.14 *(b) and (c)*

The access mode must be either `"r"` or `"rw"`. Other variations are not valid. Note that opening a file for write only is not allowed.

18.15 *(d)*

The statement `seek(length()-1)` would position the file pointer right before the last byte of the file. The `length()` method returns the number of bytes in the file, and the `seek()` method places the file pointer after the given number of bytes from the beginning of the file.

18.16 *(a)*

There are no methods defined in the `Serializable` interface. This marker interface can be used to signify that a class supports serialization.

18.17 *(c)*

The `ObjectOutputStream` can write both objects and primitive Java types. The serialization mechanism will follow object references and can write whole hierarchies of objects.

19 Javadoc Facility

19.1 *(a), (b), (d) and (e)*

Javadoc comments are recognized preceding class, interface and member declarations. No Javadoc comment is recognized in front of local variable declarations.

19.2 *(c)*

The leading white space followed by an optional sequence of asterisks is ignored. All characters after the optional sequence of asterisks is considered a part of the comment, including white space and asterisks.

19.3 *(d)*

The character sequence ". " (period, space) denotes the end of the sentence. Various workarounds can be used to make the period–space sequence appear in the generated documentation, without actually ending the sentence.

19.4 *(a), (b) and (d)*

Class names, if specified, must be fully qualified. Skipping the parameter list is allowed, since it will revert to choosing the first member matching the given name.

19.5 *(b), (c) and (e)*

The `@deprecated`, `@exception` and `@since` tags are valid. The proper name for the tag used to create hyperlinks to other relevant entries is `@see`, not `@seealso`. The proper name for the tag used to document the return value is `@return`.

19.6 *(a)*

The option `-public` ensures that only documentation for `public` elements is generated. The options `-protected`, `-package` and `-private` generate documentation for classes and members of their representative accessibility and all classes and members with less restrictive accessibility.

19.7 *(a) and (d)*

Deprecated members are included by default and can be excluded by using the `-nodeprecated` option. Showing version information and private members are off by default, and can be turned on by using the -version and -private options, respectively. There are no -noprivate, -deprecated or -noversion options.

19.8 *(b), (c) and (d)*

The @author tag is not applicable when describing a member variable. Javadoc does not provide such fine-grained control for specifying authors for member variables.

Appendix D

Solutions to Programming Exercises

1 Basics of Java programming

No programming exercises.

2 Language Fundamentals

2.1 The following program will compile and run without errors:

```
package com.acme; // Correct ordering of package and import statements.

import java.util.*;

public class Exercise1 {
    int counter; // This is rather useless

    public static void main(String args[]) { // correct main signature
        Exercise1 instance = new Exercise1();
        instance.go();
    }

    public void go() {
        int sum = 0;
        // We could just as well have written sum = 100
        // here and removed the if statement below.
        int i = 0;
        while (i<100) {
            if (i == 0) sum = 100;
            sum = sum + i;
            i++;
        }
        System.out.println(sum);
    }
}
```

2.2 The following program will compile and run without errors:

```
// Filename: Temperature.java
/* Identifiers and keywords in Java are case-sensitive. Therefore the
   case of the file name must match the class name, the keywords must
   all be written in lowercase. The name of the String class has a
   capital S. The main method must be static and take an array of
   String objects as an argument. */
public class Temperature {
    public static void main(String args[]) {  // correct method signature
        double fahrenheit = 62.5;
        // /* identifies the start of a "starred" comment.
        // */ identifies the end.
        /* Convert */
        double celsius = f2c(fahrenheit);
        // '' delimits character literals, "" delimits string literals
        System.out.println(fahrenheit + "F = " + celsius + "C");
    }

    static double f2c(double fahr) {          // Note parameter type
        return (fahr - 32) * 5 / 9;
    }
}
```

3 Operators and Assignments

3.1 The following program will compile and run without errors:

```
// Filename: Sunlight.java
public class Sunlight {
    public static void main(String args[]) {
        // Distance from sun (150 million kilometers)
        /* The max value for int is 2147483647, so using int here will
           work. */
        int kmFromSun = 150000000;

        // Again, using int for this value is OK.
        int lightSpeed = 299792458; // meters per second

        // Convert distance to meters.
        /* The result of this equation will not fit in an int. Let's
           use a long instead. We need to ensure that the values that
           are multiplied really are multiplied using long
           datatypes, not multiplied as int datatypes and later
           converted to long. The L suffix on the 1000L integer
           literal ensures this. The value of kmFromSun will
           implicitly be converted from int to long to match the
           datatype of the other factor. The conversion can be done
           implicitly by the compiler since the conversion represents
           a widening of the datatype. */
        long mFromSun = kmFromSun * 1000L;
```

```
        /* We know that the result value will fit in an int, but the
           compiler does not. We use an explicit cast to convince the
           compiler. The conversion must be specified explicitly since
           the conversion represents a narrowing of the datatype. */
        int seconds = (int) (mFromSun / lightSpeed);

        System.out.print("Light will use ");
        printTime(seconds);
        System.out.println(" to travel from the sun to the earth.");
    }

    /* We leave this method alone. */
    public static void printTime(int sec) {
        int min = sec / 60;
        sec = sec - (min*60);
        System.out.print(min + " minute(s) and " + sec + " second(s)");
    }
}
```

3.2

```
public class Binary {
    public static void main(String args[]) {
        System.out.println(makeBinaryString(42));
    }

    public static String makeBinaryString(int i) {
        /* This section could have been optimized using
           StringBuffer, but is presented in this way for the
           sake of simplicity. */
        String binary = "";
        do {
             int lowBit = (i&1);
             String newDigit = ((lowBit == 0) ? "0" : "1");
             binary = newDigit + binary;
             i >>>= 1;
        } while (i != 0);
        return binary;
    }
}
```

3.3 The following program will operate as specified in the exercise. When given no arguments, the program will not print anything.

```
public class ArgumentSkipper {
    public static void main(String args[]) {
        int count = args.length;

        // Iterate over the arguments skipping two places
        // forward between each step.
        for (int i=0; i < count; i+= 2) {
            System.out.println(args[i]);
        }
    }
}
```

4 Declarations and Access Control

4.1

```
public class EditContext {

    private Object selected;

    public void setSelected(Object newSelected) {
        selected = newSelected;
    }

    public Object getSelected() {
        return selected;
    }
}
```

4.2

```
public interface Tool {
    public void setContext(EditContext newContext);
    public boolean isActive();
}
```

4.3

```
// Filename: Database.java

// Specify package
package com.megabankcorp.system;

// Allow usage of Account class simply by referring to the name Account.
import com.megabankcorp.records.Account;

// Class must be abstract since it has abstract methods.
public abstract class Database {
    // Abstract and available from anywhere.
    public abstract void deposit(Account acc, long amount);

    // Abstract and available from anywhere.
    public abstract void withdraw(Account acc, long amount);

    // Abstract and only available from package and subclasses.
    protected abstract long amount(Account acc);

    // Unmodifiable and only available from package.
    final void transfer(Account from, Account to, long amount) {
        withdraw(from, amount);
        deposit(to, amount);
    }
}
```

5 Flow Control and Exception Handling

5.1 Finding primes using for-loops.

```
// Filename: ForPrimes.java
public class ForPrimes {
    final static int MAX = 100;
```

```
    public static void main(String args[]) {
        numbers:
        for (int num = 1; num < MAX; num++) {
            int divLim = (int) Math.sqrt(num);

            for (int div = 2; div <= divLim; div++)
                if ((num % div) == 0) continue numbers;
            System.out.println(num);
        }
    }
}
```

Finding primes using `while`-loops.

```
// Filename: WhilePrimes.java
public class WhilePrimes {
    final static int MAX = 100;

    public static void main(String args[]) {
        int num = 1;

        numbers:
        while (num < MAX) {
            int number = num++;

            int divLim = (int) Math.sqrt(number);
            int div = 2;
            while (div <= divLim)
                if ((number % div++) == 0) continue numbers;
            System.out.println(number);
        }
    }
}
```

5.2

```
/** A PowerPlant with a reactor core. */
public class PowerPlant {
    /** Each power plant has a reactor core.  This has package
        accessibility so that the Control class which is defined in
        the same package can access it. */
    Reactor core;

    /** Initialize the PowerPlant, creates a reactor core.  */
    PowerPlant() {
        core = new Reactor();
    }

    /** Sound the alarm to evacuate the power plant.  */
    public void soundEvacuateAlarm() {
        // ... implementation unspecified ...
    }

    /** Get the level of reactor output that is most desirable at
        this time. (Units are unspecified.)  */
    public int getOptimalThroughput() {
```

```
        // ... implementation unspecified ...
        return 0;
    }

    /** The main entry point of the program. Will set up a PowerPlant
        object and a Control object and let the Control object run the
        PowerPlant.  */
    public static void main(String args[]) {
        PowerPlant plant = new PowerPlant();
        Control ctrl = new Control(plant);
        ctrl.runSystem();
    }
}

/** A reactor core that has a throughput that can be either decreased or
    increased.  */
class Reactor {
    /** Get the current throughput of the reactor.  (Units are
       unspecified.)  */
    public int getThroughput() {
        // ... implementation unspecified ...
        return 0;
    }

    /** @returns true if the reactor status is critical, false otherwise.  */
    public boolean isCritical() {
        // ... implementation unspecified ...
        return false;
    }

    /** Ask the reactor to increase throughput.  */
    void increaseThroughput() throws ReactorCritical {
        // ... implementation unspecified ...
    }

    /** Ask the reactor to decrease throughput.  */
    void decreaseThroughput() {
        // ... implementation unspecified ...
    }
}

/** This exception class should be used to report that the reactor is
    critical.  */
class ReactorCritical extends Exception {}

/** A controller that will manage the power plant to make sure that the
    reactor runs with optimal throughput.  */
class Control {
    PowerPlant thePlant;

    public Control(PowerPlant p) {
        thePlant = p;
    }

    /** Run the power plant by continuously monitoring the
        optimalThroughput and the actual throughput of the reactor. If
        the throughputs differ by more than 10 units, adjust reactor
        throughput. If the reactor goes critical, the evacuate alarm is
        sounded and the reactor is shut down.
```

```
        <p>The runSystem() method does handle the reactor core directly
        but calls methods needAdjustment(), adjustThroughput() and shutdown
        instead.  */
    public void runSystem() {
        try {
            while (true) { // infinite loop
                if (needAdjustment())
                    adjustThroughput(thePlant.getOptimalThroughput());
            }
        } catch (ReactorCritical rc) {
            thePlant.soundEvacuateAlarm();
        } finally {
            shutdown();
        }
    }

    /** Reports whether the throughput of the reactor needs
        adjusting. This method should also monitor and report if the
        reactor goes critical.

        @returns true if the optimal and actual throughput values
        differ by more than 10 units.  */
    public boolean needAdjustment() throws ReactorCritical {
    /* We added the throws clause to the method declaration so that
       the method can throw a ReactorCritical exception if the reactor
       goes critical.  */
        if (thePlant.core.isCritical())
            throw new ReactorCritical();
        return (Math.abs(thePlant.getOptimalThroughput() -
                         thePlant.core.getThroughput())) > 10;
    }

    /** Adjust the throughput of the reactor by calling increaseThroughput()
        and decreaseThroughput() until the actual throughput is within 10
        units of the target throughput.  */
    public void adjustThroughput(int target) throws ReactorCritical {
    /* We added the throws clause to the method declaration so that
       the method can pass on ReactorCritical exceptions thrown by
       increaseThroughput().  We do this because the adjustThroughput
       does not want to handle the exception.  */
        while (needAdjustment()) {
            if (thePlant.getOptimalThroughput() >
                    thePlant.core.getThroughput())
                thePlant.core.increaseThroughput();
            else
                thePlant.core.decreaseThroughput();
        }
    }

    /** Shut down the reactor by lowering the throughput to 0. */
    public void shutdown() {
        while (thePlant.core.getThroughput() != 0) {
            thePlant.core.decreaseThroughput();
        }
    }
}
```

6 Object-oriented Programming

6.1

```
// Filename: Exercise1.java
interface Function {
    public int evaluate(int arg);
}

class Half implements Function {
    public int evaluate(int arg) {
        return arg/2;
    }
}

public class Exercise1 {
    public static int[] applyFunctionToArray(int[] arrIn) {
        int length = arrIn.length;
        int[] arrOut = new int[length];

        Function func = new Half();

        for (int i=0; i< length; i++)
            arrOut[i] = func.evaluate(arrIn[i]);

        return arrOut;
    }
}
```

6.2

```
// Filename: Exercise2.java
interface Function {
    public int evaluate(int arg);
}

class Half implements Function {
    public int evaluate(int arg) {
        return arg/2;
    }
}

class Print implements Function {
    public int evaluate(int arg) {
        System.out.println(arg);
        return arg;
    }
}

public class Exercise2 {
    public static void main(String args[]) {
        // Create array with values 1 .. 10
        int[] myArr = new int[10];
        for (int i=0; i<10;) myArr[i] = ++i;

        // Create a print function
        Function print = new Print();
```

```
        // Print array
        applyFunctionToArray(myArr, print);

        // Half values
        myArr = applyFunctionToArray(myArr, new Half());

        // Print array again
        applyFunctionToArray(myArr, print);
    }

    public static int[] applyFunctionToArray(int[] arrIn, Function func) {
        int length = arrIn.length;
        int[] arrOut = new int[length];

        for (int i=0; i< length; i++)
            arrOut[i] = func.evaluate(arrIn[i]);

        return arrOut;
    }
}
```

Output from the program:

```
1
2
3
4
5
6
7
8
9
10
0
1
1
2
2
3
3
4
4
5
```

7 Inner Classes

7.1

```
// Filename: Exercise3.java
interface Function {
    public int evaluate(int arg);
}

class Half implements Function {
    public int evaluate(int arg) {
        return arg/2;
    }
}
```

```
class Print implements Function {
    public int evaluate(int arg) {
        System.out.println(arg);
        return arg;
    }
}

public class Exercise3 {
    /* Inner class that applies the function, and prints the value and
       returns the result. */
    static class PrintFunc extends Print {
        PrintFunc(Function f) {
            func = f;
        }

        Function func;

        public int evaluate(int arg) {
            return super.evaluate(func.evaluate(arg));
        }
    }

    // Inner class that just returns the argument unchanged.
    /* Use this when you want a PrintFunc object to print
       the argument as-is. */
    static class NoOpFunc implements Function {
        public int evaluate(int arg) {
            return arg;
        }
    }

    public static void main(String args[]) {
        // Create array with values 1 .. 10
        int[] myArr = new int[10];
        for (int i=0; i<10;) myArr[i] = ++i;

        // Print array without modification
        applyFunctionToArray(myArr, new PrintFunc(new NoOpFunc()));

        // Print halved values
        applyFunctionToArray(myArr, new PrintFunc(new Half()));
    }

    public static int[] applyFunctionToArray(int[] arrIn, Function func) {
        int length = arrIn.length;
        int[] arrOut = new int[length];

        for (int i=0; i< length; i++)
            arrOut[i] = func.evaluate(arrIn[i]);

        return arrOut;
    }
}
```

The output when run is the same as in Exercise 6.2.

8 Object Lifetime

No programming exercises.

9 Threads

9.1

```
// Filename: Counter.java
/*
    Notice that the result of running this program
    may not be what you expect. Since both threads are
    working on full throttle it is possible that only one
    of the threads is granted CPU time.
 */
public class Counter implements Runnable {
    public static void main(String args[]) {
        Storage store = new Storage();
        new Counter(store);
        new Printer(store);
    }

    Storage storage;
    Counter(Storage target) {
        storage = target;
        new Thread(this).start();
    }

    public void run() {
        int i=0;
        while (true) {
            storage.setValue(i);
            i++;
        }
    }
}

class Printer implements Runnable {
    Storage storage;
    Printer(Storage source) {
        storage = source;
        new Thread(this).start();
    }

    public void run() {
        while (true) {
            System.out.println(storage.getValue());
        }
    }
}

class Storage {
    int value;
    void setValue(int i) { value = i; }
    int getValue() { return value; }
}
```

9.2

```
// Filename: Counter.java
/* Only the Storage class has been altered. */

/* No changes to this class */
public class Counter implements Runnable {
    public static void main(String args[]) {
        Storage store = new Storage();
        new Counter(store);
        new Printer(store);
    }

    Storage storage;
    Counter(Storage s) {
        storage = s;
        new Thread(this).start();
    }

    public void run() {
        int i=0;
        while (true) {
            storage.setValue(i);
            i++;
        }
    }
}

/* No changes to this class. */
class Printer implements Runnable {
    Storage storage;
    Printer(Storage s) {
        storage = s;
        new Thread(this).start();
    }

    public void run() {
        while (true) {
            System.out.println(storage.getValue());
        }
    }
}

/* This class now ensures that getting and setting are done
   in an alternating fashion.
 */
class Storage {
    int value;
    boolean isUnread = false;

    synchronized void setValue(int i) {
        ensureUnread(false);
        value = i;
        setUnread(true);
    }

    synchronized int getValue() {
        ensureUnread(true);
        setUnread(false);
        return value;
    }
```

```
    private void ensureUnread(boolean shouldHaveUnread) {
        while (shouldHaveUnread != isUnread)
            try { wait(); }
            catch (InterruptedException ie) {}
    }

    private void setUnread(boolean b) {
        isUnread = b;
        notify();
    }
}
```

10 Fundamental Classes

10.1

```
/**
 * Aggregate pairs of arbitrary objects.
 */
public final class Pair {
    private Object first, second;

    /** Construct a Pair object. */
    public Pair(Object one, Object two) {
        first = one;
        second = two;
    }

    /** Provides access to the first aggregated object. */
    public Object getFirst() { return first; }

    /** Provides access to the second aggregated object. */
    public Object getSecond() { return second; }

    /** @return true if the pair of objects are identical. */
    public boolean equals(Object other) {
        if (! (other instanceof Pair)) return false;
        Pair otherPair = (Pair) other;
        return first.equals(otherPair.getFirst()) &&
               second.equals(otherPair.getSecond());
    }

    /** @return a hash code for the aggregate pair. */
    public int hashCode() {
        // XORing the hash codes to create a hash code for the pair.
        return first.hashCode() ^ second.hashCode();
    }

    /** @return the textual representation of aggregated objects. */
    public String toString() {
        return "[" + first + "," + second + "]";
    }
}
```

10.2

```
public class Palindrome {
    public static void main(String args[]) {
        if (args.length != 1) {
            System.out.println("Usage: java Palindrome <word>");
            return;
        }
        String word = args[0];
        StringBuffer reverseWord = new StringBuffer(word);
        reverseWord.reverse();
        boolean isPalindrome = word.equals(reverseWord.toString());

        System.out.println("The word " + word + " is " +
                           (isPalindrome ? "" : "not ") +
                           "a palindrome");
    }
}
```

11 Collections

11.1

```
import java.util.*;

public class UniqueCharacterCounter {

    /**
     * A cache, mapping strings to count results. The count values are
     * stored as Integer objects within the map.
     */
    static Map globalCache = new HashMap();

    public static int countUniqueCharacters(String aString) {
        Object cachedResult = globalCache.get(aString);
        if (cachedResult != null)
            return ((Integer) cachedResult).intValue();

        // Result was not in the cache, calculate it.
        int length = aString.length();
        Set occurred = new TreeSet();
        Set duplicates = new TreeSet();

        // Identify occurrences and duplicates for each character in string:
        for (int i=0; i<length;i++) {
            Character character = new Character(aString.charAt(i));
            if (duplicates.contains(character)) continue;
            boolean newOccurrence = occurred.add(character);
            if (!newOccurrence) duplicates.add(character);
        }

        // Remove duplicates from occurrence count to obtain result:
        occurred.removeAll(duplicates);
        int result = occurred.size();

        // Put result in cache before returning:
        globalCache.put(aString, new Integer(result));
        return result;
    }
```

```
    /**
     * A simple main method for the purpose of demonstrating the
     * effect of the <code>countUniqueCharacters()</code>
     * method. Prints the result of applying the operation on each
     * commandline argument.
     */
    public static void main(String args[]) {
        int nArgs = args.length;
        for (int i=0; i<nArgs; i++) {
            String argument = args[i];
            int result = countUniqueCharacters(argument);
            System.out.println(argument + ": " + result);
        }
    }
}
```

12 AWT Components

12.1

```
// Filename: ShowExerciseText.java
import java.awt.*;

public class ShowExerciseText {
    public static void main(String args[]) {
        Window window = new Frame("Exercise text");

        String exercise = "Create a program that shows the text from " +
            "this exercise in a text area. Make the size of the frame " +
            "containing the text area 200 by 200 pixels. The text area " +
            "should not have any scrollbars and the text should not be " +
            "editable. Make the text appear as yellow lettering on a " +
            "black background.";

        /* The number of rows and columns we specify here for the text area
           does not matter since it will be overridden by the setSize() call on the
           window. */
        TextArea textDisplay = new TextArea(exercise, 5, 5,
                                            TextArea.SCROLLBARS_NONE);

        textDisplay.setEditable(false);
        textDisplay.setBackground(Color.black);
        textDisplay.setForeground(Color.yellow);
        window.add(textDisplay);
        window.setSize(200, 200);
        window.setVisible(true);
    }
}
```

13 Layout Managment

13.1

```
import java.awt.*;

public class Layout {
    public static void main(String args[]) {
        Window window = new Frame("A frame");
        window.add(new Button("A button"), BorderLayout.NORTH);
        Container textAreaContainer = new Panel();
        textAreaContainer.setLayout(new GridLayout(1, 2));
        textAreaContainer.add(new TextArea());
        textAreaContainer.add(new TextArea());
        window.add(textAreaContainer, BorderLayout.CENTER);
        window.pack();
        window.setVisible(true);
    }
}
```

13.2

```
import java.awt.*;

public class CornerButtons {
    public static void main(String args[]) {
        Window window = new Frame("A frame");
        window.add(
            createButtonEdgeBar(
                    new Button("NW"), new Button("NE")
            ), BorderLayout.NORTH
        );
        window.add(
            createButtonEdgeBar(
                    new Button("SW"), new Button("SE")
            ), BorderLayout.SOUTH
        );

        window.pack();
        window.setVisible(true);
    }

    static Component createButtonEdgeBar(Button left, Button right) {
        Container bar = new Panel();
        bar.setLayout(new BorderLayout());
        bar.add(left, BorderLayout.WEST);
        bar.add(right, BorderLayout.EAST);
        return bar;
    }
}
```

14 Event Handling

14.1

```
// Filename: Pad.java
import java.awt.*;
import java.awt.event.*;

/** Implements a simple note pad. */
public class Pad {
    /** Simply create an instance of Pad */
    public static void main(String args[]) {
        new Pad();
    }

    String rememberedString;
    TextArea textEditArea;
    Label status;

    public Pad() {
        Window window = new Frame("Pad");

        textEditArea   = new TextArea();
        status         = new Label();

        window.add(textEditArea, BorderLayout.CENTER);
        window.add(status, BorderLayout.SOUTH);
        window.add(createButtons(), BorderLayout.NORTH);

        // Make the application exit when the window is closed by the user.
        window.addWindowListener(
            new WindowAdapter() {
                public void windowClosing(WindowEvent e) {
                    System.exit(0);
                }
            }
        );

        window.pack();
        window.setVisible(true);
    }

    /** Create a row of command buttons. */
    public Component createButtons() {
        Panel buttonPanel = new Panel();

        Button clearButton    = new Button("Clear");
        Button rememberButton = new Button("Remember");
        Button recallButton   = new Button("Recall");

        buttonPanel.add(clearButton);
        buttonPanel.add(rememberButton);
        buttonPanel.add(recallButton);

        // Provide help for the command buttons.
        new ButtonHelp(clearButton,    "Clear text");
        new ButtonHelp(rememberButton, "Remember text");
        new ButtonHelp(recallButton,   "Recall text");
```

```
        clearButton.addActionListener(
            new ActionListener() {
                // Clear command implementation.
                public void actionPerformed(ActionEvent e) {
                    textEditArea.setText("");
                    setStatus("Text cleared");
                }
            }
        );

        rememberButton.addActionListener(
            new ActionListener() {
                // Remember command implementation.
                public void actionPerformed(ActionEvent e) {
                    rememberedString = textEditArea.getText();
                    setStatus("Text remembered");
                }
            }
        );

        recallButton.addActionListener(
            new ActionListener() {
                // Recall command implementation.
                public void actionPerformed(ActionEvent e) {
                    if (rememberedString == null) return;
                    textEditArea.setText(rememberedString);
                    setStatus("Text recalled");
                }
            }
        );

        return buttonPanel;
    }

    /** Set the message of the status line. */
    void setStatus(String msg) {
        status.setText(msg);
    }

    /** Clear any message on the status line. */
    void clearStatus() {
        setStatus("");
    }

    /**
     * A listener that will provide the user with help concerning the
     * command buttons.
     */
    class ButtonHelp extends MouseAdapter {
        ButtonHelp(Button button, String msg) {
            helpMsg = msg;
            button.addMouseListener(this);
        }

        String helpMsg;
```

```
        public void mouseEntered(MouseEvent e) {
            setStatus(helpMsg);
        }

        public void mouseExited(MouseEvent e) {
            clearStatus();
        }
    }
}
```

14.2

```
// Filename: CatchMe.java
import java.awt.event.*;
import java.awt.*;

public class CatchMe {
    Panel playPanel;
    Button wildButton;
    Point placement;

    public static void main(String args[]) {
        new CatchMe();
    }

    CatchMe() {
        Window window = new Frame("Try pressing the button");
        playPanel  = new Panel();
        wildButton = new Button("Click me");

        window.add(playPanel, BorderLayout.CENTER);

        playPanel.setLayout(null);
        playPanel.add(wildButton);

        window.setSize(400, 300);
        window.setVisible(true);

        Dimension buttonSize = wildButton.getPreferredSize();
        wildButton.setSize(buttonSize);

        placeButton();
        playPanel.addMouseMotionListener(new ButtonMover());
        wildButton.addActionListener(new CaughtListener());

        window.addWindowListener(
            new WindowAdapter() {
                public void windowClosing(WindowEvent e) {
                    System.exit(0);
                }
            }
        );
    }

    class ButtonMover extends MouseMotionAdapter {
        public void mouseMoved(MouseEvent mouseEvent) {
            int xd = Math.abs(placement.x - mouseEvent.getX());
            int yd = Math.abs(placement.y - mouseEvent.getY());
```

```
            Dimension buttonSize = wildButton.getSize();
            if ((xd < buttonSize.width) && (yd < buttonSize.height))
                placeButton();
        }
    }

    class CaughtListener implements ActionListener {
        public void actionPerformed(ActionEvent e) {
            wildButton.setLabel("Congratulations!");
            wildButton.setSize(wildButton.getPreferredSize());
            placeButton();
        }
    }

    void placeButton() {
        Dimension playRegion = playPanel.getSize();
        Dimension buttonSize = wildButton.getSize();
        int xSpan = playRegion.width  - buttonSize.width;
        int ySpan = playRegion.height - buttonSize.height;

        int x = (int) (Math.random() * xSpan);
        int y = (int) (Math.random() * ySpan);

        wildButton.setLocation(x, y);
        placement = new Point(x + buttonSize.width/2, y + buttonSize.height/2);
        playPanel.validate();
    }
}
```

15 Painting

15.1

```
// Filename: BorderPanel.java
import java.awt.*;

/**
 * A panel with a border to provide a visual clue to the grouping of the
 * components within it.
 */
public class BorderPanel extends Panel {
    static final int OUTER_PAD = 5;
    static final int INNER_PAD = 5;
    static final int PAD = OUTER_PAD + INNER_PAD;

    /**
     * Constructor corresponding to Panel()
     */
    public BorderPanel() {
        super();
    }

    /**
     * Constructor corresponding to Panel(LayoutManager)
     */
    public BorderPanel(LayoutManager layoutManager) {
        super(layoutManager);
    }
```

```
    public Insets getInsets() {
        /*
          Add additional padding to the inherited insets to
          accommodate the space occupied by the border.
         */
        Insets insets = super.getInsets();
        return new Insets(insets.top+PAD, insets.left+PAD,
                          insets.bottom+PAD, insets.right+PAD);
    }

    public void paint(Graphics gfx) {
        /*
          The paint method of Panel usually does nothing, but call
          it anyway, just to be sure.
         */
        super.paint(gfx);

        /*
          Calculate the area where the border should be painted,
          based on padding constants and inherited insets.
         */
        Insets ins = super.getInsets();
        Dimension dim = getSize();

        int x, y, w, h;
        x = ins.left + OUTER_PAD;
        y = ins.top  + OUTER_PAD;

        w = dim.width  - ins.left - ins.right  - OUTER_PAD*2 - 1;
        h = dim.height - ins.top  - ins.bottom - OUTER_PAD*2 - 1;

        /*
          Paint an etched border that matches the color of the
          panel.
         */
        gfx.setColor(getBackground());
        gfx.draw3DRect(x-1, y-1, w+2, h+2, false);
        gfx.draw3DRect(x+1, y+1, w-2, h-2, true);
    }
}
```

16 Applets

16.1

```
// Filename: DisplayString.java
import java.awt.*;
import java.applet.*;

public class DisplayString extends Applet {
    public void init() {
        setLayout(new BorderLayout());
        add(new Label(getParameter("text")), BorderLayout.CENTER);
    }

    public String getAppletInfo() {
        return "DisplayString -- displays a given string";
    }
```

```
    public String[][] getParameterInfo() {
        return paramInfo;
    }

    static final String[][] paramInfo = {
        { "text", "string", "String to be displayed" }
    };
}
```

16.2 We provide two solutions, one using the APPLET element and one using the OBJECT element.

Using transitional HTML 4.0 with the APPLET element:

```
<!DOCTYPE html PUBLIC "-//W3C//DTD HTML 4.0 Transitional//EN">
<!-- Filename: applet.html -->
<html>
  <head>
    <title>Using the Applet-element</title>
  </head>
  <body>
<h1>Using the Applet-element</h1>
<hr>

<applet code="DisplayString.class" width="400" height="100">
<param name="text" value="An applet a day keeps the browser awake">
</applet>

<hr>
</body>
</html>
```

Using strict HTML 4.0 with the OBJECT element:

```
<!DOCTYPE html PUBLIC "-//W3C//DTD HTML 4.0//EN">
<!-- Filename: object.html -->
<html>
  <head>
    <title>Using the Object-element</title>
  </head>
  <body>
<h1>Using the Object-element</h1>
<hr>

<div><object classid="DisplayString.class" width="400" height="100">
<param name="text" value="An applet a day keeps the browser awake">
</object></div>

<hr>
</body>
</html>
```

17 Swing

17.1

```
// Filename: SwingPad.java
import javax.swing.*;
import java.awt.*;
import java.awt.event.*;

/** Implements a simple note pad using Swing components. */
public class SwingPad {
    /** Simply creates an instance of SwingPad */
    public static void main(String args[]) {
        new SwingPad();
    }

    String rememberedString;
    JTextArea textEditArea;

    public SwingPad() {
        JFrame window = new JFrame("Swing pad");
        Container contentPane = window.getContentPane();

        /* Create a text area, wrap it in a scroll pane and stuff it
           in the content pane. */
        textEditArea = new JTextArea();
        JScrollPane editArea = new JScrollPane(textEditArea);
        contentPane.add(editArea, BorderLayout.CENTER);

        // Make the application exit when the window is closed by the user.
        window.addWindowListener(new WindowAdapter() {
                public void windowClosing(WindowEvent e) {
                    System.exit(0);
                }
        });

        // Create actions that the user can activate
        Action clearOperation = new AbstractAction("Clear") {
            public void actionPerformed(ActionEvent e) {
                textEditArea.setText("");
            }
        };

        Action rememberOperation = new AbstractAction("Remember") {
            public void actionPerformed(ActionEvent e) {
                rememberedString = textEditArea.getText();
            }
        };

        Action recallOperation = new AbstractAction("Recall") {
            public void actionPerformed(ActionEvent e) {
                if (rememberedString == null) return;
                textEditArea.setText(rememberedString);
            }
        };
```

```
            // Create the tool-bar and add the actions
            JToolBar toolbar = new JToolBar();
            toolbar.add(clearOperation);
            toolbar.add(rememberOperation);
            toolbar.add(recallOperation);

            contentPane.add(toolbar, BorderLayout.NORTH);

            // Create the edit menu and add the actions
            JMenu editMenu = new JMenu("Edit");
            editMenu.add(clearOperation);
            editMenu.add(rememberOperation);
            editMenu.add(recallOperation);

            // Put the menu in the menu-bar and attach it to menubar
            JMenuBar menubar = new JMenuBar();
            menubar.add(editMenu);
            window.getRootPane().setJMenuBar(menubar);

            window.pack();
            window.setVisible(true);
        }
    }
```

18 Files and Streams

18.1

```
// Filename: Convert.java
import java.io.*;

public class Convert {

    public static void main(String args[]) {
        String inEncoding  = "8859_1";
        String outEncoding = "UTF8";

        InputStream  inStream  = System.in;
        OutputStream outStream = System.out;

        try {
            try {
                inEncoding  = args[0];
                outEncoding = args[1];

                inStream  = new FileInputStream (args[2]);
                outStream = new FileOutputStream(args[3]);
            } catch (ArrayIndexOutOfBoundsException aioobe) {
                // Missing parameters are allowed.
            }

            BufferedReader reader = new BufferedReader(
                    new InputStreamReader(inStream, inEncoding)
            );

            BufferedWriter writer = new BufferedWriter(
                    new OutputStreamWriter(outStream, outEncoding)
            );
```

```
                // Transfer 512 chars at a time.
                char[] cbuf = new char[512];

                while (true) {
                     int bytesLastRead = reader.read(cbuf);
                     if (bytesLastRead == -1) break;
                     writer.write(cbuf, 0, bytesLastRead);
                     // Last two args was offset (none) and length.
                }

                reader.close();
                writer.close();

            } catch (FileNotFoundException fnfe) {
                System.err.println("File not found: " + fnfe.getLocalizedMessage());
            } catch (IOException ioe) {
                System.err.println("I/O error: " + ioe.getLocalizedMessage());
            } catch (SecurityException se) {
                System.err.println("Security Error: " + se.getLocalizedMessage());
            }
        }
    }
```

19 Javadoc Facility

19.1 The original Example 17.5 had one interface and two classes in the same compilation unit. In order for the `javadoc` tool to be able to extract the documentation, each interface and class must be placed in their own compilation unit. Also, notice that since most members have default accessibility, most of the documentation will not show up unless the `-package` option is given to the `javadoc` tool.

```
// Filename: IGeometryConstants.java

/**
 * Contains a set of constants that are used by other classes.
 * Contains a shape type enumeration and a size enumeration, and arrays
 * of strings associating the enumeration values with textual labels.
 */
interface IGeometryConstants {                                        // (1)
    int SQUARE  = 0;
    int CIRCLE  = 1;
    int ELLIPSE = 2;
    String[] shapeNames = {"Square", "Circle", "Ellipse"};

    int SMALL  = 0;
    int MEDIUM = 1;
    int LARGE  = 2;
    String[] sizeNames = {"Small", "Medium", "Large"};
}
```

```
// Filename: DemoSwingApplet.java

import javax.swing.*;
import javax.swing.border.*;
import java.awt.*;
import java.awt.event.*;
import java.applet.*;

/**
 * An applet demonstrating how GUIs are built and how event handling
 * works in Swing. This is a Swing version of an earlier AWT applet.
 *
 * <p>The user can specify the shape, size, fill and coordinates for a
 * drawing.  Clicking the draw button renders the shape according to
 * the specificatons indicated by the user.
 *
 * <p>The drawing region is implemented by the class
 * <code>DrawRegion</code>.
 *
 * @see DrawRegion
 */
public class DemoSwingApplet extends JApplet implements IGeometryConstants {

    /** Panel where the user can select the shape. */
    JPanel       shapePanel;
    /**
     * The group of radio buttons which allow the user to select the shape.
     */
    ButtonGroup  shapeGroup;
    /** For selecting the square shape. */
    JRadioButton squareRB;
    /** For selecting the circle shape. */
    JRadioButton circleRB;
    /** For selecting the ellipse shape. */
    JRadioButton ellipseRB;

    /** Panel where the user can specify x, y coordinates. */
    JPanel     xyPanel;
    JLabel     xLabel;
    /** For editing the x coordinate. */
    JTextField xInput;
    JLabel     yLabel;
    /** For editing the y coordinate. */
    JTextField yInput;

    /** Panel where the user can select size and fill. */
    JPanel    sizePanel;
    JLabel    sizeLabel;
    /** List of size choices the user can select. */
    JComboBox sizeChoices;
    JCheckBox fillCB;

    /**
     * Box for laying out the shape, coordinates, size and fill panels.
     */
    Box leftBox;
```

```
    /** Panel for the draw button, drawing region and message display. */
    JPanel      rightPanel;
    /** The button that will activate drawing of the shape. */
    JButton     drawButton;
    /**
     * A scroll pane allowing the draw region to be scrolled by the user.
     */
    JScrollPane scrollPane;
    /** The drawing region where the shape will be drawn. */
    DrawRegion  drawRegion;
    /** A text field used to report messages. */
    JTextField  messageDisplay;

    /** The top container. */
    Container topContainer;

    /**
     * Initialize the applet by creating all the GUI components.
     */
    public void init() {                                           // (3)
        makeShapePanel();
        makeXYPanel();
        makeSizePanel();
        makeLeftBox();
        makeRightPanel();

        addListeners();                                            // (4)

        topContainer = getContentPane();                           // (5)
        topContainer.add(leftBox,    BorderLayout.WEST);
        topContainer.add(rightPanel, BorderLayout.CENTER);

        try {                                                      // (6)
            UIManager.setLookAndFeel(
                UIManager.getSystemLookAndFeelClassName()
//              "com.sun.java.swing.plaf.motif.MotifLookAndFeel"
//              "com.sun.java.swing.plaf.windows.WindowsLookAndFeel"
//              "javax.swing.plaf.mac.MacLookAndFeel"
            );
        } catch (Exception e) { messageDisplay.setText(e.toString()); }
        SwingUtilities.updateComponentTreeUI(this);                // (7)
    }

    /**
     * Creates a panel with radio buttons where the user can select
     * the shape type.  Uses a <code>ButtonGroup</code> instance to
     * provide the semantics of radio buttons.  Stores the result in
     * the member variables.  This method is called by the
     * <code>init()</code> method.
     *
     * @see #shapePanel
     * @see #shapeBG
     * @see #squareRB
     * @see #ellipseRB
     * @see #init
     */
```

```
void makeShapePanel() {
    squareRB  = new JRadioButton(shapeNames[SQUARE],  true);
    circleRB  = new JRadioButton(shapeNames[CIRCLE],  false);
    ellipseRB = new JRadioButton(shapeNames[ELLIPSE], false);

    shapeGroup = new ButtonGroup();
    shapeGroup.add(squareRB);
    shapeGroup.add(circleRB);
    shapeGroup.add(ellipseRB);

    shapePanel = new JPanel();
    shapePanel.setLayout(new FlowLayout());
    shapePanel.add(squareRB);
    shapePanel.add(circleRB);
    shapePanel.add(ellipseRB);
    shapePanel.setBorder(new TitledBorder("Shapes"));
}

/**
 * Creates a panel with components where the user can specify x, y
 * coordinates.  Stores the result in the member variables.  This
 * method is called by the <code>init()</code> method.
 *
 * @see #xyPanel
 * @see #xInput
 * @see #yInput
 * @see #init
 */
void makeXYPanel() {
    xyPanel = new JPanel();

    xLabel  = new JLabel("X Coordinate:");
    yLabel  = new JLabel("Y Coordinate:");

    xInput  = new JTextField(5);
    yInput  = new JTextField(5);

    xyPanel.setLayout(new GridLayout(2,2));
    xyPanel.add(xLabel);
    xyPanel.add(xInput);
    xyPanel.add(yLabel);
    xyPanel.add(yInput);
}

/**
 * Creates a panel with components where the user can select size
 * and fill.  The size can be selected from a list of choices.
 * Stores the result in member variables.  This method is called
 * by the <code>init()</code> method.
 *
 * @see #sizePanel
 * @see #sizeChoices
 * @see #fillCB
 * @see #init
 */
```

```
    void makeSizePanel() {

        sizePanel   = new JPanel();

        sizeLabel   = new JLabel("Size:");

        sizeChoices = new JComboBox(sizeNames);
        sizeChoices.setSelectedIndex(0);

        fillCB = new JCheckBox("Fill", false);

        sizePanel.setLayout(new FlowLayout());
        sizePanel.add(sizeLabel);
        sizePanel.add(sizeChoices);
        sizePanel.add(fillCB);
    }

   /**
    * Lays out the shape, coordinates, size and fill panels vertically
    * in a box.  Stores the result in a member variable.  This method
    * is called by the <code>init()</code> method.
    *
    * @see #boxA
    * @see #init
    */
    void makeLeftBox() {
        leftBox = new Box(BoxLayout.Y_AXIS);

        leftBox.add(shapePanel);
        leftBox.add(Box.createGlue());
        leftBox.add(xyPanel);
        leftBox.add(Box.createGlue());
        leftBox.add(sizePanel);
    }

    /**
     * Lays out the draw button, drawing region and message display
     * components in a panel.  Stores the result in a member variable.
     * This method is called by the <code>init()</code> method.
     *
     * @see #rightPanel
     * @see #init
     */
    void makeRightPanel() {
        rightPanel = new JPanel();

        messageDisplay = new JTextField("MESSAGE DISPLAY");
        messageDisplay.setEditable(false);

        drawButton = new JButton("Draw");

        drawRegion = new DrawRegion();
        scrollPane = new JScrollPane(drawRegion);

        rightPanel.setLayout(new BorderLayout());
        rightPanel.add(drawButton, BorderLayout.NORTH);
        rightPanel.add(messageDisplay, BorderLayout.SOUTH);
        rightPanel.add(scrollPane, BorderLayout.CENTER);
    }
```

```
/**
 * Adds a listener to the draw button.  The only event handling
 * that takes place is when the user clicks the draw button. An
 * action listener is added to the button. It successively
 * collects all the information required to do the drawing: the
 * kind of shape, the coordinates, the size. Then it finally calls
 * the <code>doDraw()</code> method of the drawing region.  This
 * method is called by the <code>init()</code> method.
 *
 * @see DrawRegion#doDraw
 * @see #init
 */
void addListeners() {

    drawButton.addActionListener(new ActionListener() {      // (13)
        public void actionPerformed(ActionEvent evt) {

            int shape, xCoord, yCoord, width;

            messageDisplay.setText("");
            // Get the shape                                      (14)
            if (squareRB.isSelected())
                shape = SQUARE;
            else if (circleRB.isSelected())
                shape = CIRCLE;
            else if (ellipseRB.isSelected())
                shape = ELLIPSE;
            else {
                messageDisplay.setText("Unknown shape.");
                return;
            }

            // Get the coordinates                                (15)
            try {
                xCoord = Integer.parseInt(xInput.getText());
                yCoord = Integer.parseInt(yInput.getText());
            } catch (NumberFormatException e) {
                messageDisplay.setText("Illegal coordinates.");
                return;
            }

            // Get the size                                       (16)
            switch (sizeChoices.getSelectedIndex()) {
                case SMALL:  width = 30;  break;
                case MEDIUM: width = 60;  break;
                case LARGE:  width = 120; break;
                default: messageDisplay.setText("Unknown size."); return;
            }

            messageDisplay.setText("Drawing " + shapeNames[shape]);
            drawRegion.doDraw(                                 // (17)
                    shape,
                    xCoord, yCoord,
                    fillCB.isSelected(),
                    width
            );
```

```
            }
        });
    }
}
```

```
// Filename: DrawRegion.java
import javax.swing.JPanel;
import java.awt.*;

/**
 * A drawing region that can store information about and paint a shape.
 */

class DrawRegion extends JPanel implements IGeometryConstants {   // (18)

    // Values needed for drawing the shape
    private int     shape;
    private int     xCoord;
    private int     yCoord;
    private boolean fillFlag;
    private int     width;

    /**
     * Creates a new DrawRegion instance.  The region is given a
     * default size and background color.
     */
    public DrawRegion() {
        setSize(300,300);
        setBackground(Color.white);
    }

    /**
     * Requests that the size of the drawing region remains constant.
     *
     * @return The current size of the component.
     */
    public Dimension getPreferredSize() {
        return getSize();
    }

    /**
     * Stores the values of a shape and schedules a repainting of the
     * drawing region.
     *
     * @param shape The type of shape as defined by the constants in
     *              {@link IGeometryConstants}.
     * @param xCoord The x coordinate of the shape.
     * @param yCoord The y coordinate of the shape.
     * @param fillFlag <code>true</code> if the shape should be filled.
     * @param width   The width/size of the shape.
     */
    public void doDraw(int shape,
                       int xCoord, int yCoord,
                       boolean fillFlag, int width) {
```

```
        this.shape    = shape;
        this.xCoord   = xCoord;
        this.yCoord   = yCoord;
        this.fillFlag = fillFlag;
        this.width    = width;

        repaint();                                                      // (20)
    }

    /**
     * Paint the shape in the drawing region.
     *
     * @param g The graphics object that will be used to paint the shape.
     */
    public void paintComponent (Graphics g) {
        super.paintComponent(g);
        switch (shape) {
            case SQUARE:
                if (fillFlag) g.fillRect(xCoord, yCoord, width, width);
                else g.drawRect(xCoord, yCoord, width, width);
                break;
            case CIRCLE:
                if (fillFlag) g.fillOval(xCoord, yCoord, width, width);
                else g.drawOval(xCoord, yCoord, width, width);
                break;
            case ELLIPSE:
                if (fillFlag) g.fillOval(xCoord, yCoord, width, width/2);
                else g.drawOval(xCoord, yCoord, width, width/2);
                break;
        }
    }
}
```

Appendix E

Sample Exam

This is a mock exam for the Sun Certified Programmer for the Java 2 Platform. It is comprised of brand new questions, which are close to the questions that can be expected on the real exam. Working through this exam will give the reader a good indication how well he or she is prepared for the real exam, and whether any topics need further study.

Q1 Given the following class, which statements can be inserted at position 1 without causing the code to fail compilation?

```
public class Q6db8 {
    int a;
    int b = 0;
    static int c;

    public void m() {
        int d;
        int e = 0;

        // Position 1
    }
}
```

Select all valid answers.

(a) `a++;`
(b) `b++;`
(c) `c++;`
(d) `d++;`
(e) `e++;`

Q2 Which statements are true concerning the effect of the >> and >>> operators?

Select all valid answers.

(a) For non-negative values of the left operand, the >> and >>> operators will have the same effect.

(b) The result of (-1 >> 1) is 0.
(c) The result of (-1 >>> 1) is –1.
(d) The value returned by >>> will never be negative as long as the value of the right operand is not divisible by 32.
(e) When using the >> operator, the leftmost bit of the bit representation of the resulting value will always be the same bit value as the leftmost bit of the bit representation of the left operand.

Q3 What is wrong with the following code?

```
class MyException extends Exception {}

public class Qb4ab {
    public void foo() {
        try {
            bar();
        } finally {
            baz();
        } catch (MyException e) {}
    }

    public void bar() throws MyException {
        throw new MyException();
    }

    public void baz() throws RuntimeException {
        throw new RuntimeException();
    }
}
```

Select all valid answers.

(a) Since the method `foo()` does not catch the exception generated by the method `baz()`, it must declare the `RuntimeException` in its throws clause.
(b) A `try` block cannot be followed by both a `catch` and a `finally` block.
(c) An empty `catch` block is not allowed.
(d) A `catch` block cannot follow a `finally` block.
(e) A `finally` block must always follow one or more `catch` blocks.

Q4 What will be written to the standard output when the following program is run?

```
public class Qd803 {
    public static void main(String args[]) {
        String word = "restructure";
        System.out.println(word.substring(2, 3));
    }
}
```

Select the one right answer.

(a) `est`
(b) `es`

(c) `str`
(d) `st`
(e) `s`

Q5 Given that a static method `doIt()` in a class `Work` represents work to be done, what block of code will succeed in starting a new thread that will do the work?

Select all valid answers.

(a)
```
Runnable r = new Runnable() {
    public void run() {
        Work.doIt();
    }
};
Thread t = new Thread(r);
t.start();
```
(b)
```
Thread t = new Thread() {
    public void start() {
        Work.doIt();
    }
};
t.start();
```
(c)
```
Runnable r = new Runnable() {
    public void run() {
        Work.doIt();
    }
};
r.start();
```
(d)
```
Thread t = new Thread(new Work());
t.start();
```
(e)
```
Runnable t = new Runnable() {
    public void run() {
        Work.doIt();
    }
};
t.run();
```

Q6 Write a line of code that declares a variable named `layout` of type `LayoutManager` and initializes it with a new object, which when used with a container can lay out components in a rectangular grid of equal-sized rectangles, 3 components wide and 2 components high.

Fill in a single line of code.

Q7 What will be the result of attempting to compile and run the following code?

```
public class Q275d {
    static int a;
    int b;

    public Q275d() {
        int c;
        c = a;
        a++;
        b += c;
    }

    public static void main(String args[]) {
        new Q275d();
    }
}
```

Select the one right answer.

(a) The code will fail to compile, since the constructor is trying to access static members.
(b) The code will fail to compile, since the constructor is trying to use static member variable `a` before it has been initialized.
(c) The code will fail to compile, since the constructor is trying to use member variable `b` before it has been initialized.
(d) The code will fail to compile, since the constructor is trying to use local variable `c` before it has been initialized.
(e) The code will compile and run without any problems.

Q8 What will be written to the standard output when the following program is run?

```
public class Q63e3 {
    public static void main(String args[]) {
        System.out.println(9 ^ 2);
    }
}
```

Select the one right answer.

(a) `81`
(b) `7`
(c) `11`
(d) `0`
(e) `false`

Q9 Which statements are true concerning the default layout manager for containers in the `java.awt` package?

Select all valid answers.

(a) Objects instantiated from `Panel` do not have a default layout manager.
(b) Objects instantiated from `Panel` have `FlowLayout` as default layout manager.
(c) Objects instantiated from `Applet` have `BorderLayout` as default layout manager.
(d) Objects instantiated from `Dialog` have `BorderLayout` as default layout manager.
(e) Objects instantiated from `Window` have the same default layout manager as instances of `Applet`.

Q10 Which declarations will allow a class to be started as a standalone program?

Select all valid answers.

(a) `public void main(String args[])`
(b) `public void static main(String args[])`
(c) `public static main(String[] argv)`
(d) `final public static void main(String [] array)`
(e) `public static void main(String args[])`

Q11 Under which circumstances will a thread stop?

Select all valid answers.

(a) The method `waitforId()` in class `MediaTracker` is called.
(b) The `run()` method that the thread is executing ends.
(c) The call to the `start()` method of the `Thread` object returns.
(d) The `suspend()` method is called on the `Thread` object.
(e) The `wait()` method is called on the `Thread` object.

Q12 When creating a class that associates a set of keys with a set of values, which of these interfaces is most applicable?

Select the one right answer.

(a) `Collection`
(b) `Set`
(c) `SortedSet`
(d) `Map`

Q13 What does the value returned by the method `getID()` found in class `java.awt.AWTEvent` uniquely identify?

Select the one right answer.

(a) The particular event instance.
(b) The source of the event.
(c) The set of events that were triggered by the same action.
(d) The type of event.
(e) The type of component from which the event originated.

Q14 What will be written to the standard output when the following program is run?

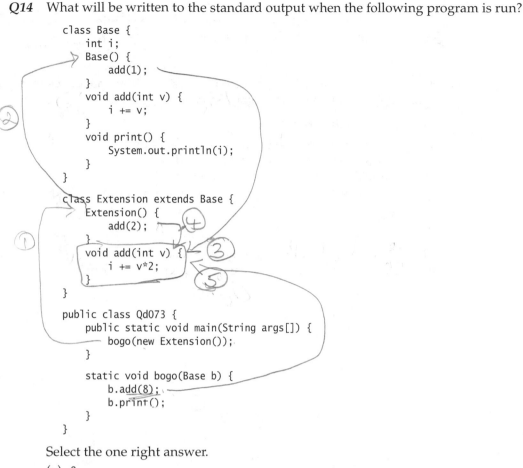

```
class Base {
    int i;
    Base() {
        add(1);
    }
    void add(int v) {
        i += v;
    }
    void print() {
        System.out.println(i);
    }
}

class Extension extends Base {
    Extension() {
        add(2);
    }
    void add(int v) {
        i += v*2;
    }
}

public class Qd073 {
    public static void main(String args[]) {
        bogo(new Extension());
    }

    static void bogo(Base b) {
        b.add(8);
        b.print();
    }
}
```

Select the one right answer.

(a) 9
(b) 18
(c) 20
(d) 21
(e) 22

Q15 Which lines of code are valid declarations of a native method when occurring within the declaration of the following class?

```
public class Qf575 {
    // insert declaration of a native method here
}
```

Select all valid answers.

(a) `native public void setTemperature(int kelvin);`
(b) `private native void setTemperature(int kelvin);`

(c) `protected int native getTemperature();`
(d) `public abstract native void setTemperature(int kelvin);`
(e) `native int setTemperature(int kelvin) {}`

Q16 How does the `weighty` property of the `GridBagConstraints` objects used in grid bag layout affect the layout of the components?

Select the one right answer.

(a) It affects which grid cell the components end up in.
(b) It affects how the extra vertical space is distributed.
(c) It affects the alignment of each component.
(d) It affects whether the components completely fill their allotted display area vertically.

Q17 Which statements can be inserted at the indicated position in the following code to make the program write 1 on the standard output when run?

```
public class Q4a39 {
    int a = 1;
    int b = 1;
    int c = 1;

    class Inner {
        int a = 2;

        int get() {
            int c = 3;
            // insert statement here
            return c;
        }
    }

    Q4a39() {
        Inner i = new Inner();
        System.out.println(i.get());
    }

    public static void main(String args[]) {
        new Q4a39();
    }
}
```

Select all valid answers.

(a) `c = b;`
(b) `c = this.a;`
(c) `c = this.b;`
(d) `c = Q4a39.this.a;`
(e) `c = c;`

Q18 Which is the earliest line in the following code after which the object created on the line marked (0) will be a candidate for being garbage collected, assuming no compiler optimizations are done?

```
public class Q76a9 {
    static String f() {
        String a = "hello";
        String b = "bye";              // (0)
        String c = b + "!";            // (1)
        String d = b;

        b = a;                         // (2)
        d = a;                         // (3)
        return c;                      // (4)
    }

    public static void main(String args[]) {
        String msg = f();
        System.out.println(msg);       // (5)
    }
}
```

Select the one right answer.

(a) The line marked (1).
(b) The line marked (2).
(c) The line marked (3).
(d) The line marked (4).
(e) The line marked (5).

Q19 Which methods from the `String` and `StringBuffer` classes modify the object on which they are called?

Select all valid answers.

(a) The `charAt()` method of the `String` class.
(b) The `toUpperCase()` method of the `String` class.
(c) The `replace()` method of the `String` class.
(d) The `reverse()` method of the `StringBuffer` class.
(e) The `length()` method of the `StringBuffer` class.

Q20 Which statements, when inserted at the indicated position in the following code, will cause a runtime exception when attempting to run the program?

```
class A {}

class B extends A {}

class C extends A {}

public class Q3ae4 {
    public static void main(String args[]) {
        A x = new A();
        B y = new B();
        C z = new C();
```

```
            // insert statement here

        }
    }
```

Select all valid answers.

(a) `x = y;`
(b) `z = x;`
(c) `y = (B) x;`
(d) `z = (C) y;`
(e) `y = (A) y;`

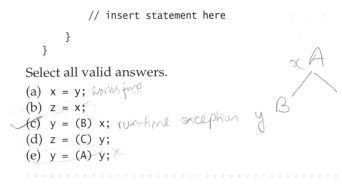

Q21 Which of these are keywords in Java?

Select all valid answers.

(a) `default`
(b) `NULL`
(c) `String`
(d) `throws`
(e) `long`

Q22 It is desirable that a certain method within a certain class can only be accessed by classes that are defined within the same package as the class of the method. How can such restrictions be enforced?

Select the one right answer.

(a) Mark the method with the keyword `public`.
(b) Mark the method with the keyword `protected`.
(c) Mark the method with the keyword `private`.
(d) Mark the method with the keyword `package`.
(e) Do not mark the method with any accessibility modifiers.

Q23 Which code fragments will succeed in initializing a two-dimensional array named `tab` with a size that will cause the expression `tab[3][2]` to access a valid element?

Select all valid answers.

(a)
```
int[][] tab = {
    { 0, 0, 0 },
    { 0, 0, 0 }
};
```
(b)
```
int tab[][] = new int[4][];
for (int i=0; i<tab.length; i++) tab[i] = new int[3];
```

(c)
```
int tab[][] = {
    0, 0, 0, 0,
    0, 0, 0, 0,
    0, 0, 0, 0,
    0, 0, 0, 0
};
```
(d) `int tab[3][2];`
(e) `int[] tab[] = { {0, 0, 0}, {0, 0, 0}, {0, 0, 0}, {0, 0, 0} };`

Q24 What will be the result of attempting to run the following program?

```
public class Qaa75 {
    public static void main(String args[]) {
        String[][][] arr = {
            { {}, null },
            { { "1", "2" }, { "1", null, "3" } },
            {},
            { { "1", null } }
        };

        System.out.println(arr.length + arr[1][2].length);
    }
}
```

Select the one right answer.

(a) The program will terminate with an `ArrayIndexOutOfBoundsException`.
(b) The program will terminate with a `NullPointerException`.
(c) 4 will be written to standard output.
(d) 6 will be written to standard output.
(e) 7 will be written to standard output.

Q25 Which expressions will evaluate to true if preceded by the following code?

```
String a = "hello";
String b = new String(a);
String c = a;
char[] d = { 'h', 'e', 'l', 'l', 'o' };
```

Select all valid answers.

(a) `(a == "Hello")`
(b) `(a == b)`
(c) `(a == c)`
(d) `a.equals(b)`
(e) `a.equals(d)`

Q26 Which statements concerning the following code are true?

```
class A {
    public A() {}

    public A(int i) { this(); }
}

class B extends A {
    public boolean B(String msg) { return false; }
}

class C extends B {
    private C() { super(); }

    public C(String msg) { this(); }

    public C(int i) {}
}
```

Select all valid answers.

(a) The code will fail to compile.
(b) The constructor in `A` that takes an `int` as an argument will never be called as a result of constructing an object of class `B` or `C`.
(c) Class `C` has three constructors.
(d) Objects of class `B` cannot be constructed.
(e) At most one of the constructors of each class is called as a result of constructing an object of class `C`.

0 or 1

Q27 Given two collection objects referenced by `col1` and `col2`, which of these statements are true?

Select all valid answers.

(a) The operation `col1.retainAll(col2)` will not modify the `col1` object.
(b) The operation `col1.removeAll(col2)` will not modify the `col2` object.
(c) The operation `col1.addAll(col2)` will return a new collection object, containing elements from both `col1` and `col2`.
(d) The operation `col1.containsAll(Col2)` will not modify the `col1` object.

Q28 Which statements concerning the relationships between the following classes are true?

```
class Foo {
    int num;
    Baz comp = new Baz();
}

class Bar {
    boolean flag;
}
```

```
class Baz extends Foo {
    Bar thing = new Bar();
    double limit;
}
```

Foo [Baz]
↳ Baz [Bar]

Select all valid answers.

(a) A Bar is a Baz.
(b) A Foo has a Bar. ✗ refer Ans
(c) A Baz is a Foo.
(d) A Foo is a Baz.
(e) A Baz has a Bar.

Q29 Which statements concerning the value of a member variable are true, when no explicit assignments have been made?

Select all valid answers.

(a) The value of an `int` is undetermined.
(b) The value of all numeric types is zero.
(c) The compiler may issue an error if the variable is used before it is initialized.
(d) The value of a `String` variable is "" (empty string).
(e) The value of all object variables is `null`.

Q30 Which statements describe guaranteed behavior of the garbage collection and finalization mechanisms?

Select all valid answers.

(a) Objects are deleted when they can no longer be accessed through any reference.
(b) The `finalize()` method will eventually be called on every object.
(c) The `finalize()` method will never be called more than once on an object.
(d) An object will not be garbage collected as long as it is possible for an active part of the program to access it through a reference.
(e) The garbage collector will use a mark and sweep algorithm.

Q31 Which code fragments will succeed in printing the last argument given on the command line to the standard output, and exit gracefully with no output if no arguments are given?

Select all valid answers.

(a)
```
public static void main(String args[]) {
    if (args.length != 0)
        System.out.println(args[args.length-1]);
}
```

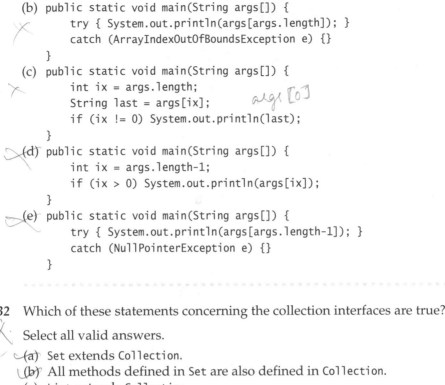

(b)
```
public static void main(String args[]) {
    try { System.out.println(args[args.length]); }
    catch (ArrayIndexOutOfBoundsException e) {}
}
```
(c)
```
public static void main(String args[]) {
    int ix = args.length;
    String last = args[ix];
    if (ix != 0) System.out.println(last);
}
```
(d)
```
public static void main(String args[]) {
    int ix = args.length-1;
    if (ix > 0) System.out.println(args[ix]);
}
```
(e)
```
public static void main(String args[]) {
    try { System.out.println(args[args.length-1]); }
    catch (NullPointerException e) {}
}
```

Q32 Which of these statements concerning the collection interfaces are true?

Select all valid answers.

(a) `Set` extends `Collection`.
(b) All methods defined in `Set` are also defined in `Collection`.
(c) `List` extends `Collection`.
(d) All methods defined in `List` are also defined in `Collection`.
(e) `Map` extends `Collection`.

Q33 Which is the legal range of values for a `short`?

Select the one right answer.

(a) -2^7 to 2^7-1
(b) -2^8 to 2^8
(c) -2^{15} to $2^{15}-1$
(d) -2^{16} to $2^{16}-1$
(e) 0 to $2^{16}-1$

Q34 What is the name of the method that threads can use to pause their execution until signalled to continue by another thread?

Fill in the name of the method (do not include a parameter list).

Q35 Given the following class definitions, which expression identifies whether the object referred to by `obj` was created by instantiating class `B` rather than classes `A`, `C` and `D`?

```
class A {}
class B extends A {}
class C extends B {}
class D extends A {}
```

Select all valid answers.

(a) `obj instanceof B`
(b) `obj instanceof A && ! (obj instanceof C)`
(c) `obj instanceof B && ! (obj instanceof C)`
(d) `!(obj instanceof C || obj instanceof D)`
(e) `! (obj instanceof A) && ! (obj instanceof C) && ! (obj instanceof D)`

Q36 What will be written to the standard output when the following program is run?

```
public class Q8499 {
    public static void main(String args[]) {
        double d = -2.9;
        int i = (int) d;
        i *= (int) Math.ceil(d);
        i *= (int) Math.abs(d);
        System.out.println(i);
    }
}
```

Select the one right answer.

(a) -12
(b) 18
(c) 8
(d) 12
(e) 27

Q37 What will be written to the standard output when the following program is run?

```
public class Qcb90 {
    int a;
    int b;
    public void f() {
        a = 0;
        b = 0;
        int[] c = { 0 };
        g(b, c);
        System.out.println(a + " " + b + " " + c[0] + " ");
    }
```

```
        public void g(int b, int[] c) {
            a = 1;
            b = 1;
            c[0] = 1;
        }

        public static void main(String args[]) {
            Qcb90 obj = new Qcb90();

            obj.f();
        }
    }
```

Select the one right answer.

(a) `0 0 0`
(b) `0 0 1`
(c) `0 1 0`
(d) `1 0 0`
(e) `1 0 1`

Q38 Which statements concerning the effect of the statement `gfx.drawRect(5, 5, 10, 10)` are true, given that `gfx` is a reference to a valid `Graphics` object?

Select all valid answers.

(a) The rectangle drawn will have a total width of 5 pixels.
(b) The rectangle drawn will have a total height of 6 pixels.
(c) The rectangle drawn will have a total width of 10 pixels.
(d) The rectangle drawn will have a total height of 11 pixels.

Q39 Given the following code, which code fragments, when inserted at the indicated location, will succeed in making the program display a button spanning the whole window area?

```
import java.awt.*;

public class Q1e65 {
    public static void main(String args[]) {
        Window win = new Frame();
        Button but = new Button("button");

        // insert code fragment here

        win.setSize(200, 200);
        win.setVisible(true);
    }
}
```

Select all valid answers.

(a)
```
win.setLayout(new BorderLayout());
win.add(but);
```

(b) `win.setLayout(new GridLayout(1, 1));`
`win.add(but);`

(c) `win.setLayout(new BorderLayout());`
`win.add(but, BorderLayout.CENTER);`

(d) `win.add(but);`

(e) `win.setLayout(new FlowLayout());`
`win.add(but);`

Q40 Which method implementations will write the given string to a file named "`file`", using UTF8 encoding?

Select all valid answers.

(a)
```
public void write(String msg) throws IOException {
     FileWriter fw = new FileWriter(new File("file"));
     fw.write(msg);
     fw.close();
}
```
Native encoding

(b)
```
public void write(String msg) throws IOException {
     OutputStreamWriter osw =
         new OutputStreamWriter(new FileOutputStream("file"), "UTF8");
     osw.write(msg);
     osw.close();
}
```

(c)
```
public void write(String msg) throws IOException {
     FileWriter fw = new FileWriter(new File("file"));
     fw.setEncoding("UTF8");
     fw.write(msg);
     fw.close();
}
```

(d)
```
public void write(String msg) throws IOException {
     FilterWriter fw = FilterWriter(new FileWriter("file"), "UTF8");
     fw.write(msg);
     fw.close();
}
```

(e)
```
public void write(String msg) throws IOException {
     OutputStreamWriter osw = new OutputStreamWriter(
         new OutputStream(new File("file")), "UTF8"
     );
     osw.write(msg);
     osw.close();
}
```

Q41 Which are valid identifiers?

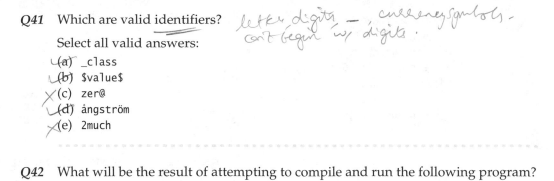

Select all valid answers:

(a) `_class`
(b) `$value$`
(c) `zer@`
(d) `ångström`
(e) `2much`

Q42 What will be the result of attempting to compile and run the following program?

```
public class Q28fd {
    public static void main(String args[]) {
        int counter = 0;
        l1:
        for (int i=10; i<0; i--) {
            l2:
            int j = 0;
            while (j < 10) {
                if (j > i) break l2;
                if (i == j) {
                    counter++;
                    continue l1;
                }
            }
            counter--;
        }
        System.out.println(counter);
    }
}
```

Select the one right answer.

(a) The program will fail to compile.
(b) The program will not terminate normally.
(c) The program will write `10` to the standard output.
(d) The program will write `0` to the standard output.
(e) The program will write `9` to the standard output.

Q43 Given the following definition, which definitions are valid?

```
interface I {
    void setValue(int val);
    int getValue();
}
```

Select all valid answers.

(a)
```
class A extends I {
    int value;
    void setValue(int val) { value = val; }
    int getValue() { return value; }
}
```
(b)
```
interface B extends I {
    void increment();
}
```
(c)
```
abstract class C implements I {
    int getValue() { return 0; }
    abstract void increment();
}
```
(d)
```
interface D implements I {
    void increment();
}
```
(e)
```
class E implements I {
    int value;
    public void setValue(int val) { value = val; }
}
```

Q44 Which statements concerning the methods `notify()` and `notifyAll()` are true?

Select all valid answers:

(a) Instances of class `Thread` have a method called `notify()`.
(b) A call to the method `notify()` will wake the thread that currently owns the monitor of the object.
(c) The method `notify()` is synchronized.
(d) The method `notifyAll()` is defined in class `Thread`.
(e) When there is more than one thread waiting to obtain the monitor of an object, there is no way to be sure which thread will be notified by the `notify()` method.

Q45 Which statements concerning the correlation between the inner and outer instances of non-static inner classes are true?

Select all valid answers.

(a) Member variables of the outer instance are always accessible to inner instances, regardless of their accessibility modifiers.
(b) Member variables of the outer instance can never be referred to using only the variable name within the inner instance.
(c) More than one inner instance can be associated with the same outer instance.
(d) All variables from the outer instance that should be accessible in the inner instance must be declared `final`.
(e) A class that is declared `final` cannot have any inner classes.

Q46 What will be the result of attempting to compile and run the following code?

```
public class Q6b0c {
    public static void main(String args[]) {
        int i = 4;
        float f = 4.3;
        double d = 1.8;
        int c = 0;
        if (i == f) c++;
        if (((int) (f + d)) == ((int) f + (int) d)) c += 2;
        System.out.println(c);
    }
}
```

Select the one right answer.

(a) The code will fail to compile.
(b) `0` will be written to the standard output.
(c) `1` will be written to the standard output.
(d) `2` will be written to the standard output.
(e) `3` will be written to the standard output.

Q47 Which operators will always evaluate all the operands?

Select all valid answers.

(a) `||`
(b) `+`
(c) `&&`
(d) `? :`
(e) `%`

Q48 Which statements concerning the `switch` construct are true?

Select all valid answers.

(a) All `switch` statements must have a `default` label.
(b) There must be exactly one label for each code segment in a `switch` statement.
(c) The keyword `continue` can never occur within the body of a `switch` statement.
(d) No `case` label may follow a `default` label within a single `switch` statement.
(e) A character literal can be used as a value for a `case` label.

Q49 Which modifiers and return types would be valid in the declaration of a working `main()` method for a Java standalone application?

Select all valid answers.

(a) `private`
(b) `final`

(c) static
(d) int
(e) abstract

Q50 What will be the appearance of an applet with the following `init()` method?

```
public void init() {
    add(new Button("hello"));
}
```

Select the one right answer.

(a) Nothing appears in the applet.
(b) A button will cover the whole area of the applet.
(c) A button will appear in the top left corner of the applet.
(d) A button will appear, centered in the top region of the applet.
(e) A button will appear in the center of the applet.

Q51 Which statements concerning the event model of the AWT are true?

Select all valid answers.

(a) At most one listener of each type can be registered with a component.
(b) Mouse motion listeners can be registered on a `List` instance.
(c) There exists a class named `ContainerEvent` in package `java.awt.event`.
(d) There exists a class named `MouseMotionEvent` in package `java.awt.event`.
(e) There exists a class named `ActionAdapter` in package `java.awt.event`.

Q52 Which statements are true, given the code `new FileOutputStream("data", true)` for creating an object of class `FileOutputStream`?

Select all valid answers.

(a) `FileOutputStream` has no constructors matching the given arguments.
(b) An `IOExeception` will be thrown if a file named "`data`" already exists.
(c) An `IOExeception` will be thrown if a file named "`data`" does not already exist.
(d) If a file named "`data`" exists, its contents will be reset and overwritten.
(e) If a file named "`data`" exists, output will be appended to its current contents.

Q53 Given the following code, write a line of code that, when inserted at the indicated location, will make the overriding method in `Extension` invoke the overridden method in class `Base` on the current object.

```
class Base {
    public void print() {
        System.out.println("base");
    }
}
```

```
class Extension extends Base {
    public void print() {
        System.out.println("extension");

        // insert line of implementation here
    }
}

public class Q294d {
    public static void main(String args[]) {
        Extension ext = new Extension();
        ext.print();
    }
}
```

Super.print();

Fill in a single line of implementation.

Q54 Given that `file` is a reference to a `File` object that represents a directory, which code fragments will succeed in obtaining a list of the entries in the directory?

Select all valid answers.

(a) `Vector filelist = ((Directory) file).getList();`
(b) `String[] filelist = file.directory();`
(c) `Enumeration filelist = file.contents();`
(d) `String[] filelist = file.list();`
(e) `Vector filelist = (new Directory(file)).files();`

Q55 What will be written to the standard output when the following program is run?

```
public class Q03e4 {
    public static void main(String args[]) {
        String space = " ";

        String composite = space + "hello" + space + space;
        composite.concat("world");

        String trimmed = composite.trim();

        System.out.println(trimmed.length());
    }
}
```

Select the one right answer.

(a) 5
(b) 6
(c) 7
(d) 12
(e) 13

Q56 Given the following code, which statements concerning the objects referenced through the member variables `i`, `j` and `k` are true, given that any thread may call the methods `a`, `b` and `c` at any time?

```
class Counter {
    int v = 0;
    synchronized void inc() { v++; }
    synchronized void dec() { v--; }
}

public class Q7ed5 {
    Counter i;
    Counter j;
    Counter k;
    public synchronized void a() {
        i.inc();
        System.out.println("a");
        i.dec();
    }

    public synchronized void b() {
        i.inc(); j.inc(); k.inc();
        System.out.println("b");
        i.dec(); j.dec(); k.dec();
    }

    public void c() {
        k.inc();
        System.out.println("c");
        k.dec();
    }
}
```

Select all valid answers.

(a) `i.v` is guaranteed always to be 0 or 1.
(b) `j.v` is guaranteed always to be 0 or 1.
(c) `k.v` is guaranteed always to be 0 or 1
(d) `j.v` will always be greater than or equal to `k.v` at any give time.
(e) `k.v` will always be greater than or equal to `j.v` at any give time.

Q57 Which statements concerning casting and conversion are true?

Select all valid answers.

(a) Conversion from `int` to `long` does not need a cast.
(b) Conversion from `byte` to `short` does not need a cast.
(c) Conversion from `float` to `long` does not need a cast.
(d) Conversion from `short` to `char` does not need a cast.
(e) Conversion from `boolean` to `int` using a cast is not possible.

Q58 Given the following code, which method declarations, when inserted at the indicated position, will not cause the program to fail compilation?

```
public class Qdd1f {
    public long sum(long a, long b) { return a + b; }

    // insert new method declaration here

}
```

Select all valid answers.

(a) `public int sum(int a, int b) { return a + b; }`
(b) `public int sum(long a, long b) { return 0; }`
(c) `abstract int sum();`
(d) `private long sum(long a, long b) { return a + b; }`
(e) `public long sum(long a, int b) { return a + b; }`

Q59 The 8859-1 character code for the uppercase letter A is 65. Which of these code fragments declare and initialize a variable of type `char` with this value?

Select all valid answers.

(a) `char ch = 65;`
(b) `char ch = '\65';`
(c) `char ch = '\0041';`
(d) `char ch = 'A';`
(e) `char ch = "A";`

Answers to Questions

Q1 *(a), (b), (c) and (e)*

Only local variables need to be explicitly initialized before use. Member variables are assigned a default value when not explicitly initialized.

Q2 *(a), (d) and (e)*

When the >> operator shifts bits to the right, it fills the new bits on the left with the bit value of the leftmost bit of the original bit pattern. When the >>> operator shifts bits to the right, it always fills the new bits on the left with a bit value of 0. Thus, the >> and the >>> operators perform the same operation when the leftmost bit of the original bit pattern has a bit value of 0. This occurs whenever the original value is non-negative.

The result of `(-1 >> 1)` is –1. In terms of bit patterns, this can be explained by saying that a bit pattern consisting of all 1s will continue to remain all 1s after being shifted by the >> operator.

The result of `(-1 >>> 1)` is 2147483647 which is $2^{31} - 1$. Shifting a bit pattern of all 1s one bit to the right using the >>> operator will yield a bit pattern of all 1s, except for the leftmost bit which will be 0. This gives the non-negative value 2147483647, which is the maximum value of type `int`.

The >>> operator will shift 0s into the bit pattern from the left, thus giving the leftmost bit a value of 0. Since a value of 0 in the leftmost bit signifies a non-negative value, the >>> operator is guaranteed to return a non-negative number if a shift has actually occurred.

Q3 *(d)*

A `try` block must be followed by at least one `catch` or `finally` block. No blocks can follow a `finally` block. Methods do not need to declare that they can throw runtime exceptions.

Q4 *(e)*

Giving `substring()` the parameters 2, 3 tells it to construct a string consisting of the characters between position 2 and position 3 of the original string. The positions are indexed in the following manner: Position 0 is immediately before the first character of the string, position 1 is between the first and the second character, position 2 is between the second and the third character, etc.

Q5 *(a)*

A `Thread` object executes the `run()` method of a `Runnable` on a separate thread when started. A `Runnable` object can be given when constructing a `Thread` object. If no `Runnable` is given, the `Thread` object will use itself as a `Runnable`. A thread is started using the `start()` method of the `Thread` object.

Q6 *Filled in:*

```
LayoutManager layout = new GridLayout(2, 3);
```

Be sure to get the order of the constructor parameters right.

Q7 *(e)*

The fact that a member variable is static does not limit access to it from non-static methods and constructors. All member variables will receive a default value when not explicitly initialized with a value. Local variables must be explicitly initialized before use. Assignment to the variable in this context constitutes initialization, not use.

Q8 *(c)*

The `^` operator will perform an XOR operation on the bit patterns `1001` and `0010` and will produce `1011`, which will be written out in decimal form as `11`.

Q9 *(b) and (d)*

`Panel` defines its default layout manager to be `FlowLayout`, so `Panel` and its subclass `Applet` have `FlowLayout` as the default layout manager.

`Window` is a subclass of `Container` but redefines its default layout manager to be `BorderLayout`, so the default layout manager for `Window` and its subclasses `Frame` and `Dialog` is `BorderLayout`.

Q10 *(d) and (e)*

The `main()` method must be `public` and `static`, and must take in an array of `String` objects. It does not return a value. The `public` and `static` modifiers must precede the return type `void`. The (b) and (c) declarations will fail to compile, due to error in the syntax of the method declaration.

Declaration (a) will compile, but will not act as a `main()` method for a standalone program. Declaration (e) is the canonical form of the `main()` method. Declaration (d) declares the method `final`, which is redundant since the method is already static. It also uses a different parameter name, but is none the less also a valid `main()` method.

Q11 *(b)*

Calls to methods `suspend()`, `sleep()` and `wait()` do not stop a thread. They only cause a thread to move out of its running state. A thread will stop when it is done executing the `run()` method.

Q12 *(d)*

The `Map` interface provides operations that map keys to values.

Q13 *(d)*

The `getId()` method of an instance of the `java.awt.AWTEvent` class returns an ID in form of an integer value that identifies the type of event. One can think of the method as identifying the cause or purpose of the event.

Q14 *(e)*

An object of class `Extension` is created. The first thing the constructor of `Extension` does is to call the constructor of `Base` using an implicit `super()` call. All calls to method `void add(int)` are dynamically bound to the `add()` method in the `Extension` class, since the actual object is of type `Extension`. So, this method is called by the constructor of `Base`, the constructor of `Extension` and the `bogo()` method with the parameters 1, 2 and 8, respectively. The instance member `i` changes values accordingly: 2, 6, and 22. The final value of 22 is printed.

Q15 *(a) and (b)*

The `native` modifier keyword can have the same placement as accessibility modifiers in method declaration. Thus the order of tokens in (a) and (b) is correct. The (c) declaration is rejected, since the `native` modifier is not allowed after the declaration of the return type. Declaration (d) is rejected, since it tries to declare an `abstract` method within a non-abstract class. The (e) declaration is rejected, since native method declarations, just like `abstract` method declarations, cannot contain a method body.

Q16 *(b)*

The `weighty` property determines how much of the extra vertical space each component is allotted.

Q17 *(a) and (d)*

Member variable `b` of the outer class is not shadowed by any local or inner class variables, thus (a) will work. Referring to `this.a` will access the member variable `a` in the inner class. Referring to `this.b` will fail, since there is no member variable `b` in the inner class. Referring to `Q4a39.this.a` will successfully access the member variable of the outer class. The statement `c = c` will only reassign the current value of the local variable `c` to itself.

Q18 *(c)*

At (1), a new string is constructed using the `"bye"` string, but no additional references to the `"bye"` string object are created. On the line below, an additional reference to `"bye"` is created. At line (2), the original reference to `"bye"` in `b` is overwritten, but `d` still contains a reference to `"bye"`. At line (3), the reference `d` also stops denoting `"bye"`. Now the `"bye"` string object cannot be referenced through any reference, and thus is a candidate for garbage collecting.

Q19 *(d)*

String objects are immutable, therefore none of the methods of the `String` class will modify the object. Methods `toUpperCase()` and `replace()` will return a new `String` object that contains the modified string of characters.

Q20 *(c)*

Statement (a) will work just fine, and (b), (d) and (e) will cause compilation errors. Statements (b) and (e) will cause compilation errors, since they attempt to assign an incompatible type to the reference. Statement (d) will cause compilation errors, since a cast from `B` to `C` is invalid, as being an instance of `B` excludes the possibility of being an instance of `C`. Statement (c) will compile, but will throw a runtime exception, since the object that is cast to `B` is not really an instance of `B`.

Q21 *(a), (d) and (e)*

`String` is a name of a class in package `java.lang`, not a keyword. Java has a keyword named `null`, but not `NULL`.

Q22 *(e)*

The desired accessibility is package accessibility, which is the default accessibility for members that have no accessibility modifier. The keyword `package` is not an access modifier and cannot be used in this context.

Q23 *(b) and (e)*

For the expression `tab[3][2]` to access a valid element of the array, the array must be at least of size 4 times 3. Actually, the length of the second dimension does not need to be uniform, but it is in all the code fragments given. Fragment (a) produces a 2 times 3 array. Fragment (c) tries to initialize a two-dimensional array as an one-dimensional array. Fragment (d) tries to specify array dimensions in a type expression.

Q24 *(a)*

The expression `arr.length` will evaluate to 4. The expression `arr[1]` will access the element `{ { "1", "2" }, { "1", null, "3" } }`, and `arr[1][2]` will try to access the third sub-element of this element. This produces an `ArrayIndexOutOfBoundsException`, since the element only has 2 sub-elements.

Q25 *(c) and (d)*

Several distinct `String` objects may contain identical sequences of characters. The `==` operator, when used on `String` object references, will only compare the object references and will return `true` only when both references point to the same object. The `equals()` method will return `true` whenever the contents of the `String` objects are identical. An array of `char` and a `String` are totally different types, and cannot be compared using the `equals()` method of `String`.

Q26 *(b) and (c)*

Statement (d) is false, since an object of `B` can be created using the implicit default constructor of the class. `B` has an implicit default constructor, since no constructor has explicitly been defined. Statement (e) is false, since the second constructor of `C` will call the first constructor of `C`.

Q27 *(b) and (d)*

The `retainAll()`, `removeAll()` and `addAll()` methods do not return a new collection object, but rather modify the collection object they were called upon. The collection object given as an argument is not affected. The `containsAll()` does not modify either of the collection objects.

Q28 *(b), (c) and (e)*

An instance of class `Baz` is also an instance of class `Foo`, since class `Baz` extends class `Foo`. `Baz` has a `Bar`, since instances of class `Baz` contain an instance of class `Bar` by reference. Since a `Foo` has a `Baz`, a `Foo` has a `Bar`.

Q29 *(b) and (e)*

Unlike local variables, all member variables are initialized with default initial values. All numeric variables are initialized to zero, `boolean` values to `false`, `char` values to `'\u0000'` and all object reference values (including references to `String` objects) to `null`.

Q30 *(c) and (d)*

Very little is guaranteed about the behavior of the garbage collection and finalization mechanisms. The (c) and (d) statements are two of the things that are guaranteed.

Q31 *(a)*

Fragment (b) will always generate and catch an `ArrayIndexOutOfBoundsException`, since it always tries to read an element with an index one higher than the highest index of the array. Fragment (c) will also try to access one index too high, but will not catch the generated exception. Fragment (d) will fail to print the argument if only one argument is given. Fragment (e) will generate an uncaught `ArrayIndexOutOfBoundsException` if no argument is given.

Q32 *(a), (b) and (c)*

`Set` and `List` both extend `Collection`. A map *is-not-a* collection and `Map` does not extend `Collection`. `Set` does not have any new methods other than those defined in `Collection`. `List` defines additional methods to the ones in `Collection`.

Q33 *(c)*

The `short` contains an 16-bit signed value and therefore has a value range from -2^{15} to $2^{15}-1$.

Q34 *Filled in:*

```
wait
```

Q35 *(c)*

The important thing to remember is that if an object is an instance of a class, then it is also an instance of all the superclasses of this class.

Q36 *(c)*

The expression `(int) d` gives –2, the expression `Math.ceil(d)` gives –2.0 and the expression `Math.abs(d)` gives 2.9, which becomes 2 when converted to `int`. Note that the behavior of the `Math.ceil()` and `Math.floor()` methods on negative numbers might seem non-intuitive.

Q37 *(e)*

Method `g()` modifies the member variable `a` which is shared by all the methods of the object. Method `g()` modifies only a local variable named `b`, since the parameter named `b` shadows the member variable named `b`. Variables are passed by value, so the change of value in parameter `b` is limited to the method `g()`. Method `g()` modifies the shared array object whose reference value has been passed as a parameter.

Q38 *(d)*

The total width of the rectangle will be 11 pixels. Note, however, that the total width would have been 10 pixels if it had been a `fillRect()` operation.

Q39 *(a), (b), (c) and (d)*

The default layout manager of a frame is `BorderLayout`. When no constraint object is given while adding a component to a container using `BorderLayout`, center placement is assumed. `FlowLayout` will give a component its preferred size, rather than utilizing all the space available.

Q40 *(b)*

Method implementation (a) will write the string to the file, but will use the native encoding. Method implementation (c) will fail to compile, since a method named `setEncoding` does not exist in class `FileWriter`. Method implementation (d) will fail to compile, since `FilterWriter` is an `abstract` class that cannot be used to translate encodings. Method implementation (e) will fail to compile, since class `OutputStream` is `abstract`.

Q41 *(a), (b) and (d)*

Both `$` and `_` are allowed as characters in identifiers. Character `@` is not allowed in identifiers. All characters considered letters in the Unicode character set are allowed. The first character of an identifier cannot be a digit.

Q42 *(a)*

The program will fail to compile, since a declaration cannot be labeled. The compiler will be unable to associate the label `l2` with any loop that the `break` statement can affect. For a label to be associated with a loop, it must immediately precede the loop construct.

Q43 *(b)*

Classes cannot extend interfaces, they must implement them. Interfaces can extend other interfaces, but cannot implement them. A class must be declared abstract if it does not provide an implementation for one of its methods. Methods declared in interfaces are implicitly `public` and classes that implement these methods must explicitly declare their implementations `public`.

Q44 *(a) and (e)*

The `notify()` and `notifyAll()` methods are declared in `Object`. Since all other classes extend `Object`, these methods are also available in instances of all other classes, including `Thread`. The method `notify()` is not synchronized but will throw an `IllegalMonitorStateException` if the current thread is not the owner of the monitor of the object.

Q45 *(a) and (c)*

Referencing of member variables of the outer instance using only the variable name works as long as the variable is not shadowed. Member variables need not be declared `final` in order to be accessible within the inner instance.

Q46 *(a)*

The code will fail to compile because the literal `4.3` has the type `double`. Assignment of a `double` value to a `float` without an explicit cast is not allowed. The code would compile and write `0` to standard output when run, if the literal `4.3` was replaced with `4.3F`.

Q47 *(b) and (e)*

The && and `||` operators exhibit short-circuit behavior. The first operand of a `? :` operator is always evaluated. Based on the result of this evaluation, either the second or the third operand is evaluated.

Q48 *(e)*

No labels are mandatory (including the `default` label) and can be placed in any order within the `switch` body. The keyword `continue` may occur within the body of a `switch` statement as long as it pertains to a loop. Any constant integral value can be used for `case` labels, as long as the type is compatible with the integral expression in the `switch` expression.

Q49 *(b) and (c)*

The `main()` method must be declared `static` and can be declared `final`. The return type of the `main()` method is `void`.

Q50 *(d)*

The default layout manager for `Applet` is `FlowLayout`. This manager will lay out the components from left to right, filling one row at a time, from top to bottom, centering each row.

Q51 *(b) and (c)*

Mouse-motion listeners can be registered on all objects that are instances of `Component`. There is no class named `MouseMotionEvent`. The events handled by mouse motion listeners are of type `MouseEvent`. The `ActionListener` interface does not have a corresponding adapter class. The reason for this is that the `ActionListener` interface only declares one method.

Q52 *(e)*

The second parameter to the constructor specifies whether the file contents should be replaced or appended when there is an existing file.

Q53 *Filled in:*

```
super.print();
```

Overridden method implementations are accessed using the `super` keyword. Statements like `print()`, `Base.print()`, `Base.this.print()`, etc. will not work.

Q54 *(d)*

An array of strings containing the file names of a directory is obtained by calling the method `list()` on the `File` object that specifies the directory.

Q55 *(a)*

Strings are immutable so the `concat()` operation has no effect on the original `String` object. The string on which the `trim()` method is called consists of 8 characters, where the first and the two last characters are spaces. The `trim()` method returns a new `String` object where the white space characters at each end have been removed. This leaves the 5 characters of the word "`hello`".

Q56 *(a) and (b)*

If a thread is executing method `b()` on an object, then it is guaranteed that no other thread executes methods `a()` and `b()` concurrently. Therefore, the invocation counters `i` and `j` will never show more than one concurrent invocation. Two threads can concurrently be executing methods `b()` and `c()`. Therefore the invocation counter `k` can easily show more than one concurrent invocation.

Q57 *(a), (b) and (e)*

Widening conversion allows conversions (a) and (b) to be done without a cast. Conversion from a floating point value to an integer value needs a cast. Conversion from a `boolean` value to an integer value is not possible.

Q58 *(a) and (e)*

Declaration (b) fails, since the method signature only differs in return type. Declaration (c) fails, since it tries to declare an `abstract` method in a non-abstract class. Declaration (d) fails, since its signature is identical to the existing method.

Q59 *(a) and (d)*

The literal `65` is parsed as type `int`. The compile-time narrowing of literal converts the `int` to a `char`. The proper syntax of a `char` literal is either as Unicode values in hexadecimal notation `'\u0041'` or for values as octal notation `'\101'`. A `char` variable cannot be assigned a string even if the string only contains one character.

Index

Symbols

" 26
* 107, 594
, 144
/* and */ 27
/** and */ 27
// 27
; 98
; 98
@-tags 596
\ 25
{} 98, 113
' 24

Numerics

2's complement 64
3D rectangle 464
8859_1 570

A

absolute layout 383, 406
absolute pathnames 550, 552
absolute values 303
abstract
  classes 109
  collection implementations 347
  interfaces 110
  methods 124
abstract pathname 550
Abstract Windowing Toolkit *see* AWT
abstraction 2, 9
access mode 583
accessibility 7, 15, 112, 510
  anonymous classes 246
  classes 108
  default 108, 118
  local classes 240
  members 109, 112, 114
  modifiers 108
  package 108
  `private` 118
  `protected` 117
  `public` 108, 115
  UML 115
action events 415
action objects 522, 535
actions performed 427
actual parameter list 75, 205
adapter classes 243, 429, 431
adaptors for collections 347
adding choices 365
adding components 384
adding to class 173
adjustment events 416
advance of characters 461
aggregation 9, 11, 175
  hierarchy 175
algorithms 324, 326
aliases 5, 60
  see also references
alignment of
  applets 492
  component rows 387
  components 532
  labels 366
alive threads 290
analyzing program code 614
anchoring in grid bag 401
and 61, 66

angle sweep 467
anonymous
  arrays 93
  collection implementations 346
  listeners 432
  string object 307
anonymous classes 243, 432
appending elements 333
applet 17, 18
  element 17
  viewer 16
`Applet` class 353, 355
applet context 488, 501
applet viewer 488
applets 353, 385, 488, 518
  alignment 492
  code base 493
  code specification 493
  context *see* applet context
  creating 488
  `destroy` method 496
  HTML element 489
  info 500
  `init` method 495
  life cycle 495
  parameters 501
  security 506
  size 491
  spacing 493
  `start` method 495
  `stop` method 496
  viewer 488
architect exam 607
arcs 467
arguments *see* parameters
arguments to main method 39
`ArithmeticException` 154
array list 334
array of arrays 87, 91
array operations 328
`ArrayIndexOutOfBoundsException` 89, 154
arrays 87, 296
  anonymous 93
  collection operations 328
  creation 93
  declarations 87
  default initialization 87, 88
  dynamic 334
  elements 87, 89
  initialization 88, 89, 91
  length 87
  objects 296
  reference 87, 89, 201
  resizable 325
ascent 460
ASCII 24, 31
assignable 205
assignments
  bitwise 67
  cascading 46
  extended operators 53, 62, 67
  implicit narrowing 47
  multiple 46
  numeric conversions 47
  operator 42, 45
  primitive values 46
  references 46
associativity 43
asynchronous 272
atomic types 29
attributes *see* properties
audio files 503
`AudioClip` class 503
`author @`-tag 597
authors 599
automatic garbage collection 251
available fonts 460
AWT 352, 510, 511
  `Button` component 360, 361, 415
  `Canvas` component 360, 362
  `Checkbox` component 360, 363, 416
  `CheckboxGroup` 364
  `CheckboxMenuItem` 378
  `Choice` component 360, 365, 416
  `Component` class 353, 354
  `Container` class 353, 355
  control components 359
  `Dialog` class 353, 357
  events 414
  `Font` class 458
  `Frame` class 353, 356
  `Graphics` class 451, 453
  `Label` component 360, 366
  `List` component 360, 367, 415, 416
  `Menu` class 378
  `MenuBar` class 377
  `MenuComponent` class 353, 377
  `MenuItem` class 415
  modal dialogs 357
  `paint` method 452

Panel component 353, 355
PopupMenu class 378
repaint method 452
Scrollbar component 360, 369, 416
TextArea component 360, 372
TextComponent component 372
TextField component 360, 372, 415
thread 475
update method 452
Window class 353, 355
see also GUI
AWT thread 273, 475
AWTException 154

B

background color 354, 454
bags 330
balanced tree 325
base 23
base class 173
baseline 458, 460
basic collection operations 327
basic map operations 338
beveled edges 464
binary
numeric promotion 45
operators 42
representations 560
search 326
shift operators 68
bit patterns 64
bit shifting 68
bitmaps 481
bitwise
and 66
assignment 67
complement 66
not 66
operators 66
or 66
shifting 68
xor 66
blank final variable 82, 123
blocked state 284
blocks 98, 113
catch 157
finally 158, 159
scope 113
try 157
see also statements
blue value 455
boolean 32
Boolean wrapper class 301
booleans 29, 32
and 61
expressions 58
literals 24
not 61
or 61
xor 61
border layout 383, 392
border regions 392
borders 454, 512, 519
bounded range model 522, 538
bounding rectangle 466, 467
bounds of components 354
box layout 531, 532
break idiom 138
break statement 137, 145
browser 355
buffer streams 575
buffering images 483
buffering streams 560, 563
building abstractions 9
building component hierarchy 407
building GUI applications 433
bulk map operations 338
bulk operations on collections 327
button labels 361
button-like components 519
buttons 360, 361, 415, 519, 520
groups 521
labels 361
models 521
byte 22, 31
byte array streams 557
byte code 14
byte streams 549

C

C 125
C++ 125
call-by-reference 79
call-by-value 79
callee 75
caller 75
canonical path 552
canvas 360

capacity of hash 330
card layout 383
cards 396, 525
carriage return 26
cascading assignments 46
cascading if-else statements 135
case labels 136, 137
case-sensitivity 21
cast operator 42
casting 43
  downcasting 178
  upcasting 176
  see also conversions
catch block 157
catch-and-throw paradigm 153
catching exceptions 153
cell editors 527, 528
cell renderers 523, 527
certification 607, 698
chained streams 549
chaining
  constructors 192
  finalizers 253
  new operator 234
change listeners 523
changing look and feel 535
char 31
character set 570
  ASCII 24, 31, 567
  ISO Latin-1 24, 31
  Latin 570
  Unicode 24, 31, 567
character streams 549, 567
character strings 307
Character wrapper class 301
characters 31, 567
  baseline 458
  drawing 458
  encoding 567
  literals 24
  searching for 312
checkboxes 360, 363, 416, 520
  group 364
  labels 364
  menu items 416
  state 363
checked exceptions 154, 162
child class 173
child threads 273, 276
choice component 365
choice control component 360, 365, 416
choice items 365
choosing between actions 134
circular arcs 467
class loader 505
ClassCastException 154, 207
classes
  abstract 109
  accessibility 108, 224
  adapters 243
  adding to 173
  anonymous 243
  as members 224
  author 597
  base 173
  child 173
  constructors 100, 187
  containers 352
  declaration context 224
  definitions 2, 4, 37, 97
  derived 173
  diagram 7
  extending 110, 173
  file name 227
  final 110
  foundation *see* JFC
  full name 226
  generalized 174
  grouping 105
  header 97, 195
  initialization 261, 267
  inner 224
  instance members 97
  instances 4
  instantiation 263
  local 238
  members 6, 97
  methods 121
  modifiers 109
  monitor 280
  mother of all 296
  name 101, 105
  nested *see* nested classes
  non-static 224, 230
  Object 296
  on-the-fly 224
  parent 173
  runtime 297
  scope 112
  specialized 174

static 224
static members 97
subclass 9, 173
superclass 9, 173
top-level 224
top-level nested 226
variables 121
version 599
wrappers 32, 296, 299
ClassLoader class 296
cleaning up 251
clean-up code 159
clicking programmatically 520
client 14
clip region 471
clipping 471
clockwise direction 467
Cloneable interface 297
cloning object 297
closed path 469
closing windows 420
code base 493
code optimizations 123
code reuse 173, 175, 220
code specification of applets 493
collapsed nodes 527
Collection interface 324
collections 206, 324, 325
abstract implementations 333, 347
adaptors 347
algorithms 326
anonymous implementations 346
array operations 328
ArrayList 334
basic operations 327, 338
bulk operations 327, 338
customizing 345
data stuctures 325
duplicate elements 330, 333
elements 324
empty constants 347
filling 326
first element 342
HashMap 339
HashSet 330
HashTable 339
immutability 345
implementations 324, 325
interfaces 324
iterators 328
last element 342
LinkedList 334
List 334
lists 333
Map 338, 339
map views 339
optional operations 327
ordered 333
range-views 333, 342
retaining elements 327
shuffle elements 326
singleton set 347
SortedMap 341
SortedSet 341, 342
sorting 326
subset 342
textual representation 333
thread-safety 334, 339, 345, 346
TreeMap 343
TreeSet 343
unsupported operations 338
Vector 334
views 334, 339, 342
collections framework 324
Collections utility class 326
color chooser 512, 529
colors 454
background 354, 454
foreground 354, 454
of text 456
of the system 456
column model 526
columns in table 526
columns of components 389
columns of text 372
combined RGB value 455
combo box 522
command
java 16
javac 15
command name 415
comments 27
common memory space 272
common subset 332
communication 6, 74
communication between threads 272
Comparable interface 342
comparable objects 341
comparator 341
Comparator interface 341

comparing objects 297, 341
  see also equality
comparison 58
compass directions 392, 401
compilation unit 106
  see source file 594
complement 66
complete methods 123
complex components 510
complex models 526
component hierarchy 407
components 353, 354
  bounds 354
  event 417
  font 354
  location 354
  size 354
  visibility 355
  see also AWT and swing
compound statement 98
concatenation of strings 311
concatenation operator 54
concurrent activities 272
conditional 58
  and 63
  expressions 71, 133
  operators 63, 71
  or 63
  statements 133
conditions 58
connecting punctuation 21
`const` 22
constant expression 258
constant values 22, 123
constants 199
constituents 11
constraints for grid bag 400
constraints for layout 384
constructing grid bag layouts 400
constructing loops 142
constructor chaining 189, 192, 265
constructors 3, 100, 187
  chaining 189, 192
  default 101
  implicit default 101
  name 101
  overloading 103
constructs 21
  high-level 21
  loops *see* iteration statements
  `synchronized` blocks 281
container events 417
container layout methods 384, 385
containers 353, 355
containment hierarchy 235
containment model 510, 512
content pane 512, 515
context switching 272
`continue` statement 147
contract 195, 197, 217, 220
contracting lists 333
control components 359
control flow
  `break` *see* `break` statement
  `continue` 147
  `do-while` 143
  exceptions *see* exceptions
  `for` 143
  `if` 133
  `if-else` 134
  iteration *see* iteration statements
  loops *see* iteration statements
  `return` 148
  statements 98, 133
  `switch` 136
  `throw` 160
  transfer statements 145
  `while` 142
control transfer 145
conventions for documentation 601
conversions 43
  cast 43
  contexts 43, 45
  explicit 43
  identity 53
  implicit 43
  implicit narrowing 53
  narrowing 43
  number systems 23, 65
  numeric promotions 44
  parameter passing 205
  parameters 75
  reference casting 206
  references 209
  string concatenation 54
  to array 328
  to strings 313, 333
  truncation 47
  type safe 205
  unsafe casts 206

widening 43
converting number systems 23, 65
coordinate system 453
coordinate translation 454
copying files 559
core interfaces 324
corners 464
counterclockwise direction 467
counter-controlled loops 143
crab 145
creating
applets 488
colors 455
files and directories 554
menus 378
objects 4, 72
threads 272, 273
currency symbol 21
cursor 334
curved rectangle corners 464
customized layout manager 407

D

daemon threads 273
dangling references 251
data models 516
data streams 558, 560
data structures 325
datatypes *see* types
date 342
dead state 284
declarations
arrays 72, 87
for initialization 144
local 98
statements 98
variables *see* variable declarations
declaring *see* declarations
decorating collections 346
decorators 346
decoupling 214
decrement operator 54
default
accessibility 108, 115, 118
character encoding 570
constructor 101
exception handler 155
label 136
layout manager 387, 395, 515
values 34, 258, 264
defining *see* definitions
definitions
classes 37, 97
constructors 101
inheritance 198
interfaces 37, 195
`main` method 39
methods 97
packages 37, 106
delegates 516
delegating requests 220
delegation objects 510
delegation of events 421, 426
deleting files or directories 554
`deprecated` @-tag 597
deprecated features 599
derived class 173
descent 460
deserialization of objects 587
designing layouts 384
desktop color scheme 456
destination of data 549
destroying objects 252
destructive collection operations 328
detail sections 602
developer exam 607, 611
device-independent interface 451
diagrams
class 3
see also UML
dialogs 353, 357
fonts 458
diameters of oval 466
dictionary 325
dictionary order 310
difference 330
dimension in grid bag 401
dimension of component 454
direct file access 583
directories 551, 553
entries 551, 553
see also files 554
disabled components 354
disjunct collections 332
displacing elements 333
disposal of resources 252
disposing graphics objects 453
disposing windows 356
distance of shift 68

dividing components 525
document base 493
document model 523
documentation 27, 594
  comment 594
  conventions 601
documentation comment 27
documenting *see* documentation
dot 105
`double` 24, 31
double buffering 519
double clicks 419
`do-while` statement 143
downcasting 44, 178
drawing
  arcs 467
  characters 458
  components 451
  context 451
  images 481
  lines 462
  ovals 466
  polygons 469
  polylines 470
  rectangles 463
  shapes 462
  text 458
  see also painting and graphics
drawing canvas 360, 362
drawing region 362, 454
drawings 362
duplicate elements 330, 333
duplicating objects 297
dynamic components 510
dynamic method binding 177
dynamic method lookup 177, 183, 214
dynamically resizable arrays 334

E

editable text 360, 372, 373
editor panes 524
elements 87, 324
  see also HTML elements
elements of collections 324
eligible for garbage collection 251
elliptical arcs 467
`else` clause matching 135
empty collections 347
empty set 330
empty statement 98
enabled components 354
encapsulation 105, 217, 225
encapsulation of implementation 220
enclosing class 224, 230
enclosing context 228, 229, 232
encoding characters 567
encoding of characters 567
end of file 556
entering monitors 279
entries in directory 551, 553
entry set 338
`EOFException` 154
equality 59, 297
  `equals` method 60, 297
  object value 60
  objects 60
  primitive values 59
  references 59
`equals` method 60, 297
equivalent collections 332
escape sequences 25
evaluation short-circuits 64
event delegation model 413, 421
event handling 352, 535
event listeners 413, 425
event objects 413
event-driven 413
events
  `ActionEvent` 415
  adapters 429
  `AdjustmentEvent` 416
  `ComponentEvent` 417
  `ContainerEvent` 417
  delegation 426
  `FocusEvent` 417
  `ID` 414
  `InputEvent` 417
  `ItemEvent` 416
  `KeyEvent` 417
  low-level 414
  `MouseEvent` 418
  objects 413
  `PaintEvent` 419
  processing methods 442
  semantic 414
  sources 421
  swing 512
  `TextEvent` 416
  `WindowEvent` 419

exam 607
exam voucher 608
exception @-tag 597
Exception class 154
exception handler 153
  see also exceptions
exceptional conditions 153
exceptions 153, 157
  ArrayIndexOutOfBoundsException 89
  checked *see* checked exceptions
  ClassCastException 207
  default handler 155
  documentation 597
  FileNotFoundException 558
  handler 153
  ignored 252
  IllegalThreadStateException 273
  IndexOutOfBoundsException 333
  NumberFormatException 300
  percolation 155
  throw 160
  throwing *see* throwing exceptions
  thrown by method 98
  throws clause 97
  types 155
  uncaught 155
  unchecked 155
  UnsupportedOperationException 327
exchanging information 75
execution paths 272
existence of files 551, 553
exiting monitors 279
expanded nodes 527
explicit
  conversions 43, 178
  freeing resources 252
  garbage collection 255
  referencing 240
exponent 24
exponential functions 304
expression statements 98
expressions 137
  boolean 58
  case labels 137
  conditional 71
  deterministic evaluation 42
  label 137
  return 149
  statements 98
  switch 137
extended assignment operators 53
extending
  adapters 432
  classes 173
  interfaces 197
  Thread 276
extends clause 173
extensions
  .class 14
  .html 18
  .jar 505
  .java 14
external encoding 568
external libraries 261
external padding 403
extracting substrings 313

F

factory methods 327, 346
fall through 136
false 24
fields *see* member variables
file 342
file chooser 512
File class 549
file name 37, 227, 549, 551
file streams 557
file system 549
files 549, 551, 553
  access 553
  aliases 555
  chooser 512
  copying 559
  creating 554
  deleting 554
  entries 553
  existence 553
  mode 583
  modification time 552
  name 551
  name filter 553
  not found 558
  path 551
  pointer 584
  random access 583
  renaming 554
  seeking 584
  size 552
  streams 558

filling collections 326
filling in grid bag 402
filter streams 560
filtering file names 553
filters 549
`final` 22
  classes 110
  members 123
  methods 181
  parameters 82
finalization mechanism 251
finalization of objects 252
finalize method 252, 297
finalizer chaining 253
finally block 158, 159
first element 342
fixed pitch font 458
fixed size separators 532
flickering 477
float 24, 31
floating-point 28
  `double` 31
  `float` 31
  literals 24
  wrapper classes 32
flow control *see* control flow
flow layout 383, 387
flushing streams 556, 571
focus events 417
`Font` class 458
font metrics 460, 461
fonts 354, 458
  baseline 460
  measurements 460
  size 459
  style 458
`for` statement 143
foreground color 354, 454
foreign methods 125
form feeds 26
formal parameters 75, 97, 100, 113, 205, 597
formatting 27
  documentation 597
foundation classes *see* JFC
fractional signed numbers 28
`Frame` class 356
frames 353
framework for collections 324
free windowing resources 356
fully qualified names 105, 199
  package 106
  short-hand 107

G

gain monitor ownership 280
gap between components 387, 390, 392, 397
garbage collection 251
general abstractions 174
general loops 143
generalized classes 174
generated events 413
generic components 362
generic data types 206
GIF 481, 503
glass pane 513
glue 532
`goto` 22, 145
grammar rules 21
graphic targets 451
graphical user interface *see* GUI
`Graphics` class 451, 453
graphics context 451, 453, 484
Graphics Interchange Format *see* GIF
graphics mode 479
graphics state 451, 479
grayed out components 354
green value 455
grid bag constraints 400
grid bag layout 383, 399
grid layout 383, 389
grid of components 389, 399
grouping 105
grouping checkboxes 363
groups of buttons 521
groups of objects 324
growth factor in grid bag 401
GUI 352, 383
  applets 353
  applications 413
  borders 519
  building 356, 433
  buttons 360, 361, 415
  checkboxes 360, 363
  choice control component 360, 365
  components 353, 354, 518
  containers 353, 355, 383
  control components 353, 359

custom rendering 452
dialogs 357
drawing canvas 360, 362
events 413
generic components 362
icons 356
labels 360, 366
layout 383
lists 360, 367, 415, 416
look and feel 534
menu-bars 513
menus 356, 377, 378, 520
pop-up menu 378
radio buttons 363
scrollbars 360, 369, 373, 416
text components 360, 372, 415
title-bar 356
windows 353, 355
GUI applications 273, 433

H

handles 30
handles *see* references
has-a relationship 175
hash codes 297
hash map 339
hash table 325, 339
`HashSet` 330
head map view 343
head set view 342
heavyweight components 511
height of applet 491
height of text 461
hiding 98
hiding internals 217
hierarchical data 526
hierarchical graphical user interfaces 355
high-level events 415
highlighted rectangle 464
horizontal font measurements 460
horizontal spacing of applets 493
hot-key 521
HTML 17, 360, 488
documentation 594
HTML elements
`a` 598
`applet` 17, 489
`b` 597
`code` 597, 601
`i` 597
`object` 488, 491
`p` 597
hyperlinks 597, 598
HyperText Markup Language *see* HTML

I

I/O buffering 560, 563, 575
I/O package 549
iconification 420
icons 356
`ID` of event 414
identifiers 21
predefined 21
reserved 21
variable 29
identity conversion 53
identity of object 4
IEEE 754-1985 32
`if-else` statement 134
ignored exceptions 252
ignoring case 310
illegal thread state 273
`IllegalArgumentException` 154
image observers 481
images 362, 481
immediate superclass 190
immutable collections 345
implementations 174, 217
collections 324
inheritance hierarchy 110
implementations of collections 325
implementing
interfaces 197
layout managers 407
models 536
implements clause 197
implicit
conversions 43
default constructor 101
inheritance 173
narrowing conversions 53
`import` 17
import
declaration 107
on demand 107
statement 37, 227
inches 459
inconsistencies 126

increment expression 143
increment operator 54
independent lifetimes 175
index bounds 333
indexed cards 396
`IndexOutOfBoundsException` 333
individual array elements 89
inequality 59
  see also equality
infinite loop 145
inheritance 9, 175
  hierarchy 174, 235
initial capacity 330, 339
initial state of object 264
initialization
  arrays 89, 91
  code 89
  default values 34
  `for` statement 143
  object references 30
  objects 4, 257
  reference variables 34
  variables 29
initializer expressions 257
initializers 257
initializing *see* initialization
inline hyperlink 597
inner classes 224, 432
  synchronization 282
  see also nested classes
input 549
input font 458
input stream 549
`InputStream` class 555
insets 403, 454
instance
  members 9, 97
  methods 9, 97, 98
  variable initialization 34
  variables 9, 29
  see also object
instance initializer block 262
instance variables 264
`instanceof` operator 72, 206
instantiation 110
  anonymous classes 245
  local classes 240
`int` 22, 31
integers 31
  and 66
  `byte` 31
  datatypes 28
  `int` 31
  literals 22
  `long` 31
  not 66
  or 66
  representation 64
  `short` 31
  types 28
  wrapper classes 32
  xor 66
integrity (maintaining) 280
interface-based 327
interfaces 195
  abstract 110
  accessibility 108
  collection core 324
  definitions 37
  extending 197
  implementing 245
  initialization 267
  top-level 224
  top-level nested 226
  variables 199
interline spacing 460
internal frames 517
internal padding 402
intersection 330
invalidating containers 385
invoke and wait 538
invoke later 538
invoking garbage collection 255
`IOException` 154
is-a relationship 174, 175, 219
ISO Latin 570
ISO Latin-1 24, 31
item events 416
item selectable component 416
iterating through elements 329
iteration statements 141
  next iteration 147
  termination 142, 146
iterators 328

J

JAR archives 494, 505
Java
  Development Kit *see* JDK

interpreter 38
Native Interface *see* JNI
program 14
java 16
Java Development Kit *see* JDK
Java Foundation Classes *see* JFC
Java Native Interface *see* JNI
Java Virtual Machine *see* JVM
javac 15, 17
javadoc comment 27
javadoc tags 594
javadoc utility 27, 594, 601
Java-enabled web browser 488
javax package 512
JDK 14, 15, 489
JFC 352, 421, 510
JNI 125
joining threads 291
Joint Photographic Experts Group *see* JPEG
JPEG 481, 503
JVM 505

K

key events 417
key objects 325
key sets 338
key sorting 343
keyboard events 417
keyboard focus 417
keyboard shortcuts 377
keys 338
keywords 21
abstract 109, 124
boolean 32
byte 31
case 136
catch 157
char 31
class 97, 195
const 22
continue 147
default 136
do 143
double 31
else 134
extends 173
final 82, 110, 123
finally 159
float 31
for 143
if 133
implements 197
import 17, 107, 227
instanceof 72, 206
int 31
interface 195
long 31
native 125
new *see* new operator
package 106
private 118
protected 117
public 115
reserved words 21
return 148
short 31
static 15, 226, 260
super 179, 183, 190
switch 136
synchronized 124, 280
this 98
throw 160
throws 162
transient 126
try 157
unused words 21
void 15
volatile 126
while 142, 143

L

labeled break statement 146
labeled continue statement 147
labels 146, 360, 366, 519
break 146
case 136
default 136
expressions 137
switch statement 136
labels of buttons 361
labels of checkboxes 364
last element 342
Latin 570
layered pane 513, 515
layout 352, 383
box 532
constraints 384
layout managers 383

BorderLayout 392
BoxLayout 531
FlowLayout 387
GridBagLayout 399
GridLayout 389
layout policy 383
LayoutManager interface 383, 385
leading 460
left
associativity 43
shift 68
leftmost bit 64
legal assignments 205
length of file 552
level of security 506
lexical tokens 21
libraries 261
life cycle of applets 495
lifetime of objects 251
lightweight components 352, 511
line segments 469
line spacing 460
line terminator 26
linear implementation inheritance 174, 195
lines 462
lines of text 574
line-separator 506, 572
link @-tag 597
LinkageError 154
linked list 325, 334
list 324, 325
list components 367, 415, 416, 522, 523
list models 523
listeners 421
listeners as inner classes 432
listing directory entries 553
lists 333, 334
iterators 333
of text items 360
literals 22
boolean 24
character 24
default type 23, 24
double 24
escape sequences 25
false 24
float 24
floating-point 24
integer 22
null 22
predefined 21
prefix 23
quoting 24
scientific notation 24
string 26
suffix 23, 24
true 24
Unicode 25
load factor 330, 339
local 35
chaining of constructors 189, 264
classes 238
declarations 98
variables 29, 113
locale 311, 579
location in grid bag 401
location of components 354, 383
logarithm 304
logical
and 61
not 61
or 61
xor 61
long 22, 31
suffix 23
look and feel 352, 510, 534
loop condition 141, 142
loops *see* iteration statements
low-level events 414, 417, 441

M

magnitude 47
main method 15, 16, 17, 38, 488
main thread 273
maintaining integrity 280
major axis 531
map 325
map views 339
mappings 325
maps 338, 339
marker interfaces 198, 588
Math class 99, 303
math constants 303
mathematical set 330
MAX_VALUE constant 301
maximum value 304
measuring angles 467
measuring fonts 460
member variables 2

members 3, 6, 97, 112
  access 98
  accessibility 109, 114
  classes 224
  default values 34
  documenting 600
  `final` 123
  inheritance 173
  instance 97
  interfaces 224
  modified 173
  modifiers 121
  of objects 6
  scope 112
  shadowed 232
  short-hand 99
  `static` 7, 97, 121
  terminology 9
memory management 251
menu components 377, 520
menu items 377, 415, 520
menu-bars 377, 513, 522
menus 356, 378
message
  passing 74
  receiver 6
method activation stack 155
method call 74, 97
method overloading 99, 181
  resolution 182
method overriding 177, 179, 181, 266
method signature 179
methods 3
  `abstract` 124
  accessibility 97
  activation stack 155
  body 97, 113
  call *see* method call
  definition 75, 97
  documenting 600
  dynamic binding 177
  dynamic lookup 177, 214
  `equals` 60, 297
  event processing 442
  exceptions 98
  `final` 181
  `finalize` 252, 297
  foreign 125
  header 97
  implementation 124
  `init` 17
  invocation *see* method call
  local declarations 98
  `main` *see* `main` method
  modifiers 97
  mutually exclusive 281
  name 75
  `native` 125
  objects 98
  overloading *see* method overloading
  `paint` 17
  parameters 97
  prototypes 195
  `return` 148
  return value 97
  signature 99, 181
  statements 98
  stubs 431
  synchronized 124, 280
  termination 148
  `throws` clause 162
  `toString` 297
  `valueOf` 314
`MIN_VALUE` constant 301
minimizing overhead 251
minimum value 304
mnemonic 521
modal dialogs 357
mode of file 583
model delegates 516, 536
modification time 552
modifiers
  `abstract` 109, 124
  accessibility 108, 114
  classes 109
  `final` 123
  `main` method 39
  `native` 125
  `static` 121
  `synchronized` 124
  `transient` 126
  `volatile` 126
monitor 279
mono spaced 458
most significant bit 64
mother of all classes 296
mouse buttons 418
mouse clicks 419
mouse events 418
mouseless operation 521

multiple assignments 46
multiple implementation inheritance 195
multiple interface inheritance 195
multiple-exclusion mechanism 521
multiple-line comment 27
multisets 330
multitasking 272
multithreaded programming 272
mutable character strings 317
mutex 279
mutually exclusive
  actions 134
  items 520
  locks 279
  operations 280

N

name 21
names of files 551
naming conventions of files 549
narrowing conversions 43
  primitive 44
  reference 44
native libraries 261
native methods 125
native peer components 511
natural logarithms 303, 304
natural order 326, 341, 342
negation 61
nested classes 224
  anonymous 243
  compiling 234
  full name 226
  importing 234
  local 238
  non-static inner 230
  synchronization 282
  top-level 226
nested containers 385
nesting components 355
neutral look and feel 535
`new` operator 4, 88, 100, 234, 243, 251, 264
newline 26, 372
next-to-last component 401
no serifs 458
not 61, 66
notifying threads 286, 287, 298
`null` reference 22
`NullPointerException` 154
`Number` class 301
number formats 579
number systems
  base 23
  converting 23, 65
  decimal 23
  hexadecimal 23
  octal 23
`NumberFormatException` 154, 300
numeric promotions 44
  assigment 47
  binary 45
  unary 44
numeric wrapper classes 301

O

object 2
`Object` class 174, 296
object references 4
object state 6, 79, 100, 264
object-oriented programming 2
objects 11, 251
  arrays 87
  callee 75
  caller 75
  class 297
  cleaning up 251
  cloning 297
  communication 74
  comparing 297, 341
  constituents 11
  constructing 264
  contract 217
  create 4
  decoupling 214
  deserialization 587
  destroying 252
  element 491
  equality 60, 297
  events 413
  exchanging information 75
  finalization 252
  HTML element 488
  identity 4
  implementation 217
  in use 251
  initial state 264
  initialization 4, 100, 257
  initializer block 262

  - internals 217
  - lifetime 251
  - members 6
  - memory 251
  - methods 98
  - monitor 279
  - `Object` class 296
  - outer 231
  - persistent 126
  - reading 587
  - resurrection 251
  - serialization 494, 587
  - services 217
  - state *see* object state
  - streams 558
  - value equality 60
  - writing 587
- observing images 481
- off-screen buffer 519
- off-screen images 481
- one-dimensional arrays 87
- on-the-fly classes 224
- open range-view operations 333
- operands 43
- operations 2
- operators 42
  - -- 54
  - ! 61
  - != 59
  - %= 53
  - & 61, 66
  - && 63
  - &= 62, 67
  - *= 53
  - + 54
  - ++ 54
  - += 53
  - . 6, 105
  - /= 53
  - < 58
  - << 68, 69
  - <<= 71
  - <= 58
  - -= 53
  - = 45
  - == 59
  - > 58
  - >= 58
  - >> 68, 70
  - >>= 71
  - >>> 68, 70
  - >>>= 71
  - ? : 71
  - ^ 61, 66
  - ^= 62, 67
  - | 61, 66
  - |= 62, 67
  - || 63
  - ~ 66
  - assignment 42, 45
  - associativity 42
  - binary 42
  - bitwise 66, 68
  - boolean 58, 59, 61
  - cast 42
  - comparisons 58
  - conditional 63, 71
  - decrement 54
  - dot 6
  - equality 59
  - extended assignment 53, 62, 67
  - increment 54
  - `instanceof` 72, 206
  - integer 66
  - logical 61
  - negation 61
  - `new` *see* `new` operator
  - postfix 42
  - precedence 42
  - relational 58
  - shift 68
  - short-circuited 63
  - string concatenation 54
  - ternary 42
  - unary 42
- option pane 529
- optional operations 327
- or 61, 66
- order of events 413
- ordered collections 87, 324, 333
- orientation of scrollbar 370
- origin of coordinate system 453
- out of bounds 333
- outer instance 228
- outer object 231
- output 549
- output stream 549
- `OutputStream` class 555
- ovals 466
- overflow 64

overloading
  constructors 103
  methods 99, 181
  resolution 182
override 163
overriding
  equals 60
  finalizers 252
  methods 177, 179, 181
  paint method 452
overwriting pixels 479
owning monitors 279

P

package accessibility 108, 115
package statement 37, 106
packages 105
  accessibility *see* package accessibility
  definition 37, 106
  hierarchy 105
  java.applet 355, 488
  java.awt 352
  java.awt.event 416
  java.io 549
  java.lang 296
  java.swing 512
  java.util 324
  javax 512
  javax.swing.table 526
  javax.swing.text 523
  members 106
  naming scheme 106
  short-hand 107
  statement *see* package statement
  swing 512
  using 107
packing components 356
Pac-man 472, 483
padding in grid bag 402
paint events 419
paint method 477
paint mode 479
painting 452
  components 362, 451
  context 451
  graphics 451
  state 451
  see also drawing
panel 521
Panel component 353, 355
panels 522
param @-tag 597
param @-tag 597
parameter list *see* formal parameters
parameters 97
  actual 75
  applets 501
  array elements 80
  arrays 79
  conversions on passing 205
  final 82
  formal *see* formal parameters
  implicit 98
  passing 74
  primitives 76
  references 77
  this 98
parent class 173
parent pathname 552
parentheses 42
parsing numeric values 302
partial implementation 197
partly synchronizing a method 281
passing
  messages 74
  parameters 74
  references 77
password fields 525
path separator 549
pathname 549, 551
paths of execution 272
peer components 511
permute elements 326
persistent objects 126
pictures 481
piped streams 558
pixels 453
pixmaps 481
PLAF 352, 512
platform-independent layout 383
playing sound 504
pluggable look and feel 352, 512
pointer position 419
points 459
points per inch 459
polygons 469
polylines 470
polymorphic algorithms 326
polymorphism 177, 201, 213, 220, 242

pop-up menu 360, 365, 378
position in file 584
position in grid 389
postfix operators 42
power 304
precedence rules 42
precision 47
predefined colors 455
predefined identifiers 21
predefined literals 21
preempted threads 285
preemptive scheduling 285
preferred size of component 385
prefix 23
  `0` 23
  `0x` 23
primitive types 11
  see also primitive values
primitive values
  assignment 46
  binary representations 560
  equality 59
  passing 76
print writers 571
printers 451
priorities 284
priority of thread 284
`private` 10
`private` members 118
process-based multitasking 272
processes 272
processing events 442
program
  applet 16
  compiling 15
  formatting 27
  running 16
  standalone application 14
programmatically clicking 520
programmer exam 607
progress bar 522
promotion 44
propagation of events 413
properties 2
  see also class members
`protected` 10
`protected` members 117
prototypes of methods 195
pseudo random number 305
`public` 15
`public` members 115
pull-down menus 378
push button 360, 361, 520

Q

questions 613
quotation marks 26
quote ' 24

R

radio buttons 360, 363, 520, 521
raised to power 304
random access 549
random access file 583
random number 305
random order 326
range
  character values 31
  floating-point values 31
  integer values 31
range-view 333, 334, 342
read access 551, 553
readers 567
reading bytes 555
reading data 549
ready-to-run state 284
reclaiming memory 251
re-creating objects 587
rectangles 463
red value 455
redo functionality 512
redrawing components 451
reducing complexity 217
reducing flicker 477
reference values 4
reference variable 4
references 4, 5, 8, 11, 30, 75
  abstract types 110
  aliases 60
  array 87, 89, 201
  assignment 46
  casting 43, 206
  converting 209
  dangling 251
  equality 59
  initialization 34
  `null` *see* `null` reference
  passing 77

super 183, 240
this 98, 240
variables 4
refreshing components 451
registering layout managers 384
registering listeners 421
relational operators 58
relative pathnames 550
relative placement 401
reloading applets 489
remove white space 313
removing components 384
renaming files or directories 554
rendering delegates 516
rendering graphics 352, 451, 453
rendering text 458
repaint method 477
repainting components 451
replacing characters 313
requesting repaint 477
reserved identifiers 21
reserved keywords 21
const 22
goto 145
reserved literals
false 24
null *see* null reference
true 24
resizable arrays 325, 334
resources 251
restricted execution 506
resurrecting objects 251
retaining elements 327
return @-tag 597
return statement 148
return value 6, 597
reuse of code 173, 175, 220
reversible graphical operation 479
RGB values 455
right associativity 43
rigid areas 532
ripple effect 220
role relationship 219
root component 512
root of component hierarchy 407
root pane 512
rounded rectangle corners 464
rounding functions 303
rounding numbers 304
round-robin scheduling 285
row-major allocation 387
rows of components 387, 389
rows of data 526
Runnable interface 273, 277
running javadoc 601
running out of memory 251
running state 284, 285
running threads 274
runtime checks 43
runtime class 297
runtime environment 251
RuntimeException 154

S

sans serifs 458
schedulers 285
scheduling repaint 477
scientific notation 24
scope 112
block 113
catch block 158
class 112
screen size 460
scroll pane 525
scrollable list 367
scrollbars 360, 369, 370, 373, 416, 522
scrolling facilities 523
searching 324
searching for elements 326
searching in string 312
security 506
security levels 506
SecurityManager class 296
seeking in files 584
selectable items 521
selected choice 365
selected text 373
selecting choices 365
selection model 516
selection statements 133
semantic definition 21
semantic events 414
semaphore 279
semicolon 98
separator components 532
separators 522, 549
sequence 324, 333
sequential I/O 549
serialization of objects 587

serialized objects 494
serifs 458
services 217
set 324, 325
shadow 98
shadowed members 232
shadowing variables 181
shapes, filled shapes 462
shared resource 279
shift
  distance 68
  left 68
  operators 68
shifting 68
short 22, 31
short-circuit 63
  evaluation 64
shortcut 521
showing windows 356
shuffle elements 326
sign fill 68
signature 99, 181
signed applets 506
signed shift 68
simple
  assignment operator 45
  `if` 133
  statement 98
simple implementation inheritance 174
`since` @-tag 597
single implementation inheritance 198
single thread rule 538
single-line comment 27
single-quotes 24
singleton set 347
single-valued maps 338
size of
  applet 491
  components 354, 383, 454
  file 552
skeletal source file 37
slack 401, 532
slack consumers 532
sleeping 284, 286
sleeping state 284, 286
sliders 360, 370, 522
soft corners 464
sorted map 325, 341
sorted set 324, 325, 341, 342
sorting 324, 326
sound 503
source
  file 14, 15, 17, 106
  file name 37
  file structure 37
source of data 549
source of events 421
space saving 525
spaces 26
spacing between lines 460
spanning multiple cells 399
spanning remainder 401
spawning threads 273
special character values 25
specialized classes 174
split pane 525
square root 305
stack 3
stack of cards 383, 396
stack trace 155
standalone applications 14, 38, 488
standard error 579
standard font names 458
standard input 579
starting threads 274
state of checkboxes 363
state of graphics context 451
state *see* object state
statements 98
  `break` 145
  compound 98
  conditional 133
  `continue` 147
  control transfer 145
  declarations 98
  `do-while` 143
  empty 98
  expression 98
  flow control 98, 133
  `for` 143
  `if` 133
  `if-else` 134
  iteration 141
  `return` 148
  selection 133
  simple 98
  simple `if` 133
  `switch` 136
  termination 98
  `throw` 160

  transfer 145
  `while` 142
static
  initializer block 260
  members *see* static members
  methods 7, 9
  variable initialization 34
  variables *see* static variables
static factory methods 346
`static` keyword 260
`static` members 8, 9, 97
`static` variables 7, 9, 29
status message 488
storing objects 126
streams 549
  files 558
  filters 549, 557, 560
  of characters 567
streams of objects 558
`String` class 307
`StringBuffer` class 317
strings 307
  appending 318
  buffers 317
  changing case 311
  `charAt` 309
  comparing 310, 342
  concatenation 54, 311
  constructing 317
  creating 307
  deleting 318
  drawing 458
  `equals` 310
  extracting substrings 313
  individual characters 309, 318
  initializing 307
  inserting 318
  `length` 309, 318, 320
  literals 26
  natural order 342
  replacing 313
  searching 312
  substrings 313
  width 460
strongly typed language 43
struts 532
stubs 431
style of font 458
style sheets 491
subclass 9, 10, 173
sublist 334
submap view 343
sub-nodes 527
subpackage 105
subset 330, 332, 342
substring searching 312
substrings 312, 313
suffix
  `D` 24
  `F` 24
  `L` 23
summary sections 602
summary sentence 594, 603
Sun Educational Services 608
`super` keyword 179, 183, 190
`super` reference 183
`super()` construct 190
superclass 9, 10, 173
superclass–subclass relationship 174, 175
superset 332
supertypes 198
sweeping angles 467
swing 352, 510
  `AbstractAction` class 536
  `AbstractButton` 519
  `Action` interfaces 535
  basic components 521
  borders 519
  box layout 531
  cell editors 527
  cell renderers 523, 527
  `ChangeListener` 523
  components 518
  content pane 512
  delegates 516
  `Document` interface 523
  event handling 517
  glass pane 513
  inheritance hierarchy 519
  internal frame listeners 517
  `JApplet` 512, 518
  `JButton` 520
  `JCheckBox` 520
  `JCheckBoxMenuItem` 520
  `JColorChooser` 529
  `JComboBox` 522
  `JComponent` 518
  `JDesktopPane` 517
  `JDialog` 512, 518
  `JEditorPane` 524

JInternalFrame 518
JLabel 519
JList 522, 523
JMenu 520
JMenuBar 522
JMenuItem 520
JOptionPane 529
JPanel 521, 522
JPasswordField 525
JProgressBar 522
JRadioButton 520
JRadioButtonMenuItem 520
JRootPane 512
JScrollBar 522
JScrollPane 525, 527
JSeparator 522
JSlider 522
JSplitPane 525
JTabbedPane 525
JTable 526
JTableHeader 527
JTextArea 523
JTextField 523
JToggleButton 520
JToolBar 522
JTree 527
JViewPort 526
JWindow 512, 518
layered pane 513
listeners 517
look and feel 534
menus 513
packages 512
redo 512
root pane 512
RootPaneContainer 514
Scrollable interface 526
single thread rule 538
SwingUtilities class 535, 538
text components 523
TextComponent 523
tool tip 519
TreeModel interface 527
TreeSelectionModel 527
UIManager 534
undo 512
see also GUI
switch 22
break 137
break idiom 138
expression 137
statement 136
switching between threads 272
Sylvan Prometric 608
symbol font 458
synchronization 273, 279
synchronized 22
blocks 281
keyword 280
methods 124, 280
syntactically legal 21
System class 296
system colors 456

T

tabbed pane 525
table 512
table component 526
table model 526
tabs 26, 525
tabulators 26
tagging interface
see marker interface
tags *see* HTML elements
tail map view 343
tail set view 342
technology architect exam 607
telephone directory order 310
terminating a GUI application 427
terminating loops 145
ternary conditional operator 42
testing locations 612
text 512
area *see* text areas
baseline 458
color 456
columns 372
components 372, 523
drawing 458
events 416
fields *see* text fields
files 571
selection 373
text areas 360, 372, 373, 523
text components 523
text fields 360, 372, 373, 415, 523
textual label 360
textual representation 297, 571
this reference 98

this() constructor call 188, 266
Thread class 273
thread of execution 272
thread-based multitasking 272
ThreadDeath 154
ThreadGroup class 296
threads 296, 497
  alive 273, 290
  AWT 273, 475
  blocked state 284
  child 273, 276
  class 273
  code executed 274
  communication 272
  constructors 274
  creation 273
  daemon 273
  dead state 284
  death 155
  extending Thread 276
  IllegalThreadStateException 273
  joining 291
  main 273
  monitor 279
  names 274
  notification 284, 286
  notifying 287, 298
  priorities 284
  ready-to-run state 284
  Runnable 273, 277
  running 274, 276
  running state 284, 285
  scheduler 284
  single thread rule 538
  sleeping 284, 286
  sleeping state 284, 286
  spawning 273
  starting 274, 276
  states 273, 283
  status 273
  switching 272
  synchronization 124, 279
  synchronized 280
  Thread class 273
  transitions 283
  user 273
  waiting 284, 298
  waiting state 284
  yielding 284, 285
threads creation 272
thread-safe collections 345, 346
throw statement 160
Throwable class 154
throwing exceptions 153, 160
throws @-tag 597
throws clause 162
time of event 418
time-sliced scheduling 285
title-bar 356
toggle buttons 360, 520
tokens 21
tool tip 519
tool-bars 522
top-level
  classes 108
  components *see* windows
  nested class 226
  package member 224
  windows 355, 385
torn-off tool-bar 538
toString method 297
total order 341
transfer statements 145
transient variables 126
translation origin 454
tree map 343
tree set 343
trees 325, 512
  component 527
  model 527
  selection model 527
trigonometry functions 305
trim 313
true literal 24
truth-values 24, 29
try block 157
try-catch-finally construct 156
two-dimensional table 526
two-state buttons 520
two-state checkbox 520
type safe 205
types
  boolean 29, 32
  byte 22, 31
  casting 43
  char 31
  classes *see* classes
  compatibility 43
  conversion 43
  double 31

exceptions 155
float 31
floating-point 28, 31
generic 206
int 22, 31
integers 28, 31
long 22, 31
parsing 302
short 22, 31
wrappers 32, 299
see also classes
typewriter spacing 458
typographic points 459

U

UCS Transformation Format 570
see also Unicode
UML 2
accessibility 115
aggregation 11
classes 3
inheritance 9
objects 4
see also diagrams
unary numeric promotion 44
unary operators 42
uncaught exceptions 155
unchangeable variables 123
unchecked exceptions 155
underflow 64
underlying windowing system 452
undo functionality 512
undocking tool-bars 522
uneditable text 372, 373
Unicode 24, 31, 567
literals 25
Unicode Transformation Format *see* UTF-8
Unified Modeling Language *see* UML
Uniform Resource Locator *see* URL
union 330
Universal Character Set *see* UCS
Universal Resource Locator *see* URL
unsafe casts 206
unsupported operations 327, 338
unused keywords 21
upcasting 44, 176
update method 477
URL 481, 489
user interface *see* GUI
user threads 273
using control components 359
using packages 107
using variables 29
UTF-8 570

V

validating containers 385
value collection 338
value objects 325
valueOf method 300, 314
values 64, 338
constants 22
conversion 43
overflow 64
underflow 64
wrap-around 64
see also variables
variable declarations 4, 29, 30, 113
variable initialization 8, 35, 264
variable pitch font 458
variable shadowing 181
variables 3, 29
blank final 82, 123
constant values 123
declarations *see* variable declarations
default values 34
final 123
hiding 98
identifiers 29
in interfaces 199
initialization *see* variable initialization
initializer expressions 257
local 113
object reference 30
parameters 75, 98
references 30
shadowing 98, 181
sharing 126
static 7
storing 126
transient 126
volatile 126
vector 334
Venn diagrams 328
version 599
version @-tag 597
vertical font measurements 460
vertical spacing of applets 493

view of list 334
view port 525
`VirtualMachineError` 154
visibility of components 355
visible card 397
`Void` class 299
`volatile` variables 126
voucher 608

W

waiting for conditions 286
waiting state 284
web browser 16
web client *see* web browser
weight in grid bag 401
while statement 142
white space 26, 313
whole–part relationship 175
widening conversions 43
  primitive 43
  reference 44
width of applet 491
width of text 460, 461
windowing system 452
windowing toolkit *see* AWT
windows 353, 355, 420
  decoration 518
  events 419
  listeners 517
wrap-around 64
wrapper classes 29, 32, 296, 299, 342
wrapping collections 346
write access 551, 553
writers 567
writing bytes 555

X

xor 61, 66
xor paint mode 479

Y

yielding 284, 285

Z

zero fill shift 68

Java™ Technology from Addison-Wesley

ISBN 0-201-37949-X

ISBN 0-201-37963-5

ISBN 0-201-60446-9

ISBN 0-201-43329-X

ISBN 0-201-48543-5

ISBN 0-201-61563-0

ISBN 0-201-30972-6

ISBN 0-201-59614-8

ISBN 0-201-18393-5

ISBN 0-201-32573-X

ISBN 0-201-32582-9

http://www.awl.com/cseng

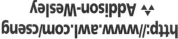

Addison-Wesley